July 20–22, 2011
Odense, Denmark

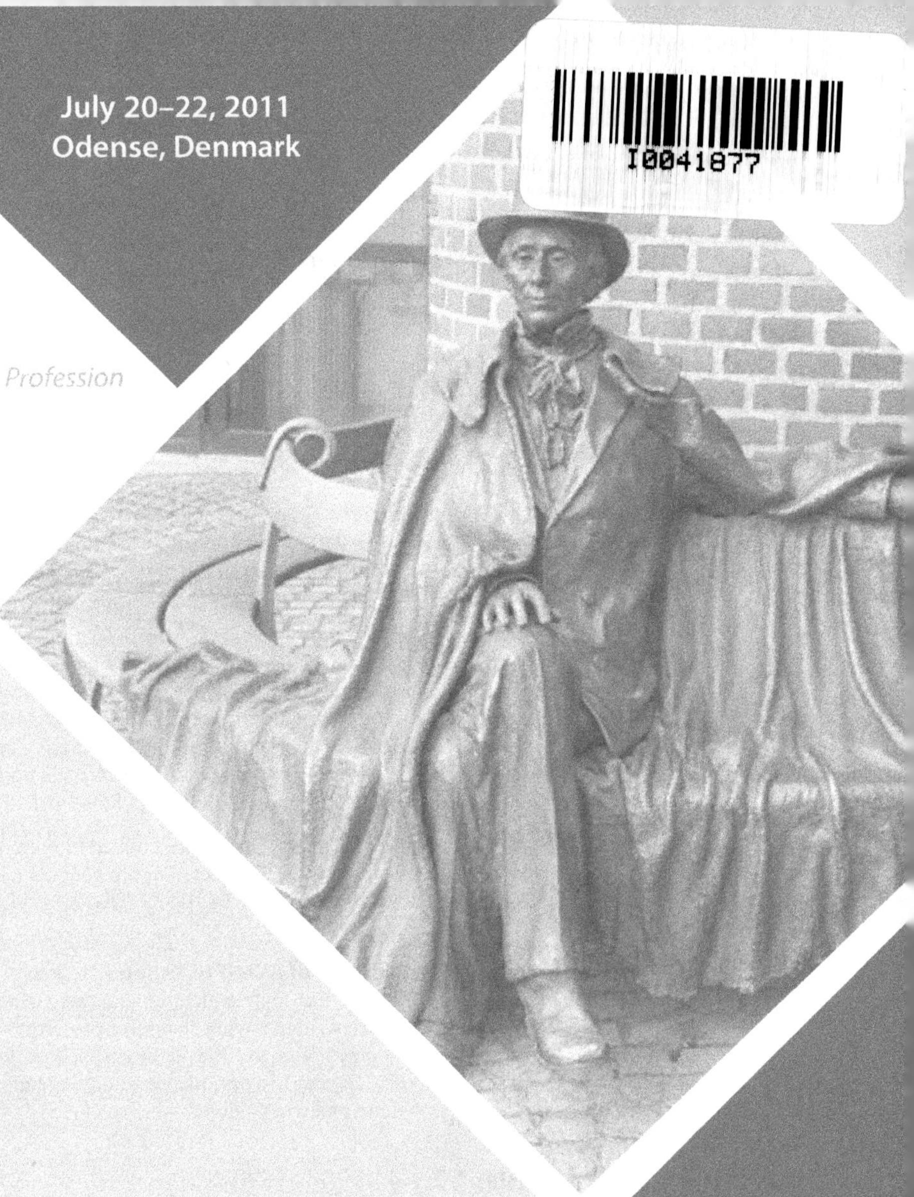

Association for
Computing Machinery

Advancing Computing as a Science & Profession

PPDP'11

Proceedings of the 2011 Symposium on
Principles and Practices of Declarative Programming

In cooperation with:

ACM SIGPLAN

Sponsored by:

University of Southern Denmark
& Danish Agency for Science Technology and Innovation

Association for
Computing Machinery

Advancing Computing as a Science & Profession

The Association for Computing Machinery
2 Penn Plaza, Suite 701
New York, New York 10121-0701

Notice to Past Authors of ACM-Published Articles
ACM intends to create a complete electronic archive of all articles and/or other material previously published by ACM. If you have written a work that has been previously published by ACM in any journal or conference proceedings prior to 1978, or any SIG Newsletter at any time, and you do NOT want this work to appear in the ACM Digital Library, please inform permissions@acm.org, stating the title of the work, the author(s), and where and when published.

ISBN: 978-1-4503-1268-4

Additional copies may be ordered prepaid from:

ACM Order Department
PO Box 30777
New York, NY 10087-0777, USA

Phone: 1-800-342-6626 (USA and Canada)
+1-212-626-0500 (Global)
Fax: +1-212-944-1318
E-mail: acmhelp@acm.org
Hours of Operation: 8:30 am – 4:30 pm ET

Printed in the USA

Foreword

This volume contains the papers presented at PPDP 2011, the 13th International ACM SIGPLAN Symposium on Principles and Practice of Declarative Programming, held in Odense, Denmark, July 20-22, 2011.

The PPDP series of conferences is a major forum for researchers and practitioners in the declarative programming communities to present results on leading edge issues of logic, constraint and functional programming, as well as related paradigms. The goal is to stimulate research in the use of logical formalisms and methods for specifying, performing, and analyzing computations, including mechanisms for mobility, modularity, concurrency, object-orientation, security, and static analysis. PPDP 2011 continued this tradition, bringing together researchers from the declarative programming communities and related areas (such as specification and theorem proving, database languages, AI languages and knowledge representation) and researchers applying declarative programming techniques to a variety of domains (for example, network security, concurrency, program analysis, language implementation, bioinformatics, etc).

This year, 36 papers were initially submitted to PPDP, and out of 29 papers reviewed the programme committee selected 16 papers for presentation in the symposium. Each submission was reviewed by at least three program committee members. The program committee used the EasyChair conference management system for handling electronic submissions, allocating reviewing duties, managing reviews, and the final discussions about all papers. In addition to regular paper sessions, the symposium included three invited talks by Fritz Henglein (University of Copenhagen, Denmark), Vitaly Lagoon (Cadence Design Systems, Boston, USA), and Andrey Rybalchenko (Technical University of Munich, Germany).

PPDP 2011 was part of the Odense Summer on Logic and Programming 2011. It was co-located with the 21st International Symposium on Logic-Based Program Synthesis and Transformation (LOPSTR 2011) with shared invited talks, the 20th International Workshop on Functional and (Constraint) Logic Programming (WFLP 2011), and 4th International Workshop on Approaches and Applications of Inductive Programming (AAIP 2011).

The symposium was organized in cooperation with ACM SIGPLAN and was sponsored by the University of Southern Denmark and the Danish Council for Independent Research & Natural Sciences. Lisa Tolles at Sheridan Printing Company managed the production of these proceedings.

We would like to thank all the authors who submitted papers to PPDP 2011. We are grateful to the program committee members and additional reviewers for their careful and efficient evaluation of the papers submitted. We are also grateful to the sponsors and local organizers, and to the invited speakers, for devoting time and effort to help make this conference a success.

Michael Hanus
PPDP 2011 Program Chair
University of Kiel, Germany

Peter Schneider-Kamp
PPDP 2011 Symposium Chair
University of Southern Denmark

Table of Contents

Session 5: Logic Programming and Constraints

Session 6: Types and Lambda Calculus

PPDP 2011 Symposium Organization

Symposium Chair: Peter Schneider-Kamp *(University of Southern Denmark)*

Program Chair: Michael Hanus *(University of Kiel, Germany)*

Steering Committee Chair: Sergio Antoy *(Portland State University, USA)*

Steering Committee:
Elvira Albert *(Spain)*
Sergio Antoy *(USA)*
Annalisa Bossi *(Italy)*
Maribel Fernández *(UK)*
Graham Hutton *(UK)*
Temur Kutsia *(Austria)*
Michael Leuschel *(Germany)*
Francisco J. López Fraguas *(Spain)*
Michael Maher *(Australia)*
Andreas Podelski *(Germany)*
Antonio Porto *(Portugal)*

Program Committee:
Peter Achten *(Radboud University Nijmegen, The Netherlands)*
Sergio Antoy *(Portland State University, USA)*
Michael Codish *(Ben-Gurion University of the Negev, Israel)*
Moreno Falaschi *(Università di Siena, Italy)*
Amy Felty *(University of Ottawa, Canada)*
Michael Hanus *(University of Kiel, Germany)*
Andy King *(University of Kent, UK)*
Hélène Kirchner *(INRIA, France)*
Francisco Javier López Fraguas *(Universidad Complutense de Madrid, Spain)*
Salvador Lucas *(Universidad Politécnica de Valencia, Spain)*
Simon Peyton Jones *(Microsoft Research, Cambridge, UK)*
Kostis Sagonas *(Uppsala University, Sweden)*
Peter Schneider-Kamp *(University of Southern Denmark, Denmark)*
Doaitse Swierstra *(Utrecht University, The Netherlands)*
Paul Tarau *(University of North Texas, USA)*
Peter Thiemann *(University of Freiburg, Germany)*
Kazunori Ueda *(Waseda University, Japan)*
Tarmo Uustalu *(Tallinn University of Technology, Estonia)*
Peter Van Roy *(Catholic University of Louvain, Belgium)*

Additional reviewers:

Demis Ballis
James Cheney
Yannick Chevalier
Jesús Correas Fernández
Iavor Diatchki
Santiago Escobar
Sebastian Fischer
Carsten Fuhs
Marco Gaboardi
Isabelle Gnaedig
Michael Grossniklaus
Petra Hofstedt
James Hook
Mathieu Jaume
Florent Kirchner
Oleg Kiselyov
Jael Kriener
Herbert Kuchen
Vitaly Lagoon
Aurelien Lemay
Sebastian Maneth
Jacopo Mauro
Keiko Nakata
Carlos Olarte
Luca Padovani
Mauro Piccolo
María José Ramírez-Quintana
Enric Rodríguez Carbonell
Carlos A. Romero-Díaz
Sabina Rossi
Fernando Saenz-Perez
Tom Schrijvers
Fausto Spoto
Jaime Sánchez-Hernández

Sponsored by:

University of Southern Denmark

Danish Agency for Science Technology and Innovation
Ministry of Science Technology and Innovation

In cooperation with:

acm SIGPLAN

The Challenges of Constraint-Based Test Generation

Vitaly Lagoon
Cadence Design Systems, USA
lagoon@cadence.com

Abstract

We describe the challenges underlying the design of a constraint-based test generator for functional verification of hardware. We show how these challenges are addressed by IntelliGen^{TM}– a constraint-based test generator by Cadence Design Systems.

Categories and Subject Descriptors B.5.3 [*Register-Transfer-Level Implementation*]: Reliability and Testing – Test Generation

General Terms Design, Verification

Keywords functional verification, constraint-based test generation, constraint debugging

Microchips can fail for variety of reasons ranging from high-level design flaws to manufacturing defects. However, logic and functional "bugs" are indisputably the most common cause of chip failures. Semiconductor industry practitioners estimate (e.g., [2]) that over 70% of re-spins are caused by functional flaws in hardware designs. Considering extremely high costs of re-spins and catastrophic costs of recalls, it is not surprising that semiconductor companies invest a large (and growing) share of R&D and financial resources into functional pre-silicone verification of their hardware designs.

It has long been recognized that manual development of tests for hardware designs in C or other traditional programming languages is inadequate. Due to vast number of states and execution paths and limited productivity of manual coding, this approach can never verify a state of the art design with an acceptable level of confidence. Thus, the effort and resources invested in verification are generally directed towards more automation, higher levels of abstraction and more sophisticated verification algorithms.

Current methods of automatic validation applied by the industry can be generally subdivided into simulation-based functionality testing and formal verification. Simulation-based testing consists in running the design in a simulated environment and checking its behavior on as many automatically produced "interesting" tests as possible. Formal verification aims to automatically prove that the design correctly implements a formal specification i.e., satisfies certain properties. Due to capacity problems, applications of formal verification are usually limited to validation of individual design components, while (inherently incomplete) simulation remains the dominant technique in validating system-wide correctness of designs.

A simulation-based verification environment for a *device-under-test* (DUT) normally includes a *test generator*, a *simulator* and a *checker*. The three components are responsible respectively for generating meaningful tests, simulating the work of the device, and checking the results of the simulation for correctness. Additional modules based on *coverage metrics* are often used to track the progress of validation.

In this talk we address the challenges underlying the design of a tool for automatic generation of tests from constraint-based models. Such models provided by verification engineers define formats of test data, control signals, and capture the architectural dependencies and test requirements for the design. We present IntelliGen^{TM} by Cadence Design Systems which is a part of the company's Specman^{TM} solution for automation of hardware verification. The central component of IntelliGen is a mechanism that generates randomized tests based on a constraint-based specification.

We demonstrate that a constraint-based test generator needs to answer to a different set of requirements compared to solvers for classic CP tasks, such as resource allocation. To name a few: (1) The test generator must be designed for repeatedly solving the same constraint problem, sometimes millions of times, possibly with respect to changing external inputs. (2) The output of the system should satisfy certain distribution requirements for the produced tests to target different aspects of the design behavior. (3) Bugs found during simulation must be reproducible and for that reason the system must be *random-stable* i.e., the same model should always generate the same series of tests for the same starting seed, even if used on different platforms or embedded in different contexts.

Additional challenges are associated with the need to adequately model class hierarchies and inheritance, dynamic arrays, data types including arbitrary-precision integers, strings and pointers. The tool needs to support various kinds of constraints such as arithmetic, logic, bitwise, as well as global constraints on arrays and special pragmas for controlling distributions. We show how all of these needs are addressed by Specman through its modeling capabilities [3] and constraint solving techniques of IntelliGen [4, 6].

Finally, we argue that a constraint debugger is a "must have" feature of a constraint-based test generator. Due to immenseness of real-life specifications, automatic tools are crucial to the engineers' ability to analyze and fix problems in test environments. Similarly to other kinds of software, constraint-based specification may contain "bugs" which lead to unexpected behavior such as (a) the specification is infeasible i.e., no solution can be found, (b) solving is too slow or runs out of time, (c) unexpected values are generated in the solutions or (d) some expected and targeted values never occur in the solutions. We present the basic concepts of GenDebugger [1, 5], a constraint debugger integrated in IntelliGen and show how it makes debugging of constraint models a manageable task.

PDPP'11, July 20–22, 2011, Odense, Denmark.
ACM 978-1-4503-0776-5/11/07.

References

[1] G. Alexandron, V. Lagoon, R. Naveh, and A. Rich. Gendebugger: An explanation-based constraint debugger. In *Third workshop on Techniques foR Implementing Constraint programming Systems (TRICS)*, 2010.

[2] T. Fitzpatrick. Building modular, reusable, transaction-level testbenches in system verilog. 2006 MAPLD International Conference, Sept. 2006. tutorial.

[3] Y. Hollander, M. Morley, and A. Noy. The e language: A fresh separation of concerns. In *38th International Conference on Technology of Object-Oriented Languages and Systems*, pages 41–50. IEEE Computer Society, 2001. ISBN 0-7695-1095-7.

[4] V. Lagoon and G. Baruch. Method for providing bitwise constraints for test generation. Patent US 6,918,076, Nov. 2009.

[5] A. Rich, G. Alexandron, and R. Naveh. An explanation-based constraint debugger. In *Proceedings of the 5th international Haifa Verification Conference*, pages 52–56. Springer-Verlag, 2009. ISBN 978-3-642-19236-4.

[6] S. Uziel, A. Noy, V. Lagoon, Y. Kinderman, and A. Gal. System and method for test generation with dynamic constraints using static analysis and multidomain constraint reduction. Patent US 7,870,523, Jan. 2011.

Towards Automatic Synthesis of Software Verification Tools

Andrey Rybalchenko
Technische Universität München
rybal@in.tum.de

Abstract

Automatically generated tools can significantly improve programmer productivity. For example, parsers can be automatically generated from declarative specifications in form of grammars, which tremendously simplifies the task of implementing a compiler. In this talk, we present a method for the automatic synthesis of software verification tools. Our synthesis procedure takes as input a description of the employed proof rule, e.g., program safety checking via inductive invariants, and produces a tool that automatically discovers the auxiliary assertions required by the proof rule, e.g., inductive loop invariants and procedure summaries. We rely on a (standard) representation of proof rules using recursive equations over the auxiliary assertions. The discovery of auxiliary assertions, i.e., solving the equations, is based on an iterative process that extrapolates solutions obtained for finitary unrollings of equations. We show how our method synthesizes automatic safety and liveness verifiers for programs with procedures, multi-threaded programs, and higher-order functional programs.

Categories and Subject Descriptors D.2.4 [*Software Engineering*]: Software/Program Verification; F.3.1 [*Logics and Meanings of Programs*]: Specifying and Verifying and Reasoning about Programs

General Terms Algorithms, Reliability, Security, Theory, Verification

Keywords Software verification, automatic tool generation, constraint solving

PDPP'11, July 20–22, 2011, Odense, Denmark.
ACM 978-1-4503-0776-5/11/07.

Incremental Checking of Well-Founded Recursive Specifications Modulo Axioms *

Felix Schernhammer
Vienna University of Technology, Austria
felixs@logic.at

José Meseguer
University of Illinois at Urbana-Champaign, USA
meseguer@uiuc.com

Abstract

We introduce the notion of well-founded recursive order-sorted equational logic (OS) theories modulo axioms. Such theories define functions by well-founded recursion and are inherently terminating. Moreover, for well-founded recursive theories important properties such as confluence and sufficient completeness are modular for so-called fair extensions. This enables us to incrementally check these properties for hierarchies of such theories that occur naturally in modular rule-based functional programs. Well-founded recursive OS theories modulo axioms contain only commutativity and associativity-commutativity axioms. In order to support arbitrary combinations of associativity, commutativity and identity axioms, we show how to eliminate identity and (under certain conditions) associativity (without commutativity) axioms by theory transformations in the last part of the paper.

Categories and Subject Descriptors F.3.1 [*LOGICS AND MEANINGS OF PROGRAMS*]: Specifying and Verifying and Reasoning about Programs; D.2.4 [*SOFTWARE ENGINEERING*]: Software/Program Verification; D.3.3 [*PROGRAMMING LANGUAGES*]: Language Constructs and Features; D.1.1 [*PROGRAMMING TECHNIQUES*]: Applicative (Functional) Programming

General Terms Theory, Verification

Keywords Well-founded recursive theory, order-sorted rewriting modulo axioms, modularity, termination, confluence, sufficient completeness

1. Introduction

Scalability is a big, unsolved challenge in formal reasoning about executable algebraic specifications. When using such specifications as programs and reasoning about their correctness, we often need to check basic properties such as confluence, termination, and sufficient completeness. This is quite manageable for small specifications, but when dealing with larger specifications corresponding to realistic programs, we can encounter severe tool performance barriers. For example, a non-built-in specification in Maude of the natural numbers, which is the exact counterpart of Maude's built-in `NAT` module, cannot be proved terminating by the MTT tool, which performs a relatively simple transformation to make the order-sorted specification unsorted and then invokes the AProVE tool with a 900 second timeout. Likewise, Mu-term cannot prove the same specification terminating with the same timeout, even though both AProVE and Mu-Term are state-of-the-art tools. In a similar way, particularly in the presence of AC axioms, a large number of critical pairs is often generated when checking the local confluence of specifications. For example, a small AC specification of hereditarily finite sets with only 26 equations already generates 1027 critical pairs when using the Maude Church-Rosser Checker [10]. Modularity is crucial.

Modular methods for termination and confluence (for a good survey up to 2002 see [24]) are certainly helpful. However: (i) some of these methods make quite strong requirements (e.g., disjointness) on the kind of modularity they allow; (ii) little seems to be known about the modularity of sufficient completeness; and (iii) the modularity results we are aware of do not deal with sorts and subsorts, nor (except for, e.g., [19, 23]) with rewriting modulo axioms, which are key features of state-of-the-art rule-based languages such as ASF+SDF [30], ELAN [5], CafeOBJ [11], and Maude [6].

Our Approach is based on the observation that in practice algebraic specifications are often *recursive function definitions* based on *constructor patterns*, and whose right-hand sides involve *recursive calls* to the same and/or previously defined functions on *smaller arguments* in the *well-founded* subterm ordering. This includes, but goes beyond, the very common case of primitive-recursive definitions. For example, the equations defining Ackerman's function,

$$A(0,n) = s(n) \qquad A(s(m),0) = A(m,1)$$
$$A(s(m),s(n)) = A(m, A(s(m),n))$$

exemplify a well-founded recursive function definition based on natural number constructor patterns which is not primitive-recursive. Such specifications define *total* (i.e., terminating) functions on the set of constructor terms. Furthermore, they naturally form *hierarchies*, so that previously-defined functions can be used to define more complex ones. For example, natural number exponentiation can be recur-

* The first author has been supported by the Austrian Academy of Sciences under grant number 22.361 and by the Austrian Marshall Plan Foundation in the Marshall Plan Scholarship Program under grant number 154.265.20.3.2010. The second author has been supported by NSF Grants CNS 07-16638 and 09-04749, and CCF 09-05584.

sively defined in terms of multiplication, which can in turn be recursively defined in terms of addition.

The main goal of this work is to reduce the checking of *confluence, termination, and sufficient completeness* for algebraic specifications based on well-founded recursive function definitions to relatively simple *incremental checks* on the module hierarchies containing such definitions. However, in order to be practically useful for rule-based languages, the notion of well-founded recursive function definition *needs to be generalized* to support: (a) mutually recursive definitions; (b) sorts, subsorts, and subsort overloading of function symbols; and (c) rewriting modulo axioms such as associativity and/or commutativity and/or identity. Such a generalization is non-trivial. Support for (a) is the least problematic, but support for (b) means that, because of subsort overloading, a function f can never be considered to be defined *once and for all:* it can always be *extended* to bigger sorts. For example, we can first define a $+$ function in a `NAT` module, and then extend its domain of definition in `INT`, `RAT`, and `COMPLEX` modules. Support for (c) is the least obvious, because the notion of "well-founded recursive function definition" does not have a straightforward extension to the modulo case. For example, if f is an associative-commutative (AC) function symbol, a definition of f based on a binary constructor g and a constructor constant a might include an equation $f(g(x,y),a) = g(f(x,y),g(a,a))$, which syntactically satisfies all the expected requirements of well-founded recursive function definitions, yet is non-AC-terminating (cf. Example 5 in Section 3). A related difficulty for axioms like AC is that the usual *syntactic* characterizations of classes of recursive functions (e.g., primitive recursive) are no longer adequate, because of the much greater flexibility in the constructor patterns that can be used. For example, the definition of the cardinality function `card` in the `MSET-NAT` module below could just as well have used an equation `card(MS,MS')= card(MS) + card(MS')` with `MS`, `MS'` of sort `MSet`, instead of the equation `card(N,MS)= s(0) + card(MS)` with `N` of sort `Nat` below. This work provides a notion of well-founded recursive function definition supporting features (a)–(b)–(c). We show in Section 3.1 that our approach generalizes an already very general notion of many-sorted well-founded recursive function.

To make the approach scalable, the cost of each incremental check should be small. This can be achieved by taking advantage of modular methodologies which ensure that in an immediate submodule inclusion $(\Sigma, E \cup Ax) \subset (\Sigma \cup \Sigma_\Delta, (E \cup E_\Delta) \cup (Ax \cup Ax_\Delta))$, while both modules *can be arbitrarily large*, the *incremental additions* Σ_Δ to the signature, E_Δ to the defining equations, and Ax_Δ to the axioms, are *small.* Such increments being big is a clear sign of bad software engineering practice, since usually a more modular design can be achieved by module refactoring. The incremental proof methods we propose are scalable precisely because they are based on checking the typically small increments $(\Sigma_\Delta, E_\Delta \cup Ax_\Delta)$ and not the, potentially very large, theory $(\Sigma \cup \Sigma_\Delta, (E \cup E_\Delta) \cup (Ax \cup Ax_\Delta))$.

A Running Example. Throughout the paper we use the following running example in Maude. Although small, it illustrates all the key features supported: mutual recursion, order-sortedness, and rewriting modulo axioms.

```
fmod NATURAL is pr TRUTH-VALUE .
 sort Nat .
 op 0 : -> Nat [ctor] .
 op s : Nat -> Nat [ctor] .
 op _+_ : Nat Nat -> Nat [comm id: 0] .
 ops even odd : Nat -> Bool .
 vars N M : Nat .
 eq s(N) + s(M) = s(s(N + M)) .
 eq even(0) = true .  eq even(s(N)) = odd(N) .
 eq odd(0) = false .  eq odd(s(N)) = even(N) .
endfm

fmod MSET-NAT is pr NATURAL .
 sort MSet .
 subsort Nat < MSet .
 op _,_ : MSet MSet -> MSet [ctor assoc comm id: null] .
 op null : -> MSet [ctor] .
 op card : MSet -> Nat .
 var MS : MSet .  var N : Nat .
 eq card(null) = 0 .
 eq card(N,MS)= s(0) + card(MS) .
endfm

fmod LIST-MSET-NAT is pr MSET-NAT .
 sorts List NeList .
 subsorts MSet < NeList < List .
 op nil : -> List [ctor] .
 op U : List -> MSet .
 op _;_ : List List -> List [assoc id: nil] .
 op _;_ : MSet NeList -> NeList [ctor assoc id: nil] .
 var MS : MSet .  var NL : NeList .
 eq U(nil) = null .  eq U(MS) = MS .
 eq U(MS ; NL) = MS, U(NL) .
endfm
```

The `NATURAL` module defines the natural numbers with addition and with `even` and `odd` predicates. The `MSET-NAT` module defines multisets of naturals and cardinality of multisets. Finally, the `LIST-MSET-NAT` module forms lists of multisets of numbers and defines a multiset union operator on such lists. Associativity, commutativity and identity axioms are specified with the `assoc`, `comm`, and `id:` attributes. All constructor operators are declared with the `ctor` keyword. As illustrated for `_;_`, an operator can be a constructor for some typing (`NeList`) and a defined symbol for a looser typing: `(0,0) ; nil` and `nil ; nil` are *not* constructor terms.

The paper is organized as follows. Section 2 gives background on order-sorted rewriting. Section 3 introduces well-founded recursive theories. Section 4 describes and justifies the incremental checking methods modulo C and AC axioms. Section 5 extends the approach to other combinations of A, C and I (identity) axioms. Finally, Section 6 discusses related work and presents some conclusions. The proofs of all theorems can be found in the long version of the paper[1].

2. Background on Order-sorted Term Rewriting

We summarize here material from [14, 21] on order-sorted algebra and order-sorted rewriting. For standard notions and notations of ordinary term rewriting we refer to [3, 4]. We start with a partially ordered set $(S, \leq)$ of *sorts*, where $s \leq s'$ is interpreted as *subsort inclusion*. The *connected components* of $(S, \leq)$ are the equivalence classes $[s]$ corresponding to the least equivalence relation $\equiv_\leq$ containing $\leq$. When a connected component $[s]$ has a top element, we will also denote by $[s]$ such a top element. An order-sorted signature $\Sigma = (S, \leq, F)$ consists of a poset of sorts $(S, \leq)$ and a $S^* \times S$-indexed family of sets $F = \{F_{w,s}\}_{(w,s)\in S^*\times S}$, which are *function symbols* with given string of argument sorts and

[1] Available as technical report from
http://www.logic.at/people/schernhammer/ and
http://www.ideals.illinois.edu/handle/2142/23865

result sort. If $f \in F_{s_1 \dots s_n, s}$, we declare the function symbol f as $f : s_1 \dots s_n \longrightarrow s$. Some of these symbols f can be *subsort-overloaded*, i.e., they can have several declarations related in the $\leq$ ordering [14].

Given an S-sorted set $\mathcal{X} = \{\mathcal{X}_s \mid s \in S\}$ of *disjoint* sets of variables and an order-sorted (OS) signature $\Sigma = (S, \leq, F)$, the set $\mathcal{T}(\Sigma, \mathcal{X})_s$ of terms of sort s is the least set such that $\mathcal{X}_s \subseteq \mathcal{T}(\Sigma, \mathcal{X})_s$; if $s' \leq s$, then $\mathcal{T}(\Sigma, \mathcal{X})_{s'} \subseteq \mathcal{T}(\Sigma, \mathcal{X})_s$; and if $f : s_1 \dots s_n \longrightarrow s$ is a declaration for symbol f and $t_i \in \mathcal{T}(\Sigma, \mathcal{X})_{s_i}$ for $1 \leq i \leq n$, then $f(t_1, \dots, t_n) \in \mathcal{T}(\Sigma, \mathcal{X})_s$. The set $\mathcal{T}(\Sigma, \mathcal{X})$ of order-sorted terms is $\mathcal{T}(\Sigma, \mathcal{X}) = \cup_{s \in S} \mathcal{T}(\Sigma, \mathcal{X})_s$. An element of any set $\mathcal{T}(\Sigma, \mathcal{X})_s$ is called a *well-formed* term. A simple syntactic condition on Σ called *preregularity* [14] ensures that each well-formed term t has always a *least-sort* possible among all sorts in S, which is denoted $ls(t)$. Furthermore, Σ is *monotonic* if for every two declarations $f : s_1 \dots s_n \longrightarrow s$ and $f : s'_1 \dots s'_n \longrightarrow s'$, $s_1 \dots s_n > s'_1 \dots s'_n$ implies $s > s'$, where $s_1, \dots, s_n > s'_1, \dots, s'_n$ means $s_i \geq s'_i$ for all $1 \leq i \leq n$ and $s_i > s'_i$ for some $1 \leq i \leq n$. Throughout this paper we assume that all order-sorted signatures are preregular and monotonic. Terms are viewed as labeled trees in the usual way. Positions $p, q, \dots$ are represented by chains of positive natural numbers used to address subterm positions of t. The set of positions of a term t is denoted $\mathcal{P}os(t)$. Positions of non-variable symbols in t are denoted as $\mathcal{P}os_\Sigma(t)$, and $\mathcal{P}os_\mathcal{X}(t)$ are the positions of variables. The subterm at position p of t is denoted as $t|_p$ and $t[u]_p$ is the term t with the subterm at position p replaced by u. We write $t \trianglerighteq u$, read *u is a subterm of t*, if $u = t|_p$ for some $p \in \mathcal{P}os(t)$ and $t \triangleright u$ if $t \trianglerighteq u$ and $t \neq u$.

An order-sorted substitution σ is an S-sorted mapping $\sigma = \{\sigma : \mathcal{X}_s \rightarrow \mathcal{T}(\Sigma, \mathcal{X})_s\}_{s \in S}$ from variables to terms. A *specialization* ν is an OS-substitution that maps a variable x of sort s to a variable x' of sort $s' \leq s$. We denote $\mathcal{D}om(\sigma)$ and $\mathcal{R}ng(\sigma)$ the domain and range of a substitution σ. An (order-sorted) rewrite rule is an ordered pair (l, r), written $l \rightarrow r$, with $l, r \in \mathcal{T}(\Sigma, \mathcal{X})$, $l \notin \mathcal{X}$, $\mathcal{V}ar(r) \subseteq \mathcal{V}ar(l)$ (and $ls(l) \equiv_\leq ls(r)$ for order-sorted rules). If for all specializations ν, $ls(\nu(l)) \geq ls(\nu(r))$, then we say that the OS-rule $l \rightarrow r$ is *sort-decreasing*. A term $t \in \mathcal{T}(\Sigma, \mathcal{X})$ rewrites to u (at position $p \in \mathcal{P}os(t)$ and using the rule $l \rightarrow r$), written $t \xrightarrow{p}_{l \rightarrow r} s$ (or just $t \rightarrow_\mathcal{R} s$ or even $t \rightarrow s$ if no confusion arises), if $t|_p = \sigma(l)$ and $s = t[\sigma(r)]_p$, for some OS-substitution σ; if $l \rightarrow r$ is *not* sort-decreasing, we also require that $t[\sigma(r)]_p$ is a well-formed term.

An *order-sorted theory* (OS theory) is a triple $\mathcal{E} = (\Sigma, B, R)$ with Σ a preregular order-sorted signature such that each connected component has a top sort, B a set of unconditional Σ-equations, and R a set of unconditional Σ-rules. In this paper B will always be a combination of associativity and/or commutativity and/or identity axioms for some of the operators in Σ. Moreover, associative and commutative operators f are always typed $f : s\, s' \longrightarrow s$ for some sorts s, s' where $s' \leq s$. By Σ_{AC} (resp. Σ_C) we denote the subsignature of Σ where all function symbols are associative and commutative but do not have an identity (resp. where all function symbols are commutative but not associative and do not have an identity). Furthermore, we assume[2] that in each equation $u = v$ in B the variables $\{x_1, \dots, x_n\} = \mathcal{V}ar(u) = \mathcal{V}ar(v)$ have *top sorts* $[s_1], \dots, [s_n]$.

Given an OS theory $\mathcal{E}$ as above, $t \rightarrow_{R/B} t'$ iff there exist u, v such that $t =_B u$ and $u \rightarrow_R v$ and $v =_B t'$. We say that (Σ, B, R) is *B-confluent*, resp. *B-terminating*, if the relation $\rightarrow_{R/B}$ is confluent, resp. terminating. By $[w]_B$ we denote that equivalence class of terms that are B-equal to w. We call an order-sorted signature *B-preregular* if the set of sorts $\{s \in S \mid \exists w' \in [w]_B \text{ s.t. } w' \in \mathcal{T}(\Sigma, \mathcal{X})_s\}$ has a least upper bound, denoted $ls[w]_B$ which can be effectively computed.[3] If (Σ, B, R) is B-confluent, B-terminating, B-preregular, and sort-decreasing, then the initial algebra $\mathcal{T}_{\Sigma/R \cup B}$, where the rules R are interpreted as equations, is isomorphic to the canonical term algebra $\mathcal{C}_{\Sigma/R,B}$, whose elements are B-equivalence classes in $\rightarrow_{R/B}$-canonical form. An order-sorted subsignature $\Omega \subseteq \Sigma$ with the same poset of sorts as Σ is called a *constructor subsignature* iff for each ground Σ-term t there is a ground Ω-term u such that $t \rightarrow^*_{R/B} u$. Terms from $\mathcal{T}(\Omega, \mathcal{X})$ are called *Ω-constructor terms*, or just constructor terms if Ω is clear from the context. We then say that (Σ, B, R) is *sufficiently complete* with respect to Ω. Intuitively this means that the functions defined by the rules R have been fully defined. For instance, the operators declared with the `ctor` attribute in our running example define a constructor subsignature, so that the specification is sufficiently complete. Assuming that (Σ, B, R) is B-confluent, B-terminating, B-preregular, and sort-decreasing, and that Ω is a constructor subsignature, if for any $t \rightarrow t'$ in R, whenever t is an Ω-term then t' is also an Ω-term, we are then guaranteed that all the elements in the canonical term algebra $\mathcal{C}_{\Sigma/R,B}$ are B-equivalence classes of ground Ω-terms. If, in addition, any ground Ω-term t is in $\rightarrow_{R/B}$-canonical form, then we call Ω a signature of *free constructors modulo B*.

Given an OS theory $\mathcal{E} = (\Sigma, B, R)$, we call an unsorted theory $\mathcal{E}' = (\Sigma', B', R')$ a *sound reflection* of $\mathcal{E}$ if there exists a mapping $\mathcal{M}$ from $\mathcal{T}(\Sigma, \mathcal{X})$ to a set of unsorted terms such that $t \rightarrow_{R/B} t' \Rightarrow \mathcal{M}(t) \rightarrow^+_{R'/B'} \mathcal{M}(t')$ for all terms $t, t' \in \mathcal{T}(\Sigma, \mathcal{X})$ (in that case we say that $\mathcal{E}'$ is a sound reflection of $\mathcal{E}$ w.r.t. $\mathcal{M}$; cf. [25]). Given a strict order $\succ$ on some domain D, the lexicographic extension of $\succ$ to n-tuples over D is defined as $\langle d_1, \dots, d_n \rangle \succ^{lex} \langle d'_1, \dots, d'_n \rangle$ if there exists an $i \leq n$ such that $d_j = d'_j$ for all $j < i$ and $d_i \succ d'_i$. Moreover, the multiset extension of $\succ$ to multisets over D is defined by $D_1 \succ^{mul} D_2$ if $D_1 \neq D_2$ and for each $d \in D_2 \setminus D_1$ there exists a $d' \in D_1 \setminus D_2$ such that $d' \succ d$.

3. Well-founded Recursive Theories

In this section we introduce the notion of well-founded recursive OS theories modulo axioms. The basic idea is to impose conditions on the equations of such theories, that guarantee finiteness of rewrite derivations. These conditions are based on the notion of *recursive dependency* of function symbols. Intuitively, a function symbol f recursively depends on g if there is a rule $f(t_1, \dots, t_n) \rightarrow r$ in the OS theory with $root(r|_p) = g$ for some position p of r.

[2] This assumption makes the technical treatment simpler, but it does not involve loss of generality and does not have to be specified explicitly: we can always assume that a new top sort $[s]$ is added to each connected component so that a binary operator f to which some axiom in B apply is overloaded for the top sort as $f : [s]\, [s] \longrightarrow [s]$. Maude adds these "kind" sorts $[s]$ automatically to any specification.

[3] Maude automatically checks the B-preregularity of a signature Σ for any combination of associativity, commutativity and identity axioms (see [6, Chapter 22.2.5]).

Definition 1 (recursive dependency). *Assume the axioms B_0 of the theory $\mathcal{E} = (\Sigma, B_0, R)$ are only commutativity and associativity-commutativity axioms.*[4]

Let G be the names of function symbols in Σ. The relation $\blacktriangleright^1_{\mathcal{E}} \subseteq G \times G$ is defined as $f \blacktriangleright^1_{\mathcal{E}} g$ whenever, there is a rule $l \to r \in R$ and a position $p \in Pos(r)$ such that $root(l) = f$ and $root(r|_p) = g$. The preorder $\blacktriangleright_{\mathcal{E}} \subseteq G \times G$ is obtained as the reflexive and transitive closure of $\blacktriangleright^1_{\mathcal{E}}$.

For order-sorted theories, and in particular in the presence of subsort overloaded function symbols, it is advantageous to distinguish between subsort overloaded variants of function symbols, because by doing so one obtains a more fine-grained notion of recursive dependency. This more fine-grained notion is needed because recursive dependencies exclusively based on the *names* of overloaded function symbols are too coarse to faithfully capture the actual dependencies involved in order-sorted rewriting.

A straightforward approach to achieve this disambiguation of subsort overloaded function symbols is to label them with the sorts of their arguments. This approach was used for instance by Ölveczky et al. ([25][Definitions 2 and 3]) to obtain an unsorted *reflection* of order-sorted rewrite systems. Unfortunately, in the presence of associativity axioms the unsorted rewrite system obtained by this labeling may not reflect the original order-sorted one.

Example 1. *Consider an OS theory $\mathcal{E}$ with sorts $A < B$, a function symbol f which is subsort overloaded with typings $f\colon A\,A \to A$, and $f\colon B\,B \to B$, a unary function symbol s with typing $s\colon B \to A$, and a constant b of sort B. The symbol f is associative and commutative and the rules are*

$$\begin{aligned} f(b,x) &\to f(s(b),s(b)) \\ f(b,s(x)) &\to f(b,x) \end{aligned}$$

where the sort of the variable x is B. By labeling the function symbols according to the sorts of their arguments in the corresponding order-sorted rewrite system, one does not obtain a sound reflection. The labeled versions of the above rules (including specializations) are

$$\begin{aligned} f_{B,B}(b,x) &\to f_{A,A}(s_B(b),s_B(b)) \\ f_{B,A}(b,x) &\to f_{A,A}(s_B(b),s_B(b)) \\ f_{B,A}(b,s_B(x)) &\to f_{B,B}(b,x) \\ f_{B,A}(b,s_A(x)) &\to f_{B,A}(b,x) \end{aligned}$$

In [25], additionally rules that decrease the sort labelings of function symbols are needed. Here, these rules are

$$\begin{aligned} f_{B,B}(x,y) &\to f_{A,B}(x,y) \\ f_{B,B}(x,y) &\to f_{B,A}(x,y) \\ f_{A,B}(x,y) &\to f_{A,A}(x,y) \\ f_{B,A}(x,y) &\to f_{A,A}(x,y) \\ s_B(x) &\to s_A(x) \end{aligned}$$

The symbols $f_{B,B}, f_{B,A}$ and $f_{A,A}$ are considered to be associative and commutative. The following cyclic reduction sequence cannot be reflected.

$$\begin{aligned} f(f(b,s(b)),b) &\to & f(f(s(b),s(b)),b) &=_{AC} \\ &=_{AC} & f(f(b,s(b)),s(b)) &\to \\ &\to & f(f(b,b),s(b)) &=_{AC} f(f(b,s(b)),b) \end{aligned}$$

In fact the labeled rewrite system is terminating (which can automatically be proved by AProVE [13]).

The reason for the inability of the labeled rewrite system to simulate correctly the order-sorted rewriting of Example 1 is the complex interaction between sorts and structural axioms. More precisely, in the term $f(f(s(b),s(b)),b)$ the sort of the arguments of the inner f symbol is A. However, in the AC-equal term $f(f(b,s(b)),s(b))$ the two arguments of the inner f symbol have sorts B and A. Hence, there is an increase in the sorts of the arguments caused by the associativity axiom. Note that in the labeled version of the term $f(f(s(b),s(b)),b)$ which is $f_{A,B}(f_{A,A}(s_B(b_B),s_B(b_B)),b_B)$ no associativity equation is applicable since $f_{A,B} \neq f_{A,A}$.

The problem, therefore, is to find a C- and AC-compatible disambiguation scheme on which we can express order-sorted recursive dependencies. The solution to this problem is to label AC function symbols not by pairs of sorts, but by the multisets of sorts of arguments of the flattened versions of the terms in question. Commutative (but not associative) function symbols are labeled by unordered pairs of sorts of their arguments.

Definition 2 ((top) flattening). *Let Σ be an unsorted signature containing free and AC-function symbols and let f be an AC symbol. Then,*

$$flat(t,f) = \begin{cases} x & \text{if } t = x, \text{ a variable} \\ g(t_1,\ldots,t_n) & \text{if } t = g(t_1,\ldots,t_n),\ g \neq f \\ f(T_1 \cup T_2) & \text{if } t = f(t_1,t_2) \end{cases}$$

where

$$T_i = \begin{cases} \{u_1,\ldots,u_m\} & \text{if } flat(t_i,f) = f(u_1,\ldots,u_m) \\ \{flat(t_i,f)\} & \text{otherwise} \end{cases}$$

Definition 3 (labeled signature, lab). *Let $\Sigma = (S,<,F)$ be an order-sorted signature containing AC, C and free function symbols. Its associated unsorted labeled signature Σ^{os} is given by*

$$\begin{aligned} \{f_\Psi \quad | \quad & f\colon A\,B \to A \in \Sigma_{AC}, \\ & \Psi \text{ a finite multiset of sorts} \leq A\} \cup \\ \{f_{[A',B']} \quad | \quad & f\colon A\,B \to C \in \Sigma_C, [A',B'] \text{ an unordered} \\ & \text{pair of sorts } A' \leq A, B' \leq B\} \cup \\ \{f_{A'_1,\ldots,A'_n} \quad | \quad & f\colon A_1 \ldots A_n \to C \in \Sigma \setminus (\Sigma_C \cup \Sigma_{AC}), \\ & A'_i \leq A_i \text{ for all } 1 \leq i \leq n\}. \end{aligned}$$

For a function symbol $f_{\mathcal{A}}$ of Σ^{os} where $\mathcal{A}$ is a multiset, an unordered pair or a sequence of sorts, we denote by $erase(f_{\mathcal{A}})$ the unlabeled function symbol f and by $lab(f_{\mathcal{A}})$ the label $\mathcal{A}$.

Note that Σ^{os} is countably infinite in general if Σ is countable. Next we define a mapping from terms over Σ to terms over the labeled signature Σ^{os}.

Definition 4 (labeling terms). *Let $\Sigma = (S,<,F)$ be an order-sorted signature containing AC, C and free function symbols which is preregular modulo the AC and C axioms. The mapping $\overline{\cdot}\colon \mathcal{T}(\Sigma,V) \to \mathcal{T}(\Sigma^{os},V)$ is defined by*

$$\bar{t} = \begin{cases} x & \text{if } t = x \in V \\ f_{ls(t_1),\ldots,ls(t_n)}(\overline{t_1},\ldots,\overline{t_n}) & \text{if } t = f(t_1,\ldots,t_n), \\ & f \in \Sigma \setminus (\Sigma_C \cup \Sigma_{AC}) \\ f_{[ls(t_1),ls(t_2)]}(\overline{t_1},\overline{t_2}) & \text{if } t = f(t_1,t_2),\ f \in \Sigma_C \\ f_\Psi(\lambda(t_1,f,\Psi),\lambda(t_2,f,\Psi)) & \text{if } t = f(v_1,v_2),\ f \in \Sigma_{AC}, \\ & flat(t,f) = f(u_1,\ldots,u_m), \\ & \Psi = \{ls(u_1),\ldots,ls(u_m)\} \end{cases}$$

[4] The subscript 0 in B_0 indicates that only C and AC axioms are present. In Section 5 below also other combinations of A, C and I axioms will be considered.

where

$$\lambda(u, f, \Psi) = f_\Psi(\lambda(u_1, f, \Psi), \lambda(u_2, f, \Psi))$$

if $u = f(u_1, u_2)$ *and* $\overline{u}$ *otherwise.*

Note that, by definition, constants are always *labeled by the empty sequence* ϵ*. Thus, for notational simplicity we omit the label of constants if no confusion arises. Slightly abusing notation, we denote by erase the inverse mapping of* $\bar{\cdot}$*, which erases the labels of function symbols and is defined for terms* $f(t_1, \ldots, t_n) \in \mathcal{T}(\Sigma^{os}, V)$ *as* $erase(f)(erase(t_1), \ldots, erase(t_n))$.

Example 2. *Consider the signature of* $\mathcal{E}$ *in Example 1. The labeled term* $\overline{f(f(s(b), s(b)), b)}$ *is*

$$f_{\{A,A,B\}}(f_{\{A,A,B\}}(s_B(b), s_B(b)), b).$$

By labeling terms in equations of an OS theory, we obtain a theory transformation that maps OS theories modulo axioms to unsorted theories modulo axioms.

Definition 5 (labeled theory)**.** *Let* $\mathcal{E} = (\Sigma, B_0, R)$ *be an OS theory with axioms* B_0 *including only C and AC axioms. By* $\overline{\mathcal{E}}$ *we denote the unsorted theory* $(\Sigma^{os}, \overline{B_0}, \overline{R})$ *where*

$$\begin{aligned} \overline{B_0} &= \{\overline{l\theta} = \overline{r\theta} \mid l = r \in B_0,\ \theta \text{ a sort specialization}\} \\ \overline{R} &= \{\overline{l\theta} \to \overline{r\theta} \mid l \to r \in R,\ \theta \text{ a sort specialization}\} \end{aligned}$$

Example 3. *Consider the module* `LIST-MSET-NAT` *of our running example of Section 1 and the equation*

```
(MS ; NL) ; L = MS ; (NL ; L)
```

that is added by the theory transformation of Section 5 below, thus eliminating the associativity axiom for ";". The sorts of the variables are MS: $MSet$, NL: $NeList$ *and* L: $List$*. Hence, the labeled version of this equation (considering the identity specialization) is*

$$\texttt{(MS}\ ;_{\texttt{MSet,NeList}}\ \texttt{NL)}\ ;_{\texttt{NeList,List}}\ \texttt{L} = \texttt{MS}\ ;_{\texttt{MSet,List}}\ \texttt{(NL}\ ;_{\texttt{NeList,List}}\ \texttt{L)}.$$

Thus, the various occurrences of the symbol ";" in the equation are explicitly disambiguated. Moreover, there are 24 specializations of this equation (including the identity), because the variables can be specialized in the following way:

$$\begin{aligned} MS &\ \text{to}\ MSet, Nat \\ NL &\ \text{to}\ NeList, MSet, Nat \\ L &\ \text{to}\ List, NeList, MSet, Nat \end{aligned}$$

Hence, according to Definition 5, our equation is transformed into 24 labeled equations given by

$$\texttt{(MS}\ ;_{X,Y}\ \texttt{NL)}\ ;_{Y,Z}\ \texttt{L} = \texttt{MS}\ ;_{X,Z}\ \texttt{(NL}\ ;_{Y,Z}\ \texttt{L)}$$
$$\text{where } X \in \{MSet, Nat\}, Y \in \{NeList, MSet, Nat\}, Z \in \{List, NeList, MSet, Nat\}.$$

As shown by Example 4 below, the theory transformation of Definition 5 is *not* a sound reflection (w.r.t. $\bar{\cdot}$). However, it can be extended to a theory transformation that is a sound reflection (w.r.t. $\bar{\cdot}$). This is detailed in the long version of this paper[5]. Nevertheless, in this short version of the paper we use labeled versions of rewrite rules exclusively to derive a "sort-aware" recursive dependency relation (cf. Definition 8 below). For this purpose, it suffices to use the simpler theory transformation of Definition 5. Hence, for the sake of simplicity, we use only this transformation in the rest of this section.

Example 4. *Consider the theory* $\mathcal{E} = (\Sigma, B_0, R)$ *of Example 1. The rules of* $\overline{\mathcal{E}} = (\Sigma^{os}, \overline{B_0}, \overline{R})$ *are*

$$\begin{aligned} f_{\{B,B\}}(b, x) &\to f_{\{A,A\}}(s_B(b), s_B(b)) \\ f_{\{A,B\}}(b, s_B(x)) &\to f_{\{B,B\}}(b, x) \\ f_{\{A,B\}}(b, x) &\to f_{\{A,A\}}(s_B(b), s_B(b)) \\ f_{\{A,B\}}(b, s_A(x)) &\to f_{\{A,B\}}(b, x) \end{aligned}$$

In the unlabeled system, we have $s = f(b, f(b, b)) \to_R f(s(b), s(b)) = t$*, but after labeling the corresponding reduction is impossible:* $\overline{s} = f_{\{B,B,B\}}(b_\epsilon, f_{\{B,B,B\}}(b_\epsilon, b_\epsilon)) \not\to_{\overline{R}} f_{\{A,A\}}(s_B(b), s_B(b)) = \overline{t}$.

Based on the notion of recursive dependency and the labeling of function symbols, we now define well-founded recursive OS theories modulo axioms. These well-founded recursive theories are guaranteed to be terminating and properties like confluence and sufficient completeness can be verified incrementally. Left-hand sides of equations in well-founded OS theories are linear *patterns*, or linear constructor terms with constructor right-hand sides in case constructors are not B_0-free ($\Omega \subseteq \Sigma$ is B_0-free iff for each specialization $l\nu \to r\nu$ with $l \to r \in R$, $l\nu$ is not an Ω-term).

Definition 6 (pattern)**.** *Let* $\mathcal{E} = (\Sigma, B_0, E)$ *be an OS theory where* $\Sigma = \mathcal{D} \uplus \Omega$ *is partitioned into defined function symbols and constructors.*[6] *A term* t *is a* pattern *if it is linear and every proper subterm is from* $\mathcal{T}(\Omega, V)$.

In order to obtain termination of well-founded recursive theories, arguments of functions called recursively by other mutually recursively dependent functions have to decrease. For example, when considering a rewrite rule $f(s_1, s_2, s_3) \to C[f(t_1, t_2, t_3)]$ for some context C, we demand that the tuple $\langle s_1, s_2, s_3 \rangle$ resp. the multiset $\{s_1, s_2, s_3\}$ is greater than $\langle t_1, t_2, t_3 \rangle$ resp. $\{t_1, t_2, t_3\}$ w.r.t. some extension of the subterm ordering to tuples or multisets that preserves well-foundedness. Whether arguments of non-commutative functions are compared as tuples (thus using a lexicographic ordering *lex*) or multisets (thus using a multiset ordering *mul* or a more specialized version *tup* for *AC* functions) is determined by a status function. This provides a maximum of flexibility, since arguments of different functions can be compared in different ways (unless the functions are mutually recursive). The idea of recursive calls to functions with smaller collections of arguments is formalized by the notion of *argument decreasing rules*, where all recursive function calls are to functions with smaller argument collections.

Definition 7 (decreasing rule)**.** *Let* $\mathcal{E} = (\Sigma, B_0, R)$ *be an OS theory where* B_0 *consists exclusively of AC and C axioms and let* $stat\colon \Sigma \to \{lex, mul\}$ *be a status function on* Σ*. Moreover, let* $l \to r$ *be a rule of* R *and* g *a function symbol such that* $root(l)$ *and* g *are either both AC or none of them is AC. We say that* $l \to r$ *is* g-argument decreasing *if* $stat(root(l)) = stat(g)$ *and for each subterm* $r|_p$ *of* r *with* $root(r|_p) = g$ *there are terms* $l' =_{B_0} l$ *and* $w' =_{B_0} r|_p$ *such that*

$$\{l''|_1, \ldots, l''|_{ar(root(l''))}\} \rhd^{tup} \{w''|_1, \ldots, w''|_{ar(root(w''))}\}$$

[5] Available as technical report from
`http://www.logic.at/people/schernhammer/` and
`http://www.ideals.illinois.edu/handle/2142/23865`

[6] But note that we can have $f\colon s_1, \ldots, s_n \to s \in \mathcal{D}$ and another $f\colon s'_1, \ldots, s'_n \to s' \in \Omega$, as illustrated for $f = \_;\_$ by our running example.

if $root(l'), root(w') \in \Sigma_{AC}$ *where* $l'' = flat(l', root(l'))$ *and* $w'' = flat(w', root(w'))$[7]*; and*

$$\{l'|_1, \ldots, l'|_{ar(root(l'))}\} \rhd^{mul} \{w'|_1, \ldots, w'|_{ar(root(w'))}\}$$

if $root(l'), root(w') \notin \Sigma_{AC}$ *and* $stat(root(l)) = mul$*; and*

$$\langle l'|_1, \ldots, l'|_{ar(root(l'))}\rangle \rhd^{lex} \langle w'|_1, \ldots, w'|_{ar(root(w'))}\rangle$$

if $root(l'), root(w') \notin \Sigma_{AC}$ *and* $stat(root(l)) = lex$.

Note that the status function does not assign the *tup* extension of the subterm ordering to non-AC function symbols, as the *mul* extension is more general and thus subsumes the use of the *tup* extension. For AC function symbols it is crucial to compare multisets of arguments by $\rhd^{tup}$ instead of $\rhd^{mul}$ in order to obtain a well-founded decrease of argument multisets. Example 5 shows that theories may be non-terminating even if multisets of mutually recursive functions decrease w.r.t $\rhd^{mul}$.

Example 5. *Consider the unsorted theory $\mathcal{E}$ (already used in Section 1) using a defined binary AC-function symbol f, a binary constructor g and a constructor constant a. The single rule is $f(g(x, y), a) \to g(f(x, y), g(a, a))$.*

We have $f \blacktriangleright_{\mathcal{E}} g$ but not $g \blacktriangleright_{\mathcal{E}} f$. Hence, we compare the arguments of $flat(f(g(x, y), a), f) = f(g(x, y), a)$ and $flat(f(x, y), f) = f(x, y)$. We have $\{g(x, y), a\} \rhd^{mul} \{x, y\}$.

Indeed, $\mathcal{E}$ is not AC-terminating:

$$\begin{array}{rcl} & f(g(f(a,a), g(a,a)), a) & \to \\ \to & g(f(f(a,a), g(a,a)), g(a,a)) & =_{AC} \\ =_{AC} & g(f(f(g(a,a),a),a), g(a,a)) & \to \\ \to & g(\underline{f(g(f(a,a), g(a,a)), a)}, g(a,a)) & \end{array}$$

Note however that $\{g(x, y), a\} \not\rhd^{tup} \{x, y\}$.

Now we are ready to define well-founded recursive OS theories modulo axioms. Ultimately, our goal is to show that well-founded recursive OS theories are compatible with a recursive path ordering that is compatible with C and AC axioms (i.e. an $ACRPO$). Due of the presence of rules like $c(c(x, y), z) \to c(x, c(y, z))$ (cf. e.g. Example 9 and Section 5 below) and commutative function symbols, it is crucial to compare arguments of some functions lexicographically and others by multiset orders. Moreover, for rules involving subsort-overloaded AC function symbols, sorts may or may not be crucial and it may even be advantageous to ignore sorts of certain function symbols (cf. Example 6 below). Hence, the notion of well-founded recursive OS theory modulo axioms is *parameterized* by two status functions *stat* and $stat_{ac}$. Note, however, that this does not compromise the syntactic and easy-to-check character of well-founded recursion, since the possible choices for these status functions are finite for each finite OS theory. However, finding working status functions may be computationally hard. To solve this problem we show in Section 4 below that these status functions can be computed incrementally when checking hierarchies of order-sorted theories for being well-founded recursive. Hence, provided that the theory extensions in such a hierarchy are small, the task of choosing suitable status functions is feasible.

[7] $A \rhd^{tup} B$ (where $\rhd$ is the proper subterm relation of terms) for multisets A and B of terms means that $A = A' \cup C$, $B = B' \cup C$, $A' \neq \emptyset$ and there is a (possibly partial) surjective mapping $\phi\colon A' \to B'$, such that $\phi(a) = b$ implies $a \rhd b$.

Definition 8 (well-founded theories)**.** *Let $\mathcal{E} = (\Sigma, B_0, R)$ be an OS theory with constructors $\Omega \subseteq \Sigma$ where the structural axioms B_0 are either AC or C axioms. Let $stat\colon \Sigma \to \{lex, mul\}$ be a status function where $stat(f) = mul$ for all $f \in \Sigma_C \cup \Sigma_{AC}$ and where $f \blacktriangleright_{\mathcal{E}} g, g \blacktriangleright_{\mathcal{E}} f$ implies $stat(f) = stat(g)$. Let $stat_{ac}\colon \Sigma_{AC} \to \{s, us\}$[8] be a status function where $f, g \in \Sigma_{AC}$ and $f \blacktriangleright_{\mathcal{E}} g, g \blacktriangleright_{\mathcal{E}} f$ implies $stat_{ac}(f) = stat_{ac}(g)$.*

$\mathcal{E}$ is well-founded recursive iff (i) $g \blacktriangleright_{\mathcal{E}} h$ and $h \blacktriangleright_{\mathcal{E}} g$ ($h, g \in \Sigma$) implies that h and g are either both AC symbols or both non-AC-symbols, and (ii) there are status function $stat$ and $stat_{ac}$ such that for each rule $l \to r$ and each specialization θ the following properties hold:

1. *Either l is a linear constructor term, or if not then l is a pattern in case $root(l) \in \Sigma \setminus \Sigma_{AC}$ and $flat(l, root(l))$ is a pattern in case $root(l) \in \Sigma_{AC}$.*
2. *If l is a constructor term, then so is r.*
3. *For every (not necessarily proper) subterm $r|_p$ of r,*

   $$root(\overline{r\theta}|_p) \blacktriangleright_{\overline{\mathcal{E}}} root(\overline{l\theta})$$

   (resp. $root(r|_p) \blacktriangleright_{\mathcal{E}} root(l) \in \Sigma_{AC}$ and $stat_{ac} = us$) implies that

   $\overline{l\theta} \to \overline{r\theta}$ is $root(\overline{r\theta}|_p)$ argument decreasing (w.r.t. stat)

   (resp. that $l \to r$ is $root(r|_p)$ argument decreasing).
4. *Assume $root(l) = root(r|_p)$ for some $p \in Pos(r)$, $root(r|_p) \blacktriangleright_{\mathcal{E}} root(l)$ and $stat_{ac}(root(l)) = s$ and consider the multiset S of arguments of $root(\overline{l\theta})$ in the term $\overline{l\theta}$ as well as the multiset T of arguments of $root(\overline{r|_p\theta})$ in the term $\overline{r|_p\theta}$. For every variable $x \in T \setminus S$, there exists a term $s \in S \setminus T$, such that $ls(s) > ls(x)$. Moreover, $lab(root(\overline{l\theta})) \geq^{mul} lab(root(\overline{r|_p\theta}))$.*
5. *If l is a constructor term and $root(l)$ is associative and commutative, then*

   $$root(flat(l, root(l))|_p) \not\blacktriangleright_{\mathcal{E}} root(l)$$

   for all positions $p \in Pos_{\Sigma}(flat(l, root(l)))$ with $p > \epsilon$.

The status function *stat* in Definition 8 determines whether arguments of function symbols are compared lexicographically or by multiset comparison. Mutually recursive function symbols must have the same status. Moreover, arguments of commutative function symbols may only be compared by multiset orders. Hence, the problem of finding suitable statuses for non-commutative functions is very similar to the problem of finding suitable statuses for functions when checking TRSs for RPOS compatibility for which efficient methods exist (cf. e.g. [28]). These methods can be used to determine the status function when checking theories for being well-founded recursive. The other status function $stat_{ac}$ determines whether sorts are taken into account when comparing arguments of AC-function symbols. The reason why we make this distinction is that in the presence of AC function symbols it is not always desirable to take sorts into account, because the labels of AC-function symbols appearing in equations may change through instantiations.

Example 6. *Consider an OS theory containing two sorts A, B with $A < B$, an AC function symbol $g\colon B, B \to B$, two*

[8] The function $stat_{ac}$ determines for an AC function symbol f whether sorts are taken into account (s for sorted) or not (us for unsorted) when comparing labeled versions $f_{\Psi}, f_{\Psi'}$ of this function in the $ACRPO$ we are going to use to prove termination of well-founded recursive theories (cf. Theorem 1 below).

unary function $h\colon B \to B$ *and* $t\colon B \to A$ *and a constant* $a : B$. *Consider a rule*

$$g(h(x), h(y)) \to g(x, y).$$

We have

$$root(\overline{g(h(x), h(y))}) = g_{\{B,B\}}$$

and indeed $root(\overline{g(h(x), h(y))\sigma}) = g_{\{B,B\}}$ *for every substitution* σ. *On the other hand, e.g.* $root(\overline{g(x, y)\sigma}) = g_{\{B,B,B\}}$ *if* $x\sigma = g(a, a), y\sigma = y$. *Hence, when instantiating the rule, there may be an increase in the multiset of sorts of the root symbol of the right-hand side compared to that of the root symbol of the left-hand side of the rule. In this case it is preferable to consider labeled occurrences of g as equal, since there is a decrease in the arguments of the recursive function call. We would have* $stat_{ac}(g) = us$ *in this case.*

On the other hand, consider a rule

$$g(a, a) \to g(h(a), h(a)).$$

We have

$$\begin{aligned} root(\overline{g(a, a)}) &= g_{\{B,B\}} \\ root(\overline{g(h(a), h(a))}) &= g_{\{A,A\}}. \end{aligned}$$

Thus, in order to orient this rule, e.g. by an (AC)RPO, it is preferable to consider the symbols $g_{\{B,B\}}$ *and* $g_{\{A,A\}}$ *as different ones, so that* $g_{\{B,B\}}$ *can be larger in the precedence of function symbols than* $g_{\{A,A\}}$. *We would have* $stat_{ac}(g) = s$ *in this case.*

The concrete value of $stat_{ac}$ for AC functions can be determined by checking a theory for possible increases in the multisets of sorts (w.r.t. the multiset extension of the subsort ordering) of the arguments in recursive calls to other (or the same) AC functions. If there are no such increases $stat_{ac}$ of the corresponding function should be set to s, otherwise it should be set to us.

Example 7. *Consider the functional Maude module* `NATURAL` *of the running example of Section 1. It contains an identity axiom so it is outside the scope of well-founded recursive theories. However, by the semantics-preserving theory transformation described in Section 5 below, we obtain the following module which, considered as an OS theory modulo C, is sort-decreasing and well-founded recursive.*

```
fmod TR-NATURAL is pr TRUTH-VALUE .
 sort Nat .
 op 0 : -> Nat [ctor] .  op s : Nat -> Nat [ctor] .
 op _+_ : Nat Nat -> Nat [comm] .
 ops even odd : Nat -> Bool .
 vars N M : Nat .
 eq N + 0 = N .
 eq s(N) + s(M) = s(s(N + M)) .
 eq even(0) = true .  eq odd(0) = false .
 eq odd(s(N)) = even(N) .  eq even(s(N)) = odd(N) .
endfm
```

Note that, since there is only one sort in this module, there are no non-trivial sort specializations and thus the equations of the labeled theory are identical with those of the unlabeled one (modulo names of function symbols; cf. Definition 5). Moreover, there are no AC axioms. Hence, the status function $stat_{ac}$ *is irrelevant. Finally, the choice of the status function stat is completely arbitrary since the module is well-founded recursive w.r.t. every choice of the status function.*

As for *stat*, mutually recursive AC function symbols have to agree on $stat_{ac}$ in well-founded recursive OS theories. In the presence of AC function symbols $f \in \Sigma$ with $stat_{ac}(f) = s$ in a well-founded recursive OS theory $\mathcal{E}$, two additional complications, compared to non-AC function symbols or those with a $stat_{ac}$ of us, may arise, but, as we explain below, these two potential complications do not cause any problems.

First, since Σ^{os} is infinite, there might be infinite decreasing $\blacktriangleright_{\overline{\mathcal{E}}}$ chains that are not looping. However, by Item (4) of Definition 8 we have $\Psi >^{mul} \Psi'$ whenever, $f_\Psi \blacktriangleright_{\overline{\mathcal{E}}} g_{\Psi'}$ ($f_\Psi \neq g_{\Psi'}$ and $f, g \in \Sigma_{AC}$) where $<$ is the (well-founded) subsort ordering. Hence, there are no infinite non-looping $\blacktriangleright_{\overline{\mathcal{E}}}$ chains.

The second potential complication is that the labeling is not-stable under substitutions as illustrated by Example 6. Item (4) of Definition 8 ensures that this stability is restored by ensuring that the sort of every variable occurring directly under an AC function symbols in the (subterm of the) right-hand side in question is dominated by a larger sort in the left-hand side.

The key result of this section is that well-founded recursive sort-decreasing OS theories modulo axioms are terminating. Therefore, our notion of well-founded recursive OS-theories provides: (i) a new formal definition that extends to the order-sorted and modulo C and AC cases the intuitive notion of "specification of a set of well-founded recursive functions"; (ii) a machine-checkable way of ascertaining whether a specification is indeed well-founded recursive; and (iii) a proof that such specifications are always terminating. Furthermore, as shown in Section 4, the checking that a specification is well-founded recursive can be made in a modular and *incremental* way. In practice, of course, we will want our well-founded recursive specifications to be also *confluent*, and *sufficiently complete* with respect to their constructors. These extra properties can also be checked incrementally, as explained in Section 4.

Theorem 1. *Let* $\mathcal{E} = (\Sigma, B_0, R)$ *be a sort-decreasing well-founded recursive OS theory where the structural axioms* B_0 *are either AC or C axioms. Then* $\mathcal{E}$ *is* B_0*-terminating.*

Note that the sort-decreasingness requirement is essential in Theorem 1, as shown by the following example.

Example 8. *Consider the following OS theory* $\mathcal{E}$ *without structural axioms. We have sorts* s_1 *and* s_2 *where* $s_1 < s_2$. *Moreover, there is a unary function symbol f typed* $f\colon s_2 \to s_2$, *another unary function symbol g typed* $g\colon s_2 \to s_1$ *and a constant a of sort* s_2. *The rules are*

$$\begin{aligned} f(a) &\to f(g(a)), \\ g(x) &\to x \end{aligned}$$

where x is a variable of sort s_2. *This theory is well-founded recursive. For the problematic first rule we have*

$$\overline{f(a)} = f_{s_2}(a_\epsilon)$$

and

$$\overline{f(g(a))} = f_{s_1}(g_{s_2}(a_\epsilon)).$$

Moreover, $f_{s_1} \not\blacktriangleright_{\overline{\mathcal{E}}} f_{s_2}$ *and* $g_{s_2} \not\blacktriangleright_{\overline{\mathcal{E}}} f_{s_2}$.

However the theory is non-terminating as is witnessed by the cyclic reduction sequence

$$f(a) \to f(g(a)) \to f(a).$$

The problem here is that $\mathcal{E}$ *is not sort-decreasing, since* $ls(g(x)) = s_1 \not\geq s_2 = ls(x)$ *for the second rule if x is of sort* s_2.

3.1 Many-Sorted Well-Founded Functions as a Special Case of Well-Founded Theories

To further explain the generality of our notion of well-founded recursive theories we show in detail how it captures as a special case a very general notion of well-founded recursive definition in the many-sorted case without axioms. In a sense this is the most general comparison we can make with previous notions, since to the best of our knowledge the notion has not been previously studied in the order-sorted and modulo cases.

To simplify the exposition we focus on the case of recursive definitions without mutual recursion. It is well-known that by adding extra data constructors, such as product types, several mutually recursive functions can be expressed as a single function.

Definition 9. *Let Ω be a many sorted signature of constructors. A* well-founded recursive tower *is a sequence*

$$(f_1 : s_1^1 \ldots s_{n_1}^1 \to s_1, R_{f_1}) \ldots (f_m : s_1^m \ldots s_{n_m}^m \to s_m, R_{f_m})$$

consisting of fresh function symbols $f_1, \ldots, f_m$ not in Ω and of sets of rules R_{f_i}, $1 \leq i \leq m$, defining each f_i such that the rules in R_{f_i} are of the form

$$f_i(t_1, \ldots, t_{n_i}) \to C[f_i(u_1^1, \ldots, u_{n_i}^1) \ldots f_i(u_1^k, \ldots, u_{n_i}^k)]$$

with $t_1, \ldots, t_{n_i}$ Ω-terms and where:

(i) $f_i(t_1, \ldots, t_{n_i})$ is linear and the right-hand side of the rule involves only variables occurring in $f(t_1, \ldots, t_{n_i})$.

(ii) The context C is a term in the signature $\Omega \cup \{f_1, \ldots, f_{i-1}\}$.

(iii) $k \geq 0$, and for each $1 \leq j \leq k$ the set $\{1, \ldots, n_i\}$ can be split into two disjoint subsets $A \uplus B = \{1, \ldots, n_i\}$ such that $1 \in A$, and

(1) for each $a \in A$, $t_a \trianglerighteq u_a^j$;

(2) for each $b \in B$, either $u_b^j \in \mathcal{T}(\Omega \cup \{f_1, \ldots, f_{i-1}\}, \mathcal{X})$ or $u_b^j = f_i(v_1^b, \ldots, v_{n_i}^b)$ with $(t_1, \ldots, t_{n_i}) \triangleright (v_1^b, \ldots v_{n_i}^b)$; and

(3) there is an $a \in A$ with $a < min(B)$ such that $(t_1, \ldots, t_a) \triangleright (u_1^j, \ldots, u_a^j)$

where by definition $(t_1, \ldots, t_l) \triangleright (t_1', \ldots, t_l')$ iff for each $1 \leq i \leq l$, $t_i \trianglerighteq t_i'$, and there is a $j \in \{1, \ldots, l\}$ such that $t_j \triangleright t_j'$.

Note that this definition includes as a special case all primitive recursive functions, where the terms $f_i(u_1^j, \ldots, u_{n_i}^j)$ are such that $(t_1, \ldots, t_{n_i}) \triangleright (u_1^j, \ldots, u_{n_i}^j)$. Note also that the equations for Ackerman's function in the introduction are a special instance of the above definition. In practice, two more conditions are required of such recursive towers:

(1) *disjoint patterns*, that is, if $f_i(t_1, \ldots, t_{n_i})$ and $f_i(t_1', \ldots, t_{n_i}')$ are two different left-hand sides in R_{f_i}, which we may assume have distinct variables, then the patterns do not unify.

(2) *sufficient completeness*, that is, the collection of patterns

$$\{(t_1, \ldots, t_{n_i}) \mid \exists t' s.t.\ f_i(t_1, \ldots, t_{n_i}) = t' \in R_{f_i}\}$$

cover the product sort $s_1^i \times \ldots \times s_{n_i}^i$ in the sense that any ground term in that product is an instance of one of the patterns.

Those are precisely the conditions of confluence and sufficient completeness that we show how to check incrementally in Section 4. The main result is now:

Theorem 2. *For any well-founded recursive tower as in Definition 9, the equational theory $(\Omega \cup \{f_1, \ldots, f_m\}, R_{f_1} \cup \ldots \cup R_{f_m})$ is a well-founded recursive many-sorted theory.*

4. Verifying Properties of OS Theories Incrementally

For well-founded recursive OS theories modulo axioms we can check important properties like termination, confluence, sort-decreasingness and sufficient completeness incrementally in the presence of theory hierarchies that satisfy reasonable conditions. These conditions are formalized in the notion of *fair extension.* The basic idea of fair extensions is that extending modules do not interfere with their base modules, i.e., they do not introduce new constructors of sorts of the base module and they do not redefine existing functions.

Definition 10 (fair extension)**.** *Assume that $\mathcal{E}_1 = (\Sigma_1, B_0^1, R_1)$ and $\mathcal{E}_2 = (\Sigma_1 \cup \Sigma_2, B_0^1 \cup B_0^2, R_1 \cup R_2)$ are OS theories where the B_0^is are C or AC axioms for $i \in \{1, 2\}$. Σ_1 and $\Sigma_1 \cup \Sigma_2$ are order-sorted signatures. We write $\Sigma_1 = (S_1, <_1, F_1)$ and $\Sigma_1 \cup \Sigma_2 = (S_1 \cup S_2, <_1 \cup <_2, F_1 \cup F_2)$. Furthermore, F_i is divided into constructors Ω_i and defined function symbols $\mathcal{D}_i$ for both $i \in \{1, 2\}$. $\mathcal{E}_2$ is a* fair extension *of $\mathcal{E}_1$ iff:*

1. every function symbol f from Σ_1 is AC (resp. C) in $\mathcal{E}_2$ iff it is AC (resp. C) in $\mathcal{E}_1$;

2. Σ_2 does not introduce subsorts of sorts of Σ_1, i.e. $s \in S_1 \wedge s' <_1 \cup <_2 s$ for some $s' \in S_1 \cup S_2$ implies $s' <_1 s$;

3. Σ_2 does not contain new constructors of some sort of S_1, i.e. $f : s_1, \ldots, s_n \to s \in \Omega_2$ implies $s \notin S_1$;

4. for every rule $l \to r \in R_2$ and every function symbol $f : s_1, \ldots, s_n \to s \in F_1$, l and $f(x_{s_1}^1, \ldots, x_{s_n}^n)$ do not unify in an order-sorted fashion modulo axioms (where x_s denotes a variable of sort s).

5. if f is a defined AC symbol in $\mathcal{E}_1$ and $f \blacktriangleright_{\mathcal{E}_1} g$, $g \not\blacktriangleright_{\mathcal{E}_1} f$, then $g \not\blacktriangleright_{\mathcal{E}_2} f$.

6. if $c \in \Omega_1$ and there is a rule $l \to r$ from R_1 such that $root(l) = c$, then l does not overlap (order-sorted modulo axioms) with the left-hand side of any rule $l' \to r'$ of R_2 in case $root(l')$ is a defined symbol in $\Sigma_1 \cup \Sigma_2$, and c does not occur below the root of l' in case $root(l')$ is an associative-commutative constructor.

The first item of Definition 10 ensures that overloaded function symbols have the same set of attached axioms. Items 2 – 4 ensure that no new subsorts and constructors of sorts of the base module are introduced and no functions of the base module are redefined. Item 5 makes sure that no additional mutual recursive dependency of *AC* symbols is introduced by the extending module, and item 6 is needed to prevent overlaps of rules from R_1 that have constructor terms as left-hand sides with rules from R_2.

In the rest of this section we denote by $\mathcal{E}_1 = (\Sigma_1, B_0^1, R_1)$ an OS theory modulo axioms B_0^1 and by $\mathcal{E}_2 = (\Sigma_1 \cup \Sigma_2, B_0^1 \cup B_0^2, R_1 \cup R_2)$ a fair extension of $\mathcal{E}_1$. By $\mathcal{E}_2'$ we denote the OS theory $(\Sigma_1 \cup \Sigma_2, B_0^1 \cup B_0^2, R_2)$. First, we show modularity of sort-decreasingness. Then we show that the property of being well-founded recursive itself is modular, provided that the base and extending theory agree on the status functions.

Theorem 3 (modularity of sort-decreasingness)**.** *If $\mathcal{E}_1$ and $\mathcal{E}_2'$ are both sort-decreasing, then so is $\mathcal{E}_2$.*

Theorem 4 (modularity of well-founded recursion). *If $\mathcal{E}_1$ and $\mathcal{E}_2'$ are well-founded recursive w.r.t. to compatible functions $stat^1, stat^1_{ac}$ and $stat^2, stat^2_{ac}$, then so is $\mathcal{E}_2$*[9].

Note that we require that the status functions of the base theory and the extending theory are compatible. In a naive mechanization of incremental checks for well-founded recursiveness this could necessitate backtracking, i.e., modifying the status function of a base module depending on an extending theory. To avoid this backtracking, we propose to compute the status functions incrementally in a "by need" fashion. This means that a specific status is assigned to a function symbol (resp. an *AC* symbol) only if this status is crucial for the theory in question to be well-founded recursive. Otherwise, the status is left open, so that it can be set later when incrementally checking an extending theory for well-founded recursiveness. For example, consider the theory of Example 7. It is well-founded recursive w.r.t. every status function *stat*. Hence, the status of functions can later be set arbitrarily when checking an extending module. A fully general implementation of this idea could, for example, compute a set of status functions for which a module is well-founded recursive. Then when checking an extending module for well-founded recursiveness one could choose suitable status functions from this set of possible ones. Next we show that confluence is modular for fair extensions of well-founded recursive theories.

Theorem 5 (modularity of confluence). *Assume $\mathcal{E}_1$ and $\mathcal{E}_2'$ are well-founded recursive w.r.t. to compatible functions $stat^1, stat^1_{ac}$ and $stat^2, stat^2_{ac}$. If $\mathcal{E}_1$ and $\mathcal{E}_2'$ are confluent then so is $\mathcal{E}_2$.*

Note that for sufficient completeness the adequate notion of modular check consists of checking the property only for *new* defined function symbols.

Theorem 6 (modularity of sufficient completeness). *Assume $\mathcal{E}_1$ and $\mathcal{E}_2'$ are well-founded recursive w.r.t. to compatible functions $stat^1, stat^1_{ac}$ and $stat^2, stat^2_{ac}$. If $\mathcal{E}_1$ is sufficiently complete and for every function $f\colon s_1, \ldots, s_n \to s \in \mathcal{D}_2 \setminus \mathcal{D}_1$ and every ground substitution σ mapping variables to irreducible constructor terms, $f(x^1_{s_1}, \ldots, x^n_{s_n})\sigma$ is either $\mathcal{E}_2$-reducible or a constructor term (x_s denotes a variable of sort s), then $\mathcal{E}_2$ is sufficiently complete.*

This way of incrementally checking sufficient completeness is compatible with existing automated methods to check the property. Roughly, the idea of these methods is to check whether ground terms rooted by a defined function symbol and having only constructor terms as proper subterms are either reducible, or constructor terms (which is possible as the root symbol might be subsort overloaded). This is done by describing the respective languages of terms by (propositional) tree automata and then reducing the problem to an emptiness problem for tree automata (we refer to [15] and [16] for more details). The method is suitable for incremental checks following Theorem 6, since it can easily be adapted to consider only terms rooted by defined function symbols of the extending theory instead of all.

Corollary 1. *Assume $\mathcal{E}_1$ and $\mathcal{E}_2'$ are well-founded recursive w.r.t. to functions $stat^1, stat^1_{ac}$ and $stat^2, stat^2_{ac}$ that are compatible. If $\mathcal{E}_1$ and $\mathcal{E}_2'$ are sort-decreasing and confluent and moreover, $\mathcal{E}_1$ is sufficiently complete and for every function $f\colon s_1, \ldots, s_n \to s \in \mathcal{D}_2 \setminus \mathcal{D}_1$ and every irreducible ground substitution σ (that maps variables only to constructor terms) $f(x^1_{s_1}, \ldots, x^n_{s_n})\sigma$ is $\mathcal{E}_2$-reducible (or a constructor term), then $\mathcal{E}_2$ is sort-decreasing, well-founded recursive (thus terminating), confluent and sufficiently complete.*

[9] Compatibility of two functions f_1 and f_2 here means that $f_1(a) = f_2(a)$ whenever $a \in Dom(f_1) \cap Dom(f_2)$.

Example 9. *Consider the running example of Section 1. In order to apply our methods to the modules of this example, the identity axioms and those axioms specifying associativity for a non-commutative function symbol have to be eliminated. Indeed, we can eliminate these problematic axioms by the theory transformation presented in Section 5. This transformation yields the module of Example 7 for the module NATURAL and the following two transformed theories for the modules MSET-NAT and LIST-MSAT-NAT.*

```
fmod TR-MSET-NAT is pr TR-NATURAL .
 sort MSet .
 subsort Nat < MSet .
 op _,_ : MSet MSet -> MSet [ctor assoc comm] .
 op null : -> MSet [ctor] .
 op card : MSet -> Nat .
 var MS : MSet .   var N : Nat .  var X : [MSet] .
 eq X , null = X .
 eq card(null) = 0 .  eq card(N) = s(0) + card(null) .
 eq card(N,MS) = s(0) + card(MS) .
endfm

fmod TR-LIST-MSET-NAT is pr TR-MSET-NAT .
 sorts List NeList .
 subsorts MSet < NeList < List .
 op nil : -> List [ctor] .
 op _;_ : List List -> List .
 op _;_ : MSet NeList -> NeList [ctor] .
 op U : List -> MSet .
 var MS : MSet .  var NL : NeList .  var L : List.
 var Y : [List] .
 eq Y ; nil = Y .  eq nil ; Y = Y .
 eq (MS ; NL) ; L = MS ; (NL ; L) .
 eq U(nil) = null .  eq U(MS) = MS .
 eq U(MS ; NL) = MS, U(NL) .
endfm
```

We already established that the TR-NATURAL module is sort-decreasing and well-founded recursive in Example 7. Moreover, it is non-overlapping and thus (by termination) confluent. Sufficient completeness can automatically be verified by the Maude sufficient completeness checker (cf. e.g. [15]). The module TR-MSET-NAT, restricted to equations explicitly defined in the module and particularly not including the ones from the TR-NATURAL module, is sort-decreasing and well-founded recursive as well. This is seen for instance by using the status functions $stat(f) = mul$ for all f and $stat_{ac}(\_,\_) = us$. Confluence of the equations of TR-MSET-NAT follows again from non-overlappingness. All ground instances of $card(x)$ are reducible. Furthermore, TR-MSET-NAT is a fair extension of TR-NATURAL. Hence, it is sort-decreasing, well-founded recursive, confluent and sufficiently complete.

Finally, consider the module TR-LIST-MSET-NAT restricted to equations explicitly defined in the module and particularly not including the ones from the TR-MSET-NAT module. It is sort-decreasing and well-founded recursive (e.g. $stat(;) = lex$ and $stat(f) = mul$ for all other functions f). Furthermore, it is confluent because all critical pairs are joinable. All ground instances of $(x_1; x_2)$ are either reducible or constructor terms and all ground instances of $U(x)$ are reducible. As TR-LIST-MSET-NAT is a fair extension of TR-MSET-NAT it is thus sort-decreasing, well-founded recursive (thus terminating), confluent and sufficiently complete.

5. A Variant-Based Theory Transformation

So far, our incremental methods for checking the sort-decreasingness, confluence, termination, and sufficient completeness of order-sorted well-founded recursive specifications modulo B have been developed for the case where B can only have commutativity and/or associativity-commutativity axioms. But we are interested in checking the confluence, termination, and sufficient completeness of more general order-sorted specifications $\mathcal{E} = (\Sigma, B, R)$ where B can have any combination of associativity and/or commutativity and/or identity axioms (with some restrictions on the case of associativity without commutativity as explained below). The extension of our method to this more general case is accomplished by an automatic theory transformation $(\Sigma, B, R) \mapsto (\Sigma, B_0, \widehat{R} \cup \Delta)$ such that: (i) B_0 only involves commutativity and associativity-commutativity axioms; (ii) the theories $R \cup B$ and $B_0 \cup \widehat{R} \cup \Delta$ are semantically equivalent (as inductive theories, see below); and (iii) (Σ, B, R) is confluent, terminating, and sufficiently complete for Ω modulo B iff $(\Sigma, B_0, \widehat{R} \cup \Delta)$ has the same properties modulo B_0. Here we summarize and extend the basic ideas of the transformation and refer to [9] for further details.

The first key idea is to decompose B as a disjoint union $B = B_0 \cup \Delta$ so that (Σ, B_0, Δ) is confluent and terminating modulo B_0, and Δ contains all its B_0-extensions (cf. e.g. [26, Definition 10.4]). The second key idea is to generate the transformed rules $\widehat{R}$ by computing the most general Δ, B-*variants* ([7]) of the left-hand sides l for the rules $l \to r$ in R. Given a term t, a Δ, B-variant of t is a Δ, B-canonical form u of an instance of t by some substitution θ; more precisely, it is a pair (u, θ). Some variants are more general than others, so that variants form a preorder in a natural way. The set $\widehat{R}$ then consists of all rules $\widehat{l} \to r\theta$ such that $(\widehat{l}, \theta)$ is a maximal variant of l for $l \to r$ a rule in R. Our transformation $(\Sigma, B, R) \mapsto (\Sigma, B_0, \widehat{R} \cup \Delta)$ is actually the composition of two simpler transformations of this kind:

$$(\Sigma, B, R) \mapsto (\Sigma, B_1, \widehat{R}_1 \cup \Delta_1) \mapsto (\Sigma, B_0, \widehat{R} \cup \Delta)$$

where B_1 is obtained by removing *all identity axioms*[10] Δ_1 from B, and B_0 is obtained by removing from B_1 all axioms that are associative but not commutative, so that Δ is the union of Δ_1 and such associativity axioms oriented (in one of the two directions) as rules. In this way, B_0 only contains commutativity and/or associativity-commutativity axioms. We then incrementally check the confluence, termination, and sufficient completeness of (Σ, B, R) modulo B by checking the same properties modulo B_0 for the semantically equivalent theory $(\Sigma, B_0, \widehat{R} \cup \Delta)$ according to the methods already developed in Sections 3 and 4.

For the first transformation $(\Sigma, B, R) \mapsto (\Sigma, B_1, \widehat{R}_1 \cup \Delta_1)$ we are always guaranteed that the set of rules $\widehat{R}_1$ is finite if R is (see [9]). However, for the second transformation $(\Sigma, B_1, \widehat{R}_1 \cup \Delta_1) \mapsto (\Sigma, B_0, \widehat{R} \cup \Delta)$, which removes associative but not commutative axioms from B_1, we cannot in general guarantee that $(\Sigma, B_0, \widehat{R} \cup \Delta)$ is a finite theory. However, the *use of subsorts* can make it often the case in practice that $(\Sigma, B_0, \widehat{R} \cup \Delta)$ is finite. We can illustrate this interesting phenomenon with our running example. The first transformation, removing identities, leaves the equation `U(MS ; NL) = MS, U(NL)` unchanged because, since `NL` has sort `NeList`, the identity rules for `_;_` cannot be applied to any instance of `MS ; NL`. By orienting the associativity axiom as a rule `(L ; P); Q` $\to$ `L; (P ; Q)`, the only variant of the equation `U(MS ; NL) = MS, U(NL)` is itself, since the left-hand side of the associativity rule fails to have an order-sorted unifier with the subterm `MS ; NL`. Therefore, the second transformation also succeeds in our running example (for the resulting transformed modules see Examples 7 and 9).

For well-founded recursive specifications containing operators f that are associative but not commutative (with or without identity) we need to impose some conditions on such f and slightly modify the version in [9] of the second transformation $(\Sigma, B_1, \widehat{R}_1 \cup \Delta_1) \mapsto (\Sigma, B_0, \widehat{R} \cup \Delta)$. There should be only one such operator per connected component, with only two overloadings, which must be

1. either of the form f : *List List* $\to$ *List*, f : *Elt NeList* $\to$ *NeList* [*ctor*], with *Elt* < *NeList* < *List*,
2. or of the form f : *List List* $\to$ *List*, f : *NeList Elt* $\to$ *NeList* [*ctor*], with *Elt* < *NeList* < *List*.

Moreover, there may be no other constructors of sort *List* or lower except those of sort *Elt* or lower. The names *Elt*, *NeList*, and *List* are immaterial and are only used to respectively suggest sorts for list elements, nonempty lists, and general lists. Furthermore, in order to make sure that the associativity equations introduced by the second transformation have constructor patterns below their top function symbol (so that the conditions in Section 3 apply to the transformed theory $(\Sigma, B_0, \widehat{R} \cup \Delta)$), instead of introducing an associativity rule

$$f(f(L, P), Q) \to f(L, f(P, Q))$$

for case (1) (resp. $f(L, f(P, Q)) \to f(f(L, P), Q))$ for case (2)) with L, P, Q of sort *List*, we introduce a more restricted rule

$$f(f(E, NL), Q) \to f(E, f(NL, Q))$$

for case (1) (resp. $f(Q, f(NL, E)) \to f(f(Q, NL), E))$ for case (2)) with E of sort *Elt*, NL of sort *NeList*, and Q of sort *List*. It is then easy to check that: (i) the left-hand sides of these more restricted rules have constructor patterns below and have no nontrivial overlaps with themselves; (ii) f so defined is sufficiently complete; and (iii) the unrestricted associativity equations are *inductive theorems* of the specification based on the more restricted associativity equations; that is, with this modified second transformation the theories $(\Sigma, B_1, \widehat{R}_1 \cup \Delta_1)$ and $(\Sigma, B_0, \widehat{R} \cup \Delta)$, although no longer equivalent as OS theories, are nevertheless *inductively equivalent* in the sense that their initial algebras $\mathcal{T}_{\Sigma, B_1 \cup \widehat{R}_1 \cup \Delta_1}$ and $\mathcal{T}_{\Sigma, B_0 \cup \widehat{R} \cup \Delta}$ are isomorphic. Indeed, we have

Lemma 1. *Under the above restrictions on the first typing of an associative operator f, the associativity equation $f(f(L, P), Q) = f(L, f(P, Q))$ is an inductive consequence of the restricted associativity equation*

$$f(f(E, NL), Q) = f(E, f(NL, Q))$$

. Likewise, under the second typing the associativity equation $f(L, f(P, Q)) = f(f(L, P), Q)$ is an inductive consequence of the restricted associativity equation

$$f(Q, f(NL, E)) = f(f(Q, NL), E))$$

[10] By adding a fresh top sort to each connected component as explained in Footnote 2, we only need to add a pair of identity rules $f(x, e) \to x$ and $f(e, x) \to x$, with x of sort $[s]$, for each connected component $[s]$ involving such axioms.

In practice these restrictions are not too strong, since we can automatically ensure typings (1) or (2) by introducing them through a *parameterized module for lists*. Furthermore, the restriction of having only one typing of type (1) or (2) per connected component for each associative f can be relaxed to allow several such typings, provided that the corresponding sorts $Elt < NeList < List$ and $Elt' < NeList' < List'$ involved in two different typings are incomparable.

Example 10. *We use our running example to illustrate the two theory transformations*

$$(\Sigma, B, R) \mapsto (\Sigma, B_1, \widehat{R}_1 \cup \Delta_1) \mapsto (\Sigma, B_0, \widehat{R} \cup \Delta)$$

The first transformation, adding identity axioms as explicit equations and computing the variants of rules with respect to identities, gives us the modules:

```
fmod TR1-NATURAL is pr TRUTH-VALUE .
 sort Nat .
 op 0 : -> Nat [ctor] .
 op s : Nat -> Nat [ctor] .
 op _+_ : Nat Nat -> Nat [comm] .
 ops even odd : Nat -> Bool .
 vars N M : Nat .
 eq N + 0 = N .
 eq s(N) + s(M) = s(s(N + M)) .
 eq even(0) = true .
 eq odd(0) = false .
 eq odd(s(N)) = even(N) .
 eq even(s(N)) = odd(N) .
endfm

fmod TR1-MSET-NAT is pr TR1-NATURAL .
 sort MSet .
 subsort Nat < MSet .
 op _,_ : MSet MSet -> MSet [ctor assoc comm] .
 op null : -> MSet [ctor] .
 op card : MSet -> Nat .
 var MS : MSet .
 var N : Nat .
 var X : [MSet] .
 eq X , null = X .
 eq card(null) = 0 .
 eq card(N)= s(0) + card(null) .
 eq card(N,MS)= s(0) + card(MS) .
endfm

fmod TR1-LIST-MSET-NAT is pr TR1-MSET-NAT .
 sorts List NeList .
 subsorts MSet < NeList < List .
 op nil : -> List [ctor] .
 op _;_ : List List -> List [assoc] .
 op _;_ : MSet NeList -> NeList [ctor assoc] .
 op U : List -> MSet .
 var MS : MSet .
 var NL : NeList .
 var L : List.
 var Y : [List] .
 eq Y ; nil = Y .
 eq nil ; Y = Y .
 eq U(nil) = null .
 eq U(MS) = MS .
 eq U(MS ; NL) = MS, U(NL) .
endfm
```

The way the variants of an equation with respect to the identities modulo the C and AC axioms are computed can be illustrated by the equation `card(N,MS)= s(0) + card(MS)` *in the original module* `MSET-NAT`. *Since the variable* `MS` *could collapse by instantiating it to the identity element* `null`, *the equation's left-hand side has two most general variants: (i) itself, so that the original equation is kept, and (ii) the term* `card(N)`, *leading to the new variant equation* `card(N)= s(0) + card(null)` *added to* `TR1-MSET-NAT`. *The result of the second stage of the theory transformation, denoted above as $(\Sigma, B_1, \widehat{R}_1 \cup \Delta_1) \mapsto (\Sigma, B_0, \widehat{R} \cup \Delta)$, has already been described in detail in Examples 7 and 9. Note that, since they do not involve associative but not commutative axioms, the modules* `TR1-NAT` *and* `TR1-MSET-NAT` *are not changed by the second transformation.*

6. Related Work and Conclusions

Our work is related to modularity methods for confluence and/or termination of TRSs. A very good survey of the literature on such methods up to 2002 can be found in [24]. One key difference is that, to the best of our knowledge, such work does not address sorts and subsorts, nor (except for, e.g., [19, 23]) rewriting modulo axioms. Another difference is that in some cases the modularity conditions imposed are quite strong, requiring for example disjointness, which is relatively rare in practical module hierarchies. Perhaps the earliest work most closely related to ours is the work on *proper extensions* of term rewriting systems of [24] (cf. also [8] and [27]). The basic idea behind proper extensions is that calls to functions f in right-hand sides of rewrite rules $l \to r$ where $root(l)$ and f are mutually recursive, do not involve defined function symbols from the base theory (or from the extending theory that recursively depend on functions from the base theory) in the arguments of the function call. Our notion of fair extensions of well-founded recursive theories is even more restrictive in this respect, since the arguments of calls to functions in right-hand sides have to be constructor terms if the function in question is mutually recursive with the root of the left-hand side of the rule. Note however, that the advantage of our more restrictive definition is not just its ability to deal with sorts and structural axioms, but also in our case general termination is modular instead of the weaker notion of $C_{\mathcal{E}}$-termination as for proper extensions.

Our work is also related to the hierarchical termination approach of Urbain and Marché ([23, 29]), with their notion of hierarchical extension being similar to ours of fair extension. In some ways our notion is more general, since for us function symbols can appear in both a submodule and a supermodule, but of course our incremental conditions are in other ways stronger so as to ensure termination, whereas in [23, 29] a modular approach to dependency pairs is developed. Furthermore [23] covers the AC case. There is also a rich body of related work on rewriting modulo axioms, e.g. [2, 17, 18, 22, 26, 31]. For termination modulo, related papers include, e.g., [1, 9, 12, 23].

When using well-founded recursive OS theories and fair extensions to create hierarchies of theories, one can verify important properties such as sort-decreasingness, termination, confluence and sufficient completeness incrementally. Hence, at a practical level, when developing equational programs (such as functional modules in Maude), one can follow a programming discipline ensuring that modules are well-founded recursive and module extensions are fair extensions. Sticking to this programming discipline then guarantees that the verification complexity of the properties in question grows roughly linearly with the number of distinct modules. This is a significant improvement compared to existing methods used for the verification of, e.g., termination where experiments show that in practice the verification complexity grows rapidly with increasing size of theories (see also [29]).

Obvious future work includes the mechanization of all the incremental checks described above in a tool, experimentation with such a tool, and the extension of our results to conditional and context-sensitive theories, which are also supported in Maude. Moreover, recent developments in the termination analysis of rewrite systems modulo axioms (cf. e.g. [1]) might allow us to relax the conditions in the notion of well-founded recursion, thus making our approach more widely applicable.

References

[1] B. Alarcón, S. Lucas, and J. Meseguer. A dependency pair framework for A∨C-termination. In P. Ölveczky editor, Proceedings of the 8th International Workshop on Rewriting Logic and its Applications (WRLA'10), *LNCS* 6381, pages 35–51. Springer, 2010.

[2] L. Bachmair and N. Dershowitz. Completion for rewriting modulo a congruence. *Theoretical Computer Science*, 67(2&3):173–201, 1989.

[3] F. Baader and T. Nipkow. *Term rewriting and All That.* Cambridge University Press, 1998.

[4] M. Bezem, J. Klop, and R. Vrijer, editors. *Term Rewriting Systems.* Cambridge Tracts in Theoretical Computer Science 55. Cambridge University Press, 2003.

[5] P. Borovanský, C. Kirchner, H. Kirchner, and P.-E. Moreau. ELAN from a rewriting logic point of view. *Theoretical Computer Science*, 285:155–185, 2002.

[6] M. Clavel, F. Durán, S. Eker, J. Meseguer, P. Lincoln, N. Martí-Oliet and C. Talcott. *All About Maude - A High-Performance Logical Framework.* LNCS 4350, 2007.

[7] H. Comon-Lundh and S. Delaune. The finite variant property: how to get rid of some algebraic properties. In J. Giesl editor, Proceedings of the 16th International Conference on Rewriting Techniques and Applications (RTA'05), LNCS 3467, 294–307, 2005.

[8] N. Dershowitz. Hierarchical termination. In N. Dershowitz and N. Lindenstrauss editors, Proceedings of the 4th International Workshop on Conditional and Typed Rewriting Systems (CTRS-94), *LNCS 968*, pages 89–105. Springer, 1995.

[9] F. Durán, S. Lucas, and J. Meseguer. Termination modulo combinations of equational theories. In S. Ghilardi and R. Sebastiani editors, Proceedings of the 7th International Symposium on Frontiers of Combining Systems (FroCoS'09), *LNAI* 5749, pages 246–262. Springer, 2009.

[10] F. Durán and J. Meseguer. A Church-Rosser checker tool for conditional order-sorted equational Maude specifications. In P. Ölveczky editor, Proceedings of the 8th International Workshop on Rewriting Logic and its Applications (WRLA'10), *LNCS* 6381, pages 69–85. Springer, 2010.

[11] K. Futatsugi and R. Diaconescu. *CafeOBJ Report.* World Scientific, AMAST Series, 1998.

[12] J. Giesl and D. Kapur. Dependency pairs for equational rewriting. In A. Middeldorp editor, Proceedings of the 12th International Conference on Rewriting Techniques and Applications (RTA'01), *LNCS* 2051, pages 93–108. Springer, 2001.

[13] J. Giesl, P. Schneider-Kamp, and R. Thiemann. AProVE 1.2: Automatic termination proofs in the dependency pair framework. In U. Furbach and N. Shankar editors, Proceedings of the 3rd International Joint Conference on Automated Reasoning (IJCAR'06), *LNCS* 4130, pages 281–286. Springer, 2006.

[14] J. Goguen and J. Meseguer. Order-sorted algebra I: Equational deduction for multiple inheritance, overloading, exceptions and partial operations. *Theoretical Computer Science*, 105:217–273, 1992.

[15] J. Hendrix, J. Meseguer, and H. Ohsaki. A sufficient completeness checker for linear order-sorted specifications modulo axioms. In U. Furbach and N. Shankar editors, Proceedings of the 3rd International Joint Conference on Automated Reasoning (IJCAR'06), *LNCS* 4130, pages 151–155. Springer, 2006.

[16] J. Hendrix, H. Ohsaki, and J. Meseguer. Sufficient completeness checking with propositional tree automata. Technical report, CS Department University of Illinois at Urbana-Champaign, 2005. `http://www.ideals.illinois.edu/handle/2142/11096`.

[17] G. Huet. Confluent reductions: Abstract properties and applications to term rewriting systems. *Journal of the Association for Computing Machinery*, 27:797–821, 1980. Preliminary version in *18th Symposium on Mathematical Foundations of Computer Science*, 1977.

[18] J.-P. Jouannaud and H. Kirchner. Completion of a set of rules modulo a set of equations. *SIAM Journal of Computing*, 15(4):1055–1094, Nov. 1986.

[19] J.-P. Jouannaud and Y. Toyama. Modular Church-Rosser modulo: the complete picture. *International Journal of Software and Informatics*, 2(1):61–75, 2008.

[20] D. Kapur and G. Sivakumar. Proving associative-communicative termination using RPO-compatible orderings. In *Selected Papers from Automated Deduction in Classical and Non-Classical Logics LNCS 1761* pages 39–61, Springer 2000.

[21] C. Kirchner, H. Kirchner, and J. Meseguer. Operational semantics of OBJ3. In T. Lepistö and A. Salomaa editors, Proceedings of the 15th International Colloquium on Automata, Languages and Programming (ICALP'88), *LNCS 317*, pages 287–301. Springer, 1988.

[22] C. Marché. Normalised rewriting and normalised completion. In Proceedings of the 9th Annual Symposium on Logic in Computer Science (LICS'94), pages 394–403. IEEE, 1994.

[23] C. Marché and X. Urbain. Modular and incremental proofs of AC-termination. *Journal of Symbolic Computation*, 38(1):873–897, 2004.

[24] E. Ohlebusch. *Advanced Topics in Term Rewriting.* Springer Verlag, 2002.

[25] P. Ölveczky and O. Lysne. Order-sorted termination: The unsorted way. In M. Hanus and M. Rodriguez-Artalejo editors, Proceedings of the 5th International Conference on Algebraic and Logic Programming (ALP'96), *LNCS 1139*, pages 92–106. Springer, 1996.

[26] G. E. Peterson and M. E. Stickel. Complete sets of reductions for some equational theories. *Journal of the ACM*, 28(2):233–264, 1981.

[27] M. R. K. K. Rao. Modular proofs for completeness of hierarchical term rewriting systems. *Theoretical Computer Science*, 151:487–512, 1995.

[28] P. Schneider-Kamp, R. Thiemann, E. Annov M. Codish and J. Giesl. Proving Termination using Recursive Path Orders and SAT Solving. In B. Konev and F. Wolter editors, Proceedings of the 6th International Symposium on Frontiers of Combining Systems (FroCoS'07), *LNCS 4720*pages 267–282, 2007.

[29] X. Urbain. Modular & incremental automated termination proofs. *J. Autom. Reasoning*, 32(4):315–355, 2004.

[30] A. van Deursen, J. Heering, and P. Klint. *Language Prototyping: An Algebraic Specification Approach.* World Scientific, 1996.

[31] P. Viry. Equational rules for rewriting logic. *Theoretical Computer Science*, 285:487–517, 2002.

Graph-Transformation Verification using Monadic Second-Order Logic

Kazuhiro Inaba *
National Institute of Informatics, Japan
kinaba@nii.ac.jp

Soichiro Hidaka
National Institute of Informatics, Japan
hidaka@nii.ac.jp

Zhenjiang Hu
National Institute of Informatics, Japan
hu@nii.ac.jp

Hiroyuki Kato
National Institute of Informatics, Japan
kato@nii.ac.jp

Keisuke Nakano
The University of Electro-Communications
ksk@cs.uec.ac.jp

Abstract

This paper presents a new approach to solving the problem of verification of graph transformation, by proposing a new static verification algorithm for the Core UnCAL, the query algebra for graph-structured databases proposed by Bunemann et al. Given a graph transformation annotated with schema information, our algorithm statically verifies that any graph satisfying the input schema is converted by the transformation to a graph satisfying the output schema. We tackle the problem by first reformulating the semantics of UnCAL into monadic second-order logic (MSO). The logic-based foundation allows to express the schema satisfaction of transformations as the validity of MSO formulas over graph structures. Then by exploiting the two established properties of UnCAL called bisimulation-genericity and compactness, we reduce the problem to the validity of MSO over trees, which has a sound and complete decision procedure. The algorithm has been efficiently implemented; all the graph transformations in this paper and the system web page can be verified within several seconds.

Categories and Subject Descriptors D.2.4 [*Software Engineering*]: Software/Program Verification; F.3.1 [*Logics and Meanings of Programs*]: Specifying and Verifying and Reasoning about Programs

General Terms Languages, Verification

Keywords Graph Transformation, UnCAL, Monadic Second-Order Logic

1. Introduction

Graphs are very useful means to describe complex structures and systems and to model concepts and ideas in a direct and intuitive way [2], and a number of languages, such as UnQL [7], Lorel [1], Graphlog [9], have been proposed for graph transformations [23]. UnCAL (Unstructured Calculus), being the underlying algebra of the graph query language UnQL, is one of the useful graph transformation languages for efficient graph transformations [6]. It is recently adopted for bidirectional model-driven software development [15, 16], where software components in different levels of abstraction are modeled as graphs, and their relation is described as graph transformations.

In these applications, it is often assumed, for each graph transformation, that its input and output graphs have some structure (*schema*) in them. However, due to the complicated structure like cyclic reference of graphs, it is not straightforward for programmers to write a transformation that produces schema-conforming outputs for every valid input. It is thus very important to provide a static verification algorithm to check if the transformation is correct with respect to the input and output schemas, which describe structural constraints of graph databases [4].

The objective of this paper is to provide a static verification algorithm for transformations in UnCAL. More specifically, what we want to solve is the following problem:

> *Verification Problem*: Given an UnCAL transformation f, an input schema φ_{IN}, and an output schema φ_{OUT}, determine whether "for any graph g satisfying φ_{IN}, the output graph $f(g)$ satisfies φ_{OUT}".

Although many efforts have been devoted to verification of tree transformations [12, 20, 21, 26], there is little work on verification of graph transformation. One challenge here is that many verification problems turn out to be undecidable when going from trees to graphs. Therefore, to deal with verification of graph transformation, we should carefully impose reasonable constraints on graphs and graph transformations.

One attempt made on verification of UnCAL transformation was to use simulation-based schemas [5] (with constraints on the schema). There, a schema itself is again a graph, and data graphs simulated by the schema graph (i.e., any traversal on the data graph can be replicated on the schema graph) are defined to conform to the schema. The advantage of such a schema is the simplicity of verification of transformations. Since the input schema itself is a graph, it can be passed as an argument to the transformation; the transformation is valid if the outcome is subsumed by the output schema. However, it has very limited expressiveness on structures of graphs. Basically, simulation can state only conjunctions of optional conditions, like "there can be an outgoing edge labeled

* Current affiliation is Google Inc.

PDPP'11, July 20–22, 2011, Odense, Denmark.

foo and there can be another edge of bar". It fails to describe a condition such as, "under the contact edge, we must have either phone edge or mail edge, but not both". Such "either one of" feature is, however, crucial for writing structural constraints; it can be seen in all the standard XML schema languages [8, 11, 29] or in the metamodeling language [3].

In this paper we propose a new approach to the verification problem based on the two important characteristics of UnCAL, *bisimulation-equivalence* of graphs and *structured recursion*, where a graph transformation in the Core UnCAL can be automatically checked against a schema in the powerful monadic second order logic (MSO). Our verification system enjoys the following features.

- Our verification system is *powerful*. First, it allows graph schemas to be described in terms of MSO. MSO (over strings and trees) has exactly the power of expressing regular languages [24], being widely used as a schema language for XML and graphs. The structural constraints expressible by commonly used graph schema language KM3 [19] is just in this category. Second, it accepts any graph transformation defined in terms of type-annotated Core UnCAL so that all the types can be fully checked.
- Our verification system is *fully automatic and decidable*. We propose an automatic algorithm that can map the type-annotated Core UnCAL to an MSO-definable graph transduction [10], and show that verification of such an MSO property on graphs can be reduced to that on infinite trees, which is decidable. In particular, if the graph transformation is *compact* [7], the problem can be reduced to verification on finite trees.

  In addition, thanks to the property that the inverse image of an MSO-definable set of graphs under an MSO-definable transduction is MSO-definable, validity of the transformation can be checked by the input-side subsumption. This makes it possible to generate a more understandable *counterexample with respect to the input* rather than on the output, which is in sharp contrast to the simulation-based approach [5].
- Our verification system is *efficient and practical* especially for *compact* [7] transformations. As not only schemas but also transformations can be described by MSO formulas, and verification of graph transformations in UnCAL can be efficiently implemented[1] with the MONA [14] MSO solver. In fact, all the examples in this paper can be verified by our system within several seconds.

The paper is structured as follows. In Section 2, we give an overview of our approach with an example for showing the taste how our verification works. In Section 3, we explain the graph data-model and transformation of Core UnCAL. In Section 4, we introduce MSO, and their usage as schema language. Section 5 is the main technical part, which shows how to translate Core UnCAL programs to MSO formula. Then in Section 6 we discuss two theorems that ensure the decidability of the generated MSO formulas. Section 7 compares the present paper with related work, and Section 8 concludes.

2. Overview

Before proceeding with the technical details, let us demonstrate through several examples how our verification works.

[1] The implementation is available at http://www.biglab.org.

2.1 A Simple Example

Consider the friend graph $\$db$ in Figure 1(a), which consists of a set of members, each member having a name, a contact information (either mail or phone), and a set of friends. The structure of this graph can be described by the following schema definition:

```
type Members = { mem : Person }
type Person  = {
  name    : Data,
  contact : MailOrPhone,
  friend  : Person    }
type MailOrPhone = Mail | Phone
type Mail  = { mail  : Data }
type Phone = { phone : Data }
```

Now suppose that we want to transform this graph by renaming mem to member, friend to knows, and flattening the contact information. This transformation can be described as *flatten* (*rename*($db)) where *flatten* and *rename* can be defined by structured recursions as follows.

$$\begin{aligned}
rename = &\ \mathbf{rec}(\lambda(\$L_1, \$G_1).\\
&\quad \&_1 := \mathbf{if}\ \$L_1 = \texttt{mem}\ \mathbf{then}\ \{\texttt{member} : \&_1\}\\
&\quad\quad \mathbf{else\ if}\ \$L_1 = \texttt{friend}\ \mathbf{then}\ \{\texttt{knows} : \&_1\}\\
&\quad\quad \mathbf{else}\ \{\$L_1 : \&_1\})\\
flatten = &\ \mathbf{rec}(\lambda(\$L_1, \$G_1).\\
&\quad \&_1 := \mathbf{if}\ \$L_1 = \texttt{contact}\ \mathbf{then}\ \$G_1\\
&\quad\quad \mathbf{else}\ \{\$L_1 : \&_1\})
\end{aligned}$$

Now our verifier can check that the above transformation is correct in the sense that if the input is of type Members, the output will always produce the graph meeting the following structure:

```
type Members2 = {member:Person2}
type Person2  = PM | PP
type PM={name:Data, mail:Data, knows:Person2}
type PP={name:Data, phone:Data, knows:Person2}
```

2.2 An Example of Verification Procedure

Our second example is to transform the friend graph to a friend-pair graph with the following structure:

```
type Pair  = { fst: Person, snd: Person }
type Pairs = { pair: Pair }
```

For instance, the graph structured data in Figure 1(a) is transformed to the table-like structure in Figure 1(b).

To make sure this transformation does generate a structure that we intuitively expect, we annotate schema information to the UnCAL code. By using this schema, we describe the expected type of each graph-variable and a return-expression of the **rec** recursion as follows, where input schema φ_{IN} corresponds to Members, and output schema φ_{OUT} corresponds to Pairs.

$$\begin{aligned}
&\mathbf{rec}(\lambda(\$L_1, \$G_1).\\
&\quad \&_1 :: \text{Pairs} := \mathbf{if}\ \$L_1 = \texttt{mem}\ \mathbf{then}\\
&\quad\quad \mathbf{rec}(\lambda(\$L_2, \$G_2).\\
&\quad\quad\quad \&_1 :: \text{Pairs} := \mathbf{if}\ \$L_2 = \texttt{friend}\ \mathbf{then}\\
&\quad\quad\quad\quad \{\texttt{pair} : \{\texttt{fst} : \$G_1 :: \text{Person}, \texttt{snd} : \$G_2 :: \text{Person}\}\}\\
&\quad\quad\quad\quad\quad \mathbf{else}\ \{\}\\
&\quad\quad)(\$G_1)\\
&\quad\quad\quad \mathbf{else}\ \{\}\\
&)(\$db :: \text{Members}) :: \text{Pairs}
\end{aligned}$$

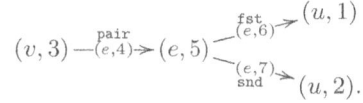

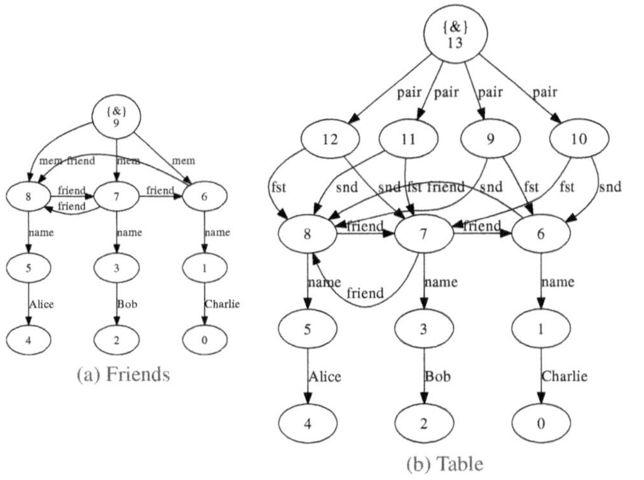

(a) Friends

(b) Table

Figure 1. Example Graph Data

Then what the verifier confirms are: (1) under the assumption $\$db$ conforms to the type Members, the node bound to $\$G_1$ during recursion always conforms to the type Person, (2) under the assumption $\$G_1$ conforms to the type Person, the node bound to $\$G_2$ during recursion always conforms to the type Person, (3) under the assumption $\$G_1$ and $\$G_2$ conforms to the type Person, the inner most recursion returns a graph conforming to Pairs for each edge, (4) under the assumption that the inner recursion returns Pairs graphs, the outer recursion returns Pairs, and (5) the whole expression evaluates to a Pairs graph. Our verifier is sound, that is, if the verifier answers that all the above conditions hold, then it does hold. Also it is complete in the sense that if it says the conditions may be broken, then there indeed is a concrete assignment of graphs to variables that breaks the conditions. In such a case, our verifier emits an instance of a counter-example variable assignment that does break the conditions imposed by the output schemas. For instance, if we forgot to write the generation of an edge $\{\texttt{pair} : \cdots\}$, the verifier reports an error with a counter-example. In this case, any input graph can be a counter-example. But the following example more appreciates the power of our contribution: the transformation extracts `contact` information, assuming it only has `Mail` information, the verifier reports the counter-example of the input having `Phone`.

$$
\begin{aligned}
&\mathbf{rec}(\lambda(\$L_1, \$G_1).\\
&\quad \&_1 :: \mathsf{Pairs} := \mathbf{if}\ \$L_1 = \texttt{mem}\ \mathbf{then}\\
&\qquad \mathbf{rec}(\lambda(\$L_2, \$G_2).\\
&\qquad\quad \&_1 :: \mathsf{Pairs} := \mathbf{if}\ \$L_2 = \texttt{contact}\ \mathbf{then}\ G_2 :: \mathsf{Mail}\\
&\qquad\qquad\qquad \mathbf{else}\ \{\})(\$G_1)\\
&\qquad\quad \mathbf{else}\ \{\})(\$db :: \mathsf{Members}) :: \mathsf{Mail}
\end{aligned}
$$

The check is carried out in the following three steps. Firstly, the schema is converted to a logic formula (more specifically, a formula of MSO logic) that exactly states the conditions that are imposed by the schema.

Secondly, the annotated UnCAL transformation is converted into a set of MSO formulas describing the transformation. For instance, from the root node of the formula, the following is the excerpt of the set of formulas generated.

$$
\begin{aligned}
&\mathbf{edge}_{\texttt{pair},3,4,5}(x, y, z) :=\\
&\quad \exists^f v, e, u.(x = y = z = e \land \mathbf{edge}_{\texttt{friend},1,1,1}(v, e, u))\\
&\mathbf{edge}_{\texttt{fst},5,6,1}(x, y, z) :=\\
&\quad \exists^f v, e, u.(x = y = e \land z = \mathsf{root} \land \mathbf{edge}_{\texttt{friend},1,1,1}(v, e, u))\\
&\mathbf{edge}_{\texttt{snd},5,7,2}(x, y, z) :=\\
&\quad \exists^f v, e, u.(x = y = e \land z = \mathsf{root} \land \mathbf{edge}_{\texttt{friend},1,1,1}(v, e, u))
\end{aligned}
$$

We assign a number (we call *copy-id*) 1 to the graph bound to the variable $\$G_1$ and the number 2 to $\$G_2$ (and 0 to $\$db$). The subformula $\mathbf{edge}_{\texttt{friend},1,1,1}(v, e, u)$ asserts that v and u are nodes of copy-id 1, and e is an edge with label `friend` connecting them. The nodes and edges created by the transformation are also numbered (in this case, we use 3 to 7).

$$
(v, 3) \xrightarrow[(e,4)]{\texttt{pair}} (e, 5) \begin{cases} \xrightarrow[(e,6)]{\texttt{fst}} (u, 1) \\ \xrightarrow[\texttt{snd}]{(e,7)} (u, 2). \end{cases}
$$

The definition of the predicate $\mathbf{edge}_{\texttt{pair},3,4,5}(x, y, z)$, for example, can be read as follows: "if 1st copy of e is an edge of label `friend`, then (and only then) an edge of label `pair` is drawn from the 3rd copy of e and 5th copy of e." This is essentially a complete description of the transformation represented by MSO.

Thirdly, the MSO formulas representing schema conformance are then expanded to formulas that only use the predicates $\mathbf{edge}_{\texttt{pair},k,k,k}(x, y, z)$ arose from the variables, (i.e., k is a copy-id assigned to a variable, not a generated output). For instance, the type annotation $\&_1 :: \mathsf{Pairs}$ asserts that the return-value of the body of the recursion must satisfy the schema formula:

$$
\begin{aligned}
&\mathit{isPairs}(x) := \exists^s \mathit{Pairs}.\ \exists^s \mathit{Pair}.\ \exists^s \mathit{Person}.\ x \in \mathit{Pairs}\\
&\quad \land\ \cdots\\
&\quad \land \forall^f y \in \mathit{Pair}. \forall^f z\ w.\ \mathbf{edge}_{\texttt{fst}}(y, z, w) \to w \in \mathit{Person}\\
&\quad \land\ \cdots).
\end{aligned}
$$

Since the body expression generates nodes and edges having the 1st to the 7th copy-id, the formula is instantiated to use $\mathbf{edge}_{\texttt{fst},3,4,5}$ etc. instead of the bare $\mathbf{edge}_{\texttt{fst}}$. The conversion is an inductive expansions of $\forall$ and $\exists$ into a finite number of $\land$s and $\lor$s, e.g., $\forall^f x.\psi(x)$ is converted to $\forall^f x.\psi_1(x) \land \ldots \land \psi_7(x)$ where ψ_i is a result for inductive transformation of the subformula ψ assuming that the variable x points to the i-th copy entity. After this process, the conditions that need to be verified can be written as a single MSO formula, which is valid on any interpretation of $\mathbf{edge}_{\_,1,1,1}$ if and only if the conditions are always satisfied.

Finally, the validity of the generated MSO formula is checked. Technical problem here is that validity of MSO on graphs is undecidable in general [27]. Fortunately, we can manage the problem by utilizing the property called bisimulation-genericity, which is shared in common for all UnCAL transformations; for bisimulation generic transformations, the validity on graphs can be reduced to the decidable validity on infinite trees [22]. Furthermore, the property called compactness that holds among a certain subset of UnCAL allows to reduce the validity problem to that on finite trees. On finite tree domain, good existing MSO solvers can be exploited for our implementation.

3. Core UnCAL: A Graph Transformation Language

We present the target language of our verification technique: a core fragment of the UnCAL graph algebra, and recall important aspects of the language (for the details, see [7]).

3.1 Graph Data Model

UnCAL deals with rooted, directed, finite-branching and edge-labeled graphs whose nodes convey no particular information. We fix the finite set *Label* of labels and the set *Data* of data values throughout the paper. We assume a special label $\varepsilon \notin \mathit{Label}$, and denote by $\mathit{Label}_\varepsilon$ the set $\mathit{Label} \cup \{\varepsilon\}$. We usually write the elements of *Label* by typewriter font like `a`, `foo`, or `name`, and write the elements of *Data* as double-quoted strings like `"John"` or `"3.14"`. A graph $g = (V, r, E)$ consists of a set V of *nodes*, a designated root node $r \in V$, and a set E of *edges* equipped with three mappings: $\mathrm{src} : E \to V$, $\mathrm{lab} : E \to \mathit{Label}_\varepsilon \cup \mathit{Data}$, and $\mathrm{dst} : E \to V$. The mappings src and dst denote the source and the destination node of the edge respectively, and lab denotes the label of the edge. We often write (v, l, u) to indicate the edge e with $\mathrm{dst}(e) = u$, $\mathrm{lab}(e) = l$, and $\mathrm{src}(e) = v$.

UnCAL's graph model has ε-edges resembling ε-transitions of automata, which work as shortcuts between nodes. Schemas and transformations will be defined to respect this intention of ε-edges. For example, the following two graphs are considered to be semantically equivalent.

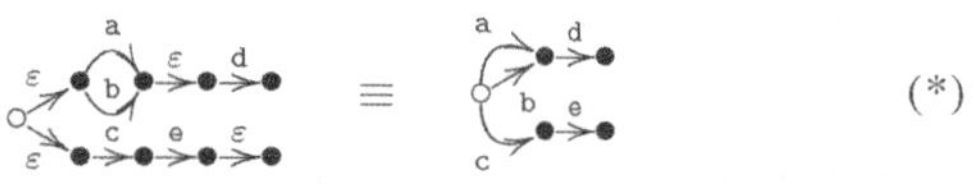

Here, the white circle $\circ$ denotes the root node of each graph. The reason for using ε-edges is to make the transformation language as simple as possible. For instance, we do not need a union operator $\tau_1 \cup \tau_2$ of two edge-sets explicitly, because it can be simulated by a construction of a new node having two outgoing ε-edges, as exemplified by the root node of the figure above. We define the set $E^{\to}(v)$ of *outgoing edges* of a node v as the set of non-ε edges reachable from v by traversing only ε-edges. That is, $e = (v', l, u) \in E^{\to}(v)$ if and only if $l \neq \varepsilon$ and there exists a sequence $v = v_0, v_1, \ldots, v_k = v'$ of nodes with $(v_i, \varepsilon, v_{i+1}) \in E$ for $i \geq 0$.

In addition, two graphs in UnCAL are considered to be equal if they are bisimilar. Graphs $g_1 = (V_1, r_1, E_1)$ and $g_2 = (V_2, r_2, E_2)$ are defined to be *bisimilar* and written $g_1 \equiv g_2$ if there exists a relation (called *(extended-)bisimulation*) $S \subseteq V_1 \times V_2$ satisfying the following conditions: (1) $(r_1, r_2) \in S$, (2) for all $(v_1, v_2) \in S$ and $(\_, l, u_1) \in E_1^{\to}(v_1)$, there exists u_2 such that $(\_, l, u_2) \in E_2^{\to}(v_2)$ and $(u_1, u_2) \in S$, and (3) for all $(v_1, v_2) \in S$ and $(\_, l, u_2) \in E_2^{\to}(v_2)$, there exists u_1 such that $(\_, l, u_1) \in E_1^{\to}(v_1)$ and $(u_1, u_2) \in S$. Here $\_$ is the wild-card pattern indicating the existence of some element whose value is arbitrary. Intuitive understanding of bisimulation is that unfolding of cycles and duplication of equivalent subgraphs are not distinguished, and the unreachable part from the root is ignored. In particular, a rooted graph always has a (possibly infinite) tree bisimilar to it; it is obtained by infinitely unfolding all the cycles and sharings. Note that bisimulation is different from a weaker notion "set of all paths from root is equal".

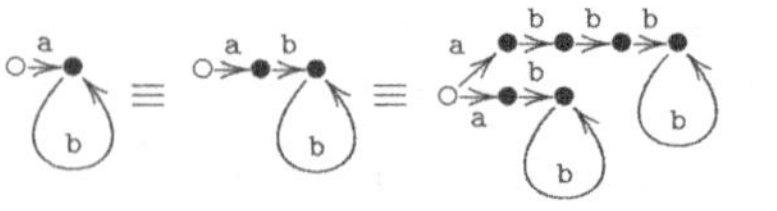

Benefits of exploiting bisimulation rather than isomorphism in the semantics are throughly discussed in [7] and not repeated here.

3.2 Core UnCAL

We define Core UnCAL, a subset of UnCAL graph algebra. The syntax is shown in Fig. 2. In addition, we syntactically restrict the uses of markers $\&_i$ (which intuitively indicate the positions where other graphs are later plugged in, as explained below). Markers do not occur globally nor directly in the argument expression τ in an expression $\mathbf{rec}(\cdots)(\tau)$; they can only appear in the body expressions of **rec**s.

The relationship between the Core UnCAL and the full UnCAL resembles that of the Core XPath [13] and XPath XML Query Language. That is, manipulation of the data values (comparison with data-values $\$l =$ `"John"` or $\$l_1 = \$l_2$ in the if-expressions, and operations on labels such as $\{$`"foo"`$ + \$l : \{\}\}$) are prohibited in Core UnCAL. Also, we have simplified the use of markers (they can only be used for connecting **rec** bodies), but this is just a syntactic difference. All the UnCAL expressions compiled from its front-end language UnQL satisfy the syntactic condition. Despite the restrictions, the full computational power of UnCAL is also available in Core UnCAL.

We hope the intuition of most of the constructs is clear. The node construction expression $\{l_1 : \tau_1, \ldots, l_n : \tau_n\}$ creates a fresh node v and edges $\{(v, l_1, r_1), \ldots, (v, l_n, r_n)\}$ where r_i is the root node of the graph obtained by evaluating the expression τ_i. Variable reference and conditional branch is defined as usual. The isEmpty Boolean expression returns true if and only if the passed node has no outgoing edge. The output marker expression $\&_i$ is used only in the body of **rec** expressions as explained below. The distinct feature of UnCAL is that basically all graph manipulations are expressed in terms of one unified and powerful construct called *structural recursion*, expressed by the $\mathbf{rec}(\ldots)$ expression.

3.2.1 Structural Recursion

Let us first explain the structural recursion in intuitive fashion by using a union operator $\cup$ for two graphs temporally for the sake of explanation. A function f on graphs is called a structural recursion if it is defined by the following equations [2]

$$
\begin{array}{lcl}
f(\{\}) & = & \{\} \\
f(\{\$l : \$g\}) & = & \omega(\$l, \$g) \odot f(\$g) \\
f(\{\$l_1 : \$g_1\} \cup \ldots \cup \{\$l_n : \$g_n\}) & & \\
 & = & f(\{\$l_1 : \$g_1\}) \cup \ldots \cup f(\{\$l_n : \$g_n\}) \ ,
\end{array}
$$

where $\odot$ is a given binary operator and the term $\omega(\$l, \$g)$ does not contain recursive calls to f. Different choices of $\odot$ define different functions. Since the first and the third equations are common in all structural recursions, we may omit them and simplify the above definition as:

$$\mathbf{sfun}\ f(\{\$l : \$g\}) = \omega(\$l, \$g) \odot f(\$g).$$

As a simple example, we may use the following structural recursion to replace all edges labeled `a` by `d` and delete the edges labeled `c` for an input graph.

$$
\begin{array}{rl}
\mathbf{sfun}\ \mathit{a2d\_xc}(\{\$l : \$g\}) = & \mathbf{if}\ \$l = \mathtt{a}\ \mathbf{then}\ \{\mathtt{d} : \mathit{a2d\_xc}(\$g)\} \\
 & \mathbf{else\ if}\ \$l = \mathtt{c}\ \mathbf{then}\ \mathit{a2d\_xc}(\$g) \\
 & \mathbf{else}\ \{\$l : \mathit{a2d\_xc}(\$g)\}
\end{array}
$$

The recursion $\mathbf{sfun}\ f\ \{\$l : \$g\} = \omega(\$l, \$g) \odot f(\$g)$ is represented in Core UnCAL by

$$\mathbf{rec}(\lambda(\$l, \$g).(\&_1 := \omega(\$l, \$g) \odot \&_1).$$

The marker $\&_1$ is used to indicate recursive calls (for mutual recursion, multiple markers $\&_1, \&_2, \ldots$ are used). For example, the structural recursive function $\mathit{a2d\_xc}$ shown in the above is represented

[2] Informally, the meaning of this definition can be considered to be a fixed point (not necessarily unique) over the graph, which is again defined by a set of equations using the three constructors $\{\}$, $:$, and $\cup$. For instance, the graph marked with $(*)$ in Section 3.1 can be considered to be the fixed point of the following equations: $G_{\mathrm{root}} = \{\mathtt{a} : G_1, \mathtt{b} : G_1\}, \mathtt{c} : \{\mathtt{e} : \{\}\}$ and $G_1 = \{\mathtt{d} : \{\}\}$.

τ	$::=$	$\{l : \tau, \ldots, l : \tau\}$	node with edges
	$\mid$	$\$g$	variable reference
	$\mid$	$\textbf{if } b \textbf{ then } \tau \textbf{ else } \tau$	conditional
	$\mid$	$\&_i$	output marker
	$\mid$	$\textbf{rec}(\lambda(\$l, \$g).\ \&_1 := \tau, \ldots, \&_n := \tau)(\tau)$	structural recursion
l	$::=$	$\$l$	label variable reference
	$\mid$	a	label ($\mathsf{a} \in \mathit{Label}_\varepsilon \cup \mathit{Data}$)
b	$::=$	$\$l = \mathsf{a}$	label comparison $\mathsf{a} \in \mathit{Label}$
	$\mid$	$\mathsf{isEmpty}(\$g)$	emptiness checking
	$\mid$	$b \mathsf{\ and\ } b \mid b \mathsf{\ or\ } b \mid \mathsf{not\ } b$	logical connectives.

Figure 2. Core UnCAL Language

v_f	$=$	$\{x, y, \ldots\}$	1st order variables
t_f	$::=$	$v_f \mid \mathsf{root}$	1st order terms
v_s	$=$	$\{X, Y, \ldots\}$	2nd order variables
t_s	$::=$	$v_s \mid t_s \cup t_s \mid t_s \cap t_s \mid \emptyset$	2nd order terms

$$\begin{array}{rcl} \varphi & ::= & \mathsf{true} \mid \mathsf{false} \\ & \mid & \neg\varphi \mid \varphi \vee \varphi \mid \varphi \wedge \varphi \mid \varphi \rightarrow \varphi \mid \varphi \leftrightarrow \varphi \\ & \mid & t_f = t_f \mid t_s = t_s \mid t_f \in t_s \mid t_s \subseteq t_s \\ & \mid & \exists^f v_f.\varphi \mid \forall^f v_f.\varphi \mid \exists^s v_s.\varphi \mid \forall^s v_s.\varphi \\ & \mid & \mathbf{vert}(t_f) \mid \mathbf{edge}_l(t_f, t_f, t_f) \end{array}$$

Figure 3. Syntax of Monadic Second-Order Logic

Schema	$::=$	*Decl* $\cdots$ *Decl*
Decl	$::=$	`type` *Name* $= \{$*Edge*$, \ldots,$ *Edge*$\}$
	$\mid$	`type` *Name* $= \{$*Edge*$, \ldots,$ *Edge*$, *\}$
Edge	$::=$	*Label* : *Type*
Type	$::=$	*Name* $\mid$ Data $\mid$ *Type* $\shortmid$ *Type*

Figure 4. Graph Schema Language $\mathcal{GS}$

by

$$\begin{array}{r} \textbf{rec}(\lambda(\$l, \$g).\&_1 := \textbf{if } \$l = \mathsf{a} \textbf{ then } \{\mathsf{d} : \&_1\} \\ \textbf{else if } \$l = \mathsf{c} \textbf{ then } \{\epsilon : \&_1\} \\ \textbf{else } \{\$l : \&_1\}). \end{array}$$

Let us show another example. Up to bisimulation, the following UnCAL expression $abab$

$$\textbf{rec}(\lambda(\$l, \$g).\ \&_1 := \{\mathsf{a} : \&_2\},\ \&_2 := \{\mathsf{b} : \&_1\})(\$db)$$

changes all edges of even distance from the root node to a, and odd distance edges to b. Here, $\$db$ is a designated variable referring to the input graph and $\tau(g)$ for any UnCAL expression τ should be read as "evaluate τ under the environment $\{\$db \mapsto g\}$".

Note that in our Core UnCAL, $\&_1$ always corresponds to the defined function.

As we have mentioned in the explanation of the graph data model, the semantics of UnCAL is carefully designed to treat bisimilar graphs equally. Indeed, it is proved that all UnCAL transformations are bisimulation-generic (Proposition 4 of [7]), that is, for any $g \equiv g'$, we have $f(g) \equiv f(g')$.

4. Graph Schema in MSO

We employ powerful monadic second-order logic (MSO) to describe a graph schema which specifies structural constrains of graphs. MSO is first-order logic extended with set quantification. It has exactly the power of expressing regular tree languages [24], being widely used as a schema language for XML and graphs.

The syntax of formulas of MSO over edge-labeled graph structure is shown in Fig. 3. We adopt a variant of MSO which is used to describe so called $(2, 2)$-*definable MSO transductions* of Courcelle [10], with customizations to adjust for our purpose, namely adding the root constant and making edge predicates $\mathbf{edge}_l$ inspect labels. For a graph $g = (V, r, E)$ and an environment Γ that maps first-order variables to $V \cup E$ and second-order variables to subsets of $V \cup E$, the entailment relation $g, \Gamma \vDash \varphi$ is defined. We present the definition of the two graph-specific primitives:

$$\begin{array}{ll} g, \Gamma \vDash \mathbf{vert}(t) & \text{if } \Gamma(t) \in V \\ g, \Gamma \vDash \mathbf{edge}_l(t_1, t_2, t_3) & \text{if } \Gamma(t_2) = (\Gamma(t_1), l, \Gamma(t_3)) \in E \end{array}$$

where Γ is extended as $\Gamma(\mathsf{root}) = r$. The other entailment relations follow the standard definition. We write $g \vDash \varphi$ when $g, \Gamma \vDash \varphi$ holds for the empty environment Γ. Note that UnCAL's semantics is defined up to bisimulation as explained in Section 3. MSO formulas that distinguish bisimilar graphs are not suitable for describing properties of UnCAL graphs. We say that a closed MSO formula φ is *bisimulation-generic*, if $g \equiv g'$ implies $g \vDash \varphi$ iff $g' \vDash \varphi$.

An MSO formula φ with one free variable can be regarded as a graph schema. For a graph $g = (V, r, E)$ and a given formula φ with one free variable x, we can say that g conforms to φ when $g, x \mapsto r \vDash \varphi$ holds. We define the bisimulation genericity of schemas in a way similar to closed formulas. We say that an MSO formula φ with one free variable x is bisimulation-generic if $g \equiv g'$ implies $g, x \mapsto v \vDash \varphi$ iff $g', x \mapsto v' \vDash \varphi$ for any nodes v in g and v' in g' where v and v' are bisimilar. In the rest of the paper, by schema we mean a bisimulation-generic MSO formula with one free variable.

Adopting MSO formulas as a front-end language of graph schemas may not be a good choice, however. In particular, it may be difficult to write correctly MSO formulas while making sure its bisimulation genericity. It would be better to provide a graph schema language which is inherently bisimulation-generic and which can be automatically translated into MSO formula. As an example, the schema language $\mathcal{GS}$ in Fig. 4 fulfills the requirements. Its concrete semantics and its translation to MSO formula can be found in [17]. For instance, the graph schema `Members` presented in Section 2 is written in $\mathcal{GS}$, and can be systematically translated into the following bisimulation-generic MSO formula:

$$
\begin{aligned}
&\exists^s X_{\texttt{Members}}.\ \exists^s X_{\texttt{Person}}.\ \exists^s X_{\texttt{MailOrPhone}}.\ \exists^s X_{\texttt{Mail}}.\ \exists^s X_{\texttt{Phone}}.\\
&\quad \mathsf{root} \in X_{\texttt{Members}} \land\\
&\quad \forall^f v.\mathbf{vert}(v) \rightarrow\\
&\qquad v \in X_{\texttt{Members}} \rightarrow \varphi_{\texttt{Members}}(v) \land\\
&\qquad v \in X_{\texttt{Person}} \rightarrow \varphi_{\texttt{Person}}(v) \land\\
&\qquad v \in X_{\texttt{MailOrPhone}} \rightarrow \varphi_{\texttt{MailOrPhone}}(v) \land\\
&\qquad v \in X_{\texttt{Mail}} \rightarrow \varphi_{\texttt{Mail}}(v) \land\\
&\qquad v \in X_{\texttt{Phone}} \rightarrow \varphi_{\texttt{Phone}}(v)
\end{aligned}
$$

where each formula $\phi_S(v)$ with a schema name S is defined using its declaration. For example, the formula $\varphi_{\texttt{Members}}(v)$ is given by

$$
\begin{aligned}
&\exists^s O.\ e\_out(v, O) \land\\
&\quad \forall^f e.\ e \in O \land \neg\mathbf{vert}(e) \rightarrow\\
&\qquad \exists^f x.\ \exists^f y.\ \mathbf{edge}_{\texttt{mem}}(x, e, y) \land y \in X_{\texttt{Person}}
\end{aligned}
$$

Here, $e\_out(v, O)$ is a predicate for checking if O is a set of non-ε edges reachable from v by traversing only ε-edges, which is implemented in a standard technique for representing transitive closures in MSO.

Note that $\mathcal{GS}$ is just an example of a front-end schema language. The results in the following sections are not specific to $\mathcal{GS}$. It is applicable to any schemas representable in MSO. For instance, in the graph schema language KM3 [19] commonly used in model-driven software development, structural constraints are expressed in terms of classes, fields, and inheritance, which just fit in this category.

5. Core UnCAL in MSO

In our verification method, not only schemas but also transformations are represented by MSO. Then, we combine the MSO formulas for transformations with those for schemas into a single MSO formula, whose validity is equivalent to the correctness of the transformation with respect to the schemas.

The difficulty here is how to map the structural recursion of UnCAL that iteratively walks through graphs to an MSO formula that declaratively represents a relationship between input and output graphs. This problem is addressed by exploiting an alternative semantics called *bulk semantics* of UnCAL [7], which more fits to logical formulation, and known to be equivalent to the usual recursive semantics.

Another challenge comes from the fact that MSO-definable transduction intentionally has been restricted its expressiveness to keep many important properties decidable. Not all Core UnCAL expressions can be translated into such a restricted class of MSO-definable transductions for the reason mentioned later. To avoid the problem and give a terminating decision procedure, we ask programmers to add several annotations on UnCAL, which provides schema information on intermediate result graphs. The annotations should be put on certain subexpressions.

This section first introduces the formalism to specify transformations in terms of MSO formula, and then shows how such formulas can be constructed from Core UnCAL.

5.1 MSO-Definable Graph Transduction

We basically adopt the formalism in [10] called *MSO-definable transduction* for specifying graph transformations in MSO. We, however, slightly generalize the formalism to what we call *MSO-definable transduction system* in order to give a simpler translation from UnCAL and an easier treatment of annotations.

Definition 1. *MSO-definable transduction system* is a tuple $\mathcal{M} = (I, S, D_{\text{v}}, D_{\text{e}})$ where I is a finite set called the set of *copy-ids*, S a nonempty subset of I called the *input set*, D_{v} a partial mapping that maps each $i \in I \setminus S$ to an *extended*-formula $\mathbf{vert}_i(y)$, and D_{e} a partial mapping that maps each $(l, i, j, k) \in \mathit{Label}_\varepsilon \times (I^3 \setminus S^3)$ to an extended-formula $\mathbf{edge}_{l,i,j,k}(x, y, z)$. Here, extended-formula is an MSO formula that has $\mathbf{vert}_i(x)$ and $\mathbf{edge}_{l,i,j,k}(x, y, z)$ for $i, j, k \in I$ and $l \in \mathit{Label}_\varepsilon$ as primitives, instead of $\mathbf{vert}(x)$ and $\mathbf{edge}_l(x, y, z)$.

In MSO-definable transductions, output graphs are considered to be constructed by first generating $|I \setminus S|$ copies of the input graph (hence the name *copy-id* is given for the set I), and then reorganizing the edge/vert relations among them according to the formulas in D_{v} and D_{e}. The essential difference of MSO-definable transduction systems as above from the original definition in [10] is that each $\mathbf{edge}_{l,i,j,k}$ and $\mathbf{vert}_i$ can be defined in terms of other $\mathbf{edge}_{l',i',j',k'}$ and $\mathbf{vert}_{i'}$. In the original version, they are only allowed to be defined in terms of the original input. This difference does not change their expressiveness of graph transductions; to obtain the original version from our system we simply expand the definitions of $\mathbf{edge}_{l',i',j',k'}$ and $\mathbf{vert}_{i'}$ inline.

We only consider *acyclic* systems. That is, there must be a total order on I such that in the definition of formulas $\mathbf{vert}_i$ and $\mathbf{edge}_{l,i,j,k}$, all the occurrences of elements of I must be strictly smaller than i and j. We often write $\mathbf{edge}_{l,i,j,k}(x, y, z) := \varphi$ to mean $D_{\text{e}}(l, i, j, k) = \varphi$, and write similarly of $\mathbf{vert}_i$.

Let us explain the idea by the following example with $I = \{0, 1, 2\}$ and $S = \{0\}$:

$$
\begin{aligned}
\mathbf{edge}_{\text{buz},2,2,2}(x, y, z) &:= \mathbf{edge}_{\text{bar},1,1,1}(x, y, z)\\
\mathbf{edge}_{\text{bar},1,1,1}(x, y, z) &:= \mathbf{edge}_{\text{foo},0,0,0}(x, y, z)\\
\mathbf{vert}_2(y) &:= \mathbf{vert}_1(y)\\
\mathbf{vert}_1(y) &:= \mathbf{vert}_0(y)
\end{aligned}
$$

The input set S denotes the set of copy-ids for input graphs of the transformation defined by this system. Thus, the formula $\mathbf{edge}_{\text{foo},0,0,0}(x, y, z)$ is read as "in the input graph, x, y, and z form an edge labeled `foo`". Intuitively speaking, in an MSO-definable transduction system, output graphs are thought to be created by copy-and-edit from the input graphs. In the above example, $|I \setminus S| = 2$ copies of the input nodes and edges are created by the system, and are reorganized to form the output graph, guided by the supplied formulas. For instance, the 1st copies of x, y, and z form a `bar` edge if and only if they are a `foo` edge in the input. The 2nd copies of them form a `buz` edge if their 1st copies form a `bar` edge, which happens only when they form a `foo` edge in the original input. In other cases, no edge is drawn. After all, if we regard $\{2\} \subseteq I$ as the output graph of this system, the transformation defined by the system is what renames all the edges `foo` to `buz` and eliminates all the other edges. If we regard $\{1\}$ as the output, it defines the transformation renaming `foo` to `bar` and eliminating others.

In general, S may not be a singleton. In such a case, the system represents a transformation taking multiple inputs $g_1, g_2, \ldots, g_{|S|}$. Even in the case, we can regard them as a single-input transformation, by assuming a virtual input graph $g = \{\texttt{elem} : g_1, \texttt{next} : \{\texttt{elem} : g_2, \texttt{next} : \cdots\}\}$ and considering each g_i as one of the output graphs from the transduction system (each g_i can be extracted by a simple subgraph extraction, and it can easily be written in a set of MSO-formulas). Hence, in the following discussion in this subsection we assume a single input $S = \{s\}$.

Formally, for a nonempty set $J \subset I$, copy-id $\rho \in J$, and graph $g = (V, r, E)$, the transduction system defines an output graph $g_{J,\rho} = (V', r'E')$ by

$$
\begin{array}{rcl}
q & ::= & \tau :: \varphi \\
\tau & ::= & \{l : \tau, \ldots, l : \tau\} \\
 & | & \textbf{if } b \textbf{ then } \tau \textbf{ else } \tau \\
 & | & \&_i \\
 & | & \textbf{rec}(\lambda(\$l, \$g).\ \&_1 :: \varphi := \tau, \ldots, \&_n :: \varphi := \tau)(\tau) \\
 & | & \$g :: \varphi
\end{array}
$$

Figure 5. Type Annotated Core UnCAL

- $V' = \{(v, i) \in (V \cup E) \times J \mid g, \{y \mapsto v\} \models \mathbf{vert}'_i(y)\}$,
- $E' = \{((v,i),(w,j),(u,m)) \in ((V \cup E) \times J)^3 \mid g, \{x \mapsto v, y \mapsto w, z \mapsto u\} \models \mathbf{edge}'_{l,i,j,m}(x,y,z)\}$, and
- $r' = (r, \rho)$

where $\mathbf{vert}'_i(y)$ is the formula obtained by recursively replacing $\mathbf{vert}_i(y)$ with $D_v(i)$ (if $D_v(i)$ is not defined, it is replaced with $\mathbf{vert}(y)$ when $i = s$ and otherwise with false) and $\mathbf{edge}_{l,i,j,k}(x,y,z)$ with $D_e(l,i,j,k)$ (if $D_e(l,i,j,k)$ is not defined, it is replaced with $\mathbf{edge}_l(x,y,z)$ when $i = j = k = s$ and otherwise with false).

The following lemma is important in MSO-definable transduction systems. The inverse image of an MSO-definable set of graphs under an MSO-definable transduction system is MSO-definable.

Lemma 1 ([10], Prop. 3.2)**.** *Let $\mathcal{M} = (I, \{s\}, D_v, D_e)$ be an MSO-definable transduction system, $J \subset I$, $\rho \in J$, and a closed MSO formula φ. Then there exists an MSO formula $\mathrm{inv}(\mathcal{M}, J, \rho, \varphi)$ such that, for any graph g, we have $g \models \mathrm{inv}(\mathcal{M}, J, \rho, \varphi)$ if and only if $g_{J,\rho} \models \varphi$.*

The lemma enables us to convert MSO formulas on output graphs into that on input graphs. Using this conversion, the verification problem that tests the assertion "for any input graph g, if it conforms to the input schema (i.e, $g \models \varphi_{\mathrm{IN}}$), then $g_{J,\rho} \models \varphi_{\mathrm{OUT}}$" can be restated as the validity of a single formula "$\varphi_{\mathrm{IN}} \to \mathrm{inv}(\mathcal{M}, J, \rho, \varphi_{\mathrm{OUT}})$" on input graphs.

One limitation of MSO-definable transduction systems is that by definition it can represent only *linear-size increase* transformations; the size $|g_{J,\rho}|$ of the nodes in the output graphs is linearly bounded by the input size $|J||g|$. In UnCAL, superlinear growth is caused only by using nested-recursions. This is exactly the reason why our verifier, as explained later, requires annotation for such cases.

5.2 Adding Annotations to Core UnCAL

Annotations are supposed to be supplied by programmers in the syntax shown in Figure 5, which we call the type annotated Core UnCAL. The nonterminal q represents the whole program. Here the programmer can specify the schema for the output database (i.e., the result of the evaluation of the whole UnCAL expression τ). In the **rec** expression, the occurrence of variables $\$g$ and the body expressions of the recursion accept the schema annotation. In conventional programming languages, this means that every function is having type annotation on its parameters and return values.

Intuitively, the annotation $\$g :: \varphi$ on parameters works for the verifier in two ways. (1) The graph pointed by the node bound to $\$g$ must conform to the schema φ: the verifier is obliged to verify the conformance. (2) In the body of the rec expression, the use of graph $\$g$ can be assumed to be bound to a node pointing to an arbitrary graph satisfying φ: the verifier can use this assumption. The annotations $\&_i :: \varphi := \tau$ on the markers also have two roles. One is to tell that the verifier must make sure that the result of evaluating this expression must conform to the schema φ. Another is to tell the verifier that the result of evaluating the whole **rec**(...) expression can be approximated as an arbitrary graph that is constructed as the union of the graphs conforming to φ_1, where φ_1 is the supplied schema annotation to the first body expression $\&_1$.

5.3 Type Annotated Core UnCAL to MSO

From now on, we consider a fixed annotated Core UnCAL program q and explain how to translate it to MSO. For the finite copy-id set I in the definition of MSO-definable transduction system, we use the set Cid of elements generated by the following BNF

$$Cid ::= CodePos \mid \langle Cid, CodePos, \mathbb{N}\rangle$$

where $CodePos$ is a set of unique identifiers assigned to each subexpression of q, and $\mathbb{N}$ is the set of natural numbers. The angle brackets $\langle\rangle$ just denote tupling. Although the set Cid is infinite, in the following construction we only use finite portion of them. More specifically, the nesting depth of $\langle\rangle$s are at most the nesting depth of recursions in the given UnCAL transformation, and the natural numbers $\mathbb{N}$ used is at most $\max(2, 2n, 2m)$ where n is the number of markers and m the maximum number of outgoing edges of the node-construction expression in the transformation.

We inductively define a procedure ft2mso that converts a type annotated Core UnCAL expression to a set of MSO formulas. It has the following form:

$$\mathrm{ft2mso}(c, \Gamma, \varphi)(\tau^p) = (\mathcal{M}, J, \rho, O, A).$$

It takes four parameters (three of them are to hold contextual information used during the conversion, and the last one is the UnCAL expression) and returns a tuple consisting of five components. The fourth parameter τ^p, which is separately parenthesized for emphasizing its special position, denotes the UnCAL expression to be converted. The superscript ^{p} denotes the code-position of the subexpression. The first parameter c is a triple (c_v, c_e, c_u) of copy-ids denoting the ids of the current edge. The meaning of this parameter should become clear when we reach to the formal definition of ft2mso that deals with **rec** expressions. The second parameter Γ is the mapping from variable names to the copy-id of the graph denoted by the variable. The third parameter φ is an MSO formula representing the condition for the current subexpression to be executed; in other words, it is a conjunction of the condition of **if** expressions enclosing the current expression.

Then it computes five components simultaneously. The first component $\mathcal{M}$ is an MSO-definable transduction system that represents the UnCAL transformation τ. The second J and the third ρ components are to denote the copy-ids of the output graph obtained by evaluating τ. The fourth O and the fifth A components are sets of MSO formulas, which represent the conditions that are *O*bligations to satisfy and that can be *A*ssumed, respectively. They correspond to the two roles of annotations as explained before. They are stored in the form of triple (J, ρ, ψ) meaning that the output graph $g_{J,\rho}$ must (or can be assumed to) satisfy ψ.

Let us show a very simple example of the translation. Consider the type-annotated UnCAL expression $\{\texttt{foo} : \$db :: \varphi_1\} :: \varphi_0$ that simply prepends an edge labeled `foo` to the input graph $\$db$. Let the code positions of the subexpressions be p, q, and r, i.e.,

$$(\{\texttt{foo} : (\$db :: \varphi_1)^r\}^q :: \varphi_0)^p.$$

Translation of the expression will yield the following MSO-definable transduction system

$$
\begin{aligned}
\mathcal{M} = (I &= \{\langle c,q,0\rangle, \langle c,q,1\rangle, \langle c,r,0\rangle, \langle c,r,1\rangle, r\}, \\
S &= \{r\}, \\
D_v &= \{\ \mathbf{vert}_{\langle c,q,0\rangle}(y) := (y = \mathsf{root}) \\
&\qquad \mathbf{vert}_{\langle c,r,0\rangle}(y) := (y = \mathsf{root})\ \}, \\
D_e &= \{\ \mathbf{edge}_{\texttt{foo},\langle c,q,0\rangle,\langle c,q,1\rangle,\langle c,r,0\rangle}(x,y,z) := \psi \\
&\qquad \mathbf{edge}_{\varepsilon,\langle c,r,0\rangle,\langle c,r,1\rangle,r}(x,y,z) := \psi\ \}\ )
\end{aligned}
$$

where $\psi \equiv \exists^f v,e,u.(x{=}e \wedge y{=}e \wedge z{=}e \wedge e{=}\mathsf{root})$ (which is equivalent to $x = y = z = \mathsf{root}$) and $c = \langle p, p, 1\rangle$. The system involves five copy-ids, and one of them, r, represents its input graph. In addition to the original input graphs, it adds to nodes $\langle c, q, 0\rangle$-th and $\langle c, r, 0\rangle$-th copies of the root node, and two edges labeled `foo` and ε (addition of ε-edge is a technical subtlety which is not important).

In addition to the system, the translation gathers the obligation and assumption formulas as follows:

$$O = \{\ (\{\langle c,q,0\rangle, \langle c,q,1\rangle, \langle c,r,0\rangle, \langle c,r,1\rangle, r\}, \langle c,q,0\rangle, \varphi_0[\mathsf{root}])\ \}.$$
$$A = \{\ (\{r\}, r, \varphi_1[\mathsf{root}])\ \}.$$

That is, the verifier must make sure that the output graph conforms to the schema φ_0, under the assumption that the input graph satisfies φ_1. Hence, the correctness of the transformation with respect to annotations are equivalent to the validity of the following MSO formula.

$$\mathrm{inv}(\mathcal{M}, \{r\}, r, \varphi_1[\mathsf{root}]) \rightarrow \mathrm{inv}(\mathcal{M}, I, \langle c, q, 0\rangle, \varphi_0[\mathsf{root}])$$

The testing procedure of this kind of MSO formula is discussed in Section 6.

Whole Program The whole program of type annotated UnCAL consists of an expression τ and a schema annotation :: φ. It is translated as follows; it first translates the body expression into the corresponding transduction system, and adds an obligation formula stating that the output graph must conform to φ.

$$\begin{aligned} &\mathrm{ft2mso}(\_,\_,\_)((\tau :: \varphi)^p) = (\mathcal{M}, J, \rho, O_0 \cup O, A)\\ &\quad \mathbf{where}(\mathcal{M}, J, \rho, O, A) = \mathrm{ft2mso}(c, \{\$db \mapsto p\}, e{=}\mathsf{root})(\tau)\\ &\qquad\qquad O_0 = \{(J, \rho, \varphi[\mathsf{root}])\}\\ &\qquad\qquad c = (\langle p,p,0\rangle, \langle p,p,1\rangle, \langle p,p,2\rangle) \end{aligned}$$

The first argument c to the recursive call of ft2mso is meant to be a three unique copy-ids that will not conflict with copy-ids used in the other place during translation (conflict avoidance is the reason why we include the code-position of the current expression in copy-ids). The second argument assigns a copy-id to the designated variable $\$db$ denoting the input graph. The third argument is a formula containing possibly three free variables v, e, and u that encodes the condition that the UnCAL expression is executed. In this case, we specify $e{=}\mathsf{root}$ to mean we start evaluation from the root node.

Theorem 1. *Let $q = \tau :: \varphi$ be a type annotated UnCAL program and $(\mathcal{M}, \_, \_, O, A) = \mathrm{ft2mso}(q)$, then $\bigwedge_{\bar{a}\in A} \mathrm{inv}(\mathcal{M}, \bar{a}) \rightarrow \bigwedge_{\bar{o}\in O} \mathrm{inv}(\mathcal{M}, \bar{o})$ is valid if and only if q never violates the schema annotation. In particular, if the formula is valid, then for any input graph, the output graph conforms to φ.*

In the remaining subsections, we give the inductive construction of the translation ft2mso in detail for each kind of UnCAL expression. Although the proof is omitted for brevity, the correctness of the construction can be shown by straightforward induction on the structure of expression, showing that it exactly represents the *bulk semantics* of UnCAL [7].

Node Construction Let us examine the rules for subexpressions one by one. The first case is the node-construction. As an exercise, let us first explain the case of node creation $\{l_1 : \tau_1\}$ with only one outgoing edge.

$$\begin{aligned} &\mathrm{ft2mso}(c, \Gamma, \varphi)(\{l_1 : \tau_1\}^p) =\\ &\quad (\ \mathcal{M}_1[(l_1, \langle c_e, p, 0\rangle\ e, \langle c_e, p, 1\rangle\ e, \rho_1\ e) \mapsto \varphi],\\ &\quad\ \ J_1 \cup \{\langle c_e, p, 0\rangle, \langle c_e, p, 1\rangle\}, \quad \langle c_e, p, 0\rangle,\\ &\quad\ \ O_1, \quad A_1\ )\\ &\mathbf{where}\ (\mathcal{M}_1, J_1, \rho_1, O_1, A_1) = \mathrm{ft2mso}(c, \Gamma, \varphi)(\tau_1) \end{aligned}$$

Since this node construction expression itself does not have any schema annotation, it does not add any obligation or assumption. Hence, the O_1 and A_1 components are the same as those of the subexpression τ_1.

The first three components describe edges and nodes generated by the current expression. The notation $\mathcal{M}[(l, i\ \alpha, j\ \beta, k\ \gamma) \mapsto \varphi]$ for $\alpha, \beta, \gamma \in \{v, e, u, \mathsf{root}\}$ is a short hand for defining a new MSO-definable transduction system (I', J, D'_v, D'_e) from $\mathcal{M} = (I, J, D_v, D_e)$ by $I' = I \cup \{i, j\}$, $D'_v = D_v \cup \{i \mapsto \exists^f xz.\psi, k \mapsto \exists^f xz.\psi\}$, and $D'_e = D_e \cup \{l, i, j, k \mapsto \psi\}$ where ψ is $\exists^f v,e,u.(x{=}\alpha \wedge y{=}\beta \wedge z{=}\gamma \wedge \varphi)$. It should be read as "$i$-th copy of α, j-th copy of β, and k-th copy of γ forms an edge in the output graph of this expression when φ holds" as the picture below:

$$(\langle c_e, p, 0\rangle\text{-th copy of } e) \xrightarrow[\langle c_e,p,1\rangle\text{-th copy of } e]{l_1} \rho\text{-th copy of } e$$

For example, in the example in Section 2, an edge labeled `pair` will be drawn for each edge labeled `friend` in the input graph. The expression $\{$`pair` : ...$\}$ generating the `pair` edge is translated by the ft2mso procedure with the parameter $\varphi = \mathbf{edge}_{\mathtt{friend}, c_v, c_e, c_u}(v, e, u)$. Then the transduction system has a definition of an edge as follows:

$$\begin{aligned} &\mathbf{edge}_{\mathtt{pair}, \langle c_e,p,0\rangle, \langle c_e,p,1\rangle, \rho_1}(x, y, z) :=\\ &\qquad \exists^1 v,e,u.(x{=}e \wedge y{=}e \wedge z{=}e \wedge \mathbf{edge}_{\mathtt{friend}, c_v, c_e, c_u}(v, e, u)). \end{aligned}$$

That is, "an edge (which is the $\langle c_e, p, 1\rangle$-th copy of e) of label pair is drawn from the $\langle c_e, p, 0\rangle$-th copy of e to the ρ_1-th copy of e, only when c-th copy of e is an edge labeled `friend`".

The actual definition of ft2mso is generalized for the case of n outgoing edges, by simply taking the union of the above construction:

$$\begin{aligned} &\mathrm{ft2mso}(c, \Gamma, \varphi)(\{l_1 : \tau_1, \ldots, l_n : \tau_n\}^p) =\\ &\qquad (\ \bigcup_{1\le i\le n} \mathcal{M}_i[(l_i, \langle c_e, p, 0\rangle\ e, \langle c_e, p, i\rangle\ e, \rho_i\ e) \mapsto \varphi],\\ &\qquad\ \ \bigcup_{1\le i\le n} (J_i \cup \{\langle c_e, p, 0\rangle, \langle c_e, p, i\rangle\}), \quad \langle c, p, 0\rangle,\\ &\qquad\ \ \bigcup_{1\le i\le n} O_i, \quad \bigcup_{1\le i\le n} A_i, \ )\\ &\quad \mathbf{where}\ (\mathcal{M}_i, J_i, \rho_i, O_i, A_i) = \mathrm{ft2mso}(c, \Gamma, \varphi)(\tau_i)\\ &\qquad\qquad \text{for each } 1 \le i \le n. \end{aligned}$$

Here, the union of transduction systems $(I, S, D_v, D_e) \cup (I', S', D'_v, D'_e)$ is defined as $(I \cup I', S \cup S', i \mapsto D_v(i) \vee D'_v(i), (l, i, j, k) \mapsto D_e(l, i, j, k) \vee D'_e(l, i, j, k))$.

If Expression In fact, **if** expression is quite similar to usual node construction $\{l_1 : \tau_1\}$; it just draws an ϵ-edge pointing to the **then** branch or **else** branch, depending on whether the condition holds or not.

$$\begin{aligned} &\mathrm{ft2mso}(c, \Gamma, \varphi)((\mathbf{if}\ b\ \mathbf{then}\ \tau_1\ \mathbf{else}\ \tau_2)^p) =\\ &\qquad (\ \mathcal{M}_1[(\epsilon, \langle c_e, p, 0\rangle\ e, \langle c_e, p, 1\rangle\ e, \rho_1\ e) \mapsto \varphi \wedge \varphi_b]\\ &\qquad\ \ \cup \mathcal{M}_2[(\epsilon, \langle c_e, p, 0\rangle\ e, \langle c_e, p, 2\rangle\ e, \rho_2\ e) \mapsto \varphi \wedge \neg\varphi_b],\\ &\qquad\ \ J_1 \cup J_2 \cup \{\langle c_e, p, 0\rangle, \langle c_e, p, 1\rangle, \langle c_e, p, 2\rangle\}, \quad \langle c_e, p, 0\rangle,\\ &\qquad\ \ O_1 \cup O_2, \quad A_1 \cup A_2\ \ )\\ &\mathbf{where}\ (\mathcal{M}_1, J_1, \rho_1, O_1, A_1) = \mathrm{ft2mso}(c, \Gamma, \varphi \wedge \varphi_b)(\tau_1)\\ &\qquad (\mathcal{M}_2, J_2, \rho_2, O_2, A_2) = \mathrm{ft2mso}(c, \Gamma, \varphi \wedge \neg\varphi_b)(\tau_2)\\ &\qquad \varphi_b = \mathrm{b2mso}(b) \end{aligned}$$

The procedure b2mso is to convert boolean condition to MSO formula in a straightforward manner. E.g., the condition $\$l = \mathbf{a}$ is converted to $\mathbf{edge}_{\mathtt{a}, c_v, c_e, c_u}(v, e, u)$. Only one complexity is in the isEmpty predicate of Core UnCAL, but it can be dealt with by the standard technique to represent transitive closure in MSO.) One thing that must be noted here is that we assume all label variables $\$l$ are always the innermost-scope variable. This assumption is satisfied by a simple program transformation; since we are now considering the case where the set $Label_\epsilon$ of labels is finite, we can eliminate nested-occurrence of $\$l$'s by first inserting an exhaustive branching **if** $\$l$ = a ⋯ **else if** $\$l$ = b **else** ⋯ to the scope where the variable $\$l$ is introduced and then instantiate $\$l$ to the concrete label constant in each body of the branching. In fact, this transformation eliminates expressions of the form $\{\$l : \tau\}$ (which we did not consider in the definition of ft2mso above), too.

Marker In type annotated UnCAL, markers are always annotated with schema in the top-level of **rec** expression. So, we assign copy-ids for markers during processing **rec** expression, and store it to the environment Γ. At the occurrence site of a marker as an expression our MSO-encoding simply generates an ε-edge and connect to the root node of the graph whose copy-id is stored in Γ. The reason we add ε-edge here is a technical and non-essential reason; we want to make every output nodes/edges copies of input edges e (not root), which make implementation and definition slightly simpler.

$$\begin{aligned}&\mathrm{ft2mso}(c,\Gamma,\varphi)(\&_i{}^p) = \\ &\quad(\ \mathcal{M}_p[(\epsilon, \langle c_e, p, 0\rangle\ e, \langle c_e, p, 1\rangle\ e, \Gamma(\&_i)\ \mathsf{root}) \mapsto \varphi], \\ &\quad\ \{\langle c_e,p,0\rangle, \langle c_e,p,1\rangle, \Gamma(\&_i)\}, \langle c_e,p,0\rangle, \{\}, \{\})\end{aligned}$$

The transduction system $\mathcal{M}_p = (\{p\}, \{p\}, \emptyset, \emptyset)$ is the empty system with the copy-id of input graphs being p.

Variable Reference (Outer Scope) There are two types of occurrences of variables in expression. One is the innermost-scope variable, which is the variable that is bound in the innermost enclosing **rec** expressions, like $\$g$ in $\mathbf{rec}(\lambda(\$l,\$g).\&_1 := \$g)$. Another case is the outer-scope variables, which are bound in the outer **rec** recursion, like $\$g_1$ in $\mathbf{rec}(\lambda(\$l_1,\$g_1).\&_1 := \mathbf{rec}(\lambda(\$l_2,\$g_2).\&_1 := \$g_1))$. The latter case (and the designated input variable $\$db$) is treated similarly as markers. That is, we simply draw an ε-edge to the root of the graph.

$$\begin{aligned}&\mathrm{ft2mso}(c,\Gamma,\varphi)(\$g :: \psi^p) = \\ &\quad(\ \mathcal{M}_p[(\varepsilon, \langle c_e, p, 0\rangle\ e, \langle c_e, p, 1\rangle\ e, \Gamma(\$g)\ \mathsf{root}) \mapsto \varphi], \\ &\quad\ \{\langle c_e,p,0\rangle, \langle c_e,p,1\rangle, \Gamma(\$g)\},\quad \langle c_e,p,0\rangle, \\ &\quad\ \{\},\quad \{\ (\{\Gamma(\$g)\}, \Gamma(\$g), \psi[\mathsf{root}])\ \}\quad)\end{aligned}$$

We also add assumption formulas here. Obligation formulas are generated in outside of this expression.

Variable Reference (Innermost Scope) Difference between variables and markers is that the type of variable can be context-dependent. Consider the expression **if** $\$l$ = contact **then** $\$g :: \psi_1$ **else** $\{\$l : \$g :: \psi_2\}$. To generate obligations for the annotation $:: \psi_1$, it must take into account that the expression is under the branching by **if**. In this case, $\$g$ must conform to ψ_1 only when $\$l$ = contact. To incorporate the information, we use the third parameter φ of ft2mso containing the conditions of translated **if** branches.

$$\begin{aligned}&\mathrm{ft2mso}(c,\Gamma,\varphi)(\$g :: \psi^p) = \\ &\quad(\ \mathcal{M}_p[(\varepsilon, \langle c_e, p, 0\rangle\ e, \langle c_e, p, 1\rangle\ e, \Gamma(\$g)\ \mathsf{root}) \mapsto \varphi], \\ &\quad\ \{\langle c_e,p,0\rangle, \langle c_e,p,1\rangle, \Gamma(\$g)\},\quad \langle c_e,p,0\rangle, \\ &\quad\ \{\ (J_0, c_u, \forall^f v, e, u.\ (\varphi \rightarrow \psi[u]))\ \}, \\ &\quad\ \{\ (\{\Gamma(\$g)\}, \Gamma(\$g), \psi[\mathsf{root}])\ \}\quad)\end{aligned}$$

where J_0 is the set of copy-ids of the argument graph of the **rec** expression introduced the variable $\$g$, which is computed while ft2mso processes the **rec** expression.

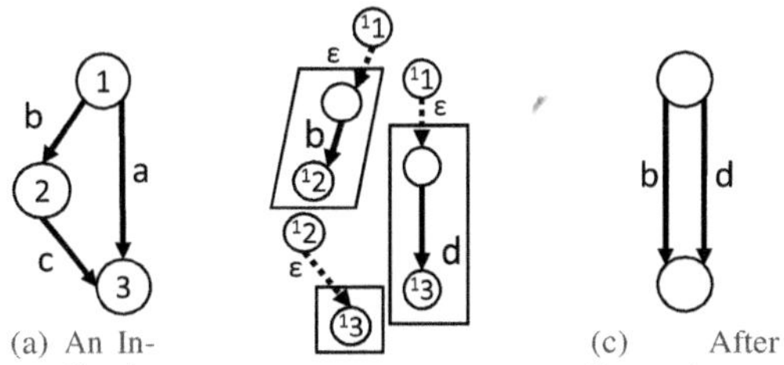

(a) An Input Graph (b) Before Removing ε-edges (c) After Removing ε-edges

Figure 6. Bulk Semantics of Structural Recursion in UnCAL

Structural Recursion The rule for recursion is the most complicated one. The difficulty here is how to map the structural recursion of UnCAL that iteratively walks through graphs to an MSO formula that declaratively represents a relationship between input and output graphs. This problem is addressed by exploiting an alternative semantics called *bulk semantics* [7] of UnCAL, which more fits to logical formulation, and known to be equivalent to the usual recursive semantics.

In bulk semantics, the structural recursion $\mathbf{rec}(\lambda(\$l,\$g).\ \&_1 := \tau_1, \ldots, \&_n := \tau_n)(\tau_0)$ is evaluated as follows: first evaluate τ_0 and obtain the argument graph, and then, for every non-ε edge (v,l,u) of it, evaluate each τ_i separately under the environment $\{\$l \mapsto l, \$g \mapsto u\}$. After that, the output marker expression $\&_j$ (if any) in τ_i is connected to the root nodes of the result graphs of the evaluation of τ_j at the edges having u as their source node. Formally, the expression $\mathbf{rec}(\lambda(\$l,\$g).\ \&_1 := \tau_1, \ldots, \&_n := \tau_n)(\tau_0)$ is evaluated as follows. First, evaluate τ_0 and obtain a graph $g_0 = (V, r, E)$. Then, generate n new nodes from ${}^1v$ to ${}^nv$ for each node $v \in V$, each corresponding to the marker $\&_i$. Then for each edge $p = (v,l,u)$ starting from v, we evaluate each body expression τ_i to obtain a graph $g_{p,i}$. If $l = \varepsilon$, we let $g_{p,i} = (\{{}^iv, {}^iu\}, {}^iv, \{({}^iv, \varepsilon, {}^iu)\})$, i.e., ε-edges are always kept unchanged. If $l \neq \varepsilon$, evaluate τ_i under the environment $\{\$l \mapsto l, \$g \mapsto u, \&_1 \mapsto {}^1u, \ldots, \&_n \mapsto {}^nu\}$ and get $g'_{p,i} = (V', r', E')$. Then we let $g_{p,i} = (V_{p,i}, r_{p,i}, E_{p,i}) = (V' \cup \{{}^iv\}, {}^iv, E' \cup \{({}^iv, \varepsilon, r')\})$, making ${}^iv$ the new root node[3]. The result graph g of the evaluation of the whole expression is the simple aggregation $g = (\bigcup_{p,i} V_{p,i}, {}^1r, \bigcup_{p,i} E_{p,i})$ of all the graphs $g_{p,i}$, making the $\&_1$ output at the root node in the input graph as the root node of the output.

The behavior is illustrated in Fig. 6. Recall the structural recursion $a2d\_xc$ defined in Sec. 3.2. Applying it to the input graph in Fig. 6(a) yields the graph in Fig. 6(b). The body of the recursion is applied to each of the three edges in the input graph and we obtain three graphs illustrated in the boxes. Then, new root nodes ${}^iv$ are added. Although depicted separately, the two ${}^1i$ nodes for each i denotes the same node and hence glued together. If we eliminate all ε-edges, we obtain a standard graph in Fig. 6(c).

Compared to the recursive interpretation, this bulk semantics rather naturally translates to our logic-based formulation as follows. For each edge (represented by $c' \in J_0 \times J_0 \times J_0$), we evaluate

[3] This ε-edge introduction will be implicit in the example and depicted as if we unified r' and ${}^iv$.

bodies e' and glue them together by simply taking union.

$$\begin{aligned}
&\text{ft2mso}(c,\Gamma,\varphi)(\\
&\quad \mathbf{rec}(\lambda(\$l,\$g :: \varphi_0).\&_1 :: \varphi_1 := \tau_1,\ldots,\&_n :: \varphi_n := \tau_n)(\tau_0)^p\\
&) =\\
&\qquad (\ \mathcal{M}_p \cup \mathcal{M}_0 \cup \bigcup_{i,c'} \mathcal{M}_i^{c'},\quad \{p\},\quad p,\\
&\qquad\quad O_\$ \cup \bigcup_{1\le i\le n} O_{\&_i} \cup O_0 \cup \bigcup_{i,c'} O_i^{c'},\\
&\qquad\quad A_p \cup A_0 \cup \bigcup_{i,c'} A_i^{c'}\quad)\\
&\mathbf{where}(\mathcal{M}_0, J_0, \rho_0, O_0, A_0) = \text{ft2mso}(c,\Gamma,\varphi)(\tau_0)\\
&\qquad (\mathcal{M}_i^{c'}, J_i^{c'}, \rho_i^{c'}, O_i^{c'}, A_i^{c'}) = \text{ft2mso}(c',\\
&\qquad\qquad \Gamma[\$g \mapsto \langle c_e, p, 0\rangle, \&_1 \mapsto \langle c_e, p, 1\rangle,\\
&\qquad\qquad\quad \ldots \&_n \mapsto \langle c_e, p, n\rangle], \mathsf{true})(\tau_i)\\
&\qquad\qquad \text{for each } 1 \le i \le n, c' \in J_0 \times J_0 \times J_0\\
&\qquad O_\$ = \{\ (J_0, c_u, \forall^f v, e, u.\ (\varphi \to \varphi_0[u]))\ |\\
&\qquad\qquad\quad \$g' :: \psi \text{ occurs in some } \tau_i \text{ for the}\\
&\qquad\qquad\quad \text{current innermost scope variable } \$g'\ \}\\
&\qquad O_{\&_i} = \{\ (J_i^{c'}, \rho_i^{c'}, \varphi_i[\mathsf{root}])\ \}\\
&\qquad A_p = \{\ (\{p\}, p, \varphi_1^*[\mathsf{root}])\ \}
\end{aligned}$$

Still, quite a few things must be taken into account. First, we need to generate obligation formulas for the current innermost scope variable, if it is used inside the body of this recursion. Second, we need to generate obligation formulas for markers. Thirdly, we need to add an assumption formula that the result of the recursion conforms to the schema φ_1^*; where φ_1^* representing a set of graphs consisting of unions of graphs satisfying φ_1. To be concrete, it is $\bigwedge_{\mathsf{a}\in Label_\epsilon}(\forall^f x, e, y.\ (\mathbf{edge}_\mathsf{a}(x,e,y) \to \exists^s Z.((x,e,y,\mathsf{root} \in Z) \wedge \phi_1^Z)))$ where ϕ_1^Z is a restriction of second-order quantification into Z.

5.4 Relaxing the Annotation Burden

In the previous section, we have treated variables $\$g$, markers $\&_i$, and **rec** expressions as something *opaque*. That is, they are assigned new copy-ids and treated as an arbitrary graph that satisfies the annotated schema.

This can be made *transparent* in many situations. For instance in $\mathbf{rec}(\lambda(\$l,\$g :: \psi).\{\texttt{foo} : \$g\})$, the destination node of the `foo` edge is not an arbitrary graph of type ψ, but it is *the* destination of the currently processed edge, whose copy-id is determined during the translation by ft2mso. In such cases, no annotation is required because our verifier can automatically connect the appropriate nodes and complete the structure information of such variables.

In the following three cases, annotations can be removed: (1) annotation $\$g :: \varphi$ to the innermost scope variables can always be omitted (2) annotation $\&_i :: \varphi$ for markers with $i \ge 2$ can always be omitted (3) annotation $\&_1 :: \varphi$ for the 1st marker of the recursion can be omitted if no other annotations are used inside the structural recursion. In particular, if the transformation never uses nested recursion variables, no annotation for intermediate graphs is required to verify the correctness. Programmers just need to specify the intended schema for the input graph $\$db$ and the output graph (i.e., result of the whole expression), our verifier can convert the UnCAL expression into MSO formula fully automatically.

Here is the excerpt of the no-annotation version of ft2mso for the case of structural recursion.

$$\begin{aligned}
&\text{ft2mso_na}(c,\Gamma,\varphi)(\\
&\quad \mathbf{rec}(\lambda(\$l,\$g).\&_1 := \tau_1,\ldots,\&_n := \tau_n)(\tau_0)^p) =\\
&\qquad (\ (\mathcal{M}_0 \cup \bigcup_{i,c'} \mathcal{M}_i^{c'})[\\
&\qquad\qquad (\varepsilon, \langle c'_v, p, 2i-1\rangle v, \langle c'_v, p, 2i-2\rangle v, \rho_i^{c'} e) \mapsto \varphi],\\
&\qquad\quad J_0 \cup \bigcup_{i,c'} J_i^{c'} \cup \{\langle c_v, p, x\rangle \mid x < 2n\},\ \langle c_v, p, 0\rangle)\\
&\quad \mathbf{where}(\mathcal{M}_0, J_0, \rho_0) = \text{ft2mso_na}(c,\Gamma,\varphi)(\tau_0)\\
&\qquad (\mathcal{M}_i^{c'}, J_i^{c'}, \rho_i^{c'}) = \text{ft2mso_na}(c',\\
&\qquad\qquad \Gamma[\$g \mapsto c'_u, \&_1 \mapsto \langle c'_u, p, 1\rangle],\\
&\qquad\qquad\quad \ldots \&_n \mapsto \langle c'_u, p, 2n-1\rangle], \mathsf{true})(\tau_i)\\
&\qquad\qquad \text{for each } 1 \le i \le n, c' \in J_0 \times J_0 \times J_0
\end{aligned}$$

The difference is, for instance, in the translation of subformulas τ_i, $\$g$ is now bound to c_u, which is exactly the copy-id of the destination node of the focused edge c' and is not the newly generated fresh id $\langle c_e, p, 0\rangle$ as in the type-annotated version. Or, $\&_i$ is bound to $\langle c'_u, p, 2i-1\rangle$, the $(2i-1)$-th copy of the destination node, which, in the definition $(\langle c'_v, p, 2i-1\rangle v, \langle c'_v, p, 2i-2\rangle v, \rho_i^{c'} e)$ of the output transduction system, is declared to be connected to the root node $\rho_i^{c'}$ of the transformation result of the destination node.

6. Decision Procedure

The verification problem of annotated Core UnCAL is now reduced to the problem of validity of a closed MSO formula. This, however, is not a trivial task. Even for first-order logic, validity of a formula is well-known to be undecidable on general graph structures [27]. Even worse, expressing schemas in logic usually requires involved features like transitive-closures (e.g., to ignore ϵ-edges) that go beyond first-order logic.

Nevertheless, we can avoid the undecidability thanks to the nice property of UnCAL, namely, the bisimulation-genericity. We prove that the MSO formula obtained by the previous section is not valid on some graph if and only if it is not satisfied on some (possibly infinite) tree, on which decidability is known in the literature. Furthermore, a vast range of UnCAL transformations falls into a category called *compact* transformations [7]. For this class of transformations, we can show that there must be a finite-tree counterexample if there are any counterexamples. The property is important for efficient implementation.

6.1 Reduction to Infinite Tree Model

To decide the validity of a bisimulation-generic formula, we only need to consider some representatives of bisimilar graphs. Formally speaking, the following lemma holds.

Lemma 2. *Let b be a function from graphs to graphs such that $g \equiv b(g)$ for any g. Let φ be a bisimulation-generic formula. Then, the claim "$g \models \varphi$ for any graph g" holds if and only if "$g \models \varphi$ for any graph g in the range of b".*

Proof. The 'only if' direction is trivial. For the 'if' direction, $g \models \varphi$ equals $b(g) \models \varphi$ by the bisimulation-genericity of φ and the latter holds because $b(g)$ is surely in the range of b. □

By taking the representative function b as the infinite unfolding function, we can focus the range of g on infinite trees rather than on arbitrary graphs. Fortunately, there is an effective procedure to check the satisfiability or validity of MSO on infinite trees [22].

Theorem 2. *The verification problem is decidable.*

The proof of the decidability resorts to the decidability of emptiness of automata. Since the emptiness test procedure easily exhibits a way to produce a counterexample in a nonempty case, our approach can generate a counterexample to the UnCAL verification problem in the case of failure.

6.2 Reduction to Finite Tree Model

Graph transformations are called *positive* if they do not use isEmpty expression that checks whether or not a node has any outgoing edge. Many useful transformations fall into this category. In the appendix of [7], a positive transformation is shown to have a property called *compactness*, by which we can reduce the problem on infinite trees to finite trees.

To formalize the notion of compactness, let us first introduce the operation cut. For trees $T_1 = (V_1, r_1, E_1)$ and $T_2 = (V_2, r_2, E_2)$, we define the prefix relation $T_1 \preceq T_2$ to hold when there is a one-to-one mapping e from V_1 to V_2 such that $e(r_1) = r_2$ and $(v_1, l, u_1) \in E_1$ iff $(e(v_1), l, e(u_1)) \in E_2$. For a possibly infinite tree T, the set of its *finite-cuts* is $cut(T) = \{t \mid t \preceq T, t \text{ is finite}\}$. For instance, the finite-cuts of an infinite tree $cut(\circ \xrightarrow{a} \bullet \xrightarrow{a} \bullet \xrightarrow{a} \bullet \cdots)$ are infinitely many finite trees $\{\circ, \circ \xrightarrow{a} \bullet, \circ \xrightarrow{a} \bullet \xrightarrow{a} \bullet, \ldots\}$.

A set C is said to *cover* T if it is a subset of $cut(T)$ and for any $t \in cut(T)$ there exists $t_c \in C$ such that $t \preceq t_c$. Intuitively, $t \preceq t'$ means that t' contains more information on the original tree T than t. When C covers T, it roughly means that C has enough information to recover T. The following property of positive UnCAL is called compactness. It means that instead of transforming an infinite tree T, we only need to transform each finite-cut for obtaining enough information to construct $f(T)$.

Lemma 3 ([7], Proposition 8). *Let T be a possibly infinite tree and f be a positive UnCAL transformation. Then, $\{unfold(f(t)) \mid t \in cut(T)\}$ covers $unfold(f(T))$.*

We can extend the notion of compactness to schemas. A schema φ is called compact if for any tree T: (1) $T \models \varphi$ implies $t \models \varphi$ for all $t \in cut(T)$, and (2) if there exists a set $C \subseteq \{t \mid t \models \varphi\}$ that covers T, we have $T \models \varphi$. When both schemas and transformation are compact, validity on infinite trees can be checked by testing only on finite trees.

Theorem 3. *If the schemas are compact and the transformation is positive, the verification problem is reducible to the validity of MSO on finite trees.*

For the detail of the proof of Theorem 3, refer to our technical report [17].

Decidability of MSO on finite trees[4] is proved in [24] by much simpler manner than the infinite case. Indeed, this simplicity is important for having more efficient implementation of the verifier. For MSO on finite trees, there exists a good practical implementation MONA [14], whose efficiency is verified in many applications. Our current prototype is implemented using MONA, leaving the infinite case as future work.

[4] Here we mean by MSO on finite trees what is called weak MSO (WSkS) in the literature. Precisely speaking, it is MSO on the *infinite* k-ary tree domain with no node/edge-labels, whose second-order variables can range over *finite sets* only. Since the finiteness restriction prohibits us to encode infinitely many labeled-edges, we call it MSO on finite trees. Similarly, we mention MSO on the infinite k-ary tree with no restriction (SkS) as MSO on infinite trees.

7. Related Work

In the original paper [7], the logical characterization of UnCAL is given using first-order logic with transitive closures (FO+TC) by showing the logic captures the full expressive power of UnCAL. The problem is that the validity of FO+TC formula including closures of relations on tuples is undecidable [25] even on finite trees. Hence, naïvely reducing the problem to FO+TC can only derive either unsound, incomplete, or possibly non-terminating verification algorithms. Rather, our approach is to start from a decidable logic (namely, MSO on trees) capturing some clearly defined fragment of UnCAL, and provide sound and terminating verification algorithm for the fragment, which we hope to be a solid basis towards the complete verification of full UnCAL.

Concerning the choice of logic, in [18], it has been shown that the bisimulation-generic subset of MSO is equivalent in expressiveness to the modal μ-calculus. This suggests that we can use μ-calculus in place of MSO. The problem is, however, there is no established method to represent *transformations* in μ-calculus. Different from predicate logics, there is no way to denote each node or edge individually in μ-calculus, which makes it hard to describe a translation in terms of things like **edge** predicates as in MSO-definable transduction. Nonetheless, if we could overcome the problem, the worst-case EXPTIME complexity of validity of μ-calculus is an attractive candidate regarding the non-elementary complexity upperbound of MSO.

Another group of related work on verification of transformations can be found in the area of XML processing, under the name *exact typechecking* [12, 20, 21, 26]. The main tool there to represent transformations is what is called a tree transducer, a kind of functional programming language. Our approach to construct the inverse image $f^{-1}(\varphi_{\text{OUT}})$ of the output-schema follows the same way as those researches on XML typechecking. Advantage of MSO-definable transduction over tree transducers is, (1) it is straightforward to generalize the notion from trees to graphs, and (2) composition (in UnCAL terminology, **rec** expression inside the argument of another **rec** expression) of transformations can be relatively easily handled. In tree transducers, the number h of composition makes the complexity of typechecking very high, namely, h-exponential (and hence recent work [12, 20] targets a single, non-compositional transducers). While in MSO, it stays single exponential. Note, however, some variants of tree transducers have higher expressiveness that allows to represent nested-recursion without annotations. It is our future work to combine those two approaches and seek a balancing point of complexity and expressiveness.

Unno et al. [28] proposes a verification method for tree processing programs using higher-order macro tree transducers utilizing annotations. Since their method can be applied to infinite-trees, it can also handle bisimulation-generic graph transformations. Compared to our method, the places for required annotations are different. Theirs does not require annotation for nested occurrence of variables (which is needed in our approach), while it requires for compositions (or generally, re-consumption of temporarily created trees), which is not needed in ours.

Finally, the simulation-based schema [5] compared with MSO in the Introduction still has some advantage over our MSO-based approach. Although it is weak for representing structural properties of graphs, it is easily adopted to express properties on data values, because its schema can have unary predicates putting constraints on data edges (like, "it must match some regular expression"), which is left as future work for our approach.

8. Conclusion and Future Work

In this paper, we have proposed a new approach to verifying graph transformations written in Core UnCAL against the specified input/output graph schemas in MSO. We show that the Core UnCAL can be represented as an MSO-definable graph transduction, where not only schemas but also transformations are described by MSO formula, and efficiently implemented with MONA [14]. Our verifier can deal with any graph transformation in the type-annotated Core UnCAL, and more advanced structural properties like "either-or" compared to existing simulation-based checking algorithm. Furthermore, when the transformation failed against the verification, our verifier can produce a counterexample with respect to the input rather than the output.

The future plan is to support data values and to broaden the verifiable transformations. Firstly, unary predicates on data values such as a test of the range of integer values or the length of string data can be rather easily incorporated into our framework, by basically regarding them as a normal label, but conformance to a schema is tested by logical subsumption. As long as the conditions are written in a decidable logic, the conformance can be decided. Then, for binary or more complex predicates such as asserting that two data values must always be equal, we plan to extend our approach by using a *nondeterministic* MSO-definable transduction and approximate complex branches by a nondeterministic choice. This technique is already used in verification of XML-transformations (see, e.g., [21]).

Acknowledgments

The research was supported in part by the Grand-Challenging Project on "Linguistic Foundation for Bidirectional Model Transformation" from the National Institute of Informatics, Grant-in-Aid for Scientific Research No. 22300012 and No. 22650007.

References

[1] S. Abiteboul, D. Quass, J. Mchugh, J. Widom, and J. Wiener. The lorel query language for semistructured data. *International Journal on Digital Libraries*, 1:68–88, 1997.

[2] R. Angles and C. Gutierrez. Survey of graph database models. *ACM Comput. Surv.*, 40:1:1–1:39, February 2008. ISSN 0360-0300.

[3] ATLAS group. KM3 manual. `http://www.eclipse.org/gmt/atl/doc/`.

[4] P. Buneman, S. Davidson, M. Fernandez, and D. Suciu. Adding structure to unstructured data. Technical Report MS-CIS-96-21, Univ. of Pennsylvania, 1996.

[5] P. Buneman, S. Davidson, M. Fernandez, and D. Suciu. Adding structure to unstructured data. In *ICDT*, pages 336–350, 1997.

[6] P. Buneman, S. Davidson, G. Hillebrand, and D. Suciu. A query language and optimization techniques for unstructured data. In *Proceedings of ACM SIGMOD international conference on Management of Data*, pages 505–516. ACM, 1996.

[7] P. Buneman, M. F. Fernandez, and D. Suciu. UnQL: a query language and algebra for semistructured data based on structural recursion. *VLDB Journal*, 9(1):76–110, 2000.

[8] J. Clark and M. Murata. RELAX NG specification. `http://www.relaxng.org/`, 2001.

[9] M. P. Consens and A. O. Mendelzon. Graphlog: a visual formalism for real life recursion. In PODS, pages 404–416, 1990.

[10] B. Courcelle. Monadic second-order definable graph transductions: A survey. *Theoretical Computer Science*, 126(1):53–75, 1994.

[11] DTD. DTD: Document Type Definition. `http://www.w3.org/XML/1998/06/xmlspec-report.htm`.

[12] A. Frisch and H. Hosoya. Towards practical typechecking for macro tree transducers. In *DBPL*, pages 246–260, 2007.

[13] G. Gottlob, C. Koch, and R. Pichler. Efficient algorithms for processing XPath queries. *ACM Trans. Database Syst.*, 30:444–491, 2005.

[14] J. G. Henriksen, J. Jensen, M. Jørgensen, N. Klarlund, R. Paige, T. Rauhe, and A. Sandholm. Mona: Monadic second-order logic in practice. In *TACAS*, pages 89–110, 1995.

[15] S. Hidaka, Z. Hu, K. Inaba, H. Kato, K. Matsuda, and K. Nakano. Bidirectionalizing graph transformations. In *ICFP*, 2010.

[16] S. Hidaka, Z. Hu, H. Kato, and K. Nakano. Towards a compositional approach to model transformation for software development. In *SAC*, pages 468–475, 2009.

[17] K. Inaba, S. Hidaka, Z. Hu, H. Kato, and K. Nakano. Sound and complete validation of graph transformations. Technical Report GRACE-TR-2010-04, GRACE Center, NII, 2010.

[18] D. Janin and I. Walukiewicz. On the expressive completeness of the propositional mu-calculus with respect to monadic second order logic. In *CONCUR*, pages 263–277, 1996.

[19] F. Jouault and J. Bézivin. KM3: A DSL for metamodel specification. In *Formal Methods for Open Object-Based Distributed Systems*, pages 171–185. LNCS 4037, Springer, 2006.

[20] S. Maneth, T. Perst, and H. Seidl. Exact XML type checking in polynomial time. In *ICDT*, pages 254–268, 2007.

[21] T. Milo, D. Suciu, and V. Vianu. Typechecking for XML transformers. *J. Comp. Syst. Sci.*, 66:66–97, 2003.

[22] M. O. Rabin. Decidability of second-order theories and automata on infinite trees. *Transactions of American Mathematical Society*, 141: 1–35, 1969.

[23] G. Rozenberg, editor. *Handbook of Graph Grammars and Computing by Graph Transformations, Volume 1: Foundations*, 1997. World Scientific.

[24] J. W. Thatcher and J. B. Wright. Generalized finite automata theory with an application to a decision problem of second-order logic. *Mathematical Systems Theory*, 2:57–81, 1968.

[25] H.-J. Tiede and S. Kepser. Monadic second-order logic and transitive closure logics over trees. In *WoLLIC*, pages 189–199, 2006.

[26] A. Tozawa. Towards static type checking for XSLT. In *DocEng*, pages 18–27, 2001.

[27] B. A. Trakhtenbrot. Impossibility of an algorithm for the decision problem for finite classes. *Doklady Akademiia Nauk SSSR*, 70:569–572, 1950.

[28] H. Unno, N. Tabuchi, and N. Kobayashi. Verification of tree-processing program via higher-order model checking. In *Asian Symposium on Programming Languages and Systems (APLAS)*, 2010.

[29] W3C XML Schema WG. W3C XML Schema. `http://www.w3c.org/XML/Schema`.

Bellman's GAP - A Declarative Language for Dynamic Programming

Georg Sauthoff Stefan Janssen Robert Giegerich

Universität Bielefeld
Technische Fakultät, 33501 Bielefeld, Germany
{gsauthof, sjanssen, robert}@techfak.uni-bielefeld.de

Abstract

Dynamic programming is a well-established technique to solve combinatorial optimization problems. In several areas of applied computer science, such as operations research, natural language processing, or biosequence analysis, dynamic programming problems arise in many variations and with a considerable degree of sophistication. The simple way dynamic programming problems are normally presented in computer science textbooks – as a set of table recurrences – scales poorly for real world problems, where the search space is deeply structured and the scoring model is elaborate. Coming up with pages of correct recurrences is difficult, implementation is error-prone, and debugging is tedious. *Algebraic* Dynamic Programming (ADP) is a language-independent, declarative approach which alleviates these problems for a relevant class of dynamic programming problems over sequence data.

Bellman's GAP implements ADP by providing a declarative language (GAP-L) with a Java-reminiscent syntax, and a compiler (GAP-C) translating declarative programs into C++ code, which is competitive to handwritten code, and arguably more reliable. This article introduces the GAP-L language, demonstrates the benefits of developing dynamic programming algorithms in a declarative framework by educational example, and reports on the practice of programming bioinformatics applications with Bellman's GAP.

Categories and Subject Descriptors D.3 [*PROGRAMMING LANGUAGES*]: Language Classifications—Specialized application languages

General Terms Languages, Algorithms

Keywords Declarative Programming, Dynamic Programming, Regular Tree Grammars, Algebras, RNA Structure Prediction

1. Introduction

Difficulties with dynamic programming Dynamic programming is a widely used technique to solve combinatorial optimization problems. Often, it allows to evaluate a search space of exponential size in polynomial time. Variations of the basic algorithm return not only an optimal solution, but may also report co- or near-optimal solutions, or compute synoptic properties of the search space as a whole, such as its size or sum of all scores. They may sample the search space stochastically, or partition it into certain classes of interest and perform either one of the above analyses class-wise, and so on.

In several areas of applied computer science, such as operations research, natural language processing, or biosequence analysis, dynamic programming problems arise in many variations and with a considerable degree of sophistication. The simple way in which dynamic programming problems are normally presented in computer science textbooks – as a handful of table recurrences – scales poorly for real world problems, where the search space is deeply structured, the scoring model elaborate, and multiple objective functions may be used in combination. Coming up with several pages of correct recurrences is difficult, their implementation is error-prone, and debugging is tedious. For efficiency reasons, optimization is a separate first phase, followed by a backtracing stage to retrieve the solution associated with the optimal score. More comprehensive analyses, such as complete backtracing for the p percent near-optimal solutions, or optimization in a class-wise fashion, considerably add to the implementation effort.

Separating concerns *Algebraic* Dynamic Programming (ADP) [9] is a language-independent, declarative approach that alleviates these problems for a relevant class of dynamic programming algorithms, namely those over sequence data. The remedy is a perfect separation of four concerns that are traditionally expressed in the recurrences in an intermingled fashion: search space definition, candidate scoring, optimization objective, and tabulation issues (the last determines runtime and space efficiency). The central idea behind the algebraic approach can be introduced by a simple example: consider two strings $x = x_1 \dots x_m$ and $y = y_1 \dots y_n$. Their edit distance can be computed via the recurrences

$$dist(0,0) = 0 \tag{1}$$

$$dist(i,0) = dist(i-1,0) + del(x_i), 1 \leq i \leq m \tag{2}$$

$$dist(0,j) = dist(0,j-1) + ins(y_j), 1 \leq j \leq n \tag{3}$$

$$dist(i,j) = \min \begin{cases} match(x_i, y_j) & + dist(i-1, j-1) \\ del(x_i) & + dist(i-1, j) \\ ins(y_j) & + dist(i, j-1) \end{cases} \tag{4}$$

Here, del and ins are the scoring functions for deletions and insertions, and $match$ scores character replacements. The boundary conditions, Equations 1-3, indicate structural recursion over the two input sequences, but where does the three-fold case distinction in Equation 4 come from? It reflects the structure of a solution candidate, i.e. an alignment that edits x into y. It recurs on an invisible data structure, which is evaluated without being constructed. To

PDPP'11, July 20–22, 2011, Odense, Denmark.

make this view explicit, the last equation can be rewritten into

$$dist(\eta) = \min\left[dist(\eta_1), dist(\eta_2), dist(\eta_3)\right] = \min \begin{cases} match(x_i, y_j) + dist(\zeta_1) \\ del(x_i) + dist(\zeta_2,) \\ ins(y_j) + dist(\zeta_3) \end{cases}$$

$$\text{where } \eta_1 = Match(x_i, \zeta_1, y_j) \quad \eta_2 = Del(x_i, \zeta_2) \quad \eta_3 = Ins(\zeta_3, y_j)$$

Here, η denotes the invisible candidate(s) for a subword, and ζ the invisible candidate on which a right-hand side call to $dist$ recurs. Note that the use of subscripts with η and ζ becomes implicit, since, if η is derived from subproblem $(x_i..., y_j...)$, it is clear in each case which characters x_i or y_j are consumed by the local case analysis, and that ζ is derived from the remaining subproblem.

The ADP approach makes the invisible candidate structure explicit. Candidates are modeled as trees. The function symbols used at inner tree nodes reflect the designer's case analysis. They are seen as tree constructors on the specification level, and will be interpreted (called) as scoring functions at runtime. They are collected in a signature which serves as the interface between two (otherwise) independent specification components: grammar and algebras.

The search space is defined by a tree grammar. Candidate scoring is done by an evaluation algebra, implementing the score functions and the optimization objective. Tabulation issues are hidden from the programmer, thus there are no subscripts any more, and hence no subscript errors. Different tree grammars may share evaluation algebras, or different evaluation algebras may be used with one grammar. In particular, products of evaluation algebras give rise to new evaluation algebras, a feature providing re-use of components and a great convenience in practice. An implementation of this approach must take responsibility to generate efficient dynamic programming code, given these declarative constituents.

The Bellman's GAP system *Bellman's GAP* implements ADP. It provides a declarative language (GAP-L) with a Java-reminiscent syntax, in which the programmer specifies tree grammars and evaluation algebras. The language provides three types of evaluation algebra products, allowing to derive more sophisticated analyses from tested components without the need for any reprogramming. Furthermore, it includes a number of pragmatic extensions to the ADP approach, such as generic evaluation algebras and multi-track input. The Bellman's GAP compiler (GAP-C) translates declarative programs into C++ code, which is competitive to handwritten code, and arguably more reliable. It performs extensive optimization to achieve optimal asymptotic space and time efficiency, with reasonable constant factors.

In this article

- we recall (in a compact form) the principles of ADP, and report on their extension by new product operations,
- we introduce the GAP-L language, which bridges the gap between the abstract definitions and the practice of ADP,
- we report on the experiences with ex-bedding ADP from Haskell,
- we demonstrate the benefits of program development in Bellman's GAP by educational example,
- we report from the practice of programming bioinformatics software in GAP-L,
- we conclude with a short list of theoretical and practical research topics which emerge from our experience with Bellman's GAP, and
- the optimizations of the GAP-C compiler are described elsewhere [10].

Relation to previous work During the early development of ADP, the approach was implemented as a combinator language in Haskell [7, 8]. Efficiency concerns with applications emerging around 2004 [12, 18, 19] motivated the implementation of a compiler, which translated the Haskell-embedded notation into more efficient C code [11]. However, the Haskell syntax turned out to be an obstacle to the wider acceptance of the method within the bioinformatics community, in spite of the evident increase in programmer productivity. Also, the fragile borders of an embedded language encouraged algorithm designers to incorporate non-ADP features from the host language, resulting in an unfortunate mixture of automated translation and subsequent hand-patching. Hence, Bellman's GAP was designed to free ADP from its Haskell embedding, and at the same time to incorporate new features that had evolved after publication of [9].

Outside the realm of the algebraic approach, related work is for example the *Dynamite* system [3] for biosequence analysis, or, in the natural language processing community, the DYNA language [5]. DYNA is based on a general, Prolog-style backtracking scheme, allowing the programmer to concentrate on the logic of the parsing algorithm, rather than its implementation. Neither of these approaches achieves a separation of search space construction and evaluation. In both cases, unfortunately, it must be said that these approaches have worked well only in the hands of their creators. Since the gain in abstractness is not large enough, they have not found more widespread use. This holds also, albeit for different reasons as described above, for our early efforts with Haskell-embedded ADP. With Bellman's GAP, we hope to break this barrier.

2. GAP-L semantics

Signatures, tree grammars and evaluation algebras This paragraph recalls, in a very terse format, the basic definitions of ADP, following the literature [9]. Let $\mathcal{A}$ be an alphabet and $\mathcal{A}^*$ be the set of strings or sequences over $\mathcal{A}$. A *signature* Σ over $\mathcal{A}$ is a set of function symbols and a datatype place holder (sort) S. The return type of an $f \in \Sigma$ is S, each argument is of type S or $\mathcal{A}$. T_Σ denotes the term language described by the signature Σ and $T_\Sigma(V)$ is the term language with variables from the set V. A *Σ-algebra* or *interpretation* $\mathcal{E}$ is a mathematical structure given by a carrier set $S_\mathcal{E}$ for S and functions operating on this set for each $f \in \Sigma$, consistent with their specified type. Interpreting a term $t \in T_\Sigma$ by $\mathcal{E}$ is denoted $\mathcal{E}(t)$ and yields a value in $S_\mathcal{E}$.

A *regular tree grammar* $\mathcal{G}$ over a signature Σ is defined as tuple $(V, \mathcal{A}, Z, P)$, where V is the set of non-terminals, $\mathcal{A}$ is an alphabet, $Z \in V$ is the axiom, and P is the set of productions. Each production is of form

$$v \rightarrow t \text{ with } v \in V, t \in T_\Sigma(V) \tag{5}$$

The *language* generated by a regular tree grammar $\mathcal{G}$ is the set of trees

$$\mathcal{L}(\mathcal{G}) = \{t \in T_\Sigma | Z \Rightarrow^* t\} \tag{6}$$

where $\Rightarrow^*$ is the reflexive transitive closure of $\rightarrow$. By construction, $\mathcal{L}(\mathcal{G}) \subseteq T_\Sigma$. Its elements are seen as trees when it comes to constructing them, and as formulas when it comes to their evaluation.

Symbols from $\mathcal{A}$ reside on the leaves of these trees. The symbol y denotes the *yield function* and is of type $T_\Sigma \rightarrow \mathcal{A}^*$. It is defined as $y(a) = a$, where $a \in \mathcal{A}$ and $y(f(x_1, \ldots, x_n)) = y(x_1) \ldots y(x_n)$, for $f \in \Sigma$ and $n \geq 0$. The yield language $\mathcal{L}_y(\mathcal{G})$ of a tree grammar $\mathcal{G}$ is defined as

$$\mathcal{L}_y(\mathcal{G}) = \{y(t) | t \in \mathcal{L}(\mathcal{G})\} \tag{7}$$

Regular tree grammars as we use here pose a special type of parsing problem: given $x \in \mathcal{A}^*$, we construct the *search space* $\{t | t \in \mathcal{L}(\mathcal{G}), y(t) = x\}$. This process - computing the inverse of y – is called *yield parsing*. A Bellman's GAP programmer does not need to care about how yield parsing works.

The candidate trees constitute the "invisible" data structure mentioned in our introductory remarks. They allow us to effectively separate search space construction from search space evaluation. Note that the candidate trees, the elements of $y^{-1}(x)$, are not parse trees. Each candidate tree *has* a parse tree by $\mathcal{G}$, but it *is* a terminal tree in $L(\mathcal{G})$. Basing candidate evaluation on parse trees directly might be feasible, but would create interdependence between search space construction and evaluation.

An *evaluation algebra* is a Σ-algebra augmented with an objective function $h : [S] \to [S]$, where the square brackets denote multisets (in theory, and lists in practice).

An *ADP problem instance* is specified by a regular tree grammar $\mathcal{G}$, evaluation algebra $\mathcal{E}$ and input sequence $x \in \mathcal{A}^*$. Its solution is defined by

$$\mathcal{G}(\mathcal{E}, x) = h_{\mathcal{E}}[\mathcal{E}(t) | t \in \mathcal{L}(\mathcal{G}), y(t) = x] \quad (8)$$

The square brackets in Equation 8 denote a multiset. This is required because in practice, we often ask for all co-optimal solutions, or all solutions within a percentage of optimality. The notation $\mathcal{G}(\mathcal{E}, x)$ suggests the use of the regular tree grammar $\mathcal{G}$ (more precisely, its yield parser) as a function called with evaluation algebra $\mathcal{E}$ and input x as parameters. Internally, however, Equation 8 is not executed literally. Rather, the application of the objective function is amalgamated with the evaluation of the candidate trees, which are not constructed explicitly. (In functional language terminology, this is a case of deforestation.) Also, tabulation of intermediates is used where appropriate, to avoid exponential blow-up. The prerequisite for correct and efficient computation of the solution in this way is Bellman's Principle of Optimality [2], which is defined by Equations 9 and 10 in the ADP framework

$$\begin{aligned} h_{\mathcal{E}}[\, f_{\mathcal{E}}(x_1, \dots, x_k) \mid x_1 \leftarrow X_1, \dots, x_k \leftarrow X_k \,] = \\ h_{\mathcal{E}}[\, f_{\mathcal{E}}(x_1, \dots, x_k) \mid x_1 \leftarrow h_{\mathcal{E}}(X_1), \dots, x_k \leftarrow h_{\mathcal{E}}(X_k) \,] \end{aligned} \quad (9)$$

$$h_{\mathcal{E}}(X_1 \cup X_2) = h_{\mathcal{E}}(\, h_{\mathcal{E}}(X_1) \cup h_{\mathcal{E}}(X_2)\,) \quad \text{and} \quad h_{\mathcal{E}}[\,] = [\,], \quad (10)$$

where X_i denote multisets. Note that these equations imply less general criteria which are found in the literature. When h is minimization or maximization, it implies (strict) monotonicity of each $f \in \Sigma$ [15]. When the evaluation algebra holds only a single, binary and commutative function f, (h, f) forms a semiring where h distributes over f [17].

When compiling an ADP algorithm coded in GAP-L, it is always assumed that the evaluation algebra used satisfies Bellman's Principle. This is the developer's responsibility. However, in some cases, the compiler can notice that this principle is violated, and issues a warning.

Example We present an ADP version of the classic optimal binary search tree algorithm [4] to demonstrate the ADP concepts from the previous paragraph. Given a set of keys and their access probabilities, the algorithm computes the binary tree with minimal mean access time. Why is this a *sequence* analysis problem at all? Because in a search tree, the order of leaves is fixed. The yield string of any search tree must hold the keys in sorted order.

With a dynamic programming approach, the minimal expected access time results from the optimization phase, the underlying optimal tree structure is derived via backtracing. With the example input sequence

$$\begin{aligned} s = [&(1, 0.05), (2, 0.05), (3, 0.40), (4, 0.10), \\ &(5, 0.20), (6, 0.01), (7, 0.19)] \end{aligned}$$

the two binary trees t_1 and t_2 have a mean access time of 2.18 and 2.98, where the access time is the number of key comparisons in a lookup operation, which corresponds to the depth of the accessed node.

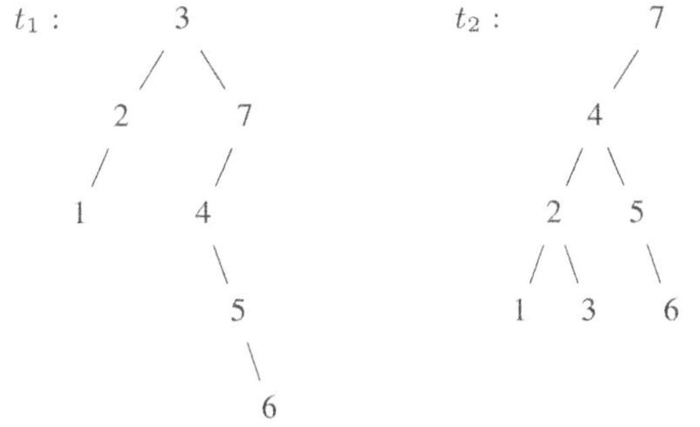

In this example, the candidates of the search space are all possible binary search trees. The *signature* requires a branching symbol br, a leaf symbol lf and a symbol that represents an empty subtree nil.

$$\begin{aligned} br &: T \times \mathcal{A} \times T && \to T \\ lf &: \mathcal{A} && \to T \\ nil &: && \to T \end{aligned}$$

Using these symbols, the following *candidate trees* represent t_1 and t_2:

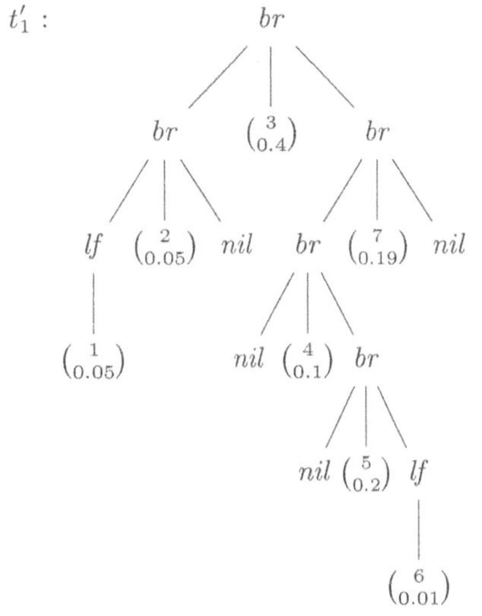

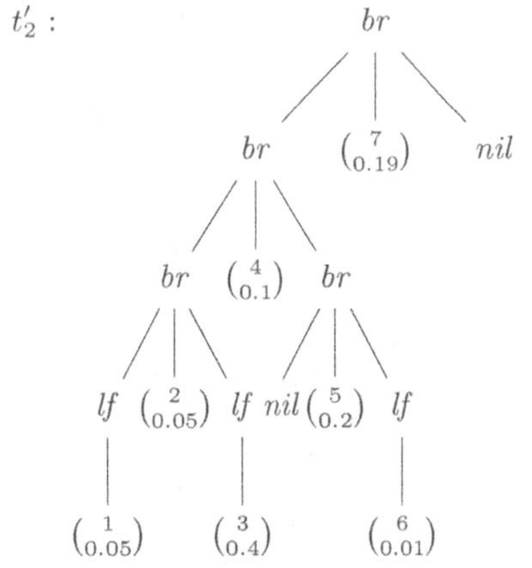

The following tree grammar *btrees* (axiom is btree) generates all possible binary search trees using the function symbols from the signature:

$$\text{btree} \rightarrow \quad br \quad | \quad lf \quad | \quad nil$$

$$\text{btree} \quad a \quad \text{btree} \qquad a$$

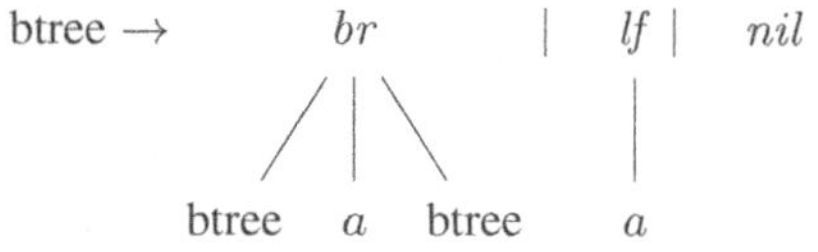

where $a \in \mathcal{A}$. The *alphabet* $\mathcal{A}$ is $K \times P$, where K is the set of keys and $P = [0, 1]$.

Computing the mean access time is done via the evaluation algebra *mean*. The place-holder (sort) T is mapped to $\mathbb{R} \times \mathbb{R}$, where the first component of a result is the mean access time of the candidate and the second component is sum of the probabilities of the yield of the candidate tree. The evaluation functions are implemented by

$$
\begin{aligned}
br(l, (k, p), r) &= \quad (l_1 + r_1 + l_2 + r_2 + p, l_2 + r_2 + p) \\
lf((k, p)) &= \qquad\qquad\qquad\qquad\qquad (p, p) \\
nil &= \qquad\qquad\qquad\qquad\qquad (0, 0) \\
h &= \qquad\qquad\qquad\qquad\qquad min
\end{aligned}
$$

The objective function h is minimization, to choose the binary tree with the minimal access time. Thus, a call to $btrees(mean, s)$ computes the minimal mean access time for the example sequence s:

$$btrees(mean, s) = [(1.96, 1)]$$

i.e. the minimal mean access time for the input sequence s is 1.96.

The non-optimizing *printing algebra*, by convention named *print*, transforms a candidate tree into a textual notation, i.e. T is mapped to the domain of character sequences.

$$
\begin{aligned}
br(l, (k, p), r) &= \quad \text{``(''} + l + \text{``)''} + str(k) + \text{``(''} + r + \text{``)''} \\
lf((k, p)) &= \qquad\qquad\qquad\qquad\qquad str(k) \\
nil &= \qquad\qquad\qquad\qquad\qquad \text{``''} \\
h &= \qquad\qquad\qquad\qquad\qquad id
\end{aligned}
$$

where str converts its argument to a string representation and $+$ means string concatenation. Note that we choose to represent only the key, not its probability.

Evaluating $btrees(print, s)$ enumerates the complete search space of 2,128 candidates, including strings for both example candidates:

$$t_1 \rightarrow ((1)2())3((()4(()5(6)))7())$$
$$t_2 \rightarrow (((1)2(3))4(()5(6)))7()$$

With a slightly more elaborate *print* algebra, we generate the LaTeX code for tree graphics as depicted above.

Computing both, minimal mean access time and the structure of the candidate which achieves it, is done via a *product algebra*: $btrees(mean * print, s)$ returns a list of optimal structures with minimal mean access time, e.g.

$$[((1.96, 1), \text{``(()1(2))3((4)5((6)7()))''})]$$

This example also demonstrates how the "separation of concerns" mentioned above is achieved in practice: The signature defines a universe of candidates, algebras define different ways to score them, objective functions capture the intended goal of the analysis, and tree grammars define the candidate space arising from given input. Efficiency concerns related to tabulation have been eliminated completely, as this issue is automated by the compiler. An immediate benefit of this separation of concerns is that we can build more sophisticated analyses from simpler ones by operations on evaluation algebras.

Products of algebras If combinatorial optimization is to be performed under multiple objectives, one could design algebras which operate on tuples of scores and apply the multiple objectives. A much faster and safer way to achieve this is often possible via *product algebras*. They allow to describe different objectives independently, and to afterwards combine them in various fashions, avoiding a lot of redundant and error-prone coding. With algebras A and B already available, one simply calls $\mathcal{G}(A * B, x)$, with no extra programming or debugging effort.

We present three kinds of products here. The "lexicographic" product has been introduced and studied in [22], the other two are new.

We need to introduce two properties of algebras, which are prerequisites for well-defined products. An algebra is called *unitary*, if its evaluation functions return lists of results holding at most one element. A *generic* algebra $A(k)$ has a parameter $k > 0$ such that it returns the k best solutions under its objective function. Naturally, $A(1)$ is unitary.

Let A and B be unitary evaluation algebras over Σ. The *cartesian product* $A \times B$ is an evaluation algebra over Σ. Its functions take arguments of the form $(a, b) \in \mathcal{S}_A \times \mathcal{S}_B$ or $z \in \mathcal{A}$. For simplicity, we define the functions of $A \times B$ for the case of a binary function f with one argument of either kind, and leave the general case to the reader.

$$f_{A \times B}((a, b), z) = (f_A(a, z), f_B(b, z))) \tag{11}$$

The objective function of $A \times B$ is

$$h_{A \times B}[(a_1, b_1), \ldots, (a_m, b_m)] = [\, (l, r) \mid l \leftarrow h_A[a_1, \ldots, a_m],$$
$$r \leftarrow h_B[b_1, \ldots, b_m] \,]. \tag{12}$$

The algebras are required to be unitary, because otherwise, Bellman's Principle would be violated and the answer sets would blow up exponentially, without adding information. The cartesian product has little use by itself, because the results returned from A and B are independent – according to Eq. 12 they are drawn from different candidates in the search space. Thus, instead of $\mathcal{G}(A \times B, x)$ one might call $\mathcal{G}(A, x)$ and $\mathcal{G}(B, x)$ separately, which gives the same result, albeit more slowly. However, in combinations with other products, we have found the cartesian product useful, and we will see examples of this later.

The *lexicographic product* $A * B$ is an evaluation algebra over Σ and has the functions

$$f_{A * B} = f_{A \times B} \tag{13}$$

for each $f \in \Sigma$, and the objective function

$$h_{A * B}[(a_1, b_1), \ldots, (a_m, b_m)] = [\, (l, r) \mid$$
$$l \leftarrow set(h_A[a_1, \ldots, a_m]),$$
$$r \leftarrow h_B[r' \mid (l', r') \leftarrow [(a_1, b_1), \ldots, (a_m, b_m)], l' = l] \,]. \tag{14}$$

Here, $set(X)$ reduces the multiset X to a set. This product gets its name from the fact that if both algebras optimize, then it implements the lexicographic ordering of the two independent criteria as its objective. However, this product is not restricted to the case of two optimizing algebras, and exhibits a surprising versatility of use [22]. For example, a product $A * P$, where P is an algebra that produces an external "print" representation of the candidate, specifies a backtracing phase after optimization with A.

Our third product combines the objective functions in a more sophisticated way. Assume we have the generic $MinPrice(k)$ algebra which returns the k cheapest pizzas in our search space, and algebra $Kind$ which evaluates pizzas as "vegetarian", "meat", "seafood", or "other", but does not make any choices. Then, the use of $(Kind \otimes MinPrice)(2)$ is defined to yield the two cheapest pizzas such that each is of a different kind.

Let A be a Σ-algebra and $B(k)$ a generic Σ-algebra. The *interleaved product* $(A \otimes B)(k)$ is a generic Σ-algebra and has the functions

$$f_{A \otimes B} = f_{A \times B} \tag{15}$$

for each $f \in \Sigma$, and the objective function

$$\begin{aligned} &h_{(A \otimes B)(k)}[(a_1, b_1), \ldots, (a_m, b_m)] = \\ &\quad [(l, r) \mid (l, r) \leftarrow U, p \leftarrow V, p = r] \\ &\text{where} \\ &\quad U = h_{A * B(1)}[(a_1, b_1), \ldots, (a_m, b_m)] \\ &\quad V = \text{set}(h_{B(k)}[v \mid (\_, v) \leftarrow U]) \end{aligned} \tag{16}$$

Further generalizations To keep the formalism short, we have ignored several features which are required to turn a concise formalism into a practical programming tool, but do not make the theory deeper. *Generic* algebras may contain parameters, to be instantiated when the algebra is applied. They are not restricted to be a number as in Eq. 16. Signatures and algebras may be many-sorted, if the result types need to be different for subproblems that arise in the input decomposition. The objective function h then splits into a separate function for each result type. Some problems, such as string edit distance, require two input strings rather than one. These issues will be discussed in our description of GAP-L.

3. The Bellman's GAP Language

The design goal of GAP-L is to make it easy to learn for ADP beginners, and powerful to use for ADP experts. To lower the entry barrier for novice programmers, GAP-L uses some concepts that are common in the widespread C/Java-like languages. A signature declaration in GAP-L is similar to an interface declaration in Java. An evaluation algebra *implements* a signature, as a Java class may implement an interface. An algebra may *extend* another algebra and overwrite existing functions, as a Java class is able to extend another class. Tree grammars are specified in a declarative style, where the right hand side of productions contain tree patterns resembling function calls. The algebra code is written as imperative code blocks. In spite of such resemblance, GAP-L is a declarative language for dynamic programming over sequence input.

Space does not allow a full presentation of GAP-L here. The interested reader is referred to [20, 21]. We demonstrate features of GAP-L in two parts. First, we show the notations for the core ADP concepts. Then we present a selection of further language features which are motivated by practical convenience and control of efficiency.

Coding signatures, grammars, algebras and instances

We demonstrate the GAP-L syntax using a simple example. Given string x, we seek a palindromic structure for it, which is optimal under some scoring scheme. This is a toy example, which we will gradually extend to show the building-block style of program development in GAP-L. *Exact* palindromes are strings which read the same forward and backward, i.e. $x = x^{-1}$. We will use several variants of the basic problem, such as approximate palindromes (allowing errors), nested palindromes, or finding the sub-string with the best palindrome score under a given scoring model.

We first decide which function symbols we need to model the candidate terms in the search space, i.e. we define the signature, and then proceed (in any order) to define algebras and grammars. Our first signature is

```
signature paliS(alphabet, answer) {
  answer match(alphabet, answer, alphabet);
  answer nil(void);
  answer turn(alphabet);
  choice [answer] h([answer]); }
```

where answer denotes the sort symbol, and function symbols are $\{match, nil, turn\}$. They cover the cases of two matching characters, and the mid-point of a palindrome of even or odd length. The signature declaration resembles a Java interface declaration and the [] brackets denote a list type. The **choice** keyword marks the function symbol h as the objective function.

We describe the search space of all palindrome candidate terms with Grammar *Pali1*, axiom is S

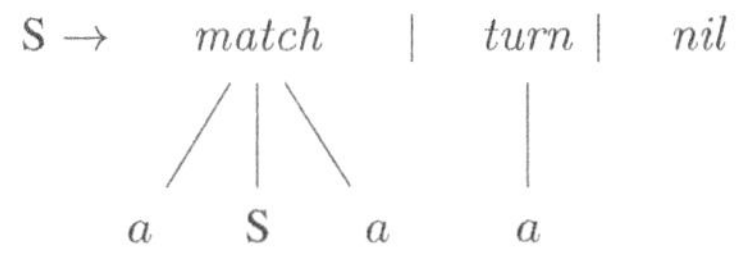

where the first two rules are shorthands for $|\mathcal{A}|$ rules each, one for each $a \in \mathcal{A}$.

In GAP-L syntax the tree patterns are written like function applications:

```
grammar Pali1 uses paliS(axiom = S) {
  S     = match(CHAR, S, CHAR) with equal |
          turn(CHAR) |
          nil(EMPTY) # h ; }
```

The underlying signature and the axiom are specified in the header of the grammar definition. The # operator specifies where the objective function should be applied to the rules' alternatives (# binds more weakly than |). While it could be applied by default with every production, there are situations which require exceptions from this default, and we decided to give the programmer full control by an explicit # operator. Terminal symbol/parser names are written in upper case, such as CHAR for a single character from the alphabet, and STRING for a string.

The first alternative of non-terminal S uses *syntactic filtering*, i.e. the left hand side of the **with** keyword is only parsed if the *equal* filter returns true for the parsed sub-word. The *equal* filter tests if the first and last character of the sub-word are equal. This filtering reduces the search space, rather than penalizing non-palindromes with a large cost. As a consequence, the *match* algebra function does not need to check the characters. Without syntactic filtering, we would need to duplicate the match rule for every character of the alphabet.

Next, we define a simple scoring scheme:

```
algebra score
    implements paliS(alphabet = char,
                     answer = int) {
  int match(char a, int b, char c)
    { return b + 3; }
  int turn(char l) { return 0; }
  choice [int] h([int] x)
    { return list(maximum(x)); } }
```

The syntax of the algebra definition resembles the definition of a Java class. The header contains the mapping between alphabet and sort symbol to concrete data types.

Perfect palindromes do not pose an optimization problem. The search space is empty if x is not a palindrome, and otherwise, it is $[t]$, with $score(t) = (|x| \; div \; 2) \cdot 3$. No dynamic programming is needed – a simple loop is sufficient that checks for character matches in x outside to inside. In fact, the optimizations within GAP-C recognize such a special case and generate a simple loop without allocating any tables.

To make the example more interesting, we want to search the input for *local* palindromes. They may hold a (non-palindromic) turn of any length, and may be embedded somewhere in a longer string. We extend the signature for this:

```
signature paliS(alphabet, answer) {
  answer match(alphabet, answer, alphabet);
  answer turn(int);
  answer sl(char, answer);
  answer sr(answer, char);
  choice [answer] h([answer]); }
```

sl and *sr* allow for leading or trailing characters around the palindrome and *turn* allows for a region of several unmatched characters.

We extend the grammar towards local palindromes:
grammar *Pali2*, axiom is *skipl*

$$skipl \rightarrow \quad sl \quad | \quad skipr \qquad skipr \rightarrow \quad sr \quad | \quad S$$

```
              / \                              / \
         char  skipl                      skipr  S
```

$$S \rightarrow \quad match \quad | \quad turn$$

```
         / | \                 |
    char  S  char           string
```

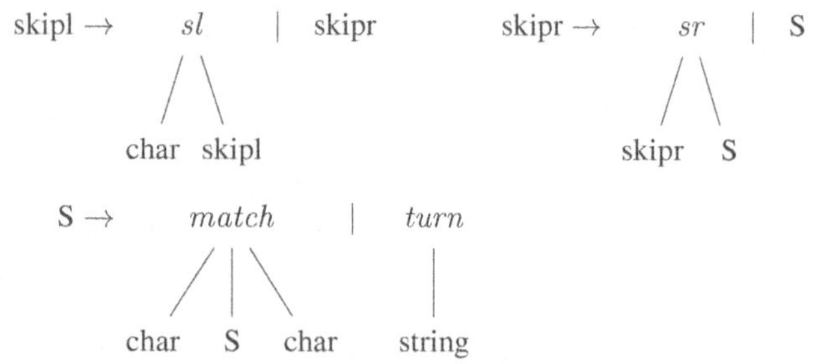

Here *string* is a terminal symbol denoting an arbitrary string over $\mathcal{A}$, and *char* denotes a character.

We write the *Pali2* grammar in GAP-L as:

```
grammar Pali2 uses paliS(axiom = skipl) {
  skipl = skipr |
          sl(CHAR, skipl)  # h ;
  skipr = skipr(sr, CHAR) |
          S                # h ;
  S     = match(CHAR, S, CHAR) with equal |
          turn(SEQ0)       # h ; }
```

The SEQ0 terminal parser accepts an arbitrary sub-word of the input and returns its length.

In our simple scoring scheme, skipping characters in the beginning or end or in the middle turn is for free:

```
algebra localscore
    implements paliS(alphabet = char,
                     answer = int) {
  int match(char a, int b, char c)
    { return b + 3; }
  int turn(int l) { return 0; }
  int sl(char c, int x) { return x; }
  int sr(int x, char c) { return x; }
  choice [int] h([int] x)
    { return list(maximum(x)); } }
```

Our scoring ignores the length of the "turn", but since SEQ0 passes the length of the subword to the function turn, we could have penalized long turns with a score of, say, $-0.2 \cdot l$.

With grammar *Pali2*, the palindromic structure of a string is no longer unique. If we depict alternative structures using parenthesis for matched characters, '+' for characters constituting the turn, and '-' for leading/trailing characters, three candidate solutions (out of many, resulting from applying *Pali2* to the source text of this article) can be depicted as

```
     partofatwotrack
p1:  -((((++++))))--

     wheisthereader
p2:  --(((++)))----

     grammar
p3:  -((()))
```

As elements of $\mathcal{L}(Pali2)$, they are represented as trees

```
p1 :        sl        p2 :        sl        p3 :    sl
          /  \                   /  \             /  \
        p    sr                w    sl          g  match
            /  \                   /  \          / | \
          sr    k                h    sr        r match r
         /  \                        /  \        / | \
      match  c                     sr    r      a match a
      / | \                       /  \          / | \
     a match a                   sr    e       m turn m
        / | \                   /  \              |
       r match r               sr    d
          / | \               /  \
         t match t          match  a
            / | \           / | \
           o turn o        e match e
              |            / | \
            fatw          r match r
                             / | \
                            e turn e
                               |
                              th
```

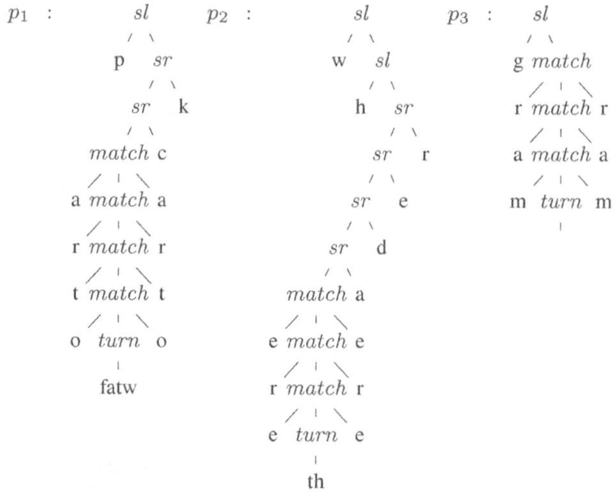

where the reader may verify (using Eq. 8) that $Pali1(score,$ "grammar") $= []$, and $Pali2(localscore,$ "grammar" $) = [9]$, where this optimal score is derived from the candidate p_3.

In many situations, the size of the search space for given input is of interest. It can be determined by a *counting* algebra, which scores every candidate by 1 and the objective function sums over all candidates. Care must be taken to write the algebra in a way such that it satisfies Bellman's Principle. Since there is a schematic way to achieve this, a counting algebra can be automatically derived from the signature. The syntax to request a counting algebra in GAP-L is:

```
algebra howMany auto count ;
```

The compiler generates an algebra named *howMany* which is equivalent to following explicit algebra definition:

```
algebra count
    implements paliS(alphabet = char,
                     answer = int) {
  int match(char a, int b, char c)
    { return b; }
  int turn(int l) { return 1; }
  int sl(char c, int x) { return x; }
  int sr(int x, char c) { return x; }
  choice [int] h([int] x)
    { return list(sum(x)); } }
```

This is a particularly simple example, but the automatic generation works for any signature.

A *print* algebra does not optimize an objective nor does it do synoptic analysis of the search space, but it specifies how a candidate structure is mapped to a string representation. The following algebra marks gaps with - characters, matches with parentheses and an unmatched position with a + character, such as -(((+++)))-. The objective function is the identity.

```
algebra print
    implements paliS(alphabet = char,
                     answer = string) {
  string match(char a, string x, char b) {
    string r; append(r, '(');
    append(r, x); append(r, ')');
    return r;
  }
  string turn(int l) {
    string r; append(r, '+', l);
    return r;
  }
  string sl(char b, string x) {
    string r; append(r, '−');
    append(r, x); return r;
  }
 string sr(string x, char b) {
    string r; append(r, x);
    append(r, '−'); return r;
  }

  choice [string] h([string] x)
    { return x; }
}
```

Bellman's GAP requires the programmer to specify in advance which combinations of grammars and algebras will be called. This is because the compiler can perform extensive optimizations and produce specialized code when the instances are known.

As part of the GAP-L program we add two instance definitions for the products we want to use:

```
instance scorecnt =
          pali2( localscore * count ) ;
instance scoreprt =
          pali2( localscore * print ) ;
```

This example displays the versatility of the lexicographic product. According to Eq. 14, the first instance computes the number of co-optimally scoring palindromes in the search space. The second instance computes the optimal palindrome score and the print string of (all) their associated candidate structures. If you ever have programmed a backtracing phase to retrieve the candidate behind the optimal score, you will appreciate getting it without programming effort in this way.

The product operators $\times$ and $\otimes$ are written as % and / characters in GAP-L.

Multi-track input GAP-L supports dynamic programming on multiple sequences. An example of a multi-track DP algorithm is the pairwise sequence alignment algorithm, i.e. the optimal sequence of edit operations to transform one sequence into the other. We write a sequence alignment grammar to exemplify the GAP-L multi-track syntax. It implements our introductory edit-distance example.

First, an input declaration specifies a two track program:

```
input < raw, raw >
```

The raw keyword means that no preprocessing of the input sequence is done. Otherwise, some character transformations may be specified.

In the grammar, the <> brackets start input track bifurcations:

```
grammar Align uses alignS(axiom = ali) {
  ali = match(<CHAR, CHAR>,   ali)  |
        ins(<EMPTY, CHAR>,    ali)  |
        del(<CHAR, EMPTY>,    ali)  |
        nil(<EMPTY, EMPTY>)          # h ; }
```

The non-terminal ali is a two-track non-terminal, i.e. it is part of a two-track context. The <> parentheses enclose as many components as the number of tracks in the current context. Each component is in a one-track context. In this example, the one-track contexts only contains terminal parser calls, but it is also possible to call one-track non-terminals from multi-track bifurcations. A use case for this is the minisatellite alignment problem [1], but the model is too complex to be included here.

The <> parentheses are also used in the signature declaration and algebra definition to access the different tracks:

```
signature alignS(alphabet, answer) {
  answer match( < alphabet, alphabet >,
                answer); ...  }
algebra affine implements
    alignS(alphabet = char, answer = int) {
  int match(<char a, char b>, int m)
  { ... } ...  }
```

Filters, parameters, and more We have already seen *syntactic filtering*, using the **with** keyword followed by filtering function defined by the programmer. This boolean function is applied to an input sub-word before it is parsed, and no parse is made if the filter is false. This implements a syntactic pruning of the search space. *Semantic filtering* is also possible using the keyword **suchthat**. It tests on values derived for a candidate by the given algebra. In this case, the candidate is parsed and scored, but may be eliminated from further consideration, for any reason we specify via the semantic filter function.

Sometimes, a grammar requires many rules with renamed non-terminal symbols, but isomorphic in structure. In this case, GAP-L allows the use of nonterminal symbols that pass parameters from the left-hand to the right-hand side.

Although subscripts are completely banned in ADP programming, sometimes scoring requires access to positions in the input, for example, when a match of two characters near the ends is to be scored more highly than near the middle. To this end, GAP-L provides a parser LOC which recognizes an empty subword and returns its position in the input. Positions so obtained become regular arguments to the algebra functions.

Finally, for programming in the large, GAP-L provides a module concept and allows to mix several algebras, signatures and grammars in one program.

4. Ex-bedding Experience

As described in the introduction, ADP was first implemented as domain specific language (DSL) embedded in Haskell. With Bellman's GAP we have chosen to ex-bed ADP from Haskell into the GAP-L language and have created the optimizing GAP-C, which translates GAP-L into efficient C++ code. [10] The reasons for the ex-bedding are threefold.

First, like with other DSLs embedded into a host language, error reporting and diagnostics are problematic in the ADP Haskell embedding. Small errors, like a missing parameter or an accidental indenting (offside rule) may lead to several screen pages of type inference errors. Effectively, to program in the embedded language one has to know how to program in Haskell and implementation details of the client language. Haskell-literacy in bioinformatics is marginal. We designed GAP-L and GAP-C with this in mind. The syntax is Java-like and algebra functions are written as imperative code. GAP-C includes some efforts for user friendly reporting of warnings and diagnostics regarding syntax and semantic errors.

Second, the performance of the Haskell embedding is limited. The runtime is several magnitudes greater in comparison with handwritten code. For several algorithms, the memory usage is

Table 1. program variations for different palindrom problems.

program	features	opt. score	answer
input $x =$ `ababdcdaaadacda`			
$Pali_1(score * print, x)$	exact palindrome	-	
$Pali_2(score * print, x)$	longer turn, free ends	6	`----((++++++))-`
$Pali_3(score * print, x)$	unmatched characters anywhere	7	`----(({{()}}))-`
$Pali_4(score * print, x)$	several adjacent palindromes	15	`(+)-(+)()((++))`
$Pali_5(score * print, x)$	nested palindromes	18	`((-)((((+))-)))`

Table 2. the results of the Pali5 grammar and two classifying example products.

grammar	Pali5$(trns * count, x)$	Pali5$(trns * score * print, x)$
input	`ababdcdaaadacda`	`ababdcdaaadacda`
results	`( 1 , 26632 )`	`( ( 1 , 15 ) , --(-((((+))-))) )`
	`( 2 , 60684 )`	`( ( 2 , 15 ) , ((+)-(((+))-)-) )`
	`( 3 , 16896 )`	`( ( 3 , 15 ) , ((+)(+)-)((++)) )`
	`( 4 , 200 )`	`( ( 4 , 10 ) , {}({}(-()(+))-) )`

very high, such that they can only be used for short sequences [10]. GAP-C includes several optimizations such that the generated imperative code is competitive with handwritten code. Since the compiler is specialized to the domain of dynamic programming, memory management is not a problem in the generated code.

Third, new language features of GAP-L, e.g. multitrack DP and filters are problematic to implement in the embedding, because of the danger of bulky parser combinators and inter-parser interactions.

However, we still maintain the Haskell embedding, because it proves to be useful in several respects. We use it as reference implementation of the ADP core. The testsuite of GAP-C includes several parallel test cases against it. Also, it is advantageous rapid prototyping of new language ideas in some cases, e.g. new product variants. Rewriting large parts of the compiler for a language extension, where it is unclear if it pays off, is not feasible.

5. Program development in Bellman's GAP

We further extend our palindrome example to demonstrate the ease of developing dynamic programming algorithms in GAP-L. See Table 1 for an overview. We rely on the reader's intuition to evaluate the extend to which such convenience carries over from our toy to real-world applications.

Four variations on palindromes Proceeding from *Pali2* to *Pali3*, we merely drop the syntactic filter, and thus leave it to the scoring functions to score two equal, or similar, characters positive, the others negative:

```
grammar Pali3 uses paliS(axiom = skipl) {
  skipl = sl(CHAR, skipl) |
          skipr             # h ;
  skipr = sr(skipr , CHAR) |
          S                 # h ;
  S = match(CHAR, S, CHAR)|
      turn(SEQ0)            # h; }
```

The *localscore* scoring algebra is changed such that mismatches are penalized:

```
int match(char a, int b, char c) {
  if (a == c) return b + 3;
          else return b - 1; }
```

Next, we change the grammar to allow for multiple successive palindromes in the input. For this, we need to add a new non-terminal to the grammar which also becomes the axiom, and we need to add another alternative rule to S to append only non-empty palindromes:

```
grammar Pali4 uses paliS(axiom = A) {
  A = skipl |
      app(skipl , S) # h ;
  ...
  S = match(CHAR, S, CHAR) |
      match(CHAR, turn(SEQ0), CHAR) # h ; }
```

The new function symbol app extends the signature. It is responsible for scoring the case of two adjacent (sub-)palindromes. We extend algebra *localscore* with a line

```
int app(int x, int y) { return x + y; }
```

Adding one more alternative rule for S, we can allow for nested palindromes, i.e. the "turn" of a palindrome can recursively contain palindromes:

```
grammar Pali5 uses paliS(axiom = A) {

  A = skipl | app(skipl , S) # h ;

  skipl = skipr                 |
          sl(CHAR, skipl) # h ;

  skipr = sr(skipr , CHAR) |
          S                # h ;

  S = match(CHAR, S, CHAR)                |
      match(CHAR, turn(SEQ), CHAR)        |
      match(CHAR, sl(CHAR, A), CHAR)      |
      match(CHAR, sr(A, CHAR), CHAR) # h; }
```

At this point, the grammar already resembles a simplified RNA secondary structure prediction grammar. We will build this in the next section on "real world" examples.

In Table 1 we give an overview of different results.

Splitting the search space into classes Let us assume we want to understand our search space more deeply, and compute several near-optimal structures, which are subject to the condition that they hold a different number of local palindromes. We leave it to the reader to design the evaluation algebra $trns$ which counts the number of "turns" in a candidate structure. (Hint: use $app(x, y) = x + y, match(a, x, b) = x$.) Using this algebra $trns$ in the two products shown in Table 2, we obtain the count of structures for each number of turns, as well as the optimal score/structure for each number.

This simple example demonstrates a general method: *any* analysis $\mathcal{G}(B, x)$ can be refined with respect to a classification attribute that can be computed by yet another algebra A, simply by calling $\mathcal{G}(A * B, x)$.

An $O(n^6)$ time, $O(n^4)$ space algorithm To give an example for an algorithm of higher complexity, let us seek optimal *joint* palindrome structures for two sequences, as exemplified by

```
MI-SSISSIPPI
+( ((+)))()
PAPPALAPAPP-
```

We extend the grammar $Align$ by a production which derives a matching character pair in either sequence, where the two pairs need not be the same. This case is scored by the new function $pmatch$. (The extended signature align2 is not shown).

```
grammar PaliJoint uses align2(axiom = pj) {
  pj = rep(<CHAR, CHAR>, pj)          |
       ins(<EMPTY, CHAR>, pj)         |
       del(<CHAR, EMPTY>, pj)         |
       nil(<EMPTY, EMPTY>)            |
       pmatch(<CHAR, CHAR>, pj,
              <CHAR, CHAR>, pj) # h ;
}
```

```
algebra score implements align2(
    alphabet = char, answer = int) {
  int rep(<char a, char b>, int x) {
    if (a==b) return x + 1;
        else  return x - 1;
  }
  int ins(<void, char b>, int x) {
    return x - 1; }
  int del(<char a, void>, int x) {
    return x - 1; }
  int nil(<void, void>) {
    return 0; }
  int pmatch(<char a1, char b1>, int x,
             <char a2, char b2>, int y) {
    if ((a1 == a2) && (b1 == b2)) {
      if (a1 == b1) return x + y + 3;
          else      return x + y + 2;
    } else { return -1000; }
  }
  choice [int] h([int] x) {
    return list(maximum(x));
  }
}
```

Here is one of the two optimal candidates for input strings "MISSISSIPPI" and "PAPPALAPAPP" with score 5.

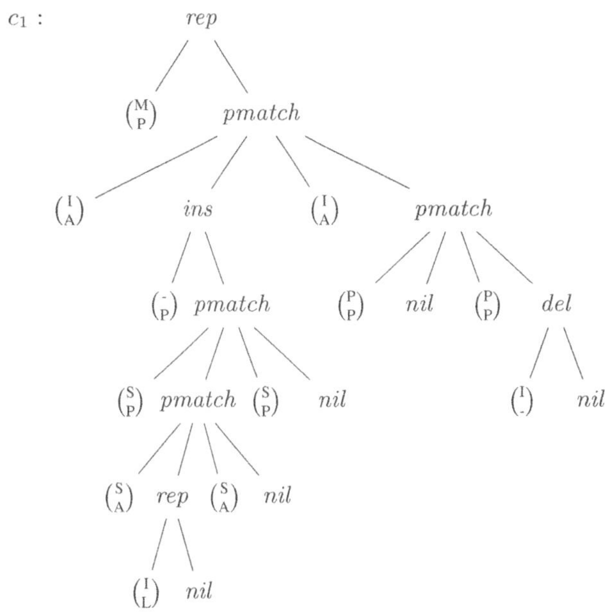

The new rule in Grammar $PaliJoint$ has the abstract form $pj \rightarrow$ '(' pj ')' pj. Due to insertions and deletions, the position of the split between the two instances of pj is independent in the two input sequences. This leads to an algorithm which requires a four-dimensional table to tabulate non-terminal pj and has asymptotics of $O(n^6)$ time and $O(n^4)$ space. This concludes our expository example series, and we turn to the real world.

6. Practice of declarative programming with Bellman's GAP

Although the Bellman's GAP system has been released just recently [10], there is already a substantial amount of practical experience. Earlier applications developed with the ADP approach were transcribed into GAP-L. Firmly based on ADP theory, recoded grammars and algebras must produce identical results in both implementations. This has been a great testbed for GAP-C. The recoded tools now enjoy the improved efficiency achieved by GAP-C, and have smoothly replaced their earlier versions available for interactive and webservice use at `http://bibiserv.cebitec.uni-bielefeld.de` [1]

In this section, we report how grammars, algebras and products interplay in practice to solve bioinformatics problems in the area of RNA structure analysis.

RNA folding RNA is a chain molecule composed from nucleotides holding the bases A (Alanine) , C (Cytosine), G (Guanine), and U (Uracil). Folding back onto it self, base pairs (A-U), (C-G), and (G-U) making hydrogen bonds create secondary structure. An RNA sequence x has a large set $F(x)$ of possible foldings, its *folding space*. Individual structures are encoded by string representations as in

```
x = AUCGUCGCAAUUGCGUCCAACGCCUUAAUG
    ..((.((((....)))...((....))..))
```

where pairing base positions are indicated by matched parentheses, and dots denote unpaired bases. "Stacks" of successive base pairs give rigidity to the folding. This class of structures resembles our palindromes described by grammar *Pali5*, now taking base pairs for matching characters. A more refined grammar is required, though,

[1] The administration pages of the server collect information about the actual usage of these tools in the bioinformatics community.

because it must accommodate a sophisticated thermodynamic scoring scheme. Based on this thermodynamic model, a structure of minimal free energy (MFE) is computed via dynamic programming, and returned as the predicted structure by established bioinformatics tools such as *Mfold* and *RNAfold* [14, 24].

RNAshapes *RNAshapes* [12] provides a grammar $\mathcal{G}_{\text{MicroStates}}$ (describing $F(x)$) as well as algebras A_{MFE} (implementing the thermodynamic energy model), and $A_{\text{dot-backet}}$ (mapping candidates to their string representations). Hence,

$$\mathcal{G}_{\text{MicroStates}}(A_{\text{MFE}} * A_{\text{dot-backet}}, x)$$

performs "classical" structure prediction by free energy minimization, akin to the aforementioned tools. The unique feature of the program *RNAshapes* is shape abstraction: candidate structures in $F(x)$ are mapped to equivalence classes called shapes, characterized by their arrangement of stacks and unpaired regions, irrespective of their length. The abstract shape of the above example structure would be represented as:

```
[[][]]
```

Shape abstraction is implemented by an algebra A_{shape}, mapping candidates to their shape. The *interleaved product* is used to compute the k best structures of different shape by a call to

$$\mathcal{G}_{\text{MicroStates}}((A_{\text{shape}} \otimes A_{\text{MFE}(k)}) * A_{\text{dot-backet}}, x).$$

This is called *simple shape analysis*.

A second function of *RNAshapes* is to re-scale folding energies into Boltzmann probabilities, which are accumulated over all structures within the same shape. This calls for a simple transformation from the A_{MFE} algebra to A_{BWE}, which computes Boltzmann-weighted energies. It requires a much more refined grammar $\mathcal{G}_{\text{MacroStates}}$ in order not to overcount candidates in the folding space. $\mathcal{G}_{\text{MacroStates}}$ has 26 non-terminal symbols and 67 productions. Trees on the right hand side of some productions have a height > 1 (which is allowed by Eq. 5 but has not occurred in our simpler examples). A call to

$$\mathcal{G}_{\text{MacroStates}}(A_{\text{shape}} * (A_{\text{MFE}} \times A_{\text{BWE}}) * A_{\text{dot-backet}}), x),$$

making use of a cartesian as well as two lexicographic products, computes the probabilities of all shapes which x can fold into, together with the minimal-free-energy structure within each shape. (For backtracing the A_{BWE} values are actually disregarded by GAP-C.) This is called *complete probabilistic shape analysis*; it provides more comprehensive information than simple shape analysis, but is more expensive to compute.

pknotsRG and pKiss So-called pseudoknots in RNA are structures which break the nested (palindromic) pattern of base pairing. Two common classes of pseudoknots, called "H-type" and "kissing hairpin" are exemplified here using different types of matching parenthesis:

```
H-type        ..[[[...{{{....]]]..}}}..
kissing HP    ..[[[...{{{....]]].<<<..}}}...>>>...
```

Such structures, in general, are not context free, but relevant subclasses thereof can be cast into a grammar which leads to recurrences of runtime $O(n^4)$. The tool *pknotsRG* [18] implements RNA folding, allowing for H-type pseudoknots where energetically favourable, and has become a widely used tool for this purpose. Its recent extension *pKiss* also allows for the kissing hairpin motif [23]. Both programs use grammars which extend $\mathcal{G}_{\text{MicroStates}}$ by special productions for pseudoknots, using syntactic filters provided in GAP-L to deal with the non-context-free features. Algebras A_{MFE} and A_{BWE} are extended by energy rules for pseudoknotted structures. We found that biologists often request to find the best structure including a pseudoknot, even when it is not near the energetic minimum. This task is solved by providing a classification algebra A_{knot}, which maps candidate structures to the value set $\{nested, knot, kiss\}$, depending on their character, with $kiss$ dominating $knot$ and $knot$ dominating $nested$. A call to

$$\mathcal{G}_{\text{pKiss}}(A_{\text{knot}} * A_{\text{MFE}} * A_{\text{dot-backet}}, x)$$

returns the structure of minimal free energy of either type.

Rapidshapes: a generator of GAP-L programs The tool *RapidShapes* marks a different type of application. It *generates* RNA folding programs coded in GAP-L. Interesting shapes p are determined by stochastic sampling. *RapidShapes* then generates so-called shape matchers coded in GAP-L, compiles them on-the-fly with GAP-C, and executes them to compute the shape probability $Prob(p)$. This takes $O(n^3)$ runtime per shape p, while complete probabilistic shape analysis (cf. above) requires $O(\alpha^n \cdot n^3)$ for $\alpha \approx 1.13$. The automatically generated grammars have up to several hundred rules, while all share the A_{MFE}, A_{BWE} and $A_{\text{dot-backet}}$ algebras from *RNAshapes*. These large GAP-L programs are typically never seen by a human programmer, and it is essential that GAP-C completely automates table design for grammars of this origin and size.

Further tools to be converted On our present agenda, there are further tools to be converted to Bellman's GAP, along with implementing planned enhancements. One is the approach of [1] for the comparison of minisatellites, which are repetitive genomic regions used in population studies. This problem is methodically interesting as it combines single-track analysis (for the construction of duplication histories of individual minisatellites) with two-track analysis (for the alignment of two minisatellite sequences) in a single grammar. This algorithm was originally coded the hard way, since ADP implementations prior to Bellman's GAP did not support single- and multitrack combinations.

The second candidate for conversion is the tool *RNAhybrid* [19], which predicts hybridization sites between a (very short) microRNA and (much longer) protein-coding RNA molecules. Today, the regulatory role of these microRNAs is intensively studied because of its medical implications, and the tool *RNAhybrid* has become the busiest tool on our server. The microRNA target prediction task is a two-track problem, with a relatively small grammar akin to $\mathcal{G}_{\text{MicroStates}}$, but with a large number of options to be set by the tool user, since the precise mechanism of interaction between microRNA and target is different between e.g. animals and plants.

7. Conclusion

Declarative dynamic programming with Bellman's GAP suggests a diverse agenda of research topics, both on the theoretical and on the practical side. Let us mention a few of these.

Theoretical questions relate to *properties of algebra products*. Products are associative (modulo re-grouping of tuples), and generally not commutative. Some conditions are known when a product preserves Bellman's Principle, especially the frequent case of $A * B$, when both are optimizing algebras, or when A computes a classification attribute. More general results are lacking. Bellman's GAP clearly states that it is the programmers's responsibility to prove that Bellman's principle is actually satisfied by a product algebra – but our programmers, who no longer have to deal with the amalgamation of search space construction and optimization, tend to forget about this fundamental prerequisite of dynamic programming.

Several *efficiency improving transformations* are known, which can reduce the runtime complexity by an order of magnitude. In general, they require a joint transformation of grammar and algebra(s); the precise preconditions have not been formulated.

As defined by Equations 6 – 10, algebraic dynamic programming is restricted to sequence input, and to a recursive pattern which follows the subword structure of the input. There are other types of recursion in dynamic programming: information flow may go from the context of a subword to the inside. Recursion may be based not on the input data structure, but on the score values achieved by candidates, e.g. with knapsack-type problems. Furthermore, the input data structure may be trees rather than strings, as occurs in RNA structure comparison. Such extensions of the algebraic approach are yet to be studied.

On the practical side, we have started to recreate the *Infernal* tool [16] in Bellman's GAP. This software creates structure-based covariance models for families of RNA sequences, which are collected in the Rfam data base [6] and widely used in RNA gene finding. Making use of product algebras, we plan to explore different, novel semantics [13] that can be associated with stochastic grammars.

Finally, as algebraic dynamic programming has started to enter (bio)informatics curricula at other universities, we feel obliged to enhance our suite of educational materials[2], migrating our collection of educational examples to GAP-L. These examples include typical problems such as the edit distance problem on strings, in many variants, optimal matrix chain multiplication, El Mamun's caravan, and satisfiability, aside from classical bioinformatics problems. We hope to solicit further examples from the community.

References

[1] M. I. Abouelhoda, R. Giegerich, B. Behzadi, and J.-M. Steyaert. Alignment of minisatellite maps based on run-length encoding scheme. *J Bioinform Comput Biol*, 7(2):287–308, 2009.

[2] R. E. Bellman. *Dynamic Programming*. Princeton University Press, 1957.

[3] E. Birney and R. Durbin. Dynamite: A flexible code generating language for dynamic programming methods used in sequence comparison. In *Proc. of the 5th ISCB*, pages 56–64, 1997.

[4] T. H. Cormen, C. E. Leiserson, R. L. Rivest, and C. Stein. *Introduction to Algorithms*. MIT Press, 2001.

[5] J. Eisner, E. Goldlust, and N. A. Smith. Compiling comp ling: Weighted dynamic programming and the Dyna language. In *Proc. of HLT-EMNLP*, pages 281–290, 2005.

[6] P. P. Gardner, J. Daub, J. G. Tate, E. P. Nawrocki, D. L. Kolbe, S. Lindgreen, A. C. Wilkinson, R. D. Finn, S. Griffiths-Jones, S. R. Eddy, and A. Bateman. Rfam: updates to the RNA families database. *Nucl. Acids Res.*, 37(suppl_1):D136–140, Jan. 2009.

[7] R. Giegerich. A systematic approach to dynamic programming in bioinformatics. *Bioinformatics*, 16:665–677, 2000.

[8] R. Giegerich and C. Meyer. Algebraic Dynamic Programming. In H. Kirchner and C. Ringeissen, editors, *AMAST 2002*, volume 2422 of *Springer Lecture Notes in Computer Science*, pages 349–364, 2002.

[9] R. Giegerich, C. Meyer, and P. Steffen. A discipline of dynamic programming over sequence data. *Science of Computer Programming*, 51(3):215–263, 2004.

[10] R. Giegerich and G. Sauthoff. Yield grammar analysis in the Bellman's GAP compiler. In *Proceedings of the Eleventh Workshop on Language Descriptions, Tools and Applications*, LDTA '11. ACM, 2011.

[11] R. Giegerich and P. Steffen. Challenges in the Compilation of a Domain Specific Language for Dynamic Programming. In H. Haddad, editor, *Proceedings of the 2006 ACM Symp. on Appl. Comp.*, 2006.

[12] R. Giegerich, B. Voß, and M. Rehmsmeier. Abstract shapes of RNA. *Nucleic Acids Research*, 32(16):4843, 2004.

[13] R. Giegerich and C. H. zu Siederdissen. Semantics and ambiguity of stochastic rna family models. *IEEE/ACM Transactions on Computational Biology and Bioinformatics*, 8(2):499–516, 2011.

[14] I. L. Hofacker, W. Fontana, P. F. Stadler, L. S. Bonhoeffer, M. Tacker, and P. Schuster. Fast folding and comparison of RNA secondary structures. *Monatshefte für Chemie*, 125(2):167–188, 1994.

[15] T. L. Morin. Monotonicity and the principle of optimality. *Journal of Mathematical Analysis and Applications*, 86:665–674, 1982.

[16] E. P. Nawrocki, D. L. Kolbe, and S. R. Eddy. Infernal 1.0: inference of RNA alignments. *Bioinformatics*, 25(10):1335–1337, May 2009.

[17] L. Pachter and B. Sturmfels. *Algebraic Statistics for Computational Biology*. Cambridge University Press, 2005.

[18] J. Reeder and R. Giegerich. Design, implementation and evaluation of a practical pseudoknot folding algorithm based on thermodynamics. *BMC Bioinformatics*, 5:104, 2004.

[19] M. Rehmsmeier, P. Steffen, M. Höchsmann, and R. Giegerich. Fast and effective prediction of microRNA/target duplexes. *RNA*, 10:1507–1517, 2004.

[20] G. Sauthoff. *Bellman's GAP: A 2nd Generation Language and System for Algebraic Dynamic Programming*. PhD thesis, Bielefeld University, 2011.

[21] G. Sauthoff and R. Giegerich. Bellman's gap language report. Technical report, Bielefeld University, 2010.

[22] P. Steffen and R. Giegerich. Versatile and declarative dynamic programming using pair algebras. *BMC Bioinformatics*, 6(1):224, 2005.

[23] C. Theis, S. Janssen, and R. Giegerich. Prediction of RNA Secondary Structure Including Kissing Hairpin Motifs. In V. Moulton and M. Singh, editors, *Algorithms in Bioinformatics*, volume 6293 of *Lecture Notes in Computer Science*, chapter 5, pages 52–64. Springer Berlin / Heidelberg, Berlin, Heidelberg, 2010.

[24] M. Zuker and P. Stiegler. Optimal computer folding of large RNA sequences using thermodynamics and auxiliary information. *Nucleic Acids Research*, 9(1):133–148, 1981.

[2] `http://bibiserv.techfak.uni-bielefeld.de/cgi-bin/dpcourse`

A Modular Semantics for Higher-Order Declarative Programming with Constraints *

Rafael del Vado Vírseda
Universidad Complutense de Madrid, Spain
rdelvado@sip.ucm.es

Fernando Pérez Morente
Universidad Complutense de Madrid, Spain
fperezmo@fdi.ucm.es

Abstract

Modularity is a key issue in the construction of large multi-paradigm declarative programs involving complex features like higher-order, polymorphism or constraints. The modular framework defined in this paper for higher-order declarative constraint programming builds complex software systems by combining and composing existing components or modules from a number of composition operations expressive enough to model typical modularization issues like export/import relationships and inheritance. The effectiveness of our approach relies on a higher-order constraint rewriting logic over a parametrically given constraint domain as the basis of a model-theoretic and fixpoint semantics for program modules, and a modular semantics given by a suitable immediate consequence operator which is compositional and fully abstract, offering the possibility of reasoning on the composition process itself. The availability of this well-founded semantics characterization for structuring and modularizing higher-order declarative constraint programs provides the ground to perform sound semantics-based transformation, analysis, debugging and verification of declarative software.

Categories and Subject Descriptors D.3.2 [*Programming Languages*]: Language Classifications—Multiparadigm languages; F.3.2 [*Logics and Meanings of Programs*]: Semantics of Programming Languages

General Terms Languages, Theory, Verification

Keywords Modular Semantics, Higher-Order Declarative Programming, Lambda Calculus, Constraints, Modules

1. Introduction

Modularity is a central issue in all programming paradigms motivated by the need of mastering the complexity inherent in the construction of large programs and systems. Building complex software systems by composing code and combining existing components is a standard methodology of software development with an incremental knowledge organization, in which programs should be developed incrementally by defining several units with their corresponding interfaces and then by composing those units. This leads to an approach to modularity based on the notion of program composition, where the effectiveness depends on the possibility of reasoning on the composition process itself. The availability of well-founded modular semantics of programs and program composition is important to perform sound semantics-based transformation [4], analysis [25], debugging [23], and verification [37].

In the multi-paradigm declarative programming setting [17], combined features like higher-order, polymorphism or constraints make essential to separate the whole task of designing a program into subtasks of manageable size. Complex declarative programs are constructed in a structured fashion by combining and modifying smaller programs or components. For instance, the constraint functional logic system $\mathcal{TOY}$ (see `http://toy.sourceforge.net`) incorporates a module system to support the main declarative programming styles and their combination: higher-order patterns, a polymorphic type system, constraints with symbolic equations and disequations, linear and non-linear arithmetic constraints over real numbers, finite domain constraints over integer numbers, and constraint domain cooperation [28]. Each module corresponds to a block of code whose external view is mediated by a signature and is defined by a file which consists of a module declaration, and import/export lists. The $\mathcal{TOY}$ module system enjoys the advantages of modularization for software development by allowing to easily interchange, add or remove predefined domain-dependent functions from the implementation by simply loading a file.

The interest in well-founded modular semantics for this class of declarative programming languages and systems has motivated a considerable research effort over the past decades and it has been the subject of an active and still open research in the theory and practice of declarative programming. A number of different approaches to modularizing declarative programming systems and languages have received theoretical treatment and have been included in practical systems [15, 20, 21, 38]. Some of them augment declarative programming with constructs for declaring and using modules, much in the spirit of conventional programming languages. In this field, a typical module consists of a body, an export interface, a list of imports and, possibly, a list of formal parameters, and typical operations with modules have to do with setting up hierarchical relationships between modules as the union of modules or deletion of signatures and the application of a parameterized module to an actual module.

In the logic programming field, several compositional semantics for logic programs have been studied by using higher-order semantics and notions such as full abstraction [13, 14, 27]. Moreover, modularity has been the objective of different proposals which basically have followed two different guidelines. One, focused on

* This work has been partially supported by the Spanish projects STAMP (TIN2008-06622-C03-01), Prometidos-CM (S2009TIC-1465) and GPD (UCM-BSCH-GR35/10-A-910502)

PDPP'11, July 20–22, 2011, Odense, Denmark.

programming-in-the-large, extends logic programming with modular constructs as a meta-linguistic mechanism [3] and gives semantics to modules with the aid of the immediate consequence operator. And the other one, focused on programming-in-the-small, enriches the theory with new logical connectives for dealing with modules [29]. Other extensions of logic programming, such as the functional and logic programming paradigm, rely on the *Constructor-based Conditional Rewriting Logic* $CRWL$ [33], a general framework for integrating first-order functional and non-constraint logic programming which gives an algebraic semantics for non-deterministic programs. In this context, [31, 32] develops a study of programs structuring and modularity in $CRWL$, based on a meta-linguistic mechanism close that developed in [2, 3].

However, in the higher-order functional and constraint logic programming framework adopted by real multi-paradigm systems such as $\mathcal{TOY}$, we do not know any study of modularity semantically well founded. Due to its expressiveness [18], higher-order declarative programming with constraints is used for specification and verification of software, hardware circuits synthesis, machine learning, theorem proving systems, and symbolic computation with complex algebraic structures in mathematics (for instance, the kernel of *Mathematica*^{TM} is a particular application of higher-order rewriting techniques with numeric constraints), providing the necessary level of abstraction for concise and natural formulations. The lack of modularity in this framework derives from the lack of compositionality in its standard semantics (i.e., the meaning of a program can be obtained from the meaning of its components).

The model-theoretic semantics recently proposed in [8] for higher-order declarative programming (without constraints) is not suitable for program modules because it is not compositional with respect to the classical operations defined over modules (union, deletion of a signature of function symbols, and renaming). With this paper we have tried to contribute to filling this gap, and has motivated our decision of developing a study of programs structuring and modularity in a higher-order logical and semantics framework with constraints useful in real declarative systems like $\mathcal{TOY}$, *Curry* (`http://www-i2.informatik.uni-kiel.de/ curry/`) or the *Teyjus* implementation (`http://teyjus.cs.umn.edu/`) of the higher-order logic programming language λ*Prolog* [24].

The paper is organized as follows. Section 2 introduces our approach by presenting a motivating example of modular hardware synthesis, intended to illustrate the main features of the higher-order declarative programming setting with constraints. In Section 3 we give a mathematical formalization of a higher-order constraint domain involving λ-terms over primitive elements. We also define the notions of program and module on a higher-order constraint domain together with a reduced set of operations on program modules, the *union* of program modules and the *deletion* of a signature in a program module. In Section 4 we introduce a higher-order constraint rewriting logic as the basis of a model-theoretic and fixpoint semantics for program modules. Section 5 provides a modular semantics, given by a suitable immediate consequence operator which is compositional and fully abstract. Finally, Section 6 summarizes some conclusions and presents a brief outline of planned future work.

2. A Motivating Example

Simple hardware circuits can be represented and computed within higher-order declarative constraint programming by simply typed λ-terms over integer numbers (int) and booleans ($bool$). As a motivation for the rest of the paper and a first impression of our higher-order programming framework, we consider an example of modular hardware synthesis adapted from [18]. Our modules consist of

- a typed signature of predefined function symbols $+ :: int \to int \to int$, $\leq :: int \to int \to bool$, etc., on a typical integer constraint domain with the usual interpretation,
- a typed signature of function symbols invoked but defined in other modules,
- an exported typed signature of defined function symbols, and
- a set of higher-order constrained program rules for the defined function symbols of the exported signature.

Let us consider a first module *Gate* to define a (first-order) specific *and*-function (or gate), a second module *Size* over integer λ-abstractions to count the number of generic gates in a circuit, and a third module *HigherOrder* with a classical higher-order function *map* for the application of a given function to a list of integers:

$$\begin{array}{ll} Gate = \langle \{\}, \{\}, \{gate :: int \to int \to int\}, \\ \qquad gate\,(0, X) \to 0 \\ \qquad gate\,(X, 0) \to 0 \\ \qquad gate\,(1, 1) \to 1 \,\rangle \end{array}$$

$$\begin{array}{l} Size = \langle \{+ :: int \to int \to int\}, \\ \qquad \{gate :: int \to int \to int\}, \\ \qquad \{size :: (int \to int \to int) \to int\}, \\ \qquad size\,(\lambda u, v.\, u) \to 0 \\ \qquad size\,(\lambda u, v.\, v) \to 0 \\ \qquad size\,(\lambda u, v.\, gate\,(F(u, v), G(u, v))) \to \\ \qquad\qquad 1 + size\,(\lambda u, v.\, F(u, v)) \\ \qquad\qquad + size\,(\lambda u, v.\, G(u, v)) \,\rangle \end{array}$$

$$\begin{array}{l} HigherOrder = \langle \{\}, \{\}, \\ \qquad \{map :: (int \to int) \to [int] \to [int]\}, \\ \qquad map\,(\lambda u.\, F(u), [\,]) \to [\,] \\ \qquad map\,(\lambda u.\, F(u), [X|Xs]) \to \\ \qquad\qquad [F(X) \mid map\,(\lambda u.\, F(u), Xs)] \,\rangle \end{array}$$

Let us consider a new module *Circuit* by joining the previous three modules

$$Circuit = Gate \cup Size \cup HigherOrder$$

as the simple union of signatures and program rules:

$$\begin{array}{l} Circuit = \langle \{+ :: int \to int \to int\}, \{\}, \\ \qquad \{gate :: int \to int \to int, \\ \qquad size :: (int \to int \to int) \to int, \\ \qquad map :: (int \to int) \to [int] \to [int]\}, \\ \qquad gate... \to ..., size... \to ..., map... \to ... \,\rangle \end{array}$$

From the module *Circuit* we are ready to compute the following goal involving integer λ-abstractions and finite domain constraints over integer numbers:

$$\begin{array}{l} map(F, [0, 1]) == [0, 1], \\ \qquad size(\lambda u, v.\, F(u)) \leq 2, \\ \qquad size(\lambda u, v.\, F(u)) \geq 1 \end{array}$$

We can apply *higher-order narrowing* [7, 18] as a suitable operational semantics to obtain the following substitution solution:

$$\{F \mapsto \lambda u, v.\, gate(u, u)\}$$

Let us also consider another module defining a specific *nand*-gate:

$$NandGate = \langle \{\}, \{\}, \{gate :: int \to int \to int\},$$

$$gate(0, X) \to 1$$
$$gate(X, 0) \to 1$$
$$gate(1, 1) \to 0 \rangle$$

From this module we could define a new module *NandCircuit* making module *Circuit* inherit from *NandGate* by means of union and deletion of the exported signature of *NandGate*:

$$NandCircuit = NandGate \cup (Circuit \setminus exp(NandGate))$$

Note that the defined function *gate*, defined in the first module *Circuit*, has been redefined in *NandCircuit* with the new version of the module *NandGate*. The rest of functions has been inherit from *Circuit*. However, if we try to compute the following higher-order constrained goal

$$\lambda x, y.\, map(F, [(0,0), (x,1), (1,y)]) == [0,1,1], \quad size(\lambda u, v.\, F(u,v)) \leq 3$$

we obtain an error with the function *map* in *NandCircuit*. This particular erroneous symptom could be mended by redefining the higher-order function *map* in a new module *HigherOrder2* (we decide to maintain the *HigherOrder* module for future higher-order programming):

$$\begin{aligned} HigherOrder2 = \langle\ & \{\}, \{\}, \\ & \{map :: (int \to int \to int) \to \\ & \quad [(int, int)] \to [int]\}, \\ & map(\lambda u, v.\, F(u,v), [\,]) \to [\,] \\ & map(\lambda u, v.\, F(u,v), [(X,Y) \mid Zs]) \to \\ & \quad [F(X,Y) \mid map(\lambda u, v.\, F(u,v), Zs)]\ \rangle \end{aligned}$$

We remove the erroneous higher-order function *map* before adding the new definition in a inherited module *NandCircuit2*:

$$\begin{aligned} & NandCircuit2 = \\ & \quad HigherOrder2 \cup (NandCircuit \setminus exp(HigherOrder2)) \end{aligned}$$

Now, we obtain by narrowing the following substitution as a solution of the last goal:

$$\{F \mapsto \lambda u, v.\, gate(gate(u,u), gate(v,v))\}$$

The availability of a well-founded modular semantics for this kind of higher-order declarative constrained programs offers the ground to perform sound semantics-based transformations, analysis, algorithmic debugging, and formal verification of hardware synthesis. In particular, the modular approach proposed in this work is important to the practical use of static analysis techniques and is fundamental to the notion of separate compilation and testing. In this paper we try to provide enough abstraction mechanisms for structuring and modularizing a higher-order framework in the constraint functional logic programming system $\mathcal{TOY}$. First, we introduce the technical background of our theoretical setting from the syntax given by the previous example.

3. Higher-Order Declarative Programming with Constraints

We briefly introduce the notions of λ-terms and patterns pertaining to simply typed λ-calculus (see e.g. [22] for more examples and motivations). As novelty in this work, we need to define lambda abstractions on a set of primitive elements $\mathcal{U}$, intended to represent some domain specific set of values, as e.g., the set of integer or real numbers. Then we introduce a mathematical formalization of higher-order constraint domains and the fundamental notions of higher-order constrained programs and modules.

3.1 Simply Typed λ-Terms and Patterns

The set of types for simply typed λ-terms is generated by a set $\mathcal{B}$ of *base types* (as e.g., *bool*, *int*) and the function type constructor "$\to$". Simply typed λ-*terms* are generated from a signature $\mathcal{F}$ of *function symbols*, a countably infinite set $\mathcal{V}$ of *variables*, and a set $\mathcal{U}$ of *primitive elements* by successive operations of abstraction and application:

$$t ::= X\ (X \in \mathcal{V}) \mid u\ (u \in \mathcal{U}) \mid f\ (f \in \mathcal{F}) \mid \lambda x.\, t\ (x \in \mathcal{V}) \mid (t\ t')$$

We also consider the enhanced signature $\mathcal{F}_\perp = \mathcal{F} \cup \texttt{Bot}$, where $\texttt{Bot} = \{\perp_b \mid b \in \mathcal{B}\}$ is a set of distinguished $\mathcal{B}$-typed constants. The constant $\perp_b$ is intended to denote an *undefined value* of type b. We employ $\perp$ as a generic notation for a constant from Bot. In this paper, we assume the following conventions of notation: X, Y, Z, R, H, possibly primed or with subscripts, denote *free variables*; f, f' denote function symbols, and a a (free or bound) variable or a constant from $\mathcal{F}$; l, r, s, t, u, possibly primed or with subscript, denote terms; $\pi, \pi', \pi_1, \pi_2, \ldots$ denote terms of base type. We also define the *arity* of $f \in \mathcal{F}$ as $ar(f) = n \geq 0$.

A sequence of syntactic objects $o_1, \ldots, o_n$, where $n \geq 0$, is abbreviated by $\overline{o_n}$. For instance, the simply typed λ-term $\lambda x_1. \cdots .\lambda x_k. (\cdots (a\ t_1)\ \cdots\ t_n)$ is abbreviated by $\lambda \overline{x_k}.\, a(\overline{t_n})$. *Substitutions* $\gamma \in Subst(\mathcal{F}_\perp, \mathcal{V}, \mathcal{U})$ are finite type-preserving mappings from variables to λ-terms, extended homomorphically to λ-terms. By convention, we write $\{\}$ for the *identity substitution*, $t\{x \mapsto s\}$ to denote the results of replacing every free occurrence of x in t by s, $t\sigma$ instead of $\sigma(t)$, and $\sigma\sigma'$ for the function composition $\sigma' \circ \sigma$.

Besides α-*conversion*, i.e. the consistent renaming of bound variables, the β-*conversion* in λ-calculus is defined as $(\lambda x.s)t =_\beta s\{x \mapsto t\}$, and the η-*conversion* as $\lambda x. (t\, x) =_\eta t$ if x is not a free variable of t. The *long* $\beta\eta$-*normal form* of a λ-term t, denoted by $t\updownarrow^\eta_\beta$, is the η-expanded form of the β-normal form of t. It is well-known that $s =_{\alpha\beta\eta} t$ if $s\updownarrow^\eta_\beta =_\alpha t\updownarrow^\eta_\beta$ [22]. Since $\beta\eta$-normal forms are always defined, we will in general assume that λ-terms are in long $\beta\eta$-normal form and are identified modulo α-conversion. For brevity, we may write variables and constants from $\mathcal{F}$ in η-normal form, e.g., X instead of $\lambda\overline{x_k}.\, X(\overline{x_k})$. We assume that the transformation into long $\beta\eta$-normal form is an implicit operation, e.g., when applying a substitution to a λ-term. With these conventions, every λ-term t has an unique long $\beta\eta$-normal form $\lambda\overline{x_k}.\, a(\overline{t_n})$, where $a \in \mathcal{F}_\perp \cup \mathcal{V} \cup \mathcal{U}$ and $a()$ coincides with a. We distinguish between the set $\mathcal{T}(\mathcal{F}_\perp, \mathcal{V}, \mathcal{U})$ of *partial* λ-terms and the set $\mathcal{T}(\mathcal{F}, \mathcal{V}, \mathcal{U})$ of *total* λ-terms. The set $\mathcal{T}(\mathcal{F}_\perp, \mathcal{V}, \mathcal{U})$ is a poset with respect to the *approximation ordering* $\sqsubseteq$, defined as the least partial ordering such that:

$$\lambda\overline{x_k}.\, \perp \sqsubseteq \lambda\overline{x_k}.\, t \qquad t \sqsubseteq t \qquad \frac{s_1 \sqsubseteq t_1 \ \cdots\ s_n \sqsubseteq t_n}{\lambda\overline{x_k}.\, a(\overline{s_n}) \sqsubseteq \lambda\overline{x_k}.\, a(\overline{t_n})}$$

A λ-term t is called a *(higher-order) pattern* if every free occurrence of a variable X in t is in a subterm $X(\overline{t_n})$ of base type of t such that the $\overline{t_n}$ are η-equivalent to a list of distinct bound variables. Moreover, if there are no other bound variables in all such subterms of t, then the pattern t is fully extended. Formally:

DEFINITION 1 (Higher-Order Patterns).

(1) A pattern is a λ-term t for which all subterms $t|_p = X(\overline{t_n})$, with $X \in \mathcal{FV}(t)$ a free variable of t and $p \in MPos(t)$ a maximal position in t (i.e., $t|_p$ is of base type), satisfy the condition that $t_1{\downarrow_\eta}, \ldots, t_n{\downarrow_\eta}$ is a sequence of distinct elements of the set $\mathcal{BV}(t, p)$ of bound variables abstracted on the path to position p in t.

(2) If all such subterms of t satisfy the additional condition $\mathcal{BV}(t,p)\setminus\{t_1{\downarrow_\eta},\ldots,t_n{\downarrow_\eta}\}=\emptyset$*, then the pattern t is fully extended.*

It is well known that unification of patterns is decidable and unitary (see e.g. [30]). Therefore, for every $t \in \mathcal{T}(\mathcal{F}_\perp,\mathcal{V},\mathcal{U})$ and pattern π, there exists at most one matcher between t and π.

EXAMPLE 1. *Examples of higher-order patterns are* $\lambda x, y.\, F(x,y)$, $\lambda x.\, f(G(\lambda z.\, x(z)))$, *and* $\lambda x, y, z.\, g(F(x,y))$, *where only the latter is not fully extended. Non-patterns are for instance* $\lambda x, y.\, F(a,y)$ *and* $\lambda x.\, G(H(x))$.

3.2 Higher-Order Constraint Domains

We propose the notion of *higher-order constraint domains* $\mathcal{D}$ as structures with carrier set ground patterns built from a set of primitive elements $\mathcal{U}$, intended to represent some domain specific values (as e.g., the set of the integer numbers), and a domain-dependent signature $\mathcal{F}_\mathcal{D}$, intended to represent domain specific primitive functions (as e.g., addition over integer numbers).

DEFINITION 2 (Higher-order constraint domain). *A* (higher-order) constraint domain *over a set of primitive elements* $\mathcal{U}$ *and a domain-dependent signature* $\mathcal{F}_\mathcal{D}$ *is any structure* $\mathcal{D}=\langle D_\mathcal{U}, \{p^\mathcal{D}\}_{p\in\mathcal{F}_\mathcal{D}}\rangle$ *such that the carrier set* $D_\mathcal{U}$ *coincides with the set of ground patterns (i.e., patterns without free variables over the set of primitive elements* $\mathcal{U}$ *and the constraint signature* $\mathcal{F}_\mathcal{D}$*), and the interpretation* $p^\mathcal{D} \subseteq (\mathcal{D}_\mathcal{U})^n \times \mathcal{D}_\mathcal{U}$ *of each* $p \in \mathcal{F}_\mathcal{D}$ *with arity n (we use the notation* $p^\mathcal{D}\overline{t_n} \to t$ *to indicate that* $(\overline{t_n},t) \in p^\mathcal{D}$*) satisfy the following requirements:*

(1) Whenever $p^\mathcal{D}\overline{t_n} \to t$, $\overline{t_n} \sqsubseteq \overline{t'_n}$ *and* $t \sqsupseteq t'$ *one also has* $p^\mathcal{D}\overline{t'_n} \to t'$.

(2) Whenever $p^\mathcal{D}\overline{t_n} \to t$ *and* $t \neq \perp$*, there is some total pattern (i.e., a pattern without* $\perp$ *occurrences)* $t' \in D_\mathcal{U}$ *such that* $p^\mathcal{D}\overline{t_n} \to t'$ *and* $t' \sqsupseteq t$.

EXAMPLE 2. *The* $\curlywedge$*-constraint domain [9] is a higher-order constraint domain built over the empty set of primitive elements, and having* $==^\curlywedge$ *as its only primitive function:*

$$\curlywedge = \langle D_\emptyset^\curlywedge, \{==^\curlywedge\}\rangle$$

such that the carrier set $D_\emptyset^\curlywedge$ *coincides with the set of ground patterns over an empty set of primitive elements, and* $==^\curlywedge \subseteq (D_\emptyset^\curlywedge)^2 \times D_\emptyset^\curlywedge$*, where* $t_1 ==^\curlywedge t_2 \to t$ *iff one of the following three cases hold:*

(1) t_1 *and* t_2 *are one and the same total* λ*-term in* $D_\emptyset^\curlywedge$*, and true* $\sqsupseteq$ *t.*

(2) t_1 *and* t_2 *have no common upper bound in* $D_\emptyset^\curlywedge$ *with respect to the approximation ordering* $\sqsupseteq$ *and false* $\sqsupseteq$ *t.*

(3) $t = \perp$.

The higher-order constraint finite domain $\mathcal{FD}$ *extends* $\curlywedge$ *with the usual primitive operators and relations over the integer set of primitive elements* $0, 1, -1, 2, -2, \ldots$ *(i.e.,* $+ :: int \to int \to int$, $\leq :: int \to int \to bool$*, etc.), the domain* $:: [int] \to int \to int \to bool$ *primitive used for constraining the possible values of a list of integer variables, and the labeling* $:: [int] \to bool$ *primitive for constraining a list of integer variables to take concrete values from its domain. Analogously, the higher-order constraint domain* $\mathcal{R}$ *extends* $\curlywedge$ *with the usual primitive operators and relations over the set of real numbers.*

The following definition introduces *$\mathcal{D}$-constraints* in a constraint domain $\mathcal{D}$ as atomic higher-order logical formulas built over the set of primitive elements $\mathcal{U}_\mathcal{D}$, identified by $\mathcal{D}$, and the constraint signature $\mathcal{F}_\mathcal{D}$.

DEFINITION 3 ($\mathcal{D}$-Constraints). *A (higher-order)* $\mathcal{D}$*-constraint has the syntactic form* $p\,\overline{t_n} \to t$*, with* $p \in \mathcal{F}_\mathcal{D}$ *of arity* $n \geq 0$, $t_i \in \mathcal{T}(\mathcal{F}_\perp,\mathcal{V},\mathcal{U}_\mathcal{D})$*, and* $t \in \mathcal{T}(\mathcal{F},\mathcal{V},\mathcal{U}_\mathcal{D})$*. In the sequel,* $p\,\overline{t_n}$ *abbreviates* $p\,\overline{t_n} \to true$.

EXAMPLE 3. *In order to illustrate* $\mathcal{FD}$*-constraints, let us consider two constraints from our running example given in Section 2:*

(a) $map\;(\lambda u.\, gate\,(u,u), [0,1]) == [1,0]$
(b) $size\;(\lambda u, v.\, gate\,(gate\,(u,u), gate\,(v,v))) \leq 3$

3.3 Higher-Order Constrained Programs and Modules

In the sequel we assume an arbitrary fixed higher-order constraint domain $\mathcal{D}$ built over a set of primitive elements $\mathcal{U}_\mathcal{D}$ and a constraint signature $\mathcal{F}_\mathcal{D}$. In our higher-order declarative programming framework with $\mathcal{D}$-constraints, *programs* are considered as a special kind of $\mathcal{D}$-constrained rewrite systems over fully extended linear patterns for defined function symbols with arity $n \geq 0$, and $\mathcal{D}$-constraints over total λ-terms in the constrained part "$\Leftarrow$" of each rewriting rule, called *program rules*.

DEFINITION 4 ($CPRS(\mathcal{D})$-programs). *A constrained pattern rewrite system* $\mathcal{P}$ *over a higher-order constraint domain* $\mathcal{D}$ *(i.e., a* $CPRS(\mathcal{D})$*-program for short) is a finite set of* $\mathcal{D}$*-constrained rewrite rules of the form* $f(\overline{l_n}) \to r \Leftarrow C$*, where:*

(1) $f(\overline{l_n})$ *and r are total* λ*-terms over* $\mathcal{U}_\mathcal{D}$ *of the same base type of* $\mathcal{B}$.

(2) $f(\overline{l_n})$ *is a fully extended linear pattern.*

(3) C is a (possibly empty) finite sequence of total $\mathcal{D}$*-constraints.*

Each $CPRS(\mathcal{D})$*-program* $\mathcal{P}$ *induces a partition of the underlying signature* $\mathcal{F}^\mathcal{P}$ *into* $\mathcal{F}^\mathcal{P}_\mathcal{D}$ *(primitive function symbols in* $\mathcal{D}$ *that appear in* $\mathcal{P}$*),* $\mathcal{F}^\mathcal{P}_d$ *(function symbols defined in* $\mathcal{P}$*), and* $\mathcal{F}^\mathcal{P}_c = \mathcal{F}^\mathcal{P} \setminus (\mathcal{F}^\mathcal{P}_\mathcal{D} \cup \mathcal{F}^\mathcal{P}_d)$ *(data constructors).*

EXAMPLE 4. *As a concrete example, we consider the following* $CPRS(\mathcal{R})$*-program defining a higher-order function diff to compute the differential of a function f at some numeric value X under some arithmetic* $\mathcal{R}$*-constraints in the conditional part of program rules.*

$diff :: (real \to real) \to real \to real$

$diff\;(\lambda u.\, u, X) \;\to\; 1$
$diff\;(\lambda u.\, ln\,(F(u)), X) \;\to\; diff\;(\lambda u.\, F(u), X)/F(X) \;\Leftarrow F(X) \neq 0$
$diff\;(\lambda u.\, sin\,(F(u)), X) \;\to\; cos\,(F(X)) * diff\;(\lambda u.\, F(u), X) \;\Leftarrow$
$\pi/4 \leq F(X) \leq \pi/2$

Programs are used to solve goals by means of a suitable *goal solving calculus* [7, 9] based on higher-order narrowing and parameterized by a constraint solver over the given constraint domain $\mathcal{D}$. A goal for a given $CPRS(\mathcal{D})$ is a set of $\mathcal{D}$-constraints. For instance, we can compute the substitution $\{F \mapsto \lambda u.\, sin\,(u)\}$ as a solution of the goal $\lambda x.\, diff\;(\lambda u. ln\,(F(u)), x) == \lambda x.\, cos\,(x)/sin\,(x)$ because the constraint $\lambda x.\, (\pi/4 \leq x \leq \pi/2 \to sin\,(x) \neq 0)$ is evaluated to *true* by an $\mathcal{R}$-constraint solver.

For designing large $CPRS(\mathcal{D})$-programs it is convenient to separate the whole task into subtasks of manageable size and construct programs in a structured fashion by combining and modifying smaller programs, as we have seen in Section 2. This idea has been extended to many programming languages giving rise to different notions of *program module*, each one being attached to a programming paradigm. In $CPRS(\mathcal{D})$-programming we are going to follow an approach close to that developed in [2, 3] for logic programming and first-order functional logic programming [31, 32]. However, in the new higher-order setting with constraints we must consider modules as open programs in the sense that function definitions in a *defined module* can be completed with definitions for the same functions in other modules or in the higher-order constraint domain $\mathcal{D}$, interpreted as a *predefined module*.

DEFINITION 5 (Defined and predefined modules).

(1) Given a signature $\mathcal{F} = \mathcal{F}_\mathcal{D} \cup \mathcal{F}_d$, a $\mathcal{D}$-defined module $\mathcal{M}$ (or $\mathcal{D}$-module for short) in $CPRS(\mathcal{D})$-programming is a tuple:

$$\mathcal{M} = \langle\, \mathcal{F}_\mathcal{D}^\mathcal{M}, \mathcal{F}^\mathcal{M}, \mathcal{F}_d^\mathcal{M}, \mathcal{P}_\mathcal{M} \,\rangle$$

where:

- *$\mathcal{P}_\mathcal{M}$ is a $CPRS(\mathcal{D})$-program.*
- *$\mathcal{F}_\mathcal{D}^\mathcal{M} \subseteq \mathcal{F}_\mathcal{D}$ are the domain-dependent primitive function symbols $p \in \mathcal{F}_\mathcal{D}$ that appear in $\mathcal{P}_\mathcal{M}$.*
- *$\mathcal{F}^\mathcal{M} \subseteq \mathcal{F}$ are the function symbols $g \in \mathcal{F}$ with no definition rule in $\mathcal{P}_\mathcal{M}$ that are invoked in $\mathcal{P}_\mathcal{M}$.*
- *$\mathcal{F}_d^\mathcal{M} \subseteq \mathcal{F}_d$ are the defined function symbols $f \in \mathcal{F}_d$ in $\mathcal{P}_\mathcal{M}$.*

$\mathcal{P}_\mathcal{M}$ is the body *of the $\mathcal{D}$-module and $\langle\, \mathcal{F}_\mathcal{D}^\mathcal{M}, \mathcal{F}^\mathcal{M}, \mathcal{F}_d^\mathcal{M} \,\rangle$ its* interface. *More precisely, $\mathcal{F}_d^\mathcal{M}$ is the exported signature of defined functions, $\mathcal{F}^\mathcal{M}$ is the parameter (imported) signature, and $\mathcal{F}_\mathcal{D}^\mathcal{M}$ is the domain-dependent (imported) signature. The interface of a $\mathcal{D}$-module could be inferred from its body and the higher-order constraint domain $\mathcal{D}$.*

(2) A $\mathcal{D}$-predefined module is a particular case of $\mathcal{D}$-module with no imported signatures in which the exported signature coincides with the constraint signature $\mathcal{F}_\mathcal{D}$ of the domain $\mathcal{D}$.

EXAMPLE 5. *As an example of $\mathcal{R}$-module for the higher-order constraint domain $\mathcal{R}$, we consider the following interface for the previous $CPRS(\mathcal{R})$-program to compute the differential of a function at some numeric value:*

$$\begin{array}{lcl} \textit{Differential} & = & \langle\ \{* :: real \to real \to real, \\ & & \quad / :: real \to real \to real, \\ & & \quad \neq :: real \to real \to bool, \\ & & \quad \leq :: real \to real \to bool\}, \\ & & \quad \{sin :: real \to real \to real, \\ & & \quad cos :: real \to real \to real, \\ & & \quad ln :: real \to real \to real\}, \\ & & \quad \{diff :: (real \to real) \to real \to real\}\ \rangle \end{array}$$

The body of the Differential module is given in Example 4.

Our modular framework defined for higher-order declarative constraint programming consists of a small number of operations over $\mathcal{D}$-modules which will be semantically justified in Section 5. We present now this set of basic operations that allow us to express typical features of modularization techniques in declarative programming. We focus on the most basic composition operations over declarative programs, the *union* of programs and the *deletion* of a signature. However, the high expressiveness of these operations enable us to model typical constructs for program modularization like export/import, instantiation, and inheritance with overriding in a simple way.

- **Union.** The union of $\mathcal{D}$-modules reflects the behavior of some programming systems that allow adding new programs stored in separate files to the main database. We define the union of two $\mathcal{D}$-modules as the $\mathcal{D}$-module obtained as the simple union of signatures and rules over the constraint domain $\mathcal{D}$. Given two $\mathcal{D}$-modules $\mathcal{M}_1 = \langle\, \mathcal{F}_\mathcal{D}^{\mathcal{M}_1}, \mathcal{F}^{\mathcal{M}_1}, \mathcal{F}_d^{\mathcal{M}_1}, \mathcal{P}_{\mathcal{M}_1} \,\rangle$ and $\mathcal{M}_2 = \langle\, \mathcal{F}_\mathcal{D}^{\mathcal{M}_2}, \mathcal{F}^{\mathcal{M}_2}, \mathcal{F}_d^{\mathcal{M}_2}, \mathcal{P}_{\mathcal{M}_2} \,\rangle$, their union $\mathcal{M}_1 \cup \mathcal{M}_2$ is defined as the $\mathcal{D}$-module:

$$\begin{array}{rl} \mathcal{M}_1 \cup \mathcal{M}_2 =_{def} \langle & \mathcal{F}_\mathcal{D}^{\mathcal{M}_1} \cup \mathcal{F}_\mathcal{D}^{\mathcal{M}_2}, \\ & (\mathcal{F}^{\mathcal{M}_1} \cup \mathcal{F}^{\mathcal{M}_2}) \setminus (\mathcal{F}_d^{\mathcal{M}_1} \cup \mathcal{F}_d^{\mathcal{M}_2}), \\ & \mathcal{F}_d^{\mathcal{M}_1} \cup \mathcal{F}_d^{\mathcal{M}_2}, \\ & \mathcal{P}_{\mathcal{M}_1} \cup \mathcal{P}_{\mathcal{M}_2} \,\rangle \end{array}$$

  Each argument in this operation is considered an open program that can be extended or completed with the other argument, possibly with additional rules for its exported function symbols.

- **Deletion.** Deletion of a signature $\mathcal{F} = \mathcal{F}_\mathcal{D} \cup \mathcal{F}_d$ in a $\mathcal{D}$-module $\mathcal{M}$ removes all $\mathcal{D}$-primitive functions $\mathcal{F}_\mathcal{D}$ in $\mathcal{F}_\mathcal{D}^\mathcal{M}$, and all rules defining function symbols $\mathcal{F}_d$ in that signature $\mathcal{F}_d^\mathcal{M}$, but maintains the occurrences of these symbols in the right hand side of the other rules. This option can be used to abstract the signature $\mathcal{F}$ from a $\mathcal{D}$-module $\mathcal{M}$, and is very useful for making generic modules from concrete ones. Formally, given a $\mathcal{D}$-module $\mathcal{M} = \langle\, \mathcal{F}_\mathcal{D}^\mathcal{M}, \mathcal{F}^\mathcal{M}, \mathcal{F}_d^\mathcal{M}, \mathcal{P}_\mathcal{M} \,\rangle$, the deletion in $\mathcal{M}$ of a signature of function symbols $\mathcal{F}$ produces the $\mathcal{D}$-module:

$$\mathcal{M} \backslash \mathcal{F} =_{def} \langle\, \mathcal{F}_\mathcal{D}^\mathcal{M} \setminus \mathcal{F}_\mathcal{D}, \mathcal{F}'^\mathcal{M}, \mathcal{F}_d^\mathcal{M} \setminus \mathcal{F}_d, \mathcal{P}_\mathcal{M} \backslash \mathcal{F}_d \,\rangle$$

  where $\mathcal{F}'^\mathcal{M}$ denotes the corresponding parameter signature, and $\mathcal{P}_\mathcal{M} \backslash \mathcal{F}_d$ denotes the set of those rules in $\mathcal{P}_\mathcal{M}$ defining function symbols not appearing in $\mathcal{F}_d$.

- **Inheritance.** From the union and deletion operations we can model an inheritance relationship between $\mathcal{D}$-modules. *Inheritance with overriding* may be captured by means of union and deletion as follows:

$$\mathcal{M} \ll \mathcal{N} =_{def} \mathcal{M} \cup (\mathcal{N} \setminus \mathcal{F}_d^\mathcal{M})$$

  This new $\mathcal{D}$-module $\mathcal{M} \ll \mathcal{N}$ inherits all functions in $\mathcal{N}$, with their rules, not defined in $\mathcal{M}$ and uses the rules of $\mathcal{M}$ for all functions defined in $\mathcal{M}$, overriding the definition rules in $\mathcal{N}$, for common functions. In this case, overriding is carried out by deleting the common signature of the inherited $\mathcal{D}$-module before adding it to the derived module.

- **Instantiation.** We can instantiate function symbols of a $\mathcal{D}$-module $\mathcal{M} = \langle\, \mathcal{F}_\mathcal{D}^\mathcal{M}, \mathcal{F}^\mathcal{M}, \mathcal{F}_d^\mathcal{M}, \mathcal{P}_\mathcal{M} \,\rangle$ with function symbols exported by other $\mathcal{D}$-module, simply by renaming suitably the functions of $\mathcal{M}$ to fit (a part of) the exported signature of $\mathcal{N}$. Thus, we obtain an instantiation operation that we denote $\mathcal{M}[\mathcal{N}, \theta]$ and define as:

$$\mathcal{M}[\mathcal{N}, \theta] =_{def} \mathcal{N} \ll \theta(\mathcal{M})$$

  where θ is the function symbol renaming that characterizes the instantiation, and $\theta(\mathcal{M}) =_{def} \langle\, \theta(\mathcal{F}_\mathcal{D}^\mathcal{M}) \setminus \theta(\mathcal{F}_d^\mathcal{M}), \theta(\mathcal{F}^\mathcal{M}) \setminus \theta(\mathcal{F}_d^\mathcal{M}), \theta(\mathcal{F}_d^\mathcal{M}), \mathcal{P}_\mathcal{M}\theta \,\rangle$. The renaming operation allows us to change function symbols with other function symbols in a signature.

Practical applications in our higher-order constraint declarative programming framework often involve more than one "pure" domain (i.e., λ, $\mathcal{R}$, $\mathcal{FD}$, etc.). The current implementation of the constraint functional logic system $\mathcal{TOY}$ offers a module system for constraint domain cooperation between the higher-order constraint domains $\mathcal{FD}$ and $\mathcal{R}$. An important idea emerging from our

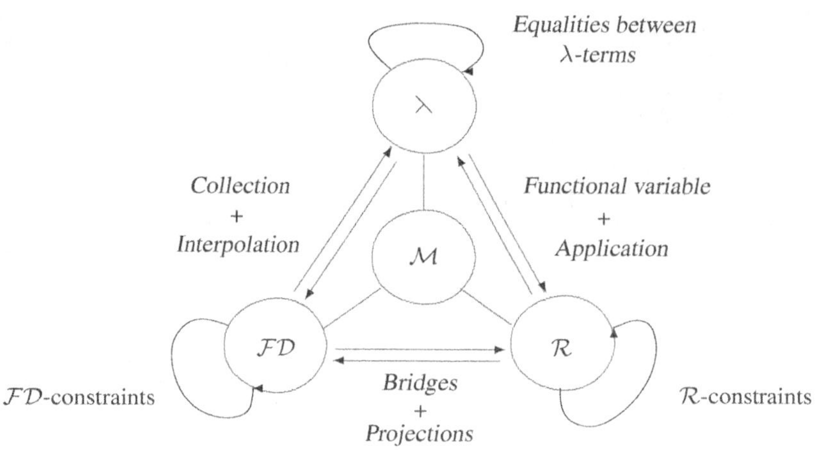

Figure 1. Modular design of the higher-order coordination constraint domain $\mathcal{C} = \mathcal{M} \oplus \lambda \oplus \mathcal{FD} \oplus \mathcal{R}$.

approach to modularity is that *hybrid constraint domains* $\mathcal{C}$, built as a combination of simpler pure domains $\mathcal{D}$, can be designed in a modular way. This modular design supports the cooperation and coordinations of the predefined $\mathcal{D}$-modules, so that more declarative and efficient solutions for practical problems can be promoted.

EXAMPLE 6 (Modular Constraint Cooperation). *A common problem in engineering is the approximation of a complicated continuous function by a simple discrete function (e.g., the approximation of GPS satellite coordinates). Suppose we know a real function (given by a lambda abstraction $\lambda u.\, F(u)$) but it is too complex to evaluate efficiently. Then we could pick a few approximated (integer) data points from the complicated function, and try to interpolate those data points to construct a simpler function, for example, a polynomial $\lambda u.\, P(u)$. We propose the following interface of a $\mathcal{C}$-module to approximate a continuous function represented by a lambda abstraction $\lambda u.\, F(u)$ over real numbers by a discrete polynomial function $\lambda u.\, P(u)$ over integer numbers:*

$$\begin{array}{lll} GPS & = & \langle\ \{domain :: [int] \to int \to int \to bool, \\ & & \quad labeling :: [int] \to bool, \\ & & \quad \rightleftharpoons :: int \to real \to bool, \\ & & \quad - :: real \to real \to real, \\ & & \quad < :: real \to real \to bool, \\ & & \quad |\cdot| :: real \to real\}, \\ & & \quad \{collection :: int \to int \to [(int, int)] \to bool, \\ & & \quad interpolation :: [(int, int)] \to (int \to int) \to bool\}, \\ & & \quad \{disc :: (real \to real) \to (int \to int)\}\ \rangle \end{array}$$

where the corresponding body of the module is:

$$\begin{array}{l} disc\,(\lambda u.\, F(u)) \ \to\ \lambda u.\, P(u) \ \Leftarrow \\ \qquad domain\ [X]\ 0\ N,\ labeling\ [X], \\ \qquad X \rightleftharpoons RX,\ Y \rightleftharpoons RY, \\ \qquad |\, F(RX) - RY\,| < 1, \\ \qquad collection\ X\ Y\ C,\ interpolation\ C\ P \end{array}$$

The $\mathcal{C}$-module *GPS* uses the predefined $\mathcal{FD}$-module to provide $\mathcal{FD}$-constraints $domain\ [X]\ 0\ N$, $labeling\ [X]$ to generate each value of the discrete interval $[0..N]$. In order to model the cooperation and communication between $\mathcal{FD}$-modules and $\mathcal{R}$-modules we use a special kind of hybrid constraints $\rightleftharpoons$ called *bridges* provided by a predefined *mediatorial domain* $\mathcal{M}$, as a key tool for communicating constraints between different higher-order numeric constraint domains [9, 28]. More precisely, the first bridge constraint $X \rightleftharpoons RX$ maps each integer value of X into an equivalent real value in RX. By applying the higher-order functional variable F to RX we obtain the $\mathcal{R}$-constraint $|\, F(RX) - RY\,| < 1$ provided by the primitive functions of the predefined $\mathcal{R}$-module. From this constraint, the $\mathcal{R}$-solver computes (infinitely many) real values for RY. However, because of the second bridge constraint $Y \rightleftharpoons RY$, each real value assigned to RY by the constraint solving process causes the variable Y to be bound only to an equivalent integer value. By means of the primitive constraint $collection\ X\ Y\ C$ provided by the predefined λ-module we can collect all the pairs (X, Y) generated by the labeling-solving process in a set C. Finally, $interpolation\ C\ P$ finds a polynomial which goes exactly through the points collected in C by means of the *Lagrange Interpolation* method. For instance, we can consider the following goal $disc\,(\lambda u.\, 4 * u - u^2) == \lambda u.\, P(u)$ involving the continuous function F as $\lambda u.\, 4 * u - u^2$ with $N = 4$. We obtain the set of integer pairs (x_i, y_i) in $C = \{(0,0), (1,3), (2,4), (3,3), (4,0)\}$. For this particular case, it is easy to check that this computed answer is simply $\{P \mapsto \lambda u.\, 4 * u - u^2\}$.

Figure 1 illustrates the modular design of the $\mathcal{TOY}$ system for the cooperation among predefined $\mathcal{D}$-modules, and the mechanisms for communication and coordination via bridges, projections, functional variable applications, interpolations, and some more ad hoc operations.

4. Model and Fixpoint Semantics

The effectiveness of our modular approach relies on a higher-order constraint rewriting logic over a parametrically given constraint domain as the basis of a model-theoretic and fixpoint semantics given by a suitable immediate consequence operator which is compositional and fully abstract, as we will see in Section 5. The ideas presented in this section extend and generalize our previous works [8, 11], now with $\mathcal{D}$-constraints on a higher-order constraint domain $\mathcal{D}$. For this reason, we focus on the main novelties and differences with respect to [8, 11] which are necessary to define our modular approach in the next section, and encourage the interested reader to visit [8, 11, 32, 33] for a more detailed explanation on the common technical notions and notations used in this extension.

4.1 A Higher-Order Proof Calculus with Constraints

We generalize the $GHRC$ proof calculus with λ-abstractions presented in [8, 11] to a new proof calculus $GHRC(\mathcal{D})$ with $\mathcal{D}$-constraints in a parameterized higher-order constraint domain $\mathcal{D}$. The purpose of this calculus is to infer the semantic validity of arbitrary reduction statements (similarly to [8, 11]) besides new

B	**Bottom**	$\lambda\overline{x_k}.\, \pi \twoheadrightarrow \lambda\overline{x_k}.\, \bot$
MN	**MoNotonicity**	$\dfrac{\lambda\overline{x_k}.\, s_1 \twoheadrightarrow \lambda\overline{x_k}.\, t_1 \;\cdots\; \lambda\overline{x_k}.\, s_n \twoheadrightarrow \lambda\overline{x_k}.\, t_n}{\lambda\overline{x_k}.\, a(\overline{s_n}) \twoheadrightarrow \lambda\overline{x_k}.\, a(\overline{t_n})}$
RF	**ReFlexivity**	$s \twoheadrightarrow s$
DF	**Defined Function**	$\dfrac{\lambda\overline{x_k}.\, s_1 \twoheadrightarrow l_1^{\updownarrow\overline{x_k}}\theta \;\cdots\; \lambda\overline{x_k}.\, s_n \twoheadrightarrow l_n^{\updownarrow\overline{x_k}}\theta \quad C^{\updownarrow\overline{x_k}}\theta \quad \pi^{\updownarrow\overline{x_k}}\theta \twoheadrightarrow u}{\lambda\overline{x_k}.\, f(\overline{s_n}) \twoheadrightarrow u}$ if $f \in \mathcal{F}_d^{\mathcal{P}}, u \neq \lambda\overline{x_k}.\, \bot$, and $(f(\overline{l_n}) \to r \Leftarrow C) \in \mathcal{P}$, with $\theta \in VSubst(\mathcal{F}_\bot, \mathcal{V}, \mathcal{U}_\mathcal{D})$.
PF	**Primitive Function**	$\dfrac{\lambda\overline{x_k}.\, s_1 \twoheadrightarrow u_1 \;\cdots\; \lambda\overline{x_k}.\, s_n \twoheadrightarrow u_n}{\lambda\overline{x_k}.\, p(\overline{s_n}) \twoheadrightarrow u}$ if $p \in \mathcal{F}_\mathcal{D}, u \neq \lambda\overline{x_k}.\, \bot$, and $p^{\mathcal{D}}\overline{u_n} \to u$ with $u_i \in Val(\mathcal{F}, \mathcal{V}, \mathcal{U}_\mathcal{D})$.

Figure 2. The $GHRC(\mathcal{D})$ proof calculus over a higher-order constraint domain $\mathcal{D}$.

constrained statements over $\mathcal{D}$ from the program rules of a given $CPRS(\mathcal{D})$-program $\mathcal{P}$:

- *reduction statements*: $s \twoheadrightarrow t$, where s, t are λ-terms on $\mathcal{U}_\mathcal{D}$ and $\mathcal{F}_\bot$ of the same type.
- *constrained statements*: $p\overline{t_n} \twoheadrightarrow t$, with $p \in \mathcal{F}_\mathcal{D}$ and λ-terms $\overline{t_n}, t$ on $\mathcal{U}_\mathcal{D}$ and $\mathcal{F}_\bot$.

We write $\mathcal{P} \vdash_\mathcal{D} \varphi$ to indicate that the reduction or constrained statement φ can be derived from $\mathcal{P}$ in the constrained higher-order rewriting calculus $GHRC(\mathcal{D})$, which consists of the inference rules given in Figure 2. The main difference with respect to the $GHRC$ calculus [8, 11] is the new rule **PF** to infer generalized constrained statements from a set of total values $Val(\mathcal{F}, \mathcal{V}, \mathcal{U}_\mathcal{D})$ (i.e., total patterns where there is no pattern matching on the left hand side of program rules in $\mathcal{P}$) instead of the particular *join rule* for equalities between λ-terms (the reader is referred to [8, 11] for more details on the technical notations used in the rules **B**, **MN**, **RF**, and **DF**).

EXAMPLE 7. *As a particular example of $GHRC(\mathcal{D})$-derivation, we can use the instance $GHRC(\mathcal{FD})$ of the proof calculus to verify that the substitution given in the example of Section 2*

$$\{F \mapsto \lambda u, v.\, gate\,(gate\,(u, u), gate\,(v, v))\}$$

is a solution of the goal

$$\lambda x, y.\, map(F, [(0,0), (x,1), (1,y)]) == [0,1,1],\quad size(\lambda u, v.\, F(u,v)) \leq 3$$

We represent the proof corresponding to the higher-order constrained statement

$$\lambda u, v.\, size\,(gate\,(gate\,(u,u), gate\,(v,v))) \leq 3$$

as the following proof tree:

PF $\lambda u, v.\, size(gate(gate(u,u), gate(v,v))) \leq 3$
  DF $\lambda u, v.\, size(gate(gate(u,u), gate(v,v))) \twoheadrightarrow 3$
    MN $\lambda u, v.\, gate(gate(u,u), gate(v,v)) \twoheadrightarrow \lambda u, v.\, gate(gate(u,u), gate(v,v))$
      MN $\lambda u, v.\, gate(u,u) \twoheadrightarrow \lambda u, v.\, gate(u,u)$
        RF $\lambda u, v.\, u \twoheadrightarrow \lambda u, v.\, u$
        RF $\lambda u, v.\, u \twoheadrightarrow \lambda u, v.\, u$
      MN $\lambda u, v.\, gate(v,v) \twoheadrightarrow \lambda u, v.\, gate(v,v)$
        RF $\lambda u, v.\, v \twoheadrightarrow \lambda u, v.\, v$
        RF $\lambda u, v.\, v \twoheadrightarrow \lambda u, v.\, v$
    PF $\lambda u, v.\, 1 + size(gate(u,v)) + size(gate(u,v)) \twoheadrightarrow 3$
      RF $\lambda u, v.\, 1 \twoheadrightarrow 1$
      DF $\lambda u, v.\, size(gate(u,v)) \twoheadrightarrow 1$
        MN $\lambda u, v.\, gate(u,v) \twoheadrightarrow \lambda u, v.\, gate(u,v)$
          RF $\lambda u, v.\, u \twoheadrightarrow \lambda u, v.\, u$
          RF $\lambda u, v.\, v \twoheadrightarrow \lambda u, v.\, v$
        PF $\lambda u, v.\, 1 + size(gate(u)) + size(gate(v)) \twoheadrightarrow 1$
          RF $\lambda u, v.\, 1 \twoheadrightarrow 1$
          DF $\lambda u, v.\, size(u) \twoheadrightarrow 0$
            RF $\lambda u, v.\, u \twoheadrightarrow \lambda u, v.\, u$
            RF $\lambda u, v.\, 0 \twoheadrightarrow 0$
          DF $\lambda u, v.\, size(v) \twoheadrightarrow 0$
            RF $\lambda u, v.\, v \twoheadrightarrow \lambda u, v.\, v$
            RF $\lambda u, v.\, 0 \twoheadrightarrow 0$
      DF $\lambda u, v.\, size(gate(u,v)) \twoheadrightarrow 1$
        MN $\lambda u, v.\, gate(u,v) \twoheadrightarrow \lambda u, v.\, gate(u,v)$
          RF $\lambda u, v.\, u \twoheadrightarrow \lambda u, v.\, u$
          RF $\lambda u, v.\, v \twoheadrightarrow \lambda u, v.\, v$
        PF $\lambda u, v.\, 1 + size(gate(u)) + size(gate(v)) \twoheadrightarrow 1$
          RF $\lambda u, v.\, 1 \twoheadrightarrow 1$
          DF $\lambda u, v.\, size(u) \twoheadrightarrow 0$
            RF $\lambda u, v.\, u \twoheadrightarrow \lambda u, v.\, u$
            RF $\lambda u, v.\, 0 \twoheadrightarrow 0$
          DF $\lambda u, v.\, size(v) \twoheadrightarrow 0$
            RF $\lambda u, v.\, v \twoheadrightarrow \lambda u, v.\, v$
            RF $\lambda u, v.\, 0 \twoheadrightarrow 0$
  RF $\lambda u, v.\, 3 \twoheadrightarrow 3$

Following [5], it is possible to represent the instantiation of our proof calculus $GHRC(\mathcal{D})$ to a particular $CPRS(\mathcal{D})$-program $\mathcal{P}$ as an equivalent *higher-order logic theory* suitable to the *Isabelle theorem prover* [36]. With this theory, it is possible to certify the validity of $GHRC(\mathcal{D})$-proofs within this theorem prover, but also to prove more complex properties about programs represented in

Higher-Order Logic (HOL). In `http://www.fdi.ucm.es/profesor/rdelvado/PPDP2011/` we briefly describe an algorithmic procedure to get a corresponding HOL-theory from the $CPRS(\mathcal{FD})$-program of Example 7, and we show how the *Isabelle theorem prover* can be used to certificate the correctness of the $GHRC(\mathcal{FD})$-derivation given in this example. The HOL-theory obtained by this procedure would allow not only to generate certificates for reduction and constrained statements, but also for more expressive and interesting properties on declarative programs.

4.2 Model-Theoretic Semantics

In order to interpret $GHRC(\mathcal{D})$-programs, the higher-order constraint domain $\mathcal{D}$ has to be extended with interpretations for the defined function symbols. The $GHRC(\mathcal{D})$-*algebras* defined below achieve this aim in a simple and straightforward way:

DEFINITION 6 (Algebras and models).

(1) Given a signature $\mathcal{F} = \mathcal{F}_\mathcal{D} \cup \mathcal{F}_d$, *a* $GHRC(\mathcal{D})$-algebra $\mathcal{A}_\mathcal{D}$ *is a structure:*

$$\mathcal{A}_\mathcal{D} = \langle\, D_{\mathcal{A}_\mathcal{D}}, \{p^\mathcal{D}\}_{p\in\mathcal{F}_\mathcal{D}}, \{f^{\mathcal{A}_\mathcal{D}}\}_{f\in\mathcal{F}_d}, \circ^{\mathcal{A}_\mathcal{D}} \,\rangle$$

where the interpretation $p^\mathcal{D}$ *of each domain-dependent primitive function* $p \in \mathcal{F}_\mathcal{D}$ *must satisfy the requirements given in Definition 2, and* $D_{\mathcal{A}_\mathcal{D}}$ *conservatively extends* $\mathcal{U}_\mathcal{D}$ *with an interpretation* $\circ^{\mathcal{A}_\mathcal{D}}$ *of an* apply operation *for classical higher-order features [8, 34], and an interpretation* $f^{\mathcal{A}_\mathcal{D}}$ *for each defined function* $f \in \mathcal{F}_d$, *which must satisfy the usual requirements given in [8, 33] and the following additional* consistency property *for all total* $\gamma \in Subst(\mathcal{F},\mathcal{V},\mathcal{U})$ *(close to the notion of* C-interpretation *considered in [12]):*

$$(f^{\mathcal{A}_\mathcal{D}}(\overline{t_n}))\gamma = \{d\gamma \mid d \in f^{\mathcal{A}_\mathcal{D}}(\overline{t_n})\} \subseteq f^{\mathcal{A}_\mathcal{D}}(\overline{t_n}\gamma)$$

(2) A valuation *over a* $GHRC(\mathcal{D})$-*algebra* $\mathcal{A}_\mathcal{D}$ *is any mapping from* $\mathcal{V}$ *to* $D_{\mathcal{A}_\mathcal{D}}$. *The evaluation* $[\![t]\!]_\eta^{\mathcal{A}_\mathcal{D}}$ *of a* λ-*term* t *over* $\mathcal{A}_\mathcal{D}$ *and a valuation* η *follows the standard ideas of the model-theoretic semantics given in [8, 33].*

(3) $\mathcal{A}_\mathcal{D}$ *satisfies a reduction statement* $s \twoheadrightarrow t$ *under a valuation* η *(i.e.,* $\mathcal{A}_\mathcal{D} \models_\eta^\mathcal{D} s \twoheadrightarrow t$*) iff* $[\![s]\!]_\eta^{\mathcal{A}_\mathcal{D}} \supseteq [\![t]\!]_\eta^{\mathcal{A}_\mathcal{D}}$. *Additionally,* $\mathcal{A}_\mathcal{D}$ *satisfies a* $\mathcal{D}$-*constraint* $p\,\overline{t_n} \to t$ *with* $p \in \mathcal{F}_\mathcal{D}$ *of arity* $n \geq 0$ *(i.e.,* $\mathcal{A}_\mathcal{D} \models_\eta^\mathcal{D} p\,\overline{t_n} \twoheadrightarrow t$*) iff* $p^\mathcal{D}\,[\![t_n]\!]_\eta^{\mathcal{A}_\mathcal{D}} \to [\![t]\!]_\eta^{\mathcal{A}_\mathcal{D}}$. *Moreover, if* C *is a finite sequence of* $\mathcal{D}$-*constraints,* $\mathcal{A}_\mathcal{D} \models_\eta^\mathcal{D} C$ *iff* $\mathcal{A}_\mathcal{D} \models_\eta^\mathcal{D} c$ *for each* $\mathcal{D}$-*constraint* $c \in C$.

(4) $\mathcal{A}_\mathcal{D}$ *is a* $GHRC(\mathcal{D})$-*model of a* $CPRS(\mathcal{D})$-*program* $\mathcal{P}$ *(i.e.,* $\mathcal{A}_\mathcal{D} \models_\eta^\mathcal{D} \mathcal{P}$*) iff* $\mathcal{A}_\mathcal{D} \models_\eta^\mathcal{D} C$ *implies* $\mathcal{A}_\mathcal{D} \models_\eta^\mathcal{D} \pi \twoheadrightarrow r$ *for every valuation* η *and* $(\pi \to r \Leftarrow C) \in \mathcal{P}$.

$GHRC(\mathcal{D})$-provability is sound and complete with respect to these notions of algebras and models when we consider *pattern models* as algebras.

DEFINITION 7 (Pattern models). *Given a* $CPRS(\mathcal{D})$-*program* $\mathcal{P}$ *with signature* $\mathcal{F}$, *the* pattern model $\mathcal{M}_\mathcal{P}^\mathcal{D}$ *is defined as follows:*

- *The carrier* $D_{\mathcal{M}_\mathcal{P}^\mathcal{D}}$ *is the poset* $Val(\mathcal{F}_\perp,\mathcal{V},\mathcal{U}_\mathcal{D})$, *with approximation ordering* $\sqsubseteq$ *(as defined in Section 3) and bottom element* $\lambda\overline{x_n}.\perp$.
- $f^{\mathcal{M}_\mathcal{P}^\mathcal{D}}(\overline{t_n}) = \{t \in Val(\mathcal{F}_\perp,\mathcal{V},\mathcal{U}_\mathcal{D}) \mid \mathcal{P} \vdash_\mathcal{D} f(\overline{t_n}) \twoheadrightarrow t\}$.

The next theorem establishes the relationship between derivability in our higher-order rewriting logic with constraints and the model-theoretic semantics presented in this section. The technical proof can be found in `http://www.fdi.ucm.es/profesor/rdelvado/PPDP2011/`.

THEOREM 1 (Adequateness of $\mathcal{M}_\mathcal{P}^\mathcal{D}$). *For each* $CPRS(\mathcal{D})$-*program* $\mathcal{P}$*:*

(1) $\mathcal{M}_\mathcal{P}^\mathcal{D}$ *is a* $GHRC(\mathcal{D})$-*model of* $\mathcal{P}$.

(2) For any statement φ, $\mathcal{P} \vdash_\mathcal{D} \varphi$ *iff* $\mathcal{A}_\mathcal{D} \models_\eta^\mathcal{D} \varphi$, *for every* $\mathcal{A}_\mathcal{D} \models_\eta^\mathcal{D} \mathcal{P}$ *and every total valuation* η.

4.3 Fixpoint Semantics

In this subsection we prove the existence of least models for $GHRC(\mathcal{D})$-programs and we characterize them as least fixpoints. As we will see in the next section, this fixpoint semantics of programs captures the information concerning possible compositions and is compositional by construction. The approach we use here is similar to that applied in the field of logic programming [1], first-order functional logic programming [32], and higher-order functional logic programming (without constraints) [8].

DEFINITION 8 (Pattern algebra transformer).

(1) The set $Alg_\mathcal{F}^\mathcal{D}$ *of pattern algebras over a higher-order constraint domain* $\mathcal{D}$ *of a signature* $\mathcal{F}$ *is a complete lattice:*

- $Alg_\mathcal{F}^\mathcal{D}$ *is a poset with partial order* $\mathcal{A}_\mathcal{D} \sqsubseteq \mathcal{B}_\mathcal{D}$ *(defined as* $f^{\mathcal{A}_\mathcal{D}} \subseteq f^{\mathcal{B}_\mathcal{D}}$ *for each* $f \in \mathcal{F}$*), for all* $\mathcal{A}_\mathcal{D}, \mathcal{B}_\mathcal{D} \in Alg_\mathcal{F}^\mathcal{D}$.
- *The poset has a bottom* $\perp_\mathcal{F}$ *and a top* $\top_\mathcal{F}$, *characterized by* $\perp$ *and* $Val(\mathcal{F}_\perp,\mathcal{V},\mathcal{U}_\mathcal{D})$, *respectively.*
- *The poset has a least upper bound* $\sqcup S$ *and a greatest lower bound* $\sqcap S$, *for all* $S \subseteq Alg_\mathcal{F}^\mathcal{D}$ *[8].*

(2) Given a $GHRC(\mathcal{D})$-*program* $\mathcal{P}$ *with an underlying signature* $\mathcal{F}$, *we can define a pattern algebra transformer* $\mathbb{T}_\mathcal{P}^\mathcal{D} : Alg_\mathcal{F}^\mathcal{D} \to Alg_\mathcal{F}^\mathcal{D}$*:*

- $f^{\mathbb{T}_\mathcal{P}^\mathcal{D}(\mathcal{A}_\mathcal{D})}$ *is the result of one step application of program rules of* $\mathcal{P}$ *defining* $f \in \mathcal{F}_\mathcal{D}^\mathcal{P}$, *satisfied in* $\mathcal{A}_\mathcal{D} \in Alg_\mathcal{F}^\mathcal{D}$.
- $\mathbb{T}_\mathcal{P}^\mathcal{D}$ *is continuous:*
$\mathcal{A}_0 {=} \perp_\mathcal{F} \sqsubseteq \ldots \sqsubseteq \mathcal{A}_{i+1} {=} \mathbb{T}_\mathcal{P}^\mathcal{D}(\mathcal{A}_i) \sqsubseteq \ldots \sqsubseteq (\mathbb{T}_\mathcal{P}^\mathcal{D})^\omega(\perp_\mathcal{F})$

The main result in this section concerns the existence of least models and their characterization as least fixpoints of the continuous pattern algebra transformer $\mathbb{T}_\mathcal{P}^\mathcal{D}$:

THEOREM 2 (Fixpoint characterization of $\mathcal{M}_\mathcal{P}^\mathcal{D}$). *For every given* $CPRS(\mathcal{D})$-*program* $\mathcal{P}$*:*

(1) A pattern algebra $\mathcal{M}^\mathcal{D}$ *is a* $GHRC(\mathcal{D})$-*model of* $\mathcal{P}$ *iff* $\mathbb{T}_\mathcal{P}^\mathcal{D}(\mathcal{M}^\mathcal{D}) \sqsubseteq \mathcal{M}^\mathcal{D}$.

(2) $\mathcal{M}_\mathcal{P}^\mathcal{D}$ *is the least fixpoint of* $\mathbb{T}_\mathcal{P}^\mathcal{D}$.

5. A Modular Semantics

In the last section of this paper we deal with a modular semantics for program modules thanks to the pattern algebra transformer defined in the previous section. This immediate consequence operator captures the information concerning possible compositions obtained by the union of signatures and rules, and the corresponding semantics is directly *compositional* by construction with respect to the union operation of program modules. However, in order to obtain the complementary property of compositionality, the so-called *full abstraction* property, the adequacy of this semantics must be established with respect to the deletion operation of a signature in a program module, used to delete a whole set of program rules defining a function. We define a compositional and fully abstract semantics for the reduced set of operations on program modules defined in Section 3, union and deletion, that are sufficient to express the most extended ways of composing modules and their relationships. The modular semantics obtained provides meanings for higher-order programs with constraints and, more generally, $\mathcal{D}$-modules defined on a higher-order constraint domain $\mathcal{D}$.

5.1 Compositional and Fully Abstract Semantics

An important aspect to be considered when a declarative language is extended for modular programming is the sound integration of the behavior of the modular operations into the semantics of the language. In this setting, the properties of *compositionality* and *full abstraction* have been recognized as two fundamental concepts in the studies on the semantics of declarative programming languages [3]. Simply stated, a semantics is compositional if semantically equivalent programs (or program modules) are indistinguishable, that is, the meaning of a program can be obtained from the meaning of its components. The compositionality of the semantics ensures that programs (or program modules) which are semantically equivalent can be replaced with other ones without affecting the intended semantics of the whole system. For instance, this property establishes a firm foundation for reasoning about programs and program transformations. Suppose that a program $\mathcal{P}$ consists of several components $\mathcal{P}_1, ..., \mathcal{P}_n$, suitable composed together. Suppose also that $\mathcal{P}'_i$ is a more efficient version of $\mathcal{P}_i$, obtained for instance by applying some program transformation technique to $\mathcal{P}_i$. If $\mathcal{P}'_i$ is equivalent to $\mathcal{P}_i$ in the chosen semantics then the property of compositionality ensures that the substitution of $\mathcal{P}'_i$ for $\mathcal{P}_i$ will not affect the meaning of the whole program $\mathcal{P}$. On the other hand, the property of full abstraction establishes that the equivalence relation induced by the semantics is the largest equivalence relation that can be used to substitute programs (or program modules) without affecting the intended semantics of the whole system. In other words, a semantics is fully abstract if indistinguishable programs (or program modules) are semantically equivalent. In this paper we adopt an approach inspired in [3, 32], where compositionality and full abstraction are defined in terms of the equivalence relation induced by the semantics:

DEFINITION 9 (Modular semantics). *Let us consider a $GHRC(\mathcal{D})$-semantic $\mathcal{S}_\mathcal{D}$ over a higher-order constraint domain $\mathcal{D}$ and its corresponding equivalence relation $\sim^{\mathcal{S}}_{\mathcal{D}}$ (i.e., two $CPRS(\mathcal{D})$-programs are $\sim^{\mathcal{S}}_{\mathcal{D}}$-equivalent iff they have the same meaning in the semantics $\mathcal{S}_\mathcal{D}$).*

(1) $\mathcal{S}_\mathcal{D}$ is compositional if:

(a) For all $CPRS(\mathcal{D})$-programs $\mathcal{P}$ and $\mathcal{Q}$:

$$\mathcal{P} \sim^{\mathcal{S}}_{\mathcal{D}} \mathcal{Q} \Rightarrow \mathcal{M}^{\mathcal{D}}_{\mathcal{P}} = \mathcal{M}^{\mathcal{D}}_{\mathcal{Q}}$$

(b) For all $CPRS(\mathcal{D})$-programs $\mathcal{P}_i$ and $\mathcal{Q}_i$, for all $i \in \{1, ..., n\}$, and all $Op \in \{\cup, (\cdot)\backslash\mathcal{F}\}$:

$$\mathcal{P}_i \sim^{\mathcal{S}}_{\mathcal{D}} \mathcal{Q}_i \Rightarrow Op(\overline{\mathcal{P}_n}) \sim^{\mathcal{S}}_{\mathcal{D}} Op(\overline{\mathcal{Q}_n})$$

(2) $\mathcal{S}_\mathcal{D}$ is fully abstract iff for all $CPRS(\mathcal{D})$-programs $\mathcal{P}$ and $\mathcal{Q}$:

$$\mathcal{M}^{\mathcal{D}}_{\mathtt{C}[\![\mathcal{P}]\!]} = \mathcal{M}^{\mathcal{D}}_{\mathtt{C}[\![\mathcal{Q}]\!]} \Rightarrow \mathcal{P} \sim^{\mathcal{S}}_{\mathcal{D}} \mathcal{Q}$$

for all context $\mathtt{C}$, where contexts $\mathtt{C}[\![\mathcal{X}]\!]$ are inductively defined as follows: the metavariable $\mathcal{X}$ and each program is a context, and for each $Op \in \{\cup, (\cdot)\backslash\mathcal{F}\}$ and $\mathtt{C}_1, \ldots, \mathtt{C}_n$ contexts, $Op(\mathtt{C}_1, \ldots, \mathtt{C}_n)$ is a context.

To find a compositional semantics we can build programs from other programs adding rules for new functions or for already defined functions, and consider them as pattern algebra transformers as done in [3]. However, to obtain full abstraction with respect to the deletion operation, we have to consider pattern models of programs obtained by deleting any signature included in the underlying signature.

DEFINITION 10 (Transformer Semantics).

(1) We define the pattern algebra transformer semantics $\mathbb{T}_\mathcal{D}$ of a $CPRS(\mathcal{D})$-program $\mathcal{P}$ by denoting the meaning of $\mathcal{P}\backslash\mathcal{F}$, for all signature $\mathcal{F}$, by its pattern algebra transformer $\mathbb{T}^{\mathcal{D}}_{\mathcal{P}\backslash\mathcal{F}}$. By applying Theorem 2:

$$[\![\mathcal{P}]\!]^{\mathcal{D}}_{\mathbb{T}} = \{\mathcal{M}^{\mathcal{D}} \mid \mathcal{M}^{\mathcal{D}} \textit{ is a pattern model of } \mathcal{P}\backslash\mathcal{F}\}$$

for all signature $\mathcal{F}$.

(2) Two $CPRS(\mathcal{D})$-programs $\mathcal{P}$ and $\mathcal{Q}$ are $\sim^{\mathbb{T}}_{\mathcal{D}}$-equivalents iff both define the same pattern algebra transformer by deleting any signature. By applying Theorem 2:

$$\mathcal{P} \sim^{\mathbb{T}}_{\mathcal{D}} \mathcal{Q} \Leftrightarrow [\![\mathcal{P}]\!]^{\mathcal{D}}_{\mathbb{T}} = [\![\mathcal{Q}]\!]^{\mathcal{D}}_{\mathbb{T}}$$

We are ready to state and prove the properties of compositionality and full abstraction of the pattern algebra transformer semantics, which justify the adoption of this semantics as the main point of our work.

THEOREM 3 (Modularity of $\mathbb{T}_\mathcal{D}$). *The pattern algebra transformer semantics $\mathbb{T}_\mathcal{D}$ over a higher-order constraint domain $\mathcal{D}$ is compositional and fully abstract with respect to the set of operations $\{\cup, (\cdot)\backslash\mathcal{F}\}$.*

PROOF 1. *We prove that the pattern algebra transformer semantics $\mathbb{T}_\mathcal{D}$ is compositional with respect to the set of operations $\{\cup, (\cdot)\backslash\mathcal{F}\}$. First, from $\mathcal{P} \sim^{\mathbb{T}}_{\mathcal{D}} \mathcal{Q}$ we deduce that $\mathcal{P}\backslash\mathcal{F}$ and $\mathcal{Q}\backslash\mathcal{F}$ have the same pattern models for all signature $\mathcal{F}$. In particular, for the empty signature, $\mathcal{P}$ and $\mathcal{Q}$ have the same least pattern models and the same least fixpoints. Thus, we conclude that $\mathcal{M}^{\mathcal{D}}_{\mathcal{P}} = \mathcal{M}^{\mathcal{D}}_{\mathcal{Q}}$. Now, we prove that the pattern algebra transformer semantics $\mathbb{T}_\mathcal{D}$ is compositional w.r.t. the union of programs: $\mathcal{P}_i \sim^{\mathbb{T}}_{\mathcal{D}} \mathcal{Q}_i$, for $i = 1, ..., n$, implies $\bigcup_{i=1}^{n} \mathcal{P}_i \sim^{\mathbb{T}}_{\mathcal{D}} \bigcup_{i=1}^{n} \mathcal{Q}_i$. Since $\mathcal{P}_i \sim^{\mathbb{T}}_{\mathcal{D}} \mathcal{Q}_i$, both define the same pattern algebra transformer $\mathbb{T}^{\mathcal{D}}_{\mathcal{P}_i\backslash\mathcal{F}} = \mathbb{T}^{\mathcal{D}}_{\mathcal{Q}_i\backslash\mathcal{F}}$ for all signature $\mathcal{F}$. Let $\mathcal{M}^{\mathcal{D}}$ be a pattern model of $\bigcup_{i=1}^{n} \mathcal{P}_i\backslash\mathcal{F}$. From Theorem 2: $\bigsqcup_{i=1}^{n} \mathbb{T}^{\mathcal{D}}_{\mathcal{P}_i\backslash\mathcal{F}} (\mathcal{M}^{\mathcal{D}}) = (\bigsqcup_{i=1}^{n} \mathbb{T}^{\mathcal{D}}_{\mathcal{P}_i\backslash\mathcal{F}}) (\mathcal{M}^{\mathcal{D}}) = \mathbb{T}^{\mathcal{D}}_{\bigcup_{i=1}^{n} \mathcal{P}_i\backslash\mathcal{F}} (\mathcal{M}^{\mathcal{D}}) \sqsubseteq \mathcal{M}^{\mathcal{D}}$. Therefore, $\mathbb{T}^{\mathcal{D}}_{\mathcal{P}_i\backslash\mathcal{F}} (\mathcal{M}^{\mathcal{D}}) \sqsubseteq \mathcal{M}^{\mathcal{D}}$ for $i = 1, ..., n$. Moreover, from $\mathcal{P}_i \sim^{\mathbb{T}}_{\mathcal{D}} \mathcal{Q}_i$ we obtain $\mathbb{T}^{\mathcal{D}}_{\mathcal{Q}_i\backslash\mathcal{F}} (\mathcal{M}^{\mathcal{D}}) \sqsubseteq \mathcal{M}^{\mathcal{D}}$ for $i = 1, ..., n$, and then $\mathbb{T}^{\mathcal{D}}_{\bigcup_{i=1}^{n} \mathcal{Q}_i\backslash\mathcal{F}} (\mathcal{M}^{\mathcal{D}}) = (\bigsqcup_{i=1}^{n} \mathbb{T}^{\mathcal{D}}_{\mathcal{Q}_i\backslash\mathcal{F}}) (\mathcal{M}^{\mathcal{D}}) = \bigsqcup_{i=1}^{n} \mathbb{T}^{\mathcal{D}}_{\mathcal{Q}_i\backslash\mathcal{F}} (\mathcal{M}^{\mathcal{D}}) \sqsubseteq \mathcal{M}^{\mathcal{D}}$. Therefore, $\mathcal{M}^{\mathcal{D}}$ is a pattern model of $\bigcup_{i=1}^{n} \mathcal{Q}_i\backslash\mathcal{F}$. By reasoning in a similar way, it can be obtained that all pattern models of $\bigcup_{i=1}^{n} \mathcal{Q}_i\backslash\mathcal{F}$ are also pattern models of $\bigcup_{i=1}^{n} \mathcal{P}_i\backslash\mathcal{F}$, and this proves that $\mathbb{T}^{\mathcal{D}}_{\bigcup_{i=1}^{n} \mathcal{P}_i\backslash\mathcal{F}} = \mathbb{T}^{\mathcal{D}}_{\bigcup_{i=1}^{n} \mathcal{Q}_i\backslash\mathcal{F}}$. Finally, since $(\bigcup_{i=1}^{n} \mathcal{P}_i)\backslash\mathcal{F} = \bigcup_{i=1}^{n} (\mathcal{P}_i\backslash\mathcal{F})$, we deduce that $\mathbb{T}^{\mathcal{D}}_{(\bigcup_{i=1}^{n} \mathcal{P}_i)\backslash\mathcal{F}} = \mathbb{T}^{\mathcal{D}}_{(\bigcup_{i=1}^{n} \mathcal{Q}_i)\backslash\mathcal{F}}$ for all signature $\mathcal{F}$, which means $\bigcup_{i=1}^{n} \mathcal{P}_i \sim^{\mathbb{T}}_{\mathcal{D}} \bigcup_{i=1}^{n} \mathcal{Q}_i$. Second, we prove that the pattern algebra transformer semantics $\mathbb{T}_\mathcal{D}$ is compositional w.r.t. the deletion of a signature in a program: $P \sim^{\mathbb{T}}_{\mathcal{D}} Q$ implies $\mathcal{P}\backslash\mathcal{F}' \sim^{\mathbb{T}}_{\mathcal{D}} \mathcal{Q}\backslash\mathcal{F}'$, for every signature $\mathcal{F}'$. Since $P \sim^{\mathbb{T}}_{\mathcal{D}} Q$, both define the same pattern algebra transformer $\mathbb{T}^{\mathcal{D}}_{\mathcal{P}\backslash(\mathcal{F}\cup\mathcal{F}')} = \mathbb{T}^{\mathcal{D}}_{\mathcal{Q}\backslash(\mathcal{F}\cup\mathcal{F}')}$ for all signatures $\mathcal{F}$ and $\mathcal{F}'$. Since $\mathcal{R}\backslash(\mathcal{F} \cup \mathcal{F}') = (\mathcal{R}\backslash\mathcal{F})\backslash\mathcal{F}'$, we deduce that $\mathbb{T}^{\mathcal{D}}_{(\mathcal{P}\backslash\mathcal{F})\backslash\mathcal{F}'} = \mathbb{T}^{\mathcal{D}}_{(\mathcal{Q}\backslash\mathcal{F})\backslash\mathcal{F}'}$ for every signatures $\mathcal{F}$ and $\mathcal{F}'$, which means that $\mathcal{P}\backslash\mathcal{F}' \sim^{\mathbb{T}}_{\mathcal{D}} \mathcal{Q}\backslash\mathcal{F}'$, for every signature $\mathcal{F}'$. Finally, to prove that the pattern algebra transformer semantics $\mathbb{T}_\mathcal{D}$ is fully abstract, we only need to prove that $\mathcal{P} \not\sim^{\mathbb{T}}_{\mathcal{D}} \mathcal{Q}$ implies that there exists a context $\mathtt{C}$ where we can discriminate the observable behavior of both programs. From $\mathcal{P} \not\sim^{\mathbb{T}}_{\mathcal{D}} \mathcal{Q}$ we deduce* *that there exists a signature $\mathcal{F}$ such that the pattern algebra transformers $\mathbb{T}^{\mathcal{D}}_{\mathcal{P}\backslash\mathcal{F}}$ and $\mathbb{T}^{\mathcal{D}}_{\mathcal{Q}\backslash\mathcal{F}}$ are different. Then there exists a context $\mathtt{C}'$ such that $\mathcal{M}^{\mathcal{D}}_{\mathtt{C}'[\![\mathcal{P}\backslash\mathcal{F}]\!]} \neq \mathcal{M}^{\mathcal{D}}_{\mathtt{C}'[\![\mathcal{Q}\backslash\mathcal{F}]\!]}$. Thus by considering the new context $\mathtt{C}[\![\mathcal{R}]\!] = \mathtt{C}'[\![\mathcal{R}\backslash\mathcal{F}]\!]$ we have that $\mathcal{M}^{\mathcal{D}}_{\mathtt{C}[\![\mathcal{P}]\!]} \neq \mathcal{M}^{\mathcal{D}}_{\mathtt{C}[\![\mathcal{Q}]\!]}$.* □

The modularity of the $\mathbb{T}_{\mathcal{D}}$ semantics is particularly relevant in declarative programming, because one of the most critical aspects in multi-paradigms declarative systems is the possibility of making a separate compilation of modules, and this can only be made in the presence of some kind of compositionality. For instance, $\mathcal{TOY}$ is a constraint functional logic system, designed to support the main declarative programming styles and their combination. The current version provides a module system involving higher-order patterns, a polymorphic type system, constraints with symbolic equations and disequations, linear and non-linear arithmetic constraints over real numbers, and finite domain constraints. For this reason, our modular semantics for higher-order declarative constraint programming can be applied to the $\mathcal{TOY}$ system in order to allow each distinct module to be compiled separately, with the effect of inlining being realized by a subsequent linking process. Moreover, modular development installs boundaries in programs that can be important to the practical use of static analysis techniques and that are fundamental to the notion of separate compilation and testing.

6. Conclusions and Future Work

In this paper we have explored one of the major limitations of actual multi-paradigm declarative programming languages and systems [16, 17, 26] deriving from the lack of mechanisms for structuring/modularizing programs and the lack of compositionality in its declarative semantics.

The current version of the constraint functional logic system $\mathcal{TOY}$ (`toy.sourceforge.net`) and their multi-paradigm declarative language have been designed to support the main declarative programming styles and their combination: functional and logic programming, higher-order patterns, a polymorphic type system, modules, arithmetic constraints over the real numbers and finite domain constraints, and the cooperation of domains in the context of several numeric constraints domains. However, the interactions between all these different declarative features are complex so that the concrete design of a multi-paradigm declarative program is non-trivial. Modular programming is a solution to this problem and can be used to break up a large program into manageable units, or to create code that can be easily re-used and maintained. Unfortunately, the lack of modularity in the declarative semantics of the current version of the $\mathcal{TOY}$ system avoids well-founded characterizations of the program composition needed to use static analysis techniques that are fundamental to the notion of separate compilation.

To tackle this problem, in this work we have presented a fully abstract and compositional modular semantics for the higher-order declarative framework with constraints underlying the $\mathcal{TOY}$ system. We now conclude this work by summarizing the main contributions and novelties of the paper:

- A new mathematical formalization of higher-order constraint domains involving lambda abstractions over primitive elements, which allows a flexible combination of domain specific values and primitive domain-dependent operators with user defined higher-order functions.

- A suitable notion of higher-order constrained program module, along with a set of reduced set of operations on program modules, the union $\cup$ of modules and the deletion $(\cdot)\backslash\mathcal{F}$ of a signature $\mathcal{F}$ in a module, enough to support typical features of modular programming such as import/export relations, inheritance, or cooperation/coordination of constraints domains.

- A higher-order constraint rewriting logic over a parametrically given constraint domain as the basis of a model-theoretic and fixpoint semantics given by suitable notions of pattern algebras and models, and an immediate consequence operator based on a pattern algebra transformer which is compositional and fully abstract.

- A modular semantics for higher-order constrained program modules by denoting programs and modules from the immediate consequence operator on the given constraint domain which is compositional and fully abstract with respect to the set of operations $\{\cup, (\cdot)\backslash\mathcal{F}\}$.

In the future we would like to improve some of the limitations of our current theoretical approach to modular multi-paradigm declarative programming. For instance, in this work we have adopted the framework of the simply typed λ-calculus in which the set of types is generated by a set of base types. However, $\mathcal{TOY}$ is a typed programming language based on the Dalmas-Milner polymorphic type system [6]. As future work we are currently working on an extension of the $GHRC(\mathcal{D})$ modular semantics with a polymorphic type system following [19, 35].

Acknowledgements

The authors are thankful to Juan Miguel Molina Bravo and Ernesto Pimentel Sánchez for their collaboration, comments and contributions during the first stages of the development of this work and for the help in preparing the final version of this paper.

References

[1] K. R. Apt. Logic programming. In *Handbook of Theoretical Computer Science, Volume B: Formal Models and Sematics (B)*, pages 493–574. 1990.

[2] A. Brogi, P. Mancarella, D. Pedreschi, and F. Turini. Modular logic programming. *ACM Trans. Program. Lang. Syst.*, 16(4):1361–1398, 1994.

[3] A. Brogi and F. Turini. Fully abstract composition semantics for an algebra of logic programs. *Theor. Comput. Sci.*, 149(2):201–209, 1995.

[4] T.-R. Chuang and J.-L. Lin. On modular transformations of structural content. In *APLAS*, pages 251–263, 2001.

[5] J. M. Cleva, J. Leach, and F. J. López-Fraguas. A logic programming approach to the verification of functional-logic programs. In *PPDP*, pages 9–19. ACM, 2004.

[6] L. Damas and R. Milner. Principal type-schemes for functional programs. In *POPL*, pages 207–212, 1982.

[7] R. del Vado Vírseda. A higher-order demand-driven narrowing calculus with definitional trees. In *ICTAC*, volume 4711 of *Lecture Notes in Computer Science*, pages 169–184, 2007.

[8] R. del Vado Vírseda. A higher-order logical framework for the algorithmic debugging and verification of declarative programs. In *PPDP*, pages 49–60. ACM, 2009.

[9] R. del Vado Vírseda. Cooperation of algebraic constraint domains in higher-order functional and logic programming. In *AMAST*, volume 6486 of *Lecture Notes in Computer Science*, pages 180–200, 2011.

[10] R. del Vado Vírseda. A Theoretical Framework for the Higher-Order Cooperation of Numeric Constraint Domains. In *LSFA*, volume 269 of *Electr. Notes Theor. Comput. Sci.*, pages 55–69, 2011.

[11] R. del Vado Vírseda and I. Castiñeiras. A theoretical framework for the declarative debugging of functional logic programs with lambda abstractions. In *WFLP*, volume 5979 of *Lecture Notes in Computer Science*, pages 162–178, 2009.

[12] M. Falaschi, G. Levi, M. Martelli, and C. Palamidessi. A model-theoretic reconstruction of the operational semantics of logic programs. *Inf. Comput.*, 103(1):86–113, 1993.

[13] M. Fitting. Enumeration operators and modular logic programming. *J. Log. Program.*, 4(1):11–21, 1987.

[14] R. Giacobazzi. Abductive analysis of modular logic programs. *J. Log. Comput.*, 8(4):457–483, 1998.

[15] R. Haemmerlé and F. Fages. Modules for prolog revisited. In *ICLP*, volume 4079, pages 41–55, 2006.

[16] M. Hanus. A unified computation model for functional and logic programming. In *POPL*, pages 80–93, 1997.

[17] M. Hanus. Multi-paradigm declarative languages. In *ICLP*, volume 4670 of *Lecture Notes in Computer Science*, pages 45–75, 2007.

[18] M. Hanus and C. Prehofer. Higher-order narrowing with definitional trees. *J. Funct. Program.*, 9(1):33–75, 1999.

[19] R. Harper, R. Milner, and M. Tofte. A type discipline for program modules. In *TAPSOFT, Vol.2*, volume 250 of *Lecture Notes in Computer Science*, pages 308–319, 1987.

[20] R. Harper and F. Pfenning. A module system for a programming language based on the lf logical framework. *J. Log. Comput.*, 8(1):5–31, 1998.

[21] P. Hill and J. W. Lloyd. The gödel programming language. In *MIT Press*, 1994.

[22] J. R. Hindley and J. P. Seldin. *Introduction to combinators and λ-calculus*. Cambridge University Press, New York, NY, USA, 1986.

[23] D. Kranzlmüller, C. Schaubschläger, M. Scarpa, and J. Volkert. A modular debbuging insfrastructure for parallel programs. In *PARCO*, volume 13 of *Advances in Parallel Computing*, pages 143–150. Elsevier, 2003.

[24] K. Kwon, G. Nadathur, and D. S. Wilson. Implementing a notion of modules in the logic programming language lambda-prolog. In *ELP*, volume 660 of *Lecture Notes in Computer Science*, pages 359–393, 1992.

[25] F. Logozzo. Cibai: An abstract interpretation-based static analyzer for modular analysis and verification of java classes. In *VMCAI*, volume 4349 of *Lecture Notes in Computer Science*, pages 283–298, 2007.

[26] F. J. López-Fraguas and J. Sánchez-Hernández. *TOY*: A multi-paradigm declarative system. In *RTA*, volume 1631 of *Lecture Notes in Computer Science*, pages 244–247, 1999.

[27] P. Mancarella and D. Pedreschi. An algebra of logic programs. In *ICLP/SLP*, pages 1006–1023, 1988.

[28] S. E. Martín, M. T. Hortalá-González, M. Rodríguez-Artalejo, R. del Vado Vírseda, F. Sáenz-Pérez, and A. J. Fernández. On the cooperation of the constraint domains $\mathcal{H}$, $\mathcal{R}$, and $\mathcal{FD}$ in $CFLP$. *TPLP*, 9(4):415–527, 2009.

[29] D. Miller. A theory of modules for logic programming. In *SLP*, pages 106–114, 1986.

[30] D. Miller. A logic programming language with lambda-abstraction, function variables, and simple unification. *J. Log. Comput.*, 1(4):497–536, 1991.

[31] J. M. Molina-Bravo and E. Pimentel. Modularity in functional-logic programming. In *ICLP*, pages 183–197, 1997.

[32] J. M. Molina-Bravo and E. Pimentel. Composing programs in a rewriting logic for declarative programming. *TPLP*, 3(2):189–221, 2003.

[33] J. C. G. Moreno, M. T. Hortalá-González, F. J. López-Fraguas, and M. Rodríguez-Artalejo. An approach to declarative programming based on a rewriting logic. *J. Log. Program.*, 40(1):47–87, 1999.

[34] J. C. G. Moreno, M. T. Hortalá-González, and M. Rodríguez-Artalejo. A higher order rewriting logic for functional logic programming. In *ICLP*, pages 153–167, 1997.

[35] J. C. G. Moreno, M. T. Hortalá-González, and M. Rodríguez-Artalejo. Polymorphic types in functional logic programming. *Journal of Functional and Logic Programming*, 2001(1), 2001.

[36] L. C. Paulson. *Isabelle - A Generic Theorem Prover (with a contribution by T. Nipkow)*, volume 828 of *Lecture Notes in Computer Science*. Springer, 1994.

[37] P. Pietrzak, J. Correas, G. Puebla, and M. V. Hermenegildo. A practical type analysis for verification of modular prolog programs. In *PEPM*, pages 61–70. ACM, 2008.

[38] D. Sannella and L. A. Wallen. A calculus for the construction of modular prolog programs. *J. Log. Program.*, 12(1&2):147–177, 1992.

Minimally Strict Polymorphic Functions

Jan Christiansen
Christian-Albrechts-Universität Kiel
Institut für Informatik
24098 Kiel, Germany
jac@informatik.uni-kiel.de

Daniel Seidel *
Rheinische Friedrich-Wilhelms-Universität Bonn
Institut für Informatik
53117 Bonn, Germany
ds@informatik.uni-bonn.de

Abstract

In this paper we show how to efficiently check whether a polymorphic function is minimally strict. A function is minimally strict if it is the minimal element of a specific less-strict ordering. We prove that we can check whether two polymorphic functions are related by the less-strict ordering by either checking it a) for an arbitrary monomorphic instance of the functions or b) for all shapes of the functions' argument type. A shape is a value of a monomorphic instance of a polymorphic data type where each polymorphic component is replaced by an element that identifies its position in the data structure. In contrast to recent publications that characterize polymorphic functions by monomorphic instances we consider non-termination and selective strictness, i.e., a language closer to Haskell.

Categories and Subject Descriptors D.2.5 [*Software*]: Software Engineering—Testing and Debugging; F.3.1 [*Theory of Computation*]: Logics and Meanings of Programs—Specifying and Verifying and Reasoning about Programs; D.3.3 [*Software*]: Programming Languages—Language Constructs and Features,Polymorphism

General Terms Languages, Theory

Keywords polymorphism, free theorems, parametricity, testing, less strictness, generic programming, selective strictness

1. Introduction

Consider the following polymorphic Haskell (Peyton Jones 2003) function, called *intersperse*, which is defined in the standard Haskell library *Data.List*. It inserts an element between all pairs of succeeding elements of a list.

$$\begin{array}{ll} \mathit{intersperse} :: \alpha \rightarrow [\alpha] \rightarrow [\alpha] & \\ \mathit{intersperse}\ \_\ \ [\,] & = [\,] \\ \mathit{intersperse}\ \_\ \ [x] & = [x] \\ \mathit{intersperse}\ \mathit{sep}\ (x : \mathit{xs}) & = x : \mathit{sep} : \mathit{intersperse}\ \mathit{sep}\ \mathit{xs} \end{array}$$

* Research supported by the DFG under grant VO 1512/1-1.

PDPP'11, July 20–22, 2011, Odense, Denmark.

In (Christiansen 2011) we have shown that this function is unnecessarily strict and that this might cause a serious space leak when processing large lists.

We can use a tool, called Sloth[1], to observe that *intersperse* is unnecessarily strict. To check a function, Sloth generates test cases, namely, elements of the argument type of *intersperse*. Therefore, we have to choose a monomorphic instance of the polymorphic function *intersperse*. Obviously, we want to choose the monomorphic instance of the polymorphic function that results in the smallest number of test cases. A candidate that might come into mind is the monomorphic instance for the unit type (), which has only a single element denoted by (). But, unfortunately, that the monomorphic unit instance of a polymorphic function is unnecessarily strict does not imply that the corresponding polymorphic function is unnecessarily strict. For example, consider the identity function $id\ x = x$. The function $id :: () \rightarrow ()$, i.e., the monomorphic unit instance of the polymorphic identity function, is unnecessarily strict. A function is unnecessarily strict if there exists a function of the same type that is less strict. For example, the function $const\ ()::() \rightarrow ()$[2] is less strict than *id* because we have $id\ \bot \equiv \bot$ but $const\ ()\ \bot \equiv ()$ and $id\ () \equiv ()$ as well as $const\ ()\ () \equiv ()$. Here $\bot$ denotes an input causing a run-time error when evaluated. That is, for the argument $\bot$ the result of *const* () is more defined than the result of *id*. But, obviously, there exists no polymorphic function of type $\alpha \rightarrow \alpha$ whose unit instance behaves like *const* ().

To check whether *intersperse* is as non-strict as possible we instantiate all occurrences of type variables by an opaque type, called A, which is provided by Sloth. If we check this instance of *intersperse* for lists up to size four Sloth reports the following counter examples.

```
> strictCheck (intersperse :: A -> [A] -> [A]) 4
3: \a (b:⊥) -> b:⊥
5: \a (b:c:⊥) -> b:a:c:⊥
Finished 5 tests.
```

The first counter-example states that $intersperse\ a\ (b : \bot)$, where a and b are arbitrary values, yields $\bot$ while there exists a less strict implementation that yields $b : \bot$ for these arguments instead. The second counter-example states that $intersperse\ a\ (b : c : \bot)$ yields $b : a : \bot$ while there exists a less strict implementation that yields $b : a : c : \bot$ instead.

If we reconsider the implementation of *intersperse* we observe that it checks whether its second argument is a list with exactly one element. Therefore, the evaluation of the application $intersperse\ a\ (b : \bot)$ yields $\bot$. But, no matter whether the argument list has exactly one element or not, *intersperse* yields the first element of the argument list as first element of the result list.

[1] Sloth is available at `www.informatik.uni-kiel.de/~jac`.

[2] Function $const :: \alpha \rightarrow \beta \rightarrow \alpha$ is defined by $const\ x\ \_ = x$.

Thus, we can define the following less strict implementation of *intersperse*, that prevents the memory leak caused by the original implementation (Christiansen 2011).

$$
\begin{array}{l}
intersperse' :: \alpha \to [\alpha] \to [\alpha] \\
intersperse'\ \_\ \ [\,] \qquad = [\,] \\
intersperse'\ sep\ (x : xs) = x : go\ xs \\
\quad \textbf{where} \\
\qquad go\ [\,] \qquad = [\,] \\
\qquad go\ (y : ys) = sep : y : go\ ys
\end{array}
$$

If we reconsider the test cases generated by Sloth we observe that Sloth has only generated five test cases to check *intersperse* for lists up to size four. In contrast, Sloth checks exponentially many test cases in the length of the list if we test any monomorphic instance of *intersperse*. As Sloth manages the same test with linearly many test cases it obviously treats the data type A in a special way. The correctness of this strategy is one of the contributions of this paper.

So, when is a function unnecessarily strict? To answer this question, we have to introduce a less-strict relation between functions. For simplicity, we do not strictly separate syntax and semantics. We identify syntactic functions with their semantics in a standard denotational semantics. This is often done in the context of equational reasoning (Danielsson and Jansson 2004; Johann and Voigtländer 2004) to prevent proofs from becoming syntactically cluttered and hard to understand. In the following, $\equiv$ denotes semantic equivalence and $\sqsupseteq$ denotes the definedness order on the semantic domain. In the considered denotational semantics domains form pointed complete partial orders w.r.t. $\sqsupseteq$, with the undefined value $\bot$ as least element.

Definition 1.1: Monomorphic functions $f :: \tau_1 \to \tau_2$ and $g :: \tau_1 \to \tau_2$ are related by $\preceq$ if the following holds.

$$f \preceq g \quad :\Longleftrightarrow \quad \forall v :: \tau_1 .\ f\ v \sqsupseteq g\ v$$

If we have $f \prec g$, i.e., $f \preceq g \wedge g \not\preceq f$, we say that f is *less strict* than g.

Note that the less-strict relation in our previous work (Christiansen 2011) additionally requires functions to agree for total arguments. For simplicity, we omit this requirement here, but we can extend all results to the original definition by considering total arguments as a special case.

Two polymorphic functions are related by the less-strict relation if and only if all their monomorphic instances are related by the less-strict relation. The instantiation of a polymorphic function f to a monomorphic type τ is denoted by f_τ.

Definition 1.2: Let f and g be polymorphic functions of equal type. The functions f and g are related by $\preceq$ if the following holds.

$$f \preceq g :\Longleftrightarrow \forall \tau :: *.\ f_\tau \preceq g_\tau$$

By $\tau :: *$ we denote that τ is a type.

Based on the less-strict relation we define minimal strictness. A function is minimally strict if it is a minimal element w.r.t. $\preceq$. In the presence of parallel, i.e., non-sequential, functions there even exists a least strict function, i.e., a least element w.r.t. $\preceq$. In contrast, in a sequential language like Haskell we are looking for minimal elements w.r.t. $\preceq$ (Christiansen 2011).

On the way to an efficient test for minimal strictness of polymorphic functions we obtain several results about polymorphic functions in Haskell with/without a strict evaluation primitive. The contributions of this paper are as follows.

- We characterize a polymorphic data structure like a list by its shape and its content (Lemma 2.3) and prove that a polymorphic function is characterized by its behavior on shapes (Lemma 2.4). This approach is similar to the container view by Bundy and Richardson (1999) and Prince et al. (2008) but in contrast we consider non-termination and the strict evaluation primitive *seq*[3].
- We employ the characterization of a polymorphic function to prove that two polymorphic functions are related by the less-strict relation if there exists a type such that the corresponding monomorphic instances are related by the less-strict relation (Theorem 2.1). We observe that this theorem breaks in the presence of *seq*.
- We show that we can check whether two polymorphic functions are related by the less-strict relation by checking the functions for all inputs where we replace the polymorphic components by integers that encode the position of the component in the data structure. This approach is similar to an approach by Bernardy et al. (2010), but again, in contrast, we consider non-termination and *seq*. Furthermore, we show that we can use a similar approach to check whether a polymorphic function is minimally strict.
- Finally, this paper can be considered as a kind of tutorial for proving statements about polymorphic functions in the presence of non-termination and *seq* by employing recently developed extensions of free theorems.

Note that the presented results are not restricted to considerations about less strictness as we can define $f \equiv g$ by $f \preceq g \wedge g \preceq f$. Furthermore, some of the lemmas presented here are useful for proving other properties about polymorphic functions besides less strictness.

In the first part of this paper (Section 2, 3, and 4) we prove the considered statements for functions of type $[\alpha] \to [\alpha]$. In this setting it is easier to develop an intuition. In Section 5 we generalize the proofs to other polymorphic data types by employing a generic representation for data types (Magalhães et al. 2010). To generalize the proofs we replace three functions on lists by corresponding functions for arbitrary data types.

2. Less Strict Functions on Lists

In this section we consider functions of type $[\alpha] \to [\alpha]$ that do not use *seq*. We show that, if any monomorphic instance of two polymorphic functions is related by the less-strict relation, then all other monomorphic instances are related as well. This result implies that two polymorphic functions are already related if one of their monomorphic instances is related. Note that this does not imply that a polymorphic function is unnecessarily strict if a monomorphic instance is unnecessarily strict. As we have observed in the introduction, there may exist a monomorphic, less strict function that does not have a polymorphic generalization.

As a first step towards the result about the less strict relation we prove for polymorphic functions $f :: [\alpha] \to [\alpha]$ and $g :: [\alpha] \to [\alpha]$ and an arbitrary type τ that $f_\tau \preceq g_\tau$ implies $f_{()} \preceq g_{()}$.

Lemma 2.1: Let $f, g :: [\alpha] \to [\alpha]$. For all types τ the following holds.

$$f_\tau \preceq g_\tau \Rightarrow f_{()} \preceq g_{()}$$

We can prove this statement by employing a free theorem and relate all elements x of type τ such that $x \not\equiv \bot$ with $()$ and $\bot_\tau$ with $\bot_{()}$. Note that the proof employs that the type τ has an inhabitant, thus, in the following we only consider non-empty types τ.

A free theorem (Wadler 1989) states a property of a (polymorphic) function that can be derived solely from the function's type.

[3] The function $seq :: \alpha \to \beta \to \beta$ satisfies the laws $seq\ \bot\ y \equiv \bot$ and $seq\ x\ y \equiv y$ if $x \not\equiv \bot$.

For example, the free theorem for a function $f :: [\alpha] \to [\alpha]$ states that $map\ g\ (f_{\tau_1}\ xs) = f_{\tau_2}\ (map\ g\ xs)$ holds for all functions $g :: \tau_1 \to \tau_2$ and all lists $xs :: [\tau_1]$. Originally free theorems were considered for languages without general recursion. But, Wadler (1989) already observed that they hold in the presence of $\perp$ if certain functions are strict. For example, g has to be strict above.

Throughout this paper we employ various free theorems without stating them explicitly. The web application *Automatic generation of free theorems*[4] can be used to generate these theorems (Böhme 2007). If a proof step is labeled with "free theorem for f" you can generate the free theorem by entering the type of f into the web application.

Focusing again on the goal of this section, we need to prove the converse of Lemma 2.1 to succeed, which is a considerably more complex task than proving Lemma 2.1. We start with the definition of a function $shape :: [\alpha] \to [Int]$ that replaces the elements of a list by their index in the list, starting with index 0. For example, we get the following results.

$$shape\ [\texttt{'c'}, \texttt{'a'}, \texttt{'b'}] \equiv [0,1,2]$$
$$shape\ (3 : 10 : \perp) \equiv 0 : 1 : \perp$$

The function $shape$ is similar to the function $template$ defined by Voigtländer (2009). While $shape$ yields only the shape of a list, $template$ additionally yields a mapping from indices to the original elements of the list. By using this mapping it is possible to reconstruct the original list. Here, we define the mapping by means of the list indexing function $(!!) :: [\alpha] \to Int \to \alpha$. The function $(!!)$ takes a list and an index in the list (where the smallest index is 0) and yields the element at the corresponding position. If the index does not exist the function yields $\perp$ instead. More importantly than the fact that we use list indexing, $shape$ can handle partially defined lists, while $template$ cannot. For example, we have $template\ (3 : 10 : \perp) \equiv \perp$. Note that this difference is essential as we want to use $shape$ to prove statements about less strictness.

The characterization of a list by means of $shape$ and $(!!)$ is similar to the container approach by Prince et al. (2008). As Prince et al. (2008) do not consider $\perp$ or seq a list is represented by its length (i.e., the shape, appearing as the parameter of a dependent type) and a function from index to element.

Definition 2.1: We define the following function that replaces the elements of a list by increasing natural numbers, starting with 0[5].

$$shape :: [\alpha] \to [Int]$$
$$shape = zipWith\ (\lambda n\ \_ \to n)\ [0\,..]$$

The expression $[0\,..]$ generates an infinite list of increasing integers starting with 0.

To prove that we can characterize a list by its $shape$ and $(!!)$ we prove the following lemma.

Lemma 2.2: For all $x :: \tau$ and $xs :: [\tau]$ the following holds.

$$map\ ((x : xs)!!)\ [1\,..] \equiv map\ (xs!!)\ [0\,..]$$

Although this statement looks quite obvious we have to use a relational free theorem to prove it. We cannot use a standard free theorem as we have to somehow incorporate that $(x : xs)!!$ on the left hand side is never applied to the index 0.

[4] The generator is available at `www-ps.iai.uni-bonn.de/ft`.

[5] The function $zipWith$ is defined as follows.

$$zipWith :: (\alpha \to \beta \to \gamma) \to [\alpha] \to [\beta] \to [\gamma]$$
$$zipWith\ f\ (a : as)\ (b : bs) = f\ a\ b : zipWith\ f\ as\ bs$$
$$zipWith\ \_\ \_\ \ \ \ \ \_ = [\,]$$

Now we can show that a list is reconstructible from its shape by employing list indexing. In the following proof we employ the free theorem for $zipWith$, which can be generated by entering "$zipWith$" into the free theorem generator. The theorem states that for all functions f, g, h, p, and q of appropriate type that satisfy

$$h\ (p\ x\ y) \equiv q\ (f\ x)\ (g\ y)$$

for all values $x :: \tau_1$ and $y :: \tau_2$, we have

$$map\ h\ (zipWith\ p\ z\ v) \equiv zipWith\ q\ (map\ f\ z)\ (map\ g\ v)$$

for all lists $z :: [\tau_1]$ and $v :: [\tau_2]$. We give a detailed proof of the following lemma as we reconsider it in the presence of seq.

Lemma 2.3: For all lists $xs :: [\tau]$ the following holds.

$$map\ (xs!!)\ (shape\ xs) \equiv xs$$

Proof: Proof by structural induction over xs.
Base Cases: If $xs \equiv \perp$ or $xs \equiv [\,]$ we reason as follows.

$$
\begin{aligned}
& map\ (xs!!)\ (shape\ xs) \\
\equiv\ & \{\text{ definition of } shape\ \} \\
& map\ (xs!!)\ (zipWith\ (\lambda n\ \_ \to n)\ [0\,..]\ xs) \\
\equiv\ & \{\text{ definition of } zipWith,\ xs \equiv \perp \text{ or } xs \equiv [\,]\ \} \\
& map\ (xs!!)\ xs \\
\equiv\ & \{\text{ definition of } map,\ xs \equiv \perp \text{ or } xs \equiv [\,]\ \} \\
& xs
\end{aligned}
$$

Inductive Case: If $xs \equiv y : ys$ we reason as follows.

$$
\begin{aligned}
& map\ ((y : ys)!!)\ (shape\ (y : ys)) \\
\equiv\ & \{\text{ definition of } shape\ \} \\
& map\ ((y : ys)!!)\ (zipWith\ (\lambda n\ \_ \to n)\ [0\,..]\ (y : ys)) \\
\equiv\ & \{\text{ definition of } [0\,..]\ \} \\
& map\ ((y : ys)!!)\ (zipWith\ (\lambda n\ \_ \to n)\ (0 : [1\,..])\ (y : ys)) \\
\equiv\ & \{\text{ definition of } zipWith\ \} \\
& map\ ((y : ys)!!)\ (0 : zipWith\ (\lambda n\ \_ \to n)\ [1\,..]\ ys) \\
\equiv\ & \{\text{ definition of } map\ \} \\
& ((y : ys)\ !!\ 0) : map\ ((y : ys)!!) \\
& \qquad\qquad (zipWith\ (\lambda n\ \_ \to n)\ [1\,..]\ ys) \\
\equiv\ & \{\text{ definition of } (!!)\ \} \\
& y : map\ ((y : ys)!!)\ (zipWith\ (\lambda n\ \_ \to n)\ [1\,..]\ ys) \\
\overset{(*)}{\equiv}\ & \{\text{ free theorem for } zipWith,\ ((y : ys)!!) \text{ strict }\} \\
& y : zipWith\ (\lambda n\ \_ \to n)\ (map\ ((y : ys)!!)\ [1\,..])\ ys) \\
\equiv\ & \{\text{ Lemma 2.2 }\} \\
& y : zipWith\ (\lambda n\ \_ \to n)\ (map\ (ys!!)\ [0\,..])\ ys) \\
\overset{(**)}{\equiv}\ & \{\text{ free theorem for } zipWith,\ (ys!!) \text{ strict }\} \\
& y : map\ (ys!!)\ (zipWith\ (\lambda n\ \_ \to n)\ [0\,..]\ ys) \\
\equiv\ & \{\text{ induction hypothesis }\} \\
& y : ys
\end{aligned}
$$

To show the use of a free theorem in detail, we exemplarily state the instantiation of the free theorem for $zipWith$ to prove the step labeled with $(*)$.

$h = ((y : ys)!!)$	$q = \lambda n\ \_ \to n$	$z = [1\,..]$
$p = \lambda n\ \_ \to n$	$f = ((y : ys)!!)$	$v = ys$
	$g = id$	

It is easy to show that we have $h\ (p\ x\ y) \equiv q\ (f\ x)\ (g\ y)$ for all appropriate x and y. We return to the steps labeled with $(*)$ and $(**)$ when we consider the presence of seq. □

The just proved characterization of lists directly allows for a characterization of polymorphic list functions via their behavior on shapes. The Int instance of the polymorphic function f may be compared with a corresponding container morphism of f (Prince et al. 2008).

The following proof employs the free theorem for functions of type $[\alpha] \to [\alpha]$, which states that for all strict functions $g :: \tau_1 \to \tau_2$ and all $xs :: [\tau_1]$ we have $f_{\tau_2}\ (map\ g\ xs) \equiv map\ g\ (f_{\tau_1}\ xs)$.

Lemma 2.4: For all functions $f :: [\alpha] \to [\alpha]$ and all lists $xs :: [\tau]$ the following holds.

$$f_\tau\ xs \equiv map\ (xs!!)\ (f_{Int}\ (shape\ xs))$$

Proof: Let $xs :: [\tau]$. We reason as follows.

$$\begin{array}{l} f_\tau\ xs \\ \equiv \quad \{\text{ Lemma 2.3 }\} \\ f_\tau\ (map\ (xs!!)\ (shape\ xs)) \\ \overset{(*)}{\equiv} \quad \{\text{ free theorem for } f,\ (xs!!) \text{ strict }\} \\ map\ (xs!!)\ (f_{Int}\ (shape\ xs)) \end{array}$$

We return to the step labeled with $(*)$ when we consider the presence of seq. □

Lemma 2.4 enables us to prove a kind of standard lemma about functions of type $[\alpha] \to [\alpha]$. It is a formalization of the intuitive explanation of the validity of free theorems.

A polymorphic function of type $[\alpha] \to [\alpha]$ can only use the elements of its argument list and $\bot$ for the elements of the result list. Therefore, for every element in the result list there exists a position in the argument list, where it is taken from, or it is $\bot$. Furthermore, because the function is polymorphic, it can distinguish argument lists only by their shape. Thus, if we apply a polymorphic function to two lists with equal shape it chooses elements from the same positions of the argument list for the result list.

The following proof employs an instance of the free theorem for functions of type $[\alpha] \to \alpha$. More precisely, for a number $n :: Int$ we consider the function $(!!n) :: [\alpha] \to \alpha$. The free theorem states that for all strict functions $g :: \tau_1 \to \tau_2$ and all $xs :: [\tau_1]$ we have $(map\ g\ xs)\ !!\ n \equiv g\ (xs\ !!\ n)$.

Lemma 2.5: Let $f :: [\alpha] \to [\alpha]$ and $xs :: [\tau_1]$, $ys :: [\tau_2]$ lists such that $shape\ xs \equiv shape\ ys$. For all $n :: Int$ there exists $k :: Int$ such that

$$(f_{\tau_1}\ xs)\ !!\ n \equiv xs\ !!\ k \quad \text{and} \quad (f_{\tau_2}\ ys)\ !!\ n \equiv ys\ !!\ k.$$

Proof: Let $xs :: [\tau_1]$ and $n :: Int$. We define

$$k = (f_{Int}\ (shape\ xs))\ !!\ n$$

and reason as follows.

$$\begin{array}{l} (f_{\tau_1}\ xs)\ !!\ n \\ \equiv \quad \{\text{ Lemma 2.4 }\} \\ (map\ (xs!!)\ (f_{Int}\ (shape\ xs)))\ !!\ n \\ \equiv \quad \{\text{ free theorem for } (!!n),\ (xs!!) \text{ strict }\} \\ xs\ !!\ ((f_{Int}\ (shape\ xs))\ !!\ n) \\ \equiv \quad \{\ k \equiv (f_{Int}\ (shape\ xs))\ !!\ n\ \} \\ xs\ !!\ k \end{array}$$

Let $ys :: [\tau_2]$ such that $shape\ xs \equiv shape\ ys$. We reason as follows.

$$\begin{array}{l} (f_{\tau_2}\ ys)\ !!\ n \\ \equiv \quad \{\text{ like above }\} \\ ys\ !!\ ((f_{Int}\ (shape\ ys))\ !!\ n) \\ \equiv \quad \{\ shape\ xs \equiv shape\ ys,\ k \equiv (f_{Int}\ (shape\ xs))\ !!\ n\ \} \\ ys\ !!\ k \end{array}$$

Note that, if n is out of bounds, then $(f_{Int}\ (shape\ xs))\ !!\ n \equiv \bot$, i.e., $k = \bot$. □

Back on the road, the following lemma is the essential lemma to prove that $f_{()} \preceq g_{()}$ implies $f_\tau \preceq g_\tau$ for all types τ, or, more precisely, to prove its contraposition, i.e., $f_\tau \not\preceq g_\tau$ implies $f_{()} \not\preceq g_{()}$. This proof relies on mapping a list $xs :: [\tau]$ such that $f_\tau\ xs \not\sqsupseteq g_\tau\ xs$ to a list $ys :: [()]$ such that $f_{()}\ ys \not\sqsupseteq g_{()}\ ys$. But, constructing a suitable map, we encounter the following problem. When we consider an arbitrary type τ, the type $[\tau]$ may contain values xs and ys such that $xs\ !!\ k \not\equiv \bot$, $ys\ !!\ k \not\equiv \bot$, and $xs\ !!\ k \sqsupset ys\ !!\ k$. This case does not occur for values of type $[()]$ as the elements of a list of type $[()]$ are either $\bot$ or $()$. By the following lemma we elude this problem. It shows that for every problematic list there exists a non-problematic list that can be considered instead.

Lemma 2.6: Let $f, g :: [\alpha] \to [\alpha]$. For every $xs :: [\tau]$ and $n :: Int$ such that

$$(f_\tau\ xs)!!n \not\equiv \bot, \quad (g_\tau\ xs)!!n \not\equiv \bot, \quad \text{and} \quad (f_\tau\ xs)!!n \not\equiv (g_\tau\ xs)!!n$$

there exists $ys :: [\tau]$ such that

$$(f_\tau\ ys)\ !!\ n \equiv \bot \text{ and } (g_\tau\ ys)\ !!\ n \not\equiv \bot.$$

Now we are ready to prove that $f_\tau \not\preceq g_\tau$ implies $f_{()} \not\preceq g_{()}$ for all types τ. We employ that we have $xs \not\sqsupseteq ys$ if and only if $shape\ xs \not\sqsupseteq shape\ ys$ or $xs\ !!\ n \not\sqsupseteq ys\ !!\ n$ for some $n :: Int$. Furthermore, if there exists a list $xs :: [\tau]$ such that $(f_\tau\ xs)!!n \not\equiv \bot$, $g_\tau\ xs!!n \not\equiv \bot$, and $(f_\tau\ xs)!!n \not\equiv (g_\tau\ xs)!!n$ by the previous lemma we can instead consider a list $ys :: [\tau]$ such that $(f_\tau\ ys)\ !!\ n \equiv \bot$ and $(g_\tau\ ys)\ !!\ n \not\equiv \bot$.

Lemma 2.7: Let $f, g :: [\alpha] \to [\alpha]$. If there exists a type τ such that $f_\tau \not\preceq g_\tau$, then $f_{()} \not\preceq g_{()}$.

Let us summarize the statements so far, namely that less strictness for any monomorphic instance implies less strictness for all other monomorphic instances.

Theorem 2.1: Let $f, g :: [\alpha] \to [\alpha]$. For all types τ_1 and τ_2 the following holds.

$$f_{\tau_1} \preceq g_{\tau_1} \Rightarrow f_{\tau_2} \preceq g_{\tau_2}$$

Proof: By Lemma 2.1 we have $f_{\tau_1} \preceq g_{\tau_1} \Rightarrow f_{()} \preceq g_{()}$ and by Lemma 2.7 we have $f_{()} \preceq g_{()} \Rightarrow f_{\tau_2} \preceq g_{\tau_2}$. □

Employing Theorem 2.1 we can check whether two polymorphic functions are related by the less-strict relation by checking whether the unit instances are related by the less-strict relation. The characterization of lists by means of *shape* allows for a statement that is even more powerful than Theorem 2.1 w.r.t. exhaustive testing. We prove that it suffices to check two polymorphic functions for all possible images of *shape* to check whether they are related by the less-strict relation. Note that, if we consider lists of length n, then there are only linearly many shapes while there are exponentially many lists of type $[\tau]$ for all non-empty types τ.

Theorem 2.2: Let $f, g :: [\alpha] \to [\alpha]$. The following holds.

$$f_{Int} \circ shape \preceq g_{Int} \circ shape \Longleftrightarrow f \preceq g$$

Proof: $\Rightarrow$: Let $xs :: [\tau]$. We reason as follows.

$$\begin{array}{l} f_\tau\ xs \\ \equiv \quad \{\text{ Lemma 2.4 }\} \\ map\ (xs!!)\ (f_{Int}\ (shape\ xs)) \\ \sqsupseteq \quad \{\text{ monotonicity, } f_{Int} \circ shape \preceq g_{Int} \circ shape\ \} \\ map\ (xs!!)\ (g_{Int}\ (shape\ xs)) \\ \equiv \quad \{\text{ Lemma 2.4 }\} \\ g_\tau\ xs \end{array}$$

$\Leftarrow$: We prove the contraposition of this implication. If there exists $xs :: [\tau]$ such that $f_{Int}\ (shape\ xs) \not\sqsupseteq g_{Int}\ (shape\ xs)$, then there exists a list $is :: [Int]$, namely $is = shape\ xs$, such that $f_{Int}\ is \not\sqsupseteq g_{Int}\ is$. Therefore, we have $f \not\preceq g$ by the definition of the less-strict relation. □

3. Less Strict Functions in the Presence of seq

In this section we consider a language that provides a strict evaluation primitive *seq*. Although Theorem 2.1, proved in the absence of *seq*, seems quite natural, it breaks when *seq* is available. In the presence of *seq* the property $f_{()} \preceq g_{()}$ does not imply $f_\tau \preceq g_\tau$ for all types τ. For example, consider the following functions of type $[\alpha] \to [\alpha]$.

$$f :: [\alpha] \to [\alpha] \qquad\qquad g :: [\alpha] \to [\alpha]$$
$$f\ (x : y : \_) = [seq\ x\ y] \qquad g\ (x : y : \_) = [seq\ y\ x]$$

If one of the first two elements of the argument list is $\bot$, then both functions yield $[\bot]$. If both elements are $()$, then both functions yield $[()]$. That is, we have $f_{()} \preceq g_{()}$, or, more precisely, we even have $f_{()} \equiv g_{()}$. But there are obviously types τ such that f_τ and g_τ are incomparable. For example, we have $f_{Bool}\ [False, True] \equiv [False]$ but $g_{Bool}\ [False, True] \equiv [True]$. This example shows that Theorem 2.1 fails in the presence of *seq*.

So, how about Theorem 2.2, does it break as well? It holds for the previous example, but it breaks for the functions $f'\ (x : y : z : \_) = [seq\ x\ z]$ and $g'\ (x{:}y{:}z{:}\ \_) = [seq\ y\ z]$. The functions f' and g' act identically on shapes but are incomparable w.r.t. the less-strict relation. Hence, Theorem 2.2 is also not valid if we consider *seq*.

In contrast to Theorem 2.1 the assertion of Theorem 2.2 directly depends on the notion of shape. Thus, maybe we can prove a similar statement when we alter *shape*. Let us track back where the current proof is corrupted by *seq*. We start with the proof of Lemma 2.4.

Lemma 2.3 is still valid because none of the considered functions uses *seq*. In this case we are quasi considering a language without *seq*. In contrast, Lemma 2.4 considers an arbitrary function f that might use *seq*. According to Johann and Voigtländer (2004) the step labeled with $(*)$ in the proof of Lemma 2.4 might not hold in the presence of *seq* as $(xs!!)$ is not total[6]. In fact, the lemma fails completely. For example, consider the function f again. We have

$$f\ [\bot, True] \equiv [\bot]$$

and, on the other hand, the following holds.

$$\begin{array}{l} map\ ([\bot, True]!!)\ (f\ (shape\ [\bot, True])) \\ \equiv \quad \{ \text{ definition of } shape \ \} \\ map\ ([\bot, True]!!)\ (f\ [0, 1]) \\ \equiv \quad \{ \text{ definition of } f \ \} \\ map\ ([\bot, True]!!)\ [1] \\ \equiv \quad \{ \text{ definition of } map \ \} \\ [[\bot, True]\ !!\ 1] \\ \equiv \quad \{ \text{ definition of } (!!) \ \} \\ [True] \end{array}$$

That is, we have $f\ xs \not\equiv map\ (xs!!)\ (f\ (shape\ xs))$.

The function f is able to distinguish the list $[\bot, True]$ from the list $[0, 1]$ by employing *seq*, although these lists have the same shape. Hence, in the presence of *seq* a polymorphic function cannot only distinguish two lists by their shape like it is defined by the function *shape*. It can also distinguish them by the occurrences of $\bot$ as list element. Thus, to take *seq* into account we have to consider a different notion of shape, implemented by the function $shape_{seq}$.

$$shape_{seq} :: [\alpha] \to [Int]$$
$$shape_{seq} = zipWith\ (\lambda n\ x \to seq\ x\ n)\ [0\,..]$$

The function $shape_{seq}$ replaces all elements x of a list with $x \not\equiv \bot$ by their position in the list. But, in contrast to *shape*, $shape_{seq}$ keeps all elements x with $x \equiv \bot$. In the remaining part of this section we prove that a theorem like Theorem 2.2 holds in the presence of *seq* if we replace *shape* by $shape_{seq}$. The proofs in particular highlight the role of free theorems.

[6] A function f is total if for all x with $x \not\equiv \bot$ we have $f\ x \not\equiv \bot$.

$$\begin{array}{l} \forall f :: \tau_1 \to \tau_2, f\ strict\ and\ total. \\ \forall g :: \tau_3 \to \tau_4, g\ strict. \\ \quad \forall xs :: [\tau_3].\ t\ xs \not\equiv \bot \iff t\ (map\ g\ xs) \not\equiv \bot \\ \quad \wedge\ \forall ys :: [\tau_1]. \\ \qquad map\ g\ (t\ xs\ y) \equiv t\ (map\ g\ xs)\ (map\ f\ ys) \end{array}$$

Figure 1. The specialized free theorem for *zipWith* where $t \equiv zipWith\ (\lambda x\ n \to seq\ x\ n)$.

If we replace *shape* by $shape_{seq}$ in Lemma 2.4 we can provide a characterization of polymorphic functions in the presence of *seq*. To prove the characterization, first we have to ensure that Lemma 2.3 also holds for $shape_{seq}$. This is not obvious, because $shape_{seq}$ uses *seq* and consequently its free theorem is more restrictive. We employ an extension of free theorems by Seidel and Voigtländer (2009) to manage the proof. According to Johann and Voigtländer (2004), in the presence of *seq*, we have to guarantee that certain functions are total. However, the extension by Seidel and Voigtländer (2009) allows for less restrictive free theorems. Given a function definition, it assigns a refined type to the function and uses this refined type to derive less restrictive free theorems.

To generate a free theorem for a specific implementation of a polymorphic function we have to define the function in a simple functional language with a fixpoint operator and a *seq* primitive. Figure 1 shows the free theorem that is generated for $zipWith\ (\lambda n\ x \to seq\ x\ n) :: [\alpha] \to [\beta] \to [\alpha]$[7]. By inspecting the implementation the generator observes that we only use *seq* on the second argument of the function passed to *zipWith*. Therefore, in contrast to the general free theorem the specialized version does not require g to be total. This enables us to prove the following adjusted version of Lemma 2.3.

Lemma 3.1: For all lists $xs :: [\tau]$ the following holds.

$$map\ (xs!!)\ (shape_{seq}\ xs) \equiv xs$$

Proof: We reason the same way as in Lemma 2.3 but replace all occurrences of *shape* by $shape_{seq}$ and all occurrences of $(\lambda n\ \_ \to n)$ by $(\lambda n\ x \to seq\ x\ n)$. Instead of the general free theorem for *zipWith* we employ the specialized free theorem for $zipWith\ (\lambda n\ x \to seq\ x\ n)$ shown in Figure 1. We replace the steps labeled with $(*)$ and $(**)$ in the proof of Lemma 2.3 by the following reasoning. We prove the step labeled with $(*)$ by instantiating the specialized free theorem as follows.

$$g = ((y : ys)!!) \qquad x = [1\,..]$$
$$f = id \qquad y = ys$$

We prove the step labeled with $(**)$ by instantiating the specialized free theorem as follows.

$$g = (ys!!) \qquad x = [0\,..]$$
$$f = id \qquad y = ys$$

Note that id is strict and total and that $((y : ys)!!)$ and $(ys!!)$ are strict. □

To complete the proof of an adjusted version of Lemma 2.4 with $shape_{seq}$, we still have to recover the step labeled with $(*)$ in the original proof. That is, we want to prove that

$$f\ (map\ (xs!!)\ (shape_{seq}\ xs)) \equiv map\ (xs!!)\ (f\ (shape_{seq}\ xs)).$$

[7] The generator is available at
`www-ps.iai.uni-bonn.de/cgi-bin/polyseq.cgi`.

If we consider Johann and Voigtländer (2004) we have to show that $(xs!!)$ is total, which is not the case. First of all the position we are projecting to might be out of bounds, for example, $[1,2]$!! 3. Furthermore, the list xs may contain $\bot$, which also breaks totality if we project to the corresponding position, for example, $[1,\bot]$!! 1. We cannot employ the extension by Seidel and Voigtländer (2009) because we do not consider a concrete function like *zipWith* before but an arbitrary function of type $[\alpha] \to [\alpha]$. Thus, we cannot weaken the requirements of a free theorem by providing a concrete implementation. But there is rescue. For a specific list the requirements proposed by Johann and Voigtländer (2004) are unnecessarily strong. For example, for the free theorem

$$map\ g\ (f\ xs) = f\ (map\ g\ xs)$$

they demand that g has to be total. But it is sufficient if g is total w.r.t. the elements of the list xs. The following theorem proves this observation by employing the relational version of the free theorem for the type $[\alpha] \to [\alpha]$.

Theorem 3.1: Let $f :: [\alpha] \to [\alpha]$. For all strict functions $g :: \tau_1 \to \tau_2$ and for all $xs :: [\tau_1]$ with

$$g\ (xs\ !!\ n) \equiv \bot \text{ if and only if } xs\ !!\ n \equiv \bot$$

for all $n :: Int$, we have

$$map\ g\ (f_{\tau_1}\ xs) \equiv f_{\tau_2}\ (map\ g\ xs).$$

Proof: Let $xs :: [\tau_1]$. We use the relational free theorem for f to prove the statement. We define a relation that relates all elements of the list xs with the image of g of this element.

$$\begin{aligned} R_{xs} := &\{(xs\ !!\ n, g\ (xs\ !!\ n)) \mid n :: Int\} \\ &\cup \{(\bigsqcup_{i \in I}(xs!!i), \bigsqcup_{i \in I} g\ (xs!!i)) \mid \langle xs!!i \rangle_{i \in I} \text{ chain}, I \subseteq Int\} \end{aligned}$$

As R_{xs} has to be a continuous relation we close the relation by relating the suprema of all possible chains.

First we show that R_{xs} is a strict, bottom-reflecting and continuous relation. For details about these concepts consider Definition A.1. We have $(xs\ !!\ \bot, g\ (xs\ !!\ \bot)) \in R_{xs}$ and $xs\ !!\ \bot \equiv \bot$ as well as $g\ (xs\ !!\ \bot) \equiv g\ \bot \equiv \bot$, i.e., R_{xs} is strict. Next we show that R_{xs} is bottom-reflecting. Let $(x, y) \in R_{xs}$.
Case 1: $x \equiv xs\ !!\ n$ and $y \equiv g\ (xs\ !!\ n)$
In this case we have $g\ (xs\ !!\ n) \equiv \bot$ if and only if $xs\ !!\ n \equiv \bot$ by precondition.
Case 2: $x \equiv \bigsqcup_{i \in I}(xs\ !!\ i)$ and $y \equiv \bigsqcup_{i \in I} g(xs\ !!\ i)$
We reason as follows.

$$\begin{aligned} \bigsqcup_{i \in I}(xs\ !!\ i) \equiv \bot &\iff \forall i \in I.\ xs\ !!\ i \equiv \bot \\ &\iff \forall i \in I.\ g\ (xs\ !!\ i) \equiv \bot \\ &\iff \bigsqcup_{i \in I} g\ (xs\ !!\ i) \equiv \bot \end{aligned}$$

Finally, we have to show that R_{xs} is continuous. Let $\langle x_i \rangle_{i \in I}$ and $\langle y_i \rangle_{i \in I}$ be chains whose elements are pair-wise related by R_{xs}. We consider the following set.

$$K = \bigcup_{i \in I} \begin{cases} \{i\} & \text{if } x_i = xs\ !!\ i \\ J & \text{if } x_i = \bigsqcup_{j \in J}(xs\ !!\ j) \end{cases}$$

We have $(\bigsqcup_{k \in K}(xs\ !!\ k), \bigsqcup_{k \in K} g\ (xs\ !!\ k)) = (\bigsqcup_{i \in I} x_i, \bigsqcup_{i \in I} y_i)$ and, by definition of R_{xs}, we have $(\bigsqcup_{k \in K} x_k, \bigsqcup_{k \in K} y_k) \in R_{xs}$. Thus, R_{xs} is continuous.

We have $(xs, map\ g\ xs) \in \text{lift}\{[]\}(R_{xs})$ where $\text{lift}\{[]\}(R)$ is the relational structural lifting defined as follows.

$$\begin{aligned} \text{lift}\{[]\}(R) = &\{(\bot,\bot), ([],[])\} \\ &\cup \{(x : xs, y : ys) \mid (x,y) \in R, (xs, ys) \in \text{lift}\{[]\})(R)\} \end{aligned}$$

Intuitively $(xs, ys) \in \text{lift}\{[]\}(R_{xs})$ means that ys is the point-wise g image of xs. Or, in other words, $ys \equiv map\ g\ xs$. Since the relational free theorem states that $(xs, map\ g\ xs) \in \text{lift}\{[]\}(R_{xs})$ implies $(f\ xs, f\ (map\ g\ xs)) \in \text{lift}\{[]\}(R_{xs})$, we obtain that $f\ (map\ g\ xs)$ is the point-wise g image of $f\ xs$, that is, $map\ g\ (f\ xs) \equiv f\ (map\ g\ xs)$. □

For proving statements about functions in the presence of *seq* the previous theorem is quite useful as we are not restricted to total functions anymore. While the previous theorem does only consider functions of type $[\alpha] \to [\alpha]$, by employing the generalization presented in Section 5, we can generalize this theorem to arbitrary first order type constructors.

Furthermore, this kind of generalization of a functional free theorem is also valuable in the absence of *seq*. For example, the standard functional free theorem for a function $f :: (\alpha \to \beta) \to [\alpha] \to [\beta]$ states that

$$h\ (p\ x) \equiv q\ (g\ x)$$

for all x of appropriate type implies

$$map\ h\ (f\ p\ xs) \equiv f\ q\ (map\ g\ xs)$$

for all xs of appropriate type. By employing the relation R_{xs} defined in the previous proof we can derive a free theorem that states for a list xs that

$$h\ (p\ (xs\ !!\ n)) \equiv q\ (g\ (xs\ !!\ n))$$

for all $n :: Int$ already implies

$$map\ h\ (f\ p\ xs) \equiv f\ q\ (map\ g\ xs).$$

Actually, we have used this statement to prove Lemma 2.2.

We want to employ Theorem 3.1 to prove

$$map\ (xs!!)\ (f\ (shape_{seq}\ xs)) \equiv f\ (map\ (xs!!)\ (shape_{seq}\ xs))$$

to fix step $(*)$ of Lemma 2.4. Thus, we have to show that xs !! $(shape_{seq}\ xs\ !!\ n) \equiv \bot$ if and only if $shape_{seq}\ xs\ !!\ n \equiv \bot$. Therefore, we show a connection between (!!) and *zipWith*, namely that

$$(zipWith\ f\ xs\ ys)\ !!\ n \equiv f\ (xs\ !!\ n)\ (ys\ !!\ n).$$

This statement is quite similar to the free theorem for (!!), which states that $(map\ f\ xs)\ !!\ n \equiv f\ (xs\ !!\ n)$. And, indeed, these statements are closely related. In the context of free theorems mostly only two-ary logical relations are considered. The connection between *zipWith* and (!!) is the functional instantiation of the relational free theorem for (!!) if we consider three-ary relations. Alternatively, we can prove the following lemma by means of structural induction.

Lemma 3.2: For all strict functions[8] $f :: \tau_1 \to \tau_2 \to \tau_3$ and all lists $xs :: [\tau_1]$, $ys :: [\tau_2]$ the following holds.

$$(zipWith\ f\ xs\ ys)\ !!\ n \equiv f\ (xs\ !!\ n)\ (ys\ !!\ n)$$

By employing the previous lemma we prove a characteristic property of $shape_{seq}$, which is not valid for *shape*. The shape of a list w.r.t. $shape_{seq}$ is $\bot$ at a certain position if and only if the "original list" is $\bot$ at that position.

[8] Here strict means $f\ x\ \bot \equiv \bot$ and $f\ \bot\ y \equiv \bot$ for all x, y.

Lemma 3.3: For all lists $xs :: [\tau]$ and all $n :: Int$ we have

$$(shape_{seq}\ xs)\ !!\ n \equiv \bot \quad \text{if and only if} \quad xs\ !!\ n \equiv \bot.$$

Proof: We reason as follows.

$$\begin{aligned}
& (shape_{seq}\ xs)\ !!\ n \\
\equiv\ & \{\text{ definition of } shape_{seq}\ \} \\
& (zipWith\ (\lambda n\ x \to seq\ x\ n)\ [0\,..]\ xs)\ !!\ n \\
\equiv\ & \{\text{ Lemma 3.2, } seq \text{ strict }\} \\
& seq\ (xs\ !!\ n)\ ([0\,..]\ !!\ n)
\end{aligned}$$

If we have $n \equiv \bot$ or $n < 0$, then $seq\ (xs\ !!\ n)\ ([0\,..]\ !!\ n) \equiv seq\ \bot\ \bot \equiv \bot$ as well as $xs\ !!\ n \equiv \bot$. If we have $n \geqslant 0$, then $seq\ (xs\ !!\ n)\ ([0\,..]\ !!\ n) \equiv seq\ (xs\ !!\ n)\ n$. That is, $(shape_{seq}\ xs)\ !!\ n \equiv \bot$ if and only if $xs\ !!\ n \equiv \bot$. □

Employing the characterization of $shape_{seq}$ we prove the analogous lemma to Lemma 2.4 in the presence of seq.

Lemma 3.4: For all functions $f :: [\alpha] \to [\alpha]$ and all lists $xs :: [\tau]$ the following holds.

$$f_\tau\ xs \equiv map\ (xs!!)\ (f_{Int}\ (shape_{seq}\ xs))$$

Proof: Let $xs :: [\tau]$. We reason as follows.

$$\begin{aligned}
& f_\tau\ xs \\
\equiv\ & \{\text{ Lemma 3.1 }\} \\
& f_\tau\ (map\ (xs!!)\ (shape_{seq}\ xs)) \\
\equiv\ & \{\text{ Theorem 3.1, Lemma 3.3 }\} \\
& map\ (xs!!)\ (f_{Int}\ (shape_{seq}\ xs))
\end{aligned}$$

Now we are ready to prove the analogue of Theorem 2.2 in the presence of seq.

Theorem 3.2: For all $f, g :: [\alpha] \to [\alpha]$ the following holds.

$$f_{Int} \circ shape_{seq} \preceq g_{Int} \circ shape_{seq} \iff f \preceq g$$

Proof: The proof is analogous to the proof of Theorem 2.2 but instead of Lemma 2.4 we employ Lemma 3.4. □

4. Minimally Strict Functions on Lists

We return to a setting without seq to consider minimal strictness. If we reconsider Theorem 2.2 one might assume that we can check whether a polymorphic function $f :: [\alpha] \to [\alpha]$ is minimally strict by checking whether there exists a function $h :: [Int] \to [Int]$ that is less strict than f_{Int} w.r.t. all shapes. Consider the following function of type $[\alpha] \to [\alpha]$ that yields a singleton list that contains the first element of its argument list.

$$\begin{aligned}
& f :: [\alpha] \to [\alpha] \\
& f\ (x{:}\ _) = [x]
\end{aligned}$$

The following function $h :: [Int] \to [Int]$ is less strict than f_{Int} w.r.t. shapes as we have $h\ \bot \equiv [0] \sqsupset \bot \equiv f_{Int}\ \bot$, for example.

$$\begin{aligned}
& h :: [Int] \to [Int] \\
& h\ _ = [0]
\end{aligned}$$

But obviously there exists no polymorphic function whose integer instance behaves like h. The function h "invents" a list element, namely 0. As Lemma 2.5 tells us the elements of the result list of a polymorphic function of type $[\alpha] \to [\alpha]$ are taken from the argument list or they are $\bot$. To prevent the monomorphic function from inventing elements we do not compare $f_{Int}\ xs$ with $h\ xs$ but with $map\ (xs!!)\ (h\ xs)$.

In the example above $h\ \bot$ is more defined than $f_{Int}\ \bot$, but $map\ (\bot!!)\ (h\ \bot)$ is as defined as $f_{Int}\ \bot$. Therefore, h is not a witness that shows that f is unnecessarily strict.

Theorem 4.1: Let $f :: [\alpha] \to [\alpha]$. The function f is not minimally strict if and only if there exists a function $h :: [Int] \to [Int]$ such that

$$g \prec f$$

where g is defined as follows.

$$\begin{aligned}
& g :: [\alpha] \to [\alpha] \\
& g\ xs = map\ (xs!!)\ (h\ (shape\ xs))
\end{aligned}$$

Proof: $\Rightarrow$: As f is not minimally strict there exists a polymorphic function $i :: [\alpha] \to [\alpha]$ that is less strict than f. By Lemma 2.4 we have

$$i\ xs \equiv map\ (xs!!)\ (i_{Int}\ (shape\ xs)).$$

That is, there exists a function $h :: [Int] \to [Int]$ with the required property, namely i_{Int}.
$\Leftarrow$: The function f is not minimally strict because $g :: [\alpha] \to [\alpha]$ is less strict than f. □

We can prove a similar theorem in the presence of seq by employing $shape_{seq}$ instead of $shape$.

Sloth uses a slightly different lemma to check whether a function is minimally strict. Instead of considering a polymorphic function g as defined in Theorem 4.1 we consider a function g that map lists of integers to lists of integers. More precisely, for a function $h :: [Int] \to [Int]$ we consider a function $g\ xs = map\ (xs!!)\ (h\ xs)$. To check whether a polymorphic function f is minimally strict we check whether we have $g \circ shape \prec f_{Int} \circ shape$. It is easy to prove this refined statement by Theorem 4.1 and Theorem 2.2. Note that Sloth indeed uses shapes similar to the shapes defined via $shape$. Thus, polymorphic functions that use seq cannot be tested using the monomorphic A instance, but in return the number of test cases is reduced.

If we check a function $f :: [A] \to [A]$ Sloth checks whether there exists a shape for which $f :: [Int] \to [Int]$ is unnecessarily strict. We can check this using the standard approach that is also used for other monomorphic functions (Christiansen 2011). If there exists a shape xs for which f is supposed to yield a more defined result ys, i.e., $ys \sqsupset f\ xs$, we check whether we have $map\ (xs!!)\ ys \sqsupset f\ xs$ as well. If this is the case xs is a counterexample that shows that f is unnecessarily strict and $map\ (xs!!)\ ys$ is the proposed result for f for the argument xs.

5. Generalization

In this section we consider polymorphic functions that do not have the type $[\alpha] \to [\alpha]$. For example, consider the following data type for binary trees.

$$\textbf{data}\ Tree\ \alpha = Empty \mid Node\ (Tree\ \alpha)\ \alpha\ (Tree\ \alpha)$$

We define a function $breadthFirst$ that enumerates the elements of a tree in breath first order. The function $partition$ takes a list of values and a list of subtrees and adds the components of a $Node$ to the corresponding lists.

$$\begin{aligned}
& partition :: Tree\ \alpha \to ([\alpha], [Tree\ \alpha]) \to ([\alpha], [Tree\ \alpha]) \\
& partition\ Empty\ \qquad level \qquad = level \\
& partition\ (Node\ l\ v\ r)\ (vs, trees) = (v : vs, l : r : trees)
\end{aligned}$$

The function $breadthLevel$ takes one level of a tree, splits the level into values and the next level by employing $partition$ and concatenates the values of the current level with the recursive result.

$$\begin{aligned}
& breadthLevel :: [Tree\ \alpha] \to [\alpha] \\
& breadthLevel\ [\,] \quad = [\,] \\
& breadthLevel\ level = values +\!\!+\ breadthLevel\ nextLevel \\
& \quad \textbf{where} \\
& \qquad (values, nextLevel) = foldr\ partition\ ([\,], [\,])\ level
\end{aligned}$$

$$\textbf{type instance}\ Gen\ Tree = U + Rec\ Tree \times P \times Rec\ Tree$$

$$\begin{array}{l}\textbf{instance}\ Representable\ Tree\ \textbf{where}\\ \quad from\ Empty \quad = Inl\ U\\ \quad from\ (Node\ l\ v\ r) =\\ \qquad Inr\ (Rec\ (from\ l) \times P\ v \times Rec\ (from\ r))\\ \quad to\ (Inl\ U) = Empty\\ \quad to\ (Inr\ (Rec\ l \times P\ v \times Rec\ r)) = Node\ (to\ l)\ v\ (to\ r)\end{array}$$

Figure 2. Instance of *Representable* for *Tree*

$$\begin{array}{l}breadthFirst :: Tree\ \alpha \to [\alpha]\\ breadthFirst\ tree = breadthLevel\ [tree]\end{array}$$

We can check whether *breadthFirst* is minimally strict by instantiating all type variables with the data type A.

```
> strictCheck (breadthFirst :: Tree A -> [A]) 3
5: \Node (Node ⊥ a ⊥) b ⊥) -> b:a:⊥
Finished 9 tests.
```

Sloth states that *breadthFirst* is unnecessarily strict. The implementation presented above does not yield any value of a certain level if any of the trees on the same level is $\bot$. To improve the implementation we simply have to replace the tuple pattern matching in *partition* by a lazy pattern matching. This minor change has a quite significant effect on the runtime of the function. For example, when we enumerate the elements of a complete binary tree of depth 22 the less strict implementation is around 9 times faster than the unnecessarily strict implementation. Furthermore, this performance gain increases with larger tree sizes.

To test whether *breadthFirst* is minimally strict Sloth uses a generalization of the results presented in Section 4. In this section we present this generalization and verify its correctness. More precisely, instead of considering functions of type $[\alpha] \to [\alpha]$ only, we consider functions of type $\varphi\ \alpha \to \psi\ \alpha$ where φ and ψ are functors that are isomorphic to a functor composed of the unit, the identity, the constant, the product, and the sum functor. The approach employed here is very similar to the approach by Magalhães et al. (2010).

To generalize the statements from the previous sections we have to define generalizations of *map*, (!!), and *shape* for arbitrary first order functors. In the following we introduce the generic representation that is used to generalize the statements.

First of all we define a type family that maps a type constructor to the isomorphic functor composed of sums and products. You can consider a type family simply as a function on the type level.

$$\textbf{type family}\ Gen\ \varphi :: * \to *$$

This type family, called *Gen*, takes an arbitrary type φ and yields a type of kind $* \to *$, i.e., a type constructor.

The type class *Representable* provides two functions. The function *from* takes a value of the original functor and yields the corresponding value of the generic representation. The function *to* takes a value of the generic representation and yields the corresponding value of the original functor.

$$\begin{array}{l}\textbf{class}\ Representable\ \varphi\ \textbf{where}\\ \quad from :: \varphi\ \alpha \to Gen\ \varphi\ \alpha\\ \quad to :: Gen\ \varphi\ \alpha \to \varphi\ \alpha\end{array}$$

Next we define the generic functors. The unit functor U represents constructors without arguments. The constant functor K takes a type τ and ignores its second argument α. The identity functor P contains a value of type α.

$$\begin{array}{l}\textbf{data}\ U\ \alpha \quad = U\\ \textbf{data}\ K\ \tau\ \alpha = K\ \tau\\ \textbf{data}\ P\ \alpha \quad = P\ \alpha\end{array}$$

To represent several constructors we use the sum functor.

$$\textbf{data}\ (\varphi + \psi)\ \alpha = Inl\ (\varphi\ \alpha) \mid Inr\ (\psi\ \alpha)$$

For example, **data** $Maybe\ \alpha = Nothing \mid Just\ \alpha$ is represented by the generic functor $U + P$.

The product functor is used to represent constructors with multiple arguments.

$$\textbf{data}\ (\varphi \times \psi)\ \alpha = (\varphi\ \alpha) \times (\psi\ \alpha)$$

For example, **data** $WithInt\ \alpha = WithInt\ Int\ \alpha$ is represented by $K\ Int \times P$.

Finally, the two-ary type constructor *Rec* is used to represent recursive components of a functor. In contrast to the definition by Magalhães et al. (2010) the constructor *Rec* contains a value of the generic representation, i.e., a value of type $Gen\ \varphi\ \alpha$ and not a value of type $\varphi\ \alpha$. This way we can prove statements about functions on generic functors by a simple structural induction.

$$\textbf{data}\ Rec\ \varphi\ \alpha = Rec\ (Gen\ \varphi\ \alpha)$$

In the following by *generic functor* we refer to an unary type constructor that is composed of the type constructors U, K, P, $+$, $\times$, and *Rec*.

As an example, Figure 2 shows an instance of *Representable* for the tree data type defined before. The product $\times$ and the sum $+$ are right associative, i.e., for example, $x \times y \times z$ stands for $x \times (y \times z)$.

The following definition states that the considered instances of *Representable* provide functions *from* and *to* that form an embedding-projection pair.

Definition 5.1: We call a type constructor φ *representable functor* if $Gen\ \varphi$ is a generic functor and φ is an instance of *Representable* that satisfies the following properties.

$$to \circ from \equiv id \qquad from \circ to \sqsubseteq id$$

In the following we assume that instances of *Representable* are representable functors. Note that Definition 5.1 implies that *from* and *to* are strict, which is employed in several of the following proofs.

To generalize free theorems from lists to representable functors we employ the type class *Functor*. The type class *Functor* provides a single function called *fmap* that is a generalization of *map* to arbitrary unary type constructors.

$$\begin{array}{l}\textbf{class}\ Functor\ \varphi\ \textbf{where}\\ \quad fmap :: (\alpha \to \beta) \to \varphi\ \alpha \to \varphi\ \beta\end{array}$$

We define instances of *Functor* for all generic functors. Besides, for every type constructor φ that is an instance of *Representable* we have to define instances for $Rec\ \varphi$[9] and φ. We abstain from defining one generic instance of *Functor* for all instances of *Representable* as this requires `UndecidableInstances`. In the following we assume that instances for representable functors are defined by means of the instances of their isomorphic generic representation. More precisely, a function $f :: \varphi\ \alpha \to \psi\ \alpha$ for representable functors φ and ψ is defined by $to \circ f \circ from$, where the latter f is an instance of the same overloaded function for the corresponding generic functors.

The free theorem for a function $f :: \varphi\ \alpha \to \psi\ \alpha$ states that we have $f\ (fmap_\varphi\ g\ x) \equiv fmap_\psi\ g\ (f\ x)$ where $fmap_\varphi :: (\alpha \to \beta) \to \varphi\ \alpha \to \varphi\ \beta$ and $fmap_\psi :: (\alpha \to \beta) \to \psi\ \alpha \to \psi\ \beta$ are structural mappings. For example, *map* is the structural mapping

[9] To define this instance we need `FlexibleInstances`.

$$
\begin{aligned}
&\textbf{instance } \mathit{Functor}\ U \textbf{ where}\\
&\quad \mathit{fmap}\ \_\ U = U\\
&\textbf{instance } \mathit{Functor}\ (K\ \tau) \textbf{ where}\\
&\quad \mathit{fmap}\ \_\ (K\ x) = K\ x\\
&\textbf{instance } \mathit{Functor}\ P \textbf{ where}\\
&\quad \mathit{fmap}\ f\ (P\ x) = P\ (f\ x)\\
&\textbf{instance } (\mathit{Functor}\ \varphi, \mathit{Functor}\ \psi) \Rightarrow \mathit{Functor}\ (\varphi + \psi) \textbf{ where}\\
&\quad \mathit{fmap}\ f\ (\mathit{Inl}\ x) = \mathit{Inl}\ (\mathit{fmap}\ f\ x)\\
&\quad \mathit{fmap}\ f\ (\mathit{Inr}\ x) = \mathit{Inr}\ (\mathit{fmap}\ f\ x)\\
&\textbf{instance } (\mathit{Functor}\ \varphi, \mathit{Functor}\ \psi) \Rightarrow \mathit{Functor}\ (\varphi \times \psi) \textbf{ where}\\
&\quad \mathit{fmap}\ f\ (x \times y) = \mathit{fmap}\ f\ x \times \mathit{fmap}\ f\ y\\
&\textbf{instance } \mathit{Functor}\ (\mathit{Rec}\ \mathit{Tree}) \textbf{ where}\\
&\quad \mathit{fmap}\ f\ (\mathit{Rec}\ x) = \mathit{Rec}\ (\mathit{fmap}\ f\ x)\\
&\textbf{instance } \mathit{Functor}\ \mathit{Tree} \textbf{ where}\\
&\quad \mathit{fmap}\ f = \mathit{to} \circ \mathit{fmap}\ f \circ \mathit{from}
\end{aligned}
$$

Figure 3. Instances of *Functor*

$$
\begin{aligned}
&\textbf{instance } \mathit{Shape}\ U \textbf{ where}\\
&\quad \mathit{gshape}'\ \_\ U = U\\
&\textbf{instance } \mathit{Shape}\ (K\ \tau) \textbf{ where}\\
&\quad \mathit{gshape}'\ \_\ (K\ x) = K\ x\\
&\textbf{instance } \mathit{Shape}\ P \textbf{ where}\\
&\quad \mathit{gshape}'\ \mathit{ds}\ (P\ \_) = P\ (\mathit{reverse}\ \mathit{ds})\\
&\textbf{instance } (\mathit{Shape}\ \varphi, \mathit{Shape}\ \psi) \Rightarrow \mathit{Shape}\ (\varphi + \psi) \textbf{ where}\\
&\quad \mathit{gshape}'\ \mathit{ds}\ (\mathit{Inl}\ x) = \mathit{Inl}\ (\mathit{gshape}'\ \mathit{ds}\ x)\\
&\quad \mathit{gshape}'\ \mathit{ds}\ (\mathit{Inr}\ x) = \mathit{Inr}\ (\mathit{gshape}'\ \mathit{ds}\ x)\\
&\textbf{instance } (\mathit{Shape}\ \varphi, \mathit{Shape}\ \psi) \Rightarrow \mathit{Shape}\ (\varphi \times \psi) \textbf{ where}\\
&\quad \mathit{gshape}'\ \mathit{ds}\ (x \times y) = \mathit{gshape}'\ (L : \mathit{ds})\ x \times \mathit{gshape}'\ (R : \mathit{ds})\ y\\
&\textbf{instance } \mathit{Shape}\ (\mathit{Rec}\ \mathit{Tree}) \textbf{ where}\\
&\quad \mathit{gshape}'\ \mathit{ds}\ (\mathit{Rec}\ x) = \mathit{Rec}\ (\mathit{gshape}'\ \mathit{ds}\ x)\\
&\textbf{instance } \mathit{Shape}\ \mathit{Tree} \textbf{ where}\\
&\quad \mathit{gshape}'\ \mathit{ds} = \mathit{to} \circ \mathit{gshape}'\ \mathit{ds} \circ \mathit{from}
\end{aligned}
$$

Figure 4. Instances of *Shape*

for the list functor. It is kind of folklore that *fmap* presented in Figure 3 is the structural mapping for a generic functor but to the best of our knowledge there is no appropriate formal treatment of this question.

To prove the following lemma we mainly replace all occurrences of *map* in the proof of Lemma 2.1 by *fmap*.

Lemma 5.1: Let $f, g :: \varphi\ \alpha \to \psi\ \alpha$. For all types τ the following holds.

$$f_\tau \preceq g_\tau \Rightarrow f_{()} \preceq g_{()}$$

To prove the generalization of Lemma 2.7 we need generalizations of the functions *shape* and (!!) to representable functors. The generalization of *shape* is called *gshape*. As it is a generalization of *shape* we can use *gshape* for lists as well. For example, consider the following applications.

$$
\begin{aligned}
\mathit{shape}\ [\texttt{'c'}, \texttt{'a'}, \texttt{'b'}] &\equiv [0, 1, 2]\\
\mathit{shape}\ [\bot, \mathit{False}] &\equiv [0, 1]\\
\mathit{shape}\ (3 : 10 : \bot) &\equiv (0 : 1 : \bot)
\end{aligned}
$$

The function *gshape* instead yields the following.

$$
\begin{aligned}
\mathit{gshape}\ [\texttt{'c'}, \texttt{'a'}, \texttt{'b'}] &\equiv [[L], [R, L], [R, R, L]]\\
\mathit{gshape}\ [\bot, \mathit{False}] &\equiv [[L], [R, L]]\\
\mathit{gshape}\ (3 : 10 : \bot) &\equiv ([L] : [R, L] : \bot)
\end{aligned}
$$

We use lists of type $[\mathit{Dir}]$ to identify positions in a polymorphic data type where *Dir* is defined as follows.

$$\textbf{data } \mathit{Dir} = L \mid R$$

A value of type $[\mathit{Dir}]$ represents a path to a polymorphic component of a data type[10]. Constructors with multiple arguments are considered as cascaded binary products.

Consider the polymorphic data type for binary trees again. For example, we have

$$
\begin{aligned}
&\mathit{gshape}\ (\mathit{Node}\ (\mathit{Node}\ \mathit{Empty}\ \texttt{'a'}\ \mathit{Empty})\\
&\qquad\qquad\qquad \texttt{'b'}\\
&\qquad\qquad\qquad (\mathit{Node}\ \mathit{Empty}\ \texttt{'c'}\ \mathit{Empty}))\\
&\equiv \mathit{Node}\ (\mathit{Node}\ \mathit{Empty}\ [L, R, L]\ \mathit{Empty})\\
&\qquad\qquad [R, L]\\
&\qquad\qquad (\mathit{Node}\ \mathit{Empty}\ [R, R, R, L]\ \mathit{Empty})
\end{aligned}
$$

[10] As we only consider total lists of type $[\mathit{Dir}]$ we can also interpret them as integers.

All paths in the left subtree of the outermost *Node* constructor start with L. The path of the value as well as all paths in the right subtree of the outermost *Node* constructor start with R as a value $\mathit{Node}\ l\ v\ r$ is represented by a product $l' \times (v' \times r')$.

To define *gshape* we define a type class *Shape* that provides a single function called gshape'. In contrast to *gshape* the function gshape' takes the path of the root position as additional argument.

$$
\begin{aligned}
&\textbf{class } \mathit{Shape}\ \varphi \textbf{ where}\\
&\quad \mathit{gshape}' :: [\mathit{Dir}] \to \varphi\ \alpha \to \varphi\ [\mathit{Dir}]
\end{aligned}
$$

We define *gshape* by means of gshape' as follows.

$$
\begin{aligned}
&\mathit{gshape} :: \mathit{Shape}\ \varphi \Rightarrow \varphi\ \alpha \to \varphi\ [\mathit{Dir}]\\
&\mathit{gshape} = \mathit{gshape}'\ [\,]
\end{aligned}
$$

Figure 4 shows the instances of *Shape* for the generic functors (Figure 3). If we discover a polymorphic component, namely an element of type $P\ \alpha$ we replace its contents with the provided path. Instead of using the list directly we reverse it because we extend paths at the front and not at the back when we apply gshape' to the components of a product. That is, we could as well not use *reverse* in the instance for P and use $\mathit{ds} +\!\!+ [L]$ and $\mathit{ds} +\!\!+ [R]$ instead of $L : \mathit{ds}$ and $R : \mathit{ds}$ in the instance for $\varphi \times \psi$. In the same way as we have defined instances of *Functor* for *Rec Tree* and *Tree* we define instances of *Shape* for these types.

The generalization of (!!) is an indexing function called *gproj* that projects to a position identified by a path.

$$
\begin{aligned}
\mathit{gproj}\ [\texttt{'c'}, \texttt{'a'}, \texttt{'b'}]\ [R, L] &\equiv \texttt{'a'}\\
\mathit{gproj}\ (3 : 10 : \bot)\ [L] &\equiv 3
\end{aligned}
$$

We define a type class *Proj* that provides a function *gproj*. The function *gproj* takes a path and projects to the corresponding component of the data structure.

$$
\begin{aligned}
&\textbf{class } \mathit{Proj}\ \varphi \textbf{ where}\\
&\quad \mathit{gproj} :: \varphi\ \alpha \to [\mathit{Dir}] \to \alpha
\end{aligned}
$$

Figure 5 shows the instances of *Proj* for generic functors. The constant *indexError* is an error message that is used when we project to a position that does not exist or does not refer to a polymorphic component. We only yield the content of a polymorphic component if the path is empty, otherwise we have projected to a non-existing position.

Next we show that we can reconstruct a data structure from a generic shape by employing *gproj*. To prove this statement we need

$$
\begin{array}{l}
\textbf{instance } \mathit{Proj}\ U \textbf{ where}\\
\quad \mathit{gproj}\ \_\ \_ = \mathit{indexError}\\
\textbf{instance } \mathit{Proj}\ (K\ \tau) \textbf{ where}\\
\quad \mathit{gproj}\ \_\ \_ = \mathit{indexError}\\
\textbf{instance } \mathit{Proj}\ P \textbf{ where}\\
\quad \mathit{gproj}\ (P\ x)\ \mathit{ds} = \textbf{if } \mathit{null}\ \mathit{ds} \textbf{ then } x \textbf{ else } \mathit{indexError}\\
\textbf{instance } (\mathit{Proj}\ \varphi, \mathit{Proj}\ \psi) \Rightarrow \mathit{Proj}\ (\varphi + \psi) \textbf{ where}\\
\quad \mathit{gproj}\ (\mathit{Inl}\ x)\ \mathit{ds}\ = \mathit{gproj}\ x\ \mathit{ds}\\
\quad \mathit{gproj}\ (\mathit{Inr}\ x)\ \mathit{ds}\ = \mathit{gproj}\ x\ \mathit{ds}\\
\textbf{instance } (\mathit{Proj}\ \varphi, \mathit{Proj}\ \psi) \Rightarrow \mathit{Proj}\ (\varphi \times \psi) \textbf{ where}\\
\quad \mathit{gproj}\ (x \times \_)\ (L : \mathit{ds}) = \mathit{gproj}\ x\ \mathit{ds}\\
\quad \mathit{gproj}\ (\_ \times x)\ (R : \mathit{ds}) = \mathit{gproj}\ x\ \mathit{ds}\\
\textbf{instance } \mathit{Proj}\ (\mathit{Rec}\ \mathit{Tree}) \textbf{ where}\\
\quad \mathit{gproj}\ (\mathit{Rec}\ x) = \mathit{gproj}\ x\\
\textbf{instance } \mathit{Proj}\ \mathit{Tree} \textbf{ where}\\
\quad \mathit{gproj} = \mathit{gproj} \circ \mathit{to}
\end{array}
$$

Figure 5. Instances of *Proj*

two standard properties of *reverse*. We consider the standard linear complexity implementation of *reverse*.

Lemma 5.2: For all total lists $xs :: [\tau]$ and $x :: \tau$ the following properties hold.

$$\mathit{reverse}\ (\mathit{reverse}\ xs) \equiv xs$$

$$x : \mathit{reverse}\ xs \equiv \mathit{reverse}\ (xs +\!\!+\ [x])$$

On basis of these statements we are able to prove the following lemma about the connection between the functions *fmap*, *gproj*, and *gshape*, which is used to prove the main lemma. We prove it by induction on the structure of generic functors.

Lemma 5.3: For all generic functors φ and ψ, all total lists $ds :: [\mathit{Dir}]$ and all $x :: \varphi\ \tau$, $y :: \psi\ \tau$, and $z :: (\varphi \times \psi)\ \tau$ the following statements hold.

$$
\begin{array}{l}
\mathit{fmap}\ (\mathit{gproj}\ (x \times y))\ (\mathit{gshape}'\ (\mathit{reverse}\ (L : ds))\ z)\\
\quad \equiv \mathit{fmap}\ (\mathit{gproj}\ x)\ (\mathit{gshape}'\ (\mathit{reverse}\ ds)\ z)\\
\mathit{fmap}\ (\mathit{gproj}\ (x \times y))\ (\mathit{gshape}'\ (\mathit{reverse}\ (R : ds))\ z)\\
\quad \equiv \mathit{fmap}\ (\mathit{gproj}\ y)\ (\mathit{gshape}'\ (\mathit{reverse}\ ds)\ z)
\end{array}
$$

Now we are ready to prove the following lemma, which is the generalization of Lemma 2.3 to generic functors. For its proof we use induction on the structure of generic functors.

Lemma 5.4: For all generic functors φ and all $x :: \varphi\ \tau$ the following holds.

$$\mathit{fmap}\ (\mathit{gproj}\ x)\ (\mathit{gshape}\ x) \equiv x$$

Finally, we prove that we can reconstruct a value from its generic shape by employing *gproj*.

Lemma 5.5: For all representable functors φ that are instances of *Shape* and *Proj* and all $x :: \varphi\ \tau$ the following holds.

$$\mathit{fmap}\ (\mathit{gproj}\ x)\ (\mathit{gshape}\ x) \equiv x$$

Proof: We reason as follows.

$$
\begin{array}{l}
\mathit{fmap}\ (\mathit{gproj}\ x)\ (\mathit{gshape}\ x)\\
\equiv \quad \{\ \varphi \text{ is an instance of } \mathit{Shape}\ \}\\
\mathit{fmap}\ (\mathit{gproj}\ x)\ (\mathit{to}\ (\mathit{gshape}\ (\mathit{from}\ x)))\\
\equiv \quad \{\ \text{definition of } \mathit{gshape}\ \}\\
\mathit{fmap}\ (\mathit{gproj}\ x)\ (\mathit{to}\ (\mathit{gshape}'\ [\,]\ (\mathit{from}\ x)))\\
\equiv \quad \{\ \varphi \text{ is an instance of } \mathit{Proj}\ \}\\
\mathit{fmap}\ (\mathit{gproj}\ (\mathit{from}\ x))\ (\mathit{to}\ (\mathit{gshape}\ [\,]\ (\mathit{from}\ x)))\\
\equiv \quad \{\ \text{free theorem for } \mathit{to}\ \}\\
\mathit{to}\ (\mathit{fmap}\ (\mathit{gproj}\ (\mathit{from}\ x))\ (\mathit{gshape}\ [\,]\ (\mathit{from}\ x)))\\
\equiv \quad \{\ \text{Lemma 5.4}\ \}\\
\mathit{to}\ (\mathit{from}\ x)\\
\equiv \quad \{\ \mathit{to} \circ \mathit{from} \equiv \mathit{id}\ \text{(Definition 5.1)}\ \}\\
x
\end{array}
$$

By employing Lemma 5.5 we can prove the same lemmas as in Section 2, 3, and 4. In fact, we only have to replace all occurrences of *map*, (!!), and *shape* by *fmap*, *gproj*, and *gshape*, respectively. The following lemma proves the generalization of Lemma 2.4 to representable functors.

Lemma 5.6: For all representable functors φ and ψ that are instances of *Shape* and *Proj* and all functions $f :: \varphi\ \alpha \to \psi\ \alpha$ and all $x :: \varphi\ \tau$ the following holds.

$$f_\tau\ x \equiv \mathit{fmap}\ (\mathit{gproj}\ x)\ (f_{\mathit{Int}}\ (\mathit{gshape}\ x))$$

Proof: Let $x :: \varphi\ \tau$. We reason as follows.

$$
\begin{array}{l}
f_\tau\ x\\
\equiv \quad \{\ \text{Lemma 5.5}\ \}\\
f_\tau\ (\mathit{fmap}\ (\mathit{gproj}\ x)\ (\mathit{gshape}\ x))\\
\equiv \quad \{\ \text{free theorem for } f\ \}\\
\mathit{fmap}\ (\mathit{gproj}\ x)\ (f_{\mathit{Int}}\ (\mathit{gshape}\ x))
\end{array}
$$

In the same manner as we have generalized the previous lemma we can generalize the other lemmas and theorems of Section 2, Section 3, and Section 4. To generalize the statements concerning *seq* we define a function $\mathit{gshape}_{\mathit{seq}}$.

$$
\begin{array}{l}
\textbf{instance } \mathit{Shape}_{\mathit{seq}}\ P \textbf{ where}\\
\quad \mathit{gshape}'_{\mathit{seq}}\ ds\ (P\ x) = P\ (\mathit{seq}\ x\ (\mathit{reverse}\ ds))
\end{array}
$$

The instances of $\mathit{Shape}_{\mathit{seq}}$ for the other generic functors are the same as the instances of *Shape*. By employing $\mathit{gshape}'_{\mathit{seq}}$ the shape of a polymorphic data structure contains $\bot$ in all polymorphic components that where $\bot$ in the "original" data structure.

6. Related Work and Conclusion

We have presented techniques for proving statements about polymorphic functions in the presence of selective strictness and non-termination. In particular we have shown how less strictness and minimal strictness of polymorphic functions is reduced to less strictness and minimal strictness of specific monomorphic instances. To the best of our knowledge the presented approach is the first to the characterization of polymorphic functions by means of monomorphic instances that considers non-termination or selective strictness.

Disregarding non-termination and selective strictness our approach is closely related to the work of Bernardy et al. (2010). Bernardy et al. (2010) prove a characterization for all functions whose type can be transformed into the form of a *canonical testing type* $(\varphi\ \alpha \to \alpha) \to (\psi\ \alpha \to \tau) \to \kappa\ \alpha$ where φ, ψ, and κ are functors and τ is a monomorphic type. For example, by employing a similar technique as Prince et al. (2008) they consider the following function, which is isomorphic to *reverse* in a setting without run-time errors and non-termination.

$$
\begin{array}{l}
\mathit{reverse}' :: (\mathit{Nat} \to \alpha) \to \mathit{Nat} \to [\alpha]\\
\mathit{reverse}'\ \mathit{proj}\ n = \mathit{map}\ \mathit{proj}\ (\mathit{reverse}_{\mathit{Nat}}\ [1\,..\,n])
\end{array}
$$

In contrast, we would consider the following function.

$$
\begin{array}{l}
\mathit{reverse}' :: (\mathit{Int} \to \alpha) \to [\mathit{Int}] \to [\alpha]\\
\mathit{reverse}'\ \mathit{proj}\ \mathit{shape} = \mathit{map}\ \mathit{proj}\ (\mathit{reverse}_{\mathit{Int}}\ \mathit{shape})
\end{array}
$$

As we take partial lists into account we cannot characterize the shape of a list by means of a natural number. Instead we consider a list of integers. Note that we never perform this transformation explicitly but use the functions *shape* and (!!) to get a similar result. That is, we consider the following definition of $reverse'$.

$$reverse' :: [\alpha] \to [\alpha]$$
$$reverse'\ xs = map\ (xs!!)\ (reverse_{Int}\ (shape\ xs))$$

While we only study first order functors, as Sloth cannot handle higher order right now anyway, the approach by Bernardy et al. (2010) works for all types that are isomorphic to the form $(\varphi\ \alpha \to \alpha) \to (\psi\ \alpha \to \tau) \to \kappa\ \alpha$. For example, they show how $filter :: (\alpha \to Bool) \to [\alpha] \to [\alpha]$ can be characterized by a monomorphic instance. To gain this extra power in the presence of $\bot$ and *seq* we can combine their approach with the characterization of a function $\varphi\ \alpha \to \psi\ \alpha$ by means of *gproj* and *gshape*. This can be considered future work as we furthermore have to adjust the proofs by Bernardy et al. (2010) to a setting with non-termination and selective strictness.

Acknowledgments

We would like to thank Janis Voigtländer for commenting a draft version of this paper.

References

J.-P. Bernardy, P. Jansson, and K. Claessen. Testing Polymorphic Properties. In *ESOP'10 Proceedings*, volume 6012, pages 125–144. Springer, 2010.

S. Böhme. Free Theorems for sublanguages of Haskell, 2007. Master's thesis, Technische Universität Dresden.

A. Bundy and J. Richardson. Proofs About Lists Using Ellipsis. In *Logic for Programming and Automated Reasoning*, volume 1705, pages 1–12. Springer, 1999.

J. Christiansen. Sloth - A Tool for Checking Minimal Strictness. In *PADL'11 Proceedings*, volume 6539, pages 160–174. Springer, 2011.

N. A. Danielsson and P. Jansson. Chasing Bottoms: A Case Study in Program Verification in the Presence of Partial and Infinite Values. In *MPC'04 Proceedings*, volume 3125, pages 85–109. Springer, 2004.

P. Johann and J. Voigtländer. Free Theorems in the Presence of seq. In *POPL'04 Proceedings*, pages 99–110. ACM, 2004.

J. P. Magalhães, A. Dijkstra, J. Jeuring, and A. Löh. A generic deriving mechanism for Haskell. In *Haskell Symposium Proceedings*, pages 37–48. ACM, 2010.

S. Peyton Jones, editor. *Haskell 98 Language and Libraries—The Revised Report*. Cambridge University Press, 2003.

R. Prince, N. Ghani, and C. McBride. Proving Properties about Lists Using Containers. In *FLOPS'08 Proceedings*, volume 4989, pages 97–112. Springer, 2008.

D. Seidel and J. Voigtländer. Taming Selective Strictness. In *ATPS'09 Proceedings*. GI, 2009.

J. Voigtländer. Bidirectionalization for Free! In *POPL'09 Proceedings*, pages 165–176. ACM, 2009.

P. Wadler. Theorems for free! In *FPCA'89 Proceedings*. ACM, 1989.

In this appendix we present some of the omitted proofs.

A. Proofs from Section 2

Definition A.1: We present some basic definitions by Johann and Voigtländer (2004).

strict A relation R is *strict* if $(\bot, \bot) \in R$.

bottom-reflecting A relation R is *bottom-reflecting* if for every $(x, y) \in R$ we have $x \neq \bot$ if and only if $y \neq \bot$.

continuous A relation R is continuous if for all chains $\langle x_i \rangle_{i \in I}$ and $\langle y_i \rangle_{i \in I}$ whose elements are pair-wise related by R we have $(\bigsqcup_{i \in I} x_i, \bigsqcup_{i \in I} y_i) \in R$.

To prove Lemma 2.2 we prove the following generalization of the functional free theorem for a function of type $f :: (\alpha \to \beta) \to [\alpha] \to [\beta]$. The standard functional free theorem states that

$$h\ (p\ x) \equiv q\ (g\ x)$$

for all $x :: \tau_1$ implies

$$map\ h\ (f\ p\ xs) \equiv f\ q\ (map\ g\ xs)$$

for all $xs :: [\tau_1]$. In contrast, the following lemma shows that we do not have to show $h\ (p\ x) \equiv q\ (g\ x)$ for all $x :: \tau_1$ but only for the elements of xs.

Lemma A.1: Let $f :: (\alpha \to \beta) \to [\alpha] \to [\beta]$. For strict functions $g :: \tau_1 \to \tau_2$, $h :: \tau_3 \to \tau_4$, $p :: \tau_1 \to \tau_3$, and $q :: \tau_2 \to \tau_4$ such that

$$h\ (p\ (xs\ !!\ n)) \equiv q\ (g\ (xs\ !!\ n))$$

for all $n :: Int$ we have

$$map\ h\ (f\ p\ xs) \equiv f\ q\ (map\ g\ xs)$$

for all $xs :: [\tau_1]$.

Proof: Let $xs :: [\tau_1]$. We define the relations

$$R_{xs} := \{(xs\ !!\ n, g\ (xs\ !!\ n)) | n :: Int\}$$
$$\cup \{(\bigsqcup_{i \in I}(xs!!i), \bigsqcup_{i \in I} g\ (xs!!i)) \mid \langle xs!!i \rangle_{i \in I} \text{ chain}, I \subseteq Int\}$$

and $S := \{(x, h\ x)\}$. Theorem 3.1 shows that R_{xs} is strict and continuous. Furthermore, S is strict and continuous because h is strict and continuous.

The relational free theorem for $f :: (\alpha \to \beta) \to [\alpha] \to [\beta]$ states that, if for all $(x, y) \in R_{xs}$ we have $(p\ x, q\ y) \in S$, then for all $(xs, ys) \in \text{lift}\{[]\}(R_{xs})$ we have $(f\ p\ xs, f\ q\ ys) \in \text{lift}\{[]\}(S)$. Let $(x, y) \in R_{xs}$. To show that $(p\ x, q\ y) \in S$ we have to show that $h\ (p\ x) \equiv q\ y$.

Case 1: $x = xs\ !!\ n$, $y = g\ (xs\ !!\ n)$

We have $h\ (p\ (xs\ !!\ n)) \equiv q\ (g\ (xs\ !!\ n)$ by precondition.

Case 2: $x = \bigsqcup xs\ !!\ i$, $y = \bigsqcup g\ (xs\ !!\ i)$

We reason as follows.

$$\begin{aligned} h\ (p\ (\bigsqcup xs\ !!\ i)) &\equiv \bigsqcup h\ (p\ (xs\ !!\ i)) && \text{continuity} \\ &\equiv \bigsqcup q\ (g\ (xs\ !!\ i)) && \text{precondition} \\ &\equiv q\ (\bigsqcup g\ (xs\ !!\ i)) && \text{continuity} \end{aligned}$$

That is, $h\ (p\ x) \equiv q\ y$.

Therefore, for all $(xs, ys) \in \text{lift}\{[]\}(R_{xs})$ we as well have $(f\ p\ xs, f\ q\ ys) \in \text{lift}\{[]\}(S)$. As we have $(xs, map\ g\ xs) \in \text{lift}\{[]\}(R_{xs})$ we get $(f\ p\ xs, f\ q\ (map\ g\ xs)) \in \text{lift}\{[]\}(S)$, i.e., $map\ h\ (f\ p\ xs) \equiv f\ q\ (map\ g\ xs)$. □

The following lemma shows a simple property about $[n\,..]$ and (!!). Here and in the following we consider $[n\,..]$ as shortform of $iterate\ (+1)\ n$.

Lemma A.2: For all $n :: Int$ and all $m :: Int$ with $m \geqslant 0$ we have $[n\,..]\ !!\ m \equiv n + m$.

Proof: By induction over m.
Base Case:

$$\begin{array}{l} iterate\ (+1)\ n\ !!\ 0 \\ \quad \equiv \quad \{ \text{definition of } iterate \} \\ (n : iterate\ (+1)\ (n+1))\ !!\ 0 \\ \quad \equiv \quad \{ \text{definition of } (!!) \} \\ n \end{array}$$

Inductive Case:

$$\begin{array}{l} iterate\ (+1)\ n\ !!\ (m+1) \\ \quad \equiv \quad \{ \text{definition of } iterate \} \\ (n : iterate\ (+1)\ (n+1))\ !!\ (m+1) \\ \quad \equiv \quad \{ \text{definition of } (!!) \} \\ iterate\ (+1)\ (n+1)\ !!\ m \\ \quad \equiv \quad \{ \text{induction hypothesis} \} \\ n+1+m \end{array}$$

Proof (of Lemma 2.2): We consider $[n\,..]$ as a shortform of $iterate\ (+1)\ n$. Let $x :: \tau$ and $xs :: [\tau]$. We reason as follows.

$$\begin{array}{l} map\ ((x : xs)!!)\ [1\,..] \\ \quad \equiv \quad \{ \text{definition of } [1\,..] \} \\ map\ ((x : xs)!!)\ (iterate\ (+1)\ 1) \\ \quad \equiv \quad \{ \text{free theorem for } iterate\text{, } (+1) \text{ strict \& total} \} \\ map\ ((x : xs)!!)\ (map\ (+1)\ (iterate\ (+1)\ 0)) \\ \quad \overset{(*)}{\equiv} \quad \{ \text{Lemma A.1 and Lemma A.2} \} \\ map\ (xs!!)\ (iterate\ (+1)\ 0) \\ \quad \equiv \quad \{ \text{definition of } [0\,..] \} \\ map\ (xs!!)\ [0\,..] \end{array}$$

To prove the step labeled with $(*)$ we have to prove the following equality.

$$(x : xs)\ !!\ ([1\,..]\ !!\ n) \equiv xs\ !!\ ([0\,..]\ !!\ n)$$

We distinguish two cases.
Case 1: $n \equiv \bot$ or $n < 0$
We have

$$\begin{array}{l} (x : xs)\ !!\ ([1\,..]\ !!\ n) \\ \quad \equiv \quad \{ \text{definition of } (!!) \} \\ (x : xs)\ !!\ \bot \\ \quad \equiv \quad \{ \text{definition of } (!!) \} \\ xs\ !!\ \bot \\ \quad \equiv \quad \{ \text{definition of } (!!) \} \\ xs\ !!\ ([0\,..]\ !!\ n) \end{array}$$

Case 2: $n \geqslant 0$

$$\begin{array}{l} (x : xs)\ !!\ ([1\,..]\ !!\ n) \\ \quad \equiv \quad \{ \text{Lemma A.2} \} \\ (x : xs)\ !!\ n+1 \\ \quad \equiv \quad \{ \text{definition of } (!!) \} \\ xs\ !!\ n \\ \quad \equiv \quad \{ \text{Lemma A.2} \} \\ xs\ !!\ ([0\,..]\ !!\ n) \end{array}$$

Proof (of Lemma 2.6): Let $xs :: [\tau]$ and $n :: Int$ such that $f_\tau\ xs\ !!\ n \not\equiv \bot$, $g_\tau\ xs\ !!\ n \not\equiv \bot$, and $f_\tau\ xs\ !!\ n \not\equiv g_\tau\ xs\ !!\ n$. By Lemma 2.5 there exist $k, l :: Int$ such that the following holds.

$$xs\ !!\ k \equiv f_\tau\ xs\ !!\ n \not\equiv g_\tau\ xs\ !!\ n \equiv xs\ !!\ l$$

This implies $k \not\equiv l$. Furthermore we have $k \not\equiv \bot$ and $l \not\equiv \bot$ because $f_\tau\ xs\ !!\ n \not\equiv \bot$ and $g_\tau\ xs\ !!\ n \not\equiv \bot$. This also implies $xs\ !!\ k \not\equiv \bot$ and $xs\ !!\ l \not\equiv \bot$.

If we replace the element of xs at position k by $\bot$ we get a list $ys :: [\tau]$ with $ys\ !!\ k \equiv \bot$ and $ys\ !!\ l \not\equiv \bot$. We have $shape\ xs \equiv shape\ ys$ and by Lemma 2.5 we get $f_\tau\ ys\ !!\ \eta \equiv ys\ !!\ k \equiv \bot$ and $g_\tau\ ys\ !!\ n \equiv ys\ !!\ l \equiv xs\ !!\ l \not\equiv \bot$. □

Proof (of Lemma 2.7): Because we have $f_\tau \not\preceq g_\tau$ there exists $xs :: [\tau]$ such that $f_\tau\ xs \not\sqsupseteq g_\tau\ xs$. We distinguish three cases.

Case 1: $shape\ (f_\tau\ xs) \not\sqsupseteq shape\ (g_\tau\ xs)$
We set $ys \equiv map\ (strictConst\ ())\ xs$ and reason as follows.

$$\begin{array}{l} shape\ (f_{()}\ ys) \\ \quad \equiv \quad \{ ys \equiv map\ (strictConst\ ())\ xs \} \\ shape\ (f_{()}\ (map\ (strictConst\ ())\ xs)) \\ \quad \equiv \quad \{ \text{free theorem for } f\text{, } strictConst\ () \text{ strict} \} \\ shape\ (map\ (strictConst\ ())\ (f_\tau\ xs)) \\ \quad \equiv \quad \{ \text{free theorem for } shape\text{, } strictConst\ () \text{ strict} \} \\ shape\ (f_\tau\ xs) \\ \quad \not\sqsupseteq \\ shape\ (g_\tau\ xs) \\ \quad \equiv \quad \{ \text{free theorem for } shape\text{, } strictConst\ () \text{ strict} \} \\ shape\ (map\ (strictConst\ ())\ (g_\tau\ xs)) \\ \quad \equiv \quad \{ \text{free theorem for } g\text{, } strictConst\ () \text{ strict} \} \\ shape\ (g_{()}\ (map\ (strictConst\ ())\ xs)) \\ \quad \equiv \quad \{ ys \equiv map\ (strictConst\ ())\ xs \} \\ shape\ (g_{()}\ ys) \end{array}$$

Therefore, there exists $ys :: [()]$ such that $shape\ (f_{()}\ ys) \not\sqsupseteq shape\ (g_{()}\ ys)$ which implies $f_{()} \not\preceq g_{()}$.

Case 2: $\exists n :: Int.\ f_\tau\ xs\ !!\ n \equiv \bot \wedge g_\tau\ xs\ !!\ n \not\equiv \bot$
We set $ys \equiv map\ (strictConst\ ())\ xs$ and reason as follows.

$$\begin{array}{l} f_{()}\ ys\ !!\ n \\ \quad \equiv \quad \{ ys \equiv map\ (strictConst\ ())\ xs \} \\ f_{()}\ (map\ (strictConst\ ())\ xs)\ !!\ n \\ \quad \equiv \quad \{ \text{free theorem for } f\text{, } strictConst\ () \text{ strict} \} \\ map\ (strictConst\ ())\ (f_\tau\ xs)\ !!\ n \\ \quad \equiv \quad \{ \text{free theorem for } (!!)\text{, } strictConst\ () \text{ strict} \} \\ strictConst\ ()\ (f_\tau\ xs\ !!\ n) \\ \quad \equiv \quad \{ \text{definition of } strictConst\text{, } f_\tau\ xs\ !!\ n \equiv \bot \} \\ \bot \end{array}$$

For g we reason the same way.

$$\begin{array}{l} g_{()}\ ys\ !!\ n \\ \quad \equiv \quad \{ ys \equiv map\ (strictConst\ ())\ xs \} \\ g_{()}\ (map\ (strictConst\ ())\ xs)\ !!\ n \\ \quad \equiv \quad \{ \text{free theorem for } g\text{, } strictConst\ () \text{ strict} \} \\ map\ (strictConst\ ())\ (g_\tau\ xs)\ !!\ n \\ \quad \equiv \quad \{ \text{free theorem for } (!!)\text{, } strictConst\ () \text{ strict} \} \\ strictConst\ ()\ (g_\tau\ xs\ !!\ n) \\ \quad \not\equiv \quad \{ \text{definition of } strictConst\text{, } g_\tau\ xs\ !!\ n \not\equiv \bot \} \\ \bot \end{array}$$

That is, there exists $ys :: [()]$ and $n :: Int$ such that $f_{()}\ ys\ !!\ n \equiv \bot$ and $g_{()}\ ys\ !!\ n \not\equiv \bot$ which implies $f_{()} \not\preceq g_{()}$.

Case 3: $\exists n :: Int.\ f_\tau\ xs\ !!\ n \not\equiv \bot \wedge g_\tau\ xs\ !!\ n \not\equiv \bot \wedge f_\tau\ xs\ !!\ n \not\equiv g_\tau\ xs\ !!\ n$
By Lemma 2.6 there exists $ys :: [\tau]$ and $n :: Int$ such that $f_\tau\ ys !! n \equiv \bot$ and $g_\tau\ ys\ !!\ n \not\equiv \bot$. That is, we reason as in Case 2. □

Protocol Analysis in Maude-NPA Using Unification Modulo Homomorphic Encryption *

Santiago Escobar
DSIC-ELP, Universidad Politécnica de Valencia, Spain
sescobar@dsic.upv.es

Deepak Kapur
University of New Mexico, Albuquerque, NM, USA
kapur@cs.unm.edu

Christopher Lynch
Clarkson University, Potsdam, NY, USA
clynch@clarkson.edu

Catherine Meadows
Naval Research Laboratory, Washington DC, USA
meadows@itd.nrl.navy.mil

José Meseguer
University of Illinois at Urbana-Champaign, USA
meseguer@illinois.edu

Paliath Narendran
University at Albany-SUNY, Albany, NY, USA
dran@cs.albany.edu

Ralf Sasse
University of Illinois at Urbana-Champaign, USA
rsasse@illinois.edu

Abstract

A number of new cryptographic protocols are being designed to secure applications such as video-conferencing and electronic voting. Many of them rely upon cryptographic functions with complex algebraic properties that must be accounted for in order to be correctly analyzed by automated tools. Maude-NPA is a cryptographic protocol analysis tool based on narrowing and typed equational unification which takes into account these algebraic properties. It has already been used to analyze protocols involving bounded associativity, modular exponentiation, and exclusive-or. All of the above can be handled by the same general *variant*-based equational unification technique. However, there are important properties, in particular homomorphic encryption, that cannot be handled by variant-based unification in the same way. In these cases the best available approach is to implement specialized unification algorithms and combine them within a modular framework. In this paper we describe how we apply this approach within Maude-NPA, with respect to encryption homomorphic over a free operator. We also describe the use of Maude-NPA to analyze several protocols using such an encryption operation. To the best of our knowledge, this is the first implementation of homomorphic encryption of any sort in a tool for verifying the security of a protocol in the presence of active attackers.

Categories and Subject Descriptors C.2.2 [*Computer-communication Networks*]: Network Protocols; D.2.4 [*Software Engineering*]: Software/Program Verification; D.3.2 [*Programming Languages*]: Language Classifications; D.4.6 [*Operating Systems*]: Security and Protection; F.3.1 [*Logics and Meanings of Programs*]: Specifying and Verifying and Reasoning about Programs

General Terms Protocol verification, unification, homomorphism

1. Introduction

With the increased use of computer networks and online transactions, more and more complex cryptographic protocols using encryption techniques with sophisticated arithmetic properties are being designed to secure applications such as video-conferencing and electronic voting. Many of these protocols are known to be secure if the arithmetic properties are not exploited, but can be broken if they are. Examples include the recursive authentication protocol proposed by Bull [11], broken by Ryan and Schneider [40] by exploiting the properties of the exclusive-or operation, and a group key protocol based on group Diffie-Hellman [5], broken by Pereira and Quisquater [39] using associative-commutative properties of modular exponentiation. Traditional Dolev-Yao modeling of protocols in which the underlying cryptographic functions are treated as a black box is thus often untrustworthy; the box must be pried open enough to account for the algebraic properties of the cryptographic functions.

Model checking has been an effective tool in cryptographic protocol analysis, and a number of model checkers have been built [4, 9, 20, 32, 35]. Cryptographic protocol analysis model checkers discover attacks by generating and analyzing the search space of possible states arising from the execution of a given protocol, taking into consideration the functions of the principals as well

* S. Escobar has been partially supported by the EU (FEDER) and the Spanish MEC/MICINN under grant TIN 2010-21062-C02-02, and by Generalitat Valenciana PROMETEO2011/052. The following authors have been partially supported by NSF: S. Escobar, J. Meseguer and R. Sasse under grants CCF 09-05584, CNS 09-04749, and CNS 09-05584 ; D. Kapur under grant CNS 09-05222; C. Lynch and C. Meadows under grant CNS 09-05378, and P. Narendran under grant CNS 09-05286.

PDPP'11, July 20–22, 2011, Odense, Denmark.

as the capabilities of the intruder(s)[1]. In this paper, we propose a symbolic approach to infinite-state, unbounded-sessions model checking based on combining unification algorithms to handle various properties of operations involved in a cryptographic protocol. Roughly speaking, a protocol is modeled as a state transition system, with a possible execution of the protocol being a sequence of state transitions; in any given state, any of the actors/principals is allowed to perform any of the operations on data in its possession.

There has been a growing body of research in extending these model checkers to reason about different types of equational theories [7, 9, 10, 13, 18, 44]. However, there has been one class of theories that has proven to be rather difficult to incorporate into protocol analysis tools. These are theories involving homomorphic operators, that is operators (usually representing encryption functions) that distribute over some other operator, which is usually associative-commutative or an Abelian group operator. Homormorphic encryption of this sort has many potential applications, including blinded signatures that can be used in electronic cash, private database retrieval, and electronic voting.

This paper describes the first steps in our research program with respect to homomorphic encryption: the adaptation of an algorithm for unification modulo an equational theory arising from encryption homomorphic over a free operator for use in Maude-NPA, and the use of the tool for analyzing protocols that satisfy this theory. Maude-NPA [21, 22] is designed to take into account the algebraic properties of cryptographic protocols. It makes use of equational unification to meet its goals. The approach of Maude-NPA up to this point has been to make use of *folding variant narrowing* [23] to perform equational unification. Suppose that the operators used in the protocol obey an equational theory $E_{\mathcal{P}}$. To do this, we divide the equational theory $E_{\mathcal{P}}$ describing the algebraic properties obeyed by the cryptosystem into $\Delta \cup Ax$, where Δ is a set of rewrite rules and Ax is a set of axioms such that Δ has the *finite variant property* modulo Ax [17, 23]. In that case, it is possible to apply a version of narrowing modulo Ax called folding variant narrowing to compute $E_{\mathcal{P}}$ unifiers. The advantage of using folding variant narrowing is that it is possible to have a general-purpose procedure that applies to many different theories. The only place we need special-purpose unification algorithms are the algorithms for Ax. We note that, when we find efficient algorithms for specific theories or combinations of theories, these theories can be moved into Ax if they satisfy the appropriate conditions, thus allowing us to increase the efficiency of our approach as fast special-purpose algorithms become available. In the most extreme case Δ could be empty.

In the past we have restricted ourselves to the case in which Ax is the free theory or associativity-commutativity (AC). In these cases we have been able to rely on unification algorithms already built into Maude [16]. However, it is well known that finite variance does not hold for homomorphic encryption, whether Ax is the free theory or AC [17]. In this case homomorphic encryption unification must be implemented in Ax. We use the unification algorithm of Anantharaman et al. [2] for this. In [2] it is applied to a procedure known as *cap unification*, which combines unification and deducibility, but it can also be used by itself, as we do here.

Contributions

The main contribution of this paper is that it demonstrates how a special-purpose unification algorithm for homomorphic encryption over a free operator is implemented and integrated with Maude-NPA. To the best of our knowledge, this represents the first implementation and integration of a special-purpose unification algorithm within a cryptographic protocol analysis tool, and the first implementation of any complete algorithm for reasoning about homomorphic encryption of any sort within a tool that can reason about protocol security in the presence of an active attacker. The only other implementation of homomorphic encryption, even over a free operator, available in a tool is in the intruder deduction tool YAPA [8], and can only prove security against passive attacks when used by itself. (See Section 2.2 for more details.)

In more detail, our implementation consists of:

1. An implementation in Full Maude of the algorithm described in [2] for homomorphic encryption. Full Maude [16] is an extension of Maude written in Maude that takes advantage of its reflective capabilities.
2. The derivation of an order-sorted unification algorithm for homomorphic encryption (see Section 6).
3. Application of the Maude-NPA infrastructure for combination of unification algorithms à la Baader and Schultz [6] (see Section 3.2) to the integration of the algorithm with the Maude-NPA search engine.
4. Testing the integration of all these new features into Maude-NPA by analyzing four protocols using homomorphic encryption (see Section 7).
5. Documenting how these four protocols behave in the Maude-NPA, which is relevant to demonstrate the feasibility of the whole approach (see Section 7).

Plan of the paper

The rest of the paper is organized as follows. In Section 2, we give a survey of the various means by which algebraic properties are addressed in automated cryptographic protocol analysis. In Section 3 we describe how equational unification is implemented in Maude-NPA. In Section 4 we provide motivating examples we will use throughout the remainder of this paper. In Section 5 we describe how Maude-NPA uses equational unification for backwards search, illustrating our explanation with examples from Section 4. In Section 6 we describe the unification algorithm we use for the homomorphic theory and its integration into Maude-NPA. In Section 7 we describe the analysis of the protocols introduced in Section 4. In Section 8 we conclude the paper and discuss future work.

2. Handling Algebraic Properties of Crypto-Algorithms

One challenge in computing the various state transitions is dealing with the algebraic properties of the cryptographic algorithms themselves. These range from the fact that decryption with a key cancels out encryption with the same key, expressible by the equation $dec(enc(m, k), k) = m$, through the Abelian group properties of algorithms based on exponentiation and/or elliptic curves, all the way to the property of homomorphism over an Abelian group possessed by many of the algorithms used for privacy-preserving computation. There are three classes of procedures that have been developed for dealing with algebraic properties: (i) augmented intruder inference rules, (ii) deducibility algorithms, and (iii) equational unification.

2.1 Augmented Inference rules

When specifying a cryptographic protocol, one normally specifies a set of inference rules that describe the operations that an intruder can perform. Thus, one would specify an inference rule that says that, if an intruder knows a message and a key, then he can construct the encryption of the message with the key. These inference rules can also be augmented to describe the consequences of equational

[1] We note that the terms "intruder" and "attacker" are used interchangeably in the literature

properties. For example, the encryption-decryption equation given above could be represented by the following inference rule:

$$\frac{enc(m,k) \in \mathcal{I}, k \in \mathcal{I}}{m \in \mathcal{I}}$$

where $\mathcal{I}$ stands for the set of terms known to the intruder.

The problem is that this method is often incomplete. Consider the following protocol:

$$1.\ A \rightarrow B : M \qquad 2.\ B \rightarrow A : dec(M, key(B))$$

The inference rule fails to predict what happens when $M = enc(X, key(B))$. In this case, A would wind up sending a cleartext message X, but this is because of the action of A's decryption operation, not because of the application of an inference rule by the intruder. Thus, the inference rules are not complete.

Although there are subclasses of protocols for which given sets of inference rules are sound (see for example [33, 37]), this must be carefully worked out for each case. However, if successful, augmented inference rules have the advantage that they can be used with tools that do not support the equational theory that the inference rules represent. Indeed, Küsters and Truderung show in [30, 31] how their inference systems for Diffie-Hellman exponentiation and exclusive-or can be used for a restricted class of protocols using Blanchet's ProVerif tool, which by itself only supports associative-commutative properties in a limited way.

We note that there is at least one example of applying augmented inference rules to homomorphic encryption. In [29], Kremer and Ryan define a set of intruder inference rules which they use, together with the ProVerif protocol analysis tool, to analyze protocols using cipher block chaining, which has a prefix homomorphism property. This approach is subject to the same incompleteness that we discussed above. However, it may be possible that completeness can be proved for the specific protocols analyzed in that paper.

2.2 Deducibility algorithms

These are algorithms for determining whether an intruder can deduce a term from a set of terms already in its possession, given that terms obey a given equational theory. In this case, one starts with a set T of terms known to the intruder, a term t the intruder is trying to learn, a set of inference rules describing operations the intruder can perform, and an equational theory E. The deducibility algorithm is a procedure for determining whether or not the intruder can derive a term from s from T such that $s \equiv_E t$. A number of algorithms have been developed for different classes of equational theories, including associative-commutative and homomorphic operators [1]. A survey of deducibility with respect to equational theories may be found in [12].

In particular, algorithms for a class of theories known as subterm convergent (convergent theories for which the right-hand side is a either an irreducible ground term or subterm of the left-hand side) have been developed in [15] and for a larger class of convergent theories that include encryption homomorphic over a free operator [8] and have been developed and implemented in the tools KISS and YAPA, respectively. These tools when used by themselves can only prove security against a passive intruder, who only spies upon message traffic but does not further interact with the protocol. However they can also be interfaced with other tools that use deducibility to reason about security against an active attacker who reads, alters, redirects, and deletes traffic as well as creating its own messages. The *intruder with caps* approach of [3] also uses deducibility algorithms for classes of equational theories that extend the subterm convergent class. The tools OFMC [7], and CL-Atse [44] all make use of deducibility and provide some support for equational theories, in the case of OFMC and CL-Atse those governing Diffie-Hellman and exclusive-or.

A limitation of using deducibility is that it requires a complete description of the terms an intruder knows at a given state. This is fine for tools that generate states in a forward fashion, but it does not work as well for tools such as Maude-NPA, which generate states on the fly in a backwards manner and thus only are aware of some of the terms the intruder knows at any point in time.

2.3 Equational Unification

Unification of two terms s and t modulo an equational theory E is the process of finding substitutions σ to the variables in s and t making them equal modulo E. We call a substitution σ to the variables in s and t an E-*unifier* of s and t, or a *unifier modulo* E, if and only if $\sigma(t) =_E \sigma(s)$, with $=_E$ the provable E-relation. We say that a set Θ of E-unifiers is a *complete set of* E-*unifiers* of s and t if for any unifier τ, there is a $\sigma \in \Theta$ such that $\tau =_E \rho\sigma$ for some substitution ρ away from the variables of s and t. Thus, a complete set of E-unifiers characterizes all the unifiers of two terms.

An advantage of E-unification over deducibility is that it can be applied even on incomplete information, since this incomplete information can be represented by variables. Thus, it applies not only to both forward and backwards search, but to constraint-based searches that can proceed from any direction (e.g. Comon-Lundh and Shmatikov's application of unification to constraint-based analysis in protocols that use exclusive-or [18], and Chevalier et al.'s use of constraints to verify presence of subterms when equational theories are present [13]). In particular, Chevalier and Rusinowitch [14] have developed a decision procedure for constraint-based protocol analysis over unions of disjoint intruder theories that is based on Baader and Schultz's [6] and Schmidt-Schauss' [42] algorithms for combining unification algorithms over disjoint theories and has similar complexity.

Early work on cryptographic protocol analysis modulo equational theories relied on existing techniques such as *narrowing*, which requires that the equational theory be expressed as a set of convergent rewrite rules. Narrowing a term consists of identifying a non-variable subterm of it that can be syntactically unified with the left-hand side of a rewrite rule and replacing it with the corresponding substitution instance of the right-hand side. This process proceeds until no further narrowing steps can be applied. Narrowing-based unification of two terms s and t is the narrowing of $eq(s,t)$ together with the rewrite rules expressing the given equations plus the additional rewrite rule $eq(x,x) \rightarrow true$. If one backtracks upon failure and upon each successful unification, one obtains a finite complete set of unifiers if the narrowing procedure terminates.

The original NRL Protocol Analyzer [35], upon which Maude-NPA is based, relied on a type of narrowing known as *basic narrowing* [26]. However, although theories such as the cancellation of encryption and decryption can be handled by basic narrowing alone, it does not apply to theories that involve associative-commutative properties. Thus, although Maude-NPA can and does make use of narrowing, it implements it in a very different way.

3. Unification in Maude-NPA

Maude-NPA employs a number of unification strategies, described below.

3.1 Folding Variant Narrowing

One way of dealing with theories containing associativity-commutativity (AC) is to split the theory E into two disjoint pieces, $E = \Delta \cup AC$, so that Δ is confluent, terminating and coherent modulo AC. However, narrowing modulo AC doesn't terminate for many theories of interest to cryptographic protocol analysis, including exclusive-or and Abelian groups. Comon and Delaune [17] have identified a property known as the *finite variant property* which is checkable under appropriate conditions [23]. Although for many theories $E = \Delta \cup AC$ narrowing modulo AC does not terminate, The *folding variant narrowing strategy* [23] computes a finite complete set of E-unifiers whenever E has the finite variant property. Folding variant narrowing (currently implemented for strongly right-irreducible theories [41]) has proved to be the backbone of Maude-NPA. Although it is not as efficient as algorithms designed specifically for a given theory, it is more widely applicable, and it is easy to combine different equational theories [41].

3.2 Typed Modular Unification in Maude-NPA

Although the ease of implementation folding variant narrowing makes it very useful for exploration and experimentation, and interesting cryptographic theories satisfy the finite variant property, ultimately we also want to be able to make use of more efficient special-purpose algorithms. Moreover, there is a class of equational theories that appears prominently in cryptographic protocols applied to privacy-preserving computation: operators that are homomorphic with respect to another, e.g., $q(X * Y) = q(X) * q(Y)$. Theories like these can be shown to lack the finite variant property whether or not $*$ is a free operator or obeys the axioms for an Abelian group.[2] In these cases folding variant narrowing does not provide a finitary E-unification algorithm, and we must seek a different method.

As a result, special-purpose algorithms are also being developed, especially for homomorphic theories. But in order to do this it is necessary to do more than just develop and implement algorithms. They must also be integrated with analysis tools like the Maude-NPA, and we must satisfy ourselves that it is possible to use the tool to specify and analyze protocols that rely upon these properties.

Integrating equational unification into protocol analysis is challenging for several reasons. First of all, in principle we need to have a different $E_{\mathcal{P}}$-unification algorithm for each protocol $\mathcal{P}$; second, experience with the Maude-NPA tool has shown the great advantages (typically leading to a much smaller search space) of *typed unification*, where variables have types (or *sorts*) and types can be arranged in *subtype hierarchies*; for example, to properly specify a protocol we may wish to distinguish different subtypes —e.g., for nonces, keys, or principal names— of a general type for messages; third, we often need to *combine* several such unification algorithms, for example when composing together various subprotocols or taking into account the associative-commutative-identity (ACU) axioms of the state constructors (see Section 5). This is made even more challenging by the fact that, in order to allow the option of verifying different kinds of implementations (e.g. the case in which a key is indistinguishable from a nonce), typing is mostly left to the discretion of the user.

Given the wide range of protocols and protocol combinations that need to be analyzed, a *modular* approach to the development of $E_{\mathcal{P}}$-unification algorithms is very much needed. Such a modular approach and its necessary infrastructure are now under development. Besides using the known techniques for combining unification algorithms for disjoint theories à la Baader and Schultz [6], Maude-NPA employs a more general methodology and associated tool infrastructure (in the Maude-NPA) in which unification algorithms can be combined and developed at three different levels and in a not necessarily disjoint way: (i) a basic library of commonly occurring theories and their combinations —currently including any combination of typed commutative, associative commutative, associative commutative and identity, or free function symbols— is efficiently supported by the Maude tool at the C++ level; (ii) unification algorithms for special-purpose cryptographic theories can be developed in a declarative way in Maude itself using its metalevel facilities as done here for the homomorphic encryption theory E_h; and (iii) it is often possible to decompose an equational theory $E_{\mathcal{P}}$ as a disjoint union $E_{\mathcal{P}} = \Delta \cup Ax$, (where Δ and Ax may share some function symbols), and where a dedicated Ax-unification algorithm exists. If Δ is viewed as a set of rewrite rules that is convergent, coherent and has the finite variant property modulo Ax, *folding variant narrowing modulo* Ax with the rules Δ provides a finitary $E_{\mathcal{P}}$-unification algorithm [23]. Finally, in the modular approach proposed in this paper it is also possible to *automatically derive* a typed (called order-sorted) $E_{\mathcal{P}}$-unification algorithm from an untyped one for which an implementation is already available. This derivation follows the methodology proposed in [25] and applies a general method by which, under mild conditions on the order-sorted theory E, an order-sorted E-unification algorithm can be automatically obtained by: (i) associating to E its unsorted version $\bar{E}$; (ii) computing a complete set of (unsorted) $\bar{E}$-unifiers for the given E-unification problem; and (iii) typing and filtering out the unsorted $\bar{E}$-unifiers to obtain a complete set of order-sorted E-unifiers using the generic *sort propagation algorithm* described in [25]. This algorithm is part of the Maude-NPA infrastructure that is applied to the homomorphic encryption algorithm described in this paper.

Finally, we combine $E_{\mathcal{P}}$-unification,with a typed version of ACU-unification. The latter is needed because Maude-NPA states are multisets of terms, which are associative-commutative and have the empty multiset as tthe identity. This combination is supported by Maude-NPA by means of an order-sorted variant of the standard combination method for disjoint theories à la Baader and Schultz [6], so that in the end typed $E_h \cup ACU$-unification is achieved. A more complete description of how this is done is given in [41].

4. Protocol Examples

In this section we include several protocols that we will use as motivating examples that are subject to attacks which we demonstrate in Maude-NPA. Because homomorphic encryption is usually used together with an operator with additional algebraic properties, there are not very many examples of protocols that rely on homomorphic encryption over an operator with no further algebraic properties that are relevant to the protocol. Thus in some cases we have devised our own. In doing this, we have attempted to cover various situations that could arise when dealing with homomorphic encryption. The first protocol is a secure two-party computation protocol that illustrates the application of homomorphic encryption to multi-party computation. The second is a version of the Needham-Schroeder-Lowe protocol using encryption in Electronic Code Book (ECB) mode, due to Cortier et al. [19], which allows us to test our implementation on an independently developed protocol. The third is an ECB version of shared key Needham-Schoeder, which allows us to check how homomorphic encryption would behave under nested encryption. The final protocol uses a homomorphic "hash function", and was designed as an example of a protocol that could not be analyzed by the application of standard intruder inference rules. The last three test protocols are not intended to be realistic, since the unsafeness of using ECB mode when message integrity is required is well known, but they serve to test the limits of our implementation.

4.1 Multi-Party Computation with Semi-Trusted Third Party

This is a protocol in which two principals, A (for Alice) and B (for Bob)want to compute a function f of their private data X and Y

[2] Comon and Delaune only prove the result for the exclusive-or case in [17], but their proof can easily be extended to the other cases.

without revealing anything about X and Y other than $f(X,Y)$. They use a trusted server to compute $f(X,Y)$, but they don't want to reveal X and Y to the server either. They make use of a public key encryption algorithm $hpke$ which is homomorphic with respect to f, i.e., it satisfies the equation $hpke(f(X,Y),Z) = f(hpke(X,Z), hpke(Y,Z))$. We assume that A and B share the same public (and corresponding private) key $pkey(A,B)$ for the homomorphic public key encryption algorithm $hpke$, so that both can decrypt data encrypted by $pkey(A,B)$. The server s also possesses a public (and private) key for a conventional public key encryption algorithm; the encryption of message M by server's key is denoted by $pke(M,S)$. All principals have digital signature keys; the digital signature of message M by principal P is denoted by $sign(M,P)$. Finally, concatenation is denoted by ;.

1. $A \rightarrow B : sign(B; N_A;$
   $pke(hpke(D_A, pkey(A,B)), S), A)$

   A starts by encrypting her data first under the homomorphic public key, then under the server's public key. She then attaches a nonce and B's name, signs it, and sends it to B.
2. $B \rightarrow A : sign(N_A; N_B;$
   $pke(hpke(D_B, pkey(A,B)), S), B)$

   B sends a similar message to A, including both his and A's nonce.
3. $A \rightarrow S : sign(A; B; N_A; N_B;$
   $pke(hpke(D_A, pkey(A,B)), S);$
   $pke(hpke(D_B, pkey(A,B)), S), A)$

   A sends a signed message containing both nonces and both encrypted data sets to S.
4. $S \rightarrow A, B : sign(A; B; N_A; N_B;$
   $f(hpke(D_A, pkey(A,B)),$
   $hpke(D_B, pkey(A,B))), S)$

   The server applies f to both encrypted data sets and sends the result to A and B.

This protocol is potentially vulnerable to an attack in which A can be led to believe that f has been applied to B's data when actually it has not. However, we can use the homomorphic property of the encryption to implement a check that prevents the attack. This attack is as follows.

1. $A \rightarrow I(B) : sign(B; N_A;$
   $pke(hpke(D_A, pkey(A,B)), S), A)$

   A initiates the protocol with B, but A's message is intercepted by I. We denote I impersonating B by $I(B)$.
2. $I \rightarrow B : sign(B; N_A; E, I)$

   I uses A's message to create a message for B. The message E could or could not be A's encrypted data. This is irrelevant to the attack.
3. $B \rightarrow A : sign(N_A; N_B;$
   $pke(hpke(D_B, pkey(I,B)), S), B)$

   B believes that he is talking to I and sends the corresponding reply message. I forwards it to A.
4. $A \rightarrow S : sign(A; B; N_A; N_B;$
   $pke(hpke(D_A, pkey(A,B)), S);$
   $pke(hpke(D_B, pkey(I,B)), S), A)$

   A now forwards both encrypted data sets to the server S, who removes the outer layer of encryption, applies f, and sends the results back to A and B.
5. $S \rightarrow A, B : sign(A; B; N_A; NB;$
   $f(hpke(D_A, pkey(A,B)),$
   $hpke(D_B, pkey(I,B)), S)$

   If A now attempts to decrypt the result of S's computation with her private key corresponding to $pkey(A,B)$, she will get nonsense, because one of the data sets was encrypted with $pkey(I,B)$.

Depending upon whether or not A can recognize that she has received nonsense, this can be used to prevent this attack. We thus specify two versions of this protocol : one in which A verifies that she has received $hpke(f(X,Y), pkey(A,B))$ for some X and Y, and one in which she does not. We do this by specifying the format of the final message that A receives. If no check is made, A will accept anything the server sends her. In this version the final message she receives in her strand is written as $sign(A; B; n(A,r); N; X1, s)$ where $X1$ is a free variable. In the version in which she checks the format, we write $hpke(f(X,Y), pkey(A,B))$ instead of $X1$. Note that the homomorphic property of the encryption is specified in both versions, but is only used in the second version, to unify the message the server sent (in which f is applied to the encrypted data) with the message Alice received (in which the encryption function is applied to the result of computing f). Note also that this check, or the lack of it, is not easy to specify in the informal, journal level style, but is straightforward to specify in Maude-NPA, in which the message the server sends and the message Alice accepts are specified separately.

4.2 Homomorphic Needham-Schroeder-Lowe

In [19] Cortier et al. give the following example of the Needham-Schroeder-Lowe protocol using public key encryption implemented in Electronic Code Book Mode, so that data is

1. $A \rightarrow B : pke(N_A; A, B)$
2. $B \rightarrow A : pke(N_A; N_B; B, A)$
3. $A \rightarrow B : pke(N_B, B)$

There are a number of ways in which either A or B can be tricked into believing that they have successfully completed a run of the protocol with another, when in fact this has not happened. Here is one of the simplest:

1. $I_A \rightarrow B : pke(N_I; A, B)$
2. $B \rightarrow I_A : pke(N_I; N_B; B, A)$

   This message is intercepted by the intruder, who, thanks to the homomorphic property, is able to extract $pke(N_B, A)$. He uses this to initiate the protocol with A, posing as B:
3. $I_B \rightarrow A : pke(N_B; B, A)$
4. $A \rightarrow I_B : pke(N_A; N_B; A, B)$

   The intruder is now able to extract $pke(N_B, B)$ and use it to complete its impersonation of A to B.
5. $I_A \rightarrow B : pke(N_B, B)$.

4.3 Homomorphic Needham-Schroeder Shared Key

This is a version of the Needham-Schroeder shared key protocol, in which a principal A requests a session key for communicating with B from a server S. The server sends A the key, encrypted under a master key shared between A and S. The message containing that key also contains the same key encrypted under a master key shared between B and S. A then forwards the encrypted key to B, after which A and B perform a handshake.

Normally the Needham-Schroeder shared key protocol is specified using only a single encryption algorithm, but here we specify three: me used for the outer encryption, e used for the inner encryption, and se used for the handshake. Only e is homomorphic over concatenation, i.e., it satisfies the equation $e(X;Y,Z) = e(X,Z);e(Y,Z)$:

1. $A \to S : A; B; N_A$

   A sends server S a request for a key to share with B.
2. $S \to A : me(N_A; B; K_{AB}; e(K_{AB}; A, K_{BS}), K_{AS})$

   S encrypts a session key K_{AB} and A's name with K_{BS} using the homomorphic e operator. It then encrypts that, along with K_{AB}, B, and N_A, with the key K_{AS} it shares with A using the me operator, and sends the result to A.
3. $A \to B : e(K_{AB}; A, K_{BS})$

   A removes the outer layer of encryption and sends the inner encrypted message to B.
4. $B \to A : se(N_B, K_{AB})$
5. $A \to B : se(s(N_B), K_{AB})$

   A and B agree that they share a key.

This protocol is vulnerable to an attack using two regular sessions in parallel, where the intruder gets $e(K_{CB}, K_{BS})$ from one regular execution between C and B and $e(A, K_{BS})$ from one regular execution between A and B.

1. $C \to S : C; B; N_C$

   C sends server S a request for a key to share with B.
2. $S \to C : me(N_C; B; K_{CB}; e(K_{CB}; C, K_{BS}), K_{CS})$

   S encrypts a session key K_{CB} and C's name with K_{BS} using the homomorphic operator e. It then encrypts that, along with K_{CB}, B, and N_C, with the key K_{CS} that it shares with C using the me operator, and sends the result to C.
3. $C \to I(B) : e(K_{CB}; C, K_{BS})$

   C removes the outer layer of encryption and sends the inner encrypted message to B. However, this is intercepted by the intruder I.
4. $I(A) \to B : e(K_{CB}; A, K_{BS})$

   Now the intruder I exploits the fact that $e(K_{CB}; C, K_{BS}) = e(K_{CB}, K_{BS}); e(C, K_{BS},)$ to obtain $e(K_{CB}, K_{BS})$. If A previously requested a key to talk to B, then the intruder could also have obtained $e(A, K_{BS})$ in the same way. He uses this to construct $e(K_{CB}, K_{BS}); e(A, K_{BS}) = e(K_{CB}; A, K_{BS})$, which he then sends to B.
5. $B \to I(A) : se(N_B, K_{CB})$
6. $I(B) \to C : se(N_B, K_{CB})$

   B responds according to the protocol, and I forwards his message to C.
7. $C \to B : se(s(N_B), K_{CB})$

   C responds according to the protocol. Now B will attribute any message from C to A.

4.4 Homomorphic Hash Protocol

In this protocol, A and B use a shared key to agree on a secret nonce N'_B. They use keyed hash functions to guarantee integrity of their messages, but let us suppose that they use a hash function h with a fatal flaw. Function h is homomorphic over concatenation, i.e., it satisfies the equation $h(X;Y,Z) = h(X,Z); h(Y,Z)$.

1. $A \to B : A; N_A$

   A starts by sending B her name and a nonce.
2. $B \to A : N_B; e(h(N_B; N'_B; N_A, K_{AB}), K_{AB});$
   $e(N'_B; N_A, K_{AB})$

   B responds with a nonce and two encrypted messages. Note that N'_B is only sent encrypted; it is intended to be a shared secret between A and B.
3. $A \to B : e(h(N_B, K_{AB}); h(N'_A, K_{AB}), K_{AB});$
   $e(N'_A, K_{AB})$

   A verifies to B that she received his message.

Now it turns out that an intruder can trick B into believing that he has completed a successful run of the protocol with A even though A is not present. This is because B can be fooled into accepting the message he sent in the second step of the protocol as the message he receives in the third step. We note that since h is homomorphic over concatenation, we have $h(N_B; N'_B; N_A, K_{AB}) = h(N_B, K_{AB}); h(N'_B; N_A, K_{AB})$. Thus we have the following attack.

1. $I(A) \to B : A; N_I$

   I starts by sending B A's name and a nonce.
2. $B \to I(A) : N_B; e(h(N_B; N'_B; N_I, K_{AB}), K_{AB});$
   $e(N'_B; N_I, K_{AB})$

   B responds to A according to the protocol. This is intercepted by I.
3. $I(A) \to B : e(h(N_B; N'_B; N_I, K_{AB}), K_{AB});$
   $e(N'_B; N_I, K_{AB})$

   I repeats B's message back to him, only leaving out the N_B at the beginning. If B has no way of telling the concatenation of two nonces from a nonce, he can mistake $N_B; N_I$ for a nonce N'_I. Thus he will mistake $e(N'_B; N_I, K_{AB})$ for $e(N'_A, K_{AB})$, and, because of the homomorphic properties of the hash function, he will mistake $e(h(N_B; N'_B; N_I, K_{AB}), K_{AB})$ for $e(h(N_B, K_{AB}); h(N'_A, K_{AB}), K_{AB})$.

5. Search in Maude-NPA

In this section we give a high-level summary of the general approach advocated in this paper for formally analyzing protocols *modulo* their algebraic properties, with particular attention to the way this approach is implemented in Maude-NPA. For further information, please see [21, 22].

Given a protocol $\mathcal{P}$, states are modeled as elements of an initial algebra $T_{\Sigma_\mathcal{P}/E_\mathcal{P}}$, where $\Sigma_\mathcal{P}$ is the signature defining the sorts and function symbols (for the cryptographic functions and for all the state constructor symbols) and $E_\mathcal{P}$ is a set of equations specifying the *algebraic properties* of the cryptographic functions and the state constructors. Therefore, a state is an $E_\mathcal{P}$-equivalence class $[t] \in T_{\Sigma_\mathcal{P}/E_\mathcal{P}}$ with t a ground $\Sigma_\mathcal{P}$-term. However, since the number of states $T_{\Sigma_\mathcal{P}/E_\mathcal{P}}$ is in general infinite, rather than exploring concrete protocol states $[t] \in T_{\Sigma_\mathcal{P}/E_\mathcal{P}}$ we explore *symbolic state patterns* $[t(x_1, \ldots, x_n)] \in T_{\Sigma_\mathcal{P}/E_\mathcal{P}}(X)$ on the free $(\Sigma_\mathcal{P}, E_\mathcal{P})$-algebra over a set of typed variables X. In this way, a state pattern $[t(x_1, \ldots, x_n)]$ represents not a single concrete state but a possibly infinite set of such states, namely all the instances of the pattern $[t(x_1, \ldots, x_n)]$ where the variables $x_1, \ldots, x_n$ have been instantiated by concrete ground terms.

In Maude-NPA [21, 22], a *state* in the protocol execution is a term t of sort *state*, $t \in T_{\Sigma_\mathcal{P}/E_\mathcal{P}}(X)_{state}$, which is a multiset. Each element in the multiset can be a strand or the intruder knowledge at that state. A *strand* [24] represents the sequence of messages sent and received by a principal executing the protocol and is indicated by a sequence of messages $[msg_1^-, msg_2^+, msg_3^-, \ldots, msg_{k-1}^-, msg_k^+]$ such that $msg_i \in T_{\Sigma_\mathcal{P}/E_\mathcal{P}}(X)_{\mathsf{Msg}}$, msg^- represents an input message, and msg^+

represents an output message. Strands are used to represent both the actions of honest principals (with a strand specified for each protocol role) and the actions of an intruder (with a strand specified for each intruder operation). In Maude-NPA, strands evolve over time; the symbol | is used to divide past and future: $[msg_1^\pm, \ldots, msg_{j-1}^\pm \mid msg_j^\pm, msg_{j+1}^\pm, \ldots, msg_k^\pm]$ where $msg_1^\pm, \ldots, msg_{j-1}^\pm$ are the past messages, and $msg_j^\pm, msg_{j+1}^\pm, \ldots, msg_k^\pm$ are the future messages ($msg_j^\pm$ is the immediate future message). The *intruder knowledge* is represented as a multiset of facts. There are two kinds of intruder facts: positive knowledge facts (the intruder knows m, i.e., $m \in \mathcal{I}$), and negative knowledge facts (the intruder *does not yet know* m but *will know it in a future state*, i.e., $m \notin \mathcal{I}$), where m is a message expression.

We illustrate the approach using the homomorphic Needham-Schroeder shared key protocol from Section 4.3. The strands associated to the five protocol steps above are given next. There are three strands, one for each principal in the protocol. Constants and function symbols are represented by small letters, and variables by capital letters, with the exception of variables of sort *Fresh* which are special variables that can't be unified with each other once they appear in a state. and are used for nonce generation. These are denoted by small letters and declared within the delimiter :: :: at the beginning of a strand. Sent messages are prefixed with a $+$, and received messages with a $-$. Note that sent messages from one strand do not always exactly with their corresponding receive messages. For example, the first message $A \rightarrow S : A; B; N_A$ is represented by a message in Alice's strand sending $(A; B; n(A, r))^+$ and another message in the Server's strand receiving $(A; B; N)^-$. When a principal cannot observe the contents of a concrete part of a received message (e.g., because a key is necessary to look inside), a generic variable is used for such part of the message in the strand (as with variable N of sort *Nonce* above). We encourage the reader to compare the protocol in strand notation to the presentation of the protocol in Section 4.3. Note that we first name the principal, then show the special variable(s) used for nonce generation (framed within ::), see below, and then the actual strand.

```
(A) :: r ::
    [ +(A ; B ; n(A,r)),
      -(me(n(A,r) ; B ; SK ; X , mkey(S, A))),
      +(X), -(se(M, SK)), +(se(succ(M), SK)) ]
(B) :: r' ::
    [ -(e(SK ; A, mkey(S,B))), +(se(n(B,r'), SK)),
      -(se(succ(n(B,r')), SK)) ]
(S) :: r'' ::
    [ -(A ; B ; N),
      +(me(N ; B ; skey(S,r'') ;
              e(skey(S,r'') ; A, mkey(S,B)),
           mkey(S,A))) ]
```

Intruder strands are also included for each function. For example, concatenation by the intruder is described by the strand $[(X)^-, (Y)^-, (X;Y)^+]$.

The protocol analysis methodology of Maude-NPA is then based on the idea of *backward reachability analysis*, where we begin with one or more state patterns corresponding to *attack states*, and want to prove or disprove that they are *unreachable* from the set of initial protocol states. In order to perform such a reachability analysis we must describe how states change as a consequence of principals performing protocol steps and of the intruder actions. This can be done by describing such state changes by means of a set $R_\mathcal{P}$ of *rewrite rules*, so that the rewrite theory $(\Sigma_\mathcal{P}, E_\mathcal{P}, R_\mathcal{P})$ characterizes the behavior of protocol $\mathcal{P}$ modulo the equations $E_\mathcal{P}$; see [21, 22] for the concrete rewrite rules.

The way to analyze *backwards* reachability is then relatively easy, namely to run the protocol "in reverse." This can be achieved by using the set of rules $R_\mathcal{P}^{-1}$, where $v \longrightarrow u$ is in $R_\mathcal{P}^{-1}$ iff $u \longrightarrow v$ is in $R_\mathcal{P}$. Reachability analysis can be performed *symbolically*, not on concrete states but on symbolic state patterns $[t(x_1, \ldots, x_n)]$ by means of *narrowing* [26, 36], where at each step of rewriting instead of *matching* a subterm t' of a concrete state t with a left-hand side v we *unify* v and the state pattern $t(x_1, \ldots, x_n)$. However, since our state patterns are not just syntactic terms $t(x_1, \ldots, x_n)$ but rather $E_\mathcal{P}$-equivalence classes $[t(x_1, \ldots, x_n)]$ we cannot just perform syntactic unification but instead should perform *semantic unification* modulo $E_\mathcal{P}$. In other words, we should perform not just syntactic narrowing for our backwards reachability analysis with $R_\mathcal{P}^{-1}$, but *narrowing modulo* $E_\mathcal{P}$ [27, 36]. Note that this is a different application of narrowing than the previous use for unification in Section 3.

$E_\mathcal{P}$-unification precisely models all the different ways in which an intruder could exploit the algebraic properties $E_\mathcal{P}$ of $\mathcal{P}$ to break the protocol; therefore, if an initial state can be shown unreachable by backwards reachability analysis modulo $E_\mathcal{P}$ from an attack state pattern, this ensures that, even if the intruder uses the algebraic properties $E_\mathcal{P}$, the attack cannot be mounted. This means that efficient support for $E_\mathcal{P}$-unification is a crucial feature of symbolic reachability analysis of protocols modulo their algebraic properties $E_\mathcal{P}$.

6. Unification modulo E_h

In this section we outline an algorithm for unification modulo the homomorphic encryption theory E_h defined by the single oriented equation $e(X; Y, Z) \rightarrow e(X, Z); e(Y, Z)$ in a signature containing symbols e, $\_;\_$, and uninterpreted function symbols. Here we only give a high-level description of the algorithm—some of the details are omitted and can be found in [2]. Since E_h can be viewed as a one-sided distributivity rule, the inference system given here can be compared to the one in [43]. We believe the algorithm we use is simpler and easier to implement, as it does not involve any cycle checking.

Over the empty theory, two terms with different top-level function symbols do not unify; but, modulo E_h, a concatenation may unify with an encryption. We extend the standard algorithm for syntactic unification by introducing additional inference rules called **Shaping**, **Parsing** and **Failure**.

Given the following E_h-unification problem: $X; Y = e(Z, k)$, the only way this can be solved is if X and Y are both encryptions with key k, so we instantiate X with $e(X', k)$ and instantiate Y with $e(Y', k)$. This idea is generalized into an inference rule called **Shaping**. Once the **Shaping** rule has been applied, everything is encrypted with key k, and then we need to remove key k and deduce that $Z = X'; Y'$. This can be generalized into an inference rule called **Parsing**.

For example, consider the E_h unification problem $X; e(Y, k_2) = e(e(Z, k_1), k_2)$. Here Z has been encrypted by k_1 followed by k_2. The pieces of the concatenation must also be encrypted by the same sequence of keys. So two applications of the **Shaping** rule will instantiate X by $e(e(X', k_1), k_2)$, and Y by $e(Y', k_1)$. The result is $e(e(X', k_1), k_2); e(e(Y', k_1), k_2) = e(e(Z, k_1), k_2)$. One application of **Parsing** removes key k_2 everywhere, resulting in $e(X', k_1); e(Y', k_1) = e(Z, k_1)$. A second application removes k_1, resulting in $Z = X'; Y'$.

To summarize, when a concatenation s is equal to an encryption t, each element of s must be a term encrypted with the same sequence of keys as t is encrypted with. The purpose of the **Shaping** rule is to guarantee that everything is encrypted by the same sequence of keys. Once everything has been encrypted by the same sequence of keys, the **Parsing** rule can be applied to remove the outermost key from each key sequence. Several applications of **Parsing** will remove all the keys.

At certain times, it can be detected that **Shaping** cannot make those key sequences to be the same. There are two rules to handle these cases and detect failure. For example, suppose we have $X; c = e(Z, k)$ or $X; e(c, k_2) = e(e(Z, k_1), k_2)$, where c is a constant. In both of these cases, the constant c cannot be instantiated, so it is impossible to make the sequence of keys the same everywhere, so we fail. This is generalized as the first **Failure** rule. A second example of failure is $X; Y = e(X, k)$ or $e(X, k_2); Y = e(e(X, k_1), k_2)$. Again here we cannot make the key sequence to be the same, because any instantiation of X on the left-hand side of the equation will also require the instantiation of X on the right hand side of the equation, so we fail. This is generalized as the second **Failure** rule.

The E_h-*Unification* procedure is defined by a don't-care nondeterministic application of the inference rules. The terms in the equations are rewritten so they are kept in E_h-normal form, thus putting concatenations over encryptions.

In a set of equality constraints, a variable x is said to be *solved* iff x appears only once and as one side of an equation. A *solved form* for E_h-Unification is a set of E_h-equalities $\{x_1 = t_1, \cdots, x_n = t_n\}$, where each x_i is a *solved variable.* The unification algorithm produces a solved form if the unification problem is solvable modulo E_h; else it returns $Fail$.

The inference rules in this section have been proved sound, complete, and terminating in [2] meaning that all solved forms created by the algorithm are correct solutions of the unification problem and that for every solution of the unification problem there is a more They also have been implemented in Full Maude and integrated into Maude-NPA, using the methods described in Section 3.2.

7. Finding attacks modulo $E_h \cup ACU$ using Maude-NPA

7.1 Multiparty Computation Protocol

We define an attack state for Alice in which the Alice strand completes, but there is no corresponding Bob strand using the same data. We do this by including Alices's strand in the final goal and putting in Bob's strand as a "never pattern" [22]. A never pattern is a pattern denoting a state with partial strand information or positive intruder knowledge that can never happen within the path from an initial state to the given attack pattern. These never patterns are checked by matching modulo $E_h \cup ACU$, i.e., if any state in a backwards reachability path matches modulo $E_h \cup ACU$ with a never pattern, then the path is discarded. Note that we do not include Bob's final received message, since it can always be blocked by the intruder. The attack pattern is as follows, written in Maude-NPA syntax [22]:

```
:: r, r' ::
[ nil, +(sign( b ; n(a,r) ;
                  pke(hpke(data(a,r'),pkey(a,b)),s),
                 a)),
       -(sign( n(a,r) ; N ; E ,b )),
       +(sign( a ; b ; n(a,r) ; N ;
                  pke(hpke (data(a,r'),pkey(a,b)),s) ; X,
                 a)),
       -(sign (a ; b ; n(a,r) ; N ; Z , s )) | nil ]
|| empty || nil || nil
|| never(*** Never Pattern for authentication
     :: r1, r2  ::
     [ nil | -(sign( b ; n(a,r) ;
                         pke(hpke(data(a,r'), pkey(a,b)),s),
                        a)),
             +(sign( n(a,r) ; N ; E ,b )),
             nil ]
     & SS:StrandSet || IK:IntruderKnowledge )
```

This pattern produces the attack we describe in Section 4.1 in ten steps, most of which involve the intruder removing the nonce from A's original message and inserting it into his own message. In our original specification of the protocol, in which encrypted messages were not typed, the tool failed to terminate, generating states in which the encrypted message field was replaced by an ever larger number of concatenated messages. Although Maude-NPA has inductive methods for avoiding such infinite sequences, they do not always work, which, given the undecidability of unbounded session protocol analysis, is not surprising. Instead, when we specified sorts for the different types of encrypted messages, the tool terminated in twelve steps (i.e., the search space was finite after twelve backwards narrowing steps, while the attack was found at step number ten). When we specified Alice's format check, Maude-NPA terminated at the fourth step without finding an attack, for the sorted version of the protocol, verifying it secure.

We also specified a corresponding attack pattern for B, in which a B strand completes without a corresponding A strand. In this case, Maude-NPA terminated in four steps without finding an attack, with and without the final check.

We note that the use of the homomorphic equational theory makes it very straightforward to specify the final check. To do something similar in the free theory we would have to either add extra deductions by A and B, or simply assume that A and B could recognize data of the form $f(hpke(X, Y))$ without specifying the reason why. Either way adds to the complexity of the analysis and detracts from the intuitive understanding of the protocol.

7.2 Homomorphic Needham-Schroeder-Lowe

For the Needham-Schroeder-Lowe protocol, we defined four attack states. In the two authentication patterns, Bob (resp. Alice) completes, apparently with the other party, but Alice (resp. Bob) does not complete with the same data. These are similar to the state defined in Section 7.1, so are omitted. In the other two , Bob (resp. Alice) completes, apparently with the other party, but the intruder learns Bob's (resp. Alice's) nonce. The secrecy pattern for Bob is as follows:

```
:: r ::
   [ nil, -(pk(a ; NA, b)), +(pk(NA ; n(b,r) ; b,a)),
          -(pk(n(b,r), b)) | nil ]
   || n(b,r) inI, empty || nil || nil || nil
```

and the pattern for Alice is similar. For the Bob authentication pattern, Maude-NPA terminated after ten steps and found three attacks (including the one described in Section 4.2). For the Bob secrecy pattern specified above, Maude-NPA terminated after thirteen steps and found three attacks. For the Alice secrecy and authentication patterns, respectively, Maude-NPA terminated after ten steps and found two attacks, and terminated after eight steps and found four attacks.

7.3 Homomorphic Needham-Schroeder

One of the purposes of this protocol was to give a "stress test" to Maude-NPA and thus at the beginning we used only one encryption algorithm for the entire protocol, which was homomorphic with respect to concatenation. We used an attack state in which Bob completes an instance of the protocol as a responder, apparently with Alice as initiator but Alice does not complete the corresponding instance of the protocol with B. This caused an enormous state explosion, and the tool did not complete or find an attack. We tried again using three cryptosystems, only one homormorphic. We again suffered from a state space explosion, but we noticed that the tool was spending much of its effort in searching for the term $\mathtt{e(A, mkey(b, s))}$. In order to eliminate this, we changed the specification to say that the intruder knows this term initially, thus eliminating the search for it. Since the production of e(A, mkey(b, s)) was the only place in which Alice's initiation of an instance of the protocol with B was needed, we could now specify a much weaker security property, in which Alice never initiates any instance of the protocol with Bob at all. This requires us to rule out not only any complete Alice strand initiated with Bob, but any aborted strands as well. In the Maude-NPA model any strand that is enabled for a send will send, so strands can only abort when they are enabled for a receive. There are two places where Alice's strand is enabled for a receive: after she has sent the initiation message, and after she has forwarded the session key to Bob. This gives us three never patterns: one for Alice's full strand, and two for the two partial strands. Our attack pattern is thus as follows:

```
:: r ::
[ nil, -(e(SKEY ; a , mkey(b,s))),+(se(n(b,r), SKEY )),
      -(se(succ(n(b,r)), SKEY)) | nil ]
|| empty || nil  || nil
|| never( *** Never Pattern for authentication
  (:: r' :: [ nil | +(a ; b ; n(a',r)),
                    -(Z), +(X), -(Y), +(W), nil ]
           & S:StrandSet || K:IntruderKnowledge )
           *** Never Pattern for authentication
  (:: r ':: [ nil | +(a ; b ; n(a,r')), -(Z), +(X), nil ]
           & S:StrandSet || K:IntruderKnowledge )
           *** Never Pattern for authentication
  (:: r' :: [ nil | +(a ; b ; n(a,r')), nil ]
           & S:StrandSet || K:IntruderKnowledge ) )
```

Maude-NPA found the attack in seven steps. However, Maude-NPA does not terminate immediately upon finding an attack, but continues to search until it has exhausted the search space. In this case, although it did find the attack, the complete search still did not terminate. Interestingly, we were not able to find evidence that Maude-NPA was generating any infinite paths in its search. Rather, the use of homomorphic encryption gave the intruder so many opportunities for generating different types of states that it overwhelmed the tool. Thus, this protocol did turn out to provide an excellent opportunity for stress testing, and likely will be useful for benchmarking in future work.

7.4 Homomorphic Hash Protocol

This protocol uses a keyed hash algorithm that is homomorphic over concatenation. This protocol was designed in order to demonstrate how Maude-NPA can reason about situations in which standard augmented intruder inference rules would not be applicable. In this protocol the homomorphic hash is hidden under a non-homomorphic encryption, so applying augmented inference rules —as explained in Section 2— that say, for example, that the intruder learns $h(X,K);h(Y;K)$ if he knows $h(X;Y,K)$ would not apply. However, the intruder can still use this property to fool honest principals, even if he can't apply it to learn anything new himself.

For this protocol we showed that a very weak security property fails to hold: Bob can execute an instance of the protocol as responder without any initiator strand executing, even a partial one. Only initiator strands are of the form `:: r1 , r2 :: [ nil | +(X) , ... ]`, so we specify the attack state as follows:

```
:: r,  r' ::
[ nil, -(a ; NA),
       +(n(b,r) ; e(h( n(b,r) ; n(b,r') ; NA, mkey(a,b)),
                     mkey(a,b))
                ; e(n(b,r') ; NA, mkey(a,b))),
       -( e( h(n(b,r), mkey(a,b)) ;
             h(NA', mkey(a,b)), mkey(A,B))
             ; e(NA', mkey(a,b)))  | nil ]
|| empty || nil || nil
|| never( *** Never Pattern for authentication
   (:: r'', r''' :: [ nil | +(X), -( Y), +(W), nil ]
   & S:StrandSet || K:IntruderKnowledge )
          *** Never Pattern for authentication
   (:: r'', r''' ::  [ nil | +(X), nil]
   & S:StrandSet || K:IntruderKnowledge))
```

This produces the attack described in Section 4.4. In this case the tool found the attack in four steps without our needing to add never patterns. However, after finding the attack, the tool demonstrated the same type of state explosion as the homomorphic Needham-Schroeder protocol. This happened as the result of several paths in which the intruder engaged in the protocol as a legitimate user of the system. The intruder thus was able to decrypt the hash and use its homomorphic property to break the hashed message into its components, resulting in a large number of states in which these parts were mixed and matched in different ways.

7.5 Discussion

As we can see, there was considerable variation in Maude-NPA's performance. It behaved well on the multi-party computation protocol, and on Cortier et al.'s ECB Needham-Schroeder-Lowe protocol. However, it suffered from combinatorial state explosion problems on the two other ECB protocols, even though their complexity was about the same as the multi-party computation protocol.

This, however, should not be a surprise. In general, extremely insecure protocols should be expected to give rise to a larger state space than more carefully designed ones, no matter what search strategy is used. There will be few possible paths through a sound protocol, while an unsound one will generate multiple paths. Thus even in the simplest ECB case, ECB Needham-Schroeder-Lowe, the tool found multiple attacks for each attack pattern.

However, even though the examples we encountered here were somewhat pathological, it can still be useful to have methods for dealing with them. Similar problems can arise when reasoning about protocols that employ long strings of concatenated messages, since the intruder can try different ways of combining different components. One possible approach to dealing with this is to employ some of the techniques that the NRL Protocol analyzer (NPA) [35] used to reduce state space size. One was the use of grammars, which are used both by the NPA and Maude-NPA to prove that certain terms could not be learned by the intruder unless they were cases of a list of excepted terms. When the NPA encountered such a term, it would unify the term with the exceptions, creating a new state for each exception [34]. Maude-NPA merely checks whether or not the condition holds [22]. This results in a cleaner model, but could contribute to increasing the size of the search space, since the tool deals with more general terms when more specific ones are available. Another feature that the NPA offered was the ability to generate lemmas about the unreachability of patterns of states encountered in a search. The identification of such patterns was manual and extremely tedious. But in Maude-NPA we have automated many procedures that were done manually in the NPA, and so these patterns may be a good topic to investigate. A third is the ability to not search for terms that can be easily be shown to be findable by the intruder, as we did for the Needham-Schroeder shared key example. This again could be specified manually in NPA, but again we can explore automated techniques to recognize, for example, terms that could be generated in an honest execution of the protocol with which the attacker does not interact.

8. Conclusions and Future Work

In this paper we described the first steps in dealing with unification-based cryptographic protocol analysis using homomorphic encryption. We developed a Maude implementation of a unification algorithm for homormorphic encryption over a free operator, and integrated it into Maude-NPA using a modular framework. Finally, we demonstrated the modular approach by applying Maude-NPA to examples and analyzed the results.

We are continuing to develop a library of dedicated unification algorithms for various cryptographic theories. Indeed, progress in this area has already been made; an efficient unification algorithm for unification modulo exclusive-or has been developed and implemented in Maude, and is currently being integrated with Maude-NPA. It is also being extended to an Abelian group unification algorithm. We plan to compare these with the folding variant narrowing approach already available in Maude-NPA.

Of particular interest, of course, is the extension of our approach to unification modulo more sophisticated homomorphic encryption theories, specifically encryption homomorphic over an Abelian group, which will allow us to apply our work to a number of realistic applications. Unfortunately the most straightforward way of achieving this in our model, via folding variant narrowing over encryption homomorphic over an AC operator, is not available to us, because unification modulo encryption homomorphic over an AC theory is known to be undecidable [38]. However, unification modulo encryption homomorphic over an Abelian group *is* decidable, giving us several ways to proceed. We could either determine if we could restrict ourselves to decidable subcases via judicious use of sorts, or we could incorporate existing unification algorithms applicable to encryption homomorphic over Abelian groups, e.g. the algorithm of Kapur et al. [28] into Maude-NPA. We are investigating these options.

References

[1] M. Abadi and V. Cortier. Deciding knowledge in security protocols under equational theories. *Theor. Comput. Sci.*, 367(1-2):2–32, 2006.

[2] S. Anantharaman, H. Lin, C. Lynch, P. Narendran, and M. Rusinowitch. Cap unification: application to protocol security modulo homomorphic encryption. In *ASIACCS*, pages 192–203. ACM, 2010.

[3] S. Anantharaman, P. Narendran, and M. Rusinowitch. Intruders with caps. In *Proc. RTA 2007*, volume 4533 of *LNCS*, pages 20–35. Springer, 2007.

[4] A. Armando, D. A. Basin, Y. Boichut, Y. Chevalier, L. Compagna, J. Cuéllar, P. H. Drielsma, P.-C. Héam, O. Kouchnarenko, J. Mantovani, S. Mödersheim, D. von Oheimb, M. Rusinowitch, J. Santiago, M. Turuani, L. Viganò, and L. Vigneron. The AVISPA tool for the automated validation of internet security protocols and applications. In *CAV*, pages 281–285, 2005.

[5] G. Ateniese, M. Steiner, and G. Tsudik. Authenticated group key agreement and friends. In *ACM Conference on Computer and Communications Security*, pages 17–26, 1998.

[6] F. Baader and K. U. Schulz. Unification in the union of disjoint equational theories: Combining decision procedures. In *CADE*, volume 607 of *LNCS*, pages 50–65. Springer, 1992.

[7] D. Basin, S. Mödersheim, and L. Viganò. An on-the-fly model-checker for security protocol analysis. In *In Proceedings of Esorics'03, LNCS 2808*, pages 253–270. Springer-Verlag, 2003.

[8] M. Baudet, V. Cortier, and S. Delaune. YAPA: A generic tool for computing intruder knowledge. In *Proc. RTA'09*, volume 5595 of *LNCS*, pages 148–163, Brasília, Brazil, June-July 2009. Springer.

[9] B. Blanchet. An efficient cryptographic protocol verifier based on prolog rules. In *CSFW*, pages 82–96. IEEE Computer Society, 2001.

[10] Y. Boichut, P.-C. Héam, and O. Kouchnarenko. Tree automata for detecting attacks on protocols with algebraic cryptographic primitives. *Electr. Notes Theor. Comput. Sci.*, 239:57–72, 2009.

[11] J. Bull. The authentication protocol. *APM Report*, 1997.

[12] S. Bursuc and H. Comon-Lundh. Protocol security and algebraic properties: Decision results for a bounded number of sessions. In *RTA*, pages 133–147, 2009.

[13] Y. Chevalier, D. Lugiez, and M. Rusinowitch. Verifying cryptographic protocols with subterms constraints. In *LPAR*, LNCS vol. 4790, pages 181–195. Springer, 2007.

[14] Y. Chevalier and M. Rusinowitch. Symbolic protocol analysis in the union of disjoint intruder theories: Combining decision procedures. *Theor. Comput. Sci.*, 411(10):1261–1282, 2010.

[15] Ş. Ciobâcă, S. Delaune, and S. Kremer. Computing knowledge in security protocols under convergent equational theories. In *Proc. CADE'09*, LNAI, pages 355–370, Montreal, Canada, 2009. Springer.

[16] M. Clavel, F. Durán, S. Eker, P. Lincoln, N. Martí-Oliet, J. Meseguer, and C. L. Talcott. *All About Maude - A High-Performance Logical Framework*, volume 4350 of *Lecture Notes in Computer Science*. Springer, 2007.

[17] H. Comon-Lundh and S. Delaune. The finite variant property: How to get rid of some algebraic properties. In *RTA*, pages 294–307, 2005.

[18] H. Comon-Lundh and V. Shmatikov. Intruder deductions, constraint solving and insecurity decision in presence of exclusive or. In *LICS*, pages 271–. IEEE Computer Society, 2003.

[19] V. Cortier, S. Delaune, and P. Lafourcade. A survey of algebraic properties used in cryptographic protocols. *Journal of Computer Security*, 14(1):1–43, 2006.

[20] C. J. F. Cremers. The Scyther tool: Verification, falsification, and analysis of security protocols. In *CAV*, pages 414–418, 2008.

[21] S. Escobar, C. Meadows, and J. Meseguer. A rewriting-based inference system for the NRL protocol analyzer and its meta-logical properties. *Theoretical Computer Science*, 367(1-2):162–202, 2006.

[22] S. Escobar, C. Meadows, and J. Meseguer. Maude-NPA: Cryptographic protocol analysis modulo equational properties. In *Foundations of Security Analysis and Design V, FOSAD 2007/2008/2009 Tutorial Lectures*, LNCS vol. 5705, pages 1–50. Springer, 2009.

[23] S. Escobar, R. Sasse, and J. Meseguer. Folding variant narrowing and optimal variant termination. *The Journal of Logic and Algebraic Programming*, 2010. In Press. Available at `http://www.dsic.upv.es/~sescobar/papers.html`.

[24] F. J. T. Fabrega, J. Herzog, and J. Guttman. Strand Spaces: What Makes a Security Protocol Correct? *Journal of Computer Security*, 7:191–230, 1999.

[25] J. Hendrix and J. Meseguer. Order-sorted equational unification revisited. *Electr. Notes Theor. Comput. Sci.*, 2008. To appear in Proc. of RULE 2008.

[26] J.-M. Hullot. Canonical forms and unification. In *CADE*, LNCS vol. 87, pages 318–334. Springer, 1980.

[27] J.-P. Jouannaud, C. Kirchner, and H. Kirchner. Incremental construction of unification algorithms in equational theories. In *Proc. ICALP*, volume 154 of *LNCS*, pages 361–373. Springer, 1983.

[28] D. Kapur, P. Narendran, and L. Wang. A unification algorithm for analysis of protocols with blinded signatures. In *Mechanizing Mathematical Reasoning*, pages 433–451. Springer, 2005.

[29] S. Kremer and M. D. Ryan. Analysing the vulnerability of protocols to produce known-pair and chosen-text attacks. In *Proceedings of SecCo'04*, ENTCS, pages 84–107, London, UK, May 2005. Elsevier Science Publishers.

[30] R. Küsters and T. Truderung. Using ProVerif to analyze protocols with Diffie-Hellman exponentiation. In *CSF*, pages 157–171. IEEE Computer Society, 2009.

[31] R. Küsters and T. Truderung. Reducing protocol analysis with xor to the xor-free case in the Horn theory based approach. *Journal of Automated Reasoning*, 2010. To appear.

[32] G. Lowe. Breaking and fixing the Needham-Schroeder public-key protocol using FDR. In *TACAS*, pages 147–166, 1996.

[33] C. Lynch and C. Meadows. On the relative soundness of the free algebra model for public key encryption. *Electr. Notes Theor. Comput. Sci.*, 125(1):43–54, 2005.

[34] C. Meadows. Language generation and verification in the nrl protocol analyzer. In *CSFW*, pages 48–61. IEEE Computer Society, 1996.

[35] C. Meadows. The NRL protocol analyzer: An overview. *J. Log. Program.*, 26(2):113–131, 1996.

[36] J. Meseguer and P. Thati. Symbolic reachability analysis using narrowing and its application to verification of cryptographic protocols. *Higher-Order and Symbolic Computation*, 20(1–2):123–160, 2007.

[37] J. K. Millen. On the freedom of decryption. *Inf. Process. Lett.*, 86(6):329–333, 2003.

[38] P. Narendran. Solving linear equations over polynomial semirings. In *LICS*, pages 466–472, 1996.

[39] O. Pereira and J.-J. Quisquater. On the impossibility of building secure cliques-type authenticated group key agreement protocols. *Journal of Computer Security*, 14(2):197–246, 2006.

[40] P. Y. A. Ryan and S. A. Schneider. An attack on a recursive authentication protocol. A cautionary tale. *Inf. Process. Lett.*, 65(1):7–10, 1998.

[41] R. Sasse, S. Escobar, J. Meseguer, and C. Meadows. Protocol analysis modulo combination of theories: A case study in Maude-NPA. In *Proc. STM 2010*. Springer, 2010.

[42] M. Schmidt-Schauß. Unification in a combination of arbitrary disjoint equational theories. *J. Symb. Comput.*, 8(1/2):51–99, 1989.

[43] E. Tidén and S. Arnborg. Unification problems with one-sided distributivity. *J. Symb. Comput.*, 3(1/2):183–202, 1987.

[44] M. Turuani. The CL-Atse protocol analyser. In *RTA*, pages 277–286, 2006.

Symbolic Analysis of Network Security Policies using Rewrite Systems

Tony Bourdier
INRIA Nancy & LORIA & Université Henri Poincaré
615 rue du Jardin Botanique
54600 Villers-lès-Nancy (France)
tony.bourdier@inria.fr

Horatiu Cirstea
INRIA Nancy & LORIA & Université Nancy 2
615 rue du Jardin Botanique
54600 Villers-lès-Nancy (France)
horatiu.cirstea@loria.fr

Abstract

First designed to enable private networks to be opened up to the outside world in a secure way, the growing complexity of organizations make firewalls indispensable to control information flow within a company. The central role they hold in the security of the organization information make their management a critical task and that is why for years many works have focused on checking and analysing firewalls. The composition of firewalls, taking into account routing rules, has nevertheless often been neglected. In this paper, we propose to specify all components of a firewall, *i.e.* filtering and translation rules, as a rewrite system. We show that such specifications allow us to handle usual problems such as comparison, structural analysis, and query analysis. We also propose a formal way to describe the composition of firewalls (including routing) in order to build a whole network security policy. The properties of the obtained rewrite system are strongly related to the properties of the specified networks and thus, classical theoretical and practical tools can be used to obtain relevant security properties of the security policies.

Categories and Subject Descriptors D.4.6 [*Operating systems*]: Security and Protection; F.1.1 [*Computation by abstract devices*]: Models of Computation; F.4.2 [*Mathematical logic and formal languages*]: Grammars and Other Rewriting Systems

General Terms Security, Theory, Verification

Keywords Security policies, firewalls, rewrite systems, tree automata

1. Introduction

Security constitutes a crucial concern in modern information systems. Several aspects are involved, such as user authentication (establishing and verifying users' identity), cryptology (changing secrets into unintelligible messages and back to the original secrets after transmission), and security policies (preventing illicit or forbidden accesses from users to information).

Due to the increasing complexity of organizations, network security policies are rarely defined as a single firewall. Most of the time, they are made up of numerous firewalls whose composition depends on the network topology and on the routing rules. That is why it is often difficult to ensure that the composition of different local security policies (*i.e.* firewalls) expresses the intended security policy. Their formal specification is thus crucial and for several years now the importance of using formal methods to specify security policies has been generally accepted. For example, to achieve high levels of certification (EAL[1] 5, 6, 7), it is necessary to provide a formal specification enabling to obtain mechanized formal proofs, to carry out techniques for test generation, or to perform static analyses ensuring required properties.

Many methods and tools have been developed for analysing and testing firewall policies. These methods are broken down into two different categories: the active methods and the passive methods. The former consist in sending packets to the network and to make a diagnosis according to the received packets. The main advantage of these methods is that they require no abstract representation of firewalls and thus no error can be introduced between the specification and the implementation. However, such methods have the major drawback of consuming bandwidth, interfering with the traffic and being non exhaustive. That is why we focused on passive methods, that is methods which send no packet and make an offline analysis. Two main categories of passive analysis are investigated in the literature: structural analysis and query analysis. Structural analysis examines the relationships that rules have with other rules within a firewall configuration or across multiple firewalls. A misconfiguration (or conflict) occurs when several rules match the same packet or when a rule can be removed without changing the behavior of the firewall. Query analysis provides a way to ask questions of the form "Which computers in the private network can receive packets from 212.12.30.25 ?". It then consists in defining a language to describe a firewall query and a way to compute its solutions. Some works [1, 2, 6, 13, 14, 22, 29] deal with structural analysis and focus on defining, detecting, and discussing misconfigurations while others [18, 24, 31] concentrate on query analysis. Some of these works abstract firewall filtering rules as one or two-dimensional ranges of IP, which does not allow to take complete advantage of the obtained results. Others assume that packets are not modified during their network traversal and then do not support network translation address capabilities. Moreover, they often focus on policies based on a single firewall or do not take into account the network topology. Some of the approaches can handle these various aspects (a detailed comparison between the different techniques could be found in [32]) but the routing aspects and especially the issues related to their combination with firewall policies are not deeply investigated. More generally, several rewrite based frameworks have

PDPP'11, July 20–22, 2011, Odense, Denmark.

[1] Evaluation Assurance Level

already been proposed for specifying and analysing security policies. In particular, [28] introduces a narrowing based method for querying rule based policies and illustrates the proposed technique by the analysis of a standalone firewall policy. This approach can be seen as a first step toward a dedicated and more complete method for rewrite based analysis of firewall security policies.

In this paper, we introduce a new framework, based on rewrite systems and automata, for specifying and analysing firewall security policies. First, we show that this approach is particularly well adapted for the efficient verification of standalone firewall rules. The particular specification we propose here is not only natural and quite close to real world firewall rules but allows also an efficient implementation. We briefly explain how this approach can be used to perform the various types of analyses described in the literature. Second, we extend this approach to take into account the network topology of the network secured by firewall security policies. We show that there is a strong relationship between relevant properties of the secured network and the properties of the rewrite systems used to specify them. We focus here on completeness, *i.e.* the ability to take a decision for any (routed) packet, and consistency, *i.e.* the coherence of the final decisions independently of the routing protocol. We consider this approach particularly interesting since the correspondence with the properties of the rewrite systems used for the specifications allowed us to use theoretical and automatic tools to perform these analyses.

The paper is structured as follows. In Section 2 we present notions and notations we use throughout this paper. Section 3 is devoted to the presentation of the rewrite-based framework for specifying and analysing (standalone) firewalls. In Section 4 we address the composition of firewalls with respect to topologies and routing rules. Finally, the last section concludes with some perspectives for further work.

2. Technical preliminaries

We suppose the reader is familiar with notions related to term algebra (terms, substitutions, positions, ...), rewriting systems (reduction relation, confluence, termination,...) [4] and tree automata [10]. In this section we recall some basic notions, present the notations we use throughout this paper and introduce the notion of constrained rewrite systems.

Term algebra. We consider in this paper many-sorted signatures of the form $(\mathcal{F}, \mathcal{S})$ consisting of a set of sorts $\mathcal{S}$ and a set of function symbols $\mathcal{F}$. Symbols of $\mathcal{F}$ are denoted by bold characters $\mathbf{f}, \mathbf{g}, \ldots$ and their profiles are denoted as follows $\mathbf{f} : \mathsf{s}_1 \times \ldots \times \mathsf{s}_n \mapsto \mathsf{s}$ where $\mathsf{s}_1, \ldots, \mathsf{s}$ are sorts of $\mathcal{S}$ and n is the arity of $\mathbf{f}$. The set of terms of sort s built out of symbols from $\mathcal{F}$ and of sorted variables from a set $\mathcal{X}$ is denoted by $\mathcal{T}^{\mathsf{s}}_{\mathcal{X}}$ and the set of ground terms of sort s is denoted by $\mathcal{T}^{\mathsf{s}}$. For any $t \in \mathcal{T}_{\mathcal{X}} = \cup_{\mathsf{s} \in \mathcal{S}} \mathcal{T}^{\mathsf{s}}_{\mathcal{X}}$, $\mathcal{V}ar(t)$ denotes the variables occurring in t. If any variable of t occurs only once in t, then t is said to be linear. A position within t is a sequence ω of integers describing the path from the root of t (seen as a finite labeled tree) to the root of the subterm at that position, denoted by $t_{|\omega}$. We use ε for the empty sequence. $|\,\omega\,|$ is the length of the position. $\mathcal{P}os(t)$ denotes the set of positions of t. $t(\omega)$ is the symbol of t at position ω and $t\,[s]_{\omega}$ the term t with the subterm at position ω replaced by s. A substitution σ is a mapping from $\mathcal{X}$ to $\mathcal{T}_{\mathcal{X}}$ which is the identity except over a finite set of variables (its domain) and which is extended to an endomorphism of $\mathcal{T}_{\mathcal{X}}$. A substitution is said to be ground if all the variables of its domain are mapped to ground terms. A term t matches a term t' iff $\sigma(t) = t'$ for some substitution σ. Two terms t and t' are unifiable iff $\sigma(t') = \sigma(t)$ from some substitution σ.

Tree automata. A *tree automaton* is a triple $A = (Q, Q_F, \Delta)$ where Q is a finite set of symbols called *states* disjoint from $\mathcal{F}$, $Q_F \subseteq Q$ is the set of *final states*, and Δ is a finite set of transitions of the form $\mathbf{f}(q_1, \ldots, q_n) \rightarrow_{\Delta} q$ where $q_1, \ldots, q_n, q \in Q$ and n is the arity of $\mathbf{f}$. $\rightarrow_{\Delta}$ is extended to $\rightarrow^*_{\Delta}$ as follows: if $\forall i, t_i \rightarrow^*_{\Delta} q_i$ and $\mathbf{f}(q_1, \ldots, q_n) \rightarrow_{\Delta} q$, then $\mathbf{f}(t_1, \ldots, t_n) \rightarrow^*_{\Delta} q$. The language recognized by $A = (Q, Q_F, \Delta)$ is $\mathcal{L}(A) = \{t \in \mathcal{T} \mid \exists q \in Q_F, t \rightarrow^*_{\Delta} q\}$. A set (or a language) of terms recognized by a tree automaton is said to be *regular*. A relation R is regular if there exists an automaton recognizing $\{\tilde{t} \mid t \in R\}$ where for any $t = (t_1, \ldots, t_n)$ and $\omega \in \cup_i \mathcal{P}os(t_i)$, $\tilde{t}(\omega) = (t_1[\omega), \ldots, t_n[\omega))$ with $t_i[\omega) = t_i(\omega)$ if $\omega \in \mathcal{P}os(t_i)$ and the special symbol Λ otherwise. Boolean operations, Cartesian product, projection, and cylindrification preserve regularity. We say that a set or a relation is effectively regular iff it is regular and we can compute an automaton which recognizes it.

Rewrite systems. A rewrite rule is a pair of terms $l \rightarrow r$ such that $Var(r) \subseteq Var(l)$. The terms l and r are respectively called the *left-hand side* and *right-hand side* of the rule. A rewrite system R is a finite set of rewrite rules. Any rewrite system R induces a binary relation over terms denoted by $\rightarrow_{\mathrm{R}}$ as follows: for any terms $t, t', t \rightarrow_{\mathrm{R}} t'$ if there exist a rule $l \rightarrow r$ of R, $\omega \in \mathcal{P}os(t)$ and a substitution σ such that $t_{|\omega} = \sigma(l)$ and $t' = t\,[\sigma(r)]_{\omega}$. A rewrite rule is linear iff its left-hand side and right-hand side are linear. A rewrite system is linear if all its rules are linear. A *growing* rewrite system (GRS) [26] is a linear rewrite system such that for every rule $l \rightarrow r$, if $l(\omega) = r(\omega') \in \mathcal{X}$ for some positions ω, ω', then $|\,\omega\,| \leq 1$.

An *ordered* rewrite system is a rewrite system in which rules are ordered. For an ordered rewrite system R, $\rightarrow_{\mathrm{R}}$ is defined as follows: for any terms t, t', $t \rightarrow_{\mathrm{R}} t'$ if there exists a rule $l \rightarrow r$ of R, $\omega \in \mathcal{P}os(t)$ and a substitution σ such that $t_{|\omega} = \sigma(l)$ and $t' = t\,[\sigma(r)]_{\omega}$ and such that there is no prior rule $l' \rightarrow r'$ such that $t_{|\omega'} = \sigma'(l')$ for some ω' and σ'.

A *constrained* rewrite system (CRS) is a rewrite system such that every rule $l \rightarrow r$ is associated to a set of membership constraints $x \in A$ where x is in $\mathcal{V}ar(l)$ and A is a regular tree language. If $l \rightarrow r$ is associated to $\{x_1 \in A_1, \ldots, x_n \in A_n\}$, we write $l \rightarrow r \;\|\; x_1 \in A_1, \ldots, x_n \in A_n$. The binary relation $\rightarrow_{\mathrm{R}}$ induced by a constrained rewrite system R is defined as follows: for any terms t, t', $t \rightarrow_{\mathrm{R}} t'$ iff there exists a rule $l \rightarrow r \;\|\; x_1 \in A_1, \ldots, x_n \in A_n$ of R, $\omega \in \mathcal{P}os(t)$ and a substitution σ such that $t_{|\omega} = \sigma(l)$ and $t' = t\,[\sigma(r)]_{\omega}$ and such that $\sigma(x_i) \in A_i$ for every i.

Given a rewrite system R, $\rightarrow^*_R$ denotes the reflexive transitive closure of the relation induced by R. For any term v, $\rightarrow^{-1}_R(v)$ denotes the set $\{u \mid u \rightarrow_R v\}$. For any set of ground terms $\mathcal{U} \subseteq \mathcal{T}$, $\rightarrow^{-1}_R(\mathcal{U})$ denotes the set $\{u \mid \exists v \in \mathcal{U}, u \rightarrow_R v\}$. A rewrite system R is *confluent* iff for any terms u, w, v, if $u \rightarrow^*_R v$ and $u \rightarrow^*_R w$, then there exists t such that $v \rightarrow^*_R t$ and $w \rightarrow^*_R t$. u is irreducible *w.r.t.* R iff there is no v such that $u \rightarrow_R v$. If $u \rightarrow^*_R v$ and v is irreducible *w.r.t.* R, then v is a *normal form* of u.

For any linear (constrained or not) rewrite system R and rule r of R, we denote by $rec(r)$ the regular set of ground terms that are reducible by r. If R is an ordered rewrite systems, we denote by $rec(r/R)$ the set of terms that are reducible by r and by no rule prior to r in R.

3. Standalone firewall specification and analysis

3.1 Short introduction to firewalls

In a network, when a host wants to transmit a message to another host, the data are encapsulated in a packet. Such a packet consists of the data that should be transmitted as well as of some additional information used to route it to the appropriate destination. The additional information, or header, mainly contains the packet's source and destination IP address, its protocol, and the source and

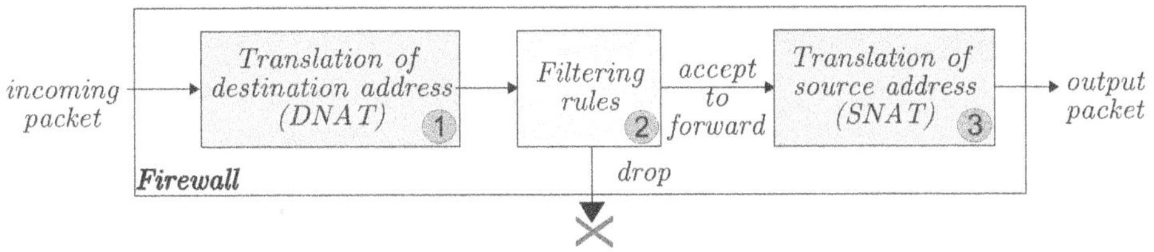

Figure 1. Firewall processing model

destination port. To control packet transmission between different subnetworks, it is common to deploy a network security policy based on a combination of firewalls. A firewall is an application that controls the forwarding of packets which cross it by using a combination of:

- *packet filtering*, which consists in inspecting each packet and either allowing it to continue its traversal or dropping it and
- *network address translation*, which consists in modifying network address information in packet headers.

Firewalls inspect incoming packets and accept or deny to forward them based on a list of decision rules which map the description of a set of packets to a decision. The most common criteria [11, 33] that firewalls use are the packet's source and destination address, its protocol, and, for TCP and UDP traffic, the port number. Moreover, firewalls often offer network address translation (NAT) functionality, which consists in rewriting the source (SNAT) or destination address (DNAT) into another address. The diagram in Figure 1 sums up the behavior of a firewall. At each step (1, 2 and 3), the packet is compared against a list of rules and the action (translation of destination address, drop or forward and translation of source address) corresponding to the first matched rule is performed.

EXAMPLE 1. *We give in Figure 2 a simple example of a firewall consisting of three rules: a filtering rule, a DNAT rule, and an SNAT rule. We use the CIDR notation [20] to denote subnetworks*[2]. *According to the rules of this firewall, any packet of protocol tcp whose destination address is* 192.168.5.130:80 *and whose source address is* 192.168.20.1:80 *(notation address:port) is forwarded by the firewall as a packet whose source address is* 121.130.1.1:80 *and whose destination address is* 121.130.1.15:80 *whereas any packet whose destination address is* 121.130.1.30:80 *is dropped by the firewall.*

3.2 Rewrite-based specification of firewalls

In this section, we present a formalization of firewalls based on rewrite systems. The ports and IP addresses are specified as terms and the firewall rules are specified as rewrite rules. Such specifications can be easily and automatically obtained from firewall configurations defined using classical firewall configuration languages such as netfilter [33].

3.2.1 Packets and subnetworks

In our approach, packets are represented as algebraic terms. For readability reasons, we consider that firewalls inspect only addresses and ports. Other information, such as protocols, TCP flags, states, could be considered without difficulty. The selected symbolic representation of packets is based on the following signature:

$\mathbf{0}, \mathbf{1}$	:	Binary	$\rightarrow$ Binary
$\#$	:		$\rightarrow$ Binary
from	:	Binary $\times$ Binary	$\rightarrow$ SrcAddr
dest	:	Binary $\times$ Binary	$\rightarrow$ DstAddress
packet	:	SrcAddr $\times$ DstAddress	$\rightarrow$ Packet

We briefly describe in this section the meaning of the above symbols and defer until Section 3.3 the discussion about the consequences of our choices.

IPv4 as well as IPv6 addresses can be equivalently seen as sequences of bits, tuples of hexadecimal numbers or integers. We have thus numerous possibilities to describe addresses as terms. However, we must keep in mind that the packet inspection performed by firewalls strongly relies on checking whether an address belongs to some given address ranges which generally correspond to subnetwork[3] domains. A special feature of subnetwork domains is that all hosts it contains are addressed with a common, identical prefix in their IP address when this address is written as a bit vector. It is thus natural to specify subnetworks as bit sequences of variable length and to use pattern matching for testing if an address belongs to a subnetwork domain.

By representing addresses as words over $\{0, 1\}$, or equivalently as terms built from monadic symbols $\mathbf{0}$ and $\mathbf{1}$, and a constant $\#$, we obtain a representation of subnetworks by linear terms built from $\mathbf{0}$ and $\mathbf{1}$. For example, the term

$$t = \mathbf{11000000\ 10101000\ 00010100}(x)$$

(we omit parentheses to keep readability) denotes the subnetwork 192.168.20.1/24 whereas

$$\mathbf{11000000\ 10101000\ 00010100\ 00000001}(\#)$$

denotes the IP address 192.168.20.1. For convenience, we will use in this paper the dot-decimal notation for addresses, the decimal notation for ports and the CIDR notation for subnetworks. When a variable occurs in the corresponding term, it will be indicated in brackets. For example t will be denoted by $192.168.20.1/24[x]$. As we will see later on, this representation allows us to efficiently build tree automata recognizing addresses that belong to given ranges and consequently to efficiently analyse firewall behavior.

Finally, packets are terms of sort Packet. For example, the term $\mathbf{packet}\begin{pmatrix} \mathbf{from}(\mathit{192.168.1.1}, \mathit{80}), \\ \mathbf{dest}(\mathit{172.20.3.1}, \mathit{80}) \end{pmatrix}$ represents a packet and $\mathbf{packet}\begin{pmatrix} \mathbf{from}(\mathit{192.168.1.1/24}[x], y), \\ \mathbf{dest}(\mathit{172.20.3.1/24}[x'], y') \end{pmatrix}$ refers to the set of packets whose source address belongs to the subnetwork 192.168.1.1/24 and whose destination address belongs to 172.20.3.1/24.

As showed in Section 3.3, explicitly identifying the source and destination addresses (using the symbols **from** and **dest**) allows

[2] The CIDR notation is a compact specification of an range of IP addresses. It consists of an IP address expressed in a dot-decimal notation and of a decimal number representing the size (in bits) of the common prefix of all the addresses in the range. The notation ip/n denotes the range of addresses whose n first bits (when addresses are expressed as binary numbers) are the same as the n first bits of the address ip. For example, 192.168.20.1/24 refers to the range [192.168.20.1, 192.168.20.255] and 121.130.1.1/28 refers to the range [121.130.1.1, 121.130.1.15].

[3] A subnetwork is a logically visible subdivision of a network characterized by an IP range (its domain).

Filtering:

IP address src	IP address dest	Protocol	Port src	Port dst	Decision
192.168.20.1/24	121.130.1.1/28	*tcp*	80	*any*	*Accept*
any	*any*	*any*	*any*	*any*	*Drop*

NAT:

Src/Dest	Address range	Port range	New address : port
Dest	192.168.5.128/25	*any*	121.130.1.15:80
Src	192.168.20.1/24	80	121.130.1.1:80

Figure 2. Example of a firewall

us to encode the firewall rules by appropriate tree automata that can be effectively used for firewall analysis.

3.2.2 Firewall rules.

To represent firewall rules, we add to the signature the following symbols:

$$\mathbf{accept}, \mathbf{drop} \quad : \quad \twoheadrightarrow \mathsf{Decision}$$

From a rewriting point of view, a filtering rule rewrites a packet into **accept** or **drop** whereas a NAT rule rewrites the source or destination address of a packet.

DEFINITION 1 (Firewall). *A firewall* $\mathfrak{f}$ *is composed of three ordered rewrite systems* $\mathrm{Pre}_\mathfrak{f}$, $\mathrm{Filter}_\mathfrak{f}$ *and* $\mathrm{Post}_\mathfrak{f}$ *such that:*

- *rules of* $\mathrm{Filter}_\mathfrak{f}$ *are of the form* $p \to d$ *where* p *is a linear term of sort* Packet *and* d *a (ground) term of sort* Decision*;*
- *rules of* $\mathrm{Pre}_\mathfrak{f}$ *and* $\mathrm{Post}_\mathfrak{f}$ *are, respectively, of the form:*

$$\begin{array}{lcl} \mathbf{dest}(ip, port) & \to & \mathbf{dest}(ip', port') \\ \mathbf{from}(ip, port) & \to & \mathbf{from}(ip', port') \end{array}$$

where ip, $port$ *are linear terms and* ip', $port'$ *are ground terms.*

EXAMPLE 2. *The firewall described in Example 1 can be specified as follows.* $\mathrm{Filter}_\mathfrak{f}$ *is the following ordered rewrite system:*

$$\left\{ \begin{array}{l} \mathbf{packet}\left(\begin{array}{l} \mathbf{from}(\mathit{192.168.20.1/24}[x], \mathit{80}) \\ \mathbf{dest}(\mathit{121.130.1.1/28}[y], z) \end{array} \right) \to \mathbf{accept} \\ \mathbf{packet}(x, y) \to \mathbf{drop} \end{array} \right.$$

while $\mathrm{Pre}_\mathfrak{f}$ *and* $\mathrm{Post}_\mathfrak{f}$ *consist, respectively, of the rules*
$\mathbf{dest}(\mathit{162.168.5.128/25}[x], y) \to \mathbf{dest}(\mathit{121.130.1.15}, \mathit{80})$
and
$\mathbf{from}(\mathit{192.168.20.1/24}[x], \mathit{80}) \to \mathbf{from}(\mathit{121.130.1.1}, \mathit{80})$.

DEFINITION 2 (Semantics). *For any firewall* $\mathfrak{f}$, *its semantics is denoted by* $[\![\mathfrak{f}]\!]$ *and defined as follows:*

$$[\![\mathfrak{f}]\!] = [\![\mathfrak{f}]\!]^{\mathrm{accept}} \cup [\![\mathfrak{f}]\!]^{\mathrm{drop}}$$

with[4]

$$[\![\mathfrak{f}]\!]^{\mathrm{accept}} = \{(t, u) \in \mathcal{T}^{\mathsf{Packet}} \times \mathcal{T}^{\mathsf{Packet}} \mid \exists v \in \mathcal{T}^{\mathsf{Packet}}, \; t \to_{\mathrm{Pre}_\mathfrak{f};\{x \to x\}} v \to_{\mathrm{Filter}_\mathfrak{f}} \mathbf{accept} \wedge v \to_{\mathrm{Post}_\mathfrak{f};\{x \to x\}} u\}$$

$$[\![\mathfrak{f}]\!]^{\mathrm{drop}} = \{(t, \mathbf{drop}) \in \mathcal{T}^{\mathsf{Packet}} \times \mathcal{T}^{\mathsf{Decision}} \mid \exists v \in \mathcal{T}^{\mathsf{Packet}}, \; t \to_{\mathrm{Pre}_\mathfrak{f};\{x \to x\}} u \to_{\mathrm{Filter}_\mathfrak{f}} \mathbf{drop}\}$$

From an abstract point of view, a firewall can be seen as a partial or total function which takes as input a packet and returns either another packet (possibly the same) or **drop**.

3.3 Analysis of firewalls

In this section, we show that this rewrite based specification allows one not only to automatically check properties concerning the semantics of a firewall but also to perform structural and query analysis over firewalls.

[4] $R; \{x \to x\}$ is the rewrite system R in which the rule $x \to x$ has been added as the last rule.

3.3.1 Firewall semantics analysis

A firewall can be seen as a decision process which associates to an incoming packet a decision which could be either drop or another packet, and thus the following properties should be verified: *consistency*, which indicates that at most one decision is taken for a given incoming packet, *termination*, which ensures that a firewall computes a decision in a finite time and *completeness*, which means that for any incoming packet, the firewall returns a decision.

As we have already said, by construction, any firewall denotes a terminating and consistent decision process and thus a function. The completeness can be thus defined as follows:

DEFINITION 3 (Completeness). *We say that a firewall* $\mathfrak{f}$ *is complete iff* $[\![\mathfrak{f}]\!]$ *is a total function.*

The particular shape of the rules defining a firewall allows us to represent the semantics of a firewall as a regular relation and consequently to verify its completeness:

PROPOSITION 1. *Completeness is decidable.*

PROOF. *The proof relies on the regularity of the relations involved in the definition of the semantics of a firewall. Indeed, since the left-hand sides of all the rewrite rules composing a firewall are linear and share no variable with their corresponding right-hand sides, we can easily show that* $\to_{\mathrm{Pre}_\mathfrak{f}}$ *and* $\to_{\mathrm{Post}_\mathfrak{f}}$ *are regular tree relations (some technical manipulations are needed to take into account the order). Since the identity is a regular relation, it follows that* $\to_{\mathrm{Pre}_\mathfrak{f};\{x\to x\}}$ *and* $\to_{\mathrm{Post}_\mathfrak{f};\{x\to x\}}$ *are also regular. By composition and restriction, we obtain that* $[\![\mathfrak{f}]\!]^{\mathrm{accept}}$ *and* $[\![\mathfrak{f}]\!]^{\mathrm{drop}}$ *are regular tree (functional) relations. Consequently,* $[\![\mathfrak{f}]\!]$ *is a regular tree (functional) relation. The completeness can be tested by checking that the first projection of* $[\![\mathfrak{f}]\!]$ *covers the (regular) set of all possible incoming packets.* □

In the case of complete firewalls, it can be important to determine if a firewall is less or more permissive than another one. A more permissive firewall allows at least the same traffic as a less permissive one. Such an order is obviously not total.

DEFINITION 4 (Order). *We define a partial order over complete firewalls* $\preceq$ *as follows: for any* $\mathfrak{f}$ *and* $\mathfrak{f}'$, $\mathfrak{f} \preceq \mathfrak{f}'$ *(*$\mathfrak{f}'$ *is more permissive than* $\mathfrak{f}$*) iff* $[\![\mathfrak{f}]\!]^{\mathrm{accept}} \subseteq [\![\mathfrak{f}']\!]^{\mathrm{accept}}$. *We write* $\mathfrak{f} \approx \mathfrak{f}'$ *iff* $\mathfrak{f} \preceq \mathfrak{f}'$ *and* $\mathfrak{f}' \preceq \mathfrak{f}$.

A firewall $\mathfrak{f}'$ is thus more permissive than a firewall $\mathfrak{f}$ if $\mathfrak{f}'$ accepts all the packets $\mathfrak{f}$ accepts and if it the result of the address translation is the same for these packets. Note that $\mathfrak{f} \approx \mathfrak{f}'$ iff $[\![\mathfrak{f}]\!] = [\![\mathfrak{f}']\!]$.

For the same reasons as before, we can decide whether a firewall is more or less permissive than another one:

PROPOSITION 2. *The order relation* $\preceq$ *is decidable.*

PROOF. *As we have already shown, for any firewall* $[\![\mathfrak{f}]\!]$, $[\![\mathfrak{f}]\!]^{\mathrm{accept}}$ *and* $[\![\mathfrak{f}]\!]^{\mathrm{drop}}$ *and* $[\![\mathfrak{f}]\!]$ *are regular relation. Consequently, the inclusion* $[\![\mathfrak{f}]\!]^{\mathrm{accept}} \subseteq [\![\mathfrak{f}']\!]^{\mathrm{accept}}$ *is decidable.* □

Note that two firewalls may have the same semantics even if their rules are different. This is particularly interesting since it allows to simplify or optimize the rules of a firewall and check if the resulted firewall has the same semantics as before.

3.3.2 Structural analysis.

Structural analysis refers to the detection of so-called misconfigurations (or anomalies) in (the rules of) a firewall. More precisely, such misconfigurations are properties expressed as relationships between the rules of a firewall. A complete survey of misconfigurations can be found in [14, 23]. Examples of anomalies are shadowing (a rule leads to decisions contradictory to decisions of prior rules), redundancy (a rule can be removed without changing the filtering result), generalization (a rule matches a superset of the set of packets matched by a prior rule with a different decision),.... We should mention that although several approaches have been developed for the detection of the above misconfigurations, this kind of anomalies are often intentionally introduced by firewall administrators in order to obtain more compact or more efficient rule sets. Detecting them is still interesting since it can outline some potential problems.

We only discuss here our approach for detecting shadowing; the other anomalies can be treated in a similar way. Let us first recall the definition of the shadowing anomaly: we say that a firewall has *shadowing* iff it contains at least one filtering rule such that all packets it accepts (resp. drops) are dropped (resp. accepted) by a prior rule. In such a case, the concerned rule is said to be *shadowed*.

The detection of the shadowed rules, as well as of the other misconfigurations, is based on the regularity of the sets of terms associated to a given rule. More precisely, each rule r is associated to several sets: $rec(r)$, denoting the set of packets matching r; $rec(r/\text{Filter}_\mathfrak{f})$, denoting the set of packets matching r that match no prior rule of $\text{Filter}_\mathfrak{f}$ (*i.e.* $rec(r) \setminus \bigcup_{r'<r} rec(r')$) and $rec(r/\text{Filter}_\mathfrak{f}[d])$ denoting the set of packets matching r that match no other rule of $\text{Filter}_\mathfrak{f}$ associated to the decision d. Since the left-hand sides of the filtering rules are linear terms, all the sets $rec(r)$ are regular; the other sets are also regular since they can be built starting from $rec(r)$ and using operations which preserve regularity. Misconfigurations can then be detected using inclusion or emptiness tests. For example, to detect if a rule r is shadowed, it suffices to check the emptiness of $rec(r/\text{Filter}_\mathfrak{f}[\mathbf{accept}])$ if the right-hand side of r is $\mathbf{drop}$ and the emptiness of $rec(r/\text{Filter}_\mathfrak{f}[\mathbf{drop}])$ otherwise.

It is well-known that the complexity of the operations over tree automata is quite high in general. In our case, the complexity of the needed operations strongly depends on the representation of packets and in particular on the representation of addresses. The choice of describing addresses as words over $\{0, 1\}$ (or equivalently as terms built from the monadic symbols $\mathbf{0}$ and $\mathbf{1}$, and the constant $\#$) was indeed made in order to obtain efficient implementations of the corresponding automata operations.

To simplify explanations, let us consider word automata; the correspondence with tree automata is straightforward. Due to the representation of address ranges, we are confronted with n-prefix (or simply prefix) languages, *i.e.* regular languages of the form $\alpha_1.\{0,1\}^* \cup \ldots \cup \alpha_n.\{0,1\}^*$. A good property of the manipulated address ranges is that corresponding minimal and deterministic automata have no loop except at their unique final state which loops over itself for any word. The main advantages of n-prefix languages are the following:

- boolean operations preserve the prefix property,
- boolean operations can be performed in $O(n)$ (where n is the number of states of the biggest operand) over the minimal deterministic automata and
- the corresponding algorithms directly produce deterministic and minimal automata (and thus there is no need to perform any determinization).

As said before, the sets of addresses of a given subnetwork are 1-prefix. It follows that $rec(r)$, $rec(r/\text{Filter}_\mathfrak{f})$, $\ldots$, are prefix languages. Consequently, misconfigurations can be efficiently detected using our approach. More details about the detection of misconfigurations using tree automata can be found in [7].

3.3.3 Query analysis

Another kind of analysis proposed by some of the firewall verification approaches [30, 31] is query analysis. This kind of analysis provides a way to assist firewall administrators in understanding the behavior of a firewall by computing the result of user-defined queries such as "Which hosts in the subnetwork 192.168.1.1/22 can receive packets from a host in the subnetwork 172.20.1.1/24 ?". We have previously shown that the semantics of a firewall is a regular relation. Thus, any query expressed as a first order formula built from:

- variables, ground terms or terms whose head is the symbol $\mathbf{packet}$ and whose subterms are variables or ground terms;
- membership constraints *w.r.t.* to one of the relations defined in Definition 2 and
- membership constraints *w.r.t.* to a linear term (which means being a ground instance of)

can be rewritten into a tree automaton recognizing the set of solutions of the query, that is values of free variables making the formula true.

4. Network security policies

A network security policy is generally deployed by using several firewalls. If each of the firewalls present in the network has the expected properties checked, for example, by performing the analyses presented in Section 3.3, this is not necessarily the case for their composition. Indeed, firewall composition introduces a new security element which could disturb the behavior of standalone firewalls after connecting them together: routing. Although routing rules can generate major security faults, these rules are often neglected in network security policy analyses. For example, they can lead to loops in the paths followed by packets and consequently to congestions and even to service denial. Moreover, the combination between the routing and the firewall rules can lead to packets handled differently depending on the route they follow and thus, to ambiguous network security policies.

Indeed, the effects induced by the interaction between the routers and the firewalls make the semantics of the global network security policy hard to understand, particularly in large networks with a complex topology. We propose in this section to go a step further in network security policies analysis and extend the approach proposed in the previous section to take into account the network topology and the routing rules.

4.1 Policy specifications

In order to analyse a network security policy, one should first specify the network topology. More precisely, one must specify the subnetworks, the location of the security hosts (*i.e.* the nodes in which firewalls, as logical entities, are deployed) and the connectivity between the subnetworks and the security hosts. A subnetwork can be seen as a logical unit consisting of a set of network hosts which can mutually communicate without going through a security host. It often corresponds to a particular section of an organization and it is usually represented by a symbolic name and by an IP address

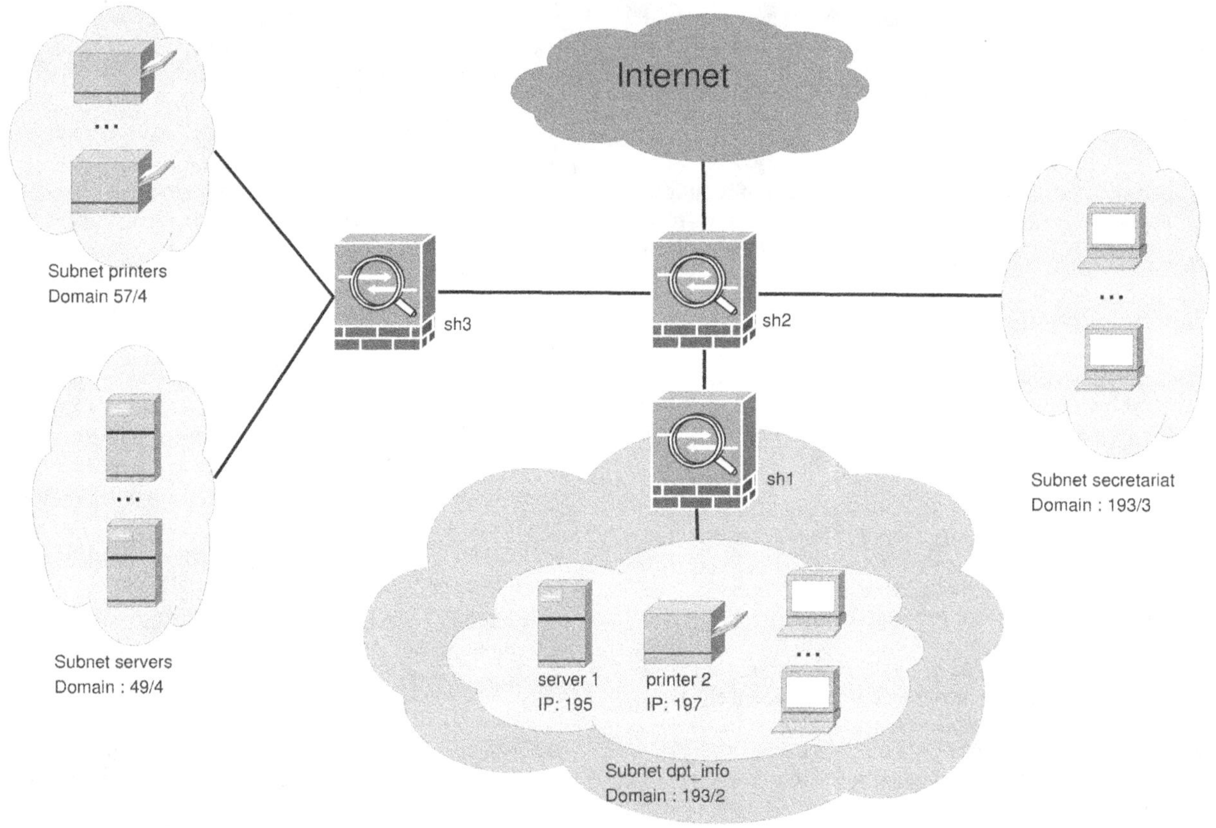

Figure 3. Example of network topology

range (called domain). Security hosts are interconnection nodes in the network which can be connected to subnetworks (a security host connected to a subnetwork is its gateway[5]) and to other security hosts. The picture in Figure 3 gives an example of a topology. For readability reasons, we consider in this figure and in the subsequent related examples that IP addresses are built from only one octet (that is 8 bits) and that the domain of Internet is $129/2$.

In order to formally specify such a topology we add to the signature given in Section 3.2 a sort Net representing subnetwork names and a sort SH representing security hosts names.

DEFINITION 5 (Network Topology). *A network topology τ is given by:*

- *a finite set* $\mathbf{net_1}, \ldots, \mathbf{net_n} : \rightarrow \mathsf{Net}$ *of subnetwork names;*
- *a finite set* $\mathrm{s}_1, \ldots, \mathrm{s}_m : \rightarrow \mathsf{SH}$ *of security host names;*

together with

- *a total map* $\Delta : \mathcal{T}^{\mathsf{Net}} \rightarrow \mathcal{T}_{\mathcal{X}}^{\mathsf{Binary}}$ *which associates any subnetwork name* $\mathbf{net_i}$ *with a linear term of* $\mathcal{T}_{\mathcal{X}}^{\mathsf{Binary}}$ *called its domain;*
- *a total map* $\mathcal{GW} : \mathcal{T}^{\mathsf{Net}} \rightarrow \mathcal{T}^{\mathsf{SH}}$ *which associates any subnetwork name* $\mathbf{net_i}$ *with a security host called its gateway such that for any security host* s *and any distinct subnetwork names* $\mathbf{net_1}, \mathbf{net_2} \in \mathcal{GW}^{-1}(\mathrm{s})$*, the terms* $\Delta(\mathbf{net_1})$ *and* $\Delta(\mathbf{net_2})$ *are not unifiable (that is to say, address ranges of subnetworks connected to the same security host must be disjoint);*
- *a relation* $\mathcal{CON}$ *over* $\mathcal{T}^{\mathsf{SH}} \times \mathcal{T}^{\mathsf{SH}}$ *describing the connection between the security hosts.*

[5] Note that without loss of generality, we can consider that any subnetwork has only one gateway. If one wants to describe a topology in which a subnetwork is connected to several security hosts, it suffices to add an intermediate security host.

EXAMPLE 3. *The topology depicted in Figure 3 is formally defined by:*

- $\mathbf{printers}, \mathbf{servers}, \mathbf{secretariat}, \mathbf{dpt\_info} : \rightarrow \mathsf{Net}$;
- $\mathbf{sh_1}, \mathbf{sh_2}, \mathbf{sh_3} : \rightarrow \mathsf{SH}$;
- $\Delta = \left\{ \begin{array}{rcl} \mathbf{printers} & \mapsto & 57/4[x] \\ \mathbf{servers} & \mapsto & 49/4[x] \\ \mathbf{secretariat} & \mapsto & 193/3[x] \\ \mathbf{dpt\_info} & \mapsto & 193/2[x] \end{array} \right\}$;
- $\mathcal{GW} = \left\{ \begin{array}{rcl} \mathbf{printers} & \mapsto & \mathbf{sh_3} \\ \mathbf{servers} & \mapsto & \mathbf{sh_3} \\ \mathbf{secretariat} & \mapsto & \mathbf{sh_2} \\ \mathbf{dpt\_info} & \mapsto & \mathbf{sh_1} \end{array} \right\}$;
- $\mathcal{CON} = \{(\mathbf{sh_1}, \mathbf{sh_2}), (\mathbf{sh_2}, \mathbf{sh_1}), (\mathbf{sh_2}, \mathbf{sh_3}), (\mathbf{sh_3}, \mathbf{sh_2})\}$.

Given a network topology, defining a network security policy consists in defining for each security host a set of NAT and filtering rules (a firewall). The firewalls associated with the security hosts describe a set of "local" policies which are combined by the topology.

DEFINITION 6 (Network security policy). *A network security policy $\wp$ over a network topology τ is a total mapping which associates any security host* $\mathbf{sh}$ *of* τ *with a firewall* $\wp(\mathbf{sh})$.

EXAMPLE 4. *Let τ be the topology defined in Example 3. We define a network security policy $\wp$ over τ as follows:*

- *the aim of the security host* $\mathbf{sh_1}$ *is to hide the private IP address space of the subnetwork* $\mathbf{dpt\_info}$ *and its machines except for the printer 2 and the server 1 which serves as a proxy for other machines of* **dpt_info**. *To achieve this goal,* $\mathbf{sh_1}$ *is associated to a firewall* $\wp(\mathbf{sh_1})$ *containing the NAT rules:*

$$\begin{cases} \mathbf{dest}(19, 515) & \rightarrow \mathbf{dest}(197, 515) \\ \mathbf{dest}(17, 8080) & \rightarrow \mathbf{dest}(195, 32) \end{cases}$$
$$\begin{cases} \mathbf{from}(197, 515) & \rightarrow \mathbf{from}(19, 515) \\ \mathbf{from}(195, 32) & \rightarrow \mathbf{from}(17, 8080) \end{cases}$$

and the following filtering rules:

$$\begin{cases} \mathbf{packet}(\mathbf{from}(197, 515), x) & \rightarrow \mathbf{accept} \\ \mathbf{packet}(\mathbf{from}(195, 32), x) & \rightarrow \mathbf{accept} \\ \mathbf{packet}(x, \mathbf{dest}(197, 515)) & \rightarrow \mathbf{accept} \\ \mathbf{packet}(x, \mathbf{dest}(195, 32)) & \rightarrow \mathbf{accept} \\ \mathbf{packet}(x, y) & \rightarrow \mathbf{drop} \end{cases}$$

The only machines accessible to the outside world are 197 (printer 2) masqueraded as 19 on the port 515 (the one associated to the Line Printer Daemon) and 195 (server 1) masqueraded as 17 on the port 32 masqueraded as 8080.

- $\mathbf{sh_2}$ *is associated to a firewall* $\wp(\mathbf{sh_2})$ *containing the following filtering rules:*

$$\begin{cases} (i) \ \mathbf{packet}\begin{pmatrix} \mathbf{from}(193/3[x], x') \\ \mathbf{dest}(129/2[y], y') \end{pmatrix} & \rightarrow \mathbf{drop} \\ (ii) \quad \mathbf{packet}(\mathbf{from}(129/2[x], x'), y) & \rightarrow \mathbf{drop} \\ (iii) \qquad \mathbf{packet}(x, y) & \rightarrow \mathbf{accept} \end{cases}$$

meaning that: (i) *the hosts in the secretariat cannot initiate an Internet communication;* (ii) *no communication can be initiated by a host outside the organization (i.e. from Internet);* (iii) *all the other packets are transmitted by the security host (as they are).*

- *The third security host* $\mathbf{sh_3}$ *focuses on traffic sent from or received by the subnetworks* **printers** *and* **servers**. *It is associated to a firewall* $\mathfrak{f}_3 = \wp(\mathbf{sh_3})$ *containing the following filtering rules:*

$$\begin{cases} (iv) \ \mathbf{packet}\begin{pmatrix} \mathbf{from}(193/3[x], x') \\ \mathbf{dest}(57/4[x], x') \end{pmatrix} & \rightarrow \mathbf{accept} \\ (v) \quad \mathbf{packet}(\mathbf{from}(97/3[x], x'), y') & \rightarrow \mathbf{accept} \\ (vi) \quad \mathbf{packet}(\mathbf{from}(17/4[x], x'), y') & \rightarrow \mathbf{accept} \\ (vii) \qquad \mathbf{packet}(x, y) & \rightarrow \mathbf{drop} \end{cases}$$

meaning that (iv) *hosts from* **secretariat** *can reach the printers but not the servers;* (v) *the security host does not block traffic sent from* $97/3 = 57/4 \cup 49/4$ *(that is from subnetworks* **printers** *and* **servers**); (vi) *packets from* **dpt_info** *(seen by* $\mathbf{sh_3}$ *as a subnetwork whose domain is* $17/4$*) are allowed and* (vii) *any other traffic is forbidden.*

To entirely characterize the network traffic under a given security policy, one must define a routing strategy to determine the paths that packets must follow to reach their destinations.

DEFINITION 7 (Routing strategy). *Given a network topology* τ*, a routing strategy is a map* $\zeta : \mathcal{T}^{\mathsf{SH}} \twoheadrightarrow \mathcal{T}_{\mathcal{X}}^{\mathsf{Binary}} \twoheadrightarrow \mathcal{T}^{\mathsf{SH}}$ *such that:*

1. *for any* $(\mathbf{sh}, t_1, \mathbf{sh_1'})$ *and* $(\mathbf{sh}, t_2, \mathbf{sh_2'}) \in \zeta$*, there is no* σ *such that* $\sigma(t_1) = \sigma(t_2)$ *and*
2. *for any* $(\mathbf{sh}, t, \mathbf{sh}') \in \zeta$*, there are no* $\mathbf{net} \in \mathcal{GW}^{-1}(\mathbf{sh})$ *and substitution* σ *such that* $\sigma(\Delta(\mathbf{net})) = \sigma(t)$.

A routing strategy ζ associates to any security host a routing map which indicates the next security host to which a given packet must be forwarded depending on its destination. We impose (i) a deterministic routing, *i.e.* all security hosts route any incoming packet to at most another one security host and (ii) that packets whose destination is a directly reachable subnetwork must be delivered (and then must not be routed to another security host). Moreover, the aim of a routing strategy is to transmit any packet from (security) host to (security) host until it reaches one which is able to take a definitive decision (*i.e.* deliver the message to its final destination or drop it). According to this point of view, a routing strategy must satisfy certain conditions. First, it must create no loop when it transmits a request (packet). Second, it must eventually transmit any packet to a (security) host which is able to take a decision if one can be taken (if no security host can take a decision, the packet is lost or, in a network jargon, the packet is non-routable). Thus, we say that a routing strategy ζ is *sound w.r.t.* a topology τ if it satisfies the conditions mentioned above. More formally, ζ is sound *w.r.t.* $\tau = (\mathsf{Net}, \mathsf{SH}, \Delta, \mathcal{GW}, \mathcal{CON})$ iff for any $t \in \bigcup_{\mathbf{net} \in \mathcal{T}^{\mathsf{Net}}} rec(\Delta(\mathbf{net}))$ and $\mathbf{sh} \in \mathcal{T}^{\mathsf{SH}}$:

- there exist a finite sequence $(\mathbf{sh_i}, t_i, \mathbf{sh_{i+1}})_{i=1\ldots n}$ of tuples from ζ and a sequence of substitutions $(\sigma_i)_{i=1\ldots n+1}$ such that $\mathbf{sh_1} = \mathbf{sh}$ and for all $1 \leq i \leq n$: $(\mathbf{sh_i}, \mathbf{sh_{i+1}}) \in \mathcal{CON}$, $t = \sigma_i(t_i)$ and $t = \sigma_{n+1}(\Delta(\mathbf{net}))$ for some $\mathbf{net}$ such that $\mathcal{GW}(\mathbf{net}) = \mathbf{sh_{n+1}}$ and
- there exist no sequence $(\mathbf{sh_i}, t_i, \mathbf{sh_{i+1}})_{i=1\ldots n}$ and $(\sigma_i)_{i=1\ldots n}$ such that $\mathbf{sh_1} = \mathbf{sh_{n+1}} = \mathbf{sh}$ and for all $1 \leq i \leq n$: $(\mathbf{sh_i}, \mathbf{sh_{i+1}}) \in \mathcal{CON}$ and $t = \sigma_i(t_i)$.

In what follows all routing strategies are considered to be sound *w.r.t.* the topology for which they are designed.

EXAMPLE 5. *Following the previous example, we define the routing strategy below:*

- $\zeta(\mathbf{sh_1}) = \begin{cases} 125/1[x] \mapsto \mathbf{sh_2} & ; 64/2[x] \mapsto \mathbf{sh_2} \\ 32/3[x] \mapsto \mathbf{sh_2} & ; \ 1/4[x] \mapsto \mathbf{sh_2} \end{cases}$

  $\zeta(\mathbf{sh_3}) = \begin{cases} 128/1[x] \mapsto \mathbf{sh_2} & ; 1/2[x] \mapsto \mathbf{sh_2} \\ 64/3[x] \mapsto \mathbf{sh_2} \end{cases}$

  specifying that any packet sent to an address which is not directly reachable from $\mathbf{sh_1}$ *(resp.* $\mathbf{sh_3}$*) is routed to* $\mathbf{sh_2}$ *and*
- $\zeta(\mathbf{sh_2}) = \{ \ 97/3[x] \mapsto \mathbf{sh_3} \ ; 17/4[x] \mapsto \mathbf{sh_1}$

The questions we are interested in are the same as for single firewalls. Which packets reach their final destination? Which ones are dropped? However, the analysis becomes more complicated in this case. Indeed, comparing to the case of a single firewall where the decision of accepting or dropping a packet is taken locally, in the case of a network topology, there is potentially an important number of intermediate steps between the moment a packet is sent and the moment it is received at its final destination (or dropped).

In other terms, a packet can be in different states: sent, received, about to be filtered by a given security host, ... The following figure represents an example of successive states in which a packet p can be:

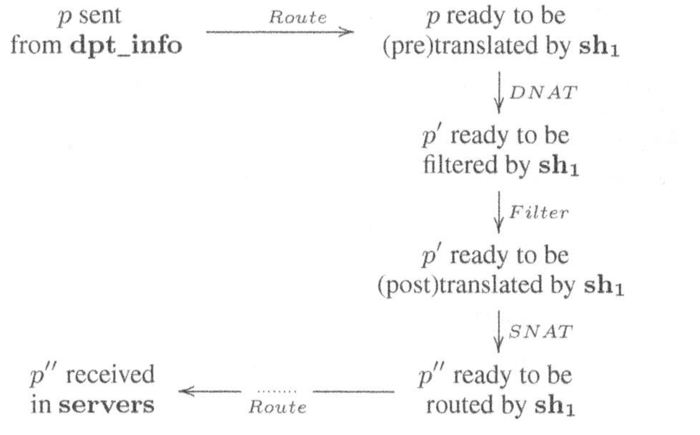

To analyse the traffic under a network security policy, our approach consists in labeling packets to indicate their current state and describing their state evolution as a rewriting process. To represent states, we introduce the following symbols:

sent	: Net × SrcAddr × DestAddr	⇀ State
received	: Net × SrcAddr × DestAddr	⇀ State
pre	: SH × SrcAddr × DestAddr	⇀ State
post	: SH × SrcAddr × DestAddr	⇀ State
filter	: SH × SrcAddr × DestAddr	⇀ State
route	: SH × SrcAddr × DestAddr	⇀ State

To conform with the classical idea that a security policy evaluates access requests to decisions, we use, for any network topology, the following vocabulary:

- network access requests refer to ground terms of the form $\mathbf{sent}(\mathbf{net}, \mathbf{from}(t_1, t_2), \mathbf{dest}(t_3, t_4))$ for some $\mathbf{net} \in \mathcal{T}^{\mathsf{Net}}$, and ground terms t_1, t_2, t_3 and t_4 such that $t_1 = \sigma(t)$ for $t = \Delta(\mathbf{net})$, and some ground substitution σ and
- decisions refer to either **drop** or ground terms of head **received**.

We denote by $\mathcal{Request}$ the set of network access requests and by $\mathcal{Decision}$ the set of decisions.

As for single firewalls, any network security policy $\wp$ is associated to a function which takes as input a packet together with the subnetwork it is sent from and returns drop (if the packet is dropped during its transmission) or the corresponding delivered packet together with the recipient subnetwork.

DEFINITION 8 (Semantics *w.r.t.* a routing strategy). *Given a network security policy $\wp$ over a topology τ and a routing strategy ζ sound w.r.t. τ, we call* semantics *of $\wp$ w.r.t. ζ and we denote by $[\![\wp]\!]_\zeta$ the (partial or total) function associating any request $r \in \mathcal{Request}$ with a decision $d \in \mathcal{Decision}$, when it exists, such that $r \xrightarrow{*}_{\mathrm{Flow}_{\wp,\zeta}} d$ with $\mathrm{Flow}_{\wp,\zeta}$ the term rewrite system defined in Figure 4.*

The rewrite system $\mathrm{Flow}_{\wp,\zeta}$ can be built for any network security policy $\wp$ and routing strategy ζ, and computes the successive states of a given packet during its traversal of the network. Note that, by construction and due to the conditions imposed on ζ, $\mathrm{Flow}_{\wp,\zeta}$ is deterministic in the sense that for any ground term t, there exists at most one t' such that $t \rightarrow_{\mathrm{Flow}_{\wp,\zeta}} t'$.

To make clear the role of each rule scheme, the figure is divided into five categories corresponding to the functionality the corresponding rules specify. The rule scheme (B) expresses that two hosts from the same subnetwork can communicate without going through a security host. (R_1) expresses that a packet which is sent from a given subnetwork net toward another subnetwork must pass through the gateway of net. (R_2) describes the packet forwarding from a security host to the one selected by the routing rules. (R_3) indicates that if no routing rule applies and if the packet destination belongs to a subnetwork connected to the current security host, then the packet must be delivered to its recipient. $(DNAT_1)$ and $(SNAT_1)$ describe the address translation process when the packet matches a NAT rule whereas $(DNAT_2)$ and $(SNAT_2)$ express that a packet that does not match any NAT rule should only change its state. Finally, (F_{drop}) (resp. (F_{accept})) specifies that a packet is dropped or forwarded according to the filtering rules of the current security host.

4.2 Policy properties

In this section, we discuss some crucial policy properties and see how the rewrite-based encoding we proposed allows us to reason about these properties.

As mentioned previously, completeness is the ability to take a decision for every network access request. In the case of a single firewall, for verifying this property it is sufficient to check that the set of filtering rules covers all possible packets. However, the case of a network security policy is more complicated. Indeed, incompleteness is obtained due to an incomplete firewall or due to the fact that a packet is never neither dropped nor delivered to its final destination (in the latter case, we say that the packet is lost).

DEFINITION 9 (Completeness). *A network security policy $\wp$ over a network topology τ is* complete *w.r.t. a routing strategy ζ, or simply ζ-*complete*, if for any $r \in \mathcal{Request}$, there exists $d \in \mathcal{Decision}$ such that $[\![\wp]\!]_\zeta (r) = d$.*

Notice that a network security policy can be complete even if the firewalls it is made of are not complete and conversely, it can be incomplete even if all the firewalls it contains are complete.

PROPOSITION 3. *For any network security policy $\wp$ and routing strategy ζ, the ζ-completeness of $\wp$ is decidable.*

More precisely, we have the following property:

PROPOSITION 4. *Given a network security policy $\wp$ over a network topology τ and a routing strategy ζ, the sets:*

- $(\rightarrow^*_{\mathrm{Flow}_{\wp,\zeta}})^{-1}(\mathbf{drop})$ *and*
- $(\rightarrow^*_{\mathrm{Flow}_{\wp,\zeta}})^{-1}(\mathcal{Decision} \setminus \mathbf{drop})$

are effectively regular.

PROOF. *The proofs of Propositions 3 and 4 are based on the fact that $\mathrm{Flow}_{\wp,\zeta}$ is a constrained growing rewrite system. The method [26] used for computing a tree automaton which recognizes the set $(\rightarrow^*_{\mathrm{R}})^{-1}(L)$ for any regular tree language L and growing rewrite system R can be extended to constrained growing rewrite systems (the proof is given in Appendix A). Since $\{\mathbf{drop}\}$ and $\mathcal{Decision} \setminus \{\mathbf{drop}\}$ are regular sets, we can build the tree automata which recognize $(\rightarrow^*_{\mathrm{Flow}_{\wp,\zeta}})^{-1}(\mathbf{drop})$ and $(\rightarrow^*_{\mathrm{Flow}_{\wp,\zeta}})^{-1}(\mathcal{Decision} \setminus \mathbf{drop})$. The completeness of a security policy can be verified by checking that the union of these two automata covers $\mathcal{Request}$.* □

Even if a routing strategy is sound, the presence of address translation rules may cause routing loops. Indeed, some packets can be caught into a loop involving two or more NAT steps which are contradictory. For example, a security host s may translate a packet p into p' and route it to s' which may translate p' into p before routing it to s. Routing loops may significantly impact the quality of traffic and may even create a denial of service. We say that a routing strategy is *safe* under a security policy if the policy creates no routing loop. It is easy to see that the size of rewritten terms is not increased during the rewriting process by $\mathrm{Flow}_{\wp,\zeta}$ and thus only loops can lead to the non-termination of the rewrite system. Consequently, we obtain:

PROPOSITION 5 (Safe routing). *Given a security policy $\wp$ over a topology τ together with a routing strategy ζ, ζ is* safe *under $\wp$ iff $\mathrm{Flow}_{\wp,\zeta}$ is terminating.*

We have considered so far only security policies *w.r.t.* static routing strategies. However, in practice, only small networks use manually configured routing. Most of the time networks have a too complex or a rapidly changing topology which makes the definition of a static routing strategy unfeasible. Moreover, with the growing complexity of networks, the notions of performance and efficiency of the routing process appear and thus, the routes should be continuously calculated to take into account the situation of the traffic and to find the best paths, that is the shortest, the most reliable or those

Broadcast

$$(B)\quad \mathbf{sent}(\mathbf{net},x,y) \to \mathbf{received}(\mathbf{net},x,y) \quad \| \quad y \in rec(\mathbf{dest}(\Delta(net),z))$$
for any $\mathbf{net} \in \mathsf{Net}$

Route

$$(R_1)\quad \mathbf{sent}(\mathbf{net},x,y) \to \mathbf{pre}(\mathbf{s},x,y) \quad \| \quad y \in \overline{rec(\mathbf{dest}(\Delta(net),z))}$$
for any $\mathbf{net} \in \mathsf{Net}$, $s = \mathcal{GW}(\mathbf{net})$

$$(R_2)\quad \mathbf{route}(\mathbf{s},x,y) \to \mathbf{pre}(\mathbf{s'},x,y) \quad \| \quad y \in rec(\mathbf{dest}(t,z))$$
for any $(s,t,s') \in \zeta$

$$(R_3)\quad \mathbf{route}(\mathbf{s},x,y) \to \mathbf{received}(\mathbf{net},x,y) \quad \| \quad y \in rec(\mathbf{dest}(\Delta(net),z))$$
for any $s \in \mathsf{SH}$, $\mathbf{net} \in \mathsf{Net}$, *such that* $\mathcal{GW}(\mathbf{net}) = s$

Destination NAT

$$(DNAT_1)\quad \mathbf{pre}(\mathbf{s},x,y) \to \mathbf{filter}(\mathbf{s},x,r) \quad \| \quad y \in rec(l \to r/\mathrm{Pre}_{\mathfrak{f}})$$
for any $s \in \mathsf{SH}$, $\mathfrak{f} = \wp(\mathbf{s})$, $l \to r \in \mathrm{Pre}_{\mathfrak{f}}$

$$(DNAT_2)\quad \mathbf{pre}(\mathbf{s},x,y) \to \mathbf{filter}(\mathbf{s},x,y) \quad \| \quad y \in \overline{\bigcup_{r \in \mathrm{Pre}_{\mathfrak{f}}} rec(r)}$$
for any $s \in \mathsf{SH}$, $\mathfrak{f} = \wp(\mathbf{s})$

Filter

$$(F_{drop})\quad \mathbf{filter}(\mathbf{s},x,y) \to \mathbf{drop} \quad \| \quad \mathbf{packet}(x,y) \in \bigcup_{l \to \mathbf{drop} \in \mathrm{Filter}_{\mathfrak{f}}} rec(l \to \mathbf{drop}/\mathrm{Filter}_{\mathfrak{f}})$$
for any $s \in \mathsf{SH}$, $\mathfrak{f} = \wp(\mathbf{s})$

$$(F_{accept})\quad \mathbf{filter}(\mathbf{s},x,y) \to \mathbf{post}(\mathbf{s},x,y) \quad \| \quad \mathbf{packet}(x,y) \in \bigcup_{l \to \mathbf{accept} \in \mathrm{Filter}_{\mathfrak{f}}} rec(l \to \mathbf{accept}/\mathrm{Filter}_{\mathfrak{f}})$$
for any $s \in \mathsf{SH}$, $\mathfrak{f} = \wp(\mathbf{s})$

Source NAT

$$(SNAT_1)\quad \mathbf{post}(\mathbf{s},x,y) \to \mathbf{route}(\mathbf{s},r,y) \quad \| \quad x \in rec(l \to r/\mathrm{Post}_{\mathfrak{f}})$$
for any $s \in \mathsf{SH}$, $\mathfrak{f} = \wp(\mathbf{s})$, $l \to r \in \mathrm{Post}_{\mathfrak{f}}$

$$(SNAT_2)\quad \mathbf{post}(\mathbf{s},x,y) \to \mathbf{route}(\mathbf{s},x,y) \quad \| \quad x \in \overline{\bigcup_{r \in \mathrm{Post}_{\mathfrak{f}}} rec(r)}$$
for any $s \in \mathsf{SH}$, $\mathfrak{f} = \wp(\mathbf{s})$

Figure 4. Rewrite system $\mathrm{Flow}_{\wp,\zeta}$ computing the traffic under a network security policy $\wp$ *w.r.t.* ζ

balancing best the network load. That is why adaptive routing, or dynamic routing, is widely used.

In this context, it is crucial that any packet has the same sort independently of the selected routing path it follows; it should be either delivered to the same recipient or dropped in all the cases. In other terms, routing should be a strategy for achieving a goal and should not alter the goal. We call consistency the property ensuring that the semantics of a security policy is the same for any (sound) routing strategy.

DEFINITION 10 (Consistency). *A network security policy* $\wp$ *over a network topology* τ *is* consistent *iff for any routing strategies* ζ *and* ζ' *sound w.r.t.* τ, $[\![\wp]\!]_{\zeta} = [\![\wp]\!]_{\zeta'}$.

We express the consistency of a policy as a property over a new rewrite system. Given a network security policy $\wp$, we define $\mathrm{Flow}_{\wp}$ as the left-linear rewrite system describing all possible packet traversal scenarios *w.r.t.* any sound routing strategy, *i.e.* which rewrites any request r into $d \in \mathcal{Decision}$ iff there exists a strategy ζ such that $[\![\wp]\!]_{\zeta}(r) = d$ and which rewrites it into a normal form which is not a decision if there exists no ζ such that $r \in \mathscr{D}([\![\wp]\!]_{\zeta})$. The rewrite system $\mathrm{Flow}_{\wp}$ is built out from the following signature:

$$
\begin{array}{lcrl}
\bot, \top & : & & \to \mathsf{Bool} \\
\langle \_, \ldots, \_ \rangle_{\_} & : & \overbrace{\mathsf{Bool} \times \ldots \times \mathsf{Bool}}^{m\ times} \times \mathsf{SH} & \to \mathsf{Context} \\
:: & : & \mathsf{Context} \times \mathsf{Trace} & \to \mathsf{Trace} \\
\# & : & & \to \mathsf{Trace} \\
\mathbf{sent} & : & \mathsf{Net} \times \mathsf{SrcAddr} \times \mathsf{DestAddr} & \to \mathsf{State} \\
\mathbf{received} & : & \mathsf{Net} \times \mathsf{SrcAddr} \times \mathsf{DestAddr} & \to \mathsf{State} \\
\mathbf{pre} & : & \mathsf{Trace} \times \mathsf{SrcAddr} \times \mathsf{DestAddr} & \to \mathsf{State} \\
\mathbf{post} & : & \mathsf{Trace} \times \mathsf{SrcAddr} \times \mathsf{DestAddr} & \to \mathsf{State} \\
\mathbf{filter} & : & \mathsf{Trace} \times \mathsf{SrcAddr} \times \mathsf{DestAddr} & \to \mathsf{State} \\
\mathbf{route} & : & \mathsf{Trace} \times \mathsf{SrcAddr} \times \mathsf{DestAddr} & \to \mathsf{State}
\end{array}
$$

where m is the number of security hosts. We modify the rewrite system presented in Figure 4 as follows (we only show modifications concerning the rewrite part of the rules - the constraints are unchanged):

(R_1) becomes $\mathbf{sent}(\mathbf{net},x,y) \to \mathbf{pre}(\langle \bot, \ldots, \bot \rangle_{\mathbf{s}}::\#, x, y)$;

(R_2) becomes $\mathbf{route}(\langle x_1, \ldots, \underbrace{\bot}_{index\ of\ \mathbf{s}'}, \ldots, x_m \rangle_{\mathbf{s}}::q, x, y) \to$

$$\mathbf{pre}(\langle x_1, \ldots, \underbrace{\top}_{index\ of\ \mathbf{s}'}, \ldots, \underbrace{\top}_{index\ of\ \mathbf{s}}, \ldots, x_m \rangle_{\mathbf{s}'}:: \langle x_1, \ldots, \underbrace{\top}_{index\ of\ \mathbf{s}'}, \ldots, x_m \rangle_{\mathbf{s}}::q, x, y)$$

(R_3) $\mathbf{route}(\langle x_1, \ldots, x_m \rangle_{\mathbf{s}}::q, x, y) \to \mathbf{received}(\mathbf{net}, x, y)$;

$(DNAT_1)$ $\mathbf{pre}(\langle x_1, \ldots, x_m \rangle_{\mathbf{s}}::q, x, y)$

$$\rightarrow \mathbf{filter}(\langle \bot, \ldots, \bot \rangle_{\mathbf{s}}::\#, x, r)$$

and $(SNAT_1)$ is built in the same way. A new rule is added:

$$(R_{back})\ \mathbf{route}(\langle \underbrace{x_1, \ldots, x_m}_{x_i = \top \text{ for each } (\mathbf{s}, \mathbf{s_i}) \in \mathcal{CON}} \rangle_{\mathbf{s}}::q, x, y) \rightarrow \mathbf{route}(q, x, y).$$

Roughly speaking, it chooses non-deterministically all the possible routes in order to reach all the possible decisions. The term $\langle t_1, \ldots, t_n \rangle_{\mathbf{s}}$ indicates that the packet is currently treated by the security host $\mathbf{s}$ and that the packet went through $\mathbf{s_i}$ iff $t_i = \top$. If the packet is translated, then the trace is reinitialized since from the network point of view this is another packet. If we have explored a path which does not lead to a decision, then the term backtracks:

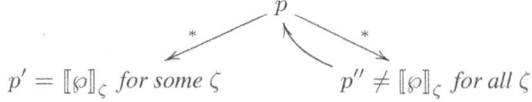

$$p \xrightarrow{*} p' = [\![\wp]\!]_\zeta \text{ for some } \zeta \qquad p \xrightarrow{*} p'' \neq [\![\wp]\!]_\zeta \text{ for all } \zeta$$

To ensure the termination of the exploration precess, packets are labeled with the set of branches they have already explored. Thus, we obtain a rewrite systems which rewrites any request into all the possible decisions according to any sound routing strategies. More precisely, we obtain a system verifying the following proposition.

PROPOSITION 6. *Let $\wp$ be a network security policy over a network topology τ.* $\mathrm{Flow}_\wp$ *is terminating iff any sound routing strategy is safe under $\wp$. In a such case, $\wp$ is consistent iff* $\mathrm{Flow}_\wp$ *is ground confluent.*

PROOF. *One can easily show that $r \xrightarrow{*}_{\mathrm{Flow}_\wp} d \in \mathcal{D}ecision$ iff there is a strategy ζ such that $[\![\wp]\!]_\zeta(r) = d$. Starting from that, the equivalence between the consistency of $\wp$ and the ground confluence of* $\mathrm{Flow}_\wp$ *stands iff for any routing strategies ζ and ζ', $\mathscr{D}([\![\wp]\!]_\zeta) = \mathscr{D}([\![\wp]\!]_{\zeta'})$. Since we consider only sound strategies, when a request cannot be solved, only two cases can occur: either the request involves a non-routable address or the strategy is not safe. In the former case, the request cannot be solved for any sound strategy. Thus, if all strategies are safe, they have all the same domain.* □

EXAMPLE 6. *Let us consider the policy described in Example 4. We can automatically prove (using A3PAT (CiME) [12] and AProVE [21]) that* $\mathrm{Flow}_\wp$ *is terminating and thus that any sound routing strategy is safe under $\wp$. We also attempted a paper proof for the consistency of $\wp$ but the property is not verified in this case. The following rewriting derivations prove that $\wp$ is not consistent.*

$$\mathbf{sent}(\mathbf{secretariat}, \mathbf{from}(195, 32), \mathbf{dest}(49, 25))$$
$$\downarrow^*$$
$$\mathbf{route}(\mathbf{sh_2}::\#, \mathbf{from}(195, 32), \mathbf{dest}(49, 25))$$
$$\downarrow^*$$
$$\mathbf{route}(\mathbf{sh_3}::\mathbf{sh_2}::\#, \mathbf{from}(195, 32), \mathbf{dest}(49, 25))$$
$$\downarrow^*$$
$$\mathbf{drop}$$

$$\mathbf{pre}(\mathbf{sh_1}::\mathbf{sh_2}::\#, \mathbf{from}(195, 32), \mathbf{dest}(49, 25))$$
$$\downarrow^*$$
$$\mathbf{route}(\mathbf{sh_1}::\#, \mathbf{from}(17, 8080), \mathbf{dest}(49, 25))$$
$$\downarrow^*$$
$$\mathbf{route}(\mathbf{sh_2}::\mathbf{sh_1}::\#, \mathbf{from}(17, 8080), \mathbf{dest}(49, 25))$$
$$\downarrow^*$$
$$\mathbf{route}(\mathbf{sh_3}::\mathbf{sh_2}::\mathbf{sh_1}::\#, \mathbf{from}(17, 8080), \mathbf{dest}(49, 25))$$
$$\downarrow^*$$
$$\mathbf{received}(\mathbf{servers}, \mathbf{from}(17, 8080), \mathbf{dest}(49, 25))$$

This above derivations show also that, under some specific routing strategy, hosts from the subnetwork **secretariat** *can exploit the server 1 to attack the subnetwork* **servers**.

We should mention that the specification of the network traffic as a rewrite system offers us two other possibilities non detailed in this paper. Indeed, semantic (dis)unification techniques [27] provide a way to perform query analyses similar to the ones briefly discussed for standalone firewalls and to detect covert channels by solving the following equation modulo $\mathrm{Flow}_\wp$:

$$\begin{aligned} &\mathbf{sent}(n, \mathbf{from}(x, x'), \mathbf{dest}(y, y')) = \mathbf{drop} \\ \wedge\ &\mathbf{sent}(n, \mathbf{from}(x_1, x_2), \mathbf{dest}(y_1, y_2)) \\ &\quad = \mathbf{received}(n', \mathbf{from}(x, x'), \mathbf{dest}(y, y')) \end{aligned}$$

In order to use specific tools and techniques to check the properties of the rewrite system $\mathrm{Flow}_\wp$, one must represent it as an unconstrained rewrite system. For that, we use the fact that automata used in our constrained rewrite systems are all based on prefix-automata. Since for any prefix-based automaton A, we can compute a finite set of linear terms $\{t_1, \ldots, t_n\}$ such that $\cup_i rec(t_i) = \mathcal{L}(A)$ and (t_i, t_j) not unifiable for any $i \neq j$, we can transform any rule of our constrained rewrite systems into an equivalent finite set of rules which do not overlap. We obtain a finite left-linear rewrite system containing only trivial overlaps (between rules corresponding to the routing).

5. Conclusion

We have proposed in this paper an approach to describe firewalls using rewrite systems and automata. We have shown that this approach can be used to perform several kinds of analyses not only for standalone firewalls but also for routed networks of firewalls. In both cases we consider firewalls that can handle NAT rules.

We have shown that this rewrite based specification of firewalls is adapted for verifying usual properties related to the semantics of a firewall (such as completeness) and to perform firewall comparisons. We can also detect the so-called misconfigurations and perform query analyses. Moreover, all these analyses can be performed in the same formalisms and using the same tools.

The same rewrite based approach has been used to specify a network topology together with routing rules and firewall policies. The obtained rewrite system provides an executable specification of the network traffic under the security policy and, because of its form (left-linear, etc.), can be used to effectively perform completeness, reachability and consistency verifications. Some properties, like the consistency, are considered *w.r.t.* a routing policy or for any routing policy.

The modeling hypotheses assumed in this paper allow us to apply the obtained results in real cases. In particular, the automata operations needed here can be performed quite efficiently. Furthermore, one of the main advantages of using rewrite systems is the possibility to use automatic tools for verifying their properties. Indeed, termination of rewrite systems can be proved using A3PAT (CiME) [12], AProVE [21] or TTT [25] for example while confluence can be checked using ACP (Automated Confluence Prover) [3] and ground confluence with CrC Maude [15]. Moreover, reachability analysis can be performed using Autowrite [16, 17] (which implements the reachability problem for left-linear growing term rewrite system) or Timbuk [19] and efficient simulations of network traffics can be done using Tom [5], ELAN [8] or Maude [9].

We have already started the implementation of the approach presented here. The rewrite systems could be automatically generated starting from a given topology and a security policy, and the preliminary results are quite promising.

There are numerous perspectives to this work. Let us just mention that we plan to extend the approach in order to take into account statefull firewalls and to model proxy abilities. More precisely, to completely model TCP connections, we will consider sequences of packets instead of single packets. This should allow us to capture other vulnerabilities such as, for example, denial of services caused by unshared memories of firewalls. Moreover, since proxy abilities essentially consist in rewriting sequences of packets, rewrite systems seem to be particularly suitable to model them.

Acknowledgment

The authors would like to thank Jean-Christophe Bach for fruitful discussions and the anonymous referees for their useful comments. This work was partially supported by the French SSURF ANR project and by a Region Lorraine fellowship.

References

[1] ABBES, T., BOUHOULA, A., AND RUSINOWITCH, M. An inference system for detecting firewall filtering rules anomalies. In *ACM Symposium on Applied Computing* (2008), ACM, pp. 2122–2128.

[2] AL-SHAER, E., HAMED, H., BOUTABA, R., AND HASAN, M. Conflict classification and analysis of distributed firewall policies. In *IEEE Journal on Selected Areas in Communications* (2005), vol. 23, pp. 2069 - 2084.

[3] AOTO, T., YOSHIDA, J., AND TOYAMA, Y. Proving confluence of term rewriting systems automatically. In *20th International Conference on Rewriting Techniques and Applications* (2009), Lecture Notes in Computer Science, Springer, pp. 93–102.

[4] BAADER, F., AND NIPKOW, T. *Term rewriting and all that.* Cambridge University Press, 1998.

[5] BALLAND, E., BRAUNER, P., KOPETZ, R., MOREAU, P.-E., AND REILLES, A. Tom: Piggybacking rewriting on java. In *18th Conference on Rewriting Techniques and Applications* (2007), Lecture Notes in Computer Science, Springer, pp. 36–47.

[6] BENELBAHRI, A., AND BOUHOULA, A. Tuple based approach for anomalies detection within firewall filtering rules. In *12th IEEE Symposium on Computers and Communications* (2007), IEEE, pp. 63–70.

[7] BOURDIER, T. Tree automata based semantics of firewalls. In *6th International Conference on Network and Information Systems Security* (2011), IEEE.

[8] BOROVANSKÝ, P., KIRCHNER, C., KIRCHNER, H., MOREAU, P.-E., AND RINGEISSEN, C. An overview of elan. In *2nd International Workshop on Rewriting Logic and its Applications* (1998), Electronic Notes in Theoretical Computer Science, Elsevier Science Publishers B. V., pp. 329–344.

[9] CLAVEL, M., ET AL., Eds. *All About Maude - A High-Performance Logical Framework* (2007), vol. 4350 of *Lecture Notes in Computer Science*, Springer.

[10] COMON, H., DAUCHET, M., GILLERON, R., JACQUEMARD, F., LUGIEZ, D., TISON, S., AND TOMMASI, M. Tree automata techniques and applications. Available on: http://gforge.inria.fr/projects/tata/, 2008.

[11] CONOBOY, B., AND FICTNER, E. Ip filter based firewalls howto. Available on: http://www.obfuscation.org/ipf/ipf-howto.pdf, 2002.

[12] CONTEJEAN, É., PASKEVICH, A., URBAIN, X., COURTIEU, P., PONS, O., AND FOREST, J. A3PAT, an approach for certified automated termination proofs. In *ACM SIGPLAN Workshop on Partial evaluation and program manipulation* (2010), ACM, pp. 63–72.

[13] CUPPENS, F., CUPPENS-BOULAHIA, N., AND GARCIA-ALFARO, J. Detection and removal of firewall misconfiguration. In *IASTED International Conference on Communication, Network and Information Security* (2005), ACTA Press.

[14] CUPPENS, F., CUPPENS-BOULAHIA, N., AND GARCIA ALFARO, J. Detection of network security component misconfiguration by rewriting and correlation. In *1st Conference on Network and Information Systems Security* (2006).

[15] DURÁN, F., AND MESEGUER, J. A Church-Rosser checker tool for conditional order-sorted equational Maude specifications. In *Rewriting Logic and Its Applications* (2010), Lecture Notes in Computer Science, Springer, pp. 69–85.

[16] DURAND, I. Autowrite: A Tool for Checking Properties of Term Rewriting Systems. In *13th Conference on Rewriting Techniques and Applications* (2002), Lecture Notes in Computer Science, Springer, pp. 371–375.

[17] DURAND, I. Autowrite version 4, 2011. http://dept-info.labri.u-bordeaux.fr/~idurand/autowrite/.

[18] ERONEN, P., AND ZITTING, J. An expert system for analyzing firewall rules. In *Nordic Work. on Secure IT Systems* (2001), pp. 100–107.

[19] FEUILLADE, G., GENET, T., AND VIET TRIEM TONG, V. Reachability analysis over term rewriting systems. In *2nd International Joint Conference on Automated Reasoning* (2004), Lecture Notes in Computer Science, Springer, pp. 341–383.

[20] FULLER, V., AND LI, T. *Classless Inter-Domain Routing (CIDR): The Internet Address Assignment and Aggregation Plan*. The Internet Society, 2006. RFC 4632.

[21] GIESL, J., SCHNEIDER-KAMP, P., AND THIEMANN, R. AProVE 1.2: Automatic termination proofs in the dependency pair framework. In *3rd International Joint Conference on Automated Reasoning* (2006), Lecture Notes in Computer Science, Springer, pp. 281–286.

[22] GOUDA, M., AND LIU, A. Firewall design: Consistency, completeness, and compactness. In *24th International Conference on Distributed Computing Systems* (2004), IEEE, pp. 320–327.

[23] HAMED, H., AND AL-SHAER, E. Taxonomy of conflicts in network security policies. *IEEE Communications Magazine 44*, 3 (2006), 134–141.

[24] HAZELHURST, S. Algorithms for analysing firewall and router access lists. Tech. Rep. TR-WITS-CS-1999-5, University of the Witwatersrand, South Africa, 2000.

[25] HIROKAWA, N., AND MIDDELDORP, A. Tyrolean termination tool. In *16th International Conference on Rewriting Techniques and Applications* (2005), Lecture Notes in Computer Science, Springer, pp. 175–184.

[26] JACQUEMARD, F. Decidable approximations of term rewriting systems. In *7th International Conference on Rewriting Techniques and Applications* (1996), Lecture Notes in Computer Science, Springer, pp. 362–376.

[27] JOUANNAUD, J.-P., AND KIRCHNER, C. Solving equations in abstract algebras: a rule-based survey of unification. In *Computational Logic: Essays in Honor of Alan Robinson*. The MIT-Press, 1991, ch. 8, pp. 257–321.

[28] KIRCHNER, C., KIRCHNER, H., AND DE OLIVEIRA, A. Analysis of rewrite-based access control policies. In *3rd International Workshop on Security and Rewriting Techniques* (2009), Electronic Notes in Theoretical Computer Science, Elsevier Science Publishers B. V., pp. 55–75.

[29] LIU, A. Formal verification of firewall policies. In *IEEE International Conference on Communications* (2008), IEEE, pp. 1494 - 1498.

[30] LIU, A., GOUDA, M., MA, H., AND NGU, A. Firewall queries. *8th International Conference on Principles of Distributed Systems* (2005), Lecture Notes in Computer Science, Springer, pp. 197–212.

[31] LIU, A. X., AND GOUDA, M. G. Firewall policy queries. *IEEE Transactions on Parallel and Distributed Systems 20*, 6 (2009), 766–777.

[32] NELSON, T., BARRATT, C., DOUGHERTY, D., FISLER, K., AND KRISHNAMURTHI, S. The margrave tool for firewall analysis. In *24th international conference on Large installation system administration* (2010), USENIX Association, pp. 1–8.

[33] RUSSELL, R. Linux 2.4 packet filtering howto. Available on: http://www.netfilter.org/documentation, 2002.

A. Reachability for CGRS

We adapt the result from [26]. Without restriction, we can consider that any CGRS is a set of rules of one of the following forms

$$x \to r[x] \quad \| \quad x \in A \tag{1}$$

$$f(x_1, \ldots, x_n) \to r[x_1, \ldots, x_n] \quad \| \quad \bigwedge_{i=1}^{n} x_i \in A_i \tag{2}$$

knowing that any unconstrained variable x can be seen as a variable constrained by $x \in A$ where A is the automaton recognizing all ground terms. Thus, we consider that any variable is constrained.

Let be L a regular language recognized by A_L and R a CGRS. The automaton recognizing $(\xrightarrow{*}_{\mathrm{R}})^{-1}(L)$ is built as follows:

$$\mathcal{R}each_0 = (Q, Q_0, \Delta_0) := \biguplus_{(l \to r \| C) \in \mathrm{R}} \left(\biguplus_{(x \in A) \in C} A \right) \uplus A_L$$

where the disjoint sum ($\uplus$) of two automata over the same signature is the automaton whose set of states, set of final states and set of rules are the union of corresponding sets of the two automata, provided that they are all disjoint. Then, we transform Δ_k ($k \geq 0$) into Δ_{k+1} by applying the following rules:

$$(i) \; \frac{\left\{ \begin{array}{l} (f(x_1, \ldots, x_n) \to g(r_1, \ldots, r_m) \| \bigwedge_i x_i \in A_i) \in \mathrm{R} \\ g(q_1, \ldots, q_m) \to q \in \Delta_k \end{array} \right.}{f(q'_1, \ldots, q'_n) \to q \in \Delta_{k+1}}$$

with the conditions:

1. for all $1 \leq i \leq n$, q'_i is a final state of A_i
2. for all $1 \leq j \leq m$, there exists a substitution $\theta : \mathcal{X} \to Q$ such that $\theta(r_j) \xrightarrow{*}_{\Delta_k} q_j$ and for each x_i occurring in $g(r_1, \ldots, r_m)$, we have $\theta(x_i) = q'_i$.

$$(ii) \; \frac{(f(x_1, \ldots, x_n) \to x \;\|\; \bigwedge_i x_i \in A_i) \in \mathrm{R} \;;\; q \in Q}{f(q'_1, \ldots, q'_n) \to q \in \Delta_{k+1}}$$

with the conditions:

1. $x = x_i$ for some $1 \leq i \leq n$
2. for all $1 \leq i \leq n$, if $x_i = x$ then $q'_i = q$, otherwise q'_i is a final state of A_i.

The desired automaton is $\mathcal{R}each = (Q, Q_L, \Delta)$ where Q_L is the set of final states of A_L.

Precision and Complexity of XQuery Type Inference

Dario Colazzo *
LRI - Université Paris Sud & Leo Team - INRIA
dario.colazzo@lri.fr

Carlo Sartiani
DMI - Università della Basilicata
sartiani@gmail.com

Abstract

A key feature of XQuery is its type system. Any language expression is statically typed and its type is used during program type-checking.

In XQuery, types of input data and functions are defined in terms of regular expression types, but it is quite easy to write queries that generate non-regular languages. As a consequence, any type system for XQuery has to rely on a *type inference* process that approximates the (possibly non-regular) output type of a query with a regular type. This approximation process, while mandatory and unavoidable, may significantly decrease the precision of the inferred types.

In this paper we will analyze the precision and the complexity of the W3C type inference algorithm. By defining an abstract model for the core of XQuery and for its type language (miniXQuery), we will identify the critical issues in the inference process and the sources of precision loss. We will also propose an alternative type inference system, used in the μXQ+ language, and show that in most cases it is more precise without any performance penalties. Finally, we will identify relevant classes of input types for which inference precision can be dramatically improved.

Categories and Subject Descriptors H.2.3 [*Information Systems*]: DATABASE MANAGEMENT—languages

General Terms Languages, Theory

Keywords XML, XQuery, Type Inference

1. Introduction

XML is a formalism for representing any kind of data, ranging from rigid and structured sources to loose semistructured data. XML diffusion is now ubiquitous and most applications leverage on XML to represent their data and to exchange them with other applications.

Many technologies for processing and manipulating XML data have been developed in the recent years. In particular, the World Wide Web Consortium (W3C) has designed a standard query language for XML data called XQuery [2]. XQuery is a functional, Turing-complete, strongly typed language that allows the programmer to navigate through an XML document (or a set of documents), to select relevant fragments of the document, and to combine them to return new documents.

A key feature of XQuery is its type system. In XQuery any language expression is statically typed and its type is used during program type-checking, even though the programmer can disable this feature.

In XQuery, types of input data and functions are defined in terms of regular expression types, but it is quite easy to write queries that generate non-regular languages. As a consequence, any type system for XQuery has to rely on a *type inference* process that approximates the (possibly non-regular) output type of a query with a regular type. This approximation process, while mandatory and unavoidable, may significantly decrease the precision of the inferred types. This is the case of the W3C proposed type system, which relies on some over-approximating rules for expressions widely used in practice (e.g., `for`-iterations). Another source of undesired over-approximation is given by rules to type horizontal and upward XPath axes, for which the type *any* is always inferred.

It is a common folklore that W3C has sacrificed precision in favor of better complexity, and that the W3C typing algorithm runs in polynomial time. An alternative and more precise approach for typing XQuery has been proposed in [6] and used as a basis for other proposals [1, 5]. This type system, used in the μXQ+ language, has a more precise type inference, at the price of a potential exponential explosion of the query output type.

Though the two above mentioned approaches are relatively well known today by the database and programming language communities, a formal, rigorous, and complete analysis showing in which cases the two proposals differ in terms of precision and complexity for type inference, is still missing. Such formal analysis could have a practical relevance as well, since it would provide important information to implementation designers.

In this paper we fill this gap by providing a first comparative analysis. Besides providing a clean and simple formalization of the main typing mechanisms of both approaches, we will formally study their complexity, show in which cases the W3C excessively over-approximates inferred types, identify cases for which inference precision can be dramatically improved, and propose new type rules to better handle these cases. We will also show that, contrary to the common belief, the W3C type system may itself infer types of exponential size wrt the query and the input size.

Paper Outline The rest of the paper is organized as follows. In Section 2 we motivate our work by showing some example of precision loss. In Section 3 we define the type language being used, while in Sections 4, 5, and 6 we present the core language miniXQuery, the W3C type system, and the μXQ+ type system. In Sections 7 and 8, then, we analyze the precision properties of the two type inference systems being studied, as well as their computational complexity. In Section 9 we discuss some related work and Section 10 concludes.

* Dario Colazzo has been partially funded by the Codex project, Agence Nationale de la Recherche, decision ANR-08- DEFIS-004.

PDPP'11, July 20–22, 2011, Odense, Denmark.

2. Motivation

Our work on the precision and the complexity of XQuery inference systems originates from the key observation that, while the type language of XQuery is based on regular expression types, it is quite easy to write queries that generate non-regular languages. This introduces approximation phenomena that may harm the result of static analysis.

Consider, for instance, the following query, where $\$db$ has type $a*$ (we use in this section a simple notation inspired by XDuce [11]):

```
<b> { for $x in $db return $x}
    { <c> </c> }
    { for $x in $db return $x}
</b>
```

This query contains two nested queries of the form `for` $\$x$ `in` $\$db$ `return` $\$x$, which iterate over a sequence of n a-element and returns each element read. The outer query returns a b-element with the following structure: $b[a^n, c, a^n]$. The language generated by the query is obviously non-regular, and is typed by the XQuery type system with $b[a*, c, a*]$. As it can be noted, this type loses the constraint between the first and the second sequence of a-elements.

While this kind of approximation phenomena cannot be avoided, as they depend on the nature of the type language, there are still other sources of approximation.

A significant example of approximation in the inference process is represented by the typing of `descendant-or-self` operations. These operations are used to recursively traverse a whole XML tree and pick all the nodes satisfying a given condition. Consider the following query, where $\$db$ has type $b, c, b*$:

```
for $x in $db::descendant-or-self::node()
return $x
```

This simple query inspects the input sequence and returns all the nodes inside the sequence. By applying the inference rules described in the W3C recommendation, we get the following type: $(b|c)*$. This type is a gross over-approximation of the real output type, as its semantics contains, for instance, c. In this case, a more precise output type would be $b, c, b*$.

Another significant source of approximation is given by the typing of `for` iterations. A `for` clause iterates over a sequence of nodes, and binds its variable to each node in the sequence. Consider the following query:

```
for $x in (<b> </b> , <c> </c> , <b> </b>)
return $x
```

This query just iterates over a sequence of three elements and returns each node in the sequence. By applying the inference rules described in the W3C specification we derive the following type: $(b \mid c)+$. In this case, the W3C inference rule for iterations over-approximates the exact output type, i.e., b, c, b, which can be derived by applying the more expensive inference rules of μXQ+. This approximation is justified by the need to keep time complexity low, hence sacrificing precision in favor of a better complexity.

The previous examples show that type inference may introduce significant approximations that may impact the development process, forcing the developer to alter correct queries, as shown by the following example.

Example 2.1 Consider the previous queries and assume they are used to populate a view with the following schema: $b+, c, b*$. When the queries are typechecked against the view schema, the compiler raises a type error in both cases, as $(b \mid c)*$ and $(b \mid c)+$ are not subtypes of $b+, c, b*$. However, the queries are perfectly legal and the error is caused by the over-approximation introduced by the inference process. ■

Types	T	::=	$()$	*empty sequence*
		|	B	*base type*
		|	$l[T]$	*element type*
		|	T, T	*sequence type*
		|	$T \mid T$	*union type*
		|	$T*$	*repetition type*
		|	$T+$	*mandatory repetition type*
		|	$T?$	*optional type*
		|	X	*type variable*
Base Type	B ::=	`String`		

Figure 1. Type language.

The previous examples, while very simple, are representative of common practical scenarios, as we will see next (Section 7), and highlight the following facts:

- low precision in type inference may be problematic;
- precision has a price to pay in terms of complexity.

In the remaining part of the paper we formally analyze features of the W3C and μXQ+ type systems that are behind the issues highlighted by previous examples. The analysis is then used to show that there is still space for improving the precision of current approaches, while keeping type inference time polynomial.

3. Type Language

The language we want to type describes forests of *unranked, node-labeled* trees and is generated by the following grammar:

$$f \quad ::= \quad () \quad | \quad b \quad | \quad l[f] \quad | \quad f, f$$

where $()$ is the empty forest; b identifies atomic values (e.g., strings and integers); $l[f]$ represents an element labeled by a label l belonging to a finite set of labels L, and having nodes in f as its children; the term f, f denotes the ordered concatenation of forests. In the following t will denote an XML tree, which can be either a base value b or an element $l[f]$

Our type language, shown in Figure 1, is based on XDuce [11] regular expression types. The language lacks full horizontal recursion and features the Kleene star $*$ operator. This restriction is canonical, and makes the type language as expressive as regular tree languages [9, 15], hence expressive enough to capture the main type mechanisms of DTD and XML Schema [3, 15, 17, 18].

To support vertical recursion, we use *type environments* and type variables. A type environment associates to each type variable a type definition; the set of variables defined by a type environment is returned by the function $\mathrm{def}(E) = \{X \mid X = T \in E\}$. The type definition associated to a given type variable can be inspected through the function $E(\cdot)$, where $E(X) = T \iff X = T \in E$.

Definition 3.1 ($E \vdash_{Def} T$) *A type T is* well-formed *in E if each variable referenced in T is defined in E.*

We restrict ourselves to element-guarded type environments, which are environments where only element-guarded vertical recursion is allowed (Definition 3.2). For example, we forbid equations such as $X = X \mid ()$ and $X = X, Y$, but allow equations such as $X = l[X \mid ()]$.

Label-Star-Variable Chains

$$e ::= \epsilon \mid l.e \mid *.e \mid X.e \qquad (e.e').e'' = e.(e'.e'') \qquad e.\epsilon = \epsilon.e = e$$

***E*-reachability**

$$l[T] \rightarrow_l^E T \qquad T* \rightarrow_*^E T$$
$$U,T \rightarrow_\epsilon^E T \qquad U,T \rightarrow_\epsilon^E U$$
$$U \mid T \rightarrow_\epsilon^E U \qquad U \mid T \rightarrow_\epsilon^E T$$

$$(X = T \in E) \Rightarrow X \rightarrow_X^E T$$
$$(T \rightarrow_e^E A \wedge A \rightarrow_{e'}^E U) \Rightarrow T \rightarrow_{e.e'}^E U$$

Figure 2. Label-Star-Variable Chains "e" and the E-reachability relation "$T \rightarrow_e^E U$".

To enforce this restriction, we require every definition of a variable X to be connected to every use of the same variable by a 'chain' of operators, one of which has to be an element type constructor $l[\_]$, where l is a label in the label set L. This is formalized by means of the relation $T \rightarrow_e^E U$ defined in Figure 2. For example, if E is $X = (m[U])*, V$, then $l[X] \rightarrow_{l.X.*.m}^E U$ holds, which means that we can reach U from $l[X]$ by crossing l, expanding X, and crossing $*$ and m (observe that $(T, U) \mid V \rightarrow_\epsilon^E U$: we do not track sequencing and union).

Definition 3.2 (Element-guarded Environments) *E is element-guarded if for each $X = T \in E$ we have $E \vdash_{Def} T$, and for each chain e we have:*

$$X \rightarrow_e^E X \Rightarrow \exists l \in L, e', e'' : e = e'.l.e''$$

The rules of the type systems being presented in this paper unfold recursive types until a tree type is met, hence element-guardedness of environments is essential to guarantee termination of these rules.

As usual, the semantics of types is defined as the minimal function that satisfies the following set of monotone equations (the function is well-defined by the Knaster-Tarski Theorem):

$$\begin{array}{lcl}
[\![()]\!]_E & \triangleq & \{()\} \\
[\![\mathsf{B}]\!]_E & \triangleq & \{b \mid b \textit{ is a base value}\} \\
[\![l[T]]\!]_E & \triangleq & \{l[f] \mid f \in [\![T]\!]_E\} \\
[\![T_1 \mid T_2]\!]_E & \triangleq & [\![T_1]\!]_E \cup [\![T_2]\!]_E \\
[\![T_1, T_2]\!]_E & \triangleq & \{f_1, f_2 \mid f_i \in [\![T_i]\!]_E\} \\
[\![X]\!]_E & \triangleq & [\![X(E)]\!]_E \\
[\![T?]\!]_E & \triangleq & [\![T \mid ()]\!]_E \\
[\![T+]\!]_E & \triangleq & [\![T]\!]_E^+ \\
[\![T*]\!]_E & \triangleq & [\![T]\!]_E^*
\end{array}$$

Subtyping is defined via type semantics, as shown below.

Definition 3.3 (Semantic subtyping) *Given two types T and U, T is a subtype of U if and only if the semantics of T is contained into the semantics of U:*

$$T \leqslant U \iff [\![T]\!]_E \subseteq [\![U]\!]_E$$

4. miniXQuery

The language miniXQuery is a minimal language modeling the FLWR core of XQuery. It contains `for`, `let`, `where`, and `return` clauses, and enables the user to specify both the child and the descendants-or-self axes. The predicate language is quite simple and comprises variable comparisons only. We distinguish between *for-variables*, e.g, $\overline{x}$, which are bound by `for` iterations, and *let-variables*, e.g., x, that are instead bound by `let` clauses. The syntax of miniXQuery is shown in Figure 3.

$$\begin{array}{lcl}
Q & ::= & () \mid b \mid l[Q] \mid Q, Q \\
 & \mid & \overline{x}\ \texttt{child} :: \textit{NodeTest} \mid \overline{x}\ \texttt{dos} :: \textit{NodeTest} \\
 & \mid & \texttt{for}\ \overline{x}\ \texttt{in}\ Q\ \texttt{return}\ Q \\
 & \mid & \texttt{for}\ \overline{x}\ \texttt{in}\ Q\ \texttt{where}\ P\ \texttt{return}\ Q \\
 & \mid & \texttt{let}\ x ::= Q\ \texttt{return}\ Q \\
 & \mid & \texttt{let}\ x ::= Q\ \texttt{where}\ P\ \texttt{return}\ Q \\
\textit{NodeTest} & ::= & \texttt{l} \mid \texttt{node()} \mid \texttt{text()}
\end{array}$$

$$\begin{array}{lcl}
P & ::= & \texttt{true} \mid \chi\ \delta\ \chi \mid \texttt{empty}(\chi) \mid P\ \texttt{or}\ P \mid \texttt{not}\ P \mid (P) \\
\chi & ::= & \overline{x} \mid x \\
\delta & ::= & = \mid <
\end{array}$$

Figure 3. The grammar of miniXQuery.

$$\begin{array}{lcl}
\texttt{true}(\rho) & \triangleq & \texttt{true} \\
(\chi\ \delta\ \chi')(\rho) & \triangleq & \exists t \in trees(\rho(\chi)), t' \in trees(\rho(\chi')).\ t\ \delta\ t' \\
(P_1\ \texttt{or}\ P_2)(\rho) & \triangleq & P_1(\rho)\ OR\ P_2(\rho) \\
\texttt{empty}((\chi))(\rho) & \triangleq & \text{if } \rho(\chi) = () \text{ then } \texttt{true} \text{ else } \texttt{false} \\
(\texttt{not}\ P)(\rho) & \triangleq & NOT\ P(\rho)
\end{array}$$

Figure 6. Predicate evaluation.

The semantics of the language and the required auxiliary functions are shown in Figures 4 and 5, where ρ is a substitution assigning a forest to each free variable in the query. We make the assumption that each ρ is well-formed, meaning that it always associates a tree t to a for-variable $\overline{x}$ it defines; also, `dos` is a shortcut for descendant-or-self. The semantics of `for` queries is defined via the operator $\prod_{t_1,\ldots,t_n} A(t_i)$, where each t_i is an XML tree, yielding the forest $A(t_1), \ldots, A(t_n)$. In Figure 4 the notation $P(\rho)$ indicates the truth value obtained by evaluating the predicate P under a variable assignment environment ρ, as indicated in Figure 6. In this figure $trees(f)$ is the set of all top-level trees of f:

$$trees(f) = \{t \mid f = f', t, f''\}$$

All the rest is self explicative.

5. W3C Type System

In this Section we will describe a core version of the W3C XQuery type system. This type system is implemented in many W3C-compliant XQuery implementations and plays a key role in the static analysis of XQuery programs.

5.1 Auxiliary definitions

The W3C inference technique relies on the notion of *prime types*. A prime type obeys the following grammar:

$$\begin{array}{lcll}
P & ::= & \mathsf{B} & \textit{base type} \\
 & \mid & l[T] & \textit{element type} \\
 & \mid & P \mid P & \textit{union type}
\end{array}$$

A prime type, hence, is a non-empty disjunction of base and element types.

Given a type T and a type environment E, we can extract a prime type from T by using the $Prime_E(T)$ function.

$$
\begin{array}{ll}
[\![b]\!]_\rho & \triangleq b \\
[\![()]\!]_\rho & \triangleq () \\
[\![\overline{x}]\!]_\rho & \triangleq \rho(\overline{x}) \\
[\![x]\!]_\rho & \triangleq \rho(x) \\
[\![Q_1, Q_2]\!]_\rho & \triangleq [\![Q_1]\!]_\rho, [\![Q_2]\!]_\rho \\
[\![l[Q]]\!]_\rho & \triangleq l[[\![Q]\!]_\rho] \\
[\![\overline{x}\ \texttt{child} :: \mathit{NodeTest}]\!]_\rho & \triangleq \mathit{childr}([\![\overline{x}]\!]_\rho) :: \mathit{NodeTest} \\
[\![\overline{x}\ \texttt{dos} :: \mathit{NodeTest}]\!]_\rho & \triangleq \mathit{dos}([\![\overline{x}]\!]_\rho) :: \mathit{NodeTest} \\
[\![\texttt{let}\ x ::= Q_1\ \texttt{return}\ Q_2]\!]_\rho & \triangleq [\![Q_2]\!]_{\rho, x \mapsto [\![Q_1]\!]_\rho}
\end{array}
$$

$$[\![\texttt{for}\ \overline{x}\ \texttt{in}\ Q_1\ \texttt{return}\ Q_2]\!]_\rho \triangleq \prod_{t_1,\ldots,t_n} [\![Q_2]\!]_{\rho, \overline{x} \mapsto t_i} \qquad \text{if } [\![Q_1]\!]_\rho = t_1, \ldots, t_n$$

$$[\![\texttt{for}\ \overline{x}\ \texttt{in}\ Q_1\ \texttt{return}\ Q_2]\!]_\rho \triangleq () \qquad \text{if } [\![Q_1]\!]_\rho = ()$$

$$[\![\texttt{let}\ x ::= Q_1\ \texttt{where}\ P\ \texttt{return}\ Q_2]\!]_\rho \triangleq \text{if } P(\rho, x \mapsto [\![Q_1]\!]_\rho) \text{ then } [\![Q_2]\!]_{\rho, x \mapsto [\![Q_1]\!]_\rho} \text{ else } ()$$

$$[\![\texttt{for}\ \overline{x}\ \texttt{in}\ Q_1\ \texttt{where}\ P\ \texttt{return}\ Q_2]\!]_\rho \triangleq \prod_{t_1,\ldots,t_n} (\text{if } P(\rho, \overline{x} \mapsto t_i) \text{ then } [\![Q_2]\!]_{\rho, \overline{x} \mapsto t_i} \text{ else } ()) \quad \text{if } [\![Q_1]\!]_\rho = t_1, \ldots, t_n$$

$$[\![\texttt{for}\ \overline{x}\ \texttt{in}\ Q_1\ \texttt{where}\ P\ \texttt{return}\ Q_2]\!]_\rho \triangleq () \qquad \text{if } [\![Q_1]\!]_\rho = ()$$

Figure 4. miniXQuery semantics.

$$
\begin{array}{llll}
\mathit{childr}(b) & \triangleq () & \mathit{childr}(l[f]) & \triangleq f \\
\mathit{dos}(b) & \triangleq b & \mathit{dos}(l[f]) & \triangleq l[f], \mathit{dos}(f) \\
\mathit{dos}(()) & \triangleq () & \mathit{dos}(f, f') & \triangleq \mathit{dos}(f), \mathit{dos}(f') \\
() :: l & \triangleq () & b :: l & \triangleq () \\
l[f] :: l & \triangleq l[f] & m[f] :: l & \triangleq () \quad m \neq l \\
(f, f') :: l & \triangleq f :: l, f' :: l & f :: \mathit{node}() & \triangleq f \\
() :: \mathit{text}() & \triangleq () & b :: \mathit{text}() & \triangleq b \\
m[f] :: \mathit{text}() & \triangleq () & (f, f') :: \mathit{text}() & \triangleq f :: \mathit{text}(), f' :: \mathit{text}()
\end{array}
$$

Figure 5. Auxiliary functions.

Definition 5.1 *$Prime_E(T)$ is inductively defined as follows:*

$$
\begin{array}{ll}
Prime_E(()) & = () \\
Prime_E(B) & = B \\
Prime_E(T_1, T_2) & = Prime_E(T_1) \mid Prime_E(T_2) \\
Prime_E(l[T]) & = l[T] \\
Prime_E(T_1 \mid T_2) & = Prime_E(T_1) \mid Prime_E(T_2) \\
Prime_E(T*) & = Prime_E(T) \\
Prime_E(T+) & = Prime_E(T) \\
Prime_E(T?) & = Prime_E(T) \\
Prime_E(X) & = Prime_E(E(X))
\end{array}
$$

Observe that, when no prime type can be extracted, this function just returns ().

Another important auxiliary function $Quant_E(T)$ returns a symbol in $\{1, +, ?, *\}$ denoting the cardinality of the type sequence of the outermost level of T.

Definition 5.2 ($Quant_E(T)$) *$Quant_E(T)$ is inductively defined as follows:*

$$
\begin{array}{ll}
Quant_E(()) & = ? \\
Quant_E(B) & = 1 \\
Quant_E(T_1, T_2) & = Quant_E(T_1), Quant_E(T_2) \\
Quant_E(l[T]) & = 1 \\
Quant_E(T_1 \mid T_2) & = Quant_E(T_1) \mid Quant_E(T_2) \\
Quant_E(T*) & = Quant_E(T).* \\
Quant_E(T+) & = Quant_E(T).+ \\
Quant_E(T?) & = Quant_E(T).? \\
Quant_E(X) & = Quant_E(E(X))
\end{array}
$$

,	1	?	+	*
1	+	+	+	+
?	+	*	+	*
+	+	+	+	+
*	+	*	+	*

|	1	?	+	*
1	1	?	+	+
?	?	?	*	*
+	+	*	+	*
*	*	*	*	*

.	1	?	+	*
1	1	?	+	*
?	?	?	*	*
+	+	*	+	*
*	*	*	*	*

Figure 7. Quantifier composition.

Quantifiers can be composed by using three operators: ',', '|', and '.'. Quantifier composition obeys the rules described in Figure 7.

A quantifier and a type can be combined by the . operator as shown below.

$$
\begin{array}{lllll}
T.1 & = & T & T.? & = & T? \\
T.+ & = & T+ & T.* & = & T*
\end{array}
$$

It will be clear from the context when . is used to combine two quantifiers together or a type and a quantifier.

It should be observed that $T \leqslant Prime_E(T).Quant_E(T)$ for any type T and any well-formed environment E.

The function $content()$ is the last auxiliary function we present here; it just extracts the content model of a given element type and it can be trivially lifted to base and union types, as shown by the following definition.

Definition 5.3 ($content()$**)** *The function content() is defined as follows:*

$$\begin{aligned} content(()) &\triangleq () \\ content(\mathsf{B}) &\triangleq () \\ content(l[T]) &\triangleq T \\ content(T_1 \mid \ldots \mid T_n) &\triangleq content(T_1) \mid \ldots \mid content(T_n) \end{aligned}$$

5.2 Judgments and variable environments

The type inference system is able to prove judgments of the form $E; \Gamma \vdash_m Q : T$, where Q is a query, Γ is an environment providing type information about the free variables of Q, and T is an upper bound for all possible values returned by Q[1]. In particular, E, Γ, and Q are intended to be the input arguments of the type inference process, while T is the output type to be inferred.

Definition 5.4 (Variable environment) *A variable environment* Γ *is a list of pairs* $\chi : T$, *where* χ *is a for-variable or a let-variable, and* T *is a type. Variable environments meet the following grammar:*

$$\textit{Variable Environments} \quad \Gamma ::= () \mid x : T, \Gamma \mid \overline{x} : T, \Gamma$$

Definition 5.5 (Variable environment variable set) *Given a variable environment* Γ, *we indicate with* $\Gamma Var(\Gamma)$ *the set of all variables defined in* Γ: $\Gamma Var(\Gamma) = \{\overline{x} \mid \overline{x} : T \in \Gamma\} \cup \{x \mid x : T \in \Gamma\}$.

A variable environment Γ is well-formed if no variable is defined twice, and if every for-variable $\overline{x}$ (i.e., a variable bound by a `for` clause) is associated to a union of tree types ($l[T']$ or B). Moreover, in the following each time we consider a variable environment Γ for a query Q, we will assume that Γ provides definitions for all free-variables of Q. $WF(E; \Gamma \vdash_m Q : U)$ means that the judgement $E; \Gamma \vdash_m Q : U$ is well-formed, that is: in Γ no variable occurs twice, and each free-variable in Q occurs (is defined) in Γ.

Beyond $E; \Gamma \vdash_m Q : T$, two auxiliary judgments are employed in our type rules. These judgments serve the purpose of keeping rules relatively simple, while allowing for a good level of precision of type inference.

The judgment $E \vdash_m S \leqslant T$ is used to test whether S is a subtype of T. The judgment $E \vdash_m T' \rightarrow_{NodeTest} U$ is used to restrict the content type T' to tree types with structure satisfying *NodeTest*. Rules to prove judgments $E \vdash_m T' \rightarrow_{NodeTest} U$ are shown in Figure 8, and their meaning is stated in the following lemma.

Lemma 5.6 (Type Filtering Checking) *For any* T:

$$E \vdash_m T \rightarrow_{NodeTest} U \Leftrightarrow [\![U]\!]_E = \{f :: \textit{NodeTest} \mid f \in [\![T]\!]_E\}$$

5.3 Type rules

The type rules for the W3C type system are shown in Figures 9 and 10. Rules in Figure 9 are shared with the μXQ+ type system, while the rules in Figure 10 are specific to the W3C type system. For reasons of space, we describe here only the most important ones.

[1] The m subscript in the judgments distinguishes the miniXQuery W3C type rules from those specific of μXQ+, which are labeled by μ.

(MATCHANYFILT)
$$\frac{}{E \vdash_m T \rightarrow_{\texttt{node()}} T}$$

(MATCHTEXTFILT)
$$\frac{}{E \vdash_m B \rightarrow_{\texttt{text()}} B}$$

(MATCHLABFILT)
$$\frac{}{E \vdash_m l[T] \rightarrow_l l[T]}$$

(NOMATCHLABFILT)
$$\frac{T = \mathsf{B} \lor T = n[T']}{E \vdash_m T \rightarrow_l ()}$$

(FORESTFILT)
$$\frac{E \vdash_m T \rightarrow_{NodeTest} T' \qquad E \vdash_m U \rightarrow_l U'}{E \vdash_m T, U \rightarrow_{NodeTest} T', U'}$$

(STARFILT)
$$\frac{E \vdash_m T \rightarrow_{NodeTest} U}{E \vdash_m T* \rightarrow_{NodeTest} U*}$$

(PLUSFILT)
$$\frac{E \vdash_m T \rightarrow_{NodeTest} U}{E \vdash_m T+ \rightarrow_{NodeTest} U+}$$

(OPTFILT)
$$\frac{E \vdash_m T \rightarrow_{NodeTest} U}{E \vdash_m T? \rightarrow_{NodeTest} U?}$$

(UNIONFILT)
$$\frac{E \vdash_m T \rightarrow_{NodeTest} T' \qquad E \vdash_m U \rightarrow_{NodeTest} U'}{E \vdash_m T \mid U \rightarrow_{NodeTest} T' \mid U'}$$

(VARFILT)
$$\frac{E \vdash_m E(X) \rightarrow_{NodeTest} U}{E \vdash_m X \rightarrow_{NodeTest} U}$$

(EMPTYFILT)
$$\frac{}{E \vdash_m () \rightarrow_{NodeTest} ()}$$

Figure 8. Filtering rules.

Rule (TYPEFOR) describes the behaviour of the type inference system when a `for`-iteration is visited. The output type is computed as follows. The rule first computes the inferred type for Q_1; from this type a *prime* type is extracted by the function $Prime_E(T_1)$, which returns the union of the uppermost base or tree types in T_1 and it can be computed in linear space and time. $Prime_E(T_1)$ is, then, bound to $\overline{x}$ in the variable environment and used to infer the output type T_2, which is further refined by the application of a quantifier in $\{1, ?, +, *\}$ ($T_2 \cdot Quant_E(T_1)$).

Rule (TYPEDOS) applies to `dos` selectors and infers a type for a $\overline{x}$ `dos` :: *NodeTest* filter. The rule essentially traverses the parse tree of T and, at each step, collects the prime types it encounters. The premise $E \vdash_m Prime_E(T_{n+1}) \leqslant Prime_E(T_1) \mid \ldots \mid Prime_E(T_n)$ is just a formal way to express the termination of the search in the parse tree and it does not involve any real subtyping operation. The rule returns a type consisting of the star-guarded union of the types collected during the exploration.

It should be observed that, while not algorithmic, these rules are deterministic. Hence, for any well-formed query Q, type environment E, and variable environment Γ, the system can infer only one type T such that $E; \Gamma \vdash_m Q : T$.

6. μXQ+ Type System

The μXQ+ specific type rules are shown in Figures 11 and 12.

$$\frac{\begin{array}{c}(\text{TYPEFOR})\\ E;\Gamma \vdash_m Q_1 : T_1 \\ E;\Gamma,\ \overline{x} : Prime_E(T_1) \vdash_m Q_2 : T_2\end{array}}{E;\Gamma \vdash_m \texttt{for}\ \overline{x}\ \texttt{in}\ Q_1\ \texttt{return}\ Q_2 : T_2.Quant_E(T_1)}$$

$$\frac{\begin{array}{c}(\text{TYPEFORWHERE})\\ E;\Gamma \vdash_m Q_1 : T_1 \\ E;\Gamma,\ \overline{x} : Prime_E(T_1) \vdash_m Q_2 : T_2\end{array}}{E;\Gamma \vdash_m \texttt{for}\ \overline{x}\ \texttt{in}\ Q_1\ \texttt{where}\ P\ \texttt{return}\ Q_2 : (T_2.Quant_E(T_1))?}$$

Figure 10. miniXQuery specific type rules.

The μXQ+ type system differs from the W3C one for the handling of `for`-iterations and `descendant-or-self` selectors. Given a query **for** $\overline{x}$ **in** Q_1 **return** Q_2, Rule (XTYPEFOR) first infers a type T_1 for Q_1. Unlike the W3C type system, where T_1 is transformed in prime form and then bound to $\overline{x}$, in the μXQ+ type system T_1 is decomposed in its basic components, and Q_2 is analyzed separately for each component of T_1. This different approach is illustrated in the following example.

Example 6.1 Consider the following basic query:

for $\overline{x}$ **in** $l[b], m[b]$
return $\overline{x}$

Rule (TYPEFOR) first infers a type $T_1 = l[\mathsf{B}], m[\mathsf{B}]$ for $l[b], m[b]$. The variable environment is, then, enriched with the binding between $\overline{x}$ and $Prime_E(T_1) = l[\mathsf{B}] \mid m[\mathsf{B}]$. As $Q_2 = \overline{x}$, the output type is just $(l[\mathsf{B}] \mid m[\mathsf{B}])+$, where $+$ is introduced by $Quant_E(T_1)$.

In the μXQ+ type system the inference process is different. Once T_1 has been inferred, Rule (TYPEINCONC) is used to infer a type for Q_2; this rule iterates over $T_1 = l[\mathsf{B}], m[\mathsf{B}]$ and returns $T_2 = l[\mathsf{B}], m[\mathsf{B}]$, without any additional $+$ or $*$ quantifier. ■

7. Precision Analysis

In this section we will compare the W3C type system and that of μXQ+ in terms of precision of the inferred types. First, we will show that the type system of μXQ+ is more precise, as it always generates a subtype of the type inferred by the W3C one. Then, we will identify some restrictions that make the two type systems equivalent in terms of precision. Finally, we will see that, if some properties are satisfied by the input type, precision can be dramatically improved.

7.1 Precision

In Example 6.1 we found that, for a very basic query iterating on a sequence of element types, the type systems being studied here behave quite differently. In particular, the W3C type system returned a type of the form $(A_1 \mid \ldots \mid A_n)+$, where A_i is an element type in the input sequence, while the μXQ+ type system inferred $A_1, \ldots, A_n$. It is straightforward to see that the latter type is a *subtype* of the former type.

This situation is not an exception. Indeed, the type inferred by μXQ+ for a query Q is always a subtype of the type inferred by the W3C system for the same query, as stated by the following theorem.

Theorem 7.1 *For each well formed* (Γ, E, Q)*:*

$$E;\Gamma \vdash_m Q : T_{w3c} \ \wedge\ E;\Gamma \vdash_\mu Q : T_\mu \ \Rightarrow\ T_\mu \leqslant T_{w3c}$$

This result tells us that the μXQ+ type system is a good and safe choice for improving the precision of inferred types, since its types are at least as precise as those returned by the W3C system.

Of course, there are several situations where the two type systems infer exactly the same type. These cases depend on both the structure of the query and the properties of the input type environment. In particular, we can identify three properties that must be satisfied to ensure the equality of the inferred types.

Definition 7.2 (Tagged-path queries) *A query Q is* tagged-path *if Q only uses XPath steps of the form* $\overline{x}$ `child` :: *NodeTest or* $\overline{x}$ `dos` :: *NodeTest with NodeTest* $\neq$ `node`().

A tagged-path query, hence, cannot use the `self` axis nor it can exploit the `node()` node test. For instance, the query of Example 6.1 is not tagged-path, as it uses the `self` axis.

Definition 7.3 (One-type environments) *Let* (Γ, E) *be well-formed. Then,* (Γ, E) *is* one-type *if, for each* $\chi : T \in \Gamma$ *and for each label* m*, there exists a type* T' *such that:*

$$\{m[U] \mid T \rightarrow^E_e m[U]\} \subseteq \{m[T']\}$$

In other words, in a one-type environment no type can contain multiple element types with the same label and different content. This property is enjoyed by DTDs, and reflects a very common scenario.

The final restriction is inspired by the notion of conflict-free types described in [8].

Definition 7.4 (Conflict-free regular expression) *A regular expression r is* conflict-free *if for each subexpression $(s \mid t)$ or (s, t): $S(s) \cap S(t) = \emptyset$, where $S(p)$ is the set of all symbols appearing in a regular expression p.*

Definition 7.5 ($RegExp_E(T)$)

$$\begin{array}{lcl} RegExp_E(()) & = & () \\ RegExp_E(B) & = & B \\ RegExp_E(l[T]) & = & l \\ RegExp_E(T*) & = & RegExp_E(T)* \\ RegExp_E(T+) & = & RegExp_E(T)+ \\ RegExp_E(T?) & = & RegExp_E(T)? \\ RegExp_E(X) & = & RegExp_E(E(X)) \\ RegExp_E(T_1, T_2) & = & RegExp_E(T_1), RegExp_E(T_2) \\ RegExp_E(T_1 \mid T_2) & = & RegExp_E(T_1) \mid RegExp_E(T_2) \end{array}$$

Definition 7.6 (Conflict-free environment) *Let* (Γ, E) *be well-formed. Then,* (Γ, E) *is* conflict-free *if for each* $X = U \in E$ *we have that* $U = l[T]$ *and* $RegExp_E(T)$ *is* conflict-free.

We can now state a theorem that sheds light on a case of equality of type inference.

(TypeEmpty)
$$\frac{\mathit{WF}(E;\Gamma \vdash_m () : ())}{E;\Gamma \vdash_m () : ()}$$

(TypeAtomic)
$$\frac{\mathit{WF}(E;\Gamma \vdash_m b : \mathsf{B})}{E;\Gamma \vdash_m b : \mathsf{B}}$$

(TypeVarLet)
$$\frac{x : T \in \Gamma \quad \mathit{WF}(E;\Gamma \vdash_m x : T)}{E;\Gamma \vdash_m x : T}$$

(TypeVarFor)
$$\frac{\overline{x} : T \in \Gamma \quad \mathit{WF}(E;\Gamma \vdash_m \overline{x} : T)}{E;\Gamma \vdash_m \overline{x} : T}$$

(TypeElem)
$$\frac{E;\Gamma \vdash_m Q : T}{E;\Gamma \vdash_m l[Q] : l[T]}$$

(TypeForest)
$$\frac{E;\Gamma \vdash_m Q_1 : T_1 \quad E;\Gamma \vdash_m Q_2 : T_2}{E;\Gamma \vdash_m Q_1, Q_2 : T_1, T_2}$$

(TypeLet)
$$\frac{\begin{array}{l} E;\Gamma \vdash_m Q_1 : T_1 \\ E;\Gamma,\ x : T_1 \vdash_m Q_2 : U \end{array}}{E;\Gamma \vdash_m \texttt{let}\ x := Q_1\ \texttt{return}\ Q_2 : U}$$

(TypeLetWhere)
$$\frac{\begin{array}{l} E;\Gamma \vdash_m Q_1 : T_1 \\ E;\Gamma,\ x : T_1 \vdash_m Q_2 : U \end{array}}{E;\Gamma \vdash_m \texttt{let}\ x ::= Q_1\ \texttt{where}\ P\ \texttt{return}\ Q_2 : U?}$$

(TypeChildNodeTest)
$$\frac{\begin{array}{l} \mathit{WF}(E;\Gamma \vdash_m \overline{x}\ \texttt{child} :: \mathit{NodeTest} : U) \\ \overline{x} : T \in \Gamma \\ (T = T'_1 \mid \ldots \mid T'_n) \wedge (T'_i = m_i[T''_i] \vee T'_i = B \vee T'_i = ()) \\ E \vdash_m \mathit{content}(T) \rightarrow_{\mathit{NodeTest}} U \end{array}}{E;\Gamma \vdash_m \overline{x}\ \texttt{child} :: \mathit{NodeTest} : U}$$

(TypeDOS)
$$\frac{\begin{array}{l} \mathit{WF}(E;\Gamma \vdash_m \overline{x}\ \texttt{dos} :: \mathit{NodeTest} : U) \\ \overline{x} : T \in \Gamma \\ (T = T'_1 \mid \ldots \mid T'_n) \wedge (T'_i = m_i[T''_i] \vee T'_i = B \vee T'_i = ()) \\ E;\Gamma \vdash_m \overline{x}\ \mathit{child} : T_1 \\ E;\Gamma,\overline{x} : \mathit{Prime}_E(T_1) \vdash_m \overline{x}\ \mathit{child} : T_2 \\ E;\Gamma,\overline{x} : \mathit{Prime}_E(T_2) \vdash_m \overline{x}\ \mathit{child} : T_3 \\ \ldots \\ E;\Gamma,\overline{x} : \mathit{Prime}_E(T_n) \vdash_m \overline{x}\ \mathit{child} : T_{n+1} \\ E \vdash_m \mathit{Prime}_E(T_{n+1}) \leqslant \mathit{Prime}_E(T_1) \mid \ldots \mid \mathit{Prime}_E(T_n) \\ U' = (\mathit{Prime}_E(T) \mid \mathit{Prime}_E(T_1) \mid \ldots \mid \mathit{Prime}_E(T_n))* \\ E \vdash_m U' \rightarrow_{\mathit{NodeTest}} U \end{array}}{E;\Gamma \vdash_m \overline{x}\ \texttt{dos} :: \mathit{NodeTest} : U}$$

Figure 9. Common type rules.

(TypeInEmpty)
$$\frac{\mathit{WF}(E;\Gamma \vdash_\mu \overline{x}\ \texttt{in}\ (\,) \rightarrow Q : (\,))}{E;\Gamma \vdash_\mu \overline{x}\ \texttt{in}\ (\,) \rightarrow Q : (\,)}$$

(TypeInAtomic)
$$\frac{E;\Gamma,\overline{x} : \mathsf{B} \vdash_\mu Q : U}{E;\Gamma \vdash_\mu \overline{x}\ \texttt{in}\ \mathsf{B} \rightarrow Q : U}$$

(TypeInEl)
$$\frac{E;\Gamma,\ \overline{x} : m[T] \vdash_\mu Q : U}{E;\Gamma \vdash_\mu \overline{x}\ \texttt{in}\ m[T] \rightarrow Q : U}$$

(TypeInConc)
$$\frac{\begin{array}{l} E;\Gamma \vdash_\mu \overline{x}\ \texttt{in}\ T_1 \rightarrow Q : T'_1 \\ E;\Gamma \vdash_\mu \overline{x}\ \texttt{in}\ T_2 \rightarrow Q : T'_2 \end{array}}{E;\Gamma \vdash_\mu \overline{x}\ \texttt{in}\ T_1, T_2 \rightarrow Q : T'_1, T'_2}$$

(TypeInStar)
$$\frac{E;\Gamma \vdash_\mu \overline{x}\ \texttt{in}\ T \rightarrow Q : U}{E;\Gamma \vdash_\mu \overline{x}\ \texttt{in}\ T* \rightarrow Q : U*}$$

(TypeInPlus)
$$\frac{E;\Gamma \vdash_\mu \overline{x}\ \texttt{in}\ T \rightarrow Q : U}{E;\Gamma \vdash_\mu \overline{x}\ \texttt{in}\ T+ \rightarrow Q : U+}$$

(TypeInOpt)
$$\frac{E;\Gamma \vdash_\mu \overline{x}\ \texttt{in}\ T \rightarrow Q : U}{E;\Gamma \vdash_\mu \overline{x}\ \texttt{in}\ T? \rightarrow Q : U?}$$

(TypeInVar)
$$\frac{E(X) = T \quad E;\Gamma \vdash_\mu \overline{x}\ \texttt{in}\ T \rightarrow Q : U}{E;\Gamma \vdash_\mu \overline{x}\ \texttt{in}\ X \rightarrow Q : U}$$

(TypeInUnion)
$$\frac{\begin{array}{l} E;\Gamma \vdash_\mu \overline{x}\ \texttt{in}\ T_1 \rightarrow Q : T'_1 \\ E;\Gamma \vdash_\mu \overline{x}\ \texttt{in}\ T_2 \rightarrow Q : T'_2 \end{array}}{E;\Gamma \vdash_\mu \overline{x}\ \texttt{in}\ T_1 \mid T_2 \rightarrow Q : T'_1 \mid T'_2}$$

Figure 11. Case analysis type rules.

(XTypeFor)
$$\frac{E;\Gamma \vdash_\mu Q_1 : T_1 \quad E;\Gamma \vdash_\mu \overline{x}\ \texttt{in}\ T_1 \rightarrow Q_2 : T_2}{E;\Gamma \vdash_\mu \texttt{for}\ \overline{x}\ \texttt{in}\ Q_1\ \texttt{return}\ Q_2 : T_2}$$

(XTypeForWhere)
$$\frac{E;\Gamma \vdash_\mu Q_1 : T_1 \quad E;\Gamma \vdash_\mu \overline{x}\ \texttt{in}\ T_1 \rightarrow Q_2 : T_2}{E;\Gamma \vdash_\mu \texttt{for}\ \overline{x}\ \texttt{in}\ Q_1\ \texttt{where}\ P\ \texttt{return}\ Q_2 : (T_2)?}$$

Figure 12. μXQ+ specific type rules.

Theorem 7.7 (Equality) *If* (Γ, E) *is one-type and conflict-free, and* Q *is tagged-path, then* $E; \Gamma \vdash_m Q : T$ *and* $E; \Gamma \vdash_\mu Q : T'$*, where* $[\![T]\!]_E = [\![T']\!]_E$.

It is interesting to observe that all these conditions are necessary to guarantee the equality of the inferred types.

Example 7.8 Consider the following query, where $\overline{db}$ has type $T = m[\mathsf{B}] \mid m[l[\mathsf{B}], n[\mathsf{B}], l[\mathsf{B}]]$.

for $\overline{x}$ **in** $\overline{db}$ **child** :: l
return $\overline{x}$

This query is tagged-path; however, the environments are not one-type and conflict-free. Rule (TYPECHILDNODETEST) computes $content(T) = \mathsf{B} \mid (l[\mathsf{B}], n[\mathsf{B}], l[\mathsf{B}])$. $content(T)$ is then filtered by using the rules of Figure 8, and $T_1 = () \mid l[\mathsf{B}], l[\mathsf{B}] = (l[\mathsf{B}], l[\mathsf{B}])?$ is returned as type for the navigational step.

Rule (TYPEFOR) binds $Prime_E(T_1) = l[\mathsf{B}]$ to $\overline{x}$ and returns $T_{w3c} = (l[\mathsf{B}]?+) = l[\mathsf{B}]*$ as result type.

Rule (XTYPEFOR), instead, navigates over $(l[\mathsf{B}], l[\mathsf{B}])?$ and returns $T_\mu = (l[\mathsf{B}], l[\mathsf{B}])?$ as result type.

As expected, $[\![T_{w3c}]\!]_E \neq [\![T_\mu]\!]_E$.

■

Example 7.9 Consider the query of the previous example and assume that $\overline{db}$ has type $T = m[l[\mathsf{B}], n[\mathsf{B}], l[\mathsf{B}]]$.

In this case, the type environments are one-type, but they fail to meet the conflict-freedom restriction.

Rule (TYPECHILDNODETEST) computes $content(T) = l[\mathsf{B}], n[\mathsf{B}], l[\mathsf{B}]$. $content(T)$ is then filtered by using the rules of Figure 8, and $T_1 = l[\mathsf{B}], l[\mathsf{B}]$ is returned as type for the navigational step.

Rule (TYPEFOR) binds $Prime_E(T_1) = l[\mathsf{B}]$ to $\overline{x}$ and returns $T_{w3c} = l[\mathsf{B}]+$ as result type.

Rule (XTYPEFOR), instead, navigates over $l[\mathsf{B}], l[\mathsf{B}]$ and returns $T_\mu = l[\mathsf{B}], l[\mathsf{B}]$ as result type.

As expected, the inferred types have different semantics. ■

Example 7.10 Consider now the query of the examples above, where $\overline{db}$ has type $T = m[l[\mathsf{B}], n[\mathsf{B}]]$. Unlike the previous examples, T is conflict-free, so we expect that the two type systems return the same type.

In this case, Rule (TYPECHILDNODETEST) returns $T_1 = l[\mathsf{B}]$. Hence, Rule (TYPEFOR) returns $T_{w3c} = l[\mathsf{B}]$ as result type, since $Quant_E(T_1) = 1$.

Rule (XTYPEFOR), instead, navigates over $l[\mathsf{B}]$ and returns $T_\mu = l[\mathsf{B}]$ as result type, as we expected. ■

As shown in the following example, situations similar to those described in the previous examples are common in real-world scenarios.

Example 7.11 Consider the following query on the well known XMark DTD [16], returning a `region` element for each region, containing the name and the number of items of the region; we assume that $\overline{x}$ is bound to the root element of an XMark instance; we use the XQuery function $name()$ returning the tag name of an XML element, and the XQuery counting function $count()$; we assume both functions returning values of type B.

```
for ȳ in x̄ child :: regions
return for z̄ in ȳ child :: node()
       return region[
                    name[name(z̄)]
                    total[count(z̄ child :: item)]]
```

In the XMark DTD, the content type of `regions` is the sequence type $(africa, asia, australia, europe, namerica, samerica)$. As a consequence, the W3C type system infers the following type: $(region[name[\mathsf{B}], total[\mathsf{B}]])+$.

However, the exact type for for this query is $region[C]$, $region[C], region[C], region[C], region[C], region[C]$, with $C = name[\mathsf{B}], total[\mathsf{B}]$. Actually this type is inferred by the μXQ+ type system, thanks to the type case analysis performed on `for`-iterations. ■

In the light of the analysis made up to now, and inspired by Theorem 7.7, we can design a new type system which mixes up advantages of the two systems being compared here. We write $E; \Gamma \vdash_H Q : T$ to indicate that the type T has been inferred from Q, Γ and E in the hybrid system. The rules of the hybrid systems are essentially those of the μXQ+ type system, with the only difference that `for`-iterations are typed by the following rules (`for-where` queries are typed in a similar way).

(TYPEFORHYBRID1)

$$\frac{\begin{array}{c} Q_1 \text{ is tagged-path} \wedge Q_2 \text{ is tagged-path} \\ (E, \Gamma) \text{ is one-type and conflict-free} \\ E; \Gamma \vdash_H Q_1 : T_1 \\ E; \Gamma,\ \overline{x} : Prime_E(T_1) \vdash_H Q_2 : T_2 \end{array}}{E; \Gamma \vdash_H \mathbf{for}\ \overline{x}\ \mathbf{in}\ Q_1\ \mathbf{return}\ Q_2 : T_2.Quant_E(T_1)}$$

(TYPEFORHYBRID2)

$$\frac{\begin{array}{c} Q_1 \text{ is not tagged-path} \vee Q_2 \text{ is not tagged-path} \vee \\ (E, \Gamma) \text{ is not one-type and conflict-free} \\ E; \Gamma \vdash_H Q_1 : T_1 \\ E; \Gamma \vdash_H \overline{x}\ \mathbf{in}\ T_1 \ \rightarrow\ Q_2 : T_2 \end{array}}{E; \Gamma \vdash_H \mathbf{for}\ \overline{x}\ \mathbf{in}\ Q_1\ \mathbf{return}\ Q_2 : T_2}$$

The resulting hybrid system has the same precision of the μXQ+ type system, but lower time consumption since the costly μXQ+ case analysis is invoked only if strictly necessary

Theorem 7.12 (Precision of the Hybrid system) *For each well formed* (Γ, E, Q)*, if* $E; \Gamma \vdash_\mu Q : T_\mu$ *and* $E; \Gamma \vdash_H Q : T_H$ *then* $[\![T_\mu]\!]_E = [\![T_H]\!]_E$.

7.2 Extensions

We found in the previous section that, under some specific circumstances, the two type systems return the same type for a given query.

In this section we will see that some restrictions on the type environment allow for an improvement of inference precision without any significant performance penalty.

7.2.1 Non-recursive Types

When the input type contains no recursive type, we can significantly improve the precision of the inferred type for `descendant-or-self` steps without affecting the computational complexity.

Indeed, given a non-recursive type T, we can define type inference for the descendant-or-self axis through the following rule:

(TYPEDOSNOREC)

$$\frac{\begin{array}{c} \overline{x} : T \in \Gamma \ \wedge\ (T = l_1[T_1'] \mid l_2[T_2'] \mid \ldots \mid l_n[T_n'] \vee T = \mathsf{B}) \\ E \vdash_m dos_E(\Gamma(\overline{x})) \rightarrow_{NodeTest} U \end{array}}{E; \Gamma \vdash_m \overline{x}\ \mathbf{dos} :: NodeTest : U}$$

where the auxiliary function $dos_E()$ mimic `dos` semantics, and is defined as follows.

Definition 7.13

$$\begin{array}{rcl} dos_E(()) & = & () \\ dos_E(B) & = & B \\ dos_E(l[T]) & = & l[T], dos_E(T) \\ dos_E(T?) & = & dos_E(T)? \\ dos_E(T*) & = & dos_E(T)* \\ dos_E(T+) & = & dos_E(T)+ \\ dos_E(T, U) & = & dos_E(T), dos_E(U) \\ dos_E(T \mid U) & = & dos_E(T) \mid dos_E(U) \\ dos_E(X) & = & dos_E(E(X)) \end{array}$$

Example 7.14 Consider the following query, where $\overline{db}$ has type $a[b[], c[()]+]$:

for $\overline{x}$ in $\overline{db}$ dos :: b
return $\$x$

By applying Rule (TYPEDOS), the system infers the type $b[()]*$ for the navigational step; by Rule (TYPEFOR), hence, the result type is just $b[()]*$.

Instead, if we apply the $dos_E()$ function to the type of $\overline{db}$, we have that $dos_E(a[b[()], c[()]+]) =$

$$\begin{array}{rl} & a[b[()], c[()]+], dos_E(b[()], c[()]+) \\ = & a[b[()], c[()]+], dos_E(b[()]), dos_E(c[()]+) \\ = & a[b[()], c[()]+], b[()], (), (c[()], ())+ \end{array}$$

Then, by using Rule (TYPEDOSNOREC), the navigational step $\overline{db}$ dos :: b is typed with $b[()]$ and the result type is $b[()].1 = b[()]$, which is a much more precise type.

■

The following theorem states the correctness of this approach.

Theorem 7.15 *For any non-recursive type T defined in E:*

$$dos_E(T) = U \quad \Rightarrow \quad \forall f \in [\![T]\!]_E.\, dos(f) \in [\![U]\!]_E$$

Proof. Trivial. ■

It is quite easy to see that Rule (TYPEDOSNOREC) always infers a subtype of that inferred by Rule (TYPEDOS).

As it can be noted from Example 7.14, $dos_E()$ satisfies the following property.

Property 7.16 *If $dos_E(T) = U$ and U contains a $*$ type at its top level, then there exists $f \in [\![T]\!]_E$ such that $dos(f) = ()$, and for each natural k there exists $f \in [\![T]\!]_E$ such that $|dos(f)| > k$.*

This property is crucial, as it states that $dos_E()$ does not introduce unnecessary $*$ type operators. Hence, unlike the general rule of the W3C system, this rule does not introduce unnecessary approximations.

It is easy to see that the following theorem holds.

Theorem 7.17 *$dos_E(T)$ can be evaluated in time $O((|T||E|)^2)$.*

8. Complexity Analysis

In this section we will analyze the complexity of the XQuery type inference in both the W3C and the μXQ+ type systems. We will prove two main results here. First, we will show that the W3C type inference algorithm may return exponentially larger output types when `let` clauses are nested in a particular way, and that it resorts to polynomial time complexity when no `let` clauses are present. Then, we will see that μXQ+ type inference system is subject to combinatorial explosion even in presence of `for` clauses only, hence leading to a worst case exponential time complexity.

8.1 Assumptions

To analyze the complexity of the type inference algorithms, we need a few assumptions about the complexity model and the basic data structures being used.

To study the complexity of our algorithms we base our analysis on the RAM (*Random Access Machine*) model. As usual, we assume that read/write operations on the RAM memory and on the input/output device are performed in unit time, as well as comparisons and arithmetic operations. Under these hypotheses, the type inference algorithms can be simulated by RAM programs with the same asymptotic complexity.

We assume here to represent E and Γ through arrays. As E is not altered by the inference process, it can be created and initialized at schema creation time, without any significant impact on the complexity of type inference. Γ, instead, is a dynamic structure that can be created and initialized at query parsing time with a $O(|\Gamma Var(\Gamma)|)$ extra cost.

We restrict our analysis to *non-recursive* queries, where one cannot navigate or output the result of a nested query, e.g., we exclude queries like

for $\overline{x}$ in $\overline{db}$ child :: a return
  for $\overline{y}$ in { for $\overline{z}$ in $\overline{db}$ dos :: c
    where $\overline{x} = \overline{z}$
    return w[$\overline{z}$] } return
  for $\overline{u}$ in $\overline{y}$ child :: d return h[$\overline{u}$]

This restriction is met by many queries used in practice and is also enforced in data integration systems using XQuery as language for expressing queries and transformations (see [10]).

8.2 Preliminary definitions

In the following we will use the terms *query size* and *type size* to denote the size of the corresponding abstract syntax tree, as shown in the following definitions.

Definition 8.1 (Query size) *Given a query Q, $|Q|$ is inductively defined as follows:*

$|()| = 1$ $\quad$ $|b| = 1$
$|l[Q]| = 1 + |Q|$ $\quad$ $|Q_1, Q_2| = |Q_1| + |Q_2|$
$|\overline{x}$ child :: *NodeTest*$| = 3$ $\quad$ $|\overline{x}$ dos :: *NodeTest*$| = 3$

$|$for $\overline{x}$ in Q_1 return $Q_2| = 2 + |Q_1| + |Q_2|$
$|$let $x ::= Q_1$ return $Q_2| = 2 + |Q_1| + |Q_2|$
$|$for $\overline{x}$ in Q_1 where P return $Q_2| = 2 + |Q_1| + |Q_2| + |P|$
$|$let $x ::= Q_1$ where P return $Q_2| = 2 + |Q_1| + |Q_2| + |P|$

$|$true$| = 1$ $\quad$ $|$false$| = 1$
$|P_1$ or $P_2| = 1 + |P_1| + |P_2|$ $\quad$ $|$not $P| = 1 + |P|$
$|(P)| = |P|$ $\quad$ $|$empty$(\chi)| = 1 + |\chi|$
$|\chi_1\ \delta\ \chi_2| = |\chi_1| + |\chi_2| + 1$ $\quad$ $|\chi| = 1$

Definition 8.2 (Type size) *Given a type T, $|T|$ is inductively defined as follows:*

$|()| = 1$ $\quad$ $|B| = 1$
$|l[T]| = 1 + |T|$ $\quad$ $|T_1, T_2| = 1 + |T_1| + |T_2|$
$|T_1 \mid T_2| = 1 + |T_1| + |T_2|$ $\quad$ $|T?| = 1 + |T|$
$|T+| = 1 + |T|$ $\quad$ $|T*| = 1 + |T|$
$|X| = 1$

Definition 8.3 (Type environment size) *Given a type environment $E = X_1 = T_1; \ldots; X_n = T_n$, $|E| = \Sigma_{i=1}^n |T_i|$ if $E \neq \emptyset$, and $|E| = 1$ if $E = \emptyset$.*

Definition 8.4 (Variable environment size) *Given a variable environment $\Gamma = x_1 : T_1, \ldots, x_n : T_n$, $|\Gamma| = \Sigma_{i=1}^n |T_i|$ if $\Gamma \neq \emptyset$, and $|\Gamma| = 1$ if $\Gamma = \emptyset$.*

We will also use the notion of *independent variables*, which is defined as follows.

Definition 8.5 *Given a query Q, $Var(Q)$ is the set of all variables occurring in Q.*

Definition 8.6 *Given a query Q and a for-variable $\overline{x} \in Var(Q)$:*

$$\begin{aligned} dep_Q(\overline{x}) &= \{\overline{y} \mid \texttt{for } \overline{x} \texttt{ in } \overline{y} \texttt{ child} :: \textit{NodeTest is in } Q\} \cup \\ &\quad \{\overline{y} \mid \texttt{for } \overline{x} \texttt{ in } \overline{y} \texttt{ dos} :: \textit{NodeTest is in } Q\} \cup \\ &\quad \{\chi \mid \texttt{for } \overline{x} \texttt{ in } \chi \textit{ is in } Q\} \end{aligned}$$

Definition 8.7 *Given a query Q and a let-variable $x \in Var(Q)$:*

$$\begin{aligned} dep_Q(x) &= \{\overline{y} \mid \texttt{let } x ::= \overline{y} \texttt{ child} :: \textit{NodeTest is in } Q\} \cup \\ &\quad \{\overline{y} \mid \texttt{let } x ::= \overline{y} \texttt{ dos} :: \textit{NodeTest is in } Q\} \cup \\ &\quad \{\chi \mid \texttt{let } x ::= \chi \textit{ is in } Q\} \end{aligned}$$

Definition 8.8 *Given a query Q and a variable $\chi \in Var(Q)$, $dep^*_Q(\chi) = \{\chi' \mid \chi' \in dep_Q(\chi) \vee \exists \chi'' \in dep_Q(\chi).\chi' \in dep^*_Q(\chi'')\}$.*

Definition 8.9 *We say that two variables χ_1, χ_2 are* independent *wrt a query Q if and only $dep^*_Q(\chi_1) \cap dep^*_Q(\chi_2) = \emptyset$.*

Definition 8.10 *Given a query Q, $\{\chi_1, \ldots, \chi_n\} \subseteq Var(Q)$ is a set of independent variables in Q if $\forall i, j = 1, \ldots, n.dep^*_Q(\chi_i) \cap dep^*_Q(\chi_j) = \emptyset$.*

8.3 Complexity of auxiliary functions

A preliminary step in the analysis of the complexity of the W3C type inference system is the analysis of the space and time complexity of auxiliary functions.

Space complexity The following lemmas show the space complexity of the auxiliary functions used in the W3C type system. Due to the presence of type variables to be unfolded, $Prime_E(T)$ and type filtering may return types bigger than the input type. As the proofs are trivial, we omit them.

Lemma 8.11 $|Prime_E(T)| \in O(|T||E|)$.

Lemma 8.12 $|Quant_T(E)| \in O(1)$.

Lemma 8.13 $|content(T)| \in O(|T|)$.

Lemma 8.14 *If* $E \vdash_m T \rightarrow_l U$, *then* $|U| \in O(|E||T|)$.

Time Complexity Once we identified the space complexity of the auxiliary functions, we can analyze their time complexity. In the following, we will use $\mathcal{C}(f)$ to denote the cost of evaluating a given function f according to the RAM complexity model. We omit the proofs of the lemmas, as they are trivial.

Lemma 8.15 $\mathcal{C}(content(T)) \in O(|T|)$.

Lemma 8.16 $\mathcal{C}(E \vdash_m T \rightarrow_l U) \in O(|E||T|)$.

Lemma 8.17 $\mathcal{C}(Prime_E(T)) \in O(|E||T|)$

Lemma 8.18 $\mathcal{C}(Quant_E(T)) \in O(|E||T|)$

8.4 Complexity of W3C type rules

To understand the complexity of the W3C type inference system, we must first analyze a few properties of the navigational operators.

Lemma 8.19 (Complexity of Rule (TYPECHILDNODETEST)) $\mathcal{C}(E; \Gamma \vdash_m \overline{x}\ \texttt{child} :: \textit{NodeTest} : U) \in O(|\Gamma(\overline{x})||E|)$.

Proof. All operators inside Rule (TYPECHILDNODETEST) have $O(1)$ complexity, except for $E \vdash_m content(T) \rightarrow_{\textit{NodeTest}} U$. This operation requires the system to compute $content(T)$ and to filter its result according to *NodeTest*. By Lemma 8.15, $content(T)$ (where $T = \Gamma(\overline{x})$) can be computed in time $O(|\Gamma(\overline{x})|)$. By Lemma 8.16, hence, Rule (TYPECHILDNODETEST) can be evaluated in $O(|\Gamma(\overline{x})||E|)$ time. ∎

The following describes the size of the type inferred by Rule (TYPEDOS).

Lemma 8.20 *If* $E; \Gamma \vdash_m \overline{x}\ \texttt{dos} :: \textit{NodeTest} : U$, *then* $|U| \in O((|E||\Gamma(\overline{x})|)^2)$.

Proof. As *NodeTest* = `node()` is the least selective node test, we analyze the size of the U when *NodeTest* = `node()`.

By the element-guardedness of type environment, we know that each type variable is unfolded only once; as a consequence, the typing rule must explore a parse tree of size $O(|E||\Gamma(\overline{x})|)$, the worst case happening when $\Gamma(\overline{x}) = l_1[X_1] \mid \ldots \mid l_n[X_n]$.

Each subtree in the parse tree is added to the result, hence $|U| \in O((|E||\Gamma(\overline{x})|)^2)$. ∎

As stated by Lemma 8.20, the typing of `descendant-or-self` may quadratically increase the size of the inferred type. This quadratic increase, however, does not lead to a combinatorial explosion, as stated by the following lemma.

Lemma 8.21 *If* $E; \Gamma \vdash_m \overline{x}\ \texttt{dos} :: \textit{NodeTest} : U$ *and* $\Gamma(\overline{x}) = C'[C[T] \mid T]$, *where* $C[\cdot]$ *and* $C'[\cdot]$ *are type contexts, then* $E; \Gamma, \overline{x} : C'[C[T]] \vdash_m \overline{x}\ \texttt{dos} :: \textit{NodeTest} : U$.

Proof. Trivial. ∎

The previous lemma states that repeated subtrees give no contribution to the output type of a `descendant-or-self` selector. By exploiting this lemma, we can prove the following result.

Lemma 8.22 *Let Q be a non-recursive query, let $\chi_0, \ldots, \chi_n$ the variables bound by Q. If $S = \{\chi_{i_0}, \ldots, \chi_{i_k}\}$ is the set of all the independent variables in Q, then, for each variable χ_i, $|\Gamma(\chi_i)| \in O((\Upsilon)^2)$, where $\Upsilon = max\{\Gamma(\chi_{i_0}), \ldots, \Gamma(\chi_{i_k})\}$.*

This lemma shows that, while a `descendant-or-self` operation can quadratically increase the size of the inferred type of a variable, no exponential explosion is possible.

This result leads to the following corollary.

Corollary 8.23 *Let $E; \Gamma \vdash_m Q : T$. Let Γ' the variable environment obtained from Γ by inferring a type for each variable $\chi_i \in Var(Q)$ such that $(\chi_i : T_i) \notin \Gamma$.Then, $|\Gamma'| \leqslant \Upsilon^2 n$, where $n = |Var(Q)|$.*

This corollary states that, during the type inference process for Q, the size of the variable environment cannot exceed $n\Upsilon^2$.

Given these results, we can now prove one of the main results of this section.

Lemma 8.24 (Complexity of Rule (TYPEDOS))
$\mathcal{C}(E; \Gamma \vdash_m \overline{x}\ \texttt{dos} :: \textit{NodeTest} : U) \in O((|\Gamma(\overline{x})||E|)^3)$.

Proof. To prove the thesis it is necessary to rewrite Rule (TYPEDOS) in a more algorithmic fashion, as shown below.

$$\frac{\begin{array}{l}\overline{x} : T \in \Gamma \ \wedge\ (T = m_1[T'_1] \mid m_2[T'_2] \mid \ldots \mid m_n[T'_n] \vee T = \mathsf{B}) \\ U' = BFSPrime(\overline{x}, \Gamma, E) \\ E \vdash_m U' \rightarrow_{\textit{NodeTest}} U\end{array}}{E; \Gamma \vdash_m \overline{x}\ \texttt{dos} :: \textit{NodeTest} : U}$$

```
BFSPrime(x̄, Γ, E)
  Queue Q ← ∅
  boolean[] expVar
  Type result ← Prime_E(Γ(x̄))
  Q ← Prime_E(Γ(x̄))
  while Q not empty
  do Type Z = S.pop()
     E; Γ, x̄ : Z ⊢_m x̄ child :: node() : Z'
     if Z' ≠ ()
        then if Z' is not a type variable
                then AddPrime(Z', Q)
        else if not expVar[Z']
                then expVar[Z'] = true
                     Q.push(Prime_E(Z'))
                     result = result | Prime_E(Z')
  return result*
```

```
AddPrime(T, Q)
  if not (genTypes contains T)
    then Q.push(Prime_E(T))
         result = result | Prime_E(T)
```

Figure 13. DFSPrime procedure.

where BFSPRIME is defined as shown in Figure 8.4.

The BFSPRIME procedure uses several auxiliary data structures. $expVar$ is a boolean array that specifies whether a given type variable has been previously unfolded, and can be initialized in $O(|Def(E)|)$ time. Q is a queue holding type terms to be visited.

ADDPRIME is an auxiliary procedure that pushes its argument into Q and adds it to the result only if its argument has never seen before (through the $genType$ map).

The algorithm is essentially a variation of the standard breadth first tree search. The number of iterations of the `while` loop is bounded by $|E||\Gamma(\overline{x})|$, as no type variable is unfolded twice and no type term is visited more than once.

During each iteration, Rule (TYPECHILDNODETEST) is invoked; as proved in Lemma 8.19, this rule can be evaluated in time $O(|\Gamma(\overline{x})||E|)$. Procedure ADDPRIME can be computed in time $O((|E||\Gamma(\overline{x}))^2)$. As a consequence, Rule (TYPEDOS) can be evaluated in time $O((|E||\Gamma(\overline{x})|)^3)$. ■

We can now state the main result of this section.

Theorem 8.25 (Complexity of type inference) *If Q has no* `let` *clauses, then $C(E;\Gamma \vdash_m Q : U) \in O(|Q|(|E|A)^3)$, where $A = max(|Q|, |E|)$.*

This theorem cannot be applied to queries with `let` clauses. Indeed, consider the following query:

```
let y1 := x̄, x̄ return
   let y2 := y1, y1 return
      ...
      let yn := yn-1, yn-1
         return yn
```

If $\overline{x}$ has type $a[\mathsf{B}]$, then y_n will have type $(a[\mathsf{B}], a[\mathsf{B}])^n$, which is exponential in the size of the query.

While this is a very uncommon situation, it shows that the W3C type inference system may degrade to an exponential complexity.

8.5 Complexity of μXQ+ Type Inference

In the previous section we discovered that, according to the W3C type rules, type inference can be performed in polynomial time and space when the query being analyzed has no `let` clauses, and that type inference may be subject to combinatorial explosion when `let` clauses are nested.

The μXQ+ type system differs from the W3C one for the treatment of `for` clauses. In μXQ+, indeed, the inference algorithm iterates over the top level element types of the for-variable, and, for each element type, infers a distinct type for Q_2. As shown in Section 7, this iterative inference approach leads to a great precision improvement over the W3C type system.

In this section we will analyze the complexity of the μXQ+ type inference. To understand the complexity issues that may arise when the μXQ+ type inference approach is used, it is worth to analyze the behaviour of the type system through an example.

Example 8.26 Consider the following query:

```
for x̄1 in l1[b], l2[b], l3[b]
return for x̄2 in l1[b], l2[b], l3[b]
       return x̄1, x̄2
```

The type inference algorithm first analyzes the outer `for` clause and infers a type for $l_1[b], l_2[b], l_3[b]$. This type ($T_1 = l_1[\mathsf{B}], l_2[\mathsf{B}], l_3[\mathsf{B}]$) is not bound to $\overline{x}$ nor it is transformed in prime form. Instead, the algorithm invokes Rule (TYPEINCONC), which analyzes the inner query for three times: one for $l_1[\mathsf{B}]$, one for $l_2[\mathsf{B}]$, and one for $l_3[\mathsf{B}]$.

The inner query is, then, analyzed exactly in same way, hence the expression $\overline{x}_1, \overline{x}_2$ is evaluated nine times.

The inferred output type, hence, is the following:

$$l_1[\mathsf{B}], l_1[\mathsf{B}], l_1[\mathsf{B}], l_2[\mathsf{B}], l_1[\mathsf{B}], l_3[\mathsf{B}],\\ l_2[\mathsf{B}], l_1[\mathsf{B}], l_2[\mathsf{B}], l_2[\mathsf{B}], l_2[\mathsf{B}], l_3[\mathsf{B}],\\ l_3[\mathsf{B}], l_1[\mathsf{B}], l_3[\mathsf{B}], l_2[\mathsf{B}], l_3[\mathsf{B}], l_3[\mathsf{B}]$$

As it can be easily seen, this type has size in $O(|T_1|^k)$, where $k = 2$ is the number of nested `for` clauses. ■

This example shows that the size of the inferred type is a polynomial whose exponent is the number of `for` clauses in the query. In the worst case scenario $k \in O(|Q|)$, which implies that the output type may have exponential size in the size of the query. This implies that case analysis may require an exponential space to precisely type a query.

Summarizing, the type inference algorithm of μXQ+ is subject to exponential explosion phenomena when the query being analyzed contains nested `for` and `let` clauses.

9. Related Works

The problem of type inference for XQuery has been studied in several recent works.

In [7], where a variant of the μXQ+ type system has been first proposed, authors deals with the problem of detecting errors wrt the source type.

In [5], Cheney proposes a new type system able to deal with XML updates, while in [4] he describes a new type system mixing a subsumption mechanism and type rules for updates. In both these papers, Cheney adopts the μXQ+ case analysis technique for typing `queries`, but in none of them he compares this approach with that of the W3C system in term of precision and complexity.

In [14], Dan Suciu et al. focus on the problem of verifying whether the output of an XML query conforms to a given type (the so-called *XML type-checking problem*). Suciu et al. show that no precise type can be inferred by using regular type languages, and base their approach on *inverse* type inference (i.e., the problem of finding, given a query Q and output type T, an input type generating T), which can be performed in a sound and complete way by relying on *k-pebble automata*. This solution, however, has *non-elementary* complexity, which strongly affects its practical applicability. Similar approaches have been described in [12, 13].

10. Conclusions

In this paper we analyzed the problem of inferring an output type for an XQuery query. By comparing two type systems we identified the main sources of precision loss, namely the generation on non-regular languages, `for`-iterations, and `descendant-or-self` navigational steps.

We compared these two type systems not only in terms of precision, but also in terms of complexity, finding that type inference can be performed in polynomial time in the W3C system if the query being analyzed has no `let` clauses, while the μXQ+ system may require exponential space.

We also showed that the precision of the W3C can be improved when particular conditions are met, without increasing the computational complexity.

As a future work, we want to further investigate the relation between precision and complexity: in particular, we want to understand how tagged-path, one-type, conflict-freedom restrictions impact on the complexity of the inference algorithms.

Finally, we want to investigate the use numerical occurrence indicators to make the inferred types more succinct.

Acknowledgments

We would like to thank all the anonymous reviewers of this paper for their insightful comments.

References

[1] V. Benzaken, G. Castagna, D. Colazzo, and K. Nguyen. Type-based XML projection. In U. Dayal, K.-Y. Whang, D. B. Lomet, G. Alonso, G. M. Lohman, M. L. Kersten, S. K. Cha, and Y.-K. Kim, editors, *VLDB*, pages 271–282. ACM, 2006.

[2] S. Boag, D. Chamberlin, M. F. Fernández, D. Florescu, J. Robie, and J. Siméon. XQuery 1.0: An XML Query Language. Technical report, World Wide Web Consortium, Jan. 2007. W3C Recommendation.

[3] T. Bray, J. Paoli, C. M. Sperberg-McQueen, E. Maler, F. Yergeau, and J. Cowan. Extensible Markup Language (XML) 1.1 (Second Edition). Technical report, World Wide Web Consortium, 2006. W3C Recommendation.

[4] J. Cheney. Regular expression subtyping for XML query and update languages. In S. Drossopoulou, editor, *ESOP*, volume 4960 of *Lecture Notes in Computer Science*, pages 32–47. Springer, 2008.

[5] J. Cheney. Flux: functional updates for XML. In J. Hook and P. Thiemann, editors, *ICFP*, pages 3–14. ACM, 2008.

[6] D. Colazzo, G. Ghelli, P. Manghi, and C. Sartiani. Types for Path Correctness of XML Queries. In *Proceedings of the 2004 International Conference on Functional Programming (ICFP), Snowbird, Utah, September 19-22, 2004*, 2004.

[7] D. Colazzo., G. Ghelli, P. Manghi., and C. Sartiani. Static analysis for path correctness of XML queries. *Journal of Functional Programming*, 16(4-5):621–661, 2006.

[8] D. Colazzo, G. Ghelli, and C. Sartiani. Efficient asymmetric inclusion between regular expression types. In *In Proceedings of the 12th International Conference on Database Theory (ICDT 2009), March 23-26 2009, Saint-Petersburg, Russia*, 2009.

[9] H. Comon, M. Dauchet, R. Gilleron, F. Jacquemard, D. Lugiez, S. Tison, and M. Tommasi. Tree Automata Techniques and Applications. Available on: `http://www.grappa.univ-lille3.fr/tata`, 1997. release October, 1rst 2002.

[10] A. Y. Halevy, Z. G. Ives, P. Mork, and I. Tatarinov. Piazza: data management infrastructure for semantic web applications. In *WWW*, pages 556–567, 2003.

[11] H. Hosoya and B. C. Pierce. Xduce: A statically typed XML processing language. *ACM Trans. Internet Techn.*, 3(2):117–148, 2003.

[12] K. Inaba, H. Hosoya, and S. Maneth. Multi-return macro tree transducers. In O. H. Ibarra and B. Ravikumar, editors, *CIAA*, volume 5148 of *Lecture Notes in Computer Science*, pages 102–111. Springer, 2008.

[13] S. Maneth, T. Perst, and H. Seidl. Exact XML type checking in polynomial time. In T. Schwentick and D. Suciu, editors, *ICDT*, volume 4353 of *Lecture Notes in Computer Science*, pages 254–268. Springer, 2007.

[14] T. Milo, D. Suciu, and V. Vianu. Typechecking for XML transformers. In *PODS*, pages 11–22. ACM, 2000.

[15] M. Murata, D. Lee, M. Mani, and K. Kawaguchi. Taxonomy of XML schema languages using formal language theory. *ACM Trans. Internet Techn.*, 5(4):660–704, 2005.

[16] A. Schmidt, F. Waas, M. L. Kersten, M. J. Carey, I. Manolescu, and R. Busse. Xmark: A benchmark for XML data management. In *VLDB*, pages 974–985. Morgan Kaufmann, 2002.

[17] J. Siméon and P. Wadler. The essence of XML. In *POPL*, pages 1–13, 2003.

[18] H. S. Thompson, D. Beech, M. Maloney, and N. Mendelsohn. XML Schema Part 1: Structures Second Edition. Technical report, World Wide Web Consortium, Oct 2004. W3C Recommendation.

A Contextual Semantics for Concurrent Haskell with Futures

David Sabel
Dept. of Computer Science and Mathematics
Goethe-University Frankfurt
60054 Frankfurt am Main, Germany
sabel@ki.informatik.uni-frankfurt.de

Manfred Schmidt-Schauß
Dept. of Computer Science and Mathematics
Goethe-University Frankfurt
60054 Frankfurt am Main, Germany
schauss@ki.informatik.uni-frankfurt.de

Abstract

In this paper we analyze the semantics of a higher-order functional language with concurrent threads, monadic IO and synchronizing variables as in Concurrent Haskell. To assure declarativeness of concurrent programming we extend the language by implicit, monadic, and concurrent futures. As semantic model we introduce and analyze the process calculus CHF, which represents a typed core language of Concurrent Haskell extended by concurrent futures. Evaluation in CHF is defined by a small-step reduction relation. Using contextual equivalence based on may- and should-convergence as program equivalence, we show that various transformations preserve program equivalence. We establish a context lemma easing those correctness proofs. An important result is that call-by-need and call-by-name evaluation are equivalent in CHF, since they induce the same program equivalence. Finally we show that the monad laws hold in CHF under mild restrictions on Haskell's seq-operator, which for instance justifies the use of the do-notation.

Categories and Subject Descriptors F.1.2 [*Computation by Abstract Devices*]: Modes of Computation—parallelism and concurrency; F.3.2 [*Logics and Meanings of Programs*]: Semantics of Programming Languages—operational semantics, process models; D.3.2 [*Language Classifications*]: Applicative (functional) languages, concurrent, distributed, and parallel languages

General Terms Languages, Theory

Keywords Contextual equivalence, Concurrency, Functional programming, Futures, Semantics

1. Introduction

Futures are variables whose value is initially not known, but becomes available in the future when the corresponding computation is finished (see e.g. [4, 13]). For functional programming languages the call-by-need evaluation implements futures (implicitly) on the functional level, since shared expressions are evaluated at the time their value is demanded. In this paper we consider *concurrent* futures on the *imperative* level in the functional programming language Haskell [26]. The futures in this paper are *concurrent*, since the computation to obtain the value of a future is performed in a *concurrent thread*. We consider the *imperative* level, since the value of a future is obtained by performing stateful programming, i.e. it is performed as a monadic computation in Haskell's `IO`-monad (see e.g. [27, 29, 44]).

One also distinguishes between *explicit* futures, i.e. where the value of a future must be explicitly forced and *implicit* futures where the value is computed automatically if the value is demanded by data dependency, i.e. there is no need to explicitly force the future.

We will see below that explicit futures can be implemented in Concurrent Haskell while implicit futures need some primitives which are outside the Concurrent Haskell language. The advantage of implicit futures is their easy use: futures can be used as a concurrency primitive without explicitly taking care about the synchronization of concurrent threads. Moreover, the futures perform this synchronization automatically. Futures can also be used in functional-logic programming to model the unknown value of logical variables as e.g in Mozart [22].

Concurrent Haskell was proposed in [30], but its current implementation in the Glasgow Haskell Compiler is slightly modified (a description can also be found in [27, 28]). We give a brief overview. Concurrent Haskell extends Haskell by a primitive `forkIO` and by synchronizing variables `MVar`. `MVar`s behave like single one-place buffers: `MVar`s are either empty or filled. The primitive operation `newEmptyMVar` creates an empty `MVar`. The operation `takeMVar` reads the value of a filled `MVar` and empties it. All threads that want to execute `takeMVar` on this empty `MVar` are blocked until the `MVar` becomes filled again. Similarly, `putMVar` v e writes the expression e into the `MVar` v, if v is empty, and blocks otherwise until the `MVar` becomes empty. The primitive for thread creation in Concurrent Haskell is `forkIO :: IO () -> IO ThreadId`. Applied to an IO-action, a concurrent thread is immediately started to compute the action concurrently. From the perspective of the calling thread, the result is a unique identifier of the concurrent thread, which for instance can be used to kill the concurrent thread using `killThread`.

Explicit Futures can be implemented in Concurrent Haskell using `forkIO` and `MVar`s:

```
type EFuture a = MVar a
efuture :: IO a → IO (EFuture a)
efuture act = do ack ← newEmptyMVar
                 forkIO (act >>= putMVar ack)
                 return ack
force :: EFuture a → IO a
force x = takeMVar x >>= (λr → putMVar x r >> return r)
```


PDPP'11, July 20–22, 2011, Odense, Denmark.

An explicit future is represented by an `MVar`. The creation of an explicit future first constructs an empty `MVar` and then starts the computation of the action corresponding to the future in a concurrent thread such that after finishing the computation the result is written into the empty `MVar`. From the view of the calling thread a future in form of an `MVar` is immediately returned. If the value of the future is needed then the future must be forced explicitly by calling `force` which reads the `MVar`. If the future's value is not computed already, then a wait situation arises until the concurrent computation is finished.

Note, that programming with explicit futures is often uncomfortable, since the programmer must be careful to explicitly force the future at the right time. It is more desirable that the future gets (automatically) forced when it is needed through data dependencies such that the programmer does not need to care about explicit forces. Unfortunately, this behavior is not implementable using explicit futures.

Implicit Futures can be implemented using a well-known technique to delay the computation of a sequential monadic IO-computation: We use Haskell's `unsafeInterleaveIO` that delays computations in the IO-monad and breaks sequentiality (i.e. it is used to implement *lazy IO*, see e.g. [27, 29]). An implementation of implicit futures is:

```
future :: IO a → IO a
future act = do ack ← newEmptyMVar
                thread ← forkIO (act >>= putMVar ack)
                unsafeInterleaveIO (do r ← takeMVar ack
                                       killThread thread
                                       return r)
```

First an empty `MVar` is created, which will be used to store the result of the concurrent computation. This computation is performed in a concurrent thread using `forkIO`. The last part consists of taking the result, killing the concurrent thread and returning the result. This part is delayed using `unsafeInterleaveIO`. Note, that without the use of `unsafeInterleaveIO` the calling thread would be blocked until the concurrent computation has finished which would not implement the desired behavior of futures. For the shown implementation the calling thread only becomes blocked if it demands the result of an unevaluated future.

Thus it is possible to implement implicit futures in Concurrent Haskell using the `unsafeInterleaveIO`-primitive (which is not included in the Haskell standard). But the general use of `unsafeInterleaveIO` breaks referential transparency, since impure effects may become visible using pure functions. Nevertheless we believe that the use in the encoding of futures is "safe". In this paper we make a first step for showing this claim by analyzing the calculus CHF (Concurrent Haskell with Futures): We will show that the usual laws like indifference of call-by-need and call-by-name evaluation and the correctness of the monad laws are valid for CHF.

The Calculus CHF. We investigate the extension of Concurrent Haskell where the above `future`-operation is built-in as a primitive using the calculus CHF as a model. CHF is a process calculus which comprises (unlike the π-calculus [20, 36]) shared memory in form of Haskell's MVars, threads (i.e. futures) and heap bindings. On the expression level we allow monadic IO-computations as well as usual pure functional expressions extending the lambda calculus by data constructors, case-expressions, recursive let-expressions, as well as Haskell's `seq`-operator for sequential evaluation. We add a monomorphic type system to CHF with recursive types where polymorphic data constructors are monomorphically instantiated. Since we want to keep the formalism and proofs simple, we keep the type system as small as possible, nevertheless we believe that our results are transferable to a calculus with a polymorphic type system. We present an operational semantics for CHF as a (call-by-need) small-step reduction relation (called *standard reduction*) where the monadic operations are performed as rewriting steps which relieves us from the issue how to implement the bind-operator in Haskell (those correctness issues are analyzed e.g. in [3]). That is we follow a suggestion made by Simon Peyton Jones in [27] and add the bind-operator as a *primitive* to the language. We show in this paper that CHF has a well-behaved semantical underpinning. Our calculus is closely related to the process calculus presented in [27] where the differences are: We provide an operational semantics for the monadic and the functional part while [27] assumes an a priori given denotational semantics for functional expressions. We do not model the `delay`-operator and external input and output, and thus use an unlabeled reduction while [27] uses a labelled transition system.

Compared to threads in Concurrent Haskell, CHF does not include a primitive to kill running threads, which is reasonable since threads are futures which may be referenced somewhere else. In CHF a *successfully evaluated* thread will become an ordinary heap binding, that is the result is kept while the thread is removed. Running threads that no longer contribute to the final result can be garbage collected.

As program equivalence we use *contextual equivalence* (see e.g. [21, 31]), that is two programs are equal iff their observable behavior is indistinguishable even if the programs are used as a subprogram of any other program (i.e. if the programs are plugged into any arbitrary context). For nondeterministic and concurrent programming languages it is usually not enough to observe termination, only. Thus we use a combination of two tests: Can a program terminate (called *may-convergence*) and does a program never lose the ability to converge (called *should-convergence*, or sometimes must-convergence, see e.g. [7, 25, 32, 33])? In the literature there is often another test used (instead of should-convergence), called must-convergence (for instance, [9]), which holds if a program terminates along all possible computation paths. The difference between should- and must-convergence is that should-convergence is insensible w.r.t. *weakly divergent* programs [23], i.e. programs that may run infinitely long but always may terminate along another computation path are should-convergent (but not must-convergent). Nevertheless this difference is small and we believe that correctness of commonly used program transformations is valid for both predicates. Some advantages of should-convergence (compared to must-convergence) are that restricting the evaluator to *fair scheduling* does not modify the predicate and also not the contextual equivalence, that the equivalence based on may- and should-convergence is invariant under a whole class of test-predicates (see [39]), and inductive reasoning is available as a tool to prove should-convergence.

Results. We provide a semantic foundation for Concurrent Haskell extended by futures. In detail we prove a context lemma for expressions which is a helpful tool for proving expressions contextually equal. We show that all reduction rules are *correct program transformations* (i.e. they do not change the contextual semantics) except for the rules which take or put an expression from or into an MVar, which are in general incorrect, but as we show are correct if the MVar access is deterministic. Using the technique of rewriting on infinite trees (see e.g. [15, 37]), we show that the (call-by-need) standard reduction can be replaced by a call-by-name reduction, which also implies that inlining of expressions is a correct program transformation. Optimizations that are based on sharing or unsharing followed by partial evaluation without take/put on MVars are thus justified by the semantics. We show that (infinite) fairness of reductions can be enforced without changing the contextual semantics based on may-and should-convergence. Finally, we show that our implementation of the IO-monad in CHF satisfies the monad laws if the `seq`-operator's first argument is restricted to non IO-

$$
\begin{array}{rcl}
e, e_i \in \mathit{Expr} & ::= & x \mid me \mid \lambda x.e \mid (e_1\ e_2) \mid \mathtt{case}_T\ e\ \mathtt{of}\ (c_{T,1}\ x_1 \ldots x_{\mathrm{ar}(c_{T,1})} \to e_1) \ldots (c_{T,|T|}\ x_1 \ldots x_{\mathrm{ar}(c_{T,|T|})} \to e_{|T|}) \\
& & \mid c\ e_1 \ldots e_{\mathrm{ar}(c)} \mid \mathtt{seq}\ e_1\ e_2 \mid \mathtt{letrec}\ x_1 = e_1\ \ldots\ x_n = e_n\ \mathtt{in}\ e \quad \text{where } n \geq 1 \\
me \in \mathit{MExpr} & ::= & \mathtt{return}\ e \mid e_1 \mathbin{\mathtt{>\!\!>=}} e_2 \mid \mathtt{future}\ e \mid \mathtt{takeMVar}\ e \mid \mathtt{newMVar}\ e \mid \mathtt{putMVar}\ e_1\ e_2
\end{array}
$$

Figure 1. Syntax of Expressions

types. This justifies the correctness of using the do-notation and its usual compilation.

Related Work. Concurrent futures in Multilisp and their applications are discussed e.g. in [4, 13]. CHF is also related to the impure (call-by-value) lambda-calculus with futures $\lambda(\mathsf{fut})$ [24] which models the core language of Alice ML [2] and has concurrent futures. In [25] a contextual equivalence with may- and should-convergence is defined for $\lambda(\mathsf{fut})$ and a set of program transformations is shown correct. In [41] variants of $\lambda(\mathsf{fut})$ are presented and their equivalence is shown.

In [10] Flanagan and Felleisen present a semantics for a (pure) call-by-value calculus extended with futures and analyze an optimization in the abstract machine, to avoid unnecessary dereferencing operations on evaluated futures (so called "touches"). Since their calculus has no side-effects and futures evaluate purely functional expressions, the futures are different from futures in CHF, but they are rather linked to Haskell's `par` operator. In [5] Baker-Finch et. al. present an operational (and a denotational) semantics for Glasgow parallel Haskell [12]. They analyze a pure functional non-strict language extended with a `par`-operator. `par` can be seen as an annotation that implements explicit parallelism i.e. in (`par` e_1 e_2) the expression e_1 can be evaluated in parallel, while e_2 is the result of the `par`-expression. Thus `par` implements futures for pure functional expressions. In contrast CHF permits to perform a monadic action to compute the value of a future. Programming with parallel Haskell using strategies was proposed in [42] and recently redesigned in [17]. Finally, [28] gives an introduction to several techniques for parallel and concurrent programming in Haskell, i.e. into Parallel Haskell, Concurrent Haskell, and Software Transactional Memory [14].

A parallel extension of Haskell using processes, but no explicit concurrency, is the programming language Eden [16].

Copying in CHF is very much like Concurrent Clean's [8] mechanism of lazy copying [43], since code parts of expressions are never copied, but referenced, whereas value parts are copied.

Outline. In Section 2 we introduce the syntax of the calculus CHF. In Section 3 we define a small-step reduction relation implementing the call-by-need strategy for CHF. In Section 4 we define contextual equivalence for CHF and show that this program equivalence remains unchanged if fair evaluation is used and we provide a context lemma. In Section 5 some first correctness results on program transformations are shown. In Section 6 we show that call-by-name evaluation is correct for CHF and prove correctness of a general copy rule. In Section 7 we use the developed techniques and results to show correctness of the monad laws in CHF. Finally, we conclude in Section 8. Missing proofs can be found in the technical report [34].

2. Syntax and Typing of CHF

In this section we present the syntax of the calculus CHF and provide a type system for the underlying language. The syntax has two layers: On the top-layer there are only processes and on the second layer there are expressions. Processes may have expressions as subterms. Let *Var* be a countably infinite set of variables. We denote variables with u, w, x, y, z (maybe indexed by natural numbers).

Processes Proc are generated by the following grammar where $e \in \mathit{Expr}$ is an arbitrary expression (defined below):

$$
\begin{array}{rcll}
P, Q, P_i, Q_i \in \mathit{Proc} & ::= & P_1 \mid P_2 & \text{(parallel composition)} \\
& \mid & x \Leftarrow e & \text{(concurrent thread)} \\
& \mid & \nu x.P & \text{(name restriction)} \\
& \mid & x\, \mathbf{m}\, e & \text{(filled MVar)} \\
& \mid & x\, \mathbf{m}\, - & \text{(empty MVar)} \\
& \mid & x = e & \text{(binding)}
\end{array}
$$

We give an informal meaning of these language constructs: Parallel composition and name restriction act like the corresponding constructs in the π-calculus, i.e. parallel composition constructs concurrently running threads (or other components) and ν-binders restrict the scope of variables. A concurrent thread $x \Leftarrow e$ evaluates the expression e and binds the result of the evaluation to the variable x. The variable x is also called the *future* x. In a process there is usually one unique distinguished thread: We assume that for a process at most one thread is labeled with "main" (i.e. as notation we use $x \overset{\mathsf{main}}{\Longleftarrow} e$). We call this thread the *main thread*. We will later see that there is no guarantee that all threads will be evaluated, while the main thread will eventually be evaluated. MVars are mutable variables which behave like one place buffers, i.e. if a thread wants to fill an already filled MVar, the thread blocks, and a thread also blocks if it tries to take something from an empty MVar. In $x\,\mathbf{m}\,e$ or $x\,\mathbf{m}\,-$ we call x the *name of the MVar*. Bindings $x = e$ model the global heap of shared expressions, where we say x is a *binding variable*. For a process P we say a variable x is an *introduced variable* if x is a future, a name of an MVar, or a binding variable. An introduced variable is visible to the whole process unless its scope is restricted by a ν-binder, i.e. in $Q \mid \nu x.P$ the scope of x is P.

For expressions we assume a set of *data constructors* c which is partitioned into sets, such that each family represents a type T. For a fixed type T we assume that the corresponding data constructors are ordered (denoted with $c_1, \ldots, c_{|T|}$, where $|T|$ is the number of constructors belonging to type T). Each data constructor c has a fixed arity $\mathrm{ar}(c) \geq 0$. For examples we assume that we have a type `Bool` with data constructors `True`, `False` and a type `List` with constructors `Nil` and `:` (written infix as in Haskell).

The syntax of expressions *Expr* is shown in Fig. 1. It comprises the constructs of a usual call-by-need lambda calculus and *monadic expressions MExpr* $\subseteq$ *Expr* which are used to model IO-operations by built-in primitives. We explain the syntactic constructs and fix some side conditions: The functional language has the usual constructs of the lambda calculus, i.e. variables, *abstractions* $\lambda x.e$, and *applications* $(e_1\ e_2)$. It is extended by *constructor applications* $(c\ e_1\ \ldots\ e_{\mathrm{ar}(c)})$ which allow constructors to occur fully saturated, only. As selectors `case`-*expressions* are part of the language, where for every type T there is one $\mathtt{case}_T$-construct. We sometimes abbreviate `case`-expressions with $\mathtt{case}_T\ e\ \mathtt{of}\ \mathit{Alts}$ where Alts are the `case`-*alternatives*. The `case`-alternatives must have exactly one alternative $(c_{T,i}\ x_1 \ldots x_{\mathrm{ar}(c_{T,i})} \to e_i)$ for every constructor $c_{T,i}$ of type T. The left hand side $c_{T,i}\ x_1 \ldots x_{\mathrm{ar}(c_{T,i})}$ of a `case`-alternative is called a *pattern* where the variables $x_1, \ldots, x_{\mathrm{ar}(c_{T,i})}$ must be pairwise distinct. In the alternative $(c_{T,i}\ x_1 \ldots x_{\mathrm{ar}(c_{T,i})} \to e_i)$ the variables x_i become bound with scope e_i. In examples we will also use `if` e `then` e_1 `else` e_2 as an abbreviation for the `case`-expression $\mathtt{case}_{\mathit{Bool}}\ e\ \mathtt{of}\ (\mathtt{True} \to e_1)\ (\mathtt{False} \to e_2)$. A further construct of the language are `seq`-*expressions* (`seq` e_1 e_2)

$$\frac{\Gamma \vdash e :: \texttt{IO}\ \tau}{\Gamma \vdash x \Leftarrow e :: \texttt{wt}} \quad \frac{\Gamma \vdash e :: \tau}{\Gamma \vdash x = e :: \texttt{wt}} \quad \frac{\Gamma \vdash P_1 :: \texttt{wt}, \quad \Gamma \vdash P_2 :: \texttt{wt}}{\Gamma \vdash P_1 \mid P_2 :: \texttt{wt}} \quad \frac{\Gamma(x) = \texttt{MVar}\ \tau, \quad \Gamma \vdash e :: \tau}{\Gamma \vdash x\,\mathbf{m}\,e :: \texttt{wt}} \quad \frac{\Gamma(x) = \texttt{MVar}\ \tau}{\Gamma \vdash x\,\mathbf{m} - :: \texttt{wt}} \quad \frac{\Gamma \vdash P :: \texttt{wt}}{\Gamma \vdash \nu x.P :: \texttt{wt}}$$

$$\frac{\Gamma \vdash e :: \tau}{\Gamma \vdash \texttt{return}\ e :: \texttt{IO}\ \tau} \quad \frac{\Gamma \vdash e_1 :: \texttt{IO}\ \tau_1, \quad \Gamma \vdash e_2 :: \tau_1 \to \texttt{IO}\ \tau_2}{\Gamma \vdash e_1 \gg\!= e_2 :: \texttt{IO}\ \tau_2} \quad \frac{\Gamma \vdash e :: \texttt{IO}\ \tau}{\Gamma \vdash \texttt{future}\ e :: \texttt{IO}\ \tau} \quad \frac{\Gamma \vdash e :: \texttt{MVar}\ \tau}{\Gamma \vdash \texttt{takeMVar}\ e :: \texttt{IO}\ \tau}$$

$$\frac{\Gamma \vdash e_1 :: \texttt{MVar}\ \tau, \quad \Gamma \vdash e_2 :: \tau}{\Gamma \vdash \texttt{putMVar}\ e_1\ e_2 :: \texttt{IO}\ ()} \quad \frac{\Gamma \vdash e :: \tau}{\Gamma \vdash \texttt{newMVar}\ e :: \texttt{IO}\ (\texttt{MVar}\ \tau)} \quad \frac{\forall i : \Gamma \vdash e_i :: \tau_i, \quad \tau_1 \to \ldots \to \tau_n \to \tau_{n+1} \in \texttt{types(c)}}{\Gamma \vdash (c\, e_1\ \ldots\ e_{\mathrm{ar}(c)}) :: \tau_{n+1}}$$

$$\frac{\forall i : \Gamma(x_i) = \tau_i, \quad \forall i : \Gamma \vdash e_i :: \tau_i, \quad \Gamma \vdash e :: \tau}{\Gamma \vdash (\texttt{letrec}\ x_1 = e_1, \ \ldots\ x_n = e_n\ \texttt{in}\ e) :: \tau} \quad \frac{\Gamma \vdash e_1 :: \tau_1 \to \tau_2, \quad \Gamma \vdash e_2 :: \tau_1}{\Gamma \vdash (e_1\ e_2) :: \tau_2} \quad \frac{\Gamma(x) = \tau_1, \quad \Gamma \vdash e :: \tau_2}{\Gamma \vdash (\lambda x.e) :: \tau_1 \to \tau_2} \quad \frac{\Gamma(x) = \tau}{\Gamma \vdash x :: \tau}$$

$$\frac{\begin{array}{c}\Gamma \vdash e_1 :: \tau_1, \quad \Gamma \vdash e_2 :: \tau_2 \\ \tau_1 = \tau_3 \to \tau_4 \text{ or } \tau_1 = (T \ldots)\end{array}}{\Gamma \vdash (\texttt{seq}\ e_1\ e_2) :: \tau_2} \quad \frac{\Gamma \vdash e :: \tau_1 \text{ and } \tau_1 = (T\ \ldots), \quad \forall i : \Gamma \vdash (c_i\, x_{1,i}\ \ldots\ x_{n_i,i}) :: \tau_1, \quad \forall i : \Gamma \vdash e_i :: \tau_2}{\Gamma \vdash (\texttt{case}_T\ e\ \texttt{of}(c_1\, x_{1,1}\ \ldots\ x_{n_1,1} \to e_1) \ldots (c_m\, x_{1,m}\ \ldots\ x_{n_m,m} \to e_m)) :: \tau_2}$$

Figure 2. Typing rules

which model Haskell's `seq`-operator for strict evaluation. Additionally, the language has `letrec`-*expressions* which implement local sharing and enables one to declare recursive bindings. In $\texttt{letrec}\ x_1 = e_1, \ldots, x_n = e_n\ \texttt{in}\ e$ the variables $x_1, \ldots, x_n$ must be pairwise distinct and the bindings $x_i = e_i$ are recursive, i.e. the scope of x_i is $e_1, \ldots, e_n$ and e. We sometimes abbreviate `letrec`-environments as *Env*, i.e. we write `letrec` *Env* `in` e. The constructs `newMVar`, `takeMVar`, and `putMVar` are used to create and access MVars. The primitive "bind" operator $\gg\!=$ implements the sequential composition of IO-operations, the `future`-operator is used for thread creation, and the `return`-operator lifts expressions to monadic expressions. All these primitives must occur with all their arguments present.

Functional values are defined as abstractions and constructor applications. The monadic expressions $(\texttt{return}\ e)$, $(e_1 \gg\!= e_2)$, $(\texttt{future}\ e)$, $(\texttt{takeMVar}\ e)$, $(\texttt{newMVar}\ e)$, $(\texttt{putMVar}\ e_1\ e_2)$ where e, e_i are arbitrary expressions are called *monadic values*. A *value* is either a functional value or a monadic value.

A process is *well-formed*, if all introduced variables are pairwise distinct, and there exists at most one main thread $x \overset{\text{main}}{\Longleftarrow} e$.

Variable binders are introduced by abstractions, `letrec`-expressions, `case`-alternatives, and for processes by the restriction $\nu x.P$. This induces a notion of free and bound variables as well as α-renaming and α-equivalence (denoted by $=_\alpha$). With $FV(P)$ ($FV(e)$, resp) we denote the free variables of process P (expression e, resp.). We assume the *distinct variable convention* to hold, i.e. free variables are distinct from bound variables, and bound variables are pairwise distinct. We assume that reductions implicitly perform α-renaming to obey this convention.

For processes we define a structural congruence to equate obviously equal processes.

Definition 2.1. *Structural congruence* $\equiv$ is the least congruence satisfying the equations:

$$\begin{array}{rcll} P_1 \mid P_2 & \equiv & P_2 \mid P_1 & \\ (P_1 \mid P_2) \mid P_3 & \equiv & P_1 \mid (P_2 \mid P_3) & \\ (\nu x.P_1) \mid P_2 & \equiv & \nu x.(P_1 \mid P_2) & \text{if } x \notin FV(P_2) \\ \nu x_1.\nu x_2.P & \equiv & \nu x_2.\nu x_1.P & \\ P_1 & \equiv & P_2 & \text{if } P_1 =_\alpha P_2 \end{array}$$

2.1 A Monomorphic Type System

In this section we provide a type system for CHF. For simplicity we choose a monomorphic type system. The use of a polymorphic type system would require more effort for correctness proofs in later sections, since types must be invariant during reduction (e.g. one could use a system F like type-system, but there are also other approaches using explicit type labels, for instance [35]).

Nevertheless we "overload" the data constructors and thus we assume that data types used in case-constructs have a fixed arity, and that the data constructors of every type have a polymorphic type according to the usual conventions. In the language the constructors are used monomorphic. The set of monomorphic types of constructor c is denoted as $\texttt{types}(c)$. The syntax of types *Typ* is:

$$\tau, \tau_i \in \mathit{Typ} ::= \texttt{IO}\ \tau \mid (T\ \tau_1\ \ldots\ \tau_n) \mid \texttt{MVar}\ \tau \mid \tau_1 \to \tau_2$$

Here $(\texttt{IO}\ \tau)$ means that an expression of type τ is packed into a monadic action, $(\texttt{MVar}\ \tau)$ stands for an `MVar`-reference with content type τ, and $\tau_1 \to \tau_2$ is a function type.

To fix the types during reduction, we assume that every variable is explicitly typed, i.e. we assume that every variable x has a built-in type. We denote the global typing function for variables with Γ, i.e. $\Gamma(x)$ is the type of variable x. The notation $\Gamma \vdash e :: \tau$ means that type τ can be derived for expression e using the global typing function Γ. For processes the notation $\Gamma \vdash P :: \texttt{wt}$ means that the process P can be well-typed using the global typing function Γ.

The typing rules are in Fig. 2. A reference type or an `IO`-type for the first argument of `seq`-expressions is forbidden. This restriction is not valid in Haskell, but is indispensable for the validity of several semantical rules and the correctness of program transformations, like the monad laws (see Section 7). Note that the type system can easily be transformed into a "more standard one" if Γ is viewed as a type environment and the rules for variable binders are adjusted such that they add type assumptions to the environment.

Definition 2.2. A process P is *well-typed* iff P is well-formed and $\Gamma \vdash P :: \texttt{wt}$ holds. An expression e is *well-typed* with type τ (written as $e :: \tau$) iff $\Gamma \vdash e :: \tau$ holds.

3. Operational Semantics of CHF

In this section we define the operational semantics of the calculus CHF as a small-step reduction relation called *standard reduction*. As a first definition we introduce *successful processes*, i.e. processes which are seen as successful outcomes of the standard reduction.

Definition 3.1. A well-formed process P is *successful*, if P has a main thread of the form $x \overset{\text{main}}{\Longleftarrow} \texttt{return}\ e$, i.e. $P \equiv \nu x_1 \ldots \nu x_n.(x \overset{\text{main}}{\Longleftarrow} \texttt{return}\ e \mid P')$.

We permit standard reductions only for well-formed processes which are not successful, i.e. successful as well as non-well-formed processes are irreducible by definition. This can be justified as follows: Non-well-formed processes can be singled out by the parser

Monadic Computations

(lunit) $y \Leftarrow \mathbb{M}[\texttt{return}\ e_1 \gg\!= e_2] \xrightarrow{sr} y \Leftarrow \mathbb{M}[e_2\ e_1]$

(tmvar) $y \Leftarrow \mathbb{M}[\texttt{takeMVar}\ x] \mid x\,\mathbf{m}\,e \xrightarrow{sr} y \Leftarrow \mathbb{M}[\texttt{return}\ e] \mid x\,\mathbf{m}\,-$

(pmvar) $y \Leftarrow \mathbb{M}[\texttt{putMVar}\ x\ e] \mid x\,\mathbf{m}\,- \xrightarrow{sr} y \Leftarrow \mathbb{M}[\texttt{return}\ ()] \mid x\,\mathbf{m}\,e$

(nmvar) $y \Leftarrow \mathbb{M}[\texttt{newMVar}\ e] \xrightarrow{sr} \nu x.(y \Leftarrow \mathbb{M}[\texttt{return}\ x] \mid x\,\mathbf{m}\,e)$

(fork) $y \Leftarrow \mathbb{M}[\texttt{future}\ e] \xrightarrow{sr} \nu z.(y \Leftarrow \mathbb{M}[\texttt{return}\ z] \mid z \Leftarrow e)$, where z is fresh and the created thread is not the main thread

(unIO) $y \Leftarrow \texttt{return}\ e \xrightarrow{sr} y = e$, if the thread is not the main-thread

Functional Evaluation

(cp) $\widehat{\mathbb{L}}[x] \mid x = v \xrightarrow{sr} \widehat{\mathbb{L}}[v] \mid x = v$, if v is an abstraction or a variable

(cpcx) $\widehat{\mathbb{L}}[x] \mid x = c\,e_1 \ldots e_n \xrightarrow{sr} \nu y_1, \ldots y_n.(\widehat{\mathbb{L}}[c\,y_1\ \ldots\ y_n] \mid x = c\,y_1\ \ldots\ y_n \mid y_1 = e_1 \mid \ldots \mid y_n = e_n)$
if c is a constructor, or `return`, `>>=`, `takeMVar`, `putMVar`, `newMVar`, or `future`

(mkbinds) $\mathbb{L}[\texttt{letrec}\ x_1 = e_1, \ldots, x_n = e_n\ \texttt{in}\ e] \xrightarrow{sr} \nu x_1, \ldots, x_n.(\mathbb{L}[e] \mid x_1 = e_1 \mid \ldots \mid x_n = e_n)$

(lbeta) $\mathbb{L}[((\lambda x.e_1)\ e_2)] \xrightarrow{sr} \nu x.(\mathbb{L}[e_1] \mid x = e_2)$

(case) $\mathbb{L}[\texttt{case}_T\ (c\,e_1\ \ldots\ e_n)\ \texttt{of}\ \ldots((c\,y_1\ \ldots\ y_n) \to e)\ldots] \xrightarrow{sr} \nu y_1, \ldots, y_n.(\mathbb{L}[e] \mid y_1 = e_1 \mid \ldots \mid y_n = e_n])$, if $n > 0$

(case) $\mathbb{L}[\texttt{case}_T\ c\ \texttt{of}\ \ldots(c \to e)\ldots] \xrightarrow{sr} \mathbb{L}[e]$

(seq) $\mathbb{L}[(\texttt{seq}\ v\ e)] \xrightarrow{sr} \mathbb{L}[e]$, if v is a functional value

Figure 3. Standard reduction rules

of a compiler, successful processes may have reducible threads (but not the main thread $x \overset{\text{main}}{\Longleftarrow} e$), but in Haskell all concurrent threads are terminated, if the main-thread terminates.

For the definition of the standard reduction we require the notion of contexts. A context is an expression with a hole $[\cdot]$. We assume that the hole $[\cdot]$ is typed and carries a type label, which we sometimes write as $[\cdot^\tau]$. The typing rules are accordingly extended by the axiom for the hole: $\Gamma \vdash [\cdot^\tau] :: \tau$. Given a context $C[\cdot^\tau]$ and an expression $e :: \tau$, $C[e]$ denotes the result of replacing the hole in C with expression e, where a variable capture is permitted. Since our syntax has different syntactic categories, we require different contexts: (i) process contexts that are processes with a hole at process position, (ii) expression contexts that are expressions with a hole at expression position, and (iii) process contexts with an expression hole.

On the process level we define the *process contexts PCtxt* as follows, where $P \in$ *Proc*:

$$\mathbb{D}, \mathbb{D}_i \in \mathit{PCtxt} ::= [\cdot] \mid \mathbb{D} \mid P \mid P \mid \mathbb{D} \mid \nu x.\mathbb{D}$$

The standard reduction rules use process contexts (together with the structural congruence) to select some components for the reductions. In general, these components are: a single thread, a thread and a (filled or empty) MVar, or a thread and a set of bindings (which are referenced and used by the selected thread).

Although we require further classes of contexts for the complete definition of the standard reduction, we introduce the standard reduction at this point. We will then explain further contexts and thereafter we explain the reduction rules in detail.

Definition 3.2. The *standard reduction rules* are given in Fig. 3 where the outer *PCtxt*-context is omitted. But we assume reductions to be closed w.r.t. *PCtxt*-contexts and w.r.t. structural congruence, i.e. the *standard reduction relation* $\xrightarrow{sr}$ is the smallest set that contains the union of the rules in Fig. 3 and if $P_1 \equiv \mathbb{D}[P_1']$ and $P_2 \equiv \mathbb{D}[P_2']$ such that $P_1' \xrightarrow{sr} P_2'$, then also $P_1 \xrightarrow{sr} P_2$.

With $\xrightarrow{sr,+}$ we denote the transitive closure of $\xrightarrow{sr}$, and with $\xrightarrow{sr,*}$ we denote the reflexive-transitive closure of $\xrightarrow{sr}$.

For the evaluation of monadic expressions we define the *monadic contexts MCtxt*. They are used to "find" the first monadic action in a sequence of actions.

$$\mathbb{M}, \mathbb{M}_i \in \mathit{MCtxt} \quad ::= \quad [\cdot] \mid \mathbb{M} \gg\!= e$$

On expressions we use usual (call-by-name) *expression evaluation contexts ECtxt* defined as follows:

$$\mathbb{E}, \mathbb{E}_i \in \mathit{ECtxt} ::= [\cdot] \mid (\mathbb{E}\ e) \mid (\texttt{case}\ \mathbb{E}\ \texttt{of}\ alts) \mid (\texttt{seq}\ \mathbb{E}\ e)$$

Sometimes, the evaluation of the (first) argument of the monadic operations `takeMVar` and `putMVar` must be forced. (i.e. before the corresponding monadic action can be performed). For example, the process

$$x \Leftarrow (\texttt{takeMVar}\ ((\lambda x.x)\ y)) \gg\!= \lambda z.(\texttt{return}\ ()) \mid y\,\mathbf{m}\,\texttt{True}$$

must first evaluate $((\lambda x.x)\ y)$ before performing the `takeMVar`-operation. To model these cases correctly (i.e. as in Haskell) we introduce the *forcing contexts FCtxt*.

$$\mathbb{F}, \mathbb{F}_i \in \mathit{FCtxt} ::= \mathbb{E} \mid (\texttt{takeMVar}\ \mathbb{E}) \mid (\texttt{putMVar}\ \mathbb{E}\ e)$$

Finally, we define the contexts *LCtxt* which model the search for a redex after one thread was already selected. The necessary reduction may either be a monadic computation, or a "functional evaluation". If the thread needs the value of a binding, then the functional evaluation may be performed inside a binding. For instance consider the process

$$x \overset{\text{main}}{\Longleftarrow} y\,0 \mid y = z\,1 \mid z = (\lambda x_1.\lambda x_2.\lambda x_3.\texttt{return}\ x_3)\ 2$$

The main-thread needs the value of y, the binding for y needs the result of z. Hence, the standard reduction is:

$$\xrightarrow{sr,\text{lbeta}} x \overset{\text{main}}{\Longleftarrow} y\,0 \mid y = z\,1 \mid \nu x_1.(z = \lambda x_2.\lambda x_3.\texttt{return}\ x_3 \mid x_1 = 2)$$

The contexts *LCtxt* model this redex search. They are defined in Fig. 4. A special class of *LCtxt*-contexts are the contexts $\widehat{LCtxt}$. They are used for the copying rules (i.e. the rules (cp) and (cpcx)) and require that the context $\mathbb{E}_1$ must not be empty. This class of contexts is necessary for the case of variable-to-variable bindings, i.e. if a thread demands the value of x and $x = y$ is a binding, then evaluation does not follow this binding, but copies the name y. For instance, for the process $z \overset{\text{main}}{\Longleftarrow} x \mid x = y \mid y = \texttt{return}\ ()$ the standard reduction proceeds as follows:

$$\xrightarrow{sr,\text{cp}} z \overset{\text{main}}{\Longleftarrow} y \mid x = y \mid y = \texttt{return}\ ()$$
$$\xrightarrow{sr,\text{cpcx}} \nu w.(z \overset{\text{main}}{\Longleftarrow} \texttt{return}\ w \mid x = y \mid y = \texttt{return}\ w \mid w = ()).$$

We now explain the standard reduction rules of Fig. 3 in detail. The first part of the rules performs monadic computations while

$$\mathbb{L}, \mathbb{L}_i \in \mathit{LCtxt} ::= (x \Leftarrow \mathbb{M}[\mathbb{F}]) \;\mid\; (x \Leftarrow \mathbb{M}[\mathbb{F}[x_n]] \mid x_n = \mathbb{E}_n[x_{n-1}] \mid \ldots \mid x_2 = \mathbb{E}_2[x_1] \mid x_1 = \mathbb{E}_1), \text{ where } \mathbb{E}_i \neq [\cdot] \text{ for } i = 2, \ldots, n.$$

$$\widehat{\mathbb{L}}, \widehat{\mathbb{L}}_i \in \widehat{\mathit{LCtxt}} ::= (x \Leftarrow \mathbb{M}[\mathbb{F}]) \;\mid\; (x \Leftarrow \mathbb{M}[\mathbb{F}[x_n]] \mid x_n = \mathbb{E}_n[x_{n-1}] \mid \ldots \mid x_2 = \mathbb{E}_2[x_1] \mid x_1 = \mathbb{E}_1), \text{ where } \mathbb{E}_i \neq [\cdot] \text{ for } i = 1, \ldots, n.$$

Figure 4. The *LCtxt*- and the $\widehat{LCtxt}$-contexts.

the second part performs functional evaluation on expressions. The *redex* is defined as follows: For (lunit), (tmvar), (pmvar), (nmvar), (fork), it is the monadic expression in the context $\mathbb{M}$, for the rule (unIO), it is $y \Leftarrow \texttt{return}\ e$, for (mkbinds), (lbeta), (case), (seq), it is the functional expression in the context $\mathbb{L}$, and for (cp), (cpcx) it is the variable x in the context $\widehat{\mathbb{L}}$.

The rule (lunit) is the direct implementation of the monadic sequencing operator `>>=`. Consider a sequence $a \gg\!= b$. If a is of the form `return` e then the monadic computation of a is finished (with the result e), hence the next computation (b) of the sequence can be started. Since the result e of the first computation may be used by b, the evaluation proceeds with $(b\ e)$.

The rules (tmvar) and (pmvar) perform a `takeMVar`- or a `putMVar`-operation on a filled (or empty, resp.) MVar. Note that there is no rule for a `takeMVar`-operation on an empty MVar (for a `putMVar`-operation on a filled MVar, resp.), which models the blocking behavior of MVars. The rule (nmvar) creates a new filled MVar. The rule (fork) spawns a new thread for a concurrent computation. In Haskell the return value of a `forkIO`-operation is a thread identifier (a number). Since CHF uses variables to identify threads, the result of a `future`-operation in CHF is the corresponding variable. The rule (unIO) binds the result of a monadic computation to a functional binding, i.e. the value of a concurrent future becomes accessible.

The rules (cp) and (cpcx) are used to inline a needed binding $x = e$. Here e must be an abstraction, a variable, a constructor application or a monadic expression. To implement call-by-need evaluation the (maybe non-value) arguments of constructor applications (and monadic expressions) are shared by new bindings, similar to lazy copying [43].

The rule (mkbinds) moves the bindings of a `letrec`-expression into the global heap bindings. ν-binders are introduced to restrict the access to the bindings of the concurrent thread only. The rule (lbeta) is the call-by-need variant of classical β-reduction, where the argument is not substituted in the body of the abstraction but shared by a new global binding. The (case)-reduction reduces a `case`-expression, where – if the scrutinee is not a constant – bindings are created to implement sharing. The (seq)-rule evaluates a `seq`-expression: If the first argument is a functional value, then the seq-expression is replaced by its second argument.

Proposition 3.3. *The following properties hold for the standard reduction* $\xrightarrow{sr}$*: (1) If* $P \xrightarrow{sr} P'$ *and* P *is well-formed, then* P' *remains well-formed. (2) If* $P \xrightarrow{sr} P'$ *and* P *is well-typed, then* P' *remains well-typed. (3) Reduction is unique for threads. I.e. if* P *contains only one thread, then for all* P_1, P_2 *with* $P \xrightarrow{sr} P_i$ *(i=1,2):* $P_1 \equiv P_2$*. (4) Reduction cannot introduce or remove a main-thread.*

Proof. (1) holds, since the reduction rules only introduce variables which are fresh and never introduce a main thread. Type preservation (2) holds since every redex keeps the type of subexpressions. (3) and (4) can be shown by induction on the process structure. □

Example 3.4. The following example shows that standard reduction is non-deterministic. Consider the process P:

$$x \stackrel{\text{main}}{\Longleftarrow} \texttt{takeMVar}\ y \mid y\,\mathbf{m}\,\texttt{True}$$
$$\mid z \Leftarrow \texttt{takeMVar}\ y \gg\!= \lambda w.(\texttt{putMVar}\ y\ \texttt{False})$$

If the main-thread is reduced, we obtain a successful process:

$$P \xrightarrow{sr,\text{tmvar}} x \stackrel{\text{main}}{\Longleftarrow} \texttt{return True} \mid y\,\mathbf{m}\,-.$$
$$\mid z \Leftarrow \texttt{takeMVar}\ y \gg\!= \lambda w.(\texttt{putMVar}\ y\ \texttt{False})$$

If the thread with identifier z is reduced four times and then the main-thread is reduced, then we also obtain a successful process, but the result is different (we omit ν-binders):

$$P \xrightarrow{sr,\text{tmvar}} x \stackrel{\text{main}}{\Longleftarrow} \texttt{takeMVar}\ y \mid y\,\mathbf{m}\,-$$
$$\mid z \Leftarrow \texttt{return True} \gg\!= \lambda w.(\texttt{putMVar}\ y\ \texttt{False})$$
$$\xrightarrow{sr,\text{lunit}} x \stackrel{\text{main}}{\Longleftarrow} \texttt{takeMVar}\ y \mid y\,\mathbf{m}\,-$$
$$\mid z \Leftarrow (\lambda w.(\texttt{putMVar}\ y\ \texttt{False}))\ \texttt{True}$$
$$\xrightarrow{sr,\text{lbeta}} x \stackrel{\text{main}}{\Longleftarrow} \texttt{takeMVar}\ y \mid y\,\mathbf{m}\,-$$
$$\mid z \Leftarrow \texttt{putMVar}\ y\ \texttt{False} \mid w = \texttt{True}$$
$$\xrightarrow{sr,\text{pmvar}} x \stackrel{\text{main}}{\Longleftarrow} \texttt{takeMVar}\ y \mid y\,\mathbf{m}\,\texttt{False}$$
$$\mid z \Leftarrow \texttt{return}\ () \mid w = \texttt{True}$$
$$\xrightarrow{sr,\text{tmvar}} x \stackrel{\text{main}}{\Longleftarrow} \texttt{return False} \mid y\,\mathbf{m}\,-$$
$$\mid z \Leftarrow \texttt{return}\ () \mid w = \texttt{True}$$

Note that after the first (sr, tmvar)-reduction the main-thread is blocked until the MVar y becomes filled.

Example 3.5. As a further example we demonstrate how a (monadic) binary amb-operator can be implemented:

$$\begin{aligned} amb = \lambda x_1, x_2.\ & \texttt{newMVar}\ x_1 \gg\!= \\ & \lambda m.\texttt{takeMVar} \gg\!= \\ & \lambda\_.(\texttt{future}\ (\texttt{seq}\ x_1\ (\texttt{putMVar}\ m\ x_1)) \gg\!= \\ & \lambda\_.(\texttt{future}\ (\texttt{seq}\ x_2\ (\texttt{putMVar}\ m\ x_2)) \gg\!= \\ & \lambda\_.\texttt{takeMVar}\ m)) \end{aligned}$$

This expression implements McCarthy's bottom-avoiding choice [19]: applied to two arguments e_1, e_2, the result of $amb\ e_1\ e_2$ is the monadic action returning the value of e_1 or e_2 (if both evaluate to a value), or the value of e_i if e_j diverges (for $(i,j) \in \{(1,2),(2,1)\}$). Using futures we can extend the binary operator for a whole list of arguments. Let $\bot$ be a closed diverging expression, e.g. $(\texttt{letrec}\ x = x\ \texttt{in}\ x)$:

$$\begin{aligned} & \texttt{letrec}\ ambList = \\ & \quad \lambda xs.\texttt{case}_{List}\ xs\ \texttt{of} \\ & \qquad (\texttt{Nil} \to \texttt{return}\ \bot), \\ & \qquad (y : ys \to \texttt{future}\ (ambList\ ys) \gg\!= \lambda ys'.amb\ y\ ys') \\ & \texttt{in}\ ambList \end{aligned}$$

4. Contextual Equivalence

In this section we introduce a notion of program equivalence for processes and for expressions. We will use contextual equivalence by observing may- and should-convergence. Subsequently, we discuss fairness of reductions and provide context lemmas which ease proofs of equivalences.

Contextual equivalence equates two processes P_1, P_2 if their observable behavior is indistinguishable if P_1 and P_2 are plugged into any process context.

For nondeterministic (and also concurrent) calculi the observation of may-convergence, i.e. the question whether or a not a process can be reduced to a successful process, is *not* sufficient to distinguish obviously different processes. It is also necessary to analyze the possibility of introducing errors or non-termination.

Thus we will observe may-convergence and a variant of must-convergence which we call should-convergence (see [32, 33]). The definitions are as follows:

Definition 4.1. A process P *may-converges* (written as $P\downarrow$), iff it is well-formed and reduces to a successful process, i.e.

$$P\downarrow \text{ iff } P \text{ is well-formed and } \exists P' : P \xrightarrow{sr,*} P' \wedge P' \text{ successful}$$

If $P\downarrow$ does not hold, then P *must-diverges* written as $P\Uparrow$. A process P *should-converges* (written as $P\Downarrow$), iff it is well-formed and remains may-convergent under reduction, i.e.

$$P\Downarrow \text{ iff } P \text{ is well-formed and } \forall P' : P \xrightarrow{sr,*} P' \implies P'\downarrow$$

If P is not should-convergent then we say P *may-diverges* written as $P\uparrow$.

Note that may-divergence can alternatively be characterized by: A process P is may-divergent if there is a finite reduction sequence $P \xrightarrow{sr,*} P'$ such that $P'\Uparrow$.

We sometimes write $P\downarrow P'$ (or $P\uparrow P'$, resp.) if $P \xrightarrow{sr,*} P'$ and P' is a successful (or must-divergent, resp.) process.

Our definition of reduction implies that non-wellformed processes are always must-divergent, since they are irreducible and never successful. Also, the process construction by $\mathbb{D}[P]$ is always well-typed if P is well-typed, since we assume that variables have a built-in type.

Definition 4.2. *Contextual approximation* $\leq_c$ and *contextual equivalence* $\sim_c$ on processes are defined as follows:

$$\begin{array}{rcll} P_1 & \leq_\downarrow & P_2 & \text{iff } \forall \mathbb{D} \in \mathit{PCtxt} : \mathbb{D}[P_1]\downarrow \implies \mathbb{D}[P_2]\downarrow \\ P_1 & \leq_\Downarrow & P_2 & \text{iff } \forall \mathbb{D} \in \mathit{PCtxt} : \mathbb{D}[P_1]\Downarrow \implies \mathbb{D}[P_2]\Downarrow \\ \leq_c & := & \leq_\downarrow \cap \leq_\Downarrow & \\ \sim_c & := & \leq_c \cap \geq_c & \end{array}$$

The previous definition only equates (or distinguishes) *processes*. We now define contextual approximation and equivalence on *expressions*. Let *CCtxt* be the class of process contexts that have their (typed) hole at an arbitrary expression position. We use $\mathbb{C}, \mathbb{C}_i$ for *CCtxt*-contexts.

Definition 4.3. Let τ be a type. Contextual approximation $\leq_{c,\tau}$ and contextual equivalence $\sim_{c,\tau}$ on expressions are defined as $\leq_{c,\tau} := \leq_{\downarrow,\tau} \cap \leq_{\Downarrow,\tau}$ and $\sim_{c,\tau} := \leq_{c,\tau} \cap \geq_{c,\tau}$, where for expressions e_1, e_2 of type τ:

$$\begin{array}{lll} e_1 \leq_{\downarrow,\tau} e_2 & \text{iff} & \forall \mathbb{C}[\cdot^\tau] \in \mathit{CCtxt} : \mathbb{C}[e_1]\downarrow \implies \mathbb{C}[e_2]\downarrow \\ e_1 \leq_{\Downarrow,\tau} e_2 & \text{iff} & \forall \mathbb{C}[\cdot^\tau] \in \mathit{CCtxt} : \mathbb{C}[e_1]\Downarrow \implies \mathbb{C}[e_2]\Downarrow \end{array}$$

Remark 4.4. An interesting fact is that closed must-divergent expressions are *not* least elements w.r.t. $\leq_c$. Let amb be defined as in Example 3.5 and let C be the context

$$z \overset{\text{main}}{\Longleftarrow} amb\ \texttt{True}\ [\cdot] \ggg= \lambda r.(\texttt{if}\ r\ \texttt{then return True else}\ \bot)$$

where $\bot$ is a closed must-divergent expression of type `Bool`. Then $C[\bot]\Downarrow$, but $C[\texttt{False}]\uparrow$ and thus $\bot \not\leq_{c,\texttt{Bool}} \texttt{False}$.

A first result is that structural congruence preserves contextual equivalence:

Proposition 4.5. *Let P_1, P_2 be well-formed processes such that $P_1 \equiv P_2$. Then $P_1 \sim_c P_2$.*

4.1 Fairness

In this section we show that contextual equivalence is unchanged if we disallow unfair reduction sequences. I.e. we assume that fair scheduling is performed for a real implementation of CHF, but since we will show that contextual equivalence is unchanged we do not need to take care about it in our further reasoning.

For a process $P \equiv \mathbb{D}[x \Leftarrow e]$ we say future x *is enabled* if there is an sr-reduction applicable to P, such that $x \Leftarrow e$ is a part of the redex or e (with its position in the thread of future x) is a superexpression of the redex. In a reduction sequence we say future x is reduced, if there exists a reduction step where x is enabled and the corresponding standard reduction for x is used.

For a process P an *infinite* reduction sequence $RED := P \xrightarrow{sr} P_1 \xrightarrow{sr} P_2 \xrightarrow{sr} \dots$ is *unfair* if there is an infinite suffix RED' of RED and there exists a future x which is enabled in infinitely many processes of RED' but never reduced. Otherwise, we say RED is a *fair* reduction sequence.

A process P is *fair* may-convergent, iff there exists a finite reduction sequence ending in a successful process.

A process P is *fair* should-convergent, iff all finite reduction sequences starting with P end in a successful process and for every fair infinite reduction sequence RED the following holds: for every finite prefix RED' of RED there exists a finite reduction sequence RED'' ending in a successful process such that RED' is a prefix of RED''.

In [34] we show that the convergence predicates (may- and should-convergence) coincide with the fair convergence predicates, and thus the following theorem holds:

Theorem 4.6. *Contextual equivalence is unchanged if unfair reduction sequences are forbidden.*

Remark 4.7. Note that must-convergence (the test whether all maximal reduction sequences are finite and end successfully) does *not* coincide with *fair* must-convergence (must-convergence restricted to fair reduction sequences, only). A counter-example is the (should-convergent) process

$$\begin{array}{r} x \overset{\text{main}}{\Longleftarrow} (\lambda x.\,\texttt{return}\ x)\ \texttt{True} \mid y \Leftarrow \mathit{forever}\ (\texttt{return}\ ()) \\ \mid \mathit{forever} = \lambda a.a \ggg= \lambda\_.(\mathit{forever}\ a) \end{array}$$

There is an unfair infinite reduction sequence: always reduce future y and ignore the main thread. On the other hand there are no infinite fair reduction sequences, since any fair reduction sequence eventually must reduce the main thread.

4.2 Context Lemmas

Context Lemmas are helpful tools, since they usually show that not all but a restricted class of contexts needs to be considered for proving two expressions (or processes) contextually equal (see also e.g. [11, 18, 38]). We first consider processes. For a process P we say P is in *prenex normal form* iff $P = \nu x_1, \dots x_n.(P_1 \mid \dots \mid P_m)$ and for $1 \leq i \leq m$: P_i does not contain ν-binders.

In [34] we prove the following lemma:

Lemma 4.8 (Prenex Context Lemma). *For all well-formed processes P_1, P_2 it holds: (1) If for all ν-free process contexts $\mathbb{D} \in \mathit{PCtxt}$ and all variable-substitutions σ: $\mathbb{D}[\sigma(P_1)]\downarrow \implies \mathbb{D}[\sigma(P_2)]\downarrow$, then $P_1 \leq_\downarrow P_2$. (2) If for all ν-free process contexts $\mathbb{D} \in \mathit{PCtxt}$ and all variable-substitutions σ: $\mathbb{D}[\sigma(P_1)]\Downarrow \implies \mathbb{D}[\sigma(P_2)]\Downarrow$, then $P_1 \leq_\Downarrow P_2$.*

In addition to the prenex-context lemma for processes, we provide a context lemma for expressions (the proof can be found in [34], and is very similar to the proof in [38]), which shows that the class of $\mathbb{D}[\mathbb{L}]$-contexts are sufficient:

Lemma 4.9 (Context Lemma for Expressions). *Let e_1, e_2 be expressions of type τ such that for all $\mathbb{D} \in \mathit{PCtxt}$ and $\mathbb{L}[\cdot^\tau] \in \mathit{LCtxt}$: $\mathbb{D}[\mathbb{L}[e_1]]\downarrow \implies \mathbb{D}[\mathbb{L}[e_2]]\downarrow$ and $\mathbb{D}[\mathbb{L}[e_1]]\Downarrow \implies \mathbb{D}[\mathbb{L}[e_2]]\Downarrow$. Then $e_1 \leq_{c,\tau} e_2$.*

5. Program Transformations

A *program transformation* γ on processes is a binary relation on processes. It is *correct* iff $\gamma \subseteq \sim_c$. A *program transformation* γ on

(dtmvar) $\nu x.\mathbb{D}[y \Leftarrow \mathbb{M}[\texttt{takeMVar}\ x] \mid x\, \mathbf{m}\, e] \quad \rightarrow \quad \nu x.\mathbb{D}[y \Leftarrow \mathbb{M}[\texttt{return}\ e] \mid x\, \mathbf{m}\, -]$
if for all $\mathbb{D}' \in \mathit{PCtxt}$ and all $\xrightarrow{sr,*}$-sequences starting with $\mathbb{D}'[\nu x.(\mathbb{D}[y \Leftarrow \mathbb{M}[\texttt{takeMVar}\ x] \mid x\, \mathbf{m}\, e])]$ the first execution of any ($\texttt{takeMVar}\ x$)-operation takes place in the y-thread

(dpmvar) $\nu x.\mathbb{D}[y \Leftarrow \mathbb{M}[\texttt{putMVar}\ x\ e] \mid x\, \mathbf{m}\, -] \quad \rightarrow \quad \nu x.\mathbb{D}[y \Leftarrow \mathbb{M}[\texttt{return}\ ()] \mid x\, \mathbf{m}\, e]$
if for all $\mathbb{D}' \in \mathit{PCtxt}$ and all $\xrightarrow{sr,*}$-sequences starting with $\mathbb{D}'[\nu x.(\mathbb{D}[y \Leftarrow \mathbb{M}[\texttt{putMVar}\ x\ e] \mid x\, \mathbf{m}\, -])]$ the first execution of any ($\texttt{putMVar}\ x\ e'$)-operation takes place in the y-thread

(gc) $\nu x_1, \ldots, x_n.(P \mid \texttt{Comp}(x_1) \mid \ldots \mid \texttt{Comp}(x_n)) \quad \rightarrow \quad P$
if for all $i \in \{1, \ldots, n\}$: $\texttt{Comp}(x_i)$ is a binding $x_i = e_i$, an MVar $x_i\, \mathbf{m}\, e_i$, or an empty MVar $x_i\, \mathbf{m}\, -$, and $x_i \notin FV(P)$.

Figure 5. Transformations for deterministic MVar-access and garbage collection

expressions is a binary relation on equally typed expressions. It is *correct* iff $\gamma \subseteq \bigcup_\tau \sim_{c,\tau}$.

We show in this section that several transformations induced by standard reductions are correct program transformations, and also that several reduction rules are correct in any context.

We write (sr, a) (or alternatively $\xrightarrow{sr,a}$) to denote the standard reduction a. For a transformation γ we write $(\mathbb{D}, \gamma)$ (or alternatively $\xrightarrow{\mathbb{D},\gamma}$) to denote the closure of γ w.r.t. *PCtxt*-contexts, i.e. $(\mathbb{D}, \gamma) := \{(\mathbb{D}[P_1], \mathbb{D}[P_2]) \mid P_1 \xrightarrow{\gamma} P_2, \mathbb{D} \in \mathit{PCtxt}\}$. We use this notation also for other context classes, e.g. $(\mathbb{D}[\mathbb{L}], \gamma)$ is the closure of the transformation γ applied inside all *PCtxt*- and *LCtxt*-contexts. We sometimes attach further information to reduction arrows, e.g. $\xrightarrow{sr,a,k}$ means k sr-reductions of type a; we use $*$ and $+$ to denote the reflexive-transitive and the transitive closure. The notation $\xrightarrow{a \vee b}$ means a reduction of kind a or of kind b.

Remark 5.1. Without typing, contextual equivalence would distinguish $\texttt{return}\ e_1 \gg\!= e_2$ and $(e_2\ e_1)$. Consider the (untyped) context

$$\mathbb{C} := x \overset{\text{main}}{\Longleftarrow} \texttt{case}_{Bool}\ [\cdot]\ \texttt{of}\ (\texttt{True} \rightarrow \texttt{True})\ (\texttt{False} \rightarrow \texttt{False}).$$

Then the expression $\mathbb{C}[\texttt{return False} \gg\!= \lambda x.\texttt{True}]$ is must-divergent, but $\mathbb{C}[(\lambda x.\texttt{True})\ \texttt{False}]{\Downarrow}$.

In [34] we show the following correctness results for the standard reduction rules:

Proposition 5.2. *The standard reductions* (sr, lunit), (sr, nmvar), (sr, fork), (unIO) *are correct transformations. The transformations* (lbeta), (case), (seq), (mkbinds) *are correct as transformation in any context (i.e. the reduction rules in Fig. 3 where the context* $\mathbb{L}$ *is replaced by an arbitrary process context* $\mathbb{C}$ *with an expression hole).*

The source of nondeterminism in CHF is the ability to concurrently access MVars from different threads. Hence, unsurprisingly the corresponding reductions are not correct:

Proposition 5.3. *The reduction rules* (sr, tmvar) *and* (sr, pmvar) *are in general not correct.*

Proof. For rule (sr, pmvar) a counter-example are the processes $P_1 \xrightarrow{sr,\text{pmvar}} P_2$ defined as:

$$P_1 := x \overset{\text{main}}{\Longleftarrow} \texttt{putMVar}\ y\ \texttt{True} \mid y\, \mathbf{m}\, - \mid z \Leftarrow \texttt{putMVar}\ y\ \texttt{True}$$
$$P_2 := x \overset{\text{main}}{\Longleftarrow} \texttt{putMVar}\ y\ \texttt{True} \mid y\, \mathbf{m}\, \texttt{True} \mid z \Leftarrow \texttt{return}\ ()$$

P_1 may-converges (if the main-thread is reduced), but P_2 is must-divergent, since the putMVar-operation of its main thread is blocked indefinitely. The counter example for (tmvar) is analogous, where all putMVar-operations are replaced by takeMVar-operations and the MVar y is filled. □

Nevertheless, if the execution of a (sr, tmvar)- or (sr, pmvar)-reduction is deterministic, it is correct. To formalize this we define further transformations related to reduction rules (we also add a rule for garbage collection):

Definition 5.4. In Fig. 5 the transformations (dtmvar), (dpmvar), and (gc) are defined, where we assume them to be closed w.r.t. structural congruence and w.r.t. *PCtxt*-contexts.

Remark 5.5. There are sufficient criteria for the applicability of (dtmvar) and (dpmvar), for example, if $\mathbb{D} = [\cdot]$, or if neither $\mathbb{M}$, e nor $\mathbb{D}$ contain occurrences of x, or if $\nu x.\mathbb{D}[\mathbb{M}[\cdot]]$ is closed and $\mathbb{D}$ does not contain any takeMVar nor putMVar.

In [34] we show:

Proposition 5.6. *The transformations* (gc), (dtmvar), *and* (dpmvar) *are correct program transformations.*

It remains to show correctness of the copy reductions (cp) and (cpcx) (i.e. the reduction rules (sr, cp) and (sr, cpcx) where the $\mathbb{L}$ is replaced by an arbitrary process context $\mathbb{C}$ with an expression hole). This proof is not straightforward and requires further proof techniques. We will show the correctness in the next section using infinite trees.

6. Call-by-Name Reduction

In this section we will introduce a call-by-name reduction, and show its semantical equivalence with call-by-need evaluation. The main technique for the proof is to use infinite terms and the corresponding reductions, which allows one to encode recursive bindings into expressions. This technique was used in [37] to show correctness of inlining in the deterministic call-by-need lambda calculus with letrec and also in [40] to show equivalence of the call-by-need lambda calculus with letrec and the lazy lambda calculus [1].

Definition 6.1. *Infinite expressions IExpr* are defined like expressions *Expr* omitting the letrec-component, adding a constant Bot, and interpreting the grammar of Fig.6 coinductively. *Infinite processes* (or *tree processes*) *IProc* are defined like usual processes *Proc* using the same (inductive) grammar (see Fig. 6) omitting bindings, with an additional process **0**, and infinite expressions instead of expressions. The process **0** is like a process without any reduction rules. Structural congruence on tree processes is defined as for processes where we add the congruence equation $\mathbf{0} \mid S \equiv S$.

Thus there are finitely many process components, but perhaps infinite expressions in threads or MVars. We say *tree* or *infinite expression* or *tree process* or *infinite process* in order to distinguish the usual notions from the ones for infinite processes. In infinite processes there are no variables for bindings, but variables corresponding to threads or MVars are there, and remain as free variables within the infinite expressions. The constant Bot in expressions is without any reduction rule. It represents cyclic binding chains where all right hand sides are variables, e.g. $x = y \mid y = x$. In

$$
\begin{array}{rcl}
s,t,s_i,t_i \in \mathit{IExpr} & ::= & x \mid ms \mid \texttt{Bot} \mid \lambda x.s \mid (s_1\ s_2) \mid c\ s_1 \ldots s_{\mathrm{ar}(c)} \mid \texttt{seq}\ s_1\ s_2 \\
 & & \mid \texttt{case}_T\ s\ \texttt{of}\ (c_{T,1}\ x_1 \ldots x_{\mathrm{ar}(c_{T,1})} \to s_1) \ldots (c_{T,|T|}\ x_1 \ldots x_{\mathrm{ar}(c_{T,|T|})} \to s_{|T|}) \\
ms \in \mathit{IMExpr} & ::= & \texttt{return}\ s \mid s_1 \ggg\!= s_2 \mid \texttt{future}\ s \mid \texttt{takeMVar}\ s \mid \texttt{newMVar}\ s \mid \texttt{putMVar}\ s_1\ s_2 \\
S,T,S_i,T_i \in \mathit{IProc} & ::= & S_1 \mid S_2 \mid x \Leftarrow s \mid \nu x.S \mid x\,\mathbf{m}\,s \mid x\,\mathbf{m}\,- \mid \mathbf{0}
\end{array}
$$

Figure 6. Infinite Expressions and Processes

the following definition we *describe* the mapping from processes to their infinite tree. In [34] we give a formal definition.

Definition 6.2. Let P be a process. The translation $IT :: \mathit{Proc} \to \mathit{IProc}$ translates a process P into its infinite tree process $IT(P)$. It recursively unfolds all bindings of `letrec`- and top-level bindings where cyclic variable chains $x_1 = x_2, \ldots, x_n = x_1$ are removed and all occurrences of x_i on other positions are replaced by the new constant `Bot`. Top-level bindings are replaced by a **0**-component. Free variables, futures, and names of MVars are kept in the tree (are not replaced). Equivalence of infinite processes is syntactic, where α-equal trees are assumed to be equivalent.

Example 6.3. The expression

$$\texttt{letrec}\ x = x, y = (\lambda z.z)\ x\ y\ \texttt{in}\ y$$

has the corresponding tree

$$((\lambda z.z)\ \texttt{Bot}\ ((\lambda z.z)\ \texttt{Bot}\ ((\lambda z.z)\ \texttt{Bot}\ \ldots))).$$

We use different classes of contexts for infinite processes and trees. In abuse of notation we use the same symbols for these contexts as for the contexts defined previously on (finite) processes and expressions.

Definition 6.4. Process contexts *IProc*, call-by-name evaluation contexts *IECtxt*, forcing contexts *IFCtxt*, and monadic contexts *IMCtxt* are defined below where all grammars are interpreted inductively and $S \in \mathit{IProc}$, $s \in \mathit{IExpr}$:

$$
\begin{array}{rl}
\mathbb{D},\mathbb{D}_i \in \mathit{IPCtxt} ::= & [\cdot] \mid \mathbb{D} \mid S \mid S \mid \mathbb{D} \mid \nu x.\mathbb{D} \\
\mathbb{M},\mathbb{M}_i \in \mathit{IMCtxt} ::= & [\cdot] \mid \mathbb{M} \ggg\!= s \\
\mathbb{F},\mathbb{F}_i \in \mathit{IFCtxt} ::= & \mathbb{E} \mid (\texttt{takeMVar}\ \mathbb{E}) \mid (\texttt{putMVar}\ \mathbb{E}\ s) \\
\mathbb{E},\mathbb{E}_i \in \mathit{IECtxt} ::= & [\cdot] \mid (\mathbb{E}\ s) \mid (\texttt{case}\ \mathbb{E}\ \texttt{of}\ alts) \mid (\texttt{seq}\ \mathbb{E}\ s)
\end{array}
$$

A *reduction context* $\mathbb{R} \in \mathit{IRCtxts}$ for infinite processes is constructed as $\mathbb{D}[x \Leftarrow \mathbb{M}[\mathbb{F}]]$.

Definition 6.5. The functional reduction rules on tree processes are allowed in any context and are as follows:

$$
\begin{array}{lll}
(\text{betaTr}) & ((\lambda x.s)\ r) \to s[r/x] & \\
(\text{seqTr}) & (\texttt{seq}\ s\ t) \ \to \ t & \text{if } s \text{ is a functional value} \\
(\text{caseTr}) & (\texttt{case}_T\ (c\ s_1 \ldots s_n)\ \texttt{of}\ \ldots (c\ x_1 \ldots x_n) \to s) & \\
 & \to\ s[s_1/x_1, \ldots, s_n/x_n] &
\end{array}
$$

The monadic computation rules are unchanged (see Fig. 3 where now $\mathbb{M}$ denotes an *IMCtxt*-context) except for the rule (unIO) which is replaced by:

(unIOTr) $\mathbb{D}[y \Leftarrow \texttt{return}\ y] \to (\mathbb{D}[\mathbf{0}])[\texttt{Bot}/y]$

(unIOTr) $\mathbb{D}[y \Leftarrow \texttt{return}\ s] \to (\mathbb{D}[\mathbf{0}])[s//y]$
if $s \neq y$; and the thread is not the main-thread where $//$ means the infinite recursive replacement of s for y; and where $\mathbb{D}$ means the whole process that is in scope of y.

Note that the substitution $P[s//y]$ is different from usual substition $P[s/y]$, since it *iteratively* replaces s by y which may generate an infinite tree if y occurs free in s. If a tree-process-reduction rule (betaTr), (caseTr), or (seqTr) is applied within an *IRCtxts*-context, or it is a monadic rule, then we call it a standard-reduction (SR-reduction) on tree processes, and write $T \xrightarrow{SR} T'$. A successful infinite process is an infinite process where the main thread exists and is of the form $y \Leftarrow \texttt{return}\ e$. We also use the convergence predicates $\downarrow, \Uparrow, \Downarrow, \uparrow$ for infinite tree processes, which are defined accordingly. The *redex* of a tree process reduction is the (infinite) subtree which is modified by the reduction rule. Note that for reduction rule (unIOTr) the redex is the whole infinite tree.

Note that $\xrightarrow{SR,\text{betaTr}}$ and $\xrightarrow{SR,\text{caseTr}}$ only reduce a single redex, but may modify infinitely many positions, since there may be infinitely many positions of the replaced variable x. E.g. a (SR, betaTr) of $IT((\lambda x.(\texttt{letrec}\ z\ =\ (z\ x)\ \texttt{in}\ z))\ r) = (\lambda x.((\ldots\ (\ldots\ x)\ x)\ x))\ r \to ((\ldots\ (\ldots\ r)\ r)\ r)$ replaces the infinite number of occurrences of x by r.

In [34] we prove the following theorem. For the proof we use a variant of infinite outside-in developments [6, 15] as a reduction on trees that may reduce infinitely many redexes in one step and show:

Theorem 6.6. *Let P be a process. Then $P\downarrow$ if and only if $IT(P)\downarrow$ and $P\uparrow$ if and only if $IT(P)\uparrow$.*

A consequence of the former theorem is that we can use infinite trees and infinite tree convergences to prove contextual equivalences. The general copy rule is defined as

$$(\text{gcp}) \qquad \mathbb{C}[x] \mid x = e \to \mathbb{C}[e] \mid x = e$$

Since (cp), (cpcx), and (gcp) applied to processes do not modify the corresponding infinite trees we immediately have:

Theorem 6.7. *The reduction rules* (cp), (cpcx) *and the general copy rule* (gcp) *are correct.*

We now present a variant of the standard reduction which uses a call-by-name instead of the call-by-need strategy. We show that the reduction does not change the convergence predicates. The call-by-name reduction is helpful for proving correctness of the monad laws in the subsequent section.

The call-by-name standard reduction is a variant of the sr-reduction where the rules (cp), (cpcx) are replaced by (cpce) and by using replacing variants of (lbeta) and (case).

Definition 6.8. The rules of the call-by-name standard reduction $\xrightarrow{src}$ are defined in Fig. 7. We assume that the rules are closed w.r.t. *PCtxt* and structural congruence, i.e. if $P \equiv \mathbb{D}[P']$, $Q \equiv \mathbb{D}[Q']$ and $P' \xrightarrow{src} Q'$ then also $P \xrightarrow{src} Q$.

We also use the convergence predicates with their obvious definitions: The predicates $\downarrow_{src}$ and $\Downarrow_{src}$ denote may- and should-convergence, and the predicates $\Uparrow_{src}$ and $\uparrow_{src}$ denote must- and may-divergence.

In [34] we first show that for all processes P: $IT(P)\downarrow \equiv P\downarrow_{src}$ and $IT(P)\Downarrow \equiv P\Downarrow_{src}$. Together with Theorem 6.6 this implies:

Theorem 6.9. *The call-by-name reduction $\xrightarrow{src}$ is equivalent to the reduction $\xrightarrow{sr}$. I.e., for every process P: $P\downarrow$ iff $P\downarrow_{src}$ and $P\Downarrow$ iff $P\Downarrow_{src}$.*

The context lemma 4.9 can be lifted to call-by-name:

Lemma 6.10 (Context Lemma for Call-By-Name). *Let e_1, e_2 be expressions of type τ such that for all $\mathbb{D} \in \mathit{PCtxt}$ and $\mathbb{L}[\cdot^\tau] \in$*

Monadic Computations

(lunit)	$y \Leftarrow \mathbb{M}[\texttt{return } e_1 \gg= e_2] \xrightarrow{src} y \Leftarrow \mathbb{M}[e_2 \, e_1]$
(tmvar)	$y \Leftarrow \mathbb{M}[\texttt{takeMVar } x] \mid x \, \mathbf{m} \, e \xrightarrow{src} y \Leftarrow \mathbb{M}[\texttt{return } e] \mid x \, \mathbf{m} \, -$
(pmvar)	$y \Leftarrow \mathbb{M}[\texttt{putMVar } x \, e] \mid x \, \mathbf{m} \, - \xrightarrow{src} y \Leftarrow \mathbb{M}[\texttt{return } ()] \mid x \, \mathbf{m} \, e$
(nmvar)	$y \Leftarrow \mathbb{M}[\texttt{newMVar } e] \xrightarrow{src} \nu x.(y \Leftarrow \mathbb{M}[\texttt{return } x] \mid x \, \mathbf{m} \, e)$
(fork)	$y \Leftarrow \mathbb{M}[\texttt{future } e] \xrightarrow{src} \nu z.(y \Leftarrow \mathbb{M}[\texttt{return } z] \mid z \Leftarrow e)$, where z is fresh and the created thread is not a main thread
(unIO)	$y \Leftarrow \texttt{return } e \xrightarrow{src} y = e$, if the thread is not the main-thread

Functional Evaluation

(cpce)	$y \Leftarrow \mathbb{M}[\mathbb{F}[x]] \mid x = e \xrightarrow{src} y \Leftarrow \mathbb{M}[\mathbb{F}[e]] \mid x = e$
(mkbinds)	$y \Leftarrow \mathbb{M}[\mathbb{F}[\texttt{letrec } x_1 = e_1, \ldots, x_n = e_n \texttt{ in } e]] \xrightarrow{src} \nu x_1, \ldots, x_n.(y \Leftarrow \mathbb{M}[\mathbb{F}[e]] \mid x_1 = e_1 \mid \ldots \mid x_n = e_n)$
(nbeta)	$y \Leftarrow \mathbb{M}[\mathbb{F}[((\lambda x.e_1) \, e_2)]] \xrightarrow{src} y \Leftarrow \mathbb{M}[\mathbb{F}[e_1[e_2/x]]]$
(ncase)	$y \Leftarrow \mathbb{M}[\mathbb{F}[\texttt{case}_T \, (c \, e_1 \ldots e_n) \texttt{ of } \ldots ((c \, y_1 \ldots y_n) \to e) \ldots]] \xrightarrow{src} y \Leftarrow \mathbb{M}[\mathbb{F}[e[e_1/y_1, \ldots, e_n/y_n]]]$
(seq)	$y \Leftarrow \mathbb{M}[\mathbb{F}[(\texttt{seq } v \, e)]] \xrightarrow{src} y \Leftarrow \mathbb{M}[\mathbb{F}[e]]$ if v is a functional value

Figure 7. Call-by-name reduction rules

$LCtxt$: $\mathbb{D}[\mathbb{L}[e_1]]\downarrow_{src} \implies \mathbb{D}[\mathbb{L}[e_2]]\downarrow_{src}$ and $\mathbb{D}[\mathbb{L}[e_1]]\Downarrow_{src} \implies \mathbb{D}[\mathbb{L}[e_2]]\Downarrow_{src}$. Then $e_1 \leq_{c,\tau} e_2$.

Proof. This follows from Lemma 4.9 and Theorem 6.9. $\qquad\square$

7. Monad Laws

The three monad laws are as follows, where (M1) is analogous to rule (lunit), but defined on expressions.

(M1)	$\texttt{return } e_1 \gg= e_2$	$=$	$e_2 \, e_1$
(M2)	$e_1 \gg= \lambda x.\texttt{return } x$	$=$	e_1
(M3)	$e_1 \gg= (\lambda x.(e_2 \, x \gg= e_3))$	$=$	$(e_1 \gg= e_2) \gg= e_3$

Note that the monad laws would be incorrect if `seq` can be used without restrictions: Assume that the first argument of `seq` is not type restricted and that the monadic operators are treated like constructors in `seq`, i.e., $(\texttt{seq } (c \ldots) \, s)$ reduces to s for the monadic operators c. This behavior can also be observed in the GHC implementation of Haskell. Let $\bot$ be a diverging closed expression. Then law (M1) does not hold under unrestricted `seq`, since e.g. $(\texttt{seq } (\texttt{return True} \gg= \bot) \, \texttt{True})$ terminates, but $(\bot \, \texttt{True})$ does not terminate. Also the law (M2) does not hold, since e.g. $(\texttt{seq } (\bot \gg= \lambda x.\texttt{return } x) \, \texttt{True})$ terminates, but $\texttt{seq } \bot \, \texttt{True}$ does not terminate.

However, due to our restriction that the first argument of `seq` cannot be of type ($\texttt{IO } a$), the monad laws are valid in CHF. For the proof we use the call-by-name reduction strategy $\xrightarrow{src}$. We define a further class of contexts: $\mathbb{A}, \mathbb{A}_i \in ACtxts ::= x \Leftarrow \mathbb{M} \mid x = \mathbb{M}$, where $\mathbb{M} \in MCtxt$.

Let (M1A) ((M2A) and (M3A), resp.) be the reduction that applies the equation (M1) ((M2) and (M3), resp.) from left to right in arbitrary $\mathbb{D}[\mathbb{A}[\cdot]]$-contexts. We write $\xrightarrow{nsr,M1A}$ iff the reduction is an (M1A)-reduction, but not an (src,lunit)-reduction. We also use $\xrightarrow{src,M1A}$ for an (src, lunit)-reduction, and $\xrightarrow{nsr,a}$ for the reduction rules of the call-by-name reduction, meaning that the reduction rule a is applied, but not as an src-reduction, since either the context is not an $\mathbb{M}$- or $\mathbb{M}[\mathbb{F}]$-context, or the process is already successful.

The type system (Fig. 2) implies:

Lemma 7.1. *If an expression $t :: \texttt{IO } \tau$ is in a $\mathbb{D}[\mathbb{L}[\cdot]]$-context, then the context is a $\mathbb{D}[\mathbb{A}[\cdot]]$-context.*

Lemma 7.2. *For all P: if $P \xrightarrow{src,a} P_1$ and $P \xrightarrow{src,b} P_2$, where the reductions have different redexes, and where a, b are not the same kind of src-reduction* (pmvar) *or* (tmvar) *on the same MVar. If neither P_1 nor P_2 are successful, then there is some P_3, such that*

$P_1 \xrightarrow{src,b} P_3$ and $P_2 \xrightarrow{src,a} P_3$. *If P_1 is successful, then there is some P_3 with $P_1 \xrightarrow{nsr,b} P_3$ and $P_2 \xrightarrow{src,a} P_3$. If P_2 is successful, then there is some P_3 with $P_1 \xrightarrow{src,b} P_3$ and $P_2 \xrightarrow{nsr,a} P_3$.*

$$\begin{array}{ccc}
P \xrightarrow{src,b} P_2 & P \xrightarrow{src,b} P_2 & P \xrightarrow{src,b} P_{2(succ.)} \\
src,a\downarrow \quad src,a\downarrow & src,a\downarrow \qquad src,a\downarrow & src,a\downarrow \qquad nsr,a\downarrow \\
P_1 \underset{src,b}{-\!\!\!\to} P_3 & P_{1(succ.)} \underset{nsr,b}{-\!\!\!\to} P_{3(succ.)} & P_1 \underset{src,b}{-\!\!\!\to} P_{3(succ.)}
\end{array}$$

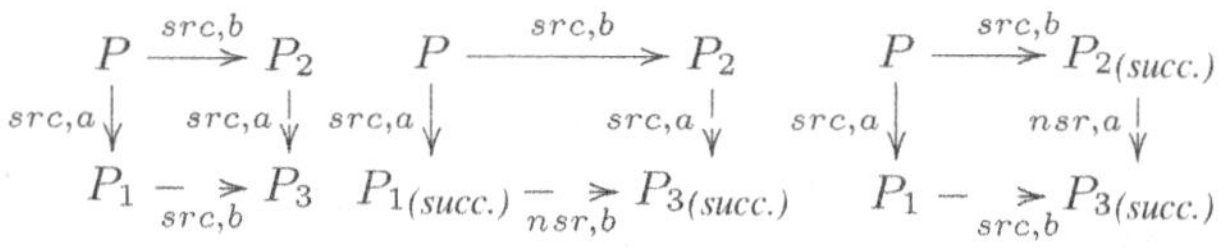

Proof. The call-by-name standard reductions are non-overlapping, since they make only changes in one thread with the exception of the MVar-modifying reductions. $\qquad\square$

By induction on k and Lemma 7.2 it follows:

Lemma 7.3. *Let $P \xrightarrow{src,b} P'$ where $b \notin \{(\text{pmvar}), (\text{tmvar})\}$, then the following holds:*

(1) If $P \xrightarrow{src,k} P_0$ where P_0 is successful, then there is some successful P_0' and $m \leq k$ with $P' \xrightarrow{src,m} P_0'$.

(2) If $P' \xrightarrow{src,k} P_0'$ where P_0' is successful, then there is some successful P_0 and $m \leq k+1$ with $P \xrightarrow{src,m} P_0$.

(3) If $P \xrightarrow{src,k} P_0$ where $P_0 \Uparrow$, then there is some must-divergent P_0' and $m \leq k$ with $P' \xrightarrow{src,m} P_0'$.

(4) If $P' \xrightarrow{src,k} P_0'$ where $P_0' \Uparrow$, then there is some must-divergent P_0 and $m \leq k+1$ with $P \xrightarrow{src,m} P_0$.

Lemma 7.4. *(M1A) overlaps with src-reductions as follows, assuming that the (M1A) and the src-reduction are different.*

$$\begin{array}{cccc}
\cdot \xrightarrow{nsr,M1A} \cdot & \cdot \xrightarrow{src,M1A} \cdot & \cdot \xrightarrow{nsr,M1A} \cdot \\
src,a\downarrow \quad src,a\downarrow' & src,a\downarrow \quad src,a\downarrow' & src,cpce\downarrow \qquad src,cpce\downarrow' \\
\cdot \underset{nsr,M1A}{-\!-\!\to} \cdot & \cdot \underset{src,M1A}{-\!-\!\to} \cdot & \cdot \underset{src,M1A}{-\!-\!\to} \cdot \underset{nsr,M1A}{-\!-\!\to} \cdot
\end{array}$$

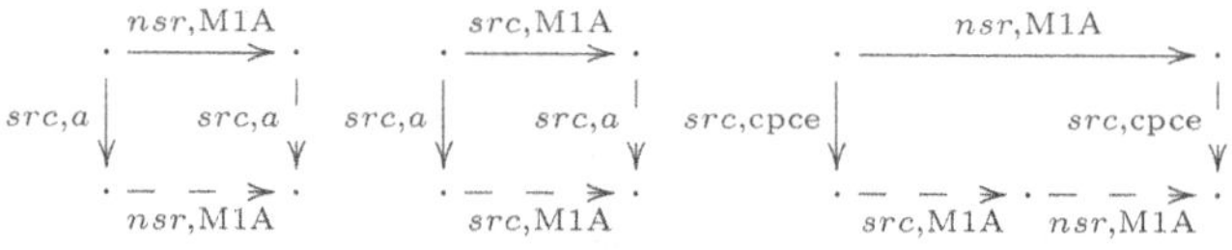

Proof. Note that occurrences of type $\texttt{IO } \tau$ are severely restricted. The only nontrivial overlap is with rule (cpce) which generates the second and last diagram. $\qquad\square$

Proposition 7.5. *The monad law (M1) is correct.*

Proof. Due to Lemma 7.1 and the context lemma (Lemma 6.10) it suffices to show four parts for processes P, P' with $P \xrightarrow{M1A} P'$:

1. $P{\downarrow} \implies P'{\downarrow}$: Let $P \xrightarrow{src,k} P_0$ where P_0 is successful. We use the diagrams in Lemma 7.4 to show that $P' \xrightarrow{src,m} P'_0$ with $m \le k$. Scanning the diagrams shows that the induction step is proved. The base case is that $P \xrightarrow{M1A} P'$ where P' is successful implies that P is successful.

2. $P'{\downarrow} \implies P{\downarrow}$: We interpret the diagrams of Lemma 7.4 as "commuting diagrams", i.e. the given sequence is $\xrightarrow{nsr,M1A}$. $\xrightarrow{src,a}$. We do not consider given $(src, M1A)$ reductions for this part and thus we omit the second diagram. By induction on the length of a successfully ending reduction sequence for P' one can show that also $P{\downarrow}$. The base case obviously holds. The induction step follows by applying the induction hypothesis first. Then either a commuting diagram is applied or the (M1A)-reduction is also an src-reduction and the claim also holds.

3. $P{\uparrow} \implies P'{\uparrow}$: Let $P \xrightarrow{src,*} P_1$ with $P_1{\uparrow}$. The diagrams in Lemma 7.4 show that there is a process P_2 with $P_1 \xrightarrow{M1A,*} P_2$, and $P' \xrightarrow{src,*} P_2$. (2) now implies that $P_2{\uparrow}$.

4. $P'{\uparrow} \implies P{\uparrow}$: Let $P' \xrightarrow{*,src} P_2$ with $P_2{\uparrow}$. An induction on the length of the sequence $P' \xrightarrow{*,src} P_2$ using the diagrams as commuting diagrams and the induction hypothesis shows that $P{\uparrow}$ where (1) covers the base case. □

Lemma 7.6. *The overlappings for (M2A) with src-reductions are:*

$$
\begin{array}{ccc}
\xrightarrow{M2A} & \xrightarrow{M2A} & \xrightarrow{M2A} \\
\Big\downarrow src,a \quad src,a & src,lunit\Big\downarrow \nearrow src,nbeta & src,cpce\Big\downarrow \quad src,cpce \\
\xrightarrow{M2A} & & \xrightarrow{\ \ } \xrightarrow{M2A\ M2A}
\end{array}
$$

Proof. One non-trivial overlap is with the $(src, cpce)$-rule similar to the diagram in 7.4, and the other nontrivial overlap is with the $(src, lunit)$-rule which generates the second diagram.

$$
\begin{array}{ccc}
\text{return } e \gg= \lambda x.\text{return } x & \xrightarrow{M2A} & \text{return } e \\
src,lunit \Big\downarrow & \nearrow src,nbeta & \\
(\lambda x.\text{return } x)\, e & &
\end{array}
$$

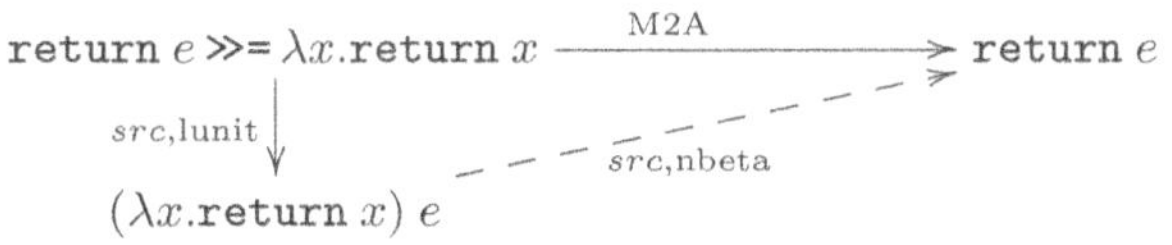

Proposition 7.7. *The monad law (M2) is correct.*

Proof. Let $P \xrightarrow{M2A} P'$. The context lemma 6.10 and Lemma 7.1 imply that the following cases suffice to prove the claim, where the diagrams in Lemma 7.6 are used for proofs by induction:

1. $P{\downarrow} \implies P'{\downarrow}$: We show a stronger claim: If $P \xrightarrow{src,k} P_0$ where P_0 is successful, then there exists a successful process P'_0 with $P' \xrightarrow{src,m} P'_0$ such that $m \le k$. The proof is by induction on k. For the base case it obviously holds that if P is successful, then P'_0 is successful. For the induction step let $P \xrightarrow{src} P_1 \xrightarrow{src,k-1} P_0$. We apply a diagram to $P_1 \xleftarrow{src} P \xrightarrow{M2A} P'$ and then apply the induction hypothesis (once for the first diagram, twice for the third diagram). The second diagram is covered by Lemma 7.2.

2. $P'{\downarrow} \implies P{\downarrow}$: We use the diagrams of Lemma 7.6 as commuting diagrams and prove the following claim: If $P' \xrightarrow{src,*} P'_0$ where P'_0 is successful and there are n $(src,cpce)$-reductions, then $P' \xrightarrow{src,*} P_0$ where P_0 is successful using at most n $(src,cpce)$-reductions. The induction is on the reduction $P' \xrightarrow{src,*} P'_0$, where the measure is the number of $(src,cpce)$-reductions, then the total number of reductions. For the third

diagram the induction hypothesis is applicable, since the number of $(src,cpce)$-reductions is strictly decreased, and thus we can apply the hypothesis twice. If the first diagram is applied, then the number of reductions is strictly decreased, and for the second, the diagram can be immediately applied. The base case holds, since process P' is successful. Then $P \equiv \mathbb{D}[x \xLeftarrow{main} \text{return } e_1 \gg= \lambda y.\text{return } y]$ and $P' \equiv \mathbb{D}[x \xLeftarrow{main} \text{return } e_1]$. The second diagram shows that $P \xrightarrow{src,(lunit)\vee(nbeta),*} P'$.

3. $P{\uparrow} \implies P'{\uparrow}$: We derive $P{\Uparrow} \iff P'{\Uparrow}$ using the first two items. If $P{\uparrow}$, then again the diagrams and a simple induction show the claim using the base case.

4. $P'{\uparrow} \implies P{\uparrow}$: Using a similar reasoning as in item (2), i.e., the corresponding induction claim and the same induction measure and using $P{\Uparrow} \iff P'{\Uparrow}$, an induction shows the claim. □

Lemma 7.8. *The overlappings for (M3A) with src-reduction are:*

$$
\begin{array}{ccc}
\xrightarrow{M3A} & \xrightarrow{M3A} & \xrightarrow{M3A} \\
src,a\Big\downarrow \quad src,a & src,lunit\Big\downarrow \quad src,lunit & src,cpce\Big\downarrow \quad src,cpce \\
\xrightarrow{M3A} & \xrightarrow{src,nbeta} & \xrightarrow{\ M3A\ \ M3A\ }
\end{array}
$$

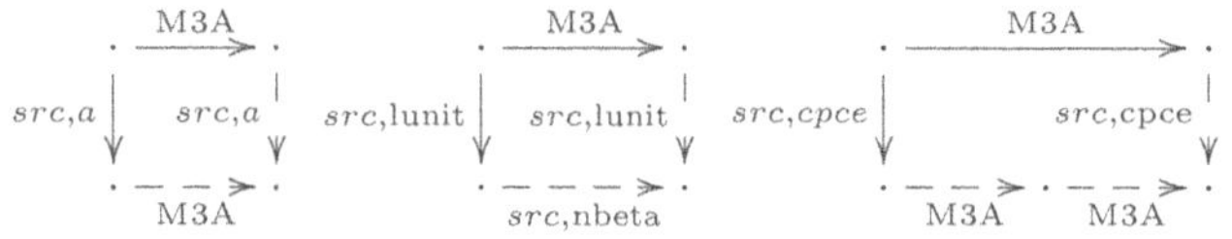

Proof. The nontrivial overlaps are with the (lunit)-rule and the (cpce)-rule.

$$
\begin{array}{ccc}
\begin{array}{l}\text{return } e_1 \\ \gg= (\lambda x.e_2\ x \gg= e_3)\end{array} & \xrightarrow{M3A} & \begin{array}{l}(\text{return } e_1 \gg= e_2) \\ \gg= e_3\end{array} \\
src,lunit \Big\downarrow & & \Big\downarrow src,lunit \\
(\lambda x.e_2\ x \gg= e_3)\, e_1 & \dashrightarrow[src,nbeta] & e_2\, e_1 \gg= e_3
\end{array}
$$

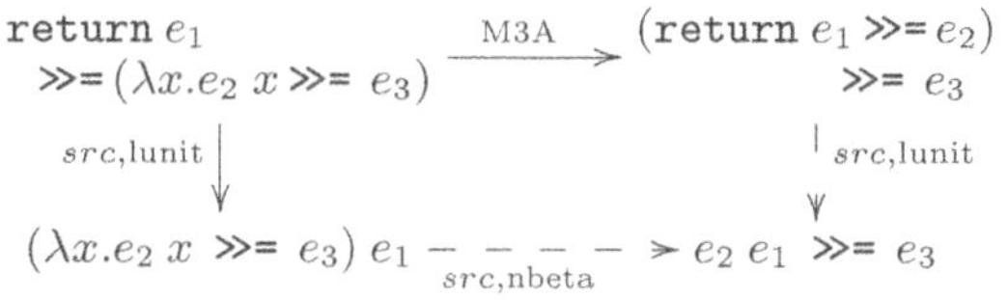

Proposition 7.9. *The monad law (M3) is correct.*

Proof. Lemmas 6.10 and 7.1 imply that it is sufficient to show that $P{\downarrow}$ iff $P'{\downarrow}$ and $P{\Downarrow}$ iff $P'{\Downarrow}$ where $P \xrightarrow{M3A} P'$.

The diagrams in Lemma 7.8 can be used for a proof by induction, very similar to the proof for (M3A) in Proposition 7.7. The following differences have to be obeyed: (M3A) cannot turn a non-successful process into a successful one, unlike (M2A), and in the second diagram an $(src,lunit)$ is there instead of an equality, which is only a minor difference. The proof is almost the same. □

Propositions 7.5, 7.7, and 7.9 show:

Theorem 7.10. *The monad laws (M1), (M2), and (M3) are correct.*

The correctness of the monad laws also ensures that the usual translation of the do-notation in Haskell is correct and behaves as expected, and thus we can use the do-notation in CHF.

8. Conclusion and Further Work

We developed the calculus CHF as a model for Concurrent Haskell extended by futures, together with a semantical foundation based on contextual semantics using may- and should-convergence. The correctness of several program transformations, the correctness of call-by-name evaluation, and the correctness of the monad-laws are proved, which opens a wide range of further (correct) program optimizations. A prerequisite is to restrict the first argument of the seq-operator to function types and constructor types, since otherwise, the monad laws are falsifiable (also in sequential Haskell). We restricted reasoning to a monomorphic type system, but we are convinced that our results can be transferred to polymorphic typing.

Ongoing work is to prove that CHF is "referential transparent", that is we try to show that pure functions that are equivalent in a pure call-by-need calculus (without IO and threads) are also equivalent in CHF.

Acknowledgments

We thank Conrad Rau for reading a version of this paper and his helpful comments. We also thank the anonymous referees for their valuable remarks.

References

[1] S. Abramsky. The lazy lambda calculus. In *Research topics in functional programming*, pages 65–116. Addison-Wesley, 1990.

[2] Alice ML. Homepage, 2011. http://www.ps.uni-saarland.de/alice/.

[3] Z. M. Ariola and A. Sabry. Correctness of monadic state: an imperative call-by-need calculus. In *Proc. of the 25th ACM symposium on Principles of programming languages*, pages 62–74. ACM, 1998.

[4] H. C. Baker, Jr. and C. Hewitt. The incremental garbage collection of processes. In *Proc. of the 1977 symposium on Artificial intelligence and programming languages*, pages 55–59. ACM, 1977.

[5] C. Baker-Finch, D. J. King, and P. Trinder. An operational semantics for parallel lazy evaluation. *SIGPLAN Not.*, 35:162–173, 2000.

[6] H. P. Barendregt. *The Lambda Calculus. Its Syntax and Semantics*. North-Holland, 1984.

[7] A. Carayol, D. Hirschkoff, and D. Sangiorgi. On the representation of McCarthy's amb in the pi-calculus. *Theoret. Comput. Sci.*, 330(3): 439–473, 2005.

[8] Concurrent Clean. Homepage, 2011. clean.cs.ru.nl/.

[9] R. De Nicola and M. Hennessy. Testing equivalences for processes. *Theoret. Comput. Sci.*, 34:83–133, 1984.

[10] C. Flanagan and M. Felleisen. The semantics of future and an application. *J. Funct. Programming*, 9:1–31, 1999.

[11] J. Ford and I. A. Mason. Formal foundations of operational semantics. *Higher Order Symbol. Comput.*, 16:161–202, 2003.

[12] Glasgow parallel Haskell. Homepage, 2011. http://www.macs.hw.ac.uk/ dsg/gph/.

[13] R. H. Halstead, Jr. Multilisp: a language for concurrent symbolic computation. *ACM Trans. Program. Lang. Syst.*, 7:501–538, 1985.

[14] T. Harris, S. Marlow, S. L. Peyton Jones, and M. Herlihy. Composable memory transactions. In *Proc. of the tenth ACM symposium on Principles and practice of parallel programming*, pages 48–60. ACM, 2005.

[15] R. Kennaway, J. W. Klop, M. R. Sleep, and F.-J. de Vries. Infinitary lambda calculus. *Theoret. Comput. Sci.*, 175(1):93–125, 1997.

[16] R. Loogen, Y. Ortega-mallén, and R. Peña marí. Parallel functional programming in eden. *J. Funct. Programming*, 15:431–475, 2005.

[17] S. Marlow, P. Maier, H.-W. Loidl, M. K. Aswad, and P. Trinder. Seq no more: better strategies for parallel haskell. In *Proc. of the third ACM Haskell symposium on Haskell*, pages 91–102. ACM, 2010.

[18] I. Mason and C. L. Talcott. Equivalence in functional languages with effects. *J. Funct. Programming*, 1(3):287–327, 1991.

[19] J. McCarthy. A Basis for a Mathematical Theory of Computation. In *Computer Programming and Formal Systems*, pages 33–70. North-Holland, Amsterdam, 1963.

[20] R. Milner. *Communicating and mobile systems - the Pi-calculus*. Cambridge University Press, 1999.

[21] J. Morris. *Lambda-Calculus Models of Programming Languages*. PhD thesis, MIT, 1968.

[22] Mozart. Homepage, 2011. http://www.mozart-oz.org/.

[23] V. Natarajan and R. Cleaveland. Divergence and fair testing. In *Proc. of the 22nd International Colloquium on Automata, Languages and Programming*, LNCS 944, pages 648–659. Springer, 1995.

[24] J. Niehren, J. Schwinghammer, and G. Smolka. A concurrent lambda calculus with futures. *Theoret. Comput. Sci.*, 364(3):338–356, 2006.

[25] J. Niehren, D. Sabel, M. Schmidt-Schauß, and J. Schwinghammer. Observational semantics for a concurrent lambda calculus with reference cells and futures. *Electron. Notes Theor. Comput. Sci.*, 173: 313–337, 2007.

[26] S. L. Peyton Jones. *Haskell 98 language and libraries: the Revised Report*. Cambridge University Press, 2003. `www.haskell.org`.

[27] S. L. Peyton Jones. Tackling the awkward squad: monadic input/output, concurrency, exceptions, and foreign-language calls in Haskell. In *Engineering theories of software construction*, pages 47–96. IOS-Press, 2001.

[28] S. L. Peyton Jones and S. Singh. A tutorial on parallel and concurrent programming in haskell. In *Advanced Functional Programming, 6th International School, Revised Lectures*, LNCS 5832, pages 267–305. Springer, 2009.

[29] S. L. Peyton Jones and P. Wadler. Imperative functional programming. In *Proc. of the 20th ACM symposium on Principles of programming languages*, pages 71–84. ACM, 1993.

[30] S. L. Peyton Jones, A. Gordon, and S. Finne. Concurrent haskell. In *Proc. of the 23rd ACM symposium on Principles of programming languages*, pages 295–308. ACM, 1996.

[31] G. D. Plotkin. Call-by-name, call-by-value, and the lambda-calculus. *Theoret. Comput. Sci.*, 1:125–159, 1975.

[32] A. Rensink and W. Vogler. Fair testing. *Inform. and Comput.*, 205(2): 125–198, 2007.

[33] D. Sabel and M. Schmidt-Schauß. A call-by-need lambda-calculus with locally bottom-avoiding choice: Context lemma and correctness of transformations. *Math. Structures Comput. Sci.*, 18(03):501–553, 2008.

[34] D. Sabel and M. Schmidt-Schauß. A contextual semantics for concurrent haskell with futures. Frank report 44, Institut für Informatik. Goethe-Universität Frankfurt am Main, 2011. http://www.ki.informatik.uni-frankfurt.de/papers/frank/.

[35] D. Sabel, M. Schmidt-Schauß, and F. Harwath. Reasoning about contextual equivalence: From untyped to polymorphically typed calculi. In *INFORMATIK 2009,4. Arbeitstagung Programmiersprachen*, LNI 154, pages 369; 2931–45, 2009.

[36] D. Sangiorgi and D. Walker. *The π-calculus: a theory of mobile processes*. Cambridge university press, 2001.

[37] M. Schmidt-Schauß. Correctness of copy in calculi with letrec. In *Term Rewriting and Applications*, LNCS 4533, pages 329–343. Springer, 2007.

[38] M. Schmidt-Schauß and D. Sabel. On generic context lemmas for higher-order calculi with sharing. *Theoret. Comput. Sci.*, 411(11-13): 1521 – 1541, 2010.

[39] M. Schmidt-Schauß and D. Sabel. Closures of may-, should- and must-convergences for contextual equivalence. *Inform. and Comput.*, 110(6):232 – 235, 2010.

[40] M. Schmidt-Schauß, D. Sabel, and E. Machkasova. Simulation in the call-by-need lambda-calculus with letrec. In *Proc. of the 21st International Conference on Rewriting Techniques and Applications*, LIPIcs 6, pages 295–310. Schloss Dagstuhl - Leibniz-Zentrum für Informatik, 2010.

[41] J. Schwinghammer, D. Sabel, M. Schmidt-Schauß, and J. Niehren. Correctly translating concurrency primitives. In *Proc. of the 2009 ACM workshop on ML*, pages 27–38. ACM, 2009.

[42] P. W. Trinder, K. Hammond, H.-W. Loidl, and S. L. Peyton Jones. Algorithm + Strategy = Parallelism. *J. Funct. Programming*, 8(1):23–60, 1998.

[43] M. C. J. D. van Eekelen, M. J. Plasmeijer, and J. E. W. Smetsers. Parallel graph rewriting on loosely coupled machine architectures. In *Proc. of the 2nd International Workshop on Conditional and Typed Rewriting Systems*, LNCS 516, pages 354–369. Springer, 1990.

[44] P. Wadler. Monads for functional programming. In *First International Spring School on Advanced Functional Programming Techniques,Tutorial Text*, LNCS 925, pages 24–52. Springer, 1995.

Nitpicking C++ Concurrency

Jasmin Christian Blanchette
T. U. München, Germany
blanchette@in.tum.de

Tjark Weber
University of Cambridge, U.K.
tjark.weber@cl.cam.ac.uk

Mark Batty
University of Cambridge, U.K.
mark.batty@cl.cam.ac.uk

Scott Owens
University of Cambridge, U.K.
scott.owens@cl.cam.ac.uk

Susmit Sarkar
University of Cambridge, U.K.
susmit.sarkar@cl.cam.ac.uk

Abstract

Previous work formalized the C++ memory model in Isabelle/HOL in an effort to clarify the proposed standard's semantics. Here we employ the model finder Nitpick to check litmus test programs that exercise the memory model, including a simple locking algorithm. Nitpick is built on Kodkod (Alloy's backend) but understands Isabelle's richer logic; hence it can be applied directly to the C++ memory model. We only need to give it a few hints, and thanks to the underlying SAT solver it scales much better than the CPPMEM explicit-state model checker. This case study inspired optimizations in Nitpick from which other formalizations can now benefit.

Categories and Subject Descriptors D.1.3 [*Programming Techniques*]: Concurrent Programming—Parallel programming; D.2.4 [*Software Engineering*]: Software/Program Verification—Model checking; D.3.3 [*Programming Languages*]: Language Constructs and Features—Concurrent programming structures; F.3.1 [*Logics and Meanings of Programs*]: Specifying and Verifying and Reasoning about Programs—Mechanical verification; F.4.1 [*Mathematical Logic and Formal Languages*]: Mathematical Logic—Logic and constraint programming

General Terms Languages, Performance, Standardization

Keywords C++ memory model, concurrency, model finding, SAT solving, higher-order logic, Isabelle/HOL, Nitpick, Kodkod

1. Introduction

Most programming languages are defined by informal prose documents that contain ambiguities, omissions, and contradictions. But for many of these, researchers have constructed rigorous, mathematical semantics after the fact and formalized them in theorem provers. The benefits of formalized semantics are well known:

- They give a rigorous (and ideally readable) description of the language that can serve as a contract between designers, implementers, and users.
- They enable machine-checked proofs of theoretical results; in particular, they are an integral part of any verified compiler.
- They can be used in conjunction with lightweight formal methods, such as model checkers and model finders, to explore the consequences of the specification.

Formal methods can be quite useful for reasoning about sequential programs, but with concurrent programming they are a vital aid because of the inherent nondeterminism. Ten-line programs can have millions of possible executions. Subtle race condition bugs can remain hidden for years despite extensive testing and code reviews before they start causing failures. Even tiny concurrent programs expressed in idealized languages with clean mathematical semantics can be amazingly subtle [9, §1.4].

In the real world, performance considerations prompt hardware designers and compiler writers to further complicate the semantics of concurrent programs. For example, at the hardware level, a write operation taking place at instant t might not yet be reflected in a read at instant $t+1$ from a different thread because of cache effects. The final authority in this matter is the processor's memory consistency model.

The Java language abstracts away the various processor memory models, and compiler reordering, behind a software memory model designed to be efficiently implementable on actual hardware. However, the original Java model was found to be flawed [25], and even the revised version had some unpleasant surprises [7, 27, 29].

The next C++ standard, tentatively called C++0x, attempts to provide a clear semantics for concurrent programs, including a memory model and library functions. In previous work [3, 4], the last four authors, together with Sewell, formalized a large fragment of the prose specification in Isabelle/HOL [23] (Sects. 2 and 3). From the Isabelle formalization, they extracted the core of a tool, CPPMEM, that can check litmus test programs—small multithreaded programs that exercise various aspects of the memory model. Using this simulator, they found flaws in the original prose specification and clarified several issues, which are now addressed by the draft standard [1]. To validate the semantics, they proved the correctness of a proposed Intel x86 implementation of the concurrency primitives.

In this paper, we are interested in tool support for verifying litmus test programs. CPPMEM exhaustively enumerates the possible program executions, checking each against the (executable) formal semantics. An attractive alternative is to apply a SAT solver to the memory model constraints and litmus tests. The MemSAT tool's success on the Java memory model [29] and our early experiments [4, §6.1] suggest that SAT solvers scale better than explicit-state model checkers, allowing us to verify more complex litmus tests.

PDPP'11, July 20–22, 2011, Odense, Denmark.

Newer Isabelle versions include an efficient SAT-based model finder, Nitpick (Sect. 4). The reduction to SAT is delegated to Kodkod [28], which also serves as a backend to MemSAT and the Alloy Analyzer [13]. Nitpick and its predecessor Refute [32] featured in several case studies [5, 6, 14, 21, 31] but were, to our knowledge, never successfully applied to a specification as complex as the C++ memory model.

Although the memory model specification was not designed with SAT solving in mind, we expected that with some adjustments it should be within Nitpick's reach. The specification is written in a fairly abstract and axiomatic style, which should favor SAT solvers. Various Kodkod optimizations help cope with large problems. Moreover, although the memory model is subtle and complicated, the specification is mostly restricted to first-order logic with sets, transitive closure, and inductive datatypes, all of which are handled efficiently in Nitpick or Kodkod.

Initially, though, we had to make drastic semantics-preserving changes to the Isabelle specification so that Nitpick would scale to handle the simplest litmus tests in reasonable time (Sect. 5). These early results had been obtained at the cost of several days of work by people who understood Nitpick's internals. Based on our experience adapting the specification by hand, we proceeded to address scalability issues directly in Nitpick (Sect. 6).

With the optimizations in place, a few minor adjustments to the original memory model specification sufficed to support efficient model finding (Sect. 7). We applied the optimized version of Nitpick to several litmus tests (Sect. 8), including a simple sequential locking algorithm, thereby increasing our confidence in the specification's adequacy. Litmus tests that were previously too large for CPPMEM can now be checked within minutes.

2. Isabelle/HOL

Isabelle [23] is a generic interactive theorem prover whose built-in metalogic is a fragment of higher-order logic [2, 8, 11]. Its HOL object logic provides a more elaborate version of higher-order logic, complete with the familiar connectives and quantifiers.

The term language consists of simply-typed λ-terms augmented with constants (of scalar or function types) and ML-style polymorphism. Function application expects no parentheses around the argument list and no commas in between, as in $f\ x\ y$. Syntactic sugar provides an infix syntax for common operators, such as $x = y$ and $x + y$. Variables may range over functions and predicates. Types are usually implicit but can be specified using a constraint $:: \tau$.

HOL's standard semantics interprets the Boolean type *bool* and the function space $\sigma \to \tau$. The function arrow associates to the right, reflecting the left-associativity of application. Predicates are functions of type $\sigma_1 \to \cdots \to \sigma_n \to bool$. HOL identifies sets with monadic predicates and provides syntactic sugar for set notations.

Inductive datatypes can be defined by specifying the constructors and the types of their arguments. The type *nat* of natural numbers is defined by the command

datatype $nat = 0 \mid Suc\ nat$

The type is generated freely from the constructors $0 :: nat$ and $Suc :: nat \to nat$. The polymorphic type $\alpha\ list$ of lists over α is defined as

datatype $\alpha\ list = Nil \mid Cons\ \alpha\ (\alpha\ list)$

Since lists are so common, Isabelle also supports the more convenient notation $[x_1, \ldots, x_n]$ for $Cons\ x_1\ (\ldots(Cons\ x_n\ Nil)\ldots)$.

Constants can be introduced by free-form axioms or, more safely, by a simple definition in terms of existing constants. In addition, Isabelle provides high-level definitional principles for inductive and coinductive predicates as well as recursive functions.

3. C++ Memory Model

The C++ Final Draft International Standard [1] defines the concurrency memory model axiomatically, by imposing constraints on the order of memory accesses in program executions. The semantics of a C++ program is then a set of allowed executions.

Here we briefly present the memory model and its Isabelle/HOL formalization [3, 4], focusing on the aspects that are necessary to understand the rest of this paper.

3.1 Introductory Example

To facilitate efficient implementations on modern parallel architectures, the C++ memory model (like other relaxed memory models) has no global linear notion of time. Program executions are not guaranteed to be *sequentially consistent* (*SC*)—that is, equivalent to a simple interleaving of threads [18].

The following program fragment is a simple example that can exhibit non-SC behavior:

```
atomic_int x = 0;
atomic_int y = 0;

{{{
    x.store(1, ord_relaxed);
    printf("y: %d\n", y.load(ord_relaxed));
|||
    y.store(1, ord_relaxed);
    printf("x: %d\n", x.load(ord_relaxed));
}}}
```

(To keep examples simple, we use the notation `{{{ ... ||| ... }}}` for parallel composition and `ord_xxx` for `memory_order_xxx`.)

Two threads write to separate memory locations `x` and `y`; then each thread reads from the other location. Can both threads read the original value of the location they read from? According to the draft standard, they can. The program has eight outputs that are permitted by the memory model:

x: 0	y: 0	x: 0	y: 0	x: 1	y: 1	x: 1	y: 1
y: 0	x: 0	y: 1	x: 1	y: 0	x: 0	y: 1	x: 1

Among these, the first two outputs exhibit the counterintuitive non-SC behavior.

3.2 Memory Actions and Orderings

From the memory model's point of view, C++ program executions consist of *memory actions*. The main actions are

L x	locking of x
U x	unlocking of x
R_{ord} x $= v$	atomic read of value v from x
W_{ord} x $= v$	atomic write of value v to x
RMW_{ord} x $= v_1/v_2$	atomic read–modify–write at x
R_{na} x $= v$	nonatomic read of value v from x
W_{na} x $= v$	nonatomic write of value v to x
F_{ord}	fence

where *ord*, an action's *memory order*, can be any of the following:

sc	`ord_seq_cst`	sequentially consistent
rel	`ord_release`	release
acq	`ord_acquire`	acquire
a/r	`ord_acq_rel`	acquire and release
con	`ord_consume`	consume
rlx	`ord_relaxed`	relaxed

Memory orders control synchronization and ordering of atomic actions. The `ord_seq_cst` ordering provides the strongest guarantees (SC), while `ord_relaxed` provides the weakest guarantees. The release/acquire discipline, where writes use `ord_release` and reads use `ord_acquire`, occupies an intermediate position on the continuum. The slightly weaker variant release/consume, with `ord_consume` for the reads, can be implemented more efficiently on hardware with weak memory ordering.

If we wanted to prohibit the non-SC executions in the program above, we could simply pass `ord_seq_cst` as argument to the `load` and `store` functions instead of `ord_relaxed`.

3.3 Isabelle/HOL Formalization

In place of a global timeline, the standard postulates several relations over different subsets of a program's memory actions. These relations establish some weak notion of time. They are not necessarily total or transitive (and can therefore be hard to understand intuitively) but must satisfy various constraints.

In the Isabelle/HOL formalization of the memory model [3, 4], a candidate execution $\mathcal{X}$ is a pair $(\mathcal{X}_{\mathsf{opsem}}, \mathcal{X}_{\mathsf{witness}})$. The component $\mathcal{X}_{\mathsf{opsem}}$ specifies the program's memory actions (*acts*), its threads (*thrs*), a simple typing of memory locations (*lk*), and four relations over actions (*sb*, *asw*, *dd*, and *cd*) that constrain their evaluation order. The other component, $\mathcal{X}_{\mathsf{witness}}$, consists of three relations: Read actions *read from* some write action (*rf*), *sequentially consistent* actions are totally ordered (*sc*), and a *modification order* (*mo*) gives a per-location linear-coherence order for atomic writes.

$\mathcal{X}_{\mathsf{opsem}}$ is given by the program's operational semantics and can be determined statically from the program source. $\mathcal{X}_{\mathsf{witness}}$ is existentially quantified. The C++ memory model imposes constraints on the components of $\mathcal{X}_{\mathsf{opsem}}$ and $\mathcal{X}_{\mathsf{witness}}$ as well as on various relations derived from them. A candidate execution is *consistent* if it satisfies these constraints. The Isabelle/HOL top-level definition of consistency is given below:

definition *consistent_execution acts thrs lk sb asw dd cd rf mo sc* ≡
well_formed_threads acts thrs lk sb asw dd cd ∧
well_formed_reads_from_mapping acts lk rf ∧
consistent_locks acts thrs lk sb asw dd cd sc ∧
let
rs = *release_sequence acts lk mo*
hrs = *hypothetical_release_sequence acts lk mo*
sw = *synchronizes_with acts sb asw rf sc rs hrs*
cad = *carries_a_dependency_to acts sb dd rf*
dob = *dependency_ordered_before acts rf rs cad*
ithb = *inter_thread_happens_before acts thrs lk sb asw dd cd sw dob*
hb = *happens_before acts thrs lk sb asw dd cd ithb*
vse = *visible_side_effect acts thrs lk sb asw dd cd hb*
in
consistent_inter_thread_happens_before acts ithb ∧
consistent_sc_order acts thrs lk sb asw dd cd mo sc hb ∧
consistent_modification_order acts thrs lk sb asw dd cd sc mo hb ∧
consistent_reads_from_mapping acts thrs lk sb asw dd cd rf sc mo hb vse

The derived relations (*rs*, *hrs*, etc.) and the various consistency conditions follow the C++ final draft standard; we omit their definitions. The complete memory model comprises approximately 1200 lines of Isabelle text.

3.4 CPPMEM

For any given $\mathcal{X}_{\mathsf{opsem}}$, there may be one, several, or perhaps no choices for $\mathcal{X}_{\mathsf{witness}}$ that give rise to a consistent execution. Since the memory model is complex, and the various consistency conditions and their interactions can be difficult to understand intuitively, tool support for exploring the model and computing the possible behaviors of C++ programs is much needed.

The CPPMEM tool [4] was designed to assist with these tasks. It consists of the following three parts: (1) a preprocessor that computes the $\mathcal{X}_{\mathsf{opsem}}$ component of a candidate execution from a C++ program's source code; (2) a search procedure that enumerates the possible values for $\mathcal{X}_{\mathsf{witness}}$; (3) a checking procedure that calculates the derived relations and evaluates the consistency conditions for each pair $(\mathcal{X}_{\mathsf{opsem}}, \mathcal{X}_{\mathsf{witness}})$.

For the second part, we refrained from implementing a sophisticated memory-model-aware search procedure in favor of keeping the code simple. CPPMEM enumerates all possible combinations for the *rf*, *mo*, and *sc* relations that respect a few basic constraints:

- *sc* only contains SC actions and is a total order over them.
- *mo* only contains pairs (a,b) such that a and b write to the same memory location; for each location, *mo* is a total order over the set of writes at this location.
- *rf* only contains pairs (a,b) such that a writes a given value to a location and b reads the same value from that location; for each read b, it contains exactly one such pair.

Because the search space grows asymptotically with $n!$ in the worst case, where n is the number of actions in the program execution, CPPMEM is mostly limited to small litmus tests, which typically involve up to eight actions. This does cover many interesting tests, but not larger parallel algorithms.

Writing a more sophisticated search procedure would require a detailed understanding of the memory model (which we hope to gain through proper tool support in the first place) and could introduce errors that are difficult to detect—unless, of course, the procedure was automatically generated from the formal specification. This is where Nitpick comes into play.

4. Nitpick

Nitpick [6] is a model finder for Isabelle/HOL based on Kodkod [28], a constraint solver for first-order relational logic (FORL) that in turn relies on the SAT solver MiniSat [10]. Given a conjecture, Nitpick searches for a standard set-theoretic model that satisfies the given formula as well as any relevant axioms and definitions. Isabelle users can invoke the tool manually at any point in an interactive proof to find models or countermodels. Unlike Isabelle itself, which adheres to the LCF "small kernel" discipline [12], Nitpick does not certify its results and must be trusted.

Nitpick's design was inspired by its predecessor Refute [32], which performs a direct reduction to SAT. The translation from HOL is parameterized by the cardinalities of the atomic types occurring in it [5]. Nitpick systematically enumerates the cardinalities, so that if the formula has a finite model, the tool eventually finds it, unless it runs out of resources.

Given finite cardinalities, the translation to FORL is straightforward, but common HOL idioms require a translation scheme tailored for SAT solving. In particular, infinite datatypes are soundly approximated by subterm-closed finite substructures [16] axiomatized in a three-valued logic.

Example. The Isabelle/HOL formula $rev\ xs = xs \wedge |set\ xs| = 2$ specifies that the list xs is a palindrome involving exactly two distinct elements. When asked to provide a model, Nitpick almost instantly finds $xs = [a_1, a_2, a_1]$. The detailed output reveals that it approximated the type α *list* with the finite substructure $\{[], [a_1], [a_2], [a_1,a_2], [a_2,a_1], [a_1,a_2,a_1]\}$.

5. First Experiments

In early experiments briefly treated elsewhere [4, §6.1], we tried out Nitpick on a previous version of the Isabelle formalization of the C++ memory model (the "post-Rapperswil model" [4]) to check whether given pairs ($\mathcal{X}_{\mathsf{opsem}}$, $\mathcal{X}_{\mathsf{witness}}$) are consistent executions of litmus test programs—a task that takes CPPMEM only a few milliseconds. Nitpick printed "Nitpicking..." but then became entangled seemingly forever in its problem-generation phase, not ever reaching Kodkod or MiniSat. What was happening?

5.1 Constant Unfolding

The first issue, a fairly technical one, was that the constant unfolding code was out of control. Nitpick has a simplistic approach to constants occurring in a satisfaction problem:

- For simple definitions $c \equiv t$, Nitpick unfolds (i.e., inlines) the constant c's definition, substituting the right-hand side t for c wherever it appears in the problem.
- Constants introduced using **primrec** or **fun**, which define recursive functions in terms of user-supplied equational specifications in the style of functional programming, are translated to FORL variables, and their equational specifications are conjoined with the problem as additional constraints to satisfy.

This approach works reasonably well for specifications featuring a healthy mixture of simple definitions and recursive functions, but it falls apart when there are too many nested simple definitions, as is the case in the C++ memory model. Simple definitions are generally of the form $c \equiv (\lambda x_1 \ldots x_n.\ u)$, and when c is applied to arguments, these are substituted for $x_1, \ldots, x_n$. The formula quickly explodes if the x_i's occur many times in the body u.

Since simple definitions are a degenerate form of recursion, we added hints to the specification telling Nitpick to treat some of the simply defined constants as if they had been recursive functions. In addition, we used the 'let' construct to store the value of an argument that is needed several times. HOL 'let' bindings are translated to an analogous FORL construct, enabling subexpression sharing all the way down to the SAT problem [28, §4.3].

5.2 Higher-Order Arguments

When we invoked Nitpick again, it produced worrisome warning messages such as the following one:

Arity 23 too large for universe of cardinality 4.

This specific message indicates that one of the free variables in the generated Kodkod problem is a 23-ary relation, whose cardinality might exceed $2^{31} - 1$ and cause arithmetic overflow in Kodkod. Nitpick detects this and warns the user.

Alloy users are taught to avoid relations of arities higher than 3 because they are very expensive in SAT: A relation over A^n requires $|A|^n$ propositional variables. HOL n-ary functions are normally translated to $(n+1)$-ary relations. Absurdly high arities arise when higher-order arguments are translated. A function from σ to τ cannot be directly passed as an argument in FORL; the workaround is to pass $|\sigma|$ arguments of type τ that encode a function table.

The memory model specification defines many constants with higher-order signatures, mainly because HOL identifies sets with their characteristic predicates. Here is one example among many:

$$
\begin{aligned}
&\mathit{synchronizes\_with} ::\\
&\quad (\mathit{act} \to \mathit{bool}) \to (\mathit{act} \times \mathit{act} \to \mathit{bool}) \to\\
&\quad (\mathit{act} \times \mathit{act} \to \mathit{bool}) \to (\mathit{act} \times \mathit{act} \to \mathit{bool}) \to\\
&\quad (\mathit{act} \times \mathit{act} \to \mathit{bool}) \to (\mathit{act} \times \mathit{act} \to \mathit{bool}) \to\\
&\quad (\mathit{act} \times \mathit{act} \to \mathit{bool}) \to \mathit{act} \to \mathit{act} \to \mathit{bool}
\end{aligned}
$$

An important optimization in Nitpick, function specialization, eliminates the most superficial higher-order arguments [6, §5.1]. A typical example is f in the definition of *map*:

primrec *map* **where**
$\mathit{map}\ f\ \mathit{Nil} = \mathit{Nil}$
$\mathit{map}\ f\ (\mathit{Cons}\ x\ \mathit{xs}) = \mathit{Cons}\ (f\ x)\ (\mathit{map}\ f\ \mathit{xs})$

Nitpick will specialize the *map* function for each admissible call site, thereby avoiding passing the argument for f altogether. At the call site, any argument whose free variables are all globally free (or are bound but less expensive to pass than the argument itself) is eligible for this optimization.

Most of the higher-order arguments in the memory model specification were eliminated this way. The remaining higher-order arguments resulted from a bad interaction between specialization and 'let'. Specifically, each 'let' introduces a higher-order bound variable, which prevents the argument from being specialized. For example, the crucial *consistent_execution* predicate's definition comprises the following 'let' bindings:

$$
\begin{aligned}
\mathit{rs} &= \mathit{release\_sequence}\ \mathit{acts}\ \mathit{lk}\ \mathit{mo}\\
\mathit{hrs} &= \mathit{hypothetical\_release\_sequence}\ \mathit{acts}\ \mathit{lk}\ \mathit{mo}\\
\mathit{sw} &= \mathit{synchronizes\_with}\ \mathit{acts}\ \mathit{sb}\ \mathit{asw}\ \mathit{rf}\ \mathit{sc}\ \mathit{rs}\ \mathit{hrs}
\end{aligned}
$$

The first two variables bound are of type $\mathit{act} \to \mathit{act} \to \mathit{bool}$. When these variables are passed to *synchronizes_with*, each of them is encoded as $|\mathit{act}|^2$ arguments of type *bool*. The easiest solution is to unfold higher-order 'let' bindings. This enables specialization to perform the essential work of keeping relation arities low, at the cost of some duplication in the generated FORL formula.

There remained one troublesome higher-order function in connection with so-called visible sequences of side-effects:

$$
\begin{aligned}
&\mathit{visible\_sequences\_of\_side\_effects\_set} ::\\
&\quad (\mathit{act} \to \mathit{bool}) \to (\mathit{thr\_id} \to \mathit{bool}) \to\\
&\quad (\mathit{loc} \to \mathit{loc\_kind}) \to (\mathit{act} \times \mathit{act} \to \mathit{bool}) \to\\
&\quad (\mathit{loc} \to \mathit{loc\_kind}) \to (\mathit{act} \times \mathit{act} \to \mathit{bool}) \to\\
&\quad (\mathit{loc} \to \mathit{loc\_kind}) \to (\mathit{act} \times \mathit{act} \to \mathit{bool}) \to\\
&\quad (\mathit{loc} \to \mathit{loc\_kind}) \to (\mathit{act} \times \mathit{act} \to \mathit{bool}) \to\\
&\quad \mathit{act} \times (\mathit{act} \to \mathit{bool}) \to \mathit{bool}
\end{aligned}
$$

The issue here is the return type $\mathit{act} \times (\mathit{act} \to \mathit{bool}) \to \mathit{bool}$: a set of pairs whose second components are sets of actions—effectively, a set of sets. We eventually found a way to completely eliminate visible sequences of side-effects without affecting the specification's semantics, as explained in Sect. 7.

5.3 Datatype Spinning

Having resolved the other problems, there remained one issue with Nitpick's handling of inductive datatypes. The memory model specification defines a few datatypes, notably a type *act* of actions:

datatype *act* =
  Lock   *act_id thr_id loc*
| *Unlock*   *act_id thr_id loc*
| *Atomic_load*   *act_id thr_id ord_order loc val*
| *Atomic_store*   *act_id thr_id ord_order loc val*
| *Atomic_rmw*   *act_id thr_id ord_order loc val val*
| *Load*   *act_id thr_id loc val*
| *Store*   *act_id thr_id loc val*
| *Fence*   *act_id thr_id ord_order*

The specification manipulates it through discriminators and selectors. An example of each follows:

definition *is_store a* ≡
  case *a* of *Store* _ _ _ _ ⇒ *True* | _ ⇒ *False*

fun *thread_id_of* **where**
$\mathit{thread\_id\_of}\ (\mathit{Lock}\ \_\ \mathit{tid}\ \_) = \mathit{tid}$
$\mathit{thread\_id\_of}\ (\mathit{Unlock}\ \_\ \mathit{tid}\ \_) = \mathit{tid}$
⋮
$\mathit{thread\_id\_of}\ (\mathit{Fence}\ \_\ \mathit{tid}\ \_) = \mathit{tid}$

Because of the type's high (in fact, infinite) cardinality, Nitpick cannot assign a distinct FORL atom to each possible *act* value. Instead, it considers only a subset of the possible values and uses a special undefined value, denoted by $\star$, to stand for the other values. Constructors and other functions sometimes return $\star$. Undefined values trickle down from terms all the way to the logical connectives and quantifiers. This leads to a Kleene three-valued logic [5, §4.2].

Which subset of *act* values should Nitpick choose? Perhaps surprisingly, it makes no specific commitment beyond fixing a cardinality for the set that approximates *act* (by default, 1, 2, and so on up to 10). It is the SAT solver's task to exhaust the possible subsets. The SAT solver finds out automatically which subset is needed. For example, if we state the conjecture

$$\mathit{length}\ xs = \mathit{length}\ ys \longrightarrow xs = ys$$

on lists, Nitpick finds the counterexample $xs = [a_1]$ and $ys = [a_2]$ with values taken from the subset $\{[], [a_1], [a_2]\}$. (The empty list is needed to build the other two lists.) Contrast this with

$$\mathit{length}\ xs < 2$$

where Nitpick instead relies on the subset $\{[], [a_1], [a_1, a_1]\}$.

This SAT-based approach to datatypes follows an established Alloy idiom [16] that typically scales up to cardinality 8 or so. However, in larger specifications such as the C++ memory model, the combinatorial explosion goes off much earlier.

And yet, for our specification, this combinatorial spinning is unnecessary: The needed actions all appear as ground terms in the litmus tests. The memory model specification inspects the actions, extracting subterms and recombining them in sets, but it never constructs new actions. Unfortunately, neither Nitpick nor Kodkod notices this, and MiniSat appears to be stumped.

Once again, we found ourselves modifying the specification to enforce the desired behavior. We first replaced the *act* datatype with an enumeration type that lists all the actions needed by a given litmus test and only those. For example:

datatype $act = a \mid b \mid c \mid d \mid e \mid f$

Then we defined the discriminators and selectors appropriately for the litmus test of interest. For example:

fun *is_store* **where**
is_store a = *True*
is_store _ = *False*

fun *thread_id_of* **where**
thread_id_of f = 1
thread_id_of _ = 0

Using this idiom, we could reuse the bulk of the memory model specification text unchanged across litmus tests. The main drawback of this approach is that each litmus test requires its own definitions for the *act* datatype and the discriminator and selector functions, on which the memory model specification rests.

The Nitpick-based empirical results presented in our previous paper [4, §6.1] employed this approach. The largest litmus test we considered (IRIW-SC) required 5 minutes using CPPMEM, but only 130 seconds using Nitpick. Other examples took Nitpick about 5 seconds. These were one-off experiments, since further changes to the original memory model were not mirrored in the Nitpick-enabled specification. The experiments were nonetheless interesting in their own right and persuaded us to optimize Nitpick further.

6. New Nitpick Optimizations

The experiments described in the previous section shed some light on areas in Nitpick that could benefit from more optimizations. Although we had come up with acceptable workarounds, we decided to improve the tool in the hope that future similar applications would require less manual work.

6.1 Heuristic Constant Unfolding

Nitpick's constant unfolding behavior, described in Sect. 5.1, left much to be desired. The notion that by default every simple definition should be unfolded was clearly misguided. If a constant is used many times and its definition is large, it should most likely be kept in the translation to facilitate reuse. Kodkod often detects shared subterms and factors them out [28, §4.3], but it does not help if Nitpick's translation phase is overwhelmed by the large terms.

We introduced a simple heuristic based on the size of the right-hand side of a definition: Small definitions are unfolded, whereas larger ones are kept as equations. It is difficult to design a better heuristic because of hard-to-predict interactions with function specialization and other optimizations occurring at later stages. We also made the unfolding more compact by heuristically introducing 'let's to bind the arguments of a constant when it is unfolded.

Nitpick provides a *nitpick_simp* hint that can be attached to a simple definition or a theorem of the right form to prevent unfolding. We now added a *nitpick_unfold* hint that can be used to forcefully unfold a larger definition, to give the user complete control.

6.2 Necessary Datatype Values

In Sect. 5.3 we explained how Nitpick's subterm-closed subset approach to inductive datatypes leads to a combinational explosion in the SAT solver. We also introduced an Isabelle idiom to prevent this "datatype spinning" when we know which values are necessary. However, the idiom requires fundamental changes to the specification, which is highly undesirable if proving and code generation (for CPPMEM) must also be catered for.

We came up with a better plan: Add an option to let users specify necessary datatype values and encode that information in the Kodkod problem. Users provide a set of datatype values as ground constructor terms, and Nitpick assigns one FORL atom to each term and subterm from that set. The atom assignment is coded as an additional constraint in the FORL problem and passed to the SAT solver, which exploits it to prune the search space.

For checking litmus tests, a convenient idiom is to first declare all the actions required as Isabelle abbreviations. For example:

abbreviation $a \equiv$ *Atomic_store* 0 0 *Ord_relaxed* 0 0
abbreviation $b \equiv$ *Atomic_rmw* 1 0 *Ord_relaxed* 0 0 1
⋮
abbreviation $f \equiv$ *Atomic_rmw* 5 1 *Ord_release* 0 2 3

If we pass the option "$\mathit{need} = a\ b\ c\ d\ e\ f$", Nitpick then generates additional constraints for these six terms and also their subterms:

$\mathsf{a}_1 = \mathit{Atomic\_store}\ 0\ 0\ \mathsf{a}_7\ 0\ 0$
$\mathsf{a}_2 = \mathit{Atomic\_rmw}\ 1\ 0\ \mathsf{a}_7\ 0\ 0\ 1$
⋮
$\mathsf{a}_6 = \mathit{Atomic\_rmw}\ 5\ 1\ \mathsf{a}_8\ 0\ 2\ 3$
$\mathsf{a}_7 = \mathit{Ord\_relaxed}$
$\mathsf{a}_8 = \mathit{Ord\_release}$

Natural numbers are left alone. The optimization makes no sense for them, since the desired cardinality k fully determines the subterm-closed subset to use, namely $\{0, \mathit{Suc}\ 0, \ldots, \mathit{Suc}^{k-1}\ 0\}$.

The resulting performance behavior is essentially the same as with the idiom presented in Sect. 5.3, but without having to restructure the specification.

We expect this optimization to be generally useful for specifications of programming language semantics. We had previously undertaken unpublished experiments with a Java compiler verified in Isabelle [19] and found that Nitpick suffered heavily from datatype spinning: Even when the program was hard-coded in the problem, the SAT solver would needlessly spin through the subterm-closed substructures of all possible Java programs.

6.3 Two-Valued Translation

There is a second efficiency issue related to Nitpick's handling of inductive datatypes. As mentioned in Sect. 5.3, attempting to construct a value that Nitpick cannot represent yields the unknown value $\star$. The ensuing partiality is handled by a Kleene three-valued logic, which is expressed in terms of Kodkod's two-valued logic as follows: At the outermost level, the FORL truth value true encodes *True* (genuine model), whereas false stands for both *False* (no model) and $\star$ (potentially spurious model). The same convention is obeyed in other positive contexts within the formula (i.e., under an even number of negations). Dually, false encodes *False* in negative contexts and true encodes *True* or $\star$.

This approach is incomplete but sound: When Kodkod finds a (finite) FORL model, it always corresponds to a (possibly infinite) HOL model. Unfortunately, the three-valued logic puts a heavy burden on the translation, which must handle $\star$ gracefully and keep track of polarities (positive and negative contexts). An operation as innocuous as equality in HOL, which we could otherwise map to FORL equality, must be translated so that it returns $\star$ if either operand is $\star$.

Formulas occurring in unpolarized, higher-order contexts (e.g., in a conditional expression or as argument to a function) are less common but all the more problematic. The conditional

$$\text{if } \varphi \text{ then } t_1 \text{ else } t_2$$

is translated to

$$\textsf{if } \widehat{\varphi}^+ \textsf{ then } \widehat{t}_1 \textsf{ else if } \neg\, \widehat{\varphi}^- \textsf{ then } \widehat{t}_2 \textsf{ else } \star$$

where $\widehat{\varphi}^+$ is the translation of φ in a positive context and $\widehat{\varphi}^-$ is its negative counterpart. The translation can quickly explode in size if φ itself contains formulas in higher-order places.

Simply stated, the root of the problem is overflow: When a constructor returns $\star$, it overflows in much the same way that IEEE n-bit floating-point arithmetic operations can yield NaN ("not a number") for large operands. Nitpick's translation to FORL detects overflows and handles them soundly. If the tool only knew that overflows are impossible, it could disable this expensive machinery and use a more direct two-valued translation [5, §4.1].

With the subterm-closed substructure approximation of inductive datatypes, overflows are a fact of life. For example, the append operator @ on lists, which is specified by the equations

$$\begin{aligned} \mathit{Nil} \mathbin{@} \mathit{ys} &= \mathit{ys} \\ (\mathit{Cons}\ x\ \mathit{xs}) \mathbin{@} \mathit{ys} &= \mathit{Cons}\ x\ (\mathit{xs} \mathbin{@} \mathit{ys}) \end{aligned}$$

will overflow if the longest representable nonempty list is appended to itself. In contrast, selectors such as *hd* (head) and *tl* (tail), which return the first and second argument of a *Cons*, cannot overflow.

The C++ memory model is a lengthy specification consisting of about 1200 lines of Isabelle/HOL definitions. On the face of it, it would be most surprising that no overflows are possible anywhere in it. But this is essentially the case. Apart from the test program and the set of possible executions, which appear in the conjecture and which we treated specially in Sect. 6.2, no overflows can occur. The whole specification is a predicate that merely inspects X_{opsem} and X_{witness} without constructing new values. Coincidentally, this design ensures the fast execution of CPPMEM, which must check thousands of potential witnesses.

To exploit this precious property of the specification, we added an option, *total_consts*, to control whether the two-valued translation without $\star$ should be used. The two-valued translation must be used with care: A single overflow in a definition can prevent the discovery of models.

Naturally, it would be desirable to implement an analysis in Nitpick to determine precisely which constants can overflow and use this information in a hybrid translation. This is future work.

7. Fine-Tuned C++ Memory Model

In parallel with our work on Nitpick, we refined the specification of the memory model in three notable ways:

- We ported the model to the custom specification language LEM; we now generate Isabelle text from that [24]. Ideally, we want to apply Nitpick directly on the generated specification.
- Reflecting recent discussions in the C++ concurrency subcommittee, in the new model SC reads cannot read from non-SC writes that happened before SC writes. This minor technical change rules out certain counterintuitive executions.
- The new model is formulated in terms of *visible side-effects* (a relation over actions) but does without the more complicated notion of *visible sequences of side-effects* (a relation between actions and sets of actions) found in the draft standard. This allows all consistency conditions to be predicates over sets and binary relations, which reduces Nitpick's search space considerably. We recently completed a formal equivalence proof for the two formulations.

With the optimizations described in Sect. 6 in place, Nitpick handles the new specification reasonably efficiently without any modifications. It nonetheless pays off to fine-tune the specification in three respects.

First, the types *act_id*, *thr_id*, *loc*, and *val*—corresponding to action IDs, thread IDs, memory locations, and values—are defined as aliases for *nat*, the type of natural numbers. This is unfortunate because it prevents us from specifying different cardinalities for the different notions. A litmus test involving eight actions, five threads, two memory locations, and two values gives rise to a much smaller SAT problem if we tell Nitpick to use the cardinalities $|act\_id| = 8$, $|thr\_id| = 5$, and $|loc| = |val| = 2$ than if all four types are set to have cardinality 8. To solve this, we replace the aliases

type_synonym *act_id* = *nat*
type_synonym *thr_id* = *nat*
type_synonym *loc* = *nat*

in the LEM specification with copies of the natural numbers:

datatype *act_id* = *A0* | *ASuc act_id*
datatype *thr_id* = *T0* | *TSuc thr_id*
datatype *loc* = *L0* | *LSuc loc*

For notational convenience, we define the following abbreviations: $a_k \equiv \mathit{ASuc}^k\ \mathit{A0}$, $t_k \equiv \mathit{TSuc}^k\ \mathit{T0}$, $\mathtt{x} \equiv \mathit{L0}$, and $\mathtt{y} \equiv \mathit{LSuc}\ \mathit{L0}$.

Second, while the unfolding heuristic presented in Sect. 6.1 allowed us to remove many *nitpick_simp* hints, we found that the heuristic was too aggressive with respect to two constants, which are better unfolded (using *nitpick_unfold*). We noticed them because they were the only relations of arity greater than 3 in the generated Kodkod problem.[1] Both were called with a higher-order argument that was not eligible for specialization. We specified the *nitpick_unfold* hints in a separate theory file that imports the LEM-generated Isabelle specification and customizes it.

Third, some of the basic definitions in the specification are gratuitously inefficient for SAT solving. The specification had its own definition of relational composition and transitive closure, but it is preferable to replace them with equivalent concepts from Isabelle's libraries, which are mapped to appropriate FORL constructs. This is achieved by providing lemmas that redefine the memory model's constants in terms of the desired Isabelle concepts:

[1] One could expect that the *act* constructors, which take between 3 and 6 arguments each, would be mapped to relations of arities 4 to 7, but Nitpick encodes constructors in terms of selectors to avoid high-arity relations [5, §5.2]. A term such as *Cons x xs* is translated to "the nonempty list *ys* such that *hd ys* = *x* and *tl ys* = *xs*," where *hd* and *tl* are coded as binary relations.

lemma [*nitpick_unfold*]: *compose R S* $= R \circ S$
lemma [*nitpick_unfold*]: *tc A R* $=$ (*restrict_relation R A*)$^+$

These lemmas are part of the separate theory file mentioned above. Similarly, we supply a more compact definition of the predicate *strict_total_order_over A R*. The original definition cleanly separates the constraints expressing the relation's domain, irreflexivity, transitivity, and totality:

$$\forall (a,b) \in R.\ a \in A \wedge b \in A$$
$$\forall x \in A.\ (x,x) \notin R$$
$$\forall x \in A.\ \forall y \in A.\ \forall z \in A.\ (x,y) \in R \wedge (y,z) \in R \longrightarrow (x,z) \in R$$
$$\forall x \in A.\ \forall y \in A.\ (x,y) \in R \vee (y,x) \in R \vee x = y$$

The optimized formulation

$$\begin{aligned}&\big(\forall x\, y.\ \text{if } (x,y) \in R \text{ then}\\&\qquad \{x,y\} \subseteq A \wedge x \neq y \wedge (y,x) \notin R\\&\quad \text{else}\\&\qquad \{x,y\} \subseteq A \wedge x \neq y \longrightarrow (y,x) \in R\big) \wedge\\&R^+ = R\end{aligned}$$

reduces the number of occurrences of A and R, both of which are higher-order arguments that are instantiated with arbitrarily large terms by the specialization optimization.

8. Litmus Tests

We evaluated Nitpick on several litmus tests designed to illustrate the semantics of the C++ memory model. The experiments were conducted on a 64-bit Mac Pro system with a Quad-Core Intel Xeon processor at 2.66 GHz clock speed, exploiting a single core. They are discussed in more detail below.

Most of these litmus tests had been checked by CPPMEM and the unoptimized version of Nitpick before [4], so it should not come as a surprise that our experiments revealed no further flaws in the C++ final draft standard. We did, however, discover many mistakes in the latest version of the formalization, such as missing parentheses and typos (e.g., $\forall$ instead of $\exists$). These mistakes had been accidentally introduced when the model was ported to LEM and had gone unnoticed even though it is used as a basis for formal proofs. Our experience illustrates once again the need to validate complex specifications, to ensure that the formal artifact correctly captures the intended semantics of the informal one (in our case, the draft standard).

8.1 Store Buffering

Our first test is simply the introductory example from Sect. 3:

```
atomic_int x = 0;
atomic_int y = 0;

{{{
    x.store(1, ord_relaxed);
    printf("y: %d\n", y.load(ord_relaxed));
|||
    y.store(1, ord_relaxed);
    printf("x: %d\n", x.load(ord_relaxed));
}}}
```

This program has six actions: two nonatomic initialization writes ($\mathsf{W_{na}}$), then one relaxed write ($\mathsf{W_{rlx}}$) and one relaxed read ($\mathsf{R_{rlx}}$) in each thread. The diagram below shows the relations *sb* and *asw*, which are part of $\mathcal{X}_{\mathsf{opsem}}$ and hence fixed by the program's operational semantics:

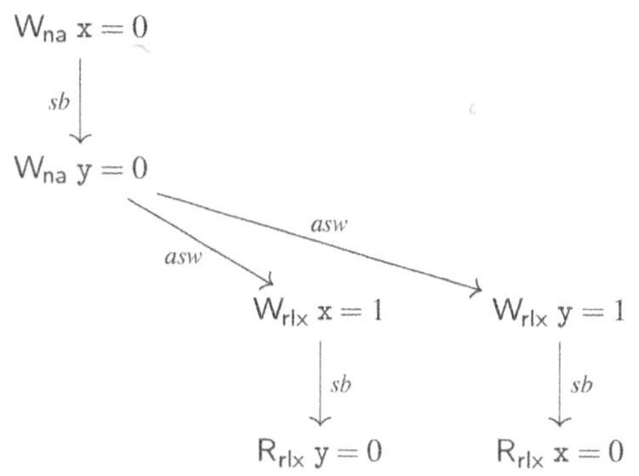

Each vertex represents an action, and an r-edge from a to b indicates that $(a,b) \in r$. The actions are arranged in three columns corresponding to the threads they belong to. For transitive relations, we omit transitive edges.

To check a litmus test with Nitpick, we must provide $\mathcal{X}_{\mathsf{opsem}}$. We can use CPPMEM's preprocessor to compute $\mathcal{X}_{\mathsf{opsem}}$ from a C++ program's source code, but for simple programs such as this one we can also translate the code manually. We first declare abbreviations for the test's actions:

abbreviation a $\equiv$ *Store* a_0 t_0 x 0
abbreviation b $\equiv$ *Store* a_1 t_0 y 0
abbreviation c $\equiv$ *Atomic_store* a_2 t_1 *Ord_relaxed* x 1
abbreviation d $\equiv$ *Atomic_load* a_3 t_1 *Ord_relaxed* y 0
abbreviation e $\equiv$ *Atomic_store* a_4 t_2 *Ord_relaxed* y 1
abbreviation f $\equiv$ *Atomic_load* a_5 t_2 *Ord_relaxed* x 0

Notice that the read actions, d and f, specify the value they expect to find as last argument to the constructor. That value is 0 for both threads because we are interested only in non-SC executions, in which the write actions c and e are ignored by the reads.

Next, we introduce the components of $\mathcal{X}_{\mathsf{opsem}}$ as constants:

definition [*nitpick_simp*]: *acts* $\equiv \{a,b,c,d,e,f\}$
definition [*nitpick_simp*]: *thrs* $\equiv \{t_0,t_1,t_2\}$
definition [*nitpick_simp*]: *lk* $\equiv$ (λ_. *Atomic*)
definition [*nitpick_simp*]: *sb* $\equiv \{(a,b),(c,d),(e,f)\}$
definition [*nitpick_simp*]: *asw* $\equiv \{(b,c),(b,e)\}$
definition [*nitpick_simp*]: *dd* $\equiv \{\}$
definition [*nitpick_simp*]: *cd* $\equiv \{\}$

Specialization implicitly propagates these values to where they are needed in the specification. To avoid clutter and facilitate subexpression sharing, we disable unfolding by specifying *nitpick_simp*.

Finally, we look for a model satisfying the constraint

consistent_execution acts thrs lk sb asw dd cd rf mo sc

where *rf*, *mo*, and *sc* are free variables corresponding to $\mathcal{X}_{\mathsf{witness}}$. The Nitpick call is shown below:

nitpick [

satisfy,	look for a model
need = a b c d e f,	the necessary actions (Sect. 6.2)
card act = 6,	six actions (a,b,c,d,e,f)
card act_id = 6,	six action IDs $(a_0,a_1,a_2,a_3,a_4,a_5)$
card thr_id = 3,	three thread IDs (t_0,t_1,t_2)
card loc = 2,	two locations (x, y)
card val = 2,	two values (0, 1)
card = 10,	maximum cardinality for other types
total_consts,	use two-valued translation (Sect. 6.3)
finitize act,	pretend *act* is finite
dont_box	disable boxing [6, §5.1]

]

With these options, Nitpick needs 4.7 seconds to find relations that witness a non-SC execution:

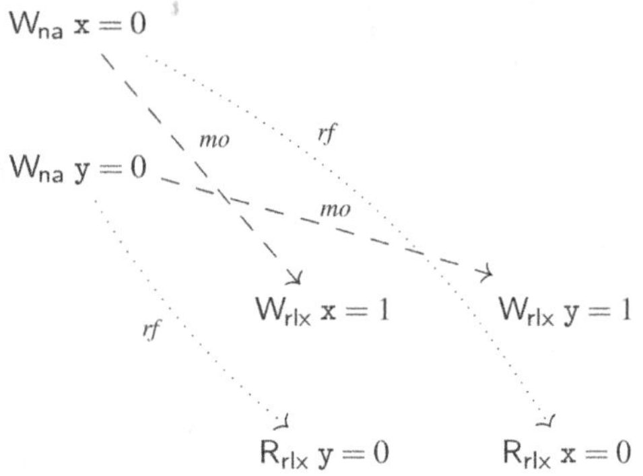

The modification-order relation (*mo*) reveals that the assignments x = 1 and y = 1 take place after the initializations to 0, but the read-from relation (*rf*) indicates that the two reads get their values from the initializations and not from the assignments.

If we replace all four relaxed memory accesses with SC atomics, such non-SC behavior is no longer possible. Nitpick verifies this in 4.0 seconds by reporting the absence of suitable witnesses. These results are consistent with our understanding of the draft standard.

8.2 Message Passing

We consider a variant of message passing where one thread writes to a data location x and then a flag y, while two reading threads read both the flag and the data. There are two initialization writes and two actions in each thread, for a total of eight actions:

```
atomic_int x = 0;
atomic_int y = 0;

{{{
    x.store(1, ord_relaxed);
    y.store(1, ord_relaxed);
|||
    printf("y1: %d\n", y.load(ord_relaxed));
    printf("x1: %d\n", x.load(ord_relaxed));
|||
    printf("x2: %d\n", x.load(ord_relaxed));
    printf("y2: %d\n", y.load(ord_relaxed));
}}}
```

Because all non-initialization actions are relaxed atomics, it is possible for the two readers to observe the writes in opposite order. Nitpick finds the following execution in 5.7 seconds:

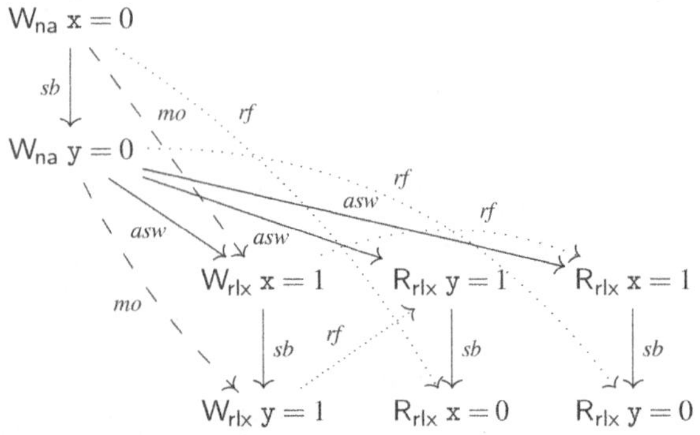

On the other hand, if the flag is accessed via a release/acquire pair, or via SC atomics, the first reader is guaranteed to observe the data written by the writer thread. Nitpick finds such an execution (without the second reader) in 4.0 seconds, and verifies the absence of a non-SC execution also in 4.0 seconds.

8.3 Load Buffering

This test is dual to the Store Buffering test. Two threads read from separate locations; then each thread writes to the other location:

```
atomic_int x = 0;
atomic_int y = 0;

{{{
    printf("x: %d\n", x.load(ord_relaxed));
    y.store(1, ord_relaxed);
|||
    printf("y: %d\n", y.load(ord_relaxed));
    x.store(1, ord_relaxed);
}}}
```

With relaxed atomics, each thread can observe the other thread's later write. Nitpick finds a witness execution in 4.2 seconds:

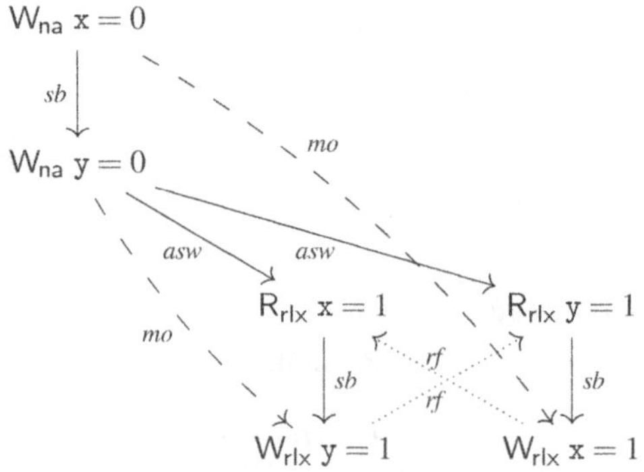

Nitpick verifies the absence of a non-SC execution with release/consume, release/acquire, and SC atomics in 4.1 seconds.

8.4 Sequential Lock

This test is more ambitious. The program models a simple sequential locking algorithm inspired by the Linux kernel's "seqlock" mechanism [17]:

```
atomic_int x = 0;
atomic_int y = 0;
atomic_int z = 0;

{{{
    for (int i = 0; i < N; i++) {
        x.store(2 * i + 1, ord_release);
        y.store(i + 1, ord_release);
        z.store(i + 1, ord_release);
        x.store(2 * i + 2, ord_release);
    }
|||
    printf("x: %d\n", x.load(ord_consume));
    printf("y: %d\n", y.load(ord_consume));
    printf("z: %d\n", z.load(ord_consume));
    printf("x: %d\n", x.load(ord_consume));
}}}
```

The program spawns a writer and a reader thread. The writer maintains a counter x; the writer's loop increments it before and after modifying the data locations y and z. Intuitively, the data is "locked" whenever the counter x is odd. The reader eventually accesses the data, but not without checking x before and after. A non-SC behavior occurs if the two reads of x yield the same even value (i.e., the lock was free during the two data reads) but $y \neq z$ (i.e., the data was observed while in an inconsistent state).

Already for $N = 1$, Nitpick finds the following non-SC execution, where the reader observes $y = 0$ and $z = 1$, in 15.8 seconds:

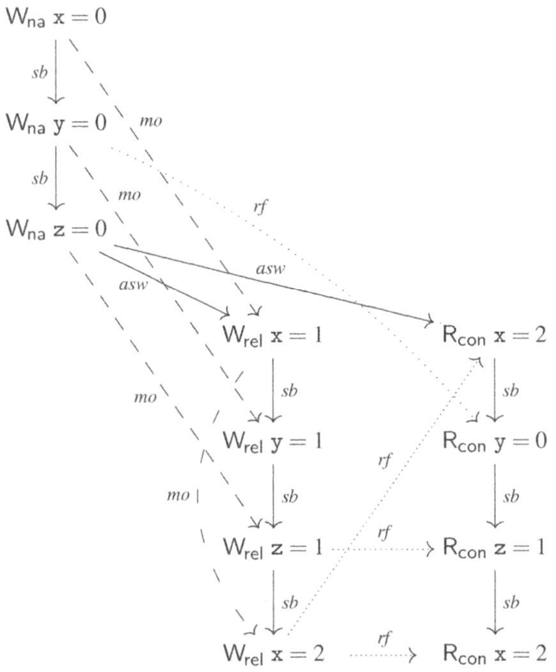

With release/acquire instead of release/consume, the algorithm should be free of non-SC behavior. Nitpick takes 15.8 seconds to exhaustively check the $N = 1$ case, 86 seconds for $N = 2$, and 378 seconds for $N = 3$. If we add a second reader thread, it takes 86 seconds for $N = 1$ and 379 seconds for $N = 2$.

Because of the loop, our analysis is incomplete: We cannot prove the absence of non-SC behavior for all bounds N (or for an arbitrary number of readers), only its presence. Nonetheless, the small-scope hypothesis, which postulates that "most bugs have small counterexamples" [13, §5.1.3], strongly suggests that the sequential locking algorithm implemented in terms of release/acquire atomics is correct for any number of iterations and reader threads.

8.5 Independent Reads of Independent Writes

Two writer threads independently write to x and y, and two readers read from both locations:

```
atomic_int x = 0;
atomic_int y = 0;

{{{
    x.store(1, ord_release);
|||
    y.store(1, ord_release);
|||
    printf("x1: %d\n", x.load(ord_acquire));
    printf("y1: %d\n", y.load(ord_acquire));
|||
    printf("y2: %d\n", y.load(ord_acquire));
    printf("x2: %d\n", x.load(ord_acquire));
}}}
```

With release/acquire, release/consume, and relaxed actions, different reader threads can observe these writes in opposite order. Nitpick finds an execution in 5.8 seconds:

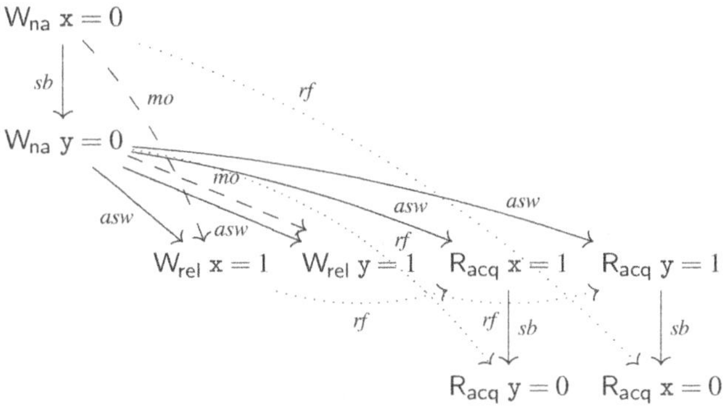

With SC actions, this behavior is not allowed, and Nitpick verifies the absence of a non-SC execution in 5.2 seconds.

8.6 Write-to-Read Causality

This test spawns three auxiliary threads in addition to the implicit initialization thread:

```
atomic_int x = 0;
atomic_int y = 0;

{{{
    x.store(1, ord_relaxed);
|||
    printf("x1: %d\n", x.load(ord_relaxed));
    y.store(1, ord_relaxed);
|||
    printf("y: %d\n", y.load(ord_relaxed));
    printf("x2: %d\n", x.load(ord_relaxed));
}}}
```

The first auxiliary thread writes to x; the second thread reads from x and writes to y; the third thread reads from y and then from x. With relaxed atomics, the third thread does not necessarily observe the first thread's write to x even if it observes the second thread's write to y and the second thread observes the first thread's write to x. Nitpick finds this execution in 4.2 seconds:

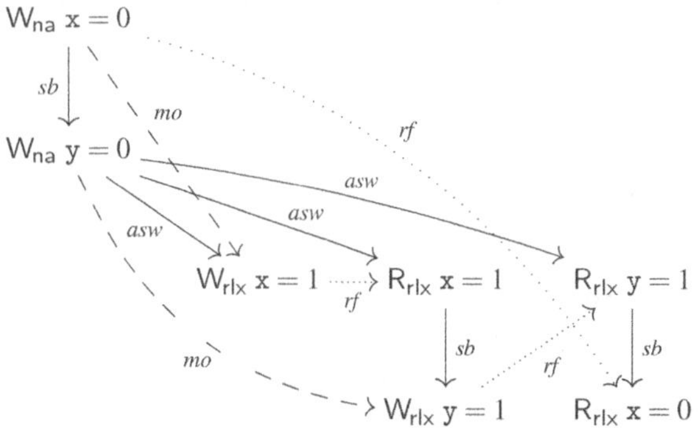

The memory model guarantees write-to-read causality for release/acquire and SC actions. Nitpick verifies the absence of a non-SC execution in 4.4 seconds.

8.7 Generalized Write-to-Read Causality

Nitpick's run-time depends on the size of the search space, which is exponential in the number of actions. To demonstrate how Nitpick scales up to larger litmus tests, we generalize the Write-to-Read Causality test from 2 to n locations. The generalized test consists of $2n$ writes (including n initializations) and $n+1$ reads, thus $3n+1$ actions in total. Since the three witness variables are binary relations over actions, the state space is of size $2^{3(3n+1)^2}$.

With relaxed atomics, there is an execution where the last thread does not observe the first thread's write. With SC atomics, no such execution exists. The Nitpick run-times are tabulated below. For comparison, we also include the CPPMEM run-times (on roughly comparable hardware).

Locations	Actions	States	CPPMEM		Nitpick	
(n)	($3n+1$)	($2^{3(3n+1)^2}$)	relaxed	SC	relaxed	SC
2	7	2^{147}	0.0 s	0.5 s	4 s	4 s
3	10	2^{300}	0.0 s	90.5 s	11 s	11 s
4	13	2^{507}	0.1 s	$>10^4$ s	41 s	40 s
5	16	2^{768}	0.2 s	$>10^4$ s	132 s	127 s
6	19	2^{1083}	0.7 s	$>10^4$ s	384 s	376 s
7	22	2^{1452}	2.5 s	$>10^4$ s	982 s	977 s

Each additional location slows down Nitpick's search by a factor of about 3. Although the search space grows with 2^{n^2}, the search time grows slightly slower than k^n, which is asymptotically better than CPPMEM's $n!$ worst-case complexity.

CPPMEM outperforms Nitpick on the relaxed version of the test because its basic constraints reduce the search space to just 2^n candidate orders for *rf* and *mo* (Sect. 3.4). On the other hand, CPPMEM scales much worse than Nitpick when the actions are SC, because it naively enumerates all $2^n \cdot (2n+1)!$ combinations for *rf*, *mo*, and *sc* that meet the basic constraints.

8.8 Further Remarks

Thanks to the optimizations presented in Sect. 6, Nitpick is about 25 times faster on medium-sized litmus tests than it was before. Verifying the absence of a consistent non-SC execution for the Independent Reads of Independent Writes test now takes about 5.2 seconds, compared with 130 seconds previously and 5 minutes using CPPMEM [4, §6.1]. Larger SC tests that cannot realistically be checked with CPPMEM are now analyzable within minutes.

On small litmus tests, Nitpick remains significantly slower than CPPMEM, which takes less than a second on some of the tests. The bottleneck is the translation of the memory model into FORL and SAT. The SAT search is extremely fast for small tests and scales much better than CPPMEM's simplistic enumeration scheme. On the largest problems we considered, Nitpick takes a few seconds, which is negligible; then about 95% of the time is spent in Kodkod, while the rest is spent in MiniSat.

For some litmus tests, CPPMEM's basic constraints reduce the search space considerably. We could probably speed up Nitpick by incorporating these constraints into the model—for example, by formalizing *rf* as a map from reads to writes, rather than as a binary relation over actions. However, this would require extensive modifications to the formalization, which we would rather avoid.

9. Related Work

The discovery of fatal flaws in the original Java memory model [25] stimulated much research in software memory models. We attempt to cover the most relevant work, focusing on tool support.

MemSAT [29] is an automatic tool based on Kodkod specifically designed for debugging axiomatic memory models. It has been used on several memory models from the literature, including the Java memory model. A noteworthy feature of MemSAT is that it produces a minimal unsatisfiable core if the model or the litmus test is overconstrained. MemSAT also includes a component that generates relational constraints from Java programs, akin to CPPMEM's preprocessor. Nitpick's main advantage over MemSAT for our case study is that it understands higher-order logic.

NemosFinder [33] is another axiomatic memory model checker. Memory models are coded as Prolog predicates and either checked using constraint logic programming or SAT solving. The tool includes a specification of the Intel Itanium memory model.

Visual-MCM [22] is a generic tool that checks and graphically displays given executions against a memory model specification. The tool was designed primarily as an aid to hardware designers.

While the above tools are generic, many tools target specific models. Manson and Pugh [20] developed two simulators for the Java memory model that enumerate the possible executions of a program. Java RaceFinder [15], an extension to Java PathFinder [30], is a modern successor. Both of these are explicit-state model checkers. Like CPPMEM (and its predecessor `memevents` [26]), they suffer from the state-explosion problem.

We refer to Batty et al. [4], Torlak et al. [29], and Yang et al. [33] for more related work.

10. Discussion and Conclusion

We applied the model finder Nitpick to our Isabelle/HOL formalization [4] of the C++ draft standard's memory model. Our experiments involved classical litmus tests and (fortunately) did not reveal any flaws in the C++ final draft standard. This is no surprise: The model has already been validated by the CPPMEM simulator on several litmus tests, and the correctness proof of the suggested Intel x86 implementation gave further evidence that the Isabelle model captures the draft standard's intended semantics.

The main challenge for a diagnosis tool such as Nitpick is that users of interactive theorem provers tend to write their specifications so as to make the actual proving easy. In contrast, if the Alloy Analyzer or MemSAT performs poorly on a specification, the tool's developers can put part of the blame on the users, arguing for example that they have "not yet assimilated the relational idiom" [16, p. 7]. We wish we could have applied Nitpick directly on the Isabelle specification of the memory model, but without changes to either Nitpick or the specification our approach would not have scaled to handle even the simplest litmus tests.

We were delighted to see that function specialization, one of the very first optimizations implemented in Nitpick [6, §5.1], proved equal to the task. By propagating arguments to where they are needed, specialization ensures that no more than two arguments ever need to be passed at a call site—a dramatic reduction from the 10 or more arguments taken by many of the memory model's functions. Without this optimization, we would have faced the unappealing prospect of rewriting the specification from scratch.

There will always be cases where more dedicated tools are called for, but it is pleasing when a general-purpose tool outperforms dedicated solutions. Our new Nitpick optimizations will be included in the next Isabelle release and should prove beneficial to other large formalizations.

Acknowledgments

This work would not have been possible without Peter Sewell, who together with the last four authors specified the C++ memory model in Isabelle/HOL. Sascha Böhme, Lukas Bulwahn, Paul Jackson, Tobias Nipkow, Peter Sewell, Mark Summerfield, Geoff Sutcliffe, and the anonymous reviewers suggested several textual improvements. We acknowledge funding from the Deutsche Forschungsgemeinschaft (grant Ni 491/11-2) and the British EPSRC (grants EP/F036345, EP/F067909, EP/H005633, EP/H027351).

References

[1] Programming languages—C++. Technical Report N3290, ISO IEC JTC1/SC22/WG21, 2011. `http://www.open-std.org/jtc1/sc22/wg21/docs/papers/2011/n3290.pdf`.

[2] P. B. Andrews. *An Introduction to Mathematical Logic and Type Theory: To Truth Through Proof (2nd Ed.)*, volume 27 of *Applied Logic*. Springer, 2002.

[3] M. Batty, S. Owens, S. Sarkar, P. Sewell, and T. Weber. Mathematizing C++ concurrency: The post-Rapperswil model. Technical Report N3132, ISO IEC JTC1/SC22/WG21, 2010. `http://www.open-std.org/jtc1/sc22/wg21/docs/papers/2010/n3132.pdf`.

[4] M. Batty, S. Owens, S. Sarkar, P. Sewell, and T. Weber. Mathematizing C++ concurrency. In T. Ball and M. Sagiv, editors, *POPL 2011*, pages 55–66. ACM, 2011.

[5] J. C. Blanchette. Relational analysis of (co)inductive predicates, (co)inductive datatypes, and (co)recursive functions. *Softw. Qual. J.* To appear.

[6] J. C. Blanchette and T. Nipkow. Nitpick: A counterexample generator for higher-order logic based on a relational model finder. In M. Kaufmann and L. Paulson, editors, *ITP 2010*, volume 6172 of *LNCS*, pages 131–146. Springer, 2010.

[7] P. Cenciarelli, A. Knapp, and E. Sibilio. The Java memory model: Operationally, denotationally, axiomatically. In R. De Nicola, editor, *ESOP 2007*, volume 4421 of *LNCS*, pages 331–346. Springer, 2007.

[8] A. Church. A formulation of the simple theory of types. *J. Symb. Log.*, 5:56–68, 1940.

[9] W.-P. de Roever, F. de Boer, U. Hannemann, J. Hooman, Y. Lakhnech, M. Poel, and J. Zwiers. *Concurrency Verification: Introduction to Compositional and Noncompositional Methods*, volume 54 of *Cambridge Tracts in Theoretical Computer Science*. Cambridge University Press, 2001.

[10] N. Eén and N. Sörensson. An extensible SAT-solver. In E. Giunchiglia and A. Tacchella, editors, *SAT 2003*, volume 2919 of *LNCS*, pages 502–518. Springer, 2004.

[11] M. J. C. Gordon and T. F. Melham, editors. *Introduction to HOL: A Theorem Proving Environment for Higher Order Logic*. Cambridge University Press, 1993.

[12] M. J. C. Gordon, R. Milner, and C. P. Wadsworth. *Edinburgh LCF: A Mechanised Logic of Computation*, volume 78 of *LNCS*. Springer, 1979.

[13] D. Jackson. *Software Abstractions: Logic, Language, and Analysis*. MIT Press, 2006.

[14] J. Jürjens and T. Weber. Finite models in FOL-based crypto-protocol verification. In P. Degano and L. Viganò, editors, *ARSPA-WITS 2009*, volume 5511 of *LNCS*, pages 155–172. Springer, 2009.

[15] K. Kim, T. Yavuz-Kahveci, and B. A. Sanders. Precise data race detection in a relaxed memory model using heuristic-based model checking. In *ASE 2009*, pages 495–499. IEEE, 2009.

[16] V. Kuncak and D. Jackson. Relational analysis of algebraic datatypes. In H. C. Gall, editor, *ESEC/FSE 2005*. ACM, 2005.

[17] C. Lameter. Effective synchronization on Linux/NUMA systems. Presented at the Gelato Conference 2005.

[18] L. Lamport. How to make a multiprocessor computer that correctly executes multiprocess programs. *IEEE Trans. Comput.*, 28(9):690–691, 1979.

[19] A. Lochbihler. Verifying a compiler for Java threads. In A. D. Gordon, editor, *ESOP 2010*, volume 6012 of *LNCS*, pages 427–447. Springer, 2010.

[20] J. Manson and W. Pugh. The Java memory model simulator. In *Formal Techniques for Java-like Programs (FTfJP) 2002*.

[21] A. McIver and T. Weber. Towards automated proof support for probabilistic distributed systems. In G. Sutcliffe and A. Voronkov, editors, *LPAR 2005*, number 3835 in LNAI, pages 534–548. Springer, 2005.

[22] A. C. Melo and S. C. Chagas. Visual-MCM: Visualising execution histories on multiple memory consistency models. In P. Zinterhof, M. Vajtersic, and A. Uhl, editors, *ACPC 1999*, volume 1557 of *LNCS*, pages 500–509. Springer, 1999.

[23] T. Nipkow, L. C. Paulson, and M. Wenzel. *Isabelle/HOL: A Proof Assistant for Higher-Order Logic*, volume 2283 of *LNCS*. Springer, 2002.

[24] S. Owens, P. Böhm, F. Zappa Nardelli, and P. Sewell. Lightweight tools for heavyweight semantics. In *ITP 2011*. Springer. To appear.

[25] W. Pugh. The Java memory model is fatally flawed. *Concurrency—Practice and Experience*, 12(6):445–455, 2000.

[26] S. Sarkar, P. Sewell, F. Zappa Nardelli, S. Owens, T. Ridge, T. Braibant, M. O. Myreen, and J. Alglave. The semantics of x86-CC multiprocessor machine code. In Z. Shao and B. C. Pierce, editors, *POPL 2009*, pages 379–391. ACM, 2009.

[27] J. Sevcík and D. Aspinall. On validity of program transformations in the Java memory model. In J. Vitek, editor, *ECOOP 2008*, volume 5142 of *LNCS*, pages 27–51. Springer, 2008.

[28] E. Torlak and D. Jackson. Kodkod: A relational model finder. In O. Grumberg and M. Huth, editors, *TACAS 2007*, volume 4424 of *LNCS*, pages 632–647. Springer, 2007.

[29] E. Torlak, M. Vaziri, and J. Dolby. MemSAT: Checking axiomatic specifications of memory models. In B. G. Zorn and A. Aiken, editors, *PLDI 2010*, pages 341–350. ACM, 2010.

[30] W. Visser, K. Havelund, G. Brat, S. Park, and F. Lerda. Model checking programs. *Autom. Softw. Eng. J.*, 10(2):203–232, 2003.

[31] T. Weber. A SAT-based Sudoku solver. In G. Sutcliffe and A. Voronkov, editors, *LPAR 2005 (Short Papers)*, pages 11–15, 2005.

[32] T. Weber. *SAT-Based Finite Model Generation for Higher-Order Logic*. Ph.D. thesis, Dept. of Informatics, T.U. München, 2008.

[33] Y. Yang, G. Gopalakrishnan, G. Lindstrom, and K. Slind. Nemos: A framework for axiomatic and executable specifications of memory consistency models. In *IPDPS 2004*. IEEE, 2004.

Maintaining Distributed Logic Programs Incrementally

Vivek Nigam
LMU, GERMANY
vivek.nigam@ifi.lmu.de

Limin Jia
CMU, USA
liminjia@cmu.edu

Boon Thau Loo
UPENN, USA
boonloo@cis.upenn.edu

Andre Scedrov
UPENN, USA
scedrov@math.upenn.edu

Abstract

Distributed logic programming languages, that allow both facts and programs to be distributed among different nodes in a network, have been recently proposed and used to declaratively program a wide-range of distributed systems, such as network protocols and multi-agent systems. However, the distributed nature of the underlying systems poses serious challenges to developing efficient and correct algorithms for evaluating these programs. This paper proposes an efficient asynchronous algorithm to compute incrementally the changes to the states in response to insertions and deletions of base facts. Our algorithm is formally proven to be correct in the presence of message reordering in the system. To our knowledge, this is the first formal proof of correctness for such an algorithm.

Categories and Subject Descriptors F.3.2 [*Semantics of Programming Languages*]: Operational Semantics

General Terms Algorithms, Theory, Correctness

Keywords Distributed Datalog, Logic Programming, Incremental Maintenance

1. Introduction

One of the most exciting developments in computer science in recent years is that computing has become increasingly distributed. Both resources and computation no longer reside in a single place. Resources can be stored in different machines possibly around the world, and computation can also be performed by different machines, *e.g.* cloud computing. Since machines usually run asynchronously and under very different environments, programming computer artifacts in such frameworks has become increasingly difficult as programs have to be at the same time correct, readable, efficient and portable. There has therefore been a recent return to using declarative programming languages, based on Prolog and Datalog, to program distributed systems such as networks and multi-agent robotic systems, *e.g.* Network Datalog (*NDlog*) [10], MELD [5], Netlog [6], DAHL [11], Dedalus [4]. When programming in these declarative languages, programmers usually do not need to specify *how* computation is done, but rather *what* is to be computed. Therefore declarative programs tend to be more readable, portable, and orders of magnitude smaller than their imperative counterpart.

Distributed systems, such as networking and multi-agent robotic systems, deal at their core with maintaining states by allowing each node (agent) to compute locally and then propagate its local states to other nodes in the system. For instance, in routing protocols, at each iteration each node computes locally its routing tables based on information it has gained so far, then distributes the set of derived facts to its neighbors. We can specify these systems as distributed logic programs, where the base facts as well as the rules are distributed among different nodes in the network.

Similarly to its centralized counterpart, one of the main challenges of implementing these distributed logic programs is to efficiently and correctly update them when the base facts change. For distributed systems, the communication costs due to updates also need to be taken consideration. For instance, in the network setting, when a new link in the network has been established or an old link has been broken, the set of derived routes need to be updated to reflect the changes in the base facts. It is impractical to recompute each node's state from-scratch when changes occur, since that would require all nodes to exchange their local states including those that have been previously propagated. For example, in the path-vector protocol used in Internet routing, recomputation from-scratch would require all nodes to exchange all routing information.

A better approach is to maintain the state of distributed logic programs incrementally. Instead of reconstructing the entire state, one only modifies previously derived facts that are affected by the changes of the base facts, while the remaining facts are left untouched. For typical network topologies, whenever a link update happens, incremental recomputation requires less bandwidth and results in much faster protocol convergence times when compared to recomputing a protocol from scratch.

This paper develops algorithms for incrementally maintaining recursive logic programs in a distributed setting. Our algorithms allow asynchronous execution among agents. No agent needs to *stop* computing because some other agent has not concluded its computation. Synchronization requires extra communication between agents, which comes at a huge performance penalty. In addition, we also allow update messages to be received out of order. We do not assume the existence of a *coordinator* in the system, which matches the realty of distributed systems. Finally, we develop techniques that ensure the termination of updates even in the presence of recursive logic programs.

PDPP'11, July 20–22, 2011, Odense, Denmark.

More concretely, we propose an asynchronous incremental logic programming maintenance algorithm, based on the *pipelined semi-naïve* (PSN) evaluation strategy proposed by Loo *et al.* [10]. PSN relaxes the traditional semi-naïve (SN) evaluation strategy for Datalog by allowing an agent to change its local state by following a local pipeline of update messages. These messages specify the insertions and deletions scheduled to be performed to the agents' local state. When an update is processed, new updates may be generated and those that have to be processed by other agents of the system are transmitted accordingly.

We discovered that existing PSN algorithms [9, 10] may produce incorrect results if the messages are received out of order. We formally prove the correctness of our PSN algorithm, which is lacking from existing work. What makes the problem hard is that we need to show that, in a distributed, asynchronous setting, the state computed by our algorithm is correct regardless of the order in which updates are processed. Unlike prior PSN proposals [9, 10], our algorithm does not require that message channels be FIFO, which is for many distributed systems an unrealistic assumption.

Guaranteeing termination is another challenge for developing an incremental maintenance algorithm for distributed recursive logic programs. Typically, in a centralized synchronous setting, algorithms, such as DRed [7], guarantee the termination of updates caused by insertion by maintaining the set of derivable facts, and discarding new derivations of previously derived facts. However, to handle updates caused by deletion properly, DRed [7] needs to first delete facts caused by deletion of base facts, then re-derive any deleted fact that has an alternative derivation. Re-derivation incurs communication costs, which degrade the performance in a distributed setting. This argues for maintaining the multiset of derivable facts, where no re-derivation of facts is needed, since nodes keep track of all possible derivations for any fact. However, termination is no longer guaranteed, as cycles in the derivation of recursive programs allow facts to be supported by infinitely many derivations.

To tackle this problem, we adapt an existing centralized solution [12] to distributed settings. For any given fact, we add annotations containing the set of base and intermediate facts used to derive that fact. These per-fact annotations are then used to detect cycles in derivations. We formally prove that in a distributed setting, the annotations are enough to detect when facts are supported by infinitely many derivations and guarantee termination of our algorithm.

This paper makes the following technical contributions, after introducing some basic definitions in Section 2:

- We propose a new PSN-algorithm to maintain distributed logic programs incrementally (Section 3). This algorithm only deals with distributed non-recursive logic programs. (Recursive programs is dealt in Section 5.)
- We formally prove that PSN is correct (Section 4). Instead of directly proving PSN maintains distributed logic programs correctly, we construct our proofs in two steps. First, we define a synchronous algorithm based on SN evaluations, and prove the synchronous SN algorithm is correct. Then, we show that any PSN execution computes the same result as the synchronous SN algorithm.
- We extend the basic algorithm by annotating each fact with information about its derivation to ensure the termination of maintaining distributed states (Section 5), and prove its correctness.
- We point out the limitations of existing maintenance algorithms in a distributed setting where channels are not necessarily FIFO (Section 6) and comment on related work (Section 7);

Finally, we conclude with some final remarks in Section 8. All proofs appear in the companion technical report [14].

2. Distributed Datalog

We present *Distributed Datalog* (*DDlog*), which extends Datalog programs by allowing Datalog rules to be distributed among different nodes. *DDlog* is the core sublanguage common to many of the distributed Datalog languages, such as *NDlog* [10], MELD [5], Netlog [6], and Dedalus [4]. Our algorithms maintain the states for *DDlog* programs.

2.1 Syntax and Evaluation

Syntax. Similar to Datalog programs, a *DDlog* program consists of a (finite) set of logic rules of the form $h(\vec{t})$:- $b_1(\vec{t_1}), \ldots, b_n(\vec{t_n})$, where the commas are interpreted as conjunctions and the symbol :- as reverse implication. Following [16], we assume a *finite* signature of predicate and constant symbols, but no function symbols. A *fact* is a ground atomic formula. For the rest of this paper, we use fact and predicate interchangeably.

We say that a predicate p depends on q if there is a rule where p appears in its head and q in its body. The *dependency graph* of a program is the transitive closure of the dependency relation using its rules. We say that a program is *(non)recursive* if there are (no) cycles in its dependency graph. We classify the predicates that do not depend on any predicates as base predicates (facts), and the remaining predicates as derived predicates.

To allow distributed computation, *DDlog* extends Datalog by augmenting its syntax with the location operator `@` [10], which specifies the location of a fact. The following *DDlog* program computes the reachability relation among nodes:

```
r1: reachable(@S,D) :- link(@S,D).
r2: reachable(@S,D) :- link(@S,Z), reachable(@Z,D).
```

It takes as input `link(@S,D)` facts, each of which represents an edge from the node itself (`S`) to one of its neighbors (`D`). The location operator `@` specifies where facts are stored. For example, `link` facts are stored based on the value of the `S` attribute.

Distributed Evaluation. Rules `r1`-`r2` recursively derive `reachable(@S,D)` facts, each of which states that the node `S` is reachable from the node `D`. Rule `r1` computes one-hop reachability, given the neighbor set of `S` stored in `link(@S,D)`. Rule `r2` computes transitive reachability as follows: if there exists a link from `S` to `Z`, and the node `D` is reachable from `Z`, then `S` can also reach `D`.

In a distributed setting, initially, each node in the system stores the link facts that are relevant to its own state. For example, the fact `link(@2,4)` is stored at the node 2. To compute all reachability relations, each node runs the exact same copy of the program above concurrently. Newly derived facts may need to be sent to the corresponding nodes as specified by the `@` operator.

Rule localization. As illustrated by the rule `r2`, the atomic formulas in the body of the rules can have different location specifiers indicating that they are stored on different nodes. To apply such a rule, facts may need to be gathered from several nodes, possibly different from where the rule resides. To have a clearly defined semantics of the program, we apply *rule localization* rewrite procedure as shown in [10] to make such communication explicit. The *rule localization* rewrite procedure transforms a program into an equivalent one (called *localized* program) where all elements in the body of a rule are located at the same location, but the head of the rule may reside at a different location than the body atoms. This procedure improves performance by eliminating the need of unnecessary communication among nodes, as a node only needs the facts locally stored to derive a new fact. For example, the followings two rules are the localized version of `r2`:

```
r2-1: reachable(@S,D) :- link(@S,Z), aux(@S,Z,D).
r2-2: aux(@S,Z,D) :- reachable(@Z,D), co-link(@Z,S).
```

Here, the predicate `aux` is a new predicate: it does not appear in the original alphabet of predicates and the fact `co-link(@Z,S)` is true if and only if `link(@S,Z)` is true. The predicate `co-link(@Z,S)` is used to denote that the node `Z` knows that the node `S` is one of its neighbors. As specified in the rule `r2-1`, these predicates are used to inform all neighbors, `S`, of node `Z` that the node `Z` can reach node `D`. It is not hard to show, by induction on the height of derivations, that this program is equivalent to the previous one in the sense that a `reachable` fact is derivable using one program if and only if it is derivable using the other. For the rest of this paper, we assume that such localization rewrite has been performed.

2.2 Multiset Semantics

The semantics of *DDlog* programs is defined in terms of the (multi)set of derivable facts (*least model*). We call such a (multi)set, the *state* of the program. In database community, it is called the *materialized view* of the program. For instance, in the following non-recursive program, `p`, `s`, and `t` are derived predicates and `u`, `q`, and `r` are base predicates.

{`p :- s,t,r;   s :- q;   t :- u;   q :-;   u :-`}.

The (multi)set of all the ground atoms that are derivable from this program, is {`s, t, q, u`}. For this example, each fact is supported by only one derivation and therefore the same state is obtained whether the state is the set, or the multiset of derivable facts. If we add, the rule `s :- u` to this program, then the state when using the multiset semantics of the resulting program would change to {`s, s, t, q, u`} where `s` appears twice. This is because there are two different ways to derive `s`: one by using `q` and the other by using `u`. Our choice of multiset-semantics is essential for correctness, which we discuss in detail in Section 6.

2.3 Incremental State Maintenance

Changes to the base predicates of a *DDlog* program will change its state. The goal of this paper is to develop a correct asynchronous algorithm that incrementally maintains the state of *DDlog* programs as updates occur in the system. The main idea of the algorithm is to first compute only the changes caused by the updates to the base predicates, then apply the changes to the state. For instance, when a base fact is inserted, the algorithm computes all the facts that were not in the state before the insertion, but are now derivable. Similarly, when a deletion occurs, the algorithm computes all the facts that were in the state before the deletion, but need to be removed. We introduce notations for defining such an algorithm here, and we formally define our algorithms and prove them correct in the next few sections starting from Section 3.

We denote an update as a pair $\langle U, p(\vec{t})\rangle$, where U is either +, denoting an insertion, or -, denoting a deletion, and $p(\vec{t})$ is a ground fact. We call an update of the form $\langle +, p(\vec{t})\rangle$ an *insertion update*; and $\langle -, p(\vec{t})\rangle$ a *deletion update*. We write $\mathcal{U}$ to denote a multiset of updates. For instance, the following multiset of updates

$$\mathcal{U} = \{\langle +, q(@1,d)\rangle, \langle -, q(@2,a)\rangle, \langle -, q(@2,a)\rangle\},$$

specifies that two copies of the fact $q(@2,a)$ should be deleted from node 2's state, while one copy of the fact $q(@1,d)$ should be inserted into node 1's state.

We use $\uplus$ as the multiset union operator, and $\setminus$ as the multiset minus operator. We write P to denote the multiset of ground atoms of the form $p(\vec{t})$ (atoms whose predicate name is p), and ΔP to denote the multiset of updates to predicate p. We write P^ν to denote the updated multiset of predicate p based on ΔP. P^ν can be computed from P and ΔP by union P with all the facts inserted by ΔP and minus the facts deleted by ΔP. For ease of presentation, we use the predicate name Δp in places where we need to use the updates, and p^ν in places where we need to use the updated multiset. For instance, if the multiset of q is $\{q(a), q(a), q(b), q(c)\}$ and we update it with $\mathcal{U}$ shown above, the resulting multiset (Q^ν) for q^ν is $\{q(b), q(c), q(d)\}$.

Rules for computing updates. The main idea of computing updates of a *DDlog* program given a multiset of updates to its base predicates is that we can modify the rules in the corresponding program to do so. Consider, for example, the rule p :- b_1, b_2 whose body contains two elements. There are the following three possible cases that one needs to consider in order to compute the changes to the predicate p: Δp :- $\Delta b_1, b_2$, Δp :- $b_1, \Delta b_2$, and Δp :- $\Delta b_1, \Delta b_2$. The first two just take into consideration the changes to the predicates b_1 and b_2 alone, while the last rule uses their combination. We call these rules *delta-rules*.

Following [1, 16], we can simplify the delta-rules above by using the state of p^ν, as defined above. The delta-rules above are changed to Δp :- $\Delta b_1, b_2$ and Δp :- $b_1^\nu, \Delta b_2$, where the second clause encompasses all updates generated by changes to new updates in both b_1 and b_2 as well as only changes to b_2.

Generalizing the notion of delta-rules described above, for each rule $h(\vec{t})$:- $b_1(\vec{t}_1), \ldots, b_n(\vec{t}_n)$ in a program, we create the following delta insertion and deletion rules, where $1 \leq i \leq n$:

$$\langle +, h(\vec{t})\rangle : -b_1^\nu(\vec{t}_1), \ldots, b_{i-1}^\nu(\vec{t}_{i-1}), \Delta b_i(\vec{t}_i), b_{i+1}(\vec{t}_{i+1}), \ldots, b_n(\vec{t}_n)$$
$$\langle -, h(\vec{t})\rangle : -b_1^\nu(\vec{t}_1), \ldots, b_{i-1}^\nu(\vec{t}_{i-1}), \Delta b_i(\vec{t}_i), b_{i+1}(\vec{t}_{i+1}), \ldots, b_n(\vec{t}_n)$$

The first rule applies when Δb_i is an insertion, and the second one applies when Δb_i is a deletion.

By distinguishing predicates with ν and without ν one does not derive the same derivation twice [7].

3. Basic PSN Algorithm for Non recursive Programs

We first present an algorithm for incremental maintenance of distributed non-recursive logic programs. We do not consider termination issues in the presence of recursive programs, which allows us to focus on proving the correctness of pipelined execution. In Section 5, we will present an improved algorithm that provably ensures termination of recursive programs.

3.1 System Assumptions

Our model of distributed systems makes two main assumptions, which are realistic for many systems, such as in networking and systems involving robots.

The first assumption, following [10], is the *bursty model*: once a burst of updates is generated, the system eventually *quiesces* (does not change) for a time long enough for all the nodes to reach a fixed point. Without the bursty model, the links in a network could be changing constantly. Due to network propagation delays, no routing protocol would be able to update routing tables to correctly reflect the latest state of the network. Similarly, if the environment where a robot is situated changes too quickly, then the robot's internal knowledge of the world would not be useful for it to construct a successful plan. The bursty model can be seen as a compromise between completely synchronized models of communication and completely asynchronous models.

The second assumption is that messages are never lost during transmission. Here, we are not interested in the mechanisms of message transmission, but we assume that any message is eventually received by the correct node specified by the location specifier @. Differently from previous work [9, 10], it is possible for messages to be reordered in our model. We do not assume that a message that is sent before another message has to necessarily arrive at its destination first. There are existing protocols which acknowledge when messages are received and have the source nodes resend the messages in the event of acknowledgments timeouts, hence en-

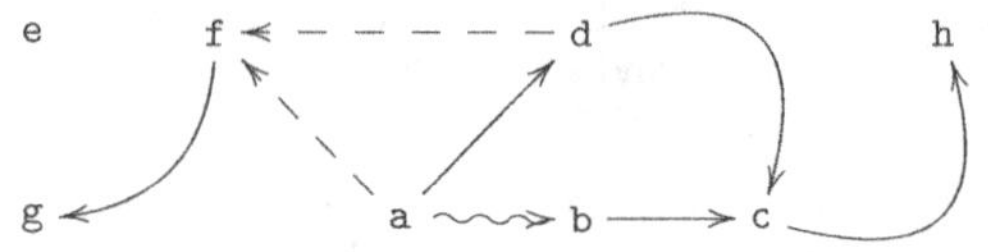

Figure 1. A simple network topology. A dashed arrow indicates an edge that is inserted, while a curly arrow an edge that is deleted. For instance, the edge from d to f is added, while the edge from a to b is deleted.

forcing that messages are not lost. Message reordering manifests itself in several practical scenarios. For instance, in addition to reordering of messages buffered at the network layer, network measurements studies have shown that packets may traverse different Internet paths for any two routers due to ISP policies [15]. In a highly disconnected environment such as in Robotics [5], messages from a given source to destination may traverse different paths due to available network connectivity during the point of transmission of each message.

3.2 PSN Algorithm

We propose Algorithm 1 for maintaining incrementally distributed states given a *DDlog* program. Algorithm 1 enhances the original pipelined evaluation strategy [10]. Since all facts are stored according to the @ operator, we can use a single multiset $\mathcal{K}$ containing the union of states of all the nodes in the system. It is clear from the @ operator where the data is stored. Similarly, we use a single multiset of updates $\mathcal{U}$ containing the updates that are in the system, but that have not yet been processed by any node.

Algorithm 1 starts with a multiset of updates $\mathcal{U}$ and the multiset $\mathcal{K}$ containing two copies of the state of all nodes in the system, one marked with ν and another without ν (see Section 2.3). The execution of one node of the system is specified by one iteration of the while-loop in Algorithm 1. In line 2, an update is *picked non-deterministically* from $\mathcal{U}$ to be processed next. However, only deletion updates whose corresponding facts are present in $\mathcal{K}$ are allowed to be picked. This is specified by the operation $removeElement(\mathcal{K})$, which avoids facts to have negative counts. Once an update is picked, the ν table is updated according to the type of update in lines 3–6. In lines 7–12, the picked update is used to *fire* delta-rules and create new updates that are then inserted into the multiset $\mathcal{U}$ (lines 13–15). This last step intuitively corresponds to a node sending new messages to other nodes, even to itself. Finally in the remaining lines, the changes to the state without ν are *committed* according to the update picked, making the table with ν and without ν have the same elements again and ready for the execution of the next iteration.

We prove that Algorithm 1 terminates for non-recursive *DDlog* programs.

LEMMA 1. *For non-recursive* DDlog *programs, PSN executions always terminate.*

The idea behind the proof is that since the dependency graph of non-recursive programs is a DAG (does not have cycles), whenever an update is picked and used to fire delta-rule, all updates created involve facts whose predicate names appear necessarily in a position "higher" in the dependency graph. Eventually, the set of updates will be empty since the dependency graph has a bounded height. Thus, the algorithm finishes. This argument is valid regardless of the order in which updates are picked.

An Example Execution. We illustrate an execution of Algorithm 1 using the topology in Figure 1 and the following program adapted

Algorithm 1 Basic pipelined semi-naïve algorithm.

1: **while** $\mathcal{U}.size > 0$ **do**
2: $\quad\delta \leftarrow \mathcal{U}.removeElement(\mathcal{K})$
3: $\quad$**if** δ is an insertion update $\langle +, p(\vec{t})\rangle$
4: $\quad\quad P^{\nu} = P \uplus \{p(\vec{t})\}$
5: $\quad$**if** δ is a deletion update $\langle -, p(\vec{t})\rangle$
6: $\quad\quad P^{\nu} = P \setminus \{p(\vec{t})\}$
7: $\quad$**if** δ is an insertion update $\langle +, b(\vec{t})\rangle$
8: $\quad\quad$execute all insertions delta-rules for b:
9: $\quad\quad\quad \langle +, h\rangle$:- $b_1^{\nu}, \ldots, b_{i-1}^{\nu}, \Delta b, b_{i+1}, \ldots, b_n$
10: $\quad$**if** δ is a deletion update $\langle -, b(\vec{t})\rangle$
11: $\quad\quad$execute all deletion delta-rules for b:
12: $\quad\quad\quad \langle -, h\rangle$:- $b_1^{\nu}, \ldots, b_{i-1}^{\nu}, \Delta b, b_{i+1}, \ldots, b_n$
13: $\quad$**for all** derived insertion (deletion) updates u **do**
14: $\quad\quad \mathcal{U}.insert(u)$
15: $\quad$**end for**
16: $\quad$**if** δ is an insertion update $\langle +, p(\vec{t})\rangle$
17: $\quad\quad P = P \uplus \{p(\vec{t})\}$
18: $\quad$**if** δ is a deletion update $\langle -, p(\vec{t})\rangle$
19: $\quad\quad P = P \setminus \{p(\vec{t})\}$
20: **end while**

from [7], which specifies two and three hop reachability:[1]

```
hop(@X,Y) :- link(@X,Z), link(@Z,Y)
tri_hop(@X,Y) :- hop(@X,Z), link(@Z,Y)
```

Here the only base predicate is link. Furthermore, assume that the state is as given below, where we elide the @ symbols. For example, the facts link(@a,b) and hop(@a,c) are in the state. Also at the beginning, the multiset of predicates with ν is the same as the multiset of predicates without ν, so we elide the former.

```
Link = {link(a,b), link(a,d), link(d,c), link(b,c),
        link(c,h), link(f,g)}
Hop = {hop(a,c), hop(a,c), hop(d,h), hop(b,h)}
Tri_hop = {tri_hop(a,h), tri_hop(a,h)}
```

In the state above some facts appear with multiplicity greater than one, which means that there are more than one derivation supporting such facts. Assume as depicted in Figure 1 that there is the following changes to the set of base facts link:

$\mathcal{U}$ = {⟨+,link(d,f)⟩, ⟨+,link(a,f)⟩, ⟨-,link(a,b)⟩}

Algorithm 1 first *picks* an update non-deterministically, for instance, the update $u = \langle +,$ link(a,f)⟩, which causes an insertion of the fact link(a,f) to the table marked with ν. Now Link$^{\nu}$ is as follows:

Link$^{\nu}$ = {link$^{\nu}$(a,b), link$^{\nu}$(a,d), link$^{\nu}$(d,c), link$^{\nu}$(b,c), link$^{\nu}$(c,h), link$^{\nu}$(f,g), link$^{\nu}$(a,f)}

Then, u is used to propagate new updates by *firing* rules, which creates a single insertion update: ⟨+, hop(a,g)⟩. Finally, the change due to the update u is committed to the table without ν. The new multiset of updates and the new multiset of the link facts are as follows:

$\mathcal{U}$ = {⟨+,hop(a,g) ⟩, ⟨+,link(d,f)⟩, ⟨-,link(a,b)⟩}
Link = {link(a,b), link(a,d), link(d,c), link(b,c), link(c,h), link(f,g), link(a,f)}

Asynchronous Execution. As previously mentioned, in a distributed setting, agents need to run as asynchronously as possible,

[1] Technically, the given program passes first through the rule localization procedure described in Section 2. However, for the purpose of illustration, we use instead this un-localized program.

since synchronization among agents involves undesired communication overhead.

Synchronized algorithms proposed in the literature admit the following invariant: in an iteration one only processes updates that insert or delete facts that are supported by derivations of some specific height. This is no longer the case for Algorithm 1: it picks updates non-deterministically. In the example above, one does not necessarily process all the updates involving `link` facts before processing `hop` or `tri_hop` facts. In fact, in the next iteration of Algorithm 1, a node is allowed to pick the update $\langle +, \texttt{hop(d,g)}\rangle$ although there are insertions and deletions of `link` facts still to be processed. However, this asynchronous behavior makes the correctness proof for Algorithm 1 much harder and forces us to proceed our correctness proofs quite differently.

Algorithm 1 sequentializes the execution of all nodes: in each iteration of the outermost while loop, one node picks an update in its queue, fires all the delta-rules and commits the changes to the state, while other nodes are idle. However this is only for the convenience of constructing the proofs of correctness. In a real implementation, nodes run Algorithm 1 concurrently. The correctness of this simplification is justified by Theorem 2 below. Intuitively, the localization procedure described in Section 2 ensures that all the predicates in the body are stored at the same location, which implies that updates on two different nodes can proceed independently, based only on their local states respectively.

Consider, as an illustrative example, the following localized program with two clauses:

(1) $p(@Y)$:- $s(@X, Y)$

(2) $s(@Y, X)$:- $q(@X), v(@X, Y)$.

Assume that there are two nodes n_1 and n_2 and that the initial state and set of updates are, respectively, $\{q(@n_1), v(@n_1, n_2)\}$ and $\{\langle +, s(@n_2, n_1)\rangle, \langle -, q(@n_1)\rangle\}$. If both nodes execute concurrently, then both updates are picked and used to fire the rules of the program. However, since the programs are localized, there is no need for the nodes n_1 and n_2 to communicate between each other during the execution of an iteration of Algorithm 1: they only need to access their own internal states. Node n_1 will fire a deletion delta-rule of rule (2) using the update $\langle -, q(@n_1)\rangle$ and the fact $v(@n_1, n_2)$, which are at node n_1. The update $\langle -, s(@n_2, n_1)\rangle$ is then created and sent to node n_2, while the fact $q(@n_1)$ is deleted from n_1's local state. Similarly, the node n_2 will fire an insertion delta-rule of rule (1) using the update $\langle +, s(@n_2, n_1)\rangle$ and creating the insertion update $\langle +, p(@n_1)\rangle$. Since the operations involved in the iterations do not interfere with each other, this concurrent execution can be replaced by a sequential execution where the node n_1 executes its iteration before the node n_2 and the resulting final state is the same.

For simplicity Theorem 2 only considers the case with two nodes running concurrently. The general case where more than two nodes running concurrently can be proved in a similar fashion.

THEOREM 2. *Let $\mathcal{P}$ be a localized* DDlog *program, and let W_I and $\mathcal{U}_I$ be an initial state and an initial multiset of updates. Let W_F and $\mathcal{U}_F$ be the state and the multiset of updates resulting from executing at different nodes two iterations, i_1 and i_2, of Algorithm 1 concurrently, where w.l.o.g. i_1 starts before or at the same time as i_2. Then the same state and multiset of updates, W_F and $\mathcal{U}_F$, are obtained after executing in a sequence i_1 and then i_2.*

4. Correctness of Basic PSN

The correctness proof relates the distributed PSN algorithm (Algorithm 1) to a synchronous SN algorithm (Algorithm 2), whose correctness is easier to show. After proving that Algorithm 2 is correct, we prove the correctness of Algorithm 1 by showing that an execution using distributed PSN can be transformed into an execution using SN.

4.1 Operational Semantics for Algorithm 1

To prove the correctness of Basic PSN, we first formally define the operational semantics of Algorithm 1 in terms of state transitions.

Algorithm 1 consists of three key operations: *pick*, *fire* and *commit*. We call them basic commands, and an informal description are given below:

pick – A node picks non-deterministically one update, u, that is not a deletion of a fact that is not (yet) in the state, from the multiset of updates $\mathcal{U}$. If u is an insertion of predicate p, p^ν is inserted into the updated state P^ν; otherwise if it is a deletion update, p^ν is deleted from P^ν. This basic command is used in lines 2–6 in Algorithm 1.

fire – This command is used to execute all the delta-rules that contain Δp in their body, where $\langle U, p(\vec{t})\rangle$ has already been selected by the *pick* command. After a rule is fired, the derived updates from firing this rule are added to the multiset $\mathcal{U}$ of updates. This basic command is used in lines 7–15 in Algorithm 1.

commit – Finally, after an update u has already been both picked and used to fire delta-rules, the change to the state caused by u is committed: if u is an insertion update of a fact p, p is inserted into the state P; otherwise, if it is a deletion update of p, p is deleted from the state P. This basic command is used in lines 16–19 in Algorithm 1.

A configuration s is a tuple $\langle \mathcal{K}, \mathcal{U}, \mathcal{P}, \mathcal{E}\rangle$, where $\mathcal{K}$ is a multiset of facts, and $\mathcal{U}$, $\mathcal{P}$ and $\mathcal{E}$ are all multisets of updates. More specifically, at each iteration of the execution, $\mathcal{K}$ is a snapshot of the derivable facts, and it contains both the multiset (P) and the updated multiset (P^ν). The multiset $\mathcal{U}$ contains all the updates that are yet to be picked for processing; $\mathcal{P}$ contains the updates that have been picked and are scheduled to fire delta-rules; and finally $\mathcal{E}$ contains the updates that have been already used to fire delta-rules, but not yet committed into the state. At the end of the execution, $\mathcal{U}$, $\mathcal{P}$ and $\mathcal{E}$ should be empty signaling that all updates have been processed, and $\mathcal{K}$ is the final state of the system.

The five functions depicted in Figure 2, that take a configuration and an update and return a new configuration, specify the semantics of the basic commands. The semantics of the *pick* command is specified by $pick_I$, when the update is an insertion; and $pick_D$, when the update is a deletion. The *pick* command moves, an update $\langle U, p(\vec{t})\rangle$ from $\mathcal{U}$ to $\mathcal{P}$, and updates the state in $\mathcal{K}$: $p^\nu(\vec{t})$ is inserted into $\mathcal{K}$ if U is +; it is deleted from $\mathcal{K}$ if U is -. Note that the rule $pick_D$ only applies when the predicate to be deleted actually exists in $\mathcal{K}$. Because messages may be re-ordered, it could happen that a deletion update message for predicate p arrives before p is derived based on some insertion updates. In an implementation, if such an update happens to be picked, we simply put it back to the update queue, and pick another update.

The rule *fire* specifies the semantics of command *fire*, where we make use of the function *firRules*. This function takes an update, $\langle U, p(\vec{t})\rangle$, the current state, $\mathcal{K}$, and the set of rules, $\mathcal{R}$, as input and returns the multiset of all updates, $\mathcal{F}$, generated from firing all delta-rules that contain Δp in their body. The multiset $\mathcal{F}$ is then added to the multiset $\mathcal{U}$ of updates to be processed later.

Finally, the last two rules, $commit_I$ and $commit_D$, specify the operation of committing the changes to the state. Similar to the rules for *pick*, they either insert into or delete from the updated multiset P a fact $p(\vec{t})$.

A *computation run* of a program $\mathcal{R}$ is a valid sequence of applications of the functions defined in Figure 2. We call the first configuration of a computation run the initial configuration and its last configuration the resulting configuration.

- $pick_I(\mathcal{S}, \langle +, p(\vec{t}) \rangle) = \langle \mathcal{K} \uplus \{p^\nu(\vec{t})\}, \mathcal{U} \setminus \{\langle +, p(\vec{t}) \rangle\}, \mathcal{P} \uplus \{\langle +, p(\vec{t}) \rangle\}, \mathcal{E} \rangle$, provided $\langle +, p(\vec{t}) \rangle \in \mathcal{U}$.
- $pick_D(\mathcal{S}, \langle -, p(\vec{t}) \rangle) = \langle \mathcal{K} \setminus \{p^\nu(\vec{t})\}, \mathcal{U} \setminus \{\langle -, p(\vec{t}) \rangle\}, \mathcal{P} \uplus \{\langle -, p(\vec{t}) \rangle\}, \mathcal{E} \rangle$, provided $\langle -, p(\vec{t}) \rangle \in \mathcal{U}$ and $p^\nu(\vec{t}) \in \mathcal{K}$.
- $commit_I(\mathcal{S}, \langle +, p(\vec{t}) \rangle) = \langle \mathcal{K} \uplus \{p(\vec{t})\}, \mathcal{U}, \mathcal{P}, \mathcal{E} \setminus \{\langle +, p(\vec{t}) \rangle\} \rangle$, provided $\langle +, p(\vec{t}) \rangle \in \mathcal{E}$.
- $commit_D(\mathcal{S}, \langle -, p(\vec{t}) \rangle) = \langle \mathcal{K} \setminus \{p(\vec{t})\}, \mathcal{U}, \mathcal{P}, \mathcal{E} \setminus \{\langle -, p(\vec{t}) \rangle\} \rangle$, provided $\langle -, p(\vec{t}) \rangle \in \mathcal{E}$.
- $fire(\mathcal{S}, u) = \langle \mathcal{K}, \mathcal{U} \uplus \mathcal{F}, \mathcal{P} \setminus \{u\}, \mathcal{E} \uplus \{u\} \rangle$, provided $u \in \mathcal{P}$ and where $\mathcal{F} = firRules(u, \mathcal{K}, \mathcal{R})$.

Figure 2. Definition for the Basic Commands. Here $\mathcal{S}$ is the configuration $\langle \mathcal{K}, \mathcal{U}, \mathcal{P}, \mathcal{E} \rangle$.

A single iteration of Algorithm 1, called *PSN-iteration*, is a sequence of these three commands. In particular, only one update is picked from $\mathcal{U}$ (lines 2–6), and used to fire delta-rules (lines 7–15), and then the change to the state (lines 16–19) is committed. For instance, in the example execution described in Section 3.2. The initial configuration is $\langle \mathcal{K}, \mathcal{U}, \emptyset, \emptyset \rangle$, where $\mathcal{K}$ and $\mathcal{U}$ are the same initial set of facts and updates shown in Section 3.2. Then the update $u = \langle +, \texttt{link(a,f)} \rangle$ from $\mathcal{U}$ is picked using the rule $pick_I$. The resulting configuration is the following, where the update u is moved to the set of picked updates:

$$\langle \mathcal{K} \uplus \{\texttt{link}^\nu\texttt{(a,f)}\}, \mathcal{U} \setminus \{u\}, \{u\}, \emptyset \rangle.$$

Then the *fire* rule is applied and creates the single update $u' = \langle +, \texttt{hop(a,g)} \rangle$, which is added to the set of updates, obtaining:

$$\langle \mathcal{K} \uplus \{\texttt{link}^\nu\texttt{(a,f)}\}, (\mathcal{U} \setminus \{u\}) \uplus \{u'\}, \emptyset, \{u\} \rangle.$$

Finally the *commit* rule is applied and the state is updated yielding:

$$\langle \mathcal{K} \uplus \{\texttt{link}^\nu\texttt{(a,f)}, \texttt{link(a,f)}\}, (\mathcal{U} \setminus \{u\}) \uplus \{u'\}, \emptyset, \emptyset \rangle.$$

which corresponds to the execution shown in Section 3.2, where the facts $\texttt{link}^\nu\texttt{(a,f)}$ and $\texttt{link(a,f)}$ are added, and the update u is removed from the original set of updates, while the propagated update u' is added to it.

The intuition above is formalized by using the more general notion of *complete-iterations*. Intuitively, a complete-iteration is a sequence of picks, fires and updates that use the same set of updates. A PSN-iteration is one special case of a complete-iteration where only one update is picked. In the example above the update used was $\langle +, \texttt{link(a,f)} \rangle$. A PSN execution is a sequence of PSN-iterations.

DEFINITION 3 (Complete-iteration).
A computation run is a complete-iteration *if it can be partitioned into a sequence of transitions using the pick commands ($pick_I$ and $pick_D$), followed by a sequence of transitions using the fire command, and finally a sequence of transitions using the commit command, such that the multiset of updates, $\mathcal{T}$, used by the sequence of $pick_I$ and $pick_D$ transitions is the same those used by the sequence of fire and those used by commit transitions.*

DEFINITION 4 (PSN-iteration). *A complete iteration is a* PSN-iteration *if the multiset of updates used by the pick commands contains only one update.*

DEFINITION 5 (PSN execution). *We call a computation run a PSN execution if it can be partitioned into a sequence of PSN-iterations, and in the last configuration $\mathcal{U}$, $\mathcal{P}$ and $\mathcal{E}$ are empty.*

4.2 Correctness of SN Evaluations

We define an incremental maintenance algorithm based on synchronous semi-naïve (SN) evaluation. This algorithm itself is not practical for any real implementation because of high synchronization costs between nodes. We only use it as an intermediary step to prove the correctness of Algorithm 1.

Algorithm 2 Basic semi-naïve algorithm (multiset semantics).

1: **while** $\mathcal{U}.size > 0$ **do**
2:   **for all** insertion updates $u = \langle +, h(\vec{t}) \rangle$ in $\mathcal{U}$ **do**
3:     $I_h.insert(h(\vec{t}))$
4:   **end for**
5:   **for all** deletion updates $u = \langle -, h(\vec{t}) \rangle$ in $\mathcal{U}$ **do**
6:     $D_h.insert(h(\vec{t}))$
7:   **end for**
8:   **for all** predicates p **do**
9:     $P^\nu \leftarrow (P \uplus I_p) \setminus D_p$
10:   **end for**
11:   **while** $\mathcal{U}.size > 0$ **do**
12:     $\delta \leftarrow \mathcal{U}.removeElement(\mathcal{K})$
13:     **if** δ is an insertion update $\langle +, b(\vec{t}) \rangle$
14:       execute all insertions delta-rules for b:
15:         $\langle +, h \rangle$:- $b_1^\nu, \ldots, b_{i-1}^\nu, \Delta b, b_{i+1}, \ldots, b_n$
16:     **if** δ is a deletion update $\langle -, b(\vec{t}) \rangle$
17:       execute all deletion delta-rules for b:
18:         $\langle -, h \rangle$:- $b_1^\nu, \ldots, b_{i-1}^\nu, \Delta b, b_{i+1}, \ldots, b_n$
19:     **for all** derived insertion (deletion) updates u **do**
20:       $\mathcal{U}^\nu.insert(u)$
21:     **end for**
22:   **end while**
23:   $\mathcal{U} \leftarrow \mathcal{U}^\nu.flush$
24:   **for all** predicates p **do**
25:     $P \leftarrow (P \uplus I_p) \setminus D_p$; $I_p \leftarrow \emptyset$; $D_p \leftarrow \emptyset$
26:   **end for**
27: **end while**

4.2.1 A Synchronous SN Algorithm

Algorithm 2 is a synchronous SN algorithm. There, all the updates in $\mathcal{U}$ (lines 2 – 10) are picked to fire delta-rules (lines 11–22) creating new updates, which are inserted in $\mathcal{U}$ (line 23), and then the changes are committed to the state (lines 24–26), where the operation *flush* in line 23 denotes that all the elements from $\mathcal{U}^\nu$ are moved to $\mathcal{U}$.

The main difference between Algorithm 1 and Algorithm 2 is that in Algorithm 2, all nodes are synchronized at the end of each iteration. In one iteration, all updates at the beginning of the iteration are processed by the corresponding nodes and updates created are sent accordingly. However, the updates that are created are not processed until the beginning of the next iteration. Nodes need to synchronize with one another so that no node is allowed to start the execution of the next iteration if there are some nodes that have not finished processing all the updates in its local queue in the current iteration or have not received all the updates generated by other nodes in the current iteration. On the other hand, Algorithm 1 allows each node to pick and process any one update available at the time of the pick.

For instance, if we apply SN to the same example discussed in Section 3.2, then all updates in $\mathcal{U}$:

$$\mathcal{U} = \{\langle +, \texttt{link(d,f)} \rangle, \langle +, \texttt{link(a,f)} \rangle, \langle -, \texttt{link(a,b)} \rangle\}$$

are necessarily picked and are used to fire delta-rules creating the following set of new updates:

$$\{\langle +, \texttt{hop(a,g)}\rangle, \langle +, \texttt{hop(d,g)}\rangle, \langle +, \texttt{hop(a,f)}\rangle, \langle -, \texttt{hop(a,c)}\rangle, \langle -, \texttt{hop(a,h)}\rangle\}$$

At the end of the while-loop, the updates picked are committed in the state. The facts `link(d,f)` and `link(a,f)` are inserted into the state, while the fact `link(a,b)` is deleted from it. The iteration repeats by using all the new updates created above.

Interestingly, the operational semantics for Algorithm 2 can also be defined in terms of the three basic commands: *pick*, *fire*, and *commit*. In particular an iteration of the outermost loop in Algorithm 2 corresponds exactly to an SN-iteration. Differently from PSN-iterations, where only a single update is picked at a time, SN-iterations are complete-iterations that pick *all* updates.

DEFINITION 6 (SN-iteration). *A complete-iteration is an* SN-iteration *if the multiset of updates used by the pick commands contains all updates in the initial configuration* $\mathcal{U}$.

DEFINITION 7 (SN execution). *We call a computation run an SN execution if it can be partitioned into a sequence of SN-iterations, and in the last configuration* $\mathcal{U}$, $\mathcal{P}$ *and* $\mathcal{E}$ *are empty.*

4.2.2 Correctness Statement

In this section we prove that the Algorithm 2 is correct. For this we need to introduce the following set of definitions.

We keep track of the multiplicity of facts by distinguishing between different occurrences of the same fact in the following form: we label different occurrences of the same base fact with different natural numbers and label each occurrence of the same derived fact with the derivation supporting it. Consider, for example, the program from Section 2.2:

```
{p :- s,t,r;   s :- q;   s :- u;    t :- u;   q :-;   u :-}.
```

The state of the above program using multiset-semantics is actually interpreted in our proofs as the set of annotated facts:

$$\{\texttt{s}^{\Xi_1}, \texttt{s}^{\Xi_2}, \texttt{t}^{\Xi_3}, \texttt{q}^1, \texttt{u}^1\}$$

. The two occurrences of `s` are distinguished by using the derivations trees Ξ_1 and Ξ_2. The former is a derivation tree with a single leaf $\texttt{q}^1$ and the latter is a derivation tree with a single leaf $\texttt{u}^1$. We elide these annotations whenever they are clear from the context. These annotations are only used in our proofs as a formal artifact to distinguish different occurrences of facts.

We use the following notation throughout the rest of this section: given a multiset of updates $\mathcal{U}$, we write $\mathcal{U}^t$ to denote the multiset of facts in $\mathcal{U}$. Given a program $\mathcal{P}$, let V be the state of a program $\mathcal{P}$ given the set of base facts E, and let V^ν be the state of $\mathcal{P}$ given the set of facts $E \uplus I^t \setminus D^t$, where I and D are, respectively, a multiset of insertion and deletion updates of base facts. We assume that $D^t \subseteq E \uplus I^t$.

We write Δ to denote the multiset of insertion and deletion updates of facts such that V^ν is the same multiset resulting from applying the insertions and deletions in Δ to V. We write $\Delta[i]$ to denote the multiset of insertion and deletion updates of facts in Δ such that $\langle U, p(\vec{t})\rangle \in \Delta[i]$ if and only if $p(\vec{t})$ is supported by a derivation of height i. In an execution of Algorithm 2, we use $\mathcal{U}[i]$ to denote the multiset of updates at the beginning of the ith iteration, and $\mathcal{U}[i,j]$ to denote the union of all multisets $\mathcal{U}[k]$ such that $i \leq k \leq j$.

Continue our example, the state of this program is the multiset of annotated facts $V = \{\texttt{s}^{\Xi_1}, \texttt{s}^{\Xi_2}, \texttt{t}^{\Xi_3}, \texttt{q}^1, \texttt{u}^1\}$. If we, for example, delete the base fact $\texttt{u}^1$, then the resulting state changes to $V^\nu = \{\texttt{s}^{\Xi_1}, \texttt{q}^1\}$, where the difference set is

$$\Delta = \{\langle -, \texttt{u}^1\rangle, \langle -, \texttt{s}^{\Xi_2}\rangle, \langle -, \texttt{t}^{\Xi_3}\rangle\},$$
$$\Delta[0] = \{\langle -, \texttt{u}^1\rangle\}, \text{ and } \Delta[1] = \{\langle -, \texttt{s}^{\Xi_2}\rangle, \langle -, \texttt{t}^{\Xi_3}\rangle\}.$$

Before proving the correctness of Algorithm 2, we formally define correctness, which is similar to the definition of *eventual consistency* used by Loo et al. [10] in defining the correctness of declarative networking protocols.

DEFINITION 8 (Correctness). *We say that an algorithm correctly maintains the state if it takes as input, a program* $\mathcal{P}$, *the state* V *based on base facts* E, *a multiset of insertion updates* I *and a multiset of deletion updates* D, *such that* $D^t \subseteq E \uplus I^t$; *and the resulting state when the algorithm finishes is the same as* V^ν, *which is the state of* $\mathcal{P}$ *given the set of facts* $E \uplus I^t \setminus D^t$.

In particular, we can prove that Algorithm 2 is indeed correct according to the definition above. It corresponds to maintenance algorithms that use semi-naïve strategies. The proofs which can be found in [14] are quite interesting. It is non-trivial to find the invariants needed for the proofs.

THEOREM 9 (Correctness of SN). *Given a non-recursive* DDlog *program* $\mathcal{P}$, *a multiset of base facts,* E, *a multiset of updates insertion updates* I *and deletion updates* D *to base facts, such that* $D^t \subseteq E \uplus I^t$, *Algorithm 2 correctly maintains the state of the program when it terminates.*

4.3 Relating SN and PSN executions

Our final goal is to prove the correctness of PSN. With the correctness result of Algorithm 2 in hand, now we are left to prove that Algorithm 1 computes the same result as Algorithm 2. At a high-level we would like to show that given any PSN execution, we can transform it into an SN execution without changing the final result of the execution. This transformation requires two operations: one is to permute two PSN-iterations so that a PSN execution can be transformed into one where the updates are picked in the same order as in an SN execution; the other is to merge several PSN-iterations into one SN-iteration. We need to show that both of these operations do not affect the final configuration of the execution.

Definitions. Let $s \xrightarrow{sn} (\mathcal{U})s'$ and $s \xrightarrow{psn} (\mathcal{U})s'$ denote, respectively, an execution from configuration s to s' using an SN iteration and a PSN iteration. We annotate the updates used in the iterations in the parenthesis after the arrow. We write $s \stackrel{a}{\Longrightarrow} s'$ to denote an execution from s to s' using multiple SN iterations, when a is *sn*; or PSN iterations, when a is *psn*. Let $s \Longrightarrow s'$ denote an execution from s to s' using multiple complete iterations. We write $\sigma_1 \rightsquigarrow \sigma_2$ if the existence of execution σ_1 implies the existence of execution σ_2. We write $\sigma_1 \leftrightsquigarrow \sigma_2$ when $\sigma_1 \rightsquigarrow \sigma_2$ and $\sigma_2 \rightsquigarrow \sigma_1$.

An update u is classified as *conflicting* if it is supported by a proof containing a base fact that was inserted (in I^t) and another fact that was deleted (in D^t). We say u and $\bar{u}$ are a pair of *complementary updates* if u is an insertion (deletion) of predicate p, and $\bar{u}$ is a deletion (insertion) of p. Intuitively, conflicting updates are temporary updates that appear in the execution of incremental maintenance algorithms but that do not affect the final configuration. The effect of a deletion update cancels the effect of the corresponding insertion update. Lemma 13 formalizes this intuition, and we will explain later in this section.

Permuting PSN-iterations. The following lemma states that permuting two PSN-iterations that are both insertion (deletion) updates leaves the final configuration unchanged. So in our example execution described in Section 3.2, it does not matter whether the update $\langle +, \texttt{link(a,f)}\rangle$ is picked before or after the update $\langle +, \texttt{link(d,f)}\rangle$. The set of updates after these two updates are picked is the same, namely the set of updates: $\{\langle +, \texttt{hop(a,g)}\rangle, \langle +, \texttt{hop(a,f)}\rangle\}$.

LEMMA 10 (Permutation – same kind).
Given an initial configuration s,

$$s \xrightarrow{psn} (\{\langle U, r_1\rangle\})s_1 \xrightarrow{psn} (\{\langle U, r_2\rangle\})s'$$
$$\leftrightsquigarrow$$
$$s \xrightarrow{psn} (\{\langle U, r_2\rangle\})s_2 \xrightarrow{psn} (\{\langle U, r_1\rangle\})s' \text{ ,where } U \in \{+,-\}.$$

The proof, given in [14], proceeds by considering all possible ways that an update can fire a rule and showing that the same set of updates are created when we permute the order in which the updates are picked.

However, permuting a PSN-iteration that picks a deletion update over a PSN-iteration that picks an insertion update might generate new updates. Consider a program consisting of the rule p :- r_1, r_2 and assume that r_2 is in the state. Furthermore, assume the updates $\{\langle +, r_1\rangle, \langle -, r_2\rangle\}$. If the deletion update is picked before the insertion update, no delta-rule is fired. However, if we pick the insertion rule first, then the rule above is fired twice, one propagating an insertion of p and the other propagating a deletion of p. However, the new updates are necessarily conflicting updates. This is formalized by the statement below. The side condition that $r_1 \neq r_2$ captures the semantics of the pick command in that deletion updates are only picked if the facts to be deleted are already in the state.

LEMMA 11 (Permutation – different kind).
Given and initial configuration s

$$s \xrightarrow{psn} (\langle +, r_1\rangle)s_1 \xrightarrow{psn} (\langle -, r_2\rangle)\langle \mathcal{K}', \mathcal{U}' \uplus \Delta, \emptyset, \emptyset\rangle$$
$$\leftrightsquigarrow$$
$$s \xrightarrow{psn} (\langle -, r_2\rangle)s_2 \xrightarrow{psn} (\langle +, r_1\rangle)\langle \mathcal{K}', \mathcal{U}', \emptyset, \emptyset\rangle,$$

where $r_1 \neq r_2$ and Δ is a (possibly empty) multiset containing pairs of complementary conflicting updates.

The proof is very similar to the proof of Lemma 10.

From PSN iterations to an SN iteration and back. The second operation we need for transforming a PSN execution into an SN execution is merging a PSN-iteration with a complete-iteration to form a bigger complete-iteration.

Similarly to the case when permuting PSN-iterations of different kinds, merging PSN iterations may change the set of conflicting updates. For example, consider a program consisting of a single rule p :- r, q, the initial state $\{q\}$, and the multiset of updates $\{\langle +, r\rangle, \langle -, q\rangle\}$. If both updates are picked in a complete-iteration, then an insertion update, $\langle +, p\rangle$, is created by firing the delta-rule $\langle +, p\rangle$:- $\Delta r, q$ using the insertion update $\langle +, r\rangle$. Similarly a deletion update $\langle -, p\rangle$ is created by firing the delta-rule $\langle -, p\rangle$:- $r^{\nu}, \Delta q$ and the deletion update $\langle -, q\rangle$. However, if we break the complete-iteration into two PSN-iterations, the first picking the deletion update and the second picking the insertion update, then no delta-rule is fired. We prove the following:

LEMMA 12 (Merging Iterations). *Let $\mathcal{U}$ be a multiset of updates such that the multiset $\{u\} \uplus \mathcal{H} \subseteq \mathcal{U}$ and let $s = \langle \mathcal{K}, \mathcal{U}, \emptyset, \emptyset\rangle$ be an initial configuration.*

$$s \Longrightarrow (\{u\} \uplus \mathcal{H})\langle \mathcal{K}', \mathcal{U}' \uplus F_1, \emptyset, \emptyset\rangle$$
$$\leftrightsquigarrow$$
$$s \Longrightarrow (\mathcal{H})\langle \mathcal{K}_2, \mathcal{U}' \uplus \{u\} \uplus F_1', \emptyset, \emptyset\rangle \xrightarrow{psn} (u)\langle \mathcal{K}', \mathcal{U}' \uplus F_2, \emptyset, \emptyset\rangle$$

Where F_1 and F_2 only differ in pairs of complementary conflicting updates.

Lemma 12 actually give us for free, the ability to break a complete SN-iteration into several PSN-iterations.

For example, we can use the lemma above to transform the SN-iteration shown in Section 4.2.1 where we pick all the updates appearing in the set of initial updates:

$$\{\langle +, \texttt{link(d,f)}\rangle, \langle +, \texttt{link(a,f)}\rangle, \langle -, \texttt{link(a,b)}\rangle\}$$

into a sequence of three PSN-iterations where these updates are picked one by one in any order. In this particular case, there are no conflicting updates created. The resulting sets of updates in both executions are the same:

$$\{\langle +, \texttt{hop(a,g)}\rangle, \langle +, \texttt{hop(d,g)}\rangle,$$
$$\langle +, \texttt{hop(a,f)}\rangle, \langle -, \texttt{hop(a,c)}\rangle, \langle -, \texttt{hop(a,h)}\rangle\}.$$

Dealing with Conflicting Update Pairs. Next, we prove that conflicting updates do not interfere with the final configuration when using PSN executions. Intuitively, we will rely on the following observations: (1) All updates generated by firing delta-rules for conflicting updates are also conflicting updates. (2) A pair of complementary conflicting updates generate pairs of complement conflicting updates. For example, consider adding the rule v :- p to the example given before Lemma 12. Then the conflicting update $\langle +, p\rangle$ would propagate the update $\langle +, v\rangle$. The latter update is also conflicting because the fact p is supported by a fact q which is to be deleted. Moreover, when the deletion of q "catches up," then the complementary update $\langle -, v\rangle$ is created and cancels the effect of the conflicting update $\langle +, v\rangle$. Consequently, a PSN execution that contains a pair of complementary conflicting updates in its initial configuration can be transformed into another PSN execution that does not contain these updates and that the final configurations of the two executions are the same. The following lemma precisely states that.

LEMMA 13. *Let $\Delta = \{\langle +, p\rangle, \langle -, p\rangle\}$ be a multiset containing a pair of complementary conflicting updates, then*

$$\langle \mathcal{K}, \mathcal{U}, \emptyset, \emptyset\rangle \overset{psn}{\Longrightarrow} s \quad \leftrightsquigarrow \quad \langle \mathcal{K}, \mathcal{U} \uplus \Delta, \emptyset, \emptyset\rangle \overset{psn}{\Longrightarrow} s.$$

Its proof relies on the termination arguments for PSN algorithm for non-recursive programs. For recursive programs, it is possible that a pair of complementary conflicting updates will generate infinite number of complementary conflicting updates; and therefore the transformation process may never terminate.

Correctness of Basic PSN. Finally, using the operations above we can prove the following theorem, which establishes that PSN is sound and complete with respect to SN.

THEOREM 14 (Correctness of PSN w.r.t. SN). *Let $s = \langle \mathcal{K}, \mathcal{U}, \emptyset, \emptyset\rangle$ be an initial configuration. Then for non-recursive programs:*

$$s \overset{psn}{\Longrightarrow} \langle \mathcal{K}, \emptyset, \emptyset, \emptyset\rangle \leftrightsquigarrow s \overset{sn}{\Longrightarrow} \langle \mathcal{K}, \emptyset, \emptyset, \emptyset\rangle.$$

The above theorem states that the same derived facts that are created by SN are also created by PSN and vice-versa. The proof idea is that we can use the operations described in Lemmas 10, 11, and 12 to transform a PSN execution into an SN one and vice-versa. In particular, we use Lemmas 10 and 11 to permute PSN iterations so that updates are picked in the same order as an SN execution. Then we use Lemma 12 to merge PSN-iterations into SN-iterations. The conflicting updates that are created in the process of using such transformations are handled by Lemma 13. Hence, from Theorem 9, PSN is correct.

COROLLARY 15 (Correctness of basic PSN). *Given a non-recursive DDlog program $\mathcal{P}$, a multiset of base facts, E, a multiset of updates insertion updates I and deletion updates D to base facts, such that $D^t \subseteq E \uplus I^t$, then Algorithm 1 correctly maintains the state of the program.*

Discussion The framework of using three basic commands: *pick*, *fire*, and *commit* to describe PSN and SN algorithms can be used for specifying and proving formal properties about other SN-like algorithms. For instance, one can easily generalize the proof above to prove the correctness of algorithms where nodes pick

- $pick_I^1(\mathcal{S}, \langle +, (p(\vec{t}), \mathcal{S}, \mathcal{H}) \rangle) = \langle \mathcal{K} \uplus \{(p^\nu(\vec{t}), \mathcal{S}, \mathcal{H}')\}, \mathcal{U} \setminus \{\langle +, (p(\vec{t}), \mathcal{S}, \mathcal{H}) \rangle\}, \mathcal{P} \uplus \{\langle +, (p(\vec{t}), \mathcal{S}, \mathcal{H}') \rangle\}, \mathcal{E} \rangle$, provided $\langle +, (p(\vec{t}), \mathcal{S}, \mathcal{H}) \rangle \in \mathcal{U}$ and $p(\vec{t}) \in \mathcal{S}$, where $\mathcal{H}' = \mathcal{H} \cup \{p(\vec{t})\}$.
- $pick_I^2(\mathcal{S}, \langle +, (p(\vec{t}), \mathcal{S}, \mathcal{H}) \rangle) = \langle \mathcal{K} \uplus \{(p^\nu(\vec{t}), \mathcal{S}, \mathcal{H})\}, \mathcal{U} \setminus \{\langle +, (p(\vec{t}), \mathcal{S}, \mathcal{H}) \rangle\}, \mathcal{P} \uplus \{\langle +, (p(\vec{t}), \mathcal{S}, \mathcal{H}) \rangle\}, \mathcal{E} \rangle$, provided $\langle +, (p(\vec{t}), \mathcal{S}, \mathcal{H}) \rangle \in \mathcal{U}$ and $p(\vec{t}) \notin \mathcal{S}$.
- $pick_D^1(\mathcal{S}, \langle -, (p(\vec{t}), \mathcal{S}, \mathcal{H}) \rangle) = \langle \mathcal{K} \setminus \{(p^\nu(\vec{t}), \mathcal{S}, \mathcal{H}')\}, \mathcal{U} \setminus \{\langle -, (p(\vec{t}), \mathcal{S}, \mathcal{H}) \rangle\}, \mathcal{P} \uplus \{\langle -, (p(\vec{t}), \mathcal{S}, \mathcal{H}') \rangle\}, \mathcal{E} \rangle$, provided $\langle -, (p(\vec{t}), \mathcal{S}, \mathcal{H}) \rangle \in \mathcal{U}$ and $p(\vec{t}) \in \mathcal{S}$, where $\mathcal{H}' = \mathcal{H} \cup \{p(\vec{t})$.
- $pick_D^2(\mathcal{S}, \langle -, (p(\vec{t}), \mathcal{S}, \mathcal{H}) \rangle) = \langle \mathcal{K} \setminus \{(p^\nu(\vec{t}), \mathcal{S}, \mathcal{H})\}, \mathcal{U} \setminus \{\langle -, (p(\vec{t}), \mathcal{S}, \mathcal{H}) \rangle\}, \mathcal{P} \uplus \{\langle -, (p(\vec{t}), \mathcal{S}, \mathcal{H}) \rangle\}, \mathcal{E} \rangle$, provided $\langle -, (p(\vec{t}), \mathcal{S}, \mathcal{H}) \rangle \in \mathcal{U}$ and $p(\vec{t}) \notin \mathcal{S}$.
- $fire(\mathcal{S}, u) = \langle \mathcal{K} \uplus \{(p(\vec{t}), \mathcal{S}, \mathcal{H})\}, \mathcal{U}, \mathcal{P}, \mathcal{E} \setminus \{\langle +, (p(\vec{t}), \mathcal{S}, \mathcal{H}) \rangle\} \rangle$, provided $u \in \mathcal{P}$, where $\mathcal{F} = firRules(u, \mathcal{K}, \mathcal{R})$.
- $commit_I(\mathcal{S}, \langle +, (p(\vec{t}), \mathcal{S}, \mathcal{H}) \rangle) = \langle \mathcal{K}, \mathcal{U} \uplus \mathcal{F}, \mathcal{P} \setminus \{u\}, \mathcal{E} \uplus \{u\} \rangle$, provided $\langle +, (p(\vec{t}), \mathcal{S}, \mathcal{H}) \rangle \in \mathcal{E}$.
- $commit_D(\mathcal{S}, \langle -, (p(\vec{t}), \mathcal{S}, \mathcal{H}) \rangle) = \langle \mathcal{K} \setminus \{(p(\vec{t}), \mathcal{S}, \mathcal{H})\}, \mathcal{U}, \mathcal{P}, \mathcal{E} \setminus \{\langle -, (p(\vec{t}), \mathcal{S}, \mathcal{H}) \rangle\} \rangle$, provided $\langle -, (p(\vec{t}), \mathcal{S}, \mathcal{H}) \rangle \in \mathcal{E}$.

Figure 3. Definitions for the basic commands that detect cycles. Here $\mathcal{S}$ is the configuration $\langle \mathcal{K}, \mathcal{U}, \mathcal{P}, \mathcal{E} \rangle$.

multiple updates per iteration instead of just one update, as in PSN-iterations; or the complete multiset of updates available, as in SN-iteration. That is, we can transform an execution with arbitrary complete iterations into an SN execution and vice-versa. One first breaks the complete-iterations into PSN-iterations, obtaining a PSN execution. Then the proof follows in exactly the same way as before. This means that when implementing such systems, a node can pick all applicable updates that are in its buffer and process them in one single iteration, instead of picking them one by one, and the resulting algorithm is still correct.

5. Extended PSN Algorithm for Recursive Programs

Algorithm 1 and 2 use multiset-semantics. As a consequence, termination is not guaranteed when they are used to maintain states of recursive programs. Consider the following recursive program.

```
p(@1) :- a(@0)     q(@2) :- p(@1)     p(@1) :- q(@2)
```

Notice that `p` and `q` form a cycle in the dependency graph. Any insertion of the fact `p(@1)` will trigger an insertion of `q(@2)` and vice versa. Given an insertion of the fact `a(@0)`, neither Algorithm 1 nor Algorithm 2 terminate because the propagation of insertion updates of `q(@2)` and `p(@1)` do not terminate. Recursively defined predicates could have infinite number of derivations because of cycles in the dependency graph. In other words, in the multiset-semantics, such facts have infinite count. Neither Algorithm 1 nor Algorithm 2 have the ability to detect cycles.

One way to detect such cycles in a centralized setting is proposed in [12]. The main idea is to remember for any fact p, the set of facts, $\mathcal{S}$, called *derivation set*, that contains all the facts that are used to derive p. While maintaining the state, the algorithm checks whether a newly derived fact p appears in the set of facts supporting it. If this is the case, then there is a cycle, and p has infinite count. Whenever a fact with infinite count is detected, we store it in a second set, $\mathcal{H}$, called *infinite count set*. Future updates of p are not propagated to avoid non-termination.[2]

The same idea is applicable to the distributed setting. We formalize this by attaching the derivation and infinite count sets, $\mathcal{S}$ and $\mathcal{H}$, to facts both in states and updates. An annotated fact is of the form $(p, \mathcal{S}, \mathcal{H})$, where p is a fact, $\mathcal{S}$ is the derivation set of p, containing all the facts used to derive p, and $\mathcal{H}$ is a subset of $\mathcal{S}$ containing all the recursive facts that belong to a cycle in the derivation and therefore cause p to have an infinite count. In the example above, the state of facts without ν of the nodes would be:

$\{$(a, $\emptyset$, $\emptyset$), (p, {a}, $\emptyset$), (q, {p,a}, $\emptyset$), (p, {a,p,q}, {p}), ...$\}$

where we elide the `(@X)` symbols. The fact `p` in `(p,{a,p,q},{p})`, also appears in the set supporting it. This means that `p` appears in a cyclic derivation, and therefore p is in the set $\mathcal{H}$.

In order to maintain correctly the state, we adapt the definition of the basic commands accordingly. A summary of the rules are shown in Figure 3. Each *pick* rule in Figure 2 is divided into two rules. Once an update $u = \langle U, (p, \mathcal{S}, \mathcal{H}) \rangle$ is picked from the multiset of updates by using either the transition rule $pick_I$ or $pick_D$, the algorithm first checks whether the fact is supported by a derivation tree that has a cycle (if $p \in \mathcal{S}$). If so, then p is added to the set $\mathcal{H}$; otherwise $\mathcal{H}$ remain unchanged. Notice that the updated state of p in $\mathcal{K}$ uses the updated $\mathcal{H}$ set. The *commit* rule is the same as before, except for the new presentation of facts.

The major changes in the operational semantics are in the *fire* rule, where the derivation set and the infinite count set need to be computed, when a delta-rule is fired and the propagation of updates to facts with infinite count need to be avoided. Given an update $\langle U, (b_i, \mathcal{S}_i, \mathcal{H}_i) \rangle$, in addition to computing all updates that are propagated from this update, the algorithm also constructs the corresponding derivation and infinite count sets, $\mathcal{S}$ and $\mathcal{H}$ as follows. Assume that the update $\langle U, p \rangle$ is propagated using a delta-rule with body $b_1^\nu, \ldots, b_i^\nu, \Delta b_i, b_{i+1}, \ldots, b_n$ and the facts $(b_j, \mathcal{S}_j, \mathcal{H}_j)$ where $1 \leq j \leq n$, then the derivation set for p is $\mathcal{S}_p = \{b_1, \ldots, b_n\} \cup \mathcal{S}_1 \cup \cdots \cup \mathcal{S}_n$ and the infinite count set $\mathcal{H}_p = \mathcal{H}_1 \cup \cdots \cup \mathcal{H}_n$. In order to avoid divergence, we also need to make sure that an update of a fact with infinite count is not re-send. To do so, the algorithm only adds the update $\langle U, (p, \mathcal{S}_p, \mathcal{H}_p) \rangle$ to the multiset of updates $\mathcal{U}$, if it is not part of cycle that has been already computed ($p \notin \mathcal{H}_p$).

Returning to the previous example, when the update inserting the fact `p(@1)` arrives for the second time at node `1`, this update would contain the derivation set $\mathcal{S}$ = `{a(@0),p(@1),q(@2)}`. Since the fact `p(@1)`$\in \mathcal{S}$, node `1` detects the cycle in the derivation and adds the fact `p(@1)` to the infinite count set $\mathcal{H}$. As `q(@2)` is not in $\mathcal{H}$, the insertion update of `q(@2)` is sent to node `2`. However, when this update is processed, creating a new insertion of `p(@1)`, this new insertion is not sent back to `1` because `p(@1)` is in the infinite count set, which means that it is part of a cycle that has already been computed. Therefore, computation terminates. In fact, the derivation set and infinite count set guarantee termination of PSN on any recursive *DDlog* program.

THEOREM 16 (Finiteness of PSN that detects cycles). *Let $\mathcal{S}$ be an initial configuration and $\mathcal{R}$ be a* DDlog *program. Then all PSN executions using $\mathcal{R}$ and from $\mathcal{S}$ have finite length.*

[2] Notice that the derivation set of a fact is not the same as the annotation used before in our proofs to distinguish different occurrences of the same fact. The former is part of the algorithm, while the latter is only used in our proofs.

Figure 4. Dependency graph of a propositional program.

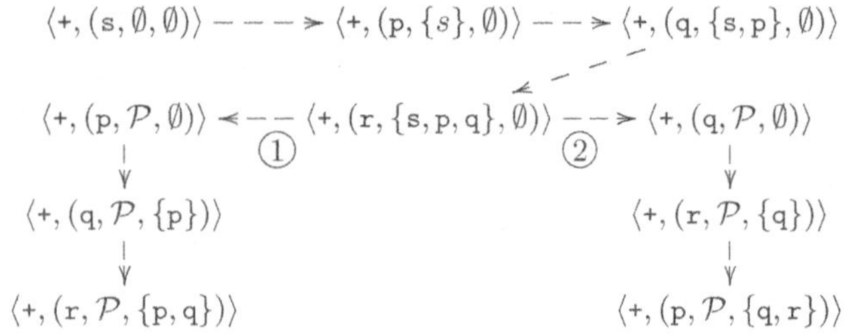

Figure 5. Sequence of updates created in an execution of PSN that detect cycles when inserting the base fact s. Here $\mathcal{P} = \{s, p, q, r\}$.

The proof of the theorem relies on the fact that while executing PSN that detects cycles, the size of the derivation set, $\mathcal{S}$ and the infinite set, $\mathcal{H}$, of updates increase. Since there are finitely many different facts in a program, there is an upper bound on the sizes of these sets. Hence, there is a global bound on the number of possible updates created in a run and therefore PSN that detects cycles terminates.

COROLLARY 17. *The PSN algorithm that detects cycles always terminates.*

Consider the following program with five clauses:

`p :- s; q :- p; r :- q; p :- r; q :- r,`

whose dependency graph is depicted in Figure 4 and contains multiple dependency cycles. Figure 5 contains the sequence of updates created when executing PSN that detects cycles starting from an update inserting the base fact s. The branches 1 and 2 are created when $\langle +, (r, \{s, p, q\}, \emptyset)\rangle$ is used to fire delta-rules. At the end of these two branches, no more updates are created. At the end of branch 1, processing the update $\langle +, (r, \mathcal{P}, \{p, q\})\rangle$ does not propagate any updates, since it could only propagate an insertion of q and of p. However, both q and p are in its infinite set, which means that they have infinite count, and therefore such updates are not created. Similarly, in the branch 2, processing the update $\langle +, (p, \mathcal{P}, \{q, r\})\rangle$ does not propagate new updates, since q is in its infinite count set. In the branches 1 and 2, the algorithm detects that all facts in $\{p, q, r\}$ have an infinite count. For instance, the first PSN-iteration in branch 1, which processes the update $\langle +, (p, \mathcal{P}, \emptyset)\rangle$, consists of the basic commands $pick_I^1$, *fire*, and $commit_I$. In the $pick_I^1$ the fact p is added to the infinite set, $\emptyset$, because p appears in the supporting set, $\mathcal{P}$. Hence, at the end of this iteration, by the $commit_I$ command, the fact $(p, \mathcal{P}, \{p\})$ is added to the state, which indicates that p has infinite count since p is in the infinite count set of this fact.

As we discuss in the companion tech report [14], the use of the annotated facts does not change the correspondence between PSN executions and SN executions. Once we show that PSN that detects cycles terminates, the same transformations used in Section 4 can be used to show that a PSN execution can be transformed into an SN execution and vice-versa, showing hence that PSN that detects cycles is correct.

COROLLARY 18 (Correctness of PSN). *Given any* DDlog *program $\mathcal{P}$, a multiset of base facts, E, a multiset of updates insertion updates I and deletion updates D to base facts, such that $D^t \subseteq E \uplus I^t$, then the PSN algorithm that detects cycles correctly maintains the state of the program.*

6. Comparison with Existing Incremental Maintenance Algorithms

We compare our algorithm with existing incremental maintenance algorithms. We discuss limitations of these existing approaches and how our algorithms improve them.

Delete and Re-derive. Gupta *et al.* proposed an algorithm in their seminal paper [7] on incrementally maintaining logic programs in a centralized setting, called DRed (Delete and Re-derive). DRed [7] maintains a state by using set-semantics. DRed does not keep track of the number of supporting derivations for any fact. Whenever a fact, p, is deleted, DRed eagerly deletes all the facts that are supported by a derivation that contains p. Since some of the deleted facts may be supported by alternative derivations that do not use p, DRed re-derives them in order to maintain a correct state.

Re-deriving facts in a distributed setting is expensive due to high communication overhead, as demonstrated in [9]. Consider, for example, the topology depicted in Figure 1, taken from [7]. There are two ways to reach the node `c` from the node `a`, one passing the node `b` and the other through the node `d`. Therefore the fact `reachable(@a,c)` is supported by two derivations. However, when using set-semantics, DRed only stores one copy of `reachable(@a,c)` at the node `a`. Assume that at some point the link from node `a` to the node `b` is broken, that is, the fact `link(@a,b)` is deleted. Then in DRed's deletion phase, the deletion of this fact propagates the deletion of `reachable(@a,b)`, which similarly will propagate the deletion of `reachable(@a,c)` and of `reachable(@a,h)`. Then DRed's re-derive phase starts, which checks which facts that were deleted in the deletion phase can be re-derived using an alternative derivation. In this case, all the deleted facts (`reachable(@a,b)`, `reachable(@a,c)`, and `reachable(@a,h)`) are re-derivable using other derivations. All the `reachable` facts derived using the path from `a` to `b` that passes through `d` have to be sent cross the network. For example `reachable(@d,c)` is send to `a` in order to re-derive the fact `reachable(@a,c)`.

Our algorithm (Algorithm 1) uses multiset-semantics to keep track of the number of supporting derivations of any fact. So, whenever a fact is deleted, such algorithm just needs to reduce its multiplicity by one, and whenever its multiplicity is zero, the fact is deleted from the state. Algorithm 1 incurs less communication than DRed. Our extended algorithm (Section 5) annotates each predicate with the set of supporting facts. Compared with DRed, this algorithm incurs higher communication overhead in a workload where there are no deletions. In the presence of deletions, our algorithm results in lower communication overhead, since the deletion of a fact does not require the construction of alternative derivations.

Original PSN algorithm. The original PSN algorithm was proposed by Loo *et al.*[10]. Our paper extends the original proposal in several ways. First, Loo *et al.* consider only linear recursive terminating Datalog programs. We consider the complete Datalog language including non-linear recursive programs. Second, we relax the assumptions in the original proposal: instead of assuming that the transmission channels are FIFO, which is unrealistic in many domains, we do not make any assumption about the order in which updates are processed. In other words, we do not assume the existence of a coordinator in the system. An important improvement is that the PSN algorithm proposed in this paper is proven to terminate and maintain states correctly. As pointed out in our previous work [13], the PSN algorithm as presented in [10] may produce unsound results and the use of the count algorithm [7] leads to non-termination. We elaborate further on the former problem of the original PSN algorithm.

The original PSN performs the following operation: whenever an update reaches a node, the update is not only stored at the end of the node's update queue, but also immediately used to update the

Node 1 :	$\{\}[\,]$	Burst	$\{\}[\,]$		$\{p\}[\langle +, p\rangle]$	Dequeue	$\{p\}[\langle +, p\rangle]$	Dequeue	$\{p\}[\,]$
Node 2 :	$\{s, t\}[\,]$	of	$\{r, s, t\}[\langle +, r\rangle]$	Dequeue	$\{r, s, t\}[\,]$	$\langle -, q\rangle$	$\{r\}[\langle -, s\rangle, \langle -, t\rangle]$	all	$\{r\}[\,]$
Node 3 :	$\{q\}[\,]$	updates.	$\{\}[\langle -, q\rangle]$	$\langle +, r\rangle$	$\{\}[\langle -, q\rangle]$	$\langle -, u\rangle$	$\{\}[\,]$	updates	$\{\}[\,]$
Node 4 :	$\{u\}[\,]$	$\longrightarrow$	$\{\}[\langle -, u\rangle]$	$\longrightarrow$	$\{\}[\langle -, u\rangle]$	$\longrightarrow$	$\{\}[\,]$	$\longrightarrow^*$	$\{\}[\,]$

Figure 6. PSN computation-run resulting in an incorrect final state. The ith row depicts the evolution of the state, in curly-brackets, and the update queue, in brackets, of node i. The updates in the arrows are the ones dequeued by PSN and used to update the state of the nodes. We also elide the (@X) in facts.

node's local state: the fact in the update is immediately inserted into or deleted from the node's state. This procedure, however, leads to unsound results if channels are not FIFO. Consider the following *DDlog* program, which is the same program as shown in Section 2.2, but now distributed over four nodes. The global state of this program is {s(@2), t(@2), q(@3), u(@4)}:

```
node2: p(@1) :- s(@2), t(@2), r(@2).
node3: s(@2) :- q(@3).
       q(@3) :-.
node4: t(@2) :- u(@4).
       u(@4) :-
```

Consider the PSN computation-run depicted in Figure 6 (based on the original algorithm). At the first transition, there is a burst of updates inserting the base fact r and deleting the base facts q and u, where we elide the (@X) symbols. When these updates are created, they are not only stored in the nodes' queues but also used to update the state of the nodes (first transition in Figure 6). Then when the update $\langle +, r\rangle$ is dequeued and processed, a new update inserting p is created (second transition in Figure 6). When the updates $\langle -, q\rangle$ and $\langle -, u\rangle$ are processed, they create the updates $\langle -, s\rangle$ and $\langle -, t\rangle$ (third transition in Figure 6). In the final transitions, none of the updates deleting s or t trigger the deletion of p because t and u are no longer in node 2's state and the bodies of the respective deletion rules are not satisfied. Hence, the predicate p is entailed after the original PSN terminates although it is not supported by any derivation.

Our algorithms correct this error by delaying updates to the facts until after updates are processed.

PSN with annotated facts. After the original PSN algorithm, Liu *et al.* proposed in [9] a new PSN algorithm where facts are annotated in order to handle the known problem that the original PSN does not terminate. Differently from our approach, Liu *et al.* only track the base facts used in the derivation, while our *derivation set* contains all facts (including intermediate derived facts) used for each derivation. Moreover, as with the original PSN algorithm, Liu *et al.* also assume the existence of coordinator in the system enforcing that all transmission channels are FIFO. Under this assumption, Liu *et al.* show that their PSN algorithm terminates.

However, by using only base facts, it is not possible, without assuming that the transmission channels used are FIFO, to differentiate an update that is the result of computing a cyclic derivation from an update that arrived out-of-order. When messages are processed out of order, the algorithm proposed in [9] yields unsound results, illustrated below.

Consider the following program also used in Section 5 that contains cycles and for which original PSN does not terminate:

```
a(@0) :-; p(@1) :- a(@0); q(@2) :- p(@1); p(@1) :- q(@2)
```

In [9], the state of this program is represented as the set {(a,{a}), (p,{a}), (q,{a})} where we elide the (@X) symbols. All facts are derived by only using the base fact a and therefore their annotations consist only of the base fact a. An update inserting (p,{a}) could be derived due to a derivation with no cycles or due to a cyclic derivation obtained by using the last two rules of the program. In order to avoid divergence, the latter type of updates resulting from cyclic derivations need to be discarded. Assume that there is a deletion of a, represented by a deletion update $\langle$-, (a,{a})$\rangle$. When this update is processed, node 1 creates $\langle$-, (p,{a})$\rangle$, which is processed by node 2, creating the update $\langle$-, (q,{a})$\rangle$. Finally, node 2 processes the latter, creating again the deletion update $\langle$-, (p,{a})$\rangle$. When this update is received by node 1, the fact (p,{a}) is not in the state, as it was deleted by the first deletion update. Therefore, node 1 can safely conclude, under the assumption of FIFO channels, that the latter update is due to a cyclic derivation. Hence it just discards it and the algorithm terminates.

It is easy to show that discarding eagerly such deletion updates yields unsound results when one relaxes the assumption of FIFO channels. Consider the same program above, but two conflicting updates: $\langle$-, (a,{a})$\rangle$ and $\langle$+, (a,{a})$\rangle$. If the deletion update is processed first by node 0, it will be discarded since the fact (a,{a}) is not present in its state. The insertion update on the other hand would be processed, generating eventually new insertion updates for all the facts in the program. Hence, the final state obtained by their algorithm is (a,{a}), (p,{a}), (q,{a}), whereas the correct state is the empty set.

Our algorithm annotates each predicate with all the predicates used to derive it, which include not only the base predicates, but also intermediate predicates. We have shown in Section 5 that we can detect cycles properly, even in the presence of message re-ordering. Finally, Liu *et al.*'s algorithm is only experimentally evaluated but not formally proven correct.

7. Additional Related Work

In contrast to our approach, MELD [5] simply attaches to each fact the height of the supporting derivation. Although they are able to perform many optimizations with such type of annotations, simply attaching the height of derivations to facts is not enough to detect cycles in derivations and therefore it is not enough to avoid divergence by itself. They address this problem by synchronizing nodes and not allowing nodes to compute until they receive the response from other nodes that all the deletions propagated from a deletion of a base fact have been processed. As expected, performance can be greatly affected since an unbounded number of nodes might need to be synchronized at the same time due to cascading derivations. We believe that their work can directly leverage the results in this paper.

In an attempt to generalize Loo *et al.*'s work [10], Dedalus [4] relaxes the set of assumptions above by no longer assuming that messages always reach their destination. The main difficulty when considering message loss is that the semantics does not relate well with the semantics in the Datalog literature. Depending on whether a message is lost or not, the final states computed by their evaluation algorithms can be considerably different. Therefore, it is not clear what is the notion of correctness in such systems. We believe that probabilistic models where messages are lost with certain probability can be used, and we leave this for future work.

In the agent programming community, several languages that allow for the update of knowledge bases have been proposed. For instance, [3] proposes a logic programming language that allows updates not only to base facts, but also to rules themselves. Differently from this paper, however, their work considers only a centralized setting. Moreover, a central difference from our work is that while [3] is concerned in extending logic programming languages so that programmers can specify updates, here we focus on algorithms that efficiently maintain states of distributed Datalog programs. An interesting direction for future work would be extend our results to also allow rule updates in a distributed setting.

Adjiman *et al.* in [2] use classical propositional logic to specify knowledge bases of agents in a peer-to-peer setting. They prove correct a distributed algorithm that computes the consequences of inserting a literal, that is, an atom or its negation, to a node (or peer). Since they use resolution in their algorithm, they are able to deduce not only the atomic formulas that are derivable when an insertion is made, but propositional formulas in general. While they are mainly interested in finding the resulting state from inserting a formula, we are interested in efficiently maintaining a state was previously computed. It is not clear how their approach can be used to update the consequences when a sequence of insertions and deletions are made to the knowledge base.

8. Conclusions and Future Work

Besides the correctness of the algorithm itself, our ultimate goal is to prove interesting properties about programs written in distributed Datalog. The correctness results in this paper allow us to first formally verify high-level properties of programs prior to actual deployment by relying on the well established semantics for centralized Datalog, then the verified properties carry over to the distributed deployment, because semantics for Distributed Datalog and centralized Datalog coincide.

In particular, we are interested in formal verification of implementations of networking protocols prior to actual deployment in declarative network setting [19, 20]. In order to do so, we need to extend this work to include additional language features present in declarative networking including function symbols and aggregates. Since Datalog programs with arbitrary functions symbols may not terminate, we are investigating if we can extend existing analysis techniques [8] developed for centralized Datalog with function symbols to determine when *DDlog* programs with function symbols terminate. It turns out that it is not an easy task to develop efficient and correct algorithms that maintain logic programs incrementally in the presence of aggregate functions. We are looking into adapting existing work, such as [17] in incremental view maintenance in a centralized setting to fit our needs.

Acknowledgements We would like to thank Iliano Cervesato, Dale Miller, Juan Antonio Navarro Pérez, Frank Pfenning Andrey Rybalchenko, Val Tannen, and Anduo Wang for helpful discussions.

This material is based upon work supported by the MURI program under AFOSR Grant No: FA9550-08-1-0352 and by the NSF Grants IIS-0812270 and CNS-0845552. Additional support for Scedrov and Nigam from ONR Grant N00014-07-1-1039 and from NSF Grants CNS-0524059 and CNS-0830949. Nigam was also supported by the Alexander von Humboldt Foundation. Scedrov was also partially supported by ONR grant N000141110555.

References

[1] S. Abiteboul, R. Hull, and V. Vianu. *Foundations of Databases*. Addison-Wesley, 1995.

[2] P. Adjiman, P. Chatalic, F. Goasdoué, M.-C. Rousset, and L. Simon. Distributed reasoning in a peer-to-peer setting: application to the semantic web. *J. Artif. Int. Res.*, 25(1):269–314, 2006.

[3] J. J. Alferes, J. A. Leite, L. M. Pereira, H. Przymusinska, and T. C. Przymusinski. Dynamic logic programming. In *KR*, pages 98–111, 1998.

[4] P. Alvaro, W. Marczak, N. Conway, J. M. Hellerstein, D. Maier, and R. C. Sears. Dedalus: Datalog in time and space. Technical Report UCB/EECS-2009-173, EECS Department, University of California, Berkeley, December 2009.

[5] M. P. Ashley-Rollman, S. C. Goldstein, P. Lee, T. C. Mowry, and P. Pillai. Meld: A declarative approach to programming ensembles. In *IEEE International Conference on Intelligent Robots and Systems (IROS)*, October 2007.

[6] S. Grumbach and F. Wang. Netlog, a rule-based language for distributed programming. In *International Symposium on Practical Aspects of Declarative Languages (PADL)*, January 2010.

[7] A. Gupta, I. S. Mumick, and V. S. Subrahmanian. Maintaining views incrementally. In *Proceedings of the 1993 ACM SIGMOD International Conference on Management of Data (SIGMOD)*, June 1993.

[8] R. Krishnamurthy, R. Ramakrishnan, and O. Shmueli. A framework for testing safety and effective computability. *J. Comput. Syst. Sci.*, 52(1):100–124, 1996.

[9] M. Liu, N. E. Taylor, W. Zhou, Z. G. Ives, and B. T. Loo. Recursive computation of regions and connectivity in networks. In *Proceedings of the 2009 IEEE International Conference on Data Engineering (ICDE)*, March 2009.

[10] B. T. Loo, T. Condie, M. Garofalakis, D. E. Gay, J. M. Hellerstein, P. Maniatis, R. Ramakrishnan, T. Roscoe, and I. Stoica. Declarative Networking: Language, Execution and Optimization. In *Proceedings of the 2006 ACM SIGMOD International Conference on Management of Data (SIGMOD)*, June 2006.

[11] N. P. Lopes, J. A. Navarro, A. Rybalchenko, and A. Singh. Applying Prolog to develop distributed systems. In *Proceedings of the Twenty-sixth International Conference on Logic Programming (ICLP)*, July 2010.

[12] I. S. Mumick and O. Shmueli. Finiteness properties of database queries. In *Australian Database Conference*, pages 274–288, 1993.

[13] V. Nigam, L. Jia, A. Wang, B. T. Loo, and A. Scedrov. An operational semantics for network datalog. In *Third International Workshop on Logics, Agents, and Mobility (LAM)*, July 2010.

[14] V. Nigam, L. Jia, B. T. Loo, and A. Scedrov. Maintaining Distributed Recursive Views Incrementally. Technical Report No. MS-CIS-11-06, UPENN, 2011.

[15] V. Paxson. End-to-end routing behavior in the internet. In *SIGCOMM*, August 1996.

[16] R. Ramakrishnan and J. D. Ullman. A Survey of Research on Deductive Database Systems. *Journal of Logic Programming*, 23(2):125–149, 1993.

[17] R. Ramakrishnan, K. A. Ross, D. Srivastava, and S. Sudarshan. Efficient incremental evaluation of queries with aggregation. In *Proceedings of the 1994 International Symposium on Logic programming (SLP)*, 1994.

[18] G. Ramalingam and T. W. Reps. On the computational complexity of dynamic graph problems. *Theor. Comput. Sci.*, 158(1&2):233–277, 1996.

[19] A. Wang, P. Basu, B. T. Loo, and O. Sokolsky. Declarative network verification. In *International Symposium on Practical Aspects of Declarative Languages (PADL)*, Jan. 2009.

[20] A. Wang, L. Jia, C. Liu, B. T. Loo, O. Sokolsky, and P. Basu. Formally Verifiable Networking. In *SIGCOMM HotNets-VIII*, 2009.

CLP Projection for Constraint Handling Rules

Rémy Haemmerlé
Technical University of Madrid

Pedro Lopez-Garcia
IMDEA Software Institute &
Spanish National Research Council

Manuel V. Hermenegildo
IMDEA Software Institute &
Technical University of Madrid

Abstract

This paper introduces and studies the notion of CLP projection for Constraint Handling Rules (CHR). The CLP projection consists of a naive translation of CHR programs into Constraint Logic Programs (CLP). We show that the CLP projection provides a safe operational and declarative approximation for CHR programs. We demonstrate moreover that a confluent CHR program has a least model, which is precisely equal to the least model of its CLP projection (closing hence a ten year-old conjecture by Abdennadher et al.). Finally, we illustrate how the notion of CLP projection can be used in practice to apply CLP analyzers to CHR. In particular, we show results from applying AProVE to prove termination, and CiaoPP to infer both complexity upper bounds and types for CHR programs.

Keywords CHR, CLP, Complexity, Declarative Semantics, Static Analysis, Termination, Types.

Categories and Subject Descriptors F.3.1 [*LOGICS AND MEANINGS OF PROGRAMS*]: Semantics of Programming Languages

General Terms Theory

1. Introduction

Constraint Handling Rules (CHR) [15] is a concurrent, committed-choice, rule-based programming language introduced in the 1990s by Frühwirth. CHR was originally designed for the design and implementation of constraint solvers, initially in the context of Constraint Logic Programming (CLP) [28], but it has since come into use as a general-purpose concurrent programming language.

It is well-known that CLP can be encoded into CHR (see, for instance Section 6.3.1 in Frühwirth's Book [15]). Operationally the encoding is sound and complete. From the logical point of view the encoding is an under-approximation, since the CHR encoding in CLP corresponds to the Clark completion [8]. Conversely, CLP has been from the beginning an implementation vehicle for CHR programs [14, 26, 39], since, as mentioned before, one of the initial objectives of CHR was precisely to encode constraint solving algorithms meant to run within CLP systems. However, the translations produce too low-level code to be easily analyzed by CLP analyzers, typically using attributed variables [25] and imperative assignments.

PDPP'11, July 20–22, 2011, Odense, Denmark.

However, and perhaps surprisingly, few attempts can be found in the literature to perform a direct translation of CHR into (pure) CLP. Such an encoding can be interesting in order to relate the CLP and CHR theoretical foundations, and to be able to use the many tools available for the semantic analysis of CLP programs in the context of CHR.

With this objective in mind in this paper we introduce the notion of CLP projection. CLP projection consists of a naive translation of CHR programs into (pure) CLP. We show that CLP projection provides a safe operational and declarative approximation for CHR programs. In particular, we show that:

- A CHR program is operationally simulated by its CLP projection.
- The logical models of a CHR program are under-approximated by the least model of its projection. We show moreover that the least model of a confluent CHR program is precisely the least model of its CLP projection (closing hence a ten year-old conjecture by Abdennadher et al. [4]).
- The success set with respect to a CHR program can be characterized by the successes of its projection.

Finally, we also illustrate how the notion of CLP projection can be used in practice to apply CLP analyzers to CHR. In particular, we show results from applying the AProVE analyzer [17] to prove termination, and the Ciao preprocessor (CiaoPP) [22] to infer both complexity upper bounds and types for CHR programs.

To the best of our knowledge the only attempt to translate CHR programs into Prolog is the so-called transformational approach of Pilozzi's et al [34, 35]. It consists of a Prolog meta-interpreter that preserves store accessibility. As the CLP projection, it provides an over-approximation of the CHR operational semantics, and has been used to prove termination and to infer types for CHR programs. The meta-level nature of this approach has the main advantage of making the notion of user-defined store explicit, but it also makes the task for Prolog/CLP analyzers much more complex, since it is a well-known fact that high levels of meta-interpretation can result in loss of precision for analyzes based on approximations. Furthermore it seems more difficult to relate the declarative semantics using a meta-interpreted approach.

The rest of the paper is structured as follows: Section 2 recalls basic notation, definitions, and results for fixpoints, reductions, and first-order logic. Then, Section 3 presents the syntax and both the operational and the declarative semantics for CLP frameworks. Section 4 similarly presents the CHR framework. Then, Section 5 formally introduces the notion of CLP projection. In Section 6, we illustrate the relevance of the CLP projection approach for the static analysis of CHR programs through different applications ranging from termination proofs to type inference through complexity upper bounds. Finally, in Section 7 we present our conclusions.

2. Preliminaries

In this section, we recall the theoretical framework of CLP.

2.1 Notations

We assume as given a denumerable set $\mathcal{V}$ of variables (denoted by $X, Y, Z \ldots$), a denumerable set Σ_f of function and constant symbols, and a set of predicate symbols Σ_p (denoted by characters or words in teletype font, such as c or p). Symbols of both kinds are assumed given with their respective arity. The set of first-order terms built from $\mathcal{V}$ and Σ_f will be denoted by $\mathcal{T}$, its elements by $t, s, \ldots$. Sets (resp. sequences) of variables and terms will be distinguished by a bar (resp. arrow) above, as, for instance, $\bar{X}$ and $\bar{t}$ (resp. $\vec{X}$ and $\vec{t}$). Atomic propositions built from $\mathcal{T}$ and Σ_p are denoted by $a, b, c, d, \ldots$. By a slight abuse of notation we will use interchangeably conjunction and multiset of atomic propositions, forget braces around multisets, and use comma for multiset union. Conjunctions and multisets will be denoted by capital blackboard letters, such as $\mathbb{A}$ or $\mathbb{C}$.

For an arbitrary formula ϕ, we use $\mathrm{fv}(\phi)$ to denote the set of free variables occurring in ϕ, and $\phi[\vec{X}\backslash\vec{t}]$ to represent ϕ in which the free occurrences of variables $\vec{X}$ have been replaced by terms $\vec{t}$ (with the usual renaming of bound variables, avoiding variable clashes). The notation $\exists\phi$ represents the existential closure of the formula ϕ. Similarly, $\exists_{-\psi}\phi$ denotes the existential closure of the formula ϕ with the exception of variables free in the formula ψ, which remain free.

In this paper, we assume that the set of predicate symbols Σ_p is partitioned into two: Σ_b, the set of *(built-in) constraint* symbols, Σ_a the set of *(user-defined) atom* symbols. Naturally, atomic propositions built from Σ_b will be called *(built-in) constraints* while atomic propositions built from Σ_b will be called *(user-defined) atoms*. Finally, we assume that there is a given consistent (first-order) axiomatic theory $\mathcal{C}$ describing the meaning of constraints.

2.2 Preliminaries on Fixpoints

Here, we recall some definitions and results about fixpoints in an arbitrary complete lattice $(\mathcal{L}, \supseteq, \cap, \cup, \top, \bot)$. We will say that a function $f : \mathcal{L} \to \mathcal{L}$ is *monotonic* if $f(\mathcal{X}) \supseteq f(\mathcal{Y})$ whenever $\mathcal{X} \supseteq \mathcal{Y}$. The *upward (ordinal) power* of a function $f : \mathcal{L} \to \mathcal{L}$ is defined by the transfinite induction:

- $f\uparrow 0 = \bot$
- $f\uparrow\alpha = f(f\uparrow(\alpha - 1))$ if α is a successor ordinal,
- $f\uparrow\alpha = \bigcup\{f\uparrow\beta \mid \beta < \alpha\}$ if α is a limit ordinal.

An element $\mathcal{X} \in \mathcal{L}$ is a *fixpoint* for $f : \mathcal{L} \to \mathcal{L}$ if $f(\mathcal{X}) = \mathcal{X}$. $\mathcal{X}$ is a *least fixpoint* for f if it is a fixpoint and $\mathcal{Y} \supseteq \mathcal{X}$ whenever $\mathcal{Y}$ is a fixpoint for f. We use $\mu\mathcal{X}.f(\mathcal{X})$ to denote such a fixpoint.

Theorem 1 (Knaster–Tarski). *If f is a monotonic function on $\mathcal{L}$, then f has a least fixpoint. Furthermore there exists a limit ordinal α such that:*

$$\mu X.f(X) = \bigcap\{X \in \mathcal{L} | X = f(X)\} = f\uparrow\alpha.$$

2.3 Preliminaries on Rewrite Relation

A *rewrite relation* is a binary relation defined over some given set $\mathcal{A}$. To stress that we are interested in the direction of rewrite relations, we use arrow-like notations like $\rightarrow$ and $\twoheadrightarrow$ to denote them. Let us assume some rewrite relations $\rightarrow$, $\twoheadrightarrow$ defined over the same set $\mathcal{A}$. We shall use the following notations and definitions:

- $\circ$ is the composition: $(\rightarrow \circ \twoheadrightarrow) = \{(a, b) \mid \exists c \in \mathcal{A}\ (a \rightarrow c \wedge c \twoheadrightarrow b)\}$;
- $\rightarrow^0 = \{a \rightarrow a \mid a \in \mathcal{A}\}$ and $\rightarrow^n = \rightarrow \circ \rightarrow^{n-1}$ for $n \geq 1$;
- $\rightarrow^* = \cup_{i \geq 0} \rightarrow^i$ is the transitive-reflexive closure of $\rightarrow$;
- $\rightarrow$ is *terminating* if there is no infinite sequence $e_0 \rightarrow e_1 \rightarrow \ldots$;
- $\rightarrow$ is *confluent* if for any element $a, b, c \in \mathcal{A}$ such that $a \rightarrow^* b$ and $a \rightarrow^* c$ there exists an element $d \in \mathcal{A}$ such that $b \rightarrow^* d$ and $c \rightarrow^* d$.

2.4 Preliminaries on First-Order Logic

In this subsection we recall some basics about model theoretic semantics of first-order logic.

2.4.1 First-Order Models

Let $\mathcal{L}_p$ be the first-order language built from the set $\mathcal{T}$ of first-order terms and the set of predicate symbols Σ_p. An *interpretation* of $\mathcal{L}_p$ is a tuple $I = \langle D, [\,] \rangle$, composed of an *interpretation domain* D together with a semantics function $[\,]$, which associates to each function symbol $f \in \Sigma_f$ of arity m a function $[f] : D^m \to D$, and to each predicate symbol $p \in \Sigma_p$ of arity n a function $[p] : D^n \to \{\top, \bot\}$. For a given interpretation I, an *I-valuation* is a function $\rho : \mathcal{V} \to D$. An *I-instance* of a term t (resp. a formula ϕ) is the tuple $t\rho$ (resp. $\phi\rho$), where ρ is an I-valuation.

Let I be an interpretation of $\mathcal{L}_p$. The *assignment* (with respect to I) of *I-instances* of terms and atomic propositions in $\mathcal{L}_p$ is the function $[\,]_I$ defined by structural induction as:

- $[X\rho]_I = \rho(X)$ if $X \in \mathcal{V}$;
- $[f(t_1, \ldots, t_n)\rho]_I = [f]([t_1\rho]_I, \ldots, [t_n\rho]_I)$ if $f \in \Sigma_f$;
- $[\mathtt{c}(t_1, \ldots, t_n)\rho]_I = [\mathtt{c}]([t_1\rho]_I, \ldots, [t_n\rho]_I)$ if $\mathtt{c} \in \Sigma_p$.

The assignment (with respect to I) is extended to logical formulas in $\mathcal{L}_p$ by applying the truth table of the logical connectors and the following rules for the quantifiers:

- $[(\forall X\phi)\rho]_I = \top$ if and only if for all elements $d \in D$, $[\phi(\rho \circ [X\backslash d])]_I = \top$;
- $[(\exists X\phi)\rho]_I = \top$ if and only if there exists an element $d \in D$, $[\phi(\rho \circ [X\backslash d])]_I = \top$.

An interpretation I of $\mathcal{L}_p$ is a *model* for a formula $\phi \in \mathcal{L}_p$, if for all I-valuations ρ, $[\phi\rho]_I = \top$. Naturally, an interpretation I of $\mathcal{L}_p$ is a *model* of a theory $\mathcal{T}$ if I is a model of all of its axioms. A formula ϕ is *satisfiable within a theory* $\mathcal{T}$ (or, more briefly, *$\mathcal{T}$-satisfiable*) if there is a model of $\mathcal{T}$ which is a model of $\exists\phi$ as well. In the following, we use the notation $\mathcal{T} \models \phi$ to express that any model of a theory $\mathcal{T}$ is as well a model of the formula ϕ (in other words, that ϕ is valid in $\mathcal{T}$).

2.4.2 Model with respect to a Constraint Theory

In this subsection, we introduce the classical notion of constrained atoms with respect to a constraint theory $\mathcal{C}$. Sets of constrained atoms will be called $\mathcal{C}$-interpretations. For a given interpretation limited to constraints, a $\mathcal{C}$-interpretation represents an interpretation for the whole set of propositions (including both constraints and atoms). $\mathcal{C}$-interpretations have the advantage with respect to classical interpretations (presented in the previous section) that they are sets of syntactic objects while classical interpretations are not. (For instance the domain of real numbers contains elements which cannot be represented syntactically.) Hence, it appears that in many cases manipulating $\mathcal{C}$-interpretations is simpler than manipulating the classical ones.

Definition 2 ($\mathcal{C}$-base). *A* constrained atom *is a pair* $(a|\mathbb{C})$, *where* a *is a user-defined atom and* $\mathbb{C}$ *is a conjunction of built-in constraints. The set of constrained atoms is called* $\mathcal{C}$-base *and is denoted by* $\mathcal{B}_\mathcal{C}$.

For the sake of simplicity, we will work always with sets of constrained atoms closed by the closure operator $\Downarrow_{\mathcal{C}}$ defined next. This operator returns the set of all atoms more constrained than the ones given as input.

Definition 3. *The closure operator* $\Downarrow_{\mathcal{C}} : 2^{\mathcal{B}_\mathcal{C}} \to 2^{\mathcal{B}_\mathcal{C}}$ *is defined as:*

$$\Downarrow_{\mathcal{C}}(\mathcal{Z}) = \{(a|\mathbb{C}) \in \mathcal{B}_\mathcal{C} \mid \exists\, (b|\mathbb{D}) \in \mathcal{Z} \text{ s.t. } \mathcal{C} \models \mathbb{C} \to \exists_{\text{-}a}(a = b \wedge \mathbb{D})\}$$

In the following, we use the notation $(a_1, \ldots, a_n|\mathbb{C})$ *for the set of constrained atoms* $\{(a_1|\mathbb{C}), \ldots (a_n|\mathbb{C})\}$.

Example 4. *Assume that* $\mathcal{C}$ *defines the order* $<$ *on integers. Let* $\mathtt{p}$ *and* $\mathtt{q}$ *be two constrained symbols and let* $\mathcal{Z} = \Downarrow_{\mathcal{C}}(\mathtt{p}(X)|0 < X \wedge X < 4)$. *For instance, we have:*

- $(\mathtt{p}(1)|\top)$, $(\mathtt{p}(X)|1 < X \wedge X < 4)$, *and* $(\mathtt{q}(Y)|\bot)$ *are in* $\mathcal{Z}$.
- *neither* $(\mathtt{p}(5)|\top)$ *nor* $(\mathtt{p}(Y)|5 < Y)$ *are in* $\mathcal{Z}$.

We define the $\mathcal{C}$-model of a formula ϕ, as a set of constrained atoms that validate ϕ without contradicting any model of $\mathcal{C}$.

Definition 5 ($\mathcal{C}$-model). *For a given interpretation* I *of* $\mathcal{C}$, *the assignment of* I*-instances associated to a set* $\mathcal{Z}$ *of constrained atoms is defined as:*

$$[\![\mathcal{Z}]\!]_I(a\rho) = \begin{cases} [\mathbb{C}\rho]_I & \text{if } (a|\mathbb{C}) \in \mathcal{Z} \\ \bot & \text{otherwise} \end{cases}$$

A set $\mathcal{Z}$ *of constrained atoms is a* $\mathcal{C}$-model *of a first-order formula* ϕ *in* $\mathcal{L}_p$, *if for any model* $I = \langle D, [\,]\rangle$ *of* $\mathcal{C}$, $\langle D, [\,] \cup [\![\mathcal{Z}]\!]_I\rangle$ *is a model of* ϕ.

Obviously, a formula is satisfiable in any interpretation of $\mathcal{C}$ if and only if it has a $\mathcal{C}$-model. The following technical lemma will be useful later to prove that a set of constrained atoms is a model of an implication.

Lemma 6. *Let* $\mathcal{Z}$ *be a set of constrained atoms,* $\mathbb{A}$ *and* $\mathbb{B}$ *be two conjunctions of user-defined atoms,* $\mathbb{C}$ *and* $\mathbb{D}$ *be two sets of built-in constraints, and* $\vec{X}$ *a sequence of variables not free in* $(\mathbb{A} \wedge \mathbb{C})$. *If for any conjunction* $\mathbb{E}$ *of built-in constraints satisfying* $\vec{X} \cap \mathrm{fv}(\mathbb{E}) = \emptyset$, $(\mathbb{A}|\mathbb{C} \wedge \mathbb{E}) \in \mathcal{Z}$ *implies* $(\mathbb{B}|\mathbb{C} \wedge \mathbb{D} \wedge \mathbb{E}) \in \mathcal{Z}$ *together with* $\mathcal{C} \models (\mathbb{C} \wedge \mathbb{E}) \to \exists\vec{X}(\mathbb{C} \wedge \mathbb{D} \wedge \mathbb{E})$, *then* $\mathcal{Z}$ *is a* $\mathcal{C}$*-model for the implication* $(\mathbb{A} \wedge \mathbb{C}) \to \exists\vec{X}(\mathbb{B} \wedge \mathbb{D})$.

Proof. Let $I = \langle D, [\,]\rangle$ be a model of $\mathcal{C}$ and $[\,]_\mathcal{Z} = ([\,] \cup [\![\mathcal{Z}]\!]_I)$. We have to show that $\langle D, [\,]_\mathcal{Z}\rangle$ is a model for $(\mathbb{A} \wedge \mathbb{C}) \to \exists X.(\mathbb{B} \wedge \mathbb{D})$, that is, for any I-valuation ρ, if $[(\mathbb{A} \wedge \mathbb{C})\rho]_\mathcal{Z} = \top$ then there exists a sequence of terms $\vec{d} \in D$ such that $[(\mathbb{A} \wedge \mathbb{C})(\rho \circ [\vec{X}\backslash\vec{d}])]_\mathcal{Z} = \top$. Let us assume some I-valuation ρ satisfying $[(\mathbb{A} \wedge \mathbb{C})\rho]_\mathcal{Z} = \top$. We have:

$$\begin{aligned}
& [(\mathbb{A} \wedge \mathbb{C})\rho]_\mathcal{Z} = \top \\
\Longrightarrow\ & [\mathbb{A}\rho]_\mathcal{Z} = \top \text{ and } [\mathbb{C}\rho]_\mathcal{Z} = \top && (1) \\
\Longrightarrow\ & (\mathbb{A}|\mathbb{E}) \in \mathcal{Z},\ [\mathbb{E}\rho]_I = \top, \text{ and } [\mathbb{C}\rho]_I = \top \text{ for some } \mathbb{E} && (2) \\
\Longrightarrow\ & [(\mathbb{C} \wedge \mathbb{E})\rho]_I = \top && (3) \\
\Longrightarrow\ & (\mathbb{A}|\mathbb{C} \wedge \mathbb{E}) \in \mathcal{Z} && (4) \\
\Longrightarrow\ & (\mathbb{B}|\mathbb{C} \wedge \mathbb{E}) \in \mathcal{Z} \text{ and } \mathcal{C} \models (\mathbb{C} \wedge \mathbb{E}) \to \exists\vec{X}(\mathbb{D} \wedge \mathbb{E}) && (5) \\
\Longrightarrow\ & \text{there exist } \vec{d} \in D \text{ s.t. } \left[(\mathbb{D} \wedge \mathbb{E})\left(\rho \circ \left[\vec{X}\backslash\vec{d}\right]\right)\right]_I = \top && (6) \\
\Longrightarrow\ & \left[\mathbb{B}\left(\rho \circ \left[\vec{X}\backslash\vec{d}\right]\right)\right]_\mathcal{Z} \text{ and } \left[(\mathbb{D} \wedge \mathbb{E})\left(\rho \circ \left[\vec{X}\backslash\vec{d}\right]\right)\right]_\mathcal{Z} = \top && (7) \\
\Longrightarrow\ & \left[(\mathbb{B} \wedge \mathbb{F})\left(\rho \circ \left[\vec{X}\backslash\vec{d}\right]\right)\right]_\mathcal{Z} && (8)
\end{aligned}$$

(1) is by definition of $[\,]_\mathcal{Z}$. (2) is by definition of $[\![\mathcal{Z}]\!]_I$. (Without loss of generality we assume $\vec{X} \cap \mathrm{fv}(\mathbb{E}) = \emptyset$.) (3) is by definition of $[\,]_I$. (4) is by definition of $[\![\mathcal{Z}]\!]_I$. (5) is by hypothesis. (6) is because I is a model of $\mathcal{C}$. (7) is by definition of $[\![\mathcal{Z}]\!]_I$. (8) is by definition of $[\,]_\mathcal{Z}$. □

3. Constraint Logic Programming

Here we recall basic definitions and results for CLP.

3.1 Syntax

In CLP, we distinguish two syntactical categories, the clauses that form the programs and the goals that are rewritten by the programs.

A *(CLP) clause* is a logical formula of the form:

$$\forall\, (a \vee \neg a_1 \ldots \neg a_m \vee \neg c_1 \vee \ldots \neg c_n),$$

where the a and a_i's are atoms and the c_i's are constraints. This formula is noted in a simpler way as: $(a \leftarrow \mathbb{A} \mid \mathbb{C})$, where $\mathbb{A}$ is the multiset of the a_i's and $\mathbb{C}$ is the conjunction of the c_i's. Empty constraints (i.e., $\top$) can be omitted together with the symbol $|$. A *CLP program* is a finite set of clauses.

A *(CLP) goal* is a logical formula of the form:

$$\forall\, (\neg a_1 \ldots \neg a_n \vee \neg c_1 \vee \ldots \neg c_m),$$

where the a_i's are atoms and the c_i's are constraints. This formula is noted in a simpler way as: $\langle \mathbb{A} \mid \mathbb{C}\rangle$, where $\mathbb{A}$ is the multiset of the a_i's and $\mathbb{C}$ is the conjunction of the c_i's.

3.2 Operational Semantics

The operational semantics of CLP is given by CSLD resolution, that we present briefly in the following.

For a given program $\mathcal{P}$, the transition relation $\xrightarrow{\mathcal{P}}$ over goals is defined as the least rewrite relation satisfying the following principle of resolution:

$$\frac{(b \leftarrow \mathbb{B} \mid \mathbb{D}) \in \mathcal{P}\theta \qquad \mathbb{D} \text{ is } \mathcal{C}\text{-satisfiable}}{\langle \mathbb{A}, a \mid \mathbb{C}\rangle \xrightarrow{\mathcal{P}} \langle \mathbb{A}, \mathbb{B} \mid \mathbb{C} \wedge a = b \wedge \mathbb{D}\rangle}$$

where θ is a renaming with fresh variables (i.e., θ satisfies $\mathrm{fv}(b, \mathbb{B}, \mathbb{D}) \cap \mathrm{fv}(\mathbb{A}, a, \mathbb{C}) = \emptyset$).

A *success* for a CLP program $\mathcal{P}$ is a goal that has a consistent answer with respect to $\mathcal{P}$ (i.e., that can be derived by $\mathcal{P}$ to a goal of the form $\langle \emptyset \mid \mathbb{C}\rangle$ where $\mathbb{C}$ is $\mathcal{C}$-satisfiable).

We state next a straightforward result about CLP transitions that we will use later in the paper:

Proposition 7. *Let* $\langle \mathbb{A} \mid \mathbb{C}\rangle$, $\langle \mathbb{A}' \mid \mathbb{C}'\rangle$, *and* $\langle \mathbb{B} \mid \mathbb{D}\rangle$ *be three CLP goals satisfying* $\mathrm{fv}(\mathbb{A}', \mathbb{C}') \cap \mathrm{fv}(\mathbb{B}, \mathbb{D}) \subseteq \mathrm{fv}(\mathbb{A}, \mathbb{C})$.

$$\textit{If } \langle \mathbb{A} \mid \mathbb{C}\rangle \xrightarrow{\mathcal{P}} \langle \mathbb{A}' \mid \mathbb{C}'\rangle \textit{ and } (\mathbb{C} \wedge \mathbb{D}) \textit{ is } \mathcal{C}\textit{-satisfiable,}$$
$$\textit{then } \langle \mathbb{A}, \mathbb{B} \mid \mathbb{C} \wedge \mathbb{D}\rangle \xrightarrow{\mathcal{P}} \langle \mathbb{A}', \mathbb{B} \mid \mathbb{C}' \wedge \mathbb{D}\rangle.$$

3.3 Fixpoint Semantics

In this section we recall the fixpoint semantics of CLP.

Definition 8 (Immediate Consequence Operator). *For any CLP program* $\mathcal{P}$, *the* immediate consequence operator $T^\mathcal{C}_\mathcal{P} : 2^{\mathcal{B}_\mathcal{C}} \to 2^{\mathcal{B}_\mathcal{C}}$ *is defined as:*

$$T^\mathcal{C}_\mathcal{P}(\mathcal{X}) = \{(a|\mathbb{C} \wedge \mathbb{D}) \in \mathcal{B}_\mathcal{C} \mid (a \leftarrow \mathbb{A} \mid \mathbb{C}) \in \mathcal{P} \wedge (\mathbb{A}|\mathbb{D}) \in \mathcal{X}\}$$

Both $T^\mathcal{C}_\mathcal{P}$ and $\Downarrow_\mathcal{C}$ being obviously monotonous, Tarski's theorem ensures that the function $\lambda\mathcal{X}.\Downarrow_\mathcal{C}(T^\mathcal{C}_\mathcal{P}(\mathcal{X}))$ has a least and greatest fixpoint.

Theorem 9 (Least $\mathcal{C}$-models [28]). *Let* $\{M_i\}_{i \in I}$ *be the set of all* $\mathcal{C}$*-models of a CLP program* $\mathcal{P}$. $\mathcal{P}$ *has a least model, which satisfies:*

$$M^\mathcal{C}_\mathcal{P} = \bigcap_{i \in I} M_i = \mu\mathcal{X}.\Downarrow_\mathcal{C}\left(T^\mathcal{C}_\mathcal{P}(\mathcal{X})\right)$$

4. Constraint Handling Rules

In this section we introduce the syntax, the equivalence-based operational semantics ω_e, and the declarative semantics of CHR.

4.1 Syntax

We recall first the syntax of the language.

4.1.1 Programs

A *Constraint Handling Rule* (CHR) is a rule of the form:

$$r \ @ \ \mathbb{K}\backslash\mathbb{H} \Longleftrightarrow \mathbb{G} \mid \mathbb{A}, \mathbb{C}$$

where $\mathbb{K}$ and $\mathbb{H}$ are multisets of user-defined atoms, called *kept head* and *removed head* respectively, $\mathbb{G}$ is a conjunction of built-in constraints called *guard*, $\mathbb{C}$ is a conjunction of built-in constraints, $\mathbb{A}$ is a multiset of user-defined atoms, and r is an arbitrary identifier assumed unique in the program and called *rule name*. Rules where both heads are empty are prohibited. The empty guard $\top$ can be omitted together with the symbol $|$. The *local variables* of the rule are the variables occurring in the guard and in the body but not in the head (i.e., $\text{lv}(r) = \text{fv}(\mathbb{G}, \mathbb{A}, \mathbb{C}) \setminus \text{fv}(\mathbb{K}, \mathbb{H})$).

CHR programs are finite sets of CHR rules. We use CHR_1 to denote the CHR language limited to single-headed rules (i.e., rules with a single head atom).

Example 10. *Assume that the user-defined atom* $\mathtt{a}(I, X)$ *represents the* I^{th} *cell of an array containing arbitrary data* X*. Now, consider* $\mathcal{P}_{10}$ *to be the following classical CHR program [15] consisting of the following single rule:*

$$\mathtt{a}(I, X), \mathtt{a}(J, Y) \Longleftrightarrow I > J, X < Y \mid \mathtt{a}(I, Y), \mathtt{a}(J, X)$$

This rule sorts the array by swapping values at positions that are in the wrong order.

4.1.2 States

A *CHR state* is a tuple $\langle \mathbb{A}; \mathbb{C}; \bar{X} \rangle$ where $\mathbb{A}$ and $\mathbb{C}$ are multisets of atoms and constraints, respectively, and $\bar{X}$ is a set of variables, called *global variables*. The global variables represent the variables which are free in the initial goal.

Following Raiser et al. [37], we will consider CHR states modulo a structural equivalence. Formally, the *CHR state equivalence* is the least equivalence relation $\equiv_{\mathcal{C}}$ over states satisfying the following rules:

- $\langle \mathbb{A}; \mathbb{C}; \bar{X} \rangle \equiv_{\mathcal{C}} \langle \mathbb{A}; \mathbb{D}; \bar{X} \rangle$ if $\mathcal{C} \vDash \exists_{\text{-}(\mathbb{A}, \bar{X})}(\mathbb{C}) \leftrightarrow \exists_{\text{-}(\mathbb{A}, \bar{X})}(\mathbb{D})$
- $\langle \mathbb{A}; \bot; \bar{X} \rangle \equiv_{\mathcal{C}} \langle \mathbb{B}; \bot; \bar{X} \rangle$
- $\langle \mathbb{A}, c; \mathbb{C} \wedge c = d; \bar{X} \rangle \equiv_{\mathcal{C}} \langle \mathbb{A}, d; \mathbb{C} \wedge c = d; \bar{X} \rangle$
- $\langle \mathbb{A}; \mathbb{C}; \bar{X} \rangle \equiv_{\mathcal{C}} \langle \mathbb{A}; \mathbb{C}; \{Y\} \cup \bar{X} \rangle$ if $Y \notin \text{fv}(\mathbb{A}, \mathbb{C})$.

will say that a state is *consistent* if its built-in store $\mathbb{C}$ is $\mathcal{C}$-satisfiable, and *inconsistent* otherwise.

To give some intuition about this structural equivalence we recall some examples by Fraiser et al.

Example 11 ([37]). *Let $\mathcal{C}$ be an arbitrary constraint theory and* $\mathtt{p}$ *a unary user-defined atom symbol. We have:*

$$\begin{aligned}
\langle \mathtt{p}(X); \top; \emptyset \rangle &\equiv_{\mathcal{C}} \langle \mathtt{p}(Y); \top; \emptyset \rangle \\
\langle \mathtt{p}(X); X = 0; \{X\} \rangle &\equiv_{\mathcal{C}} \langle \mathtt{p}(0); X = 0; \{X\} \rangle \\
\langle \emptyset; X \leq 0 \wedge X \geq 0 \wedge Y = 0; \{X\} \rangle &\equiv_{\mathcal{C}} \langle \emptyset; X = 0; \{X\} \rangle \\
\langle \mathtt{p}(0); \top; \{X\} \rangle &\equiv_{\mathcal{C}} \langle \mathtt{p}(0); \top; \emptyset \rangle \\
\langle \mathtt{p}(X); \top; \{X\} \rangle &\not\equiv_{\mathcal{C}} \langle \mathtt{p}(Y); \top; \{Y\} \rangle
\end{aligned}$$

We recall a useful result on structural equivalence.

Theorem 12 ([37]). *Let* $R = \langle \mathbb{A}; \mathbb{C}; \bar{X} \rangle$ *and* $S = \langle \mathbb{B}; \mathbb{D}; \bar{Y} \rangle$ *be CHR states, such that* $(\text{fv}(\mathbb{A}, \mathbb{C}) \cap \text{fv}(\mathbb{B}, \mathbb{D})) \subseteq (\bar{X} \cap \bar{Y})$.

$$R \equiv_{\mathcal{C}} S \text{ if and only if } \begin{cases} \mathcal{C} \models \exists_{\text{-}\bar{X}}(\mathbb{C}) \leftrightarrow \exists_{\text{-}\bar{Y}}(\mathbb{D}), \\ \mathcal{C} \models \mathbb{C} \rightarrow \exists_{\text{-}\bar{Y}}(\mathbb{A} = \mathbb{B}), \text{ and} \\ \mathcal{C} \models \mathbb{D} \rightarrow \exists_{\text{-}\bar{X}}(\mathbb{A} = \mathbb{B}). \end{cases}$$

4.2 Operational Semantics

Once state equivalence has been stated, the *equivalence-based* operational semantics ω_e of Raiser et al. [37] can be defined by a single inference rule. The resulting operational semantics is very similar to the *very abstract* semantics ω_a [15], the most general operational semantics of CHR. The equivalence-based style is preferred here, because the use of a notion of equivalence will simplify many formulations.

The *CHR transition* $\xrightarrow{\mathcal{P}}$ is the least rewrite relation satisfying the two rules:

$$\frac{(r \ @ \ \mathbb{K}\backslash\mathbb{H} \Longleftrightarrow \mathbb{G}|\mathbb{B}, \mathbb{C}) \in \mathcal{P}\theta \qquad (\mathbb{G} \wedge \mathbb{D}) \text{ is } \mathcal{C}\text{-satisfiable}}{\langle \mathbb{H}, \mathbb{K}, \mathbb{A}; \mathbb{G} \wedge \mathbb{D}; \bar{X} \rangle \xrightarrow{\mathcal{P}} \langle \mathbb{B}, \mathbb{K}, \mathbb{A}; \mathbb{G} \wedge \mathbb{C} \wedge \mathbb{D}; \bar{X} \rangle}$$

where θ renames apart the local variables of r, i.e., θ satisfies $\text{lv}(r) \cap \text{fv}(\mathbb{A}, \mathbb{D}, \bar{X}) = \emptyset$.

We will say that a state S is *data-sufficient* with respect to a program $\mathcal{P}$, if there is a computation ending with a state of the form $\langle \emptyset; \mathbb{C}; \bar{X} \rangle$ (i.e., $S \xrightarrow{\mathcal{P}} \langle \emptyset; \mathbb{C}; \bar{X} \rangle$). Similarly to CLP, a *success* for a CHR program $\mathcal{P}$ is a state that has a consistent answer with respect to $\mathcal{P}$ (i.e., that can be derived by $\mathcal{P}$ to a goal of the form $\langle \emptyset; \mathbb{C}; \bar{X} \rangle$ where $\mathbb{C}$ is $\mathcal{C}$-satisfiable).

Example 13. *The operational behavior of the program* $\mathcal{P}_{10}$ *given in Example 10 can be illustrated by the following derivation:*

$$\begin{aligned}
&\langle \mathtt{a}(0,1), \mathtt{a}(1,5), \mathtt{a}(2,7), \underline{\mathtt{a}(3,9)}, \underline{\mathtt{a}(4,2)}; \top; \emptyset \rangle \\
\xrightarrow{\mathcal{P}_{10}} &\langle \mathtt{a}(0,1), \mathtt{a}(1,5), \underline{\mathtt{a}(2,7)}, \underline{\mathtt{a}(3,2)}, \mathtt{a}(4,9); \top; \emptyset \rangle \\
\xrightarrow{\mathcal{P}_{10}} &\langle \mathtt{a}(0,1), \underline{\mathtt{a}(1,5)}, \underline{\mathtt{a}(2,2)}, \mathtt{a}(3,7), \mathtt{a}(4,9); \top; \emptyset \rangle \\
\xrightarrow{\mathcal{P}_{10}} &\langle \mathtt{a}(0,1), \mathtt{a}(1,2), \mathtt{a}(2,5), \mathtt{a}(3,7), \mathtt{a}(4,9); \top; \emptyset \rangle
\end{aligned}$$

In each state, the atoms selected to perform the next transition are underlined. In a sorted array, any pair of cells $a(I, X)$ *and* $a(J, Y)$ *such that* $I > J$ *satisfies* $X \geq \mathtt{Y}$*. The program* $\mathcal{P}_{10}$ *ensures that this property holds by exchanging the value if necessary. Hence if the program cannot be applied anymore, the final state is sorted.*

The following straightforward technical lemma about CHR transitions will be used later in the paper.

Lemma 14. *If* $\langle \mathbb{A}; \mathbb{C}; \bar{X} \rangle \xrightarrow{\mathcal{P}}{}^{*} \langle \mathbb{B}; \mathbb{D}; \bar{Y} \rangle$ *is a valid CHR derivation, then* $\mathcal{C} \vDash \exists_{\text{-}Y}(\mathbb{D}) \rightarrow \exists_{\text{-}X}(\mathbb{C})$ *holds.*

Proof. By induction on the length of the derivation. □

4.3 Confluent and Completable Programs

Confluence is an important property for CHR programs, which ensures that any computation for a state results in the same final state no matter which of the applicable rules are used.

In the following, we will say that a program $\mathcal{P}$ is *confluent* if so is $\xrightarrow{\mathcal{P}}$. Moreover, we will say that a program $\mathcal{P}$ is *completable* if it can be made confluent by adding new rules, or in other words if there exists a program $\mathcal{Q}$ such that $(\mathcal{P} \cup \mathcal{Q})$ is confluent. The following example exhibits programs satisfying such properties.

Example 15. *Consider the program $\mathcal{P}_{10}$ given in Example 10 and the following states:*

$$S \equiv_{\mathcal{C}} \langle \mathtt{a}(I,X),\mathtt{a}(J,Y),\mathtt{a}(K,Z); I>K \wedge X<Z \wedge J>K \wedge Y<Z; \emptyset\rangle$$
$$S_1 \equiv_{\mathcal{C}} \langle \mathtt{a}(I,X),\mathtt{a}(J,Y),\mathtt{a}(K,Z); I>K \wedge X<Z \wedge J>K \wedge Y<Z; \emptyset\rangle$$
$$S_2 \equiv_{\mathcal{C}} \langle \mathtt{a}(I,X),\mathtt{a}(J,Y),\mathtt{a}(K,Z); I>K \wedge X<Z \wedge J>K \wedge Y<Z; \emptyset\rangle$$

We have $S \xrightarrow{\mathcal{P}_{10}} S_1$ and $S \xrightarrow{\mathcal{P}_{10}} S_2$ but $S_1 \not\xrightarrow{\mathcal{P}_{10}}$, $S_1 \not\xrightarrow{\mathcal{P}_{10}}$, and $S_1 \not\equiv_{\mathcal{C}} S_2$, that is, $\mathcal{P}_{10}$ is not confluent.

Consider now the following program $\mathcal{Q}_{15}$, which reverses any application of the program $\mathcal{P}_{10}$.

$$\mathtt{a}(I,X), \mathtt{a}(J,Y) \Longleftrightarrow I > J, X > Y \mid \mathtt{a}(I,Y), \mathtt{a}(J,X)$$

The resulting program $(\mathcal{P}_{10} \cup \mathcal{Q}_{15})$ is confluent (it is indeed strongly confluent *[20]). $\mathcal{P}_{10}$ is therefore completable. Note that $\mathcal{P}_{10}$ could also be completed using Abdennadher and Frühwirth's technique for terminating programs [3].*

As illustrated by the following example, there exists non-completable programs.

Example 16. *Consider the program $\mathcal{P}_{16}$ consisting of the following two rules:*

$$\mathtt{q} \Longleftrightarrow \top \qquad\qquad \mathtt{q} \Longleftrightarrow \bot$$

For any program $\mathcal{Q}$, both transitions $\langle \mathtt{q}; \top; \emptyset\rangle \xrightarrow{\mathcal{P}_{16}\cup\mathcal{Q}} \langle \emptyset; \top; \emptyset\rangle$ and $\langle \mathtt{q}; \top; \emptyset\rangle \xrightarrow{\mathcal{P}_{16}\cup\mathcal{Q}} \langle \emptyset; \bot; \emptyset\rangle$ hold, but there is no state R such that $\langle \emptyset; \top; \emptyset\rangle \xrightarrow{\mathcal{P}_{16}\cup\mathcal{Q}}{}^{*} R$ and $\langle \emptyset; \bot; \emptyset\rangle \xrightarrow{\mathcal{P}_{16}\cup\mathcal{Q}}{}^{*} R$. Hence $\mathcal{P}_{16}$ is not completable.

4.4 Declarative Semantics

We state now the declarative semantics of CHR. The *logical reading* of a rule:

$$(\mathbb{K} \backslash \mathbb{H} \Longleftrightarrow \mathbb{G} \mid \mathbb{B}, \mathbb{C})$$

is the following guarded equivalence:

$$\forall\big((\mathbb{K} \wedge \mathbb{G}) \rightarrow (\mathbb{H} \leftrightarrow \exists_{\text{-}(\mathbb{K},\mathbb{H})}(\mathbb{G} \wedge \mathbb{B} \wedge \mathbb{C}))\big)$$

or, equivalently, the conjunction of implications:

$$\forall\big((\mathbb{K} \wedge \mathbb{H} \wedge \mathbb{G}) \rightarrow \exists_{\text{-}(\mathbb{K},\mathbb{H})}(\mathbb{G} \wedge \mathbb{B} \wedge \mathbb{C})\big) \wedge$$
$$\forall\big((\mathbb{K} \wedge \mathbb{G} \wedge \mathbb{B} \wedge \mathbb{C}) \rightarrow \mathbb{H}\big)$$

The *logical reading* of a program $\mathcal{P}$ within a constraint theory $\mathcal{C}$ is the theory $\mathcal{C}$ extended with the logical readings of the rules of $\mathcal{P}$. The *logical reading* of a state $\langle \mathbb{A}; \mathbb{C}; \bar{X}\rangle$ is the first-order formula: $\exists_{\text{-}\bar{X}}(\mathbb{A} \wedge \mathbb{C})$.

Example 17. *The logical reading of the program $\mathcal{P}_{10}$ given in Example 10 is equivalent to the conjunction of the two following implications:*

$$\forall(I > J \wedge X > Y \wedge \mathtt{a}(I,X), \mathtt{a}(J,Y)) \rightarrow (\mathtt{a}(I,Y), \mathtt{a}(J,X))$$
$$\forall(I > J \wedge X > Y \wedge \mathtt{a}(I,Y), \mathtt{a}(J,X)) \rightarrow (\mathtt{a}(I,X), \mathtt{a}(J,Y))$$

The logical reading above says that all arrays containing the same set of values are equivalent. Nonetheless it does not describe the nature of the preferred order between array cells, because the logical equivalence can be applied in both directions. Even if the logical meaning of $\mathcal{P}_{10}$ can seem weak, it carries some meaningful information such as the fact that the values in the array are never created or deleted during the executions of the program.

Note that contrary to that of $\mathcal{P}_{10}$, the logical reading of the program $\mathcal{P}_{16}$ given in Example 16 is completely nonsensical (it is in fact logically inconsistent).

The theorem we give next summarizes basic results about soundness and completeness of *data-sufficient states* with respect to the declarative meaning of a program.

Theorem 18. *Let $\mathcal{P}$ be a CHR program with a consistent logical reading, and $\langle \mathbb{A}; \mathbb{C}; \bar{X}\rangle \xrightarrow{\mathcal{P}}{}^{*} \langle \emptyset; \mathbb{D}; Y\rangle$ be a valid CHR derivation. $(\mathbb{A} \wedge \mathbb{C})$ is satisfiable with respect to the logical reading of $\mathcal{P}$ if and only if $\mathcal{P}, \mathcal{C} \models \exists_{\text{-}\bar{X}}(\mathbb{A} \wedge \mathbb{C}) \leftrightarrow \exists_{\text{-}\bar{X}}(\mathbb{D})$.*

Proof. Direct by the Soundness and Stronger Completeness of failed computations Theorems (refer to Theorems 3.21 and 3.25 in Frühwirth's book [15]). □

5. CLP Projection

In this section, we introduce and formally study the CLP projection for CHR programs. In the next section, we will see some direct applications.

5.1 Definition

As explained in Section 4.4, the logical reading of a simplification rule is an equivalence. The basis of the CLP projection is to ignore the right-to-left implication part of the equivalence and consider only the left-to-right part. Indeed, one can consider the implication $c_1 \wedge \cdots \wedge c_n \leftarrow \exists Z(\mathbb{K} \wedge \mathbb{G} \wedge \mathbb{B})$ as the conjunction of the n implications $(c_1 \leftarrow \exists Z(\mathbb{K} \wedge \mathbb{G} \wedge \mathbb{B})), \ldots, (c_n \leftarrow \exists Z(\mathbb{G} \wedge \mathbb{B} \wedge \mathbb{K}))$. Formally the CLP projection can be defined as follows:

Definition 19 (CLP Projection)**.** *The* (CLP) projection *of a CHR program $\mathcal{P}$ is the set $\pi(\mathcal{P})$ of CLP clauses defined as:*

$$\pi(\mathcal{P}) = \{\, (a \leftarrow \mathbb{K}, \mathbb{B} \mid \mathbb{G} \wedge \mathbb{C}) \mid$$
$$(\mathbb{K} \backslash \mathbb{H} \Longleftrightarrow \mathbb{G} \mid \mathbb{B}, \mathbb{C}) \in \mathcal{P} \text{ and } a \in (\mathbb{H}, \mathbb{K})\}$$

The (CLP) projection *of a CHR state is defined in a straightforward way, i.e.:*

$$\pi(\langle \mathbb{A}; \mathbb{C}; \bar{X}\rangle) = \langle \mathbb{A} \mid \mathbb{C}\rangle$$

We illustrate now the result of a CLP projection.

Example 20. *Consider the program $\mathcal{P}_{10}$ given in Example 10. The CLP projection of $\mathcal{P}_{10}$ consists of the following CLP clauses:*

$$\mathtt{a}(I,X) \leftarrow \mathtt{a}(I,Y), \mathtt{a}(J,X) \mid I > J \wedge X < Y$$
$$\mathtt{a}(J,Y) \leftarrow \mathtt{a}(I,Y), \mathtt{a}(J,X) \mid I > J \wedge X < Y$$

5.2 Operational Approximation of CHR

In this subsection, we show that the CLP projection provides an operational approximation for CHR programs.

5.2.1 Operational Approximation of Multi-headed Programs

In this section, we relate the operational behavior of a general CHR program and its CLP projection. To state the result of the section, we first introduce two relations of state subsumption.

Definition 21 (State subsumption relation)**.** *The relation $\sqsubseteq_{\mathcal{C}}$ is defined as the least transitive relations containing $\equiv_{\mathcal{C}}$ and satisfying*

$$\langle \mathbb{A}; \mathbb{C} \wedge \mathbb{D}; \bar{X} \cup \bar{Y}\rangle \sqsubseteq_{\mathcal{C}} \langle \mathbb{A}, \mathbb{B}; \mathbb{C}; \bar{X}\rangle$$

where $\mathbb{B}$ stands for an arbitrary multiset of atoms, $\mathbb{D}$ stands for an arbitrary conjunction of constraints, and $\bar{Y}$ stands for an arbitrary set of variables.

The theorem we give next states that the operational semantics of a CHR program can be simulated by its projection. We will use this theorem, which establishes that the termination of $\pi(\mathcal{P})$ implies the termination of $\mathcal{P}$, in Section 6.1.

Theorem 22. *For any CHR program $\mathcal{P}$, we have:*

For all states R, R', S if $R \xrightarrow{\mathcal{P}} R'$ and $R \sqsubseteq_{\mathcal{C}} S$, then

there exists a state S' such that $\pi(S) \xrightarrow{\pi(\mathcal{P})} \pi(S')$ and $R' \sqsubseteq_{\mathcal{C}} S'$.

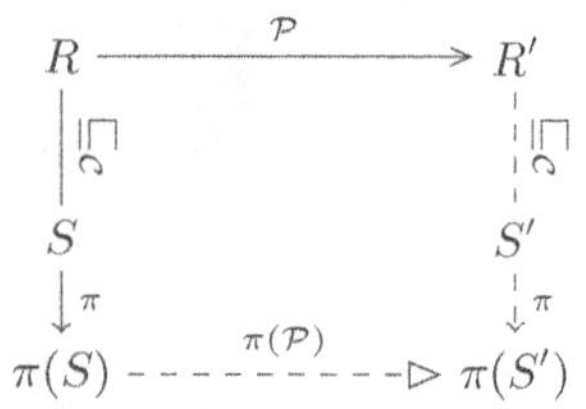

Figure 1. Simulation diagram for a CHR program $\mathcal{P}$.

The theorem is graphically represented by the diagram of Figure 1. Following standard diagrammatic notation, solid edges stand for universally-quantified relations (i.e., the premise), and the dashed edges stand for existentially-quantified relations (i.e., the conclusions). CHR states are nodes in the upper side and CLP goals are nodes in the lower side.

Before formally proving the theorem, we illustrate it on our running example.

Example 23. *Consider the program $\mathcal{P}_{10}$ given in Example 10. Applying the rule* sort, *we infer the possible transition:*

$$R = \langle \mathtt{a}(0,7), \mathtt{a}(1,5); \top; \emptyset\rangle \xrightarrow{\mathcal{P}_{10}} \langle \mathtt{a}(0,5), \mathtt{a}(1,7); \top; \emptyset\rangle = R'$$

It is straightforward to verify that using the projection of $\mathcal{P}_{10}$ (given explicitly in Example 20) that the following derivation is valid with respect to $\pi(\mathcal{P}_{10})$:

$$\langle \mathtt{a}(0,7), \mathtt{a}(1,5) \mid \top\rangle \xrightarrow{\pi(\mathcal{P}_{10})}$$
$$\langle \mathtt{a}(I,7), \mathtt{a}(0,X), \mathtt{a}(1,5) \mid I > 0 \wedge X < 7\rangle$$

Note that it holds that R' is included (with respect to $\sqsubseteq_{\mathcal{C}}$) in the state:

$$\langle \mathtt{a}(I,7), \mathtt{a}(0,X), \mathtt{a}(1,5); I > 0 \wedge X < 7; \emptyset\rangle$$

Proof. Assume that r is of the form

$$\mathbb{K}\backslash\mathbb{H} \Longleftrightarrow \mathbb{G}|\mathbb{B}, \mathbb{C}$$

Without loss of generality we can assume that the states R, R' and S satisfy:

$$R \equiv_{\mathcal{C}} \langle \mathbb{K}', \mathbb{H}', c, \mathbb{A}; \mathbb{G} \wedge \mathbb{D} \wedge \mathbb{D}'; \bar{X} \cup \bar{Y}\rangle$$
$$S \equiv_{\mathcal{C}} \langle \mathbb{K}', \mathbb{H}', c, \mathbb{A}, \mathbb{A}'; \mathbb{D}'; \bar{X}\rangle$$
$$R' \equiv_{\mathcal{C}} \langle \mathbb{B}, \mathbb{K}, \mathbb{A}; \mathbb{C} \wedge \mathbb{G} \wedge \mathbb{D} \wedge \mathbb{D}'; \bar{X} \cup \bar{Y}\rangle$$

with $(\mathbb{K}, \mathbb{H}) = (\mathbb{K}', \mathbb{H}', c)$.

Let θ be a renaming with fresh variables. Hence, we have:

$$\pi(S) \xrightarrow{\pi(\mathcal{P})} (\mathbb{K}\theta, \mathbb{B}\theta, \mathbb{K}', \mathbb{H}', \mathbb{A}, \mathbb{A}'|\mathbb{D}' \wedge c = (c\theta) \wedge \mathbb{G}\theta \wedge \mathbb{C}\theta)$$

To conclude it is sufficient to notice that:

$$R' \sqsubseteq_{\mathcal{C}} \langle \mathbb{K}\theta, \mathbb{B}\theta, \mathbb{K}', \mathbb{H}', \mathbb{A}, \mathbb{A}'; \mathbb{D}' \wedge c = (c\theta) \wedge \mathbb{G}\theta \wedge \mathbb{C}\theta; \bar{X}\rangle. \quad \square$$

5.2.2 Operational Approximation of Single-headed Programs

In fact, one can prove a more precise correspondence in the case of single-headed simplifications. This second theorem is graphically represented by the diagram of Figure 2.

Theorem 24. *For any CHR$_1$ program $\mathcal{P}$, we have:*

For all states S, S' if $S \xrightarrow{\mathcal{P}} S'$, then $\pi(S) \xrightarrow{\pi(\mathcal{P})} \pi(S')$

Proof. Assume r is of the form:

$$c \Longleftrightarrow \mathbb{G}|\mathbb{B}, \mathbb{C}$$

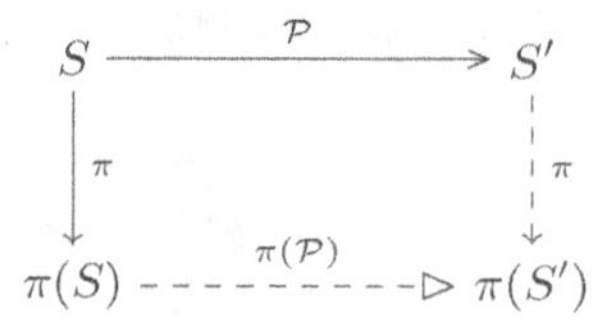

Figure 2. Simulation diagram for a CHR$_1$ program $\mathcal{P}$.

Without loss of generality we can assume that the states R, R' and S satisfy:

$$S \equiv_{\mathcal{C}} \langle c, \mathbb{A}; \mathbb{G} \wedge \mathbb{D}; \bar{X}\rangle$$
$$S' \equiv_{\mathcal{C}} \langle \mathbb{A}, \mathbb{B}; \mathbb{G} \wedge \mathbb{D} \wedge \mathbb{C}; \bar{X}\rangle$$

Let θ be a renaming with fresh variables. By definition of CHR transition, we know that $(\mathbb{G} \wedge \mathbb{D} \wedge \mathbb{D}')$ is $\mathcal{C}$-satisfiable, i.e., $(\mathbb{D}' \wedge c = (c\theta) \wedge \mathbb{G}\theta \wedge \mathbb{C}\theta)$ is $\mathcal{C}$-satisfiable. By definition of the CLP projection and the CSLD, we get straightforwardly:

$$\pi(S) \xrightarrow{\pi(\mathcal{P})} \left(\mathbb{A}, \mathbb{B}\theta|\mathbb{D}' \wedge \mathbb{G}\theta \wedge c = (c\theta) \wedge \mathbb{C}\theta\right)$$

To conclude it is sufficient to notice that:

$$S' \equiv_{\mathcal{C}} \langle \mathbb{A}, \mathbb{B}\theta; \mathbb{D}' \wedge \mathbb{G}\theta \wedge c = (c\theta) \wedge \mathbb{C}\theta; \bar{X}\rangle. \quad \square$$

In general the theorems do not hold in the reverse direction. Indeed we show through the following counter-example that a program does not simulate is projection.

Example 25. *Consider the program $\mathcal{P}_{10}$ given in Example 10 and its projection $\pi(\mathcal{P}_{10})$ given explicitly in Example 20. The CLP transition:*

$$\langle \mathtt{a}(0,5) \mid \top\rangle \xrightarrow{\pi(\mathcal{P}_{10})} \langle \mathtt{a}(I,5), \mathtt{a}(0,X), \mid I > 0 \wedge X < 5\rangle$$

is valid with respect to the CLP projection of $\mathcal{P}_{10}$. Nevertheless $\langle \mathtt{a}(0,5); \top; \emptyset\rangle$ cannot be derived by $\mathcal{P}_{10}$. The reason for this dichotomy is that $\mathcal{P}_{10}$ is a terminating program while $\pi(\mathcal{P}_{10})$ is not – in fact, $\pi(\mathcal{P}_{10})$ has no terminating derivations.

5.3 Declarative Approximation of CHR

In this section, we relate the model of a CHR program with that of its projection.

5.3.1 Declarative Approximation of General Programs

The following proposition states that the logical model of a CHR program is bounded by the least model of its projection in the lattice of $\mathcal{C}$-interpretations.

Proposition 26. *Let $\mathcal{P}$ be a CHR program. For any $\mathcal{C}$-model $\mathcal{M}$ of $\mathcal{P}$, we have:*

$$\mu\mathcal{X}.\Downarrow_{\mathcal{C}}\left(T^{\mathcal{C}}_{\pi(\mathcal{P})}(\mathcal{X})\right) \subseteq \mathcal{M}$$

Proof. If $\mathcal{P}$ has no $\mathcal{C}$-model, then the result is direct. Otherwise, let $\mathcal{M}$ be a $\mathcal{C}$-model of $\mathcal{P}$. Obviously $\pi(\mathcal{P})$ is a logical consequence of $\mathcal{P}$ (i.e., $\mathcal{C} \models \mathcal{P} \rightarrow \pi(\mathcal{P})$), hence $\mathcal{M}$ is a $\mathcal{C}$-model for $\pi(\mathcal{P})$. The conclusion is then direct using Theorem 9. $\square$

As shown by the following examples this approximation is in general quite imprecise.

Example 27. *Consider the program $\mathcal{P}_{27}$ comprising the following rules:*

$$\mathtt{c} \Longleftrightarrow \top \qquad \mathtt{c} \Longleftrightarrow \mathtt{d} \qquad \mathtt{e} \Longleftrightarrow \mathtt{e}$$

The projection of $\mathcal{P}_{27}$ consists of the following clauses:

$$\mathtt{c} \leftarrow \top \qquad \mathtt{c} \leftarrow \mathtt{d} \qquad \mathtt{e} \leftarrow \mathtt{e}$$

The least $\mathcal{C}$-model of $\pi(\mathcal{P}_{27})$ is $\Downarrow_{\mathcal{C}}((\mathtt{c}|\top))$, but the least $\mathcal{C}$-model of $\mathcal{P}_{27}$ is $\Downarrow_{\mathcal{C}}((\mathtt{c},\mathtt{d}|\top))$.

5.3.2 Declarative Approximating of Confluent Programs

We show now that in the case that $\mathcal{P}$ is confluent, the least fixpoint of $T^{\mathcal{C}}_{\pi(\mathcal{P})}$ provides a logical model for $\mathcal{P}$.

Theorem 28. *Let $\mathcal{P}$ be a confluent program. $\mu\mathcal{X}.\Downarrow_{\mathcal{C}}(T^{\mathcal{C}}_{\pi(\mathcal{P})}(\mathcal{X}))$ is the least $\mathcal{C}$-model of $\mathcal{P}$.*

The proof of the proposition relies on two main lemmas. The first one states that if a state R can be derived to a consistent state S which has a projection included in a fixpoint of $\lambda\mathcal{X}.\Downarrow_{\mathcal{C}}(T^{\mathcal{C}}_{\pi(\mathcal{P})}(\mathcal{X}))$, then there is a consistent state R' more constrained than R which is the same fixpoint.

Lemma 29. *Let $\mathcal{P}$ be a program, $\mathcal{Y}$ a set of constrained atoms, and $\langle\mathbb{A};\mathbb{C};\bar{X}\rangle \xrightarrow{\mathcal{P}}{}^{*} \langle\mathbb{B};\mathbb{D};\bar{X}\rangle$ a valid derivation such that $\mathrm{fv}(\mathbb{A},\mathbb{C}) \subseteq \bar{X}$. If $\mathcal{Y}$ is a fixpoint of $\lambda\mathcal{X}.\Downarrow_{\mathcal{C}}(T^{\mathcal{C}}_{\pi(\mathcal{P})}(\mathcal{X}))$ and $(\mathbb{B}|\mathbb{D}) \subseteq \mathcal{Y}$, then $(\mathbb{A}|\mathbb{C}\wedge\mathbb{D}) \subseteq \mathcal{Y}$.*

Proof. We prove only the case of the one-step derivation, the general case will follow directly by reflexivity and transitivity of the inclusion. Let $r@(\mathbb{K}\backslash\mathbb{H} \Longleftrightarrow \mathbb{G}|\mathbb{F},\mathbb{E})$ be the rule of $\mathcal{P}$ used for the transition. We have for some $\mathbb{A}'$, $\mathbb{C}'$, and $\bar{X}'$:

$$\langle\mathbb{A};\mathbb{C};\bar{X}\rangle \equiv_{\mathcal{C}} \langle\mathbb{H},\mathbb{K},\mathbb{A}';\mathbb{G}\wedge\mathbb{C}';\bar{X}\rangle \quad (1)$$
$$\langle\mathbb{F},\mathbb{K},\mathbb{A}';\mathbb{E}\wedge\mathbb{G}\wedge\mathbb{C}';\bar{X}\rangle \equiv_{\mathcal{C}} \langle\mathbb{B};\mathbb{D};\bar{Y}\rangle \quad (2)$$
$$\Longrightarrow (\mathbb{F},\mathbb{A}',\mathbb{K}|\mathbb{E}\wedge\mathbb{G}\wedge\mathbb{C}') \subseteq \mathcal{Z} \quad (3)$$
$$\Longrightarrow (\mathbb{H}|\mathbb{E}\wedge\mathbb{G}\wedge\mathbb{C}') \subseteq T^{\mathcal{C}}_{\pi(\mathcal{P})}(\mathcal{Z}) \quad (4)$$
$$\Longrightarrow (\mathbb{H},\mathbb{K},\mathbb{A}'|\mathbb{E}\wedge\mathbb{G}\wedge\mathbb{C}') \subseteq \mathcal{Z} \quad (5)$$

(1) and (2) are by the definition of $\xrightarrow{\mathcal{P}}$. (3) is by Theorem 12 and idempotence of a closure operator. (4) is by the definition of $T^{\mathcal{C}}_{\pi(\mathcal{P})}$. (5) combines (4) with (3) and uses the fact that $\mathcal{Z}$ is a fixpoint of $\lambda\mathcal{X}.\Downarrow_{\mathcal{C}}(T^{\mathcal{C}}_{\pi(\mathcal{P})}(\mathcal{X}))$.

On the other hand we have:

$$\mathcal{C}\models\mathbb{D}\rightarrow\mathbb{C} \text{ and } \mathcal{C}\models\mathbb{D}\rightarrow\exists_{-\bar{X}}(\mathbb{E}\wedge\mathbb{G}\wedge\mathbb{C}') \quad (6)$$
$$\mathcal{C}\models\mathbb{D}\rightarrow\mathbb{C} \text{ and } (\mathbb{H},\mathbb{K},\mathbb{A}'|\mathbb{D}) \subseteq \mathcal{Z} \quad (7)$$
$$\mathcal{C}\models\mathbb{D}\rightarrow\mathbb{C} \text{ and } (\mathbb{A}|\mathbb{D}) \subseteq \mathcal{Z} \quad (8)$$
$$(\mathbb{A}|\mathbb{C}\wedge\mathbb{D}) \subseteq \mathcal{Z} \quad (9)$$

The left hand side of (6) is by Lemma 14, the right hand side is inferred form (2) by Theorem 12. (7) is inferred from (5) because $\mathcal{Z}$ is closed by $\Downarrow_{\mathcal{C}}$. Finally, 8 combines the left and right hand sides in a straightforward way. □

The second lemma says that any state derived from a consistent state which has a CLP projection in a fixpoint of $\lambda\mathcal{X}.\Downarrow_{\mathcal{C}}(T^{\mathcal{C}}_{\pi(\mathcal{P})}(\mathcal{X}))$, has a CLP projection in the same fixpoint. Contrary to the previous lemma, the core of the proof relies on the confluence of the considered CHR program.

Lemma 30. *Let $\mathcal{P}$ be a confluent program. For any ordinal α, if $\langle\mathbb{A};\mathbb{C};\bar{X}\rangle \xrightarrow{\mathcal{P}}{}^{*} \langle\mathbb{A}';\mathbb{C}';\bar{X}\rangle$, $\mathrm{fv}(\mathbb{A}) \subseteq X$, and $(\mathbb{A}|\mathbb{C}) \subseteq \lambda\mathcal{X}.\Downarrow_{\mathcal{C}}(T^{\mathcal{C}}_{\pi(\mathcal{P})}(\mathcal{X}))\uparrow\alpha$, then $(\mathbb{A}'|\mathbb{C}') \subseteq \mu\mathcal{X}.\Downarrow_{\mathcal{C}}(T^{\mathcal{C}}_{\pi(\mathcal{P})}(\mathcal{X}))$ and $\mathcal{C}\models\mathbb{C}\rightarrow\exists_{-X}\mathbb{C}'$.*

Proof. Let F denote the function $\lambda\mathcal{X}.\Downarrow_{\mathcal{C}}(T^{\mathcal{C}}_{\pi(\mathcal{P})}(\mathcal{X}))$. The proof is by transfinite induction on α:

- The base case, $\alpha = 0$ is trivial.
- For a successor ordinal, we have:

$$(\mathbb{A}|\mathbb{C}) \subseteq F\uparrow(\alpha+1) = \Downarrow_{\mathcal{C}}\Big(T^{\mathcal{C}}_{\pi(\mathcal{P})}(F\uparrow\alpha)\Big) \quad (1)$$
$$\Longrightarrow \mathbb{A} \text{ is of the form } \{a_1,\dots,a_n\} \text{for } i\in 1,\dots,n$$
$$r_i@(\mathbb{K}_i\backslash a_i,\mathbb{H}_i \Longleftrightarrow \mathbb{G}_i \mid \mathbb{B}_i,\mathbb{C}_i) \in \rho_i(\mathcal{P}), \quad (2)$$
$$(\mathbb{K}_i,\mathbb{B}_i|\mathbb{C}_i) \subseteq F\uparrow\alpha, \text{ and} \quad (3)$$
$$\mathcal{C}\models\mathbb{C}\rightarrow\exists_{-c_i}(\mathbb{G}_i\wedge\mathbb{B}_i\wedge\mathbb{D}_i) \quad (4)$$

(1) is by definition of upward power. (2) to (4) are by definition of $T^{\mathcal{C}}_{\pi(\mathcal{P})}$ and $\Downarrow_{\mathcal{C}}$.

Assuming $\vec{A}$ is an abbreviation for any sequence of constraints of the form $A_i,\dots,A_n$ and $Y = X\cup\mathrm{fv}\big(\vec{\mathbb{K}},\vec{\mathbb{H}}\big)$, we have:

$$\Longrightarrow \langle\mathbb{A},\bar{\mathbb{H}},\bar{\mathbb{K}};\mathbb{C}\wedge\bar{\mathbb{C}}\wedge\bar{\mathbb{G}};\bar{Y}\rangle \xrightarrow{\mathcal{P}}{}^{*} \langle\mathbb{A}',\bar{\mathbb{H}},\bar{\mathbb{K}};\mathbb{C}'\wedge\bar{\mathbb{C}}\wedge\bar{\mathbb{G}};\bar{Y}\rangle \quad (5)$$
$$\langle\mathbb{A},\bar{\mathbb{H}},\bar{\mathbb{K}};\mathbb{C}\wedge\bar{\mathbb{C}}\wedge\bar{\mathbb{G}};\bar{Y}\rangle \xrightarrow{\mathcal{P}}{}^{*} \langle\bar{\mathbb{B}},\bar{\mathbb{K}};\mathbb{C}\wedge\bar{\mathbb{C}}\wedge\bar{\mathbb{G}}\wedge\bar{\mathbb{D}};\bar{Y}\rangle \quad (6)$$
$$\Longrightarrow \text{there is } \langle\mathbb{B}';\mathbb{D}';\bar{Y}\rangle \text{ s.t. :}$$
$$\langle\mathbb{A}',\bar{\mathbb{H}},\bar{\mathbb{K}};\mathbb{C}'\wedge\bar{\mathbb{C}}\wedge\bar{\mathbb{G}};\bar{Y}\rangle \xrightarrow{\mathcal{P}}{}^{*} \langle\mathbb{B}';\mathbb{D}';\bar{Y}\rangle \text{ and} \quad (7)$$
$$\langle\bar{\mathbb{B}},\bar{\mathbb{K}};\mathbb{C}\wedge\bar{\mathbb{C}}\wedge\bar{\mathbb{G}}\wedge\bar{\mathbb{D}};\bar{Y}\rangle \xrightarrow{\mathcal{P}}{}^{*} \langle\mathbb{B}';\mathbb{D}';\bar{Y}\rangle \quad (8)$$
$$\Longrightarrow (\mathbb{B}'|\mathbb{D}') \subseteq \mu\mathcal{X}.F(\mathcal{X}) \text{ with}$$
$$\mathcal{C}\models(\mathbb{C}\wedge\bar{\mathbb{C}}\wedge\bar{\mathbb{G}}\wedge\bar{\mathbb{D}})\rightarrow\exists_{-Y}\mathbb{D}' \quad (9)$$
$$\Longrightarrow (\mathbb{A}'|\mathbb{C}\wedge\bar{\mathbb{C}}\wedge\bar{\mathbb{G}}\wedge\bar{\mathbb{D}}) \subseteq \mu\mathcal{X}.F(\mathcal{X}) \quad (10)$$

(5) is by monotonicity of CHR derivation (Lemma 4.2 in [15]). (6) is by applying the r_i rules. (7) and (8) are by confluence of $\xrightarrow{\mathcal{P}}$. (9) is inferred from (3), (8), induction hypothesis, and the fact that $F\uparrow\alpha$ is closed by $\Downarrow_{\mathcal{C}}$. (10) is by Lemma 29.

On the other hand we have:

$$\Longrightarrow \mathcal{C}\models\mathbb{D}'\rightarrow\exists_{-\bar{Y}}\mathbb{C}' \quad (11)$$
$$\mathcal{C}\models\mathbb{C}\rightarrow\exists_{-\bar{Y}}(\mathbb{C}\wedge\bar{\mathbb{C}}\wedge\bar{\mathbb{G}}\wedge\bar{\mathbb{D}}) \quad (12)$$
$$\Longrightarrow \mathcal{C}\models\mathbb{C}\rightarrow\exists_{-\bar{Y}}\mathbb{C}' \quad (13)$$

Thanks to Lemma 14, (11) is inferred from (8). (12) is straightforward from (4). Finally (13) is obtained from (11), (12) and (9) using transitivity of the implication.

- For a limit ordinal, we have $T^{\mathcal{C}}_{\pi(\mathcal{P})}\uparrow\alpha = \bigcup_{\beta<\alpha}F\uparrow\beta$. Using monotonicity of $\lambda\mathcal{X}.(\mathcal{Y}\cup T^{\mathcal{C}}_{\pi(\mathcal{P})}(\mathcal{X}))$ and the fact that $\mathbb{D}$ is finite, there exists obviously an ordinal $\beta<\alpha$ such that $\mathbb{D}\rho \in \lambda\mathcal{X}.(\mathcal{Y}\cup T^{\mathcal{C}}_{\pi(\mathcal{P})}(\mathcal{X}))\uparrow\beta$. The conclusion is then direct using induction hypothesis. □

Proof of Theorem 28. Assume that the following rule is in $\mathcal{P}$:

$$r \;@\; \mathbb{K}\backslash\mathbb{H} \Longleftrightarrow \mathbb{G} \mid \mathbb{B},\mathbb{C}$$

Let θ be a renaming of $\mathrm{fv}(\mathbb{G},\mathbb{B},\mathbb{C}) \setminus \mathrm{fv}(\mathbb{K},\mathbb{H})$ with fresh variables (in particular $(\mathbb{K},\mathbb{H})\theta = (\mathbb{K},\mathbb{H})$) and let $\bar{Y} = \mathrm{fv}(\mathbb{G}\theta,\mathbb{B}\theta,\mathbb{C}\theta)$. The logical reading of r is logically equivalent to the two following implications:

$$\forall((\mathbb{K}\wedge\mathbb{H}\wedge\mathbb{G})\rightarrow\exists_{-\bar{Y}}(\mathbb{G}\theta\wedge\mathbb{B}\theta\wedge\mathbb{C}\theta))$$
$$\forall((\mathbb{K}\wedge\mathbb{G}\wedge\mathbb{B}\wedge\mathbb{C})\rightarrow\mathbb{H})$$

Thanks to Lemma 6, in order to prove that $\mathcal{Z} = \mu\mathcal{X}.\Downarrow_{\mathcal{C}}(T^{\mathcal{C}}_{\pi(\mathcal{P})}(\mathcal{X}))$ is a model for $\mathcal{P}$, we know it is sufficient to show that:

(i) For any conjunction of constraints $\mathbb{E}$ such that $\mathrm{fv}(\mathbb{E})\cap\bar{Y} = \emptyset$, $(\mathbb{K},\mathbb{H}|\mathbb{C}\wedge\mathbb{E}) \in \mathcal{Z}$ implies $(\mathbb{K},\mathbb{B}|\mathbb{G}\theta\wedge\mathbb{B}\theta\wedge\mathbb{C}\theta) \in \mathcal{Z}$ and $\mathcal{C}\models(\mathbb{C}\wedge\mathbb{E})\rightarrow\exists\bar{Y}(\mathbb{G}\theta\wedge\mathbb{C}\theta\wedge\mathbb{E})$

(ii) For any conjunction of constraints $\mathbb{E}$, $(\mathbb{K},\mathbb{B}|\mathbb{G}\wedge\mathbb{C}\wedge\mathbb{E}) \in \mathcal{Z}$ implies $(\mathbb{H}|\mathbb{G}\wedge\mathbb{C}\wedge\mathbb{E}) \in \mathcal{Z}$

Since we have obviously

$$\langle \mathbb{K}, \mathbb{H}; \mathbb{G} \wedge \mathbb{E}; \bar{X} \rangle \xrightarrow{\mathcal{P}} \langle \mathbb{K}, \mathbb{B}\theta; \mathbb{G} \wedge \mathbb{E} \wedge \mathbb{G}\theta \wedge \mathbb{C}\theta; \bar{X} \rangle$$

(i) follows by Lemma 29 and (ii) by Lemma 30 together with the Knaster–Tarski Theorem. Hence, we know that $\mu\mathcal{X}.\Downarrow_{\mathcal{C}}(T^{\mathcal{C}}_{\pi(\mathcal{P})}(\mathcal{X}))$ is a model of $\mathcal{P}$, its minimality being guaranteed by Proposition 26. □

As a direct corollary, we get that any confluent (or, more generally, completable) program is consistent. We close hence a conjecture of Abdennadher et al. about consistency of general confluent CHR programs [4], the original proof being limited to range-restricted programs (i.e., programs without local variables). Note furthermore that our theorem does not assume that the constraint theory is ground complete. Consequently, it is possible to strengthen existing results about CHR declarative semantics, especially the completeness of operational semantics with respect to failure where both conditions of range restriction and ground completeness of the constraint system can be dropped (refer to Corollary 5.19 in Früwirth's book). This improvement is important, since we identified in a recent publication a class of confluent programs (the so-called coinductive constraint solvers) which by construction are not range restricted [19].

Corollary 31. *Any completable CHR program $\mathcal{P}$ is consistent.*

The following example illustrates that a confluent CHR program may not have a unique greatest $\mathcal{C}$-model. This comes from the non-compositionality of the declarative semantics of CHR (i.e., if the logical readings of two states are independently consistent, then one cannot ensure that so is their conjunction).

Example 32. *Let $\mathcal{P}_{32}$ be the program consisting of the following rule:*

$$p, q \Longleftrightarrow \bot$$

$\Downarrow_{\mathcal{C}}(\{p|\top\})$ and $\Downarrow_{\mathcal{C}}(\{q|\top\})$ are two greatest incomparable $\mathcal{C}$-models for $\mathcal{P}_{32}$.

An interesting consequence is that the logical semantics of both formalisms coincide on data-sufficient states.

Theorem 33. *A data-sufficient state is a success for a confluent CHR program $\mathcal{P}$ if and only if it is a success for $\pi(\mathcal{P})$.*

Proof. Let $S = \langle \mathbb{A}; \mathbb{C}; \bar{X} \rangle$ be a data-sufficient state with respect to P. By Theorem 18, S is a success of $\mathcal{P}, \mathcal{C}$ if and only if $\mathcal{P}, \mathcal{C} \vdash \exists(\mathbb{A} \wedge \mathbb{C}) \rightarrow \exists\mathbb{D}$ for some $\mathcal{C}$-satisfiable conjunction $\mathbb{D}$. Since $\mathcal{P}$ and $\mathcal{P}, \mathcal{C}$ have the same least model S is a success of $\mathcal{P}, \mathcal{C}$ if and only if $\mathcal{P}, \mathcal{C} \vdash \exists(\mathbb{A} \wedge \mathbb{C}) \rightarrow \exists_{-\bar{X}}(\mathbb{D})$ for some $\mathcal{C}$-satisfiable conjunction $\mathbb{D}$. Then, by soundness and completeness of the CSLD resolution [28] S is a success of $\mathcal{P}, \mathcal{C}$ if and only if $\pi(S)$ is a success for $\pi(\mathcal{P})$. □

Note that this result does not contradict Di Giusto et al.'s results [18] about the greater expressiveness of multi-headed programs with respect to single-headed programs. Indeed, even though any multi-headed program has the same CLP projection as some single-headed program, the two CHR programs do not have the same set of data-sufficient states.

6. Application to CHR Programs Analysis

In this section, we illustrate how the notion of CLP projection can be used in practice to apply CLP analyzers to CHR.

6.1 Termination of CHR$_1$ Programs using AProVe

Theorem 22 ensures that if the CLP projection of a CHR program $\mathcal{P}$ terminates (with respect to the CLP operational semantics), then $\mathcal{P}$ terminates (with respect to the CHR operational semantics). Hence, in order to prove the termination of a CHR program, it is sufficient to prove the termination of its projection, which can be done using tools such as AProVE [17]. AProVE is a system for automated termination of term rewrite systems (TRS) that also handles several other formalisms such as logic programs (Prolog). It is recognized as one of the most powerful tools for termination of TRSs and Prolog [1].

Bench.	Trans.	Proj.	Bench.	Trans.	Proj.
ackerman	−	+	factorial	+	+
average	+	+	lex*		+
binlog[1]	+	+	modulo	+	+
booland	+	+	oddeven	+	+
boolcard	+	+	power	+	+
convert	−	+	revlist	+	+
derivative*		+	toyama	+	+
diff	+	+	weight	−	+

Table 1. CHR$_1$ termination comparison.

Nonetheless, as pointed out by Example 25 there exist terminating CHR programs that have non-terminating projections. The reason for this dichotomy resides in two possible weaknesses of the projection:

- Information about multiplicity of linear atoms is lost.
- The guard conditions are ignored.

Consequently, the CLP projection cannot be used to prove termination of programs when they rely on the multiplicity of atoms in the store (as illustrated by Example 25) or on the non-entailment of guard conditions (as illustrated by the following example).

Example 34. *Consider the program $\mathcal{P}_{34}$ consisting of the single rule:*

$$\mathtt{f}(0) \Longleftrightarrow \mathtt{f}(Y)$$

Its projection, $\pi(\mathcal{P}_{34})$, is made up of the following rule:

$$\mathtt{f}(0) \leftarrow \mathtt{f}(Y)$$

It is straightforward to verify that any CHR state has only a finite derivation with respect to $\mathcal{P}_{34}$. For instance, the following derivation cannot be extended:

$$\langle \mathtt{f}(0); \top; \emptyset \rangle \xrightarrow{\mathcal{P}_{34}} \langle \mathtt{f}(X_0); \top; \emptyset \rangle \not\xrightarrow{\mathcal{P}_{34}}$$

but unconstrained CLP goals $\langle \mathtt{f}(X_0) \mid \top \rangle$ have an infinite derivation with respect to the projection of $\mathcal{P}_{34}$:

$$\langle \mathtt{f}(X_0) \mid \top \rangle \xrightarrow{\pi(\mathcal{P}_{34})} \cdots \langle \mathtt{f}(X_i) \mid X_0{=}0 \wedge \cdots \wedge X_{i\text{-}1}{=}0 \rangle \xrightarrow{\pi(\mathcal{P}_{34})} \cdots$$

In spite of its weaknesses in treating guarded multi-headed programs – indeed the termination of most of multi-headed programs relies on the multiplicity of atoms in the constraints store – the CLP projection is a powerful notion for tackling the termination analysis of single-headed programs. For instance, Table 1 compares the termination of single-headed programs as inferred by the AProVE system using Pilozzi et al.'s transformation [34] (column **Trans.**) and using the CLP projection (column **Proj.**). In the table, '+' indicates a positive termination inference, while '−' stands for a negative one. All the results in the **Trans.** column are reported as given by Pilozzi et al. [34]. Out of a list of twenty four programs [34], the CLP projection-based approach is able to prove termination of all of the fourteen single-headed programs,[2] but fails on the ten

[1] The problem of proving termination of `booland` is decidable, since this program is single-headed and does not use function symbols [16].

[2] These favorable results suggest that widely-used benchmarks tend not to include programs as the one of Example 34 whose termination relies on non-entailment of guard conditions.

multi-headed programs while Pilozzi et al.'s approach is able to infer termination of nine of them. The table also contains two extra single-head programs (marked with a star $\star$) not presented in [34]: *lex* [15], a lexicographic order constraint solver and *derivative* [19], which calculates the derivative form of a regular expression.

In fact, transforming CHR rules into Prolog clauses has the advantage with respect to the meta-interpreter approach of Pilozzi et al. that user-defined atoms are converted to predicate names, and thus become control points. This allows using techniques that reduce the problem of global termination to several local termination problems [9] for which it is simpler to synthesize a ranking function. For instance, it is not clear what is the global ranking function for the Ackerman program, while the termination of the Prolog program can be proven easily by systems such as AProVE or TerminWeb [9].

It goes without saying that there exist today ad-hoc CHR analyzers that provide better results than Pilozzi et al.'s transformation-based approach. For instance, Pilozzi's CHRisTA system [33] can prove the termination of *convert* and *weight*. Nevertheless, to the best of our knowledge, the CLP projection together with AProVE provides the first automatic termination proof for the CHR implementation of *ackerman*.

6.2 Analysis of CHR_1 Programs using CiaoPP

In this section, we show how the CLP projection can be used to apply the CiaoPP analyzer to infer both types and complexity upper bounds for CHR programs. In the following, we briefly describe the Ciao/CiaoPP system prior to explaining some analysis examples.

6.2.1 The Ciao/CiaoPP System

Ciao [6, 21, 23, 24] is a modern, multiparadigm programming language with an advanced programming environment (CiaoPP). An important aspect of Ciao is that, in addition to supporting logic programming (and, in particular, Prolog), it provides the programmer with a large number of useful features from different programming paradigms and styles, and that the use of each of these features (including those of Prolog) can be turned on and off at will for each program module. Thus, a given module may be using, e.g., higher-order functions and constraints, while another module may be using imperative operations, predicates, Prolog meta-programming builtins, and concurrency. Furthermore, the language is designed to be extensible in a simple and modular way. This is possible thanks to the Ciao module system [7] which allows the definition of language extensions (*packages*) by grouping together syntactic definitions, compilation options, and plugins to the compiler. Packages allow Ciao to support multiple programming paradigms and styles in a single program. The different source-level sub-languages are supported by a compilation process stated by the corresponding package, typically via a set of rules defining *source-to-source* transformations into the kernel language. This kernel language is essentially pure Prolog plus a number of basic, instrumental additional functionalities (such as the cut, non-logical predicates such as `var/1` or `assert/1`, threads, attributed variables, etc.), all of which are in principle not visible to the user but can be used if needed at the kernel level to support higher-level functionality.

Another important aspect of Ciao is its programming environment, which provides a powerful preprocessor, CiaoPP, (with an associated assertion language) capable of statically finding non-trivial bugs, verifying that programs comply with specifications (given as assertions), inferring a wide range of interesting program properties, and performing many types of program optimizations (including automatic parallelization). The environment also includes a powerful auto-documenter and a unit testing framework, both closely integrated with the assertion system. Such assertion system allows the uniform integration of different functionalities (e.g., static verification, run-time checking, unit testing, debugging, and optimization).

Ciao assertions are linguistic constructs which allow expressing properties of programs. Syntactically they appear as an extended set of declarations, and semantically they allow talking about preconditions, (conditional-) postconditions, whole executions, program points, etc. Analysis results are given using also the assertion language, to ensure interoperability and make them understandable by the programmer. In this paper we describe the assertions as they appear in the examples analyzed with CiaoPP, and refer the reader to [6, 36] for a detailed description of the full assertion language.

The CiaoPP analyzers can infer properties on the (values of) variables in the computation of predicates, i.e., *state properties*, as well as global properties of such computations, i.e., *non-functional properties*. In CiaoPP *state properties* can be expressed by predicates. A particular case of *state properties* are *regular types* [10]. Regular types can be defined in libraries, defined by the user, or automatically inferred by the system. Modes and types are inferred using different methods including [30, 31] for modes and [38, 40] for types. Other examples of inferred program properties are independence among program variables [30, 31], or upper and lower bounds on the sizes of data structures. Examples of global (non-functional) computational properties are, non-failure [5], determinacy [29], the absence of side effects, and lower and upper bounds on the computational cost of predicates [11–13], including user-defined resources [32]. Such cost bounds are expressed as functions on the sizes of the input arguments.

Because of the considerations above, we have implemented the CLP projection as a Ciao *package* very easily. This in turn, has made it possible to transparently analyze CHR programs using CiaoPP.

6.2.2 Type Analysis of CHR Programs

In Section 5.3, we have shown that the success set of a confluent program $\mathcal{P}$ can be characterized by the success of the projection of $\mathcal{P}$. Consequently, any safe approximation of properties about the success set of a Prolog program inferred via static analysis is also a safe approximation of the projection of a confluent program. As an illustration, we analyze the CLP projection of some confluent programs using CiaoPP [22].

For instance, consider the following module implementing the *oddeven* program:

```
:- module(oddeven, [oddeven/2], [clp_projection]).

oddeven(0,B) <=> B=even.
oddeven(1,B) <=> B=odd.
oddeven(A,B) <=> A > 2 |
    App is A - 2, oddeven(App,B).
```

In Ciao the first and second arguments of a `module` declaration (first line of the program) hold the module name and list of exports in the standard way. The third argument declares a list of packages to be loaded (`clp_projection` in this case). This package applies the CLP projection transformation so that if the CHR program above is given as input to CiaoPP, CiaoPP sees the CLP projection of that program. The following assertions are part of the output resulting from applying CiaoPP's type analysis to the program above:

```
:- true success oddeven(A,B)
        => ( arithexpression(A), rt5(B) ).
:- regtype rt5/1.
rt5(even).
rt5(odd).
```

The first assertion expresses that on success, the first argument of `oddeven/2` is an arithmetic expression, while the second one is of type `rt5/1` (i.e., is either `even` or `odd`). The prefix `true` in this assertion expresses that it is a safe approximation automatically inferred by the analysis. In fact, it over-approximates the success set of predicate `oddeven/2`.

The *assertion* "`:- regtype rt5/1`" indicates that the `rt5/1` predicate is a regular type. The regular type `arithexpression/1` is defined in a system library and expresses that its argument is an ISO Prolog arithmetic expression [27]. However, the definition of the regular type `rt5/1` has been inferred by CiaoPP's `eterms` type (shape) analyzer, which is based on abstract interpretation and a regular type abstraction with widening [40].

As another example, consider the *weight* module:

```
:- module(weight, [weight/2], [clp_projection]).

 weight([A,B|C], E) <=>
     sumlist([A,B|C],S), weight([S|C],E).
 weight([C], D) <=> D is C.
 sumlist([A|C], S) <=>
     sumlist(C, T), S is A + T.
 sumlist([], S) <=> S is 0.
```

Similarly to the present example, the CiaoPP system infers the following assertions:

```
 :- true success weight(X,Y)
         => ( rt1(X), num(Y) ).
 :- true success sumlist(_1,S)
         => ( list(_1,arithexpression), num(S) ).
 :- regtype rt1/1.
 rt1([A|B]) :-
         arithexpression(A),
         list(B,arithexpression).
```

The parametric (regular) type `list/2` (defined in the system libraries) is used by the type analysis to express the success type automatically inferred for the first argument of `sumlist/2`: a list of arithmetic expressions (`list(_1,arithexpression)`, where the previously commented regular type `arithexpression/1` is used as a value of the type parameter). The regular type `rt1/1` is also automatically inferred by the analysis and represents a non-empty list of arithmetic expressions. The (regular) type `num` refers to the ISO numbers (i.e., floating point or integer numbers).

CiaoPP is also able to analyze confluent multi-headed programs. For instance, consider the following rules, forming part of an arc consistent finite domain solver (see section 8.2.3 in Früwirth's book [15]).

```
inconsistency @ X in A:B <=> A > B | false.
intersection  @ X in A:B, X in C:D <=>
    X in max(A, C):min(B, D).
instantiation @ X in A:A <=> X is A.
```

CiaoPP inferred the expected assertions:

```
:- true pred X in _2
        => ( number(X), rt0(_2) ).

:- regtype rt0/1.
rt0(A:B) :-
        arithexpression(A),
        arithexpression(B).
```

Note that the type analyses we can perform on CLP projections are complementary to the ones we could perform on the Pilozzi et al.'s transformation. Indeed, while the CLP projection preserves the success set, Pilozzi et al's transformation preserves the call set but not the set of successes [34].

6.2.3 Upper Bound Resource Usage Analysis for CHR_1

Theorem 22 ensures that the least upper bound complexity (in number of derivation steps) for a CLP projection provides a safe upper bound for the projected CHR program.Consequently, we can infer complexity upper bounds for a CHR program from its projection. Although this approach is in practice limited to single-headed programs – for the same reason as in Section 6.1 – it provides the first automatic tool for obtaining complexity upper bounds for CHR.

Once again, we can use the CiaoPP system, which is able to infer such bounds for CLP programs [32]. For example, consider the `oddeven` module given in the previous section. To infer interesting bounds, the system needs an `entry` assertion to describe the calls from outside the module.[3]

For instance, the following assertion informs the CiaoPP analyzers that in all external calls to `oddeven/2`, the first argument will be a number and the second one a free variable.

```
:- entry oddeven(X,Y)
        : ( num(X), var(B) ).
```

Once this `entry` assertion has been added to the original program file, and using only the information specified in it, the CiaoPP resource analysis infers the following assertion:

```
:- true pred oddeven(X,Y)
   : ( num(X), var(B) )
  => ( num(X), rt5(Y),
       size_ub(X,int(X)), size_ub(Y,1) )
  + steps_ub(0.25*exp(-1.0,int(X))+0.5*int(X)+0.75).
```

This assertion includes a lot of information: the second line after the colon (`:`) contains the *preconditions*, and states that the condition specified by the `entry` declaration (`num(X), var(B)`) also holds for the recursive calls to `oddeven/2`. The third and fourth lines, after the double arrow (`=>`), show the *postconditions* including the type of the arguments as inferred in the previous subsection together with a size upper bound for the arguments on success (`int(X)` stands for the integer value of `X`). CiaoPP currently uses some predefined metrics for measuring the "size" of an input, such as list length, term size, term depth, or integer value. These are automatically assigned to the predicate arguments involved in the size and cost analysis according to the previously inferred type information. A new, experimental version of the size analyzers is in development that can deal with user-defined size metrics (i.e., predicates) and is also able to synthesize automatically size metrics.

Finally, the field in the fifth line (after the `+`) shows the inferred complexity upper bound (in number of CSLD steps). Thanks to Theorem 24 we know that this upper bound provides a safe upper bound for the longest derivation with respect to the original, which is as precise as it is for the projection.

Similarly, we can analyze the *weight* module and obtain:

```
:- true pred weight(A,B)
   : ( list(A,arithexpression), var(B) )
  => ( rt5(A), num(B),
       size_ub(A,length(A)), size_ub(B,bot) )
  + steps_ub(0.5*exp(length(A),2)+2.5*length(A)-2.0).
:- true pred sumlist(_1,S)
   : ( list(_1,arithexpression), var(S) )
```

[3] Note that in CiaoPP the `pred` assertions of exported predicates can be used optionally instead of `entry`.

```
=> ( list(_1,arithexpression), num(S),
     size_ub(_1,length(_1)), size_ub(S,bot) )
 + steps_ub(length(_1)+1).
```

where `length(A)` stands for the length of the list `A`.

Note that obtaining a finite upper bound on cost also implies proving *termination* of the predicate. This result underlines once again the advantage of the direct translation of CHR_1 programs into CLP with respect to the meta-interpreter approach of Pilozzi. Indeed, we were able to infer a bound for the *weight* program from the CLP projection, while Table 1 illustrates it is already difficult to prove its termination using Pilozzi's translation.

7. Conclusions

We have introduced and studied the notion of CLP projection for Constraint Handling Rules (CHR). We have shown that the CLP projection provides a safe operational and declarative approximation for CHR programs. We have also shown that the least fixpoint of a confluent program is the same that the one of its projection (and in doing so we have made some contributions to the logical foundations of CHR).

We have hopefully demonstrated that the CLP projection is a promising theoretical (and also practical) tool for the study and analysis of CHR programs. The CLP projection provides a good semantic approximation that is complementary to previous work. In particular, existing analyzers are good for the analysis of termination properties when the latter rely on multiplicity of atoms in the store. On the other hand the use of the CLP projection for termination proofs appears advantageous when termination does not relies on multiplicity of atoms in the store. Furthermore, our approach provides the first method (to the best of our knowledge) for providing cost bounds for CHR programs.

As future work it seems interesting to explore, within the CLP projection approach, the possibility of adding information about the multiplicity of atoms in store and the propagation history to be able to prove termination of multi-headed programs considered within the theoretical semantic[4] [2].

Acknowledgments

The research leading to these results has received funding from the Madrid Regional Government under the CM project P2009/TIC/1465 (PROMETIDOS), the Spanish Ministry of Science under the MEC project TIN-2008-05624 (DOVES), and the E.U. Seventh Framework Programme FP/2007-2013 under grant agreement 215483 (S-CUBE).

References

[1] Annual international termination competition. http://termcomp.uibk.ac.at.

[2] S. Abdennadher. Operational semantics and confluence of Constraint Propagation Rules. In *Proc. of International Conference on Principles and Practice of Constraint Programming (CP)*, volume 1330 of *LNCS*, pages 252–266. Springer, 1997.

[3] S. Abdennadher and T. Frühwirth. On completion of Constraint Handling Rules. In *Proc. of International Conference on Principles and Practice of Constraint Programming (CP)*, volume 1520 of *LNCS*, pages 25–39. Springer, 1998.

[4] S. Abdennadher, T. Frühwirth, and H. Meuss. Confluence and semantics of Constraint Simplification Rules. *Constraints*, 4 (2):133–165, 1999.

[5] F. Bueno, P. López-García, and M. Hermenegildo. Multivariant non-failure analysis via standard abstract interpretation. In *Proc. of Symposium on Functional and Logic Programming (FLOPS)*, volume 2998 of *LNCS*, pages 100–116. Springer, 2004.

[6] F. Bueno, D. Cabeza, M. Carro, M. Hermenegildo, P. López-García, and G. Puebla-(Eds.). The Ciao system. ref. manual (v1.13). Technical report, School of Computer Science, T.U. of Madrid (UPM), 2011. Available at http://www.ciaohome.org.

[7] D. Cabeza and M. Hermenegildo. A new module system for Prolog. In *Proc. of International Conference on Computational Logic (CL)*, volume 1861 of *LNAI*, pages 131–148. Springer, July 2000.

[8] K. L. Clark. Negation as failure. In *Logic and Data Bases*. Plenum, 1978.

[9] M. Codish and C. Taboch. A semantic basis for the termination analysis of logic programs. *J. Log. Program.*, 41(1): 103–123, 1999.

[10] P. Dart and J. Zobel. A regular type language for logic programs. In *Types in Logic Programming*, pages 157–187. MIT Press, 1992.

[11] S. K. Debray and N. W. Lin. Cost analysis of logic programs. *ACM Trans. Program. Lang. Syst.*, 15(5):826–875, November 1993.

[12] S. K. Debray, N.-W. Lin, and M. Hermenegildo. Task granularity analysis in logic programs. In *Proc. of Conference on Programming Language Design and Implementation (PLDI)*, pages 174–188. ACM, June 1990.

[13] S. K. Debray, P. López-García, M. Hermenegildo, and N.-W. Lin. Lower bound cost estimation for logic programs. In *Proc. of International Logic Programming Symposium (ILPS)*. MIT Press, 1997.

[14] G. J. Duck. *Compilation of Constraint Handling Rules*. PhD thesis, University of Melburne, 2005.

[15] T. Frühwirth. *Constraint Handling Rules*. Cambridge University Press, 2009.

[16] M. Gabbrielli, J. Mauro, M. C. Meo, and J. Sneyers. Decidability properties for fragments of CHR. *TPLP*, 10(4-6):611–626, 2010.

[17] J. Giesl, P. Schneider-Kamp, and R. Thiemann. AProVE 1.2: Automatic termination proofs in the dependency pair framework. In *Proc. of International Joint Conference on Automated Reasoning (IJCAR)*, volume 4130 of *LNCS*, pages 281–286. Springer, 2006.

[18] C. D. Giusto, M. Gabbrielli, and M. Meo. On the expressive power of multiple heads in CHR. *To appear in ACM Transactions on Computational Logic.*

[19] R. Haemmerlé. (Co)-inductive semantics of Constraint Handling Rules. *To appear in TPLP (ICLP'11 Special Issue)*, 2011.

[20] R. Haemmerlé and F. Fages. Abstract critical pairs and confluence of arbitrary binary relations. In *Proc. of International Conference on Rewriting Techniques and Applications (RTA)*, volume 4533 of *LNCS*, pages 214–228. Springer, 2007.

[21] M. Hermenegildo and The Ciao Development Team. Why Ciao? –an overview of the Ciao system's design philosophy.

[4] This semantics includes a partial control that prevents the trivial looping of propagation rules by restricting their firing only once on same instances.

Technical Report CLIP7/2006.0, School of Computer Science, T.U. of Madrid (UPM), 2006.

[22] M. Hermenegildo, G. Puebla, F. Bueno, and P. López-García. Integrated program debugging, verification, and optimization using abstract interpretation (and the Ciao system preprocessor). *Science of Computer Programming*, 58(1–2), 2005.

[23] M. Hermenegildo et al. Some methodological issues in the design of CIAO - a generic, parallel, concurrent constraint system. In *Proc. of International Conference on Principles and Practice of Constraint Programming (CP)*, LNCS, pages 123–133. Springer, 1994.

[24] M. Hermenegildo et al. The CIAO multi-dialect compiler and system: An experimentation workbench for future (C)LP systems. In *Parallelism and Implementation of Logic and Constraint Logic Programming*, pages 65–85. Nova Science, 1999.

[25] C. Holzbaur. Metastructures vs. attributed variables in the context of extensible unification. In *Proc. of International Symposium on Programming Language Implementation and Logic Programming (PLIP)*, volume 631 of *LNCS*, pages 260–268. Springer, August 1992.

[26] C. Holzbaur and T. W. Frühwirth. Compiling Constraint Handling Rules into Prolog with attributed variables. In *Proc. of International Conference on Principles and Practice of Declarative Programming (PPDP)*, volume 1702 of *LNCS*, pages 117–133. Springer, 1999.

[27] *Information technology – Programming languages – Prolog – Part 1: General core.* International Organization for Standardiztion, 1995. ISO/IEC 13211-1.

[28] J. Jaffar and J.-L. Lassez. Constraint Logic Programming. In *Proc. of Symposium on Principles of Programming Languages (POPL)*, pages 111–119. ACM, 1987.

[29] P. López-García, F. Bueno, and M. Hermenegildo. Automatic inference of determinacy and mutual exclusion for logic programs using mode and type information. *New Generation Computing*, 28(2):117–206, 2010.

[30] K. Muthukumar and M. Hermenegildo. Combined determination of sharing and freeness of program variables through abstract interpretation. In *Proc. of International Conference on Logic Programming (ICLP)*, pages 49–63. MIT Press, June 1991.

[31] K. Muthukumar and M. Hermenegildo. Compile-time derivation of variable dependency using abstract interpretation. *J. Log. Program.*, 13(2/3):315–347, July 1992.

[32] J. Navas, E. Mera, P. López-García, and M. Hermenegildo. User-definable resource bounds analysis for logic programs. In *Proc. of International Conference on Logic Programming (ICLP)*, volume 4670 of *LNCS*, pages 348–363. Springer, 2007.

[33] P. Pilozzi and D. D. Schreye. Proving termination by invariance relations. In *Proc. of International Conference on Logic Programming (ICLP)*, volume 5649 of *LNCS*, pages 499–503. Springer, 2009.

[34] P. Pilozzi, T. Schrijvers, and D. De Schreye. Proving termination of CHR in Prolog: A transformational approach. In *Proc. of International Workshop on Termination (WST)*, 2007.

[35] P. Pilozzi, T. Schrijvers, and M. Bruynooghe. A transformational approach for proving properties of the CHR constraint store. In *Proc. of International Symposium on Logic Program Synthesis and Transformation (LOPSTR)*, volume 3037 of *LNCS*, pages 22–36. Springer, 2009.

[36] G. Puebla, F. Bueno, and M. Hermenegildo. An assertion language for constraint logic programs. In *Analysis and Visualization Tools for Constraint Programming*, volume 1870 of *LNCS*, pages 23–61. Springer, 2000.

[37] F. Raiser, H. Betz, and T. Frühwirth. Equivalence of CHR states revisited. In *Proc. of Workshop on Constraint Handling Rules (CHR)*, Report CW 555, pages 34–48. Kath. Univ. Leuven, 2009.

[38] H. Saglam and J. Gallagher. Approximating constraint logic programs using polymorphic types and regular descriptions. Technical Report CSTR-95-17, Dep. of Computer Science, U. of Bristol, Bristol BS8 1TR, 1995.

[39] T. Schrijvers and B. Demoen. The K. U. Leuven CHR system: Implementation and application. In *Proc. of Workshop on Constraint Handling Rules (CHR)*, pages 1–5, 2004.

[40] C. Vaucheret and F. Bueno. More precise yet efficient type inference for logic programs. In *Proc. of International Static Analysis Symposium (SAS)*, volume 2477 of *LNCS*, pages 102–116. Springer, September 2002.

Typing Control Operators in the CPS Hierarchy

Małgorzata Biernacka
Institute of Computer Science
University of Wrocław
mabi@cs.uni.wroc.pl

Dariusz Biernacki
Institute of Computer Science
University of Wrocław
dabi@cs.uni.wroc.pl

Sergueï Lenglet *
Institute of Computer Science
University of Wrocław
serguei.lenglet@gmail.com

Abstract

The CPS hierarchy of Danvy and Filinski is a hierarchy of continuations that allows for expressing nested control effects characteristic of, e.g., non-deterministic programming or certain instances of normalization by evaluation. In this article, we present a comprehensive study of a typed version of the CPS hierarchy, where the typing discipline generalizes Danvy and Filinski's type system for control operators shift and reset. To this end, we define a typed family of control operators that give access to delimited continuations in the CPS hierarchy and that are slightly more flexible than Danvy and Filinski's family of control operators shift_i and reset_i, but, as we show, are equally expressive. For this type system, we prove subject reduction, soundness with respect to the CPS translation, and termination of evaluation. We also show that our results scale to a type system for even more flexible control operators expressible in the CPS hierarchy.

Categories and Subject Descriptors D.3.3 [*Programming Languages*]: Languages Constructs and Features—Control Structures; F.3.3 [*Logics and Meanings of Programs*]: Studies of Program Constructs

General Terms Languages, Theory

Keywords Delimited Continuation, CPS Hierarchy, Type System

1. Introduction

In the recent years delimited continuations have been recognized as an important concept in the landscape of eager functional programming, with new practical [15, 16, 18, 19], theoretical [1, 2, 4, 13, 20, 24, 27], and implementational [17, 21] advances in the field. Of the numerous control operators for delimited continuations, the so-called static control operators shift and reset introduced by Danvy and Filinski in their seminal work [8] occupy a special position, primarily due to the fact that their definition has been based on the well-known concept of the Continuation-Passing Style (CPS) [23]. As such, shift and reset have solid semantic foundations [5, 8, 10], they are fundamentally related to other computational effects [10, 11] and their use is guided by CPS [5, 8]. A typical application of shift and reset, motivating their definition, are algorithms that non-deterministically generate elements of some collection, based on the success-failure continuation model of backtracking [8].

When iterated, the CPS translation leads to a hierarchy of continuations, generalizing the concept of the continuation and meta-continuation used to define the semantics of shift and reset. In terms of so defined CPS hierarchy, Danvy and Filinski proposed a hierarchy of control operators shift_i and reset_i $(i \geq 1)$ that generalize shift and reset, and that make it possible to separate computational effects that should exist independently in a program [8]. For example, in order to collect the solutions found by a backtracking algorithm implemented with shift_1 and reset_1, one has to employ shift_2 and reset_2, so that there is no interference between searching and emitting the results of the search. The CPS hierarchy was also envisaged to account for nested computations in hierarchical structures. Indeed, as shown by the first two authors and Danvy [5], the hierarchy naturally accounts for normalization by evaluation algorithms for hierarchical languages of units and products, generalizing the problem of computing disjunctive or conjunctive normal forms in propositional logic.

So far, the CPS hierarchy has been studied mainly in the untyped setting. Danvy and Filinski defined it in terms of an untyped CPS translation and a valuation function of a denotational semantics [8], Danvy and Yang introduced an operational semantics for the hierarchy and built an SML implementation of the hierarchy based on this semantics [9], Kameyama presented an axiomatization for the hierarchy that is sound and complete with respect to the CPS translation [14], and Biernacka et al. derived abstract machines and reduction semantics for the hierarchy from the definitional evaluator [5].

A byproduct of Danvy and Yang's implementation in ML is a rather restrictive type system for the hierarchy, where at each level, the answer type of the continuation is fixed once and for all. This type system generalizes Filinski's type system for shift and reset [10], but it has not been investigated on a formal ground. Formal type systems for the hierarchy appear in Murthy's [22] and in Shan's [25] work. Murthy proposes a more relaxed typing discipline than that of Danvy and Yang in that it allows the delimited continuations of level i to have varying answer types, provided the answer type agrees with the type expected by the continuation at level $i + 1$. Shan's type system, in turn, generalizes Danvy and Filinski's type system [7] which is the most expressive monomorphic type system for shift and reset. In Danvy and Filinski's type system, control effects can modify the answer type of the context (i.e., a first-order representation of the continuation) in which they occur, so statically, the answer type of the continuation at level i can be different from the argument type of the continuation at level $i+1$. Shan's work is driven by applications in linguistic theory and the hierarchy he considers is organized differently from the original CPS hierarchy of Danvy and Filinski (level 0 in his hierarchy is the highest whereas it is the lowest in the original hierarchy). Fur-

* The author is supported by the Alan Bensoussan Fellowship program.

PDPP'11, July 20–22, 2011, Odense, Denmark.

thermore, no metatheoretic properties of the presented system are considered in Shan's work.

In this article, we propose a type system which also generalizes Danvy and Filinski's type system but which has been derived directly from the iterated CPS translation that defines the original CPS hierarchy. Furthermore, the control operators we consider are slightly more flexible, although equally expressive, than the original shift$_i$ and reset$_i$ family in that they capture the subsequent continuations to separate continuation variables and allow for throwing to tuples of continuations, where the continuations may come from different captures. Such control operators arise naturally from the structure of CPS if one considers the operations of capturing continuations and throwing to captured continuations independently.

We would like to stress that it is our intention not to limit the type system for control operators in the CPS hierarchy in any way and to offer the programmer the full power of the simply-typed CPS, even though the resulting type system is rather complex. One of the goals of this work is precisely to explain the most naturally typed version of the CPS hierarchy as it is. Moreover, it has already been observed by Shan [25] that the most general types à la Danvy and Filinski are necessary in some practical applications, for instance, to deal with quantifier scope ambiguity in linguistics. Also, there exist examples that require answer type modification at the first level of the hierarchy, for instance, listing list prefixes [5] or the printf function [2], and there are potentially many more that live higher in the hierarchy waiting to be discovered. A typical scenario in which a mismatch between the answer type at level i and the type expected at level $i+1$ may arise involves a rather standard operation when programming in CPS—aborting computation of type α at level i and returning a value of a different type β to level $i+1$.

The overall goal of this article is to establish type-theoretic foundations of the CPS hierarchy and to build a general framework for studying typed control operators definable in the CPS hierarchy. The contributions of this work can be summarized as follows:

- the definition of a new family of control operators in the CPS hierarchy that are slightly more flexible than the shift$_i$ and reset$_i$ family, given in terms of a CPS translation and reduction semantics provably sound with respect to the CPS translation (Sections 3.1 and 3.2);
- a type system à la Danvy and Filinski for the proposed operators, with proofs of subject reduction and soundness of the typing with respect to the CPS translation (Section 3.3);
- a proof of termination of evaluation in reduction semantics, using a context-based method of reducibility predicates (Section 3.4);
- a simulation of the presented operators with the original family of shift$_i$ and reset$_i$ (Section 3.5);
- a generalization of the presented results to a hierarchy of even more flexible control operators expressible in the CPS hierarchy (Section 4).

2. A Programming Example

Before proceeding to the proper part of the present article, let us briefly discuss a representative example of programming in the CPS hierarchy. A typical application of the CPS hierarchy is nondeterministic programming with two layers of continuations (success and failure) on top of which there is some mechanism emitting or collecting the generated objects [8]. In order to separate searching for solutions from collecting them one uses shift$_1$/reset$_1$ for the former and shift$_2$/reset$_2$ for the latter. Here are the definitions of the standard backtracking primitives written in SML, using Danvy and Yang's implementation of the CPS hierarchy [9]:

```
fun fail ()
    = shift_1 (fn k => ())

fun amb c1 c2
    = shift_2 (fn k =>
          (reset_1 (fn () => k (c1 ()));
           reset_1 (fn () => k (c2 ()))))

fun emit v
    = shift2 (fn k => v :: (k ()))

fun collect c
    = reset_2 (fn () =>
          let val () = reset_1 (fn () => emit (c ()))
          in nil end)
```

Given the types of `shift_i` and `reset_i`:

```
shift_i : (('a -> ans_i) -> ans_i) -> 'a
reset_i : (unit -> ans_i) -> ans_i
```

for fixed types `ans_i` for each `i`, if we fix `ans_1` to `unit` and `ans_2` to `int list list` we can, for example, write a program that lists list prefixes as follows:

```
fun prefixes xs
    = let fun walk nil
              = fail ()
            | walk (x :: xs)
              = amb (fn () => x :: nil)
                    (fn () => x :: (walk xs))
      in collect (fn () => walk xs) end
```

The semantics of the control operators shift$_i$/reset$_i$ is given by an iterated CPS translation, where the number of iterations is greater than i [8]. So, in order to see what is going on in the above code, let us CPS transform the backtracking primitives and the function `prefixes` using three layers of continuations (η-reducing them where possible to avoid clutter):

```
fun fail () k1 k2
    = k2 ()

fun amb c1 c2 k1 k2
    = c1 () k1 (fn () => c2 () k1 k2)

fun emit v k1 k2
    = k1 ()
          (fn () => fn k3 =>
                k2 () (fn u => k3 (v :: u)))

fun collect c
    = c ()
         (fn v => emit v (fn u => fn k2 => k2 u))
         (fn () => fn k3  => k3 nil)
         (fn vs => vs)

fun prefixes xs
= let fun walk nil
          = fail ()
        | walk (x :: xs)
          = amb (fn () => fn k1 => k1 (x :: nil))
                (fn () =>
                   fn k1 => walk xs
                              (fn vs => k1 (x :: vs)))
  in collect (fn () => walk xs) end
```

In this model of backtracking the first level serves to generate the current solution, the second level remembers non-deterministic-choice points, and the third level is responsible for storing the generated solutions. Since in the above example there is always at most one choice point, we can write its simpler version, where the second level collects the prefixes and, therefore, the third level is not needed any more [5]:

```
fun prefixes xs
= let fun walk nil k1 k2
          = k2 nil
        | walk (x :: xs) k1 k2
          = k1 (x :: nil)
               (fn vs =>
                 walk xs (fn vs => k1 (x :: vs))
                         (fn vss => k2 (vs :: vss)))
  in walk xs (fn vs => fn k2 => k2 vs)
             (fn vss => vss) end
```

This simplification has an interesting consequence for the types of the continuations used in this program. We can observe that while the answer type of `k1` is `int list`, the argument type of `k2` is `int list list`. We face here a phenomenon known as answer-type modification [2, 5, 7], i.e., a continuation of answer type `int list` is used through a control effect to construct a value of type `int list list`. A direct-style counterpart of this program is the following familiar function [5]:

```
fun prefixes xs
= let fun walk nil
          = shift_1 (fn k => nil)
        | walk (x::xs)
          = shift_1
              (fn k =>
                 (k (x :: nil)) ::
                 (reset_1 (fn () => k (x :: (walk xs)))))
  in reset_1 (fn () => walk xs) end
```

Due to the answer-type modification, this program type-checks neither in Danvy and Yang's type system [9] nor in Murthy's type system [22]. It requires a type system à la Danvy and Filinski [7, 25], where programs have types derived from their CPS semantics and where computations can modify the answer type of continuations. The rest of this article is devoted to such a type system.

3. Flexible Control Operators

In this section, we present a hierarchy of flexible delimited-control operators and we define a type system for it. We then show that it enjoys the standard correctness properties, such as subject reduction, soundness with respect to the CPS translation, and termination of evaluation. We also discuss the link between these operators and the original hierarchy of control operators due to Danvy and Filinski [8].

3.1 Syntax

The language of terms at an arbitrary level n of the hierarchy extends the usual lambda terms with delimited-control operators *capture* $\mathcal{L}_n$, *reset* $\langle\cdot\rangle_n$, and *throw* $\hookleftarrow_n$, for $n \in \mathcal{N}_+$. At any level n, all operators inherited from lower levels $j < n$ are also available. In the following, we assume we have a set of term variables, ranged over by x, separate from n pairwise disjoint sets of continuation variables, ranged over by $k_1, \ldots, k_n$. The syntax of terms at level n is defined as follows (where $1 \leq i \leq n$):

$$\begin{array}{rcl} t & ::= & x \mid \lambda x.t \mid t\,t \mid \mathcal{L}_i(k_1,\ldots,k_i).t \mid \langle t\rangle_i \mid \\ & & (h_1,\ldots,h_i) \hookleftarrow_i t \\ h_i & ::= & k_i \mid \ulcorner E_i \urcorner \\ v & ::= & \lambda x.t \end{array}$$

and the syntax of (call-by-value) evaluation contexts is given by (where $2 \leq i \leq n+1$):

$$\begin{array}{rcl} E_1 & ::= & \bullet_1 \mid v\,E_1 \mid E_1\,t \mid (\ulcorner E_1 \urcorner,\ldots,\ulcorner E_i \urcorner) \hookleftarrow_i E_1 \\ E_i & ::= & \bullet_i \mid E_i.E_{i-1} \end{array}$$

$\mathcal{L}_i(k_1,\ldots,k_i).t$ are capture operators, each $\langle\cdot\rangle_i$ delimits the scope of the corresponding capture operator, and the throw constructs $(h_1,\ldots,h_i) \hookleftarrow_i t$ (similar to that of SML/NJ [12]) are used for applying a tuple of continuation variables or evaluation contexts to a term (or, *throwing* the term to the tuple).

In the original hierarchy of control operators [8], the shift$_i$ construct $\mathcal{S}_i k.t$ binds only one continuation variable instead of a tuple, and continuations are applied as regular functions, without any throw construct. Independently from this work, a throw construct $k \overset{\mathcal{S}}{\hookleftarrow}_i t$ can be introduced to distinguish continuation applications in the original hierarchy for typing purposes, as discussed in [4] (and in Section 3.3). Translating a term written with operators $\mathcal{S}_i$ and $\overset{\mathcal{S}}{\hookleftarrow}_i$ to fit our system amounts to replacing singular variables k by tuples of continuation variables of size i.

In a source program, a term can be thrown only to a tuple of continuation variables $(k_1,\ldots,k_i)$, and the programmer does not handle evaluation contexts explicitly. However, they can be introduced during evaluation, when some of the variables $k_1,\ldots,k_i$ are replaced by contexts captured by an operator $\mathcal{L}_j$. Therefore, we distinguish *plain terms*, i.e., terms that contain only throw constructs of the form $(k_1,\ldots,k_i) \hookleftarrow_i t$.

An abstraction $\lambda x.t$ binds x in t and a capture construct $\mathcal{L}_i(k_1,\ldots,k_i).t$ binds the variables $k_1,\ldots,k_i$ in t. The sets of free term and continuation variables are defined as usual, and we say a term is *closed* if it does not contain any free variables of any kind. A context is closed if and only if all terms occurring in it are closed. We equate terms up to α-conversion of their bound variables.

Contexts E_i can be seen as terms with a hole. We represent contexts inside-out, i.e., $\bullet_1$ represents the empty context of level 1, $v\ E_1$ represents the "term with a hole" $E_1[v\ [\ ]]$, $E_1\ \ t$ represents $E_1[[\ ]\ t]$, and $(\ulcorner E_1 \urcorner,\ldots,\ulcorner E_i \urcorner) \hookleftarrow_i E_1'$ represents $E_1'[(\ulcorner E_1 \urcorner,\ldots,\ulcorner E_i \urcorner) \hookleftarrow_i [\ ]]$. A context of level i for $i = 2,\ldots,n+1$ is a stack of contexts of level $i-1$ separated by a delimiter $\langle\cdot\rangle_{i-1}$. Therefore the empty context $\bullet_i$ of level i stands for the term with a hole $\langle[\ ]\rangle_{i-1}$, and $E_i.E_{i-1}$ represents $E_i[\langle E_{i-1}[\ ]\rangle_{i-1}]$. Formally, the function $plug_i$ ($1 \leq i \leq n+1$) gives the term obtained by putting a term t within a context E_i. We define $plug_1$ as follows:

$$\begin{array}{rcl} plug_1\,(t,\bullet_1) & = & t \\ plug_1\,(t, v\,E_1) & = & plug_1\,(v\,t, E_1) \\ plug_1\,(t_0, E_1\,t_1) & = & plug_1\,(t_0\,t_1, E_1) \\ plug_1\,(t, (\ulcorner E_1 \urcorner,\ldots,\ulcorner E_i \urcorner) \hookleftarrow_i E_1') & = & \\ & & plug_1\,((\ulcorner E_1 \urcorner,\ldots,\ulcorner E_i \urcorner) \hookleftarrow_i t, E_1') \end{array}$$

and for $i = 2,\ldots,n+1$ we define:

$$\begin{array}{rcl} plug_i\,(t,\bullet_i) & = & t \\ plug_i\,(t, E_i.E_{i-1}) & = & plug_i\,(\langle plug_{i-1}\,(t, E_{i-1})\rangle_{i-1}, E_i) \end{array}$$

We write $E_i[t]$ for the term $plug_i\,(t, E_i)$.

We choose the inside-out representation of contexts (rather than the outside-in representation) because inside-out contexts arise naturally as defunctionalized continuations, i.e., they are first-order counterparts of continuations seen as higher-order functions. Consequently, continuations can be obtained by *refunctionalizing* inside-out contexts, as shown in Figure 1.

In the following, we represent terms as *programs* in order to keep the layers of contexts delimited by the reset operators $\langle\cdot\rangle_i$ explicit. Such a representation is useful when writing reduction rules, where we have to decompose a term and locate its redex. It is also well suited for defining reducibility predicates to prove termination of well-typed terms (cf. Section 3.4).

CPS translation of terms

$$
\begin{array}{rcl}
\overline{x} & = & \lambda k_1 \ldots k_{n+1}.k_1\, x\, k_2 \ldots\, k_{n+1} \\
\overline{\lambda x.t} & = & \lambda k_1 \ldots k_{n+1}.k_1\, (\lambda x k'_1 k'_2 \ldots k'_{n+1}.\overline{t}\, k'_1\, k'_2 \ldots k'_{n+1})\, k_2 \ldots k_{n+1} \\
\overline{t_0\, t_1} & = & \lambda k_1 \ldots k_{n+1}.\overline{t_0}\, (\lambda v_0 k'_2 \ldots k'_{n+1}.\overline{t_1}\, (\lambda v_1 k''_2 \ldots k''_{n+1}.v_0\, v_1\, k_1\, k''_2 \ldots k''_{n+1})\, k'_2 \ldots k'_{n+1}) \\
 & & \qquad k_2 \ldots k_{n+1} \\
\overline{\langle t \rangle_i} & = & \lambda k_1 \ldots k_{n+1}.\overline{t}\, \theta_1 \ldots \theta_i (\lambda v_0 k'_{i+2} \ldots k'_{n+1}.k_1\, v_0\, k_2 \ldots k_{i+1}\, k'_{i+2} \ldots k'_{n+1})\, k_{i+2} \ldots k_{n+1} \\
\overline{\mathcal{L}_i(k'_1, \ldots, k'_i).t} & = & \lambda k_1 \ldots k_{n+1}.\overline{t}\{k_1/k'_1, \ldots, k_i/k'_i\}\, \theta_1 \ldots \theta_i\, k_{i+1} \ldots k_{n+1} \\
\overline{(h_1, \ldots, h_i) \hookleftarrow_i t} & = & \lambda k_1 \ldots k_{n+1}.\overline{t}\, (\lambda v_0 k'_2 \ldots k'_{n+1}.[\![h_1]\!]\, v_0\, [\![h_2]\!] \ldots [\![h_i]\!] (\lambda v_1 k''_{i+2} \ldots k''_{n+1}.k_1\, v_1\, k'_2 \ldots k'_{i+1}\, k''_{i+2} \ldots k''_{n+1}) \\
 & & \qquad k'_{i+2} \ldots k'_{n+1})\, k_2 \ldots k_{n+1} \\
\text{where}\quad \theta_i & = & \lambda x k_{i+1} \ldots k_{n+1}.k_{i+1}\, x\, k_{i+2} \ldots\, k_{n+1} \quad \text{for } i = 1, \ldots, n
\end{array}
$$

Refunctionalization of contexts

$$
\begin{array}{rcl}
[\![k_i]\!] & = & k_i \\
 & & \\
[\![\bullet_i]\!] & = & \theta_i \\
[\![E_1\ t]\!] & = & \lambda v_0 k_2 \ldots k_{n+1}.\overline{t}\, (\lambda v_1 k'_2 \ldots k'_{n+1}.v_0\, v_1\, [\![E_1]\!]\, k'_2 \ldots k'_{n+1})\, k_2 \ldots k_{n+1} \\
[\![v_0\ E_1]\!] & = & \lambda v_1 k_2 \ldots k_{n+1}.{v_0}^*\, v_1\, [\![E_1]\!]\, k_2 \ldots k_{n+1} \\
[\![(\ulcorner E_1 \urcorner, \ldots, \ulcorner E_i \urcorner) \hookleftarrow_i E'_1]\!] & = & \lambda v_0 k_2 \ldots k_{n+1}.[\![E_1]\!]\, v_0\, [\![E_2]\!] \ldots [\![E_i]\!]\, (\lambda v_1 k'_{i+2} \ldots k'_{n+1}.[\![E'_1]\!]\, v_1\, k_2 \ldots k_{i+1}\, k'_{i+2} \ldots k'_{n+1}) \\
 & & \qquad k_{i+2} \ldots k_{n+1} \\
[\![E_i.E_{i-1}]\!] & = & \lambda v k_{i+1} \ldots k_{n+1}.[\![E_{i-1}]\!]\, v\, [\![E_i]\!]\, k_{i+1} \ldots k_{n+1} \\
 & & \\
\lambda x.t^* & = & \lambda x.\overline{t}
\end{array}
$$

Figure 1. CPS translation

Formally, a program at level n of the hierarchy is defined as follows:

$$p ::= \langle t, E_1, \ldots, E_{n+1} \rangle.$$

The program $\langle t, E_1, \ldots, E_{n+1} \rangle$ represents the term

$$plug_{n+1}\,(\langle \ldots \langle plug_2\,(\langle plug_1\,(t, E_1) \rangle_1, E_2) \rangle_2 \ldots \rangle_n, E_{n+1}),$$

which can also be written as

$$E_{n+1}[\langle \ldots \langle E_2[\langle E_1[t] \rangle_1] \rangle_2 \ldots \rangle_n].$$

It can be seen from this definition that each term that we represent as a program at level n, will be implicitly enclosed by the reset operators of each level from 1 to n. For example, the term $\lambda x.t$ will be represented as the program $\langle \lambda x.t, \bullet_1, \ldots, \bullet_{n+1} \rangle$ that yields $\langle \ldots \langle \lambda x.t \rangle_1 \ldots \rangle_n$ after plugging. From the operational point of view, such a sequence of delimiters surrounding a term is superfluous, since it is enough to replace them by the reset of the highest level. Therefore we introduce another definition of the *plug* function—one that introduces fewer delimiters—defined on programs, which is shown in Figure 2. The idea is that the new *plug* function when operating on entire programs can detect sequences of empty contexts when it is enough to introduce only one delimiter of the highest level, rather than all of them (this behavior is captured by the last two clauses of *plug*). This definition relies on the fact that the first context E_{i+1} that is not empty has necessarily the form $E_{i+1}.(E_i.(\ldots(E_2.E_1)\ldots))$, as it can only be obtained by pushing a sequence of contexts from level 1 to i onto E_{i+1} (as a result of decomposition or reduction). We will use this definition when reconstructing a term from a program. For technical reasons, also the definitions of $plug_i$ functions will be used in the remainder of the article.

A term (which we consider in its representation as a program) can have many different *decompositions* into the term part and the context part; consequently different programs can represent the same term. For example, for $n = 2$, the program $\langle (\lambda x.t)\ \ v, \bullet_1, E_2.E_1, E_3 \rangle$ can be also decomposed as $\langle \lambda x.t, \bullet_1\ v, E_2.E_1, E_3 \rangle$, or as $\langle \langle (\lambda x.t)\ v \rangle_1, E_1, E_2, E_3 \rangle$. We identify all decompositions of the same term by defining an equivalence relation on programs, as follows:

$$p \sim p' := plug\,(p) = plug\,(p')$$

and considering programs up to this equivalence. Informally, the way to decompose a program is to read the definition of *plug* from right to left. In particular, in order to decompose a term enclosed in a level-i *reset*, we need to push the current i contexts onto the level-$i+1$ context. For example, the term $\langle \langle \langle t \rangle_1\ s \rangle_2, \bullet_1, \bullet_2, \bullet_3 \rangle$ can be decomposed into $\langle \langle t \rangle_1\ s, \bullet_1, \bullet_2, \bullet_3.\bullet_2.\bullet_1 \rangle$ and further into $\langle \langle t \rangle_1, \bullet_1\ s, \bullet_2, \bullet_3.\bullet_2.\bullet_1 \rangle$ and then into $\langle t, \bullet_1, \bullet_2.\bullet_1\ s, \bullet_3.\bullet_2.\bullet_1 \rangle$.

3.2 CPS Translation and Semantics

We first define a CPS translation for our language, and then we derive the reduction semantics from it, using the same approach as Biernacka et al. [5]. The CPS translation, presented in Figure 1, extends the standard call-by-value CPS translation for the lambda calculus, and it uses the function $[\![\cdot]\!]$ which transforms contexts into continuations they represent (leaving continuation variables unchanged).

The CPS translation is defined with respect to a fixed (but arbitrary) level n of the hierarchy. It means that the control constructs may interact with up to n surrounding contexts, and consequently, we introduce $n+1$ layers of continuations in the translation. In the case when a CPS-translated term does not touch some of its outer contexts, it results in the introduction of a number of eta redexes that could be reduced away. However, we prefer to keep them in

$$
\begin{aligned}
plug\ \langle t, v\ E_1, E_2, \ldots, E_{n+1}\rangle &= plug\ \langle v\ t, E_1, E_2, \ldots, E_{n+1}\rangle \\
plug\ \langle t_0, E_1\ t_1, E_2, \ldots, E_{n+1}\rangle &= plug\ \langle t_0\ t_1, E_1, E_2, \ldots, E_{n+1}\rangle \\
plug\ \langle t, (\ulcorner E_1 \urcorner, \ldots, \ulcorner E_i \urcorner) \hookleftarrow_i E'_1, E_2, \ldots, E_{n+1}\rangle &= plug\ \langle (\ulcorner E_1 \urcorner, \ldots, \ulcorner E_i \urcorner) \hookleftarrow_i t, E'_1, E_2, \ldots, E_{n+1}\rangle \\
plug\ \langle t, \bullet_1, \ldots, \bullet_i, E_{i+1}.(E_i.(\ldots(E_2.E_1)\ldots)), E_{i+2}, \ldots, E_{n+1}\rangle &= plug\ \langle \langle t\rangle_i, E_1, \ldots, E_i, E_{i+1}, E_{i+2}, \ldots, E_{n+1}\rangle \\
plug\ \langle t, \bullet_1, \ldots, \bullet_{n+1}\rangle &= \langle t\rangle_n
\end{aligned}
$$

Figure 2. Plug function for programs at level n

$$
\begin{array}{llll}
(\beta_v) & \langle (\lambda x.t)\ v, E_1, \ldots, E_{n+1}\rangle & \rightarrow_{\mathrm{v}} & \langle t\{v/x\}, E_1, \ldots, E_{n+1}\rangle \\
(capture_i) & \langle \mathcal{L}_i(k_1, \ldots, k_i).t, E_1, \ldots, E_{n+1}\rangle & \rightarrow_{\mathrm{v}} & \langle t\{\ulcorner E_1 \urcorner/k_1, \ldots, \ulcorner E_i \urcorner/k_i\}, \bullet_1, \ldots, \bullet_i, E_{i+1}, \ldots, E_{n+1}\rangle \\
(reset_i) & \langle \langle v\rangle_i, E_1, \ldots, E_{n+1}\rangle & \rightarrow_{\mathrm{v}} & \langle v, E_1, \ldots, E_{n+1}\rangle \\
(throw_i) & \langle (\ulcorner E'_1 \urcorner, \ldots, \ulcorner E'_i \urcorner) \hookleftarrow_i v, E_1, \ldots, E_{n+1}\rangle & \rightarrow_{\mathrm{v}} & \langle v, E'_1, \ldots, E'_i, E_{i+1}.(E_i.\ldots(E_2.E_1)\ldots), E_{i+2}, \ldots, E_{n+1}\rangle \\
 & & & \text{for } 1 \le i \le n
\end{array}
$$

Figure 3. Reduction rules

order to be uniform, and to exhibit the relationship with the type system of Section 3.3.

The call-by-value reduction semantics is shown in Figure 3. We write $t\{s/x\}$ for the usual capture-avoiding substitution of s for the variable x in t, and we write $t\{E_1/k_1\}\ldots\{E_i/k_i\}$ for the simultaneous capture-avoiding substitutions of contexts $E_1, \ldots, E_i$ for variables $k_1, \ldots, k_i$ in t. Terms $(\lambda x.t)\ v$ are the standard β-redexes of the call-by-value λ-calculus (the rule (β_v)). The reduction of a term $\mathcal{L}_i(k_1, \ldots, k_i).t$ within contexts $E_1, \ldots, E_{n+1}$ consists in capturing the first i contexts $E_1, \ldots, E_i$ and substituting them for the variables $k_1, \ldots, k_i$ (the rule $(capture_i)$). When a value is thrown to a tuple of contexts $(E'_1, \ldots, E'_i)$ using a level-i throw construct within contexts $E_1, \ldots, E_{n+1}$, then the new contexts $E'_1, \ldots, E'_i$ are reinstated as the current contexts, and the then-current contexts $E_1, \ldots, E_i$ are stacked on the context E_{i+1} (the rule $(throw_i)$). Finally, if a value is surrounded by a reset of any level, then the delimiter is no longer needed and can be removed using the rule $(reset_i)$.

A *redex* is the first component (a term) of the program occurring on the left-hand side of each of the reduction rules above. A *potential redex* is either a proper redex or a stuck term, i.e., a term that neither is a value nor can be further reduced. The type system we propose in Section 3.3 ensures that a well-typed program cannot generate a stuck term in the course of its reduction. Because of the unique-decomposition property of the calculus, the relation $\rightarrow_{\mathrm{v}}$ is deterministic.

We define the evaluation relation as the reflexive and transitive closure of $\rightarrow_{\mathrm{v}}$. The result of the evaluation is a program value of the form $p_v := \langle v, \bullet_1, \ldots, \bullet_{n+1}\rangle$. Hence, a program value is a term value surrounded by the (implicit) reset operators $\langle\cdot\rangle_i$ for $i = 1, \ldots, n$.

PROPOSITION 1 (Unique-decomposition property). *For all programs p, p either is a program value, or it decomposes uniquely into contexts $E_1, \ldots, E_{n+1}$ and a potential redex r such that*

$$p = \langle r, E_1, \ldots, E_{n+1}\rangle.$$

Note that the semantics of the original shift$_i$ can be retrieved by allowing only throws to tuples $E_1, \ldots, E_i$ captured by an operator $\mathcal{L}_i(k_1, \ldots, k_i).t$, i.e., by forbidding throws to tuples built from different captures or to tuples of size i built from a capture of size $j > i$.

Let us illustrate the evaluation with an example. Consider the program $\langle(\mathcal{L}_2(k_1, k_2).(k_1, k_2) \hookleftarrow_2 \langle v\rangle_1)\ (\lambda x.x), \bullet_1, \bullet_2, \bullet_3\rangle$. First, we decompose it and locate the redex:

$$\langle \mathcal{L}_2(k_1, k_2).(k_1, k_2) \hookleftarrow_2 \langle v\rangle_1, \bullet_1\ (\lambda x.x), \bullet_2, \bullet_3\rangle,$$

then we reduce it according to rule $(capture_i)$ and obtain:

$$\langle (\ulcorner \bullet_1\ (\lambda x.x) \urcorner, \ulcorner \bullet_2 \urcorner) \hookleftarrow_2 \langle v\rangle_1, \bullet_1, \bullet_2, \bullet_3\rangle.$$

Again, we decompose and find the next redex:

$$\langle \langle v\rangle_1, (\ulcorner \bullet_1\ (\lambda x.x) \urcorner, \ulcorner \bullet_2 \urcorner) \hookleftarrow_2 \bullet_1, \bullet_2, \bullet_3\rangle.$$

According to rule $(reset_i)$ we reduce it, and decompose again:

$$\langle (\ulcorner \bullet_1\ (\lambda x.x) \urcorner, \ulcorner \bullet_2 \urcorner) \hookleftarrow_2 v, \bullet_1, \bullet_2, \bullet_3\rangle.$$

Finally, we reduce it to

$$\langle v, \bullet_1\ (\lambda x.x), \bullet_2, \bullet_3.\ \bullet_2\ .\bullet_1\rangle$$

according to rule $(throw_i)$, and then we decompose it to find the (β_v)-redex which reduces to:

$$\langle v, \bullet_1, \bullet_2, \bullet_3.\ \bullet_2\ .\bullet_1\rangle.$$

Finally, we decompose it to

$$\langle \langle v\rangle_2, \bullet_1, \bullet_2, \bullet_3\rangle$$

and apply $(reset_i)$ again, which yields the result

$$\langle v, \bullet_1, \bullet_2, \bullet_3\rangle.$$

We can show that reductions in the hierarchy are sound with respect to the CPS translation:

PROPOSITION 2 (Soundness of reduction wrt. CPS). *If $p \rightarrow_{\mathrm{v}} p'$, then $\overline{p} =_{\beta\eta} \overline{p'}$.*

Proposition 2 is proved using a characterization of the CPS-image of a program in terms of its CPS-translated components:

PROPOSITION 3 (Characterization of CPS image). *If $p = \langle t, E_1, \ldots, E_n\rangle$, then*

$$\overline{p} =_{\beta\eta} \lambda k_1 \ldots k_{n+1}.\overline{t}\ [\![E_1]\!] \ldots [\![E_n]\!](\lambda v_0.k_1\ v_0\ k_2 \ldots k_{n+1}).$$

Proposition 3 states that the CPS translation of a program is convertible to the CPS term obtained first, by CPS translating the term component t of the program, then applying it to continuations obtained by refunctionalizing the successive contexts E_i, and finally applying it to a continuation of the highest level that collects all the current continuations k_i (as a refunctionalized stack of lower-level contexts/continuations).

Terms ($1 \le i \le n$):

$$\frac{}{\Gamma, x : S; \Delta \vdash_n x : S \rhd C_2 \ldots \rhd C_{n+1}, C_2, \ldots, C_{n+1}}$$

$$\frac{\Gamma, x : S; \Delta \vdash_n t : C'_1, \ldots, C'_{n+1} \qquad C_1 = T \rhd \ldots}{\Gamma; \Delta \vdash_n \lambda x.t : (S \to [C'_1, \ldots, C'_{n+1}]) \rhd C_2 \ldots \rhd C_{n+1}, C_2, \ldots, C_{n+1}}$$

$$\frac{\Gamma; \Delta \vdash_n t_0 : (S \to [C_1, \ldots, C_{n+1}]) \rhd C''_2 \ldots \rhd C''_{n+1}, C'_2, \ldots, C'_{n+1} \qquad \Gamma; \Delta \vdash_n t_1 : S \rhd C_2 \ldots \rhd C_{n+1}, C''_2, \ldots, C''_{n+1}}{\Gamma; \Delta \vdash_n t_0\, t_1 : C_1, C'_2, \ldots, C'_{n+1}}$$

$$\frac{\mathcal{I}_1(D_1) \qquad \ldots \qquad \mathcal{I}_i(D_i) \qquad \Gamma; \Delta \vdash_n t : D_1, \ldots, D_i, (S \rhd C_{i+2} \ldots \rhd C_{n+1}), C'_{i+2}, \ldots, C'_{n+1}}{\Gamma; \Delta \vdash_n \langle t \rangle_i : S \rhd C_2 \ldots \rhd C_{n+1}, C_2, \ldots, C_{i+1}, C'_{i+2}, \ldots, C'_{n+1}}$$

$$\frac{\mathcal{I}_1(D_1) \qquad \ldots \qquad \mathcal{I}_i(D_i) \qquad \Gamma; \Delta, k_1 : C_1, \ldots, k_i : C_i \vdash_n t : D_1, \ldots, D_i, C_{i+1}, \ldots, C_{n+1}}{\Gamma; \Delta \vdash_n \mathcal{L}_i(k_1, \ldots, k_i).t : C_1, C_2, \ldots, C_{n+1}}$$

$$\frac{\begin{array}{c} C_1 = S \rhd C_2 \ldots \rhd C_{n+1} \qquad C_{i+1} = T \rhd C'_{i+2} \ldots \rhd C'_{n+1} \\ \Gamma; \Delta \vdash_n h_1 : C_1 \qquad \ldots \qquad \Gamma; \Delta \vdash_n h_i : C_i \\ \Gamma; \Delta \vdash_n t : S \rhd C''_2 \rhd \ldots C''_{i+1} \rhd C_{i+2} \rhd \ldots C_{n+1}, D_2, \ldots, D_{n+1} \end{array}}{\Gamma; \Delta \vdash_n (h_1, \ldots, h_i) \hookleftarrow_i t : T \rhd C''_2 \rhd \ldots C''_{i+1} \rhd C'_{i+2} \rhd \ldots C'_{n+1}, D_2, \ldots, D_{n+1}}$$

Contexts and continuation variables:

$$\frac{\mathcal{I}_i(C_i) \qquad 1 \le i \le n+1}{\Gamma; \Delta \vdash_n \bullet_i : C_i} \qquad\qquad \frac{}{\Gamma; \Delta, k_i : C_i \vdash_n k_i : C_i}$$

$$\frac{\Gamma; \Delta \vdash_n E_i : C_i \qquad \Gamma; \Delta \vdash_n E_{i-1} : S \rhd C_i \ldots \rhd C_{n+1} \qquad 2 \le i \le n+1}{\Gamma; \Delta \vdash_n E_i.E_{i-1} : S \rhd C_{i+1} \ldots \rhd C_{n+1}}$$

$$\frac{\Gamma; \Delta \vdash_n E_1 : C_1 \qquad \Gamma; \Delta \vdash_n t_1 : S \rhd C_2 \ldots \rhd C_{n+1}, C''_2, \ldots, C''_{n+1}}{\Gamma; \Delta \vdash_n E_1\, t : (S \to [C_1, \ldots, C_{n+1}]) \rhd C''_2 \ldots \rhd C''_{n+1}}$$

$$\frac{\Gamma; \Delta \vdash_n v : (S \to [C_1, \ldots, C_{n+1}]) \rhd C''_2 \ldots \rhd C''_{n+1}, C''_2, \ldots, C''_{n+1} \qquad \Gamma; \Delta \vdash_n E_1 : C_1}{\Gamma; \Delta \vdash_n v\, E_1 : S \rhd C_2 \ldots \rhd C_{n+1}}$$

$$\frac{\begin{array}{c} C_1 = S \rhd C_2 \ldots \rhd C_{n+1} \qquad C_{i+1} = T \rhd C'_{i+2} \ldots \rhd C'_{n+1} \\ \Gamma; \Delta \vdash_n E_1 : C_1 \qquad \ldots \qquad \Gamma; \Delta \vdash_n E_i : C_i \\ \Gamma; \Delta \vdash_n E_1{}' : T \rhd C''_2 \rhd \ldots C''_{i+1} \rhd C'_{i+2} \rhd \ldots C'_{n+1} \end{array}}{\Gamma; \Delta \vdash_n (\ulcorner E_1 \urcorner, \ldots, \ulcorner E_i \urcorner) \hookleftarrow_i E_1{}' : S \rhd C''_2 \rhd \ldots C''_{i+1} \rhd C_{i+2} \rhd \ldots C_{n+1}}$$

Programs:

$$\frac{\Gamma; \Delta \vdash_n E_{n+1}[\langle \ldots E_1[t] \ldots \rangle_n] : S \rhd C_2 \ldots \rhd C_{n+1}, C_2, \ldots, C_{n+1}}{\Gamma; \Delta \vdash_n \langle t, E_1, \ldots, E_{n+1} \rangle : S}$$

Figure 4. A type system for the level n of the CPS hierarchy

3.3 Type System

We propose a type system for the CPS hierarchy. It is a conservative extension of the type system given by Biernacka and Biernacki for the first level of the hierarchy for shift and reset [4], which is itself a refinement of the classical type system of Danvy and Filinski [7]. The typing rules have been derived from the CPS image of the language (shown in Figure 1). We assume that we have a set of base type variables, ranged over by b. We let S, T range over types for terms, and C_i, D_i range over types for contexts E_i, for all $i = 1, \ldots, n+1$. The syntax of types for terms and contexts is given below, where $1 \le i \le n$:

$$\begin{array}{rcl} S & ::= & b \mid S \to [C_1, \ldots, C_{n+1}] \\ C_{n+1} & ::= & \neg S \\ C_i & ::= & S \rhd C_{i+1} \ldots \rhd C_{n+1} \end{array}$$

As in Danvy and Filinski's system, arrow types contain type annotations $S \to [C_1, \ldots, C_{n+1}]$: a function with such a type can be applied to an argument of type S within contexts of types

$C_1, \ldots, C_{n+1}$. For $n = 1$, the Danvy and Filinski's type $S\ _U \rightarrow_V T$ corresponds to $S \rightarrow [T \rhd U, \neg V]$.

In Danvy and Filinski's original type system, continuations are treated as regular functions; they are applied without any throw operator, and they are typed with regular (annotated) arrow types. As discussed in [4], this approach is too restrictive to type some interesting examples. In particular, it lacks context answer type polymorphism, which can be retrieved by representing captured continuations as contexts, and by using an explicit throw construct. Following this idea, we assign types to contexts C_i that are not function types; a context of type $S \rhd C_{i+1} \ldots \rhd C_{n+1}$ can be plugged with a term of type S, and it can be put within contexts of types $C_{i+1}, \ldots, C_{n+1}$, respectively.

A type environment for term variables Γ is a list of pairs $x : S$, and a type environment for continuation variables Δ is a list of pairs $k_i : C_i$. We derive typing judgments of the form $\Gamma; \Delta \vdash_n t : C_1, \ldots, C_{n+1}$ for terms, and typing judgments of the form $\Gamma; \Delta \vdash_n E_i : C_i$ for contexts. If $\Gamma; \Delta \vdash_n t : C_1, \ldots, C_{n+1}$, then, under the assumptions Γ, Δ, the term t can be plugged into contexts of types $C_1, \ldots, C_{n+1}$. We do not need to mention explicitly the type of the term in the judgment, because we can retrieve it from the type C_1 of the first enclosing context, if needed. If $C_1 = S \rhd C'_2 \ldots \rhd C'_{n+1}$, then t is of type S.

Danvy and Filinski's typing judgment $\Gamma; \Delta \mid T \vdash t : S \mid U$ corresponds to the judgment $\Gamma; \Delta \vdash_1 t : S \rhd T, \neg U$ in our system.

The typing rules are presented in Figure 4. We now briefly explain them and sketch how they were derived from the CPS translation of the language (of Figure 1).

The CPS defining equations are usually of the form $\overline{op(t)} = \lambda k_1 \ldots k_{n+1}.\overline{t}\, k'_1 \ldots k'_{n+1}$ for a given operator op, and we want to generate a typing rule of the form

$$\frac{\Gamma'; \Delta' \vdash_n t : C'_1, \ldots, C'_{n+1}}{\Gamma; \Delta \vdash_n op(t) : C_1, \ldots, C_{n+1}}.$$

To this end, we annotate the CPS equation with the most liberal types, and we then deduce the types $C_1, \ldots, C_{n+1}$ from the types of $k_1, \ldots, k_{n+1}$, and $C'_1, \ldots, C'_{n+1}$ from the types of $k'_1, \ldots, k'_{n+1}$. For example, consider the CPS translation for term variables:

$$\overline{x} = \lambda k_1 \ldots k_{n+1}.k_1\, x\, k_2 \ldots\, k_{n+1}$$

The type of k_1 has to match those of $x, k_2, \ldots, k_{n+1}$ to make the application typable. No other constraints on types can be deduced for this equation, so we can derive the following typing rule for term variables:

$$\frac{}{\Gamma, x : S; \Delta \vdash_n x : S \rhd C_2 \ldots \rhd C_{n+1}, C_2, \ldots, C_{n+1}}$$

Consider now the CPS translation for reset:

$$\overline{\langle t \rangle_i} = \lambda k_1 \ldots k_{n+1}.\overline{t}\, \theta_1 \ldots \theta_i\, k'_{i+1}\, k_{i+2} \ldots k_{n+1}$$

with

$$k'_{i+1} = (\lambda v_0 k'_{i+2} \ldots k'_{n+1}.k_1\, v_0\, k_2 \ldots\, k_{i+1}\, k'_{i+2} \ldots k'_{n+1})$$

Assume that we type k_1 with $S \rhd C_2 \ldots \rhd C_{n+1}$. To be able to type the continuation k'_{i+1} we have to assign types $C_2, \ldots, C_{n+1}$ to continuations $k_2, \ldots, k_{i+1}, k'_{i+2}, \ldots, k'_{n+1}$ and the type S to v_0. Consequently, the continuation k'_{i+1} has type $S \rhd C_{i+2} \ldots \rhd C_{n+1}$. We do not have any constraints on the types of the continuation $k_{i+2}, \ldots, k_{n+1}$. Finally, we have to assign valid types $D_1, \ldots, D_i$ to the initial continuations $\theta_1, \ldots, \theta_i$. Let us recall the definition of the initial continuation:

$$\theta_j = \lambda x k_{j+1} \ldots k_{n+1}.k_{j+1}\, x\, k_{j+2} \ldots\, k_{n+1}.$$

Therefore, a type $D_j = T \rhd D'_{j+1} \ldots \rhd D'_{n+1}$ is valid for θ_j iff $D'_{j+1} = T \rhd D'_{j+2} \ldots \rhd D'_{n+1}$. We check this condition by defining a family of predicates $\mathcal{I}_j$ $(1 \leq j \leq n)$ on context types as follows:

$$\mathcal{I}_j(C_j) := \exists S, C_{j+2}, \ldots, C_{n+1}.$$
$$C_j = S \rhd (S \rhd C_{j+2} \ldots \rhd C_{n+1}) \rhd C_{j+2} \rhd \ldots C_{n+1}$$

and $\mathcal{I}_{n+1}(C_{n+1}) = True$. We now have enough information to write the typing rule for $\langle \cdot \rangle_i$. Similarly, we derive typing rules for the remaining term constructors.

The typing rules for contexts can be derived by inspecting the equations defining the function $[\![\cdot]\!]$. For example, because $[\![\cdot]\!]$ translates $\bullet_i$ into the initial continuation θ_i, the empty context of level i can be typed with any type C_i provided that $\mathcal{I}_i(C_i)$ holds. Note that we use the same typing judgment for continuation variables $\Gamma; \Delta \vdash_n k_i : C_i$ as for contexts; it is just to make the typing rule for throw easier to write.

We point out that the typing rule for the original shift$_i$ $\mathcal{S}_i$, (and for reset$_i$ and throw $\overset{\mathcal{S}}{\hookleftarrow}_i$, respectively) is the same as the rule for $\mathcal{L}_i$ (and for reset$_i$, throw $\hookleftarrow_i$, respectively).

Asai and Kameyama [2] defined a notion of pure term (i.e., a term free from control effects) in the polymorphic type system they designed for the level-1 shift and reset. Using Danvy and Filinski's typing judgment, a typable term t is pure iff we can derive $\Gamma; \Delta \mid T \vdash t : S \mid T$ for any type T. We can generalize this notion to an arbitrary level n of the CPS hierarchy. We see that for $i = n$ the typing rule for reset becomes

$$\frac{\mathcal{I}_1(D_1) \quad \ldots \quad \mathcal{I}_n(D_n) \qquad \Gamma; \Delta \vdash_n t : D_1, \ldots, D_n, \neg S}{\Gamma; \Delta \vdash_n \langle t \rangle_i : S \rhd C_2 \ldots \rhd C_{n+1}, C_2, \ldots, C_{n+1}}.$$

We notice that in the conclusion of this rule as well as in the conclusion of the rules for term variable and lambda abstraction, the types $C_2, \ldots, C_{n+1}$ are arbitrary, and the type of the first enclosing context is of the form $S \rhd C_2 \ldots \rhd C_{n+1}$. Therefore, we say that a typable term t is pure iff we can derive $\Gamma; \Delta \vdash_n t : S \rhd C_2 \ldots \rhd C_{n+1}, C_2, \ldots, C_{n+1}$ for any $C_2, \ldots, C_{n+1}$.

We now state the main properties of the type system. First, we prove subject reduction: if a program p is typable and reduces to p', then p' is typable with the same type. To this end, we will need to derive types for t and $E_1, \ldots, E_{n+1}$ from the typing judgment $\Gamma; \Delta \vdash_n \langle t, E_1, \ldots, E_{n+1} \rangle : S$. We will need a few lemmas:

LEMMA 1. *If* $\Gamma; \Delta \vdash_n E_1[t] : D_1, C_2, \ldots, C_{n+1}$ *and* $\mathcal{I}_1(D_1)$ *hold, then* $\Gamma; \Delta \vdash_n E_1[\langle t \rangle_1] : C_1, C_2, \ldots, C_{n+1}$ *and* $\Gamma; \Delta \vdash_n E_1 : C_1$ *hold for some* C_1.

The proof is a straightforward structural induction on E_1.

LEMMA 2. *For* $i = 2, \ldots, n$, *the following properties hold:*

1. *If* $\Gamma; \Delta \vdash_n E_i[\langle t \rangle_{i-1}] : D_1, \ldots, D_i, C_{i+1}, \ldots, C_{n+1}$ *and* $\mathcal{I}_j(D_j)$ *for all* $j = 1, \ldots, j$, *then there exists* C_i *such that* $\Gamma; \Delta \vdash_n E_i : C_i$ *and*
$$\Gamma; \Delta \vdash_n t : D'_1, \ldots, D'_{i-1}, C_i, C_{i+1}, \ldots, C_{n+1}$$
with $\mathcal{I}_l(D'_l)$ *for all* $l = 1, \ldots, i-1$.
2. *If* $\Gamma; \Delta \vdash_n E_i[\langle t \rangle_j] : D_1, \ldots, D_i, C_{i+1}, \ldots, C_{n+1}$, $\mathcal{I}_l(D_l)$ *holds for all* $l = 1, \ldots, i$, *and* $j \geq i$, *then*
$$\Gamma; \Delta \vdash_n t : D'_1, \ldots, D'_j, S \rhd C'_{j+2} \ldots \rhd C'_{n+1}, C_{j+2}, \ldots, C_{n+1}$$
with $\mathcal{I}_l(D'_l)$ *for all* $l = 1, \ldots, j$ *and*
$$\Gamma; \Delta \vdash_n E_i : S \rhd C_{i+1} \rhd \ldots \rhd C_{j+1} \rhd C'_{j+2} \rhd \ldots \rhd C'_{n+1}.$$

The main difficulty in proving subject reduction was to write down and prove Lemma 2 (and its counterpart for reconstruction, Lemma 6). The two properties stated in the lemma are proved simultaneously by induction on i and on E_i.

LEMMA 3. *If*

$$\Gamma; \Delta \vdash_n E_{n+1}[\langle t \rangle_n] : S \rhd C_2 \ldots \rhd C_{n+1}, C_2, \ldots, C_{n+1}$$

and $E_{n+1} = \bullet_{n+1}.E_n^1.\ldots.E_n^m$, *then*

$$\Gamma; \Delta \vdash_n t : D_1, \ldots, D_n, \neg T$$

with $\mathcal{I}_l(D_l)$ *for all* $l = 1, \ldots, n$, $\Gamma; \Delta \vdash_n E_n^1 : T' \rhd \neg S$, *and* $\Gamma; \Delta \vdash_n E_{n+1} : \neg T$.

The proof is a straightforward structural induction on E_{n+1}. With these three lemmas, we can decompose a typed program as follows:

LEMMA 4. *If* $\Gamma; \Delta \vdash_n \langle t, E_1, \ldots, E_{n+1} \rangle : S$ *and* $E_{n+1} = \bullet_{n+1}.E_n^1.\ldots.E_n^m$, *then there exist* $C_1, \ldots, C_{n+1}$ *such that* $\Gamma; \Delta \vdash_n E_i : C_i$ *for all* $i = 1, \ldots, n+1$, *and* $\Gamma; \Delta \vdash_n t : C_1, \ldots, C_{n+1}$. *Furthermore,* $\Gamma; \Delta \vdash_n E_n^1 : T' \rhd \neg S$ *is derivable for some* T'.

We now state auxiliary lemmas needed to perform the reverse operation: from a typed term t and typed contexts $E_1, \ldots, E_{n+1}$, we want to deduce the type of the program $\langle t, E_1, \ldots, E_{n+1} \rangle$.

LEMMA 5. *If* $\Gamma; \Delta \vdash_n t : C_1, \ldots, C_{n+1}$ *and* $\Gamma; \Delta \vdash_n E_1 : C_1$, *then* $\Gamma; \Delta \vdash_n E_1[t] : D_1, C_2, \ldots, C_{n+1}$ *is derivable and* $\mathcal{I}_1(D_1)$ *holds.*

LEMMA 6. *The following properties hold:*

1. *If*

   $$\Gamma; \Delta \vdash_n t : D_1, \ldots, D_{i-1}, C_i, \ldots, C_{n+1},$$

   $\mathcal{I}_l(D_l)$ *hold for all* $l = 1, \ldots, i-1$, *and* $\Gamma; \Delta \vdash_n E_i : C_i$, *then*

   $$\Gamma; \Delta \vdash_n E_i[\langle t \rangle_{i-1}] : D'_1, \ldots, D'_i, C_{i+1}, \ldots, C_{n+1}$$

   and $\mathcal{I}_l(D'_l)$ *hold for all* $l = 1, \ldots, i$.
2. *If*

   $$\Gamma; \Delta \vdash_n t : D_1, \ldots, D_j, C_{j+1}, \ldots, C_{n+1},$$

   $\mathcal{I}_l(D_l)$ *hold for all* $l = 1, \ldots, j$, $C_{j+1} = S \rhd C'_{j+2} \ldots \rhd C'_{n+1}$, *and*

   $$\Gamma; \Delta \vdash_n E_i : S \rhd C_{i+1} \rhd \ldots \rhd C_{j+1} \rhd C'_{j+2} \rhd \ldots \rhd C'_{n+1},$$

   then

   $$\Gamma; \Delta \vdash_n E_i[\langle t \rangle_j] : D'_1, \ldots, D'_i, C_{i+1}, \ldots, C_{n+1}$$

   and $\mathcal{I}_l(D'_l)$ *hold for all* $l = 1, \ldots, i$.

LEMMA 7. *If* $\Gamma; \Delta \vdash_n t : D_1, \ldots, D_n, \neg T$, $\mathcal{I}_l(D_l)$ *hold for all* $l = 1, \ldots, n$, $E_{n+1} = \bullet_{n+1}.E_n^1.\ldots.E_n^m$, $\Gamma; \Delta \vdash_n E_{n+1} : \neg T$, *and* $\Gamma; \Delta \vdash_n E_n^1 : T' \rhd \neg S$, *then*

$$\Gamma; \Delta \vdash_n E_{n+1}[\langle t \rangle_n] : S \rhd C_2 \ldots \rhd C_{n+1}, C_2, \ldots, C_{n+1}.$$

LEMMA 8. *If* $\Gamma; \Delta \vdash_n t : C_1, \ldots, C_{n+1}$, $\Gamma; \Delta \vdash_n E_i : C_i$ *for all* $i = 1, \ldots, n+1$, $E_{n+1} = \bullet_{n+1}.E_n^1.\ldots.E_n^m$, *and* $\Gamma; \Delta \vdash_n E_n^1 : T' \rhd \neg S$, *then* $\Gamma; \Delta \vdash_n \langle t, E_1, \ldots, E_{n+1} \rangle : S$ *is derivable.*

As usual, we need a substitution lemma to deal with the (β_v) and $(capture_i)$ reduction rules.

LEMMA 9 (Substitution lemma). *The following hold:*

1. *If* $\Gamma, x : S; \Delta \vdash_n t : C_1, \ldots, C_{n+1}$ *and* $\Gamma; \Delta \vdash_n v : S \rhd C'_2 \ldots \rhd C'_{n+1}$, *then* $\Gamma; \Delta \vdash_n t\{v/x\} : C_1, \ldots, C_{n+1}$.
2. *If* $\Gamma; \Delta, K : D_1 \rhd \ldots \rhd D_i \vdash_n t : C_1, \ldots, C_{n+1}$ *and* $\Gamma; \Delta \vdash_n E_j : D_j$ *for all* $j \in 1, \ldots, i$, *then* $\Gamma; \Delta \vdash_n t\{(E_1, \ldots, E_i)/K\} : C_1, \ldots, C_{n+1}$.

Using these lemmas, we can prove subject reduction.

THEOREM 1 (Subject reduction). *If* $\Gamma; \Delta \vdash_n p : S$ *and* $p \rightarrow_v p'$ *then* $\Gamma; \Delta \vdash_n p' : S$.

We now state the correctness of the type system with respect to the CPS translation. To this end, we first introduce a translation of the types of terms and contexts into simple types as follows:

$$\begin{aligned}
\overline{b} &= b \\
\overline{S \rightarrow [C_1 \ldots C_{n+1}]} &= \overline{S} \rightarrow \overline{C_1} \rightarrow \ldots \rightarrow \overline{C_{n+1}} \rightarrow o \\
\overline{C_i} &= \overline{S \rhd C_{i+1} \ldots \rhd C_{n+1}} \\
&= \overline{S} \rightarrow \overline{C_{i+1}} \rightarrow \ldots \rightarrow \overline{C_{n+1}} \rightarrow o \\
\overline{C_{n+1}} &= \overline{\neg S} = \overline{S} \rightarrow o
\end{aligned}$$

where o is an abstract answer type.

We also define a translation on typing contexts in the usual way, i.e., $\overline{\Gamma}$ (resp., $\overline{\Delta}$) is obtained from Γ (resp., Δ) by translating all types occurring in Γ (resp., Δ).

PROPOSITION 4 (Soundness of typing wrt. CPS). *The following implications ensure the soundness of the typing of the hierarchy with respect to the CPS translation, where* $\vdash$ *denotes the standard typing judgments deriving simple types for pure lambda terms:*

1. *If* $\Gamma; \Delta \vdash_n t : C_1, \ldots, C_{n+1}$, *then* $\overline{\Gamma}; \overline{\Delta} \vdash \overline{t} : \overline{C_1} \rightarrow \ldots \rightarrow \overline{C_{n+1}} \rightarrow o$.
2. *If* $\Gamma; \Delta \vdash_n E_i : C_i$, *then* $\overline{\Gamma}; \overline{\Delta} \vdash [\![E_i]\!] : \overline{C_i}$, *for all* $i = 1, \ldots, n$.

3.4 Termination of Evaluation

We prove termination for call-by-value evaluation, extending the method used by Biernacka and Biernacki [4] for level-1 shift and reset to the level n of the hierarchy. The proof technique is a context-based variant of Tait's reducibility predicates [26]. For simplicity, we restrict ourselves to closed terms, but the result can be extended to open terms.

We define mutually inductive families of predicates on terms and contexts as shown in Figure 5. The predicate $\mathcal{R}_S$, indexed by term types, is defined on values, and the predicates $\mathcal{K}_{C_i}$, indexed by context types, are defined on evaluation contexts for all $i = 1, \ldots, n+1$. A value of a function type is reducible iff the program obtained by applying this value to a reducible value and put within reducible contexts normalizes (i.e., it evaluates to a program value). In turn, a context E_i of level i is reducible iff the program $\langle v, \bullet_1, \ldots, \bullet_{i-1}, E_i, E_{i+1}, \ldots, E_{n+1} \rangle$ built from any reducible value v and any reducible contexts $E_{i+1}, \ldots, E_{n+1}$ of the appropriate types normalizes. The predicate $\mathcal{N}$ is defined on closed programs: $\mathcal{N}(p)$ holds iff p evaluates to a program value in the call-by-value strategy (the strategy is enforced by the grammar of contexts E_1).

In the following, for any closed value v we write $\vdash v : S$ iff there exist $C_2, \ldots, C_{n+1}$ such that $\cdot; \cdot \vdash_n v : S \rhd C_2 \ldots \rhd C_{n+1}, C_2, \ldots, C_{n+1}$. Because v is pure, we do not care about the specific $C_2, \ldots, C_{n+1}$, as discussed in Section 3.3.

In order to prove termination, we need the following two lemmas.

LEMMA 10. *If* $\mathcal{I}_i(C_i)$, *then* $\mathcal{K}_{C_i}(\bullet_i)$.

LEMMA 11. *Let* t *be a plain term such that* $\Gamma; \Delta \vdash_n t : C_1, \ldots, C_{n+1}$, *where* $\Gamma = x_1 : T_1, \ldots, x_n : T_n$ *and* $\Delta = k_{i_1}^1 : D_{i_1}^1, \ldots, k_{i_m}^m : D_1^m$. *Let* $\vec{v}$ *be closed values such that* $\vdash v_i : T_i$ *and* $\mathcal{R}_{T_i}(v_i)$ *for all* $i = 1, \ldots, n$. *Let* $\vec{E_i}$ *be closed contexts such that* $\cdot; \cdot \vdash_n E_{i_j}^j : D_{i_j}^j$ *and* $\mathcal{K}_{D_{i_j}^j}(E_{i_j}^j)$. *Let* $E'_1, \ldots, E'_{n+1}$

$$
\begin{array}{rcl}
\mathcal{R}_b(v) & := & \mathit{True} \\
\mathcal{R}_{S \to [C_1,\ldots,C_{n+1}]}(v_0) & := & \forall v_1.\, \mathcal{R}_S(v_1) \to \forall E_1.\, \mathcal{K}_{C_1}(E_1) \to \ldots \to \forall E_{n+1}.\, \mathcal{K}_{C_{n+1}}(E_{n+1}) \to \mathcal{N}(\langle v_0\ v_1, E_1, \ldots, E_{n+1}\rangle) \\
\\
\mathcal{K}_{\neg S}(E_{n+1}) & := & \forall v.\, \mathcal{R}_S(v) \to \mathcal{N}(\langle v, \bullet_1, \ldots, \bullet_n, E_{n+1}\rangle) \\
\mathcal{K}_{S \rhd C_{i+1} \ldots \rhd C_{n+1}}(E_i) & := & \forall v.\, \mathcal{R}_S(v) \to \forall E_{i+1}.\, \mathcal{K}_{C_{i+1}}(E_{i+1}) \to \ldots \to \forall E_{n+1}.\, \mathcal{K}_{C_{n+1}}(E_{n+1}) \\
 & & \qquad \to \mathcal{N}(\langle v, \bullet_1, \ldots, \bullet_{i-1}, E_i, E_{i+1}, \ldots, E_{n+1}\rangle) \\
\mathcal{N}(p) & := & \exists v.\, p \to_{\mathrm{v}}^{*} \langle v, \bullet_1, \ldots, \bullet_{n+1}\rangle
\end{array}
$$

Figure 5. Reducibility predicates

be closed contexts such that $\cdot;\cdot \vdash_n E'_i : C_i$ *and* $\mathcal{K}_{C_i}(E'_i)$. *Then* $\mathcal{N}(\langle t\{\vec{v}/\vec{x}, \vec{E_i}/\vec{k_i}\}, E'_1, \ldots, E'_{n+1}\rangle)$ *holds.*

The proof of Lemma 11 is similar to the one of the analogous lemma in [4]; this lemma is used to prove the following result:

THEOREM 2 (Termination of evaluation). *Let* t *be a closed plain term such that* $\cdot;\cdot \vdash_n t : C_1, \ldots, C_{n+1}$, *and* $\mathcal{I}_i(C_i)$ *hold for all* $i = 1, \ldots, n+1$. *Then* $\mathcal{N}(\langle t, \bullet_1, \ldots, \bullet_{n+1}\rangle)$ *holds.*

Theorem 2 is stated for plain terms only, since it is only for such terms that we are able to control the reducibility property of captured contexts occurring in them (here, it can only happen by substituting a reducible context for a continuation variable).

3.5 Expressiveness

In this section, we prove that the hierarchy of operators $\mathcal{L}_i$ and $\hookleftarrow_i$ is as expressive as the hierarchy of the original operators *shift* $\mathcal{S}_i$ and throw $\overset{\mathcal{S}}{\hookleftarrow}_i$ [8]. We also consider an alternative throw operator $\overset{\mathcal{C}}{\hookleftarrow}_i$ and compare it with $\hookleftarrow_i$.

Regular shift and throw operators Because the original hierarchy of shift$_i$ and reset$_i$ operators with the addition of a throw$_i$ operator can be embedded in our hierarchy, the typing rules and the associated results carry over to the original hierarchy.

We now show how to express $\mathcal{L}_i$ and $\hookleftarrow_i$ with the regular shift and throw. We define a translation $(\cdot)^\circ$ which rewrites terms with $\mathcal{L}_i$ and $\hookleftarrow_i$ into terms with $\mathcal{S}_i$ and $\overset{\mathcal{S}}{\hookleftarrow}_i$ in the following way:

$$
\begin{array}{rcl}
x^\circ & = & x \\
(\lambda x.t)^\circ & = & \lambda x.t^\circ \\
(t_0\, t_1)^\circ & = & t_0^\circ\, t_1^\circ \\
\langle t\rangle_i^\circ & = & \langle t^\circ\rangle_i \\
(\mathcal{L}_i(k_1, \ldots, k_i).t)^\circ & = & \mathcal{S}_1 k_1^\circ.\mathcal{S}_2 k_2^\circ.\ldots\mathcal{S}_i k_i^\circ.t^\circ \\
((h_1, \ldots, h_i) \hookleftarrow_i t)^\circ & = & \\
\multicolumn{3}{r}{(\lambda x.\langle h_i^\circ \overset{\mathcal{S}}{\hookleftarrow}_i \ldots \langle h_2^\circ \overset{\mathcal{S}}{\hookleftarrow}_2 \langle h_1^\circ \overset{\mathcal{S}}{\hookleftarrow}_1 x\rangle_1\rangle_2 \ldots\rangle_i)\, t^\circ} \\
E_i^\circ & = & (\bullet_1, \bullet_2, \ldots, \bullet_{i-1}, E_i) \\
k_i^\circ & = & (k_1^i, \ldots, k_i^i)
\end{array}
$$

We assume that the translation of continuation variables k_i° is deterministic (i.e., it generates always the same tuple of variables, written $(k_i^\circ(1), \ldots, k_i^\circ(i))$) and that the translation of two different variables generates disjoint tuples. The idea of the translation is to perform successive shifts, in order to capture tuples of contexts of the form $(\bullet_1, \bullet_2, \ldots, \bullet_{i-1}, E_i)$. In the translation of $\hookleftarrow_i$, the contexts E_i are then restored successively by throwing to these tuples. Note that in the translated terms, we always throw to a tuple of contexts captured by a singular shift, therefore we respect the semantics of $\mathcal{S}_i$.

In order to prove the soundness of the translation with respect to CPS, we define a function $\widehat{\cdot}$, which returns the CPS translation of h_i°.

$$
\begin{array}{rcl}
\widehat{E_i^\circ} & = & [\![E_i]\!] \\
\widehat{k_i^\circ} & = & \lambda x k_{i+1} \ldots k_{n+1}.k_i^\circ(1)\, x\, k_i^\circ(2) \ldots k_i^\circ(i)\, k_{i+1} \ldots k_{n+1}
\end{array}
$$

In the following, we write $t\{(k'_1, \ldots, k'_i)/k_i^\circ\}$ as a shorthand for $t\{k'_1/k_i^\circ(1), \ldots, k'_i/k_i^\circ(i)\}$.

LEMMA 12. *The following equalities hold for all* $1 \leq j \leq i$:

$$
\begin{array}{rcl}
\overline{\mathcal{S}_j k_j^\circ.\ldots\mathcal{S}_i k_i^\circ.t} & =_{\beta\eta} & \lambda k_1 \ldots k_{n+1}. \\
\multicolumn{3}{r}{\overline{t}\{(\theta_1 \ldots \theta_{i-1}, k_i)/k_i^\circ, \ldots, (k_1 \ldots k_j)/k_j^\circ\}} \\
\multicolumn{3}{r}{\theta_1 \ldots \theta_i\, k_{i+1} \ldots k_{n+1}} \\
\overline{\langle h_i^\circ \overset{\mathcal{S}}{\hookleftarrow}_j \ldots \langle h_1^\circ \overset{\mathcal{S}}{\hookleftarrow}_1 x\rangle_1\rangle_j} & =_{\beta\eta} & \lambda k_1 \ldots k_{n+1}.\widehat{h_1^\circ}\, x\, \widehat{h_2^\circ} \ldots \widehat{h_j^\circ} \\
\multicolumn{3}{r}{(\lambda v_0 k'_{j+2} \ldots k'_{n+1}.k_1\, v_0\, k_2 \ldots k_{j+1} k'_{j+2} \ldots k'_{n+1})} \\
\multicolumn{3}{r}{k_{j+2} \ldots k_{n+1}} \\
\widehat{k_i^\circ}\{(\theta_1 \ldots \theta_{i-1}, k'_i)/k_i^\circ\} & =_{\beta\eta} & k'_i
\end{array}
$$

Using this lemma, we can prove the simulation theorem below.

THEOREM 3. *Let* t *be a term (written with* $\mathcal{L}_i$ *and* $\hookleftarrow_i$ *) and let* $k_{i_1}^1, \ldots, k_{i_j}^j$ *be its free continuation variables. Then* $\overline{t^\circ} =_{\beta\eta} \overline{t}\{\widehat{k_{i_1}^{1\,\circ}}/k_{i_1}^1, \ldots, \widehat{k_{i_j}^{j\,\circ}}/k_{i_j}^j\}$.

In particular, for closed terms we have $\overline{t^\circ} =_{\beta\eta} \overline{t}$.

The translation preserves typing judgments, except that we have to take into account the fresh variables generated by the translation of a continuation variable. To this end, we translate the type assignment $(k_1 : C_i)^\circ = k_i^\circ(1) : D_1 \ldots, k_i^\circ(i-1) : D_{i_1}, k_i^\circ(i) : C_i$, where $D_1 \ldots D_{i-1}$ are arbitrary types such that $\mathcal{I}_j(D_j)$ holds for $j \in 1 \ldots i-1$. We then have the following result.

LEMMA 13. *If* $\Gamma; \Delta \vdash_n t : C_1 \ldots C_{n+1}$ *then* $\Gamma; \Delta^\circ \vdash_n t^\circ : C_1 \ldots C_{n+1}$.

An alternative throw operator In some cases we may want to consider an alternative throw operator $\overset{\mathcal{C}}{\hookleftarrow}_i$, which restores saved contexts and discards the current ones without storing them. Formally, its CPS translation is defined as follows:

$$
\begin{array}{l}
\overline{(h_1, \ldots, h_i) \overset{\mathcal{C}}{\hookleftarrow}_i t} = \lambda k_1 \ldots k_{n+1}. \\
\quad \overline{t}\,(\lambda v_0 k'_2 \ldots k'_{n+1}.[\![h_1]\!]\, v_0\, [\![h_2]\!] \ldots [\![h_i]\!]\, k'_{i+1} \ldots k'_{n+1}) \\
\hfill k_2 \ldots k_{n+1}
\end{array}
$$

and the corresponding reduction rule is:

$$
\begin{array}{l}
\langle (E'_1, \ldots, E'_i) \overset{\mathcal{C}}{\hookleftarrow}_i v, E_1, \ldots, E_{n+1}\rangle \to_{\mathrm{v}} \\
\hfill \langle v, E'_1, \ldots, E'_i, E_{i+1}, \ldots, E_{n+1}\rangle
\end{array}
$$

The operators $\overset{\mathcal{C}}{\hookleftarrow}_i$ and $\hookleftarrow_i$ can be defined one in terms of the other as follows:

$$\begin{aligned}(h_1,\ldots,h_i) \overset{\mathcal{C}}{\hookleftarrow}_i t &= (\lambda x.\mathcal{L}_i(k'_1,\ldots,k'_i).(h_1,\ldots,h_i) \hookleftarrow_i x)\, t\\ &\quad \text{where } \{k'_1,\ldots,k'_i\} \cap \{h_1,\ldots,h_i\} = \emptyset\\ (h_1,\ldots,h_i) \hookleftarrow_i t &= (\lambda x.\langle (h_1,\ldots,h_i) \overset{\mathcal{C}}{\hookleftarrow}_i x\rangle_i)\, t\end{aligned}$$

The idea behind the first equality is to capture and destroy the current contexts with $\mathcal{L}_i$; when the throw $\hookleftarrow_i$ is performed, only empty contexts are pushed on the context of level $i+1$. In the second equation, the delimiter $\langle\cdot\rangle_i$ effectively pushes the current contexts up to level i on the context of level $i+1$, and the throw $\overset{\mathcal{C}}{\hookleftarrow}_i$ restores the captured contexts, discarding only the empty contexts $\bullet_1,\ldots,\bullet_i$ in the process. One can check that both equations are sound with respect to the CPS translation.

We can derive a typing rule for $\overset{\mathcal{C}}{\hookleftarrow}_i$ from the type system of Figure 4 using the equation above, or directly from its CPS translation:

$$\frac{\begin{array}{c} C_1 = S \rhd C_2 \ldots \rhd C_{n+1}\\ \Gamma;\Delta \vdash_n h_1 : C_1 \quad \ldots \quad \Gamma;\Delta \vdash_n h_i : C_i\\ D'_1 = S \rhd C'_2 \rhd \ldots C'_i \rhd C_{i+1} \rhd \ldots C_{n+1}\\ \Gamma;\Delta \vdash_n t : D'_1, D_2,\ldots,D_{n+1}\end{array}}{\Gamma;\Delta \vdash_n (h_1,\ldots,h_i) \overset{\mathcal{C}}{\hookleftarrow}_i t : D_1, D_2,\ldots,D_{n+1}}$$

As in the previous case, the properties of subject reduction, soundness w.r.t. the CPS translation, and termination of evaluation hold for the new system, therefore one can use interchangeably the two throw operators.

3.6 Reflecting instead of throwing

As observed in [5], in practical applications it is often more convenient to specify continuation of the computation rather than to throw a value of this computation to the continuation. Such an operation $(h_1,\ldots,h_i) \hookrightarrow_i t$ of installing a tuple of continuations as the current continuations of a given computation can be defined via CPS translation as follows:

$$\begin{aligned}\overline{(h_1,\ldots,h_i) \hookrightarrow_i t} = \lambda k_1 \ldots k_{n+1}.\overline{t}\, [\![h_1]\!] \ldots [\![h_i]\!]\\ (\lambda v k'_{i+2} \ldots k'_{n+1}.k_1\, v\, k_2 \ldots k_{i+1} k'_{i+2} \ldots k'_{n+1})\\ k_{i+2} \ldots k_{n+1}\end{aligned}$$

Following the leads of this section it is then possible to derive the reduction and typing rules for this construct and to prove their expected properties.

4. More Flexible Control Operators

In this section we consider some variants of the operators introduced in Section 3. Instead of capturing and throwing to continuous sequences of contexts starting from 1 ($E_1,\ldots,E_i$), we allow capture and throw to any sequence of contexts $E_{i_1},\ldots,E_{i_j}$, where $1 \le i_1 < i_2 < \ldots < i_j \le n$. The syntax of terms is now defined as follows:

$$\begin{aligned} t \;::=\; & x \mid \lambda x.t \mid t\,t \mid \mathcal{L}^*(k_{i_1},\ldots,k_{i_j}).t \mid \langle t\rangle_i \mid\\ & (h_{i_1},\ldots,h_{i_j}) \overset{*}{\hookleftarrow} t,\end{aligned}$$

the syntax of level-1 contexts is adjusted accordingly:

$$E_1 \;::=\; \bullet_1 \mid v\,E_1 \mid E_1\,t \mid (\ulcorner E_{i_1}\urcorner,\ldots,\ulcorner E_{i_j}\urcorner) \hookleftarrow_i E_1$$

and the remaining syntactic categories are defined as before. The CPS translation, reduction rules, and typing rules for the operators $\mathcal{L}^*$ and $\overset{*}{\hookleftarrow}$ are summarized in Figure 6. Notice that when we consider captures and throws to consecutive sets of variables starting from 1 ($k_1 \ldots k_i$), we obtain the same definitions and rules as in Section 3.

Using the same proof techniques as in the previous section, we can also prove the following results.

THEOREM 4 (Subject reduction). *If* $\Gamma;\Delta \vdash_n p : S$ *and* $p \to_{\mathrm{v}} p'$ *then* $\Gamma;\Delta \vdash_n p' : S$.

PROPOSITION 5 (Soundness of typing wrt. CPS). *The following implications hold:*

1. *If* $\Gamma;\Delta \vdash_n t : C_1,\ldots,C_{n+1}$, *then* $\overline{\Gamma};\overline{\Delta} \vdash \overline{t} : \overline{C_1} \to \ldots \to \overline{C_{n+1}} \to o$.
2. *If* $\Gamma;\Delta \vdash_n E_i : C_i$, *then* $\overline{\Gamma};\overline{\Delta} \vdash [\![E_i]\!] : \overline{C_i}$, *for all* $i = 1,\ldots,n$.

PROPOSITION 6 (Soundness of reduction wrt. CPS). *If* $p \to_{\mathrm{v}} p'$, *then* $\overline{p} =_{\beta\eta} \overline{p'}$.

THEOREM 5 (Termination of evaluation). *Let t be a closed plain term such that* $\cdot;\cdot \vdash_n t : C_1,\ldots,C_{n+1}$ *and* $\mathcal{I}_i(C_i)$ *hold for all* $i = 1,\ldots,n+1$. *Then* $\mathcal{N}(\langle t,\bullet_1,\ldots,\bullet_{n+1}\rangle)$ *holds.*

Expressiveness We first show how to simulate the operators $\mathcal{L}_i$ and $\overset{*}{\hookleftarrow}$ with $\mathcal{S}_i$ and $\overset{\mathcal{S}}{\hookleftarrow}_i$. We use the same translation as in Section 3.5, except that we translate $\overset{*}{\hookleftarrow}$ in the following way:

$$\begin{aligned}&((h_{i_1},\ldots,h_{i_j}) \overset{*}{\hookleftarrow} t)^\circ =\\ &\quad (\lambda x.\langle K_{i_j} \overset{\mathcal{S}}{\hookleftarrow}_{i_j} \ldots \langle K_2 \overset{\mathcal{S}}{\hookleftarrow}_2 \langle K_1 \overset{\mathcal{S}}{\hookleftarrow}_1 x\rangle_1\rangle_2 \ldots\rangle_{i_j})\, t^\circ\end{aligned}$$

with $K_l = h_l^\circ$ if $l \in \{i_1,\ldots,i_j\}$ and $K_l = (\bullet_1,\ldots,\bullet_l)$ otherwise. In the translation, if $l \notin \{h_{i_1},\ldots,h_{i_j}\}$, then we restore the empty context $\bullet_l$ as the current context of level l by throwing to $\bullet_l$ (in fact to the tuple $(\bullet_1,\ldots,\bullet_l)$, but only the last context matters). Otherwise, we throw to h_l°, as in the translation for $\hookleftarrow_i$. Because the translation of $\mathcal{L}_i$ remains unchanged, we still throw to tuples of contexts captured by a singular shift, as required by the semantics of shift. Expressing $\mathcal{L}^*$ with $\mathcal{S}_i$ seems more difficult, because $\mathcal{L}^*$ may capture some contexts and leave the first one unchanged, while $\mathcal{S}_i$ always captures a tuple of contexts, starting from the first one. We conjecture that $\mathcal{L}^*$ cannot be expressed with $\mathcal{S}_i$.

As in Section 3.5, we may consider an alternative throw operator $\overset{\mathcal{C}*}{\hookleftarrow}$, such that $(E_{i_1},\ldots,E_{i_j}) \overset{\mathcal{C}*}{\hookleftarrow} v$ replaces the current contexts at positions $i_1,\ldots,i_j$ by $E_{i_1},\ldots,E_{i_j}$, and leaves the other ones unchanged. We define this operator via its CPS translation:

$$\begin{aligned}&\overline{(h_{i_1},\ldots,h_{i_j}) \overset{\mathcal{C}*}{\hookleftarrow} t} = \lambda k_1 \ldots k_{n+1}.\\ &\quad \overline{t}\,(\lambda v_0 k'_2 \ldots k'_{n+1}.c_1\, v_0\, c_2 \ldots c_{i_j}\, k'_{i_j+1} \ldots k'_{n+1})\\ &\qquad\qquad k_2 \ldots k_{n+1}\end{aligned}$$

where $c_l = [\![h_l]\!]$ if $l \in \{i_1,\ldots,i_j\}$ and $c_l = k_l$ otherwise. The corresponding reduction rule is:

$$\begin{aligned}&\langle (E'_1,\ldots,E'_i) \overset{\mathcal{C}*}{\hookleftarrow} v, E_1,\ldots,E_{n+1}\rangle \to_{\mathrm{v}}\\ &\qquad \langle v, E''_1,\ldots,E''_{i_j}, E_{i_j+1},\ldots,E_{n+1}\rangle\end{aligned}$$

where $E''_l = E'_l$ if $l \in \{i_1,\ldots,i_j\}$ and $E''_l = E_l$ otherwise. We can express $\overset{*}{\hookleftarrow}$ with $\overset{\mathcal{C}*}{\hookleftarrow}$ as follows:

$$(h_{i_1},\ldots,h_{i_j}) \overset{*}{\hookleftarrow} t = (\lambda x.\langle (h_{i_1},\ldots,h_{i_j}) \overset{\mathcal{C}*}{\hookleftarrow} x\rangle_{i_j})\, t$$

Roughly, the delimiter $\langle\cdot\rangle_{i_j}$ pushes the current contexts on E_{i_j+1}, and the captured contexts are then restored with $\overset{\mathcal{C}*}{\hookleftarrow}$. However, simulating $\overset{\mathcal{C}*}{\hookleftarrow}$ with $\overset{*}{\hookleftarrow}$ seems difficult, mainly because

CPS translation

$$\overline{\mathcal{L}^*(k'_{i_1},\ldots,k'_{i_j}).t} = \lambda k_1 \ldots k_{n+1}.\overline{t}\{k'_{i_1}/k_{i_1},\ldots,k'_{i_j}/k_{i_j}\}\, c_1 \ldots c_{i_j}\, k_{i_j+1} \ldots k_{n+1}$$

$$\text{where } c_l = \begin{cases} \theta_l & \text{if } j \in \{i_1,\ldots,i_l\} \\ k_l & \text{otherwise} \end{cases} \quad \text{for all } 1 \le l \le i_j$$

$$\overline{(h_{i_1} \ldots h_{i_j}) \overset{*}{\hookleftarrow} t} = \lambda k_1 \ldots k_{n+1}.\overline{t}\,(\lambda v_0 k'_2 \ldots k'_{n+1}.[\![h_{i_1}]\!]\, v_0\, d_{i_1+1} \ldots d_{i_j}\, (\lambda v_1 k''_{i_j+2} \ldots k''_{n+1}.k_1\, v_1\, k'_2 \ldots k'_{i_j+1}\, k''_{i_j+2} \ldots k''_{n+1})\, k'_{i_j+2} \ldots k'_{n+1})\, k_2 \ldots k_{n+1}$$

$$\text{where } d_l = \begin{cases} [\![h_l]\!] & \text{if } j \in \{i_1,\ldots,i_l\} \\ \theta_l & \text{otherwise} \end{cases} \quad \text{for all } i_1 \le l \le i_j$$

Reduction rules

$$(\mathit{capture}*) \quad \langle \mathcal{L}^*(k_{i_1},\ldots,k_{i_j}).t, E_1,\ldots,E_{n+1}\rangle \to_{\mathrm{v}} \langle t\{E_1/k_{i_1},\ldots,E_{i_j}/k_{i_j}\}, E'_1,\ldots,E'_{i_j}, E_{i_j+1},\ldots,E_{n+1}\rangle$$

$$\text{where } E'_l = \begin{cases} \bullet_l & \text{if } j \in \{i_1,\ldots,i_l\} \\ E_l & \text{otherwise} \end{cases} \quad \text{for all } 1 \le l \le i_j$$

$$(\mathit{throw}*) \quad \langle (E'_{i_1},\ldots,E'_{i_j}) \overset{*}{\hookleftarrow} v, E_1,\ldots,E_{n+1}\rangle \to_{\mathrm{v}} \langle v, E''_1,\ldots,E''_{i_j}, E_{i_j+1}.(E_{i_j}.,\ldots,(E_2.E_1),\ldots,), E_{i_j+2},\ldots,E_{n+1}\rangle$$

$$\text{where } E''_l = \begin{cases} E'_l & \text{if } j \in \{i_1,\ldots,i_l\} \\ \bullet_l & \text{otherwise} \end{cases} \quad \text{for all } i_1 \le l \le i_j$$

Typing rules

$$\frac{\mathcal{I}_l(D_l) \text{ if } l \in \{i_1,\ldots,i_j\} \qquad D_l = C_l \text{ if } l \notin \{i_1,\ldots,i_j\} \qquad \Gamma;\Delta,\, k_{i_1} : C_{i_1} \ldots, k_{i_j} : C_{i_j} \vdash_n t : D_1,\ldots,D_{i_j}, C_{i_j+1} \ldots C_{n+1}}{\Gamma;\Delta \vdash_n \mathcal{L}^*(k_{i_1},\ldots,k_{i_j}).t : C_1, C_2,\ldots,C_{n+1}}$$

$$\frac{\begin{array}{c} C_{i_1} = S \rhd C_{i_1+1} \ldots \rhd C_{n+1} \qquad C_{i_j+1} = T \rhd C'_{i_j+2} \ldots \rhd C'_{n+1} \qquad \mathcal{I}_l(C_l) \text{ if } l \notin \{i_1,\ldots,i_j\} \text{ and } i_1 \le l \le i_j \\ \Gamma;\Delta \vdash_n h_{i_1} : C_{i_1} \quad \ldots \quad \Gamma;\Delta \vdash_n h_{i_j} : C_{i_j} \\ \Gamma;\Delta \vdash_n t : S \rhd C''_2 \rhd \ldots C''_{i+1} \rhd C_{i+2} \rhd \ldots C_{n+1}, D_2,\ldots,D_{n+1} \end{array}}{\Gamma;\Delta \vdash_n (h_{i_1},\ldots,h_{i_j}) \hookleftarrow_i t : T \rhd C''_2 \rhd \ldots C''_{i_j+1} \rhd C'_{i_j+2} \rhd \ldots C'_{n+1}, D_2,\ldots,D_{n+1}}$$

Figure 6. CPS translation, reduction rules, and typing rules for $\mathcal{L}^*$ and $\overset{*}{\hookleftarrow}$

$(E_{i_1},\ldots,E_{i_j}) \overset{\mathcal{C}*}{\hookleftarrow} v$ leaves contexts E_l such that $l \le i_j$ and $l \notin \{i_1,\ldots,i_j\}$ unchanged, while $(E_{i_1},\ldots,E_{i_j}) \overset{*}{\hookleftarrow} v$ replaces them with $\bullet_1$. We conjecture that $\overset{\mathcal{C}*}{\hookleftarrow}$ cannot be expressed with $\overset{*}{\hookleftarrow}$.

5. Conclusion and Perspectives

We have developed the most expressive monomorphic type system for a family of control operators in the CPS hierarchy and for this type system we have proved subject reduction, soundness with respect to CPS, and termination of evaluation. We believe that the present article, as a sequel to the operational foundations of the CPS hierarchy built by the first two authors and Danvy, is another step towards better understanding of the CPS hierarchy, and consequently, that it can inspire new theoretical and practical applications of this beautiful but complex computational structure.

There are several directions for future research related to the present work. First of all, as opposed to the type systems of Danvy and Yang [9] and of Murthy [22] the type system presented in this work allows for computations that modify the answer type of continuations at an arbitrary level of the hierarchy, which should open new possibilities for practical applications that otherwise could only be expressed in an untyped setting.

Building an experimental implementation of the hierarchy with types à la Danvy and Filinski as presented in this article is another task. In particular, one can use the syntactic correspondence between context-based reduction semantics and abstract machines [6] to obtain an abstract machine equivalent with the reduction semantics of this article, or one could adjust the existing abstract machine for the hierarchy [5] accordingly and prove its correctness with respect to the reduction semantics. Devising a type reconstruction algorithm for the hierarchy should not pose any serious problems. A more ambitious goal is to marry the type system from this work with ML-polymorphism, which could be done along the lines presented by Asai and Kameyama [2].

Another improvement would be to allow for level polymorphism. Before typing a program with our system, we have to fix the number of hierarchy levels n, which can be problematic in practice. The whole program has to be typed using the $n + 1$ levels, even if only a few parts are actually using high-level control operators. If we use a library in various programs, each with its own hierarchy level, we have to type the library several times, which goes against modularity. These issues could be fixed by allowing for level polymorphism: from a level n typing judgment, it should be possible to obtain a level $n + 1$ judgment, as in Shan's type system [25].

It would be interesting to formalize the proof of termination of evaluation in the CPS hierarchy in a logical framework such as the Calculus of Inductive Constructions of Coq. As has been shown before [3, 4], normalization proofs by Tait's context-based method yield, through program extraction from proofs, non-trivial evaluators in CPS and the program extraction mechanism of Coq could be helpful for this task.

The present article focuses on the CPS hierarchy under the call-by-value reduction strategy. A natural next step is to see how the type system à la Danvy and Filinski for call-by-name shift and reset introduced by the first two authors [4] generalizes to a call-by-name hierarchy. It would be instructive to relate such a hierarchy to the one recently presented by Saurin [24].

Finally, the still open question of the logical interpretation of delimited continuations through the Curry-Howard isomorphism carries over from *shift* and *reset* to the hierarchy.

Acknowledgments

We thank the anonymous reviewers for thorough comments on the presentation of this article and for excellent suggestions for future work.

References

[1] Z. M. Ariola, H. Herbelin, and A. Sabry. A proof-theoretic foundation of abortive continuations. *Higher-Order and Symbolic Computation*, 20(4):403–429, 2007.

[2] K. Asai and Y. Kameyama. Polymorphic delimited continuations. In *Proceedings of the Fifth Asian symposium on Programming Languages and Systems, APLAS'07*, number 4807 in Lecture Notes in Computer Science, pages 239–254, Singapore, Dec. 2007.

[3] M. Biernacka and D. Biernacki. A context-based approach to proving termination of evaluation. In *Proceedings of the 25th Annual Conference on Mathematical Foundations of Programming Semantics(MFPS XXV)*, Oxford, UK, Apr. 2009.

[4] M. Biernacka and D. Biernacki. Context-based proofs of termination for typed delimited-control operators. In F. J. López-Fraguas, editor, *Proceedings of the 11th ACM-SIGPLAN International Conference on Principles and Practice of Declarative Programming (PPDP'09)*, Coimbra, Portugal, Sept. 2009. ACM Press.

[5] M. Biernacka, D. Biernacki, and O. Danvy. An operational foundation for delimited continuations in the CPS hierarchy. *Logical Methods in Computer Science*, 1(2:5):1–39, Nov. 2005. A preliminary version was presented at the Fourth ACM SIGPLAN Workshop on Continuations (CW'04).

[6] M. Biernacka and O. Danvy. A syntactic correspondence between context-sensitive calculi and abstract machines. *Theoretical Computer Science*, 375(1-3):76–108, 2007.

[7] O. Danvy and A. Filinski. A functional abstraction of typed contexts. DIKU Rapport 89/12, DIKU, Computer Science Department, University of Copenhagen, Copenhagen, Denmark, July 1989.

[8] O. Danvy and A. Filinski. Abstracting control. In M. Wand, editor, *Proceedings of the 1990 ACM Conference on Lisp and Functional Programming*, pages 151–160, Nice, France, June 1990. ACM Press.

[9] O. Danvy and Z. Yang. An operational investigation of the CPS hierarchy. In S. D. Swierstra, editor, *Proceedings of the Eighth European Symposium on Programming*, number 1576 in Lecture Notes in Computer Science, pages 224–242, Amsterdam, The Netherlands, Mar. 1999. Springer-Verlag.

[10] A. Filinski. Representing monads. In H.-J. Boehm, editor, *Proceedings of the Twenty-First Annual ACM Symposium on Principles of Programming Languages*, pages 446–457, Portland, Oregon, Jan. 1994. ACM Press.

[11] A. Filinski. Representing layered monads. In A. Aiken, editor, *Proceedings of the Twenty-Sixth Annual ACM Symposium on Principles of Programming Languages*, pages 175–188, San Antonio, Texas, Jan. 1999. ACM Press.

[12] R. Harper, B. F. Duba, and D. MacQueen. Typing first-class continuations in ML. *Journal of Functional Programming*, 3(4):465–484, Oct. 1993. A preliminary version was presented at the Eighteenth Annual ACM Symposium on Principles of Programming Languages (POPL 1991).

[13] H. Herbelin and S. Ghilezan. An approach to call-by-name delimited continuations. In P. Wadler, editor, *Proceedings of the Thirty-Fifth Annual ACM Symposium on Principles of Programming Languages*, pages 383–394. ACM Press, Jan. 2008.

[14] Y. Kameyama. Axioms for control operators in the CPS hierarchy. *Higher-Order and Symbolic Computation*, 20(4):339–369, 2007. A preliminary version was presented at the Fourth ACM SIGPLAN Workshop on Continuations (CW'04).

[15] Y. Kameyama, O. Kiselyov, and C. Shan. Shifting the stage: Staging with delimited control. In G. Puebla and G. Vidal, editors, *Proceedings of the 2009 ACM SIGPLAN Symposium on Partial Evaluation and Semantics-Based Program Manipulation (PEPM 2009)*, pages 111–120, Savannah, GA, Jan. 2009. ACM Press.

[16] O. Kiselyov. Call-by-name linguistic side effects. In *Proceedings of the 2008 Workshop on Symmetric Calculi and Ludics for the Semantic Interpretation*, Hamburg, Germany, Aug. 2008.

[17] O. Kiselyov. Delimited control in ocaml, abstractly and concretely: System description. In M. Blume and G. Vidal, editors, *Functional and Logic Programming, 10th International Symposium, FLOPS 2010*, number 6009 in Lecture Notes in Computer Science, pages 304–320, Sendai, Japan, Apr. 2010. Springer.

[18] O. Kiselyov and Chung-chieh. Embedded probabilistic programming. In W. Taha, editor, *Domain-Specific Languages, DSL 2009*, number 5658 in Lecture Notes in Computer Science, pages 360–384, Oxford, UK, July 2009. Springer.

[19] O. Kiselyov and C. Shan. Delimited continuations in operating systems. In B. Kokinov, D. C. Richardson, T. R. Roth-Berghofer, and L. Vieu, editors, *Modeling and Using Context, 6th International and Interdisciplinary Conference, CONTEXT 2007*, number 4635 in Lecture Notes in Artificial Intelligence, pages 291–302, Roskilde, Denmark, Aug. 2007. Springer.

[20] O. Kiselyov and C. Shan. A substructural type system for delimited continuations. In S. R. D. Rocca, editor, *Typed Lambda Calculi and Applications, 8th International Conference, TLCA 2007*, number 4583 in Lecture Notes in Computer Science, pages 223–239, Paris, France, June 2007. Springer-Verlag.

[21] M. Masuko and K. Asai. Direct implementation of shift and reset in the MinCaml compiler. In A. Rossberg, editor, *Proceedings of the ACM SIGPLAN Workshop on ML, ML'09*, pages 49–60, Edinburgh, UK, Aug. 2009.

[22] C. R. Murthy. Control operators, hierarchies, and pseudo-classical type systems: A-translation at work. In O. Danvy and C. L. Talcott, editors, *Proceedings of the First ACM SIGPLAN Workshop on Continuations (CW'92)*, Technical report STAN-CS-92-1426, Stanford University, pages 49–72, San Francisco, California, June 1992.

[23] G. D. Plotkin. Call-by-name, call-by-value and the λ-calculus. *Theoretical Computer Science*, 1:125–159, 1975.

[24] A. Saurin. A hierarchy for delimited continuations in call-by-name. In L. Ong, editor, *Foundations of Software Science and Computation Structures, 13th International Conference, FOSSACS 2010*, number 6014 in Lecture Notes in Computer Science, pages 374–388, Paphos, Cyprus, Mar. 2010. Springer-Verlag.

[25] C. Shan. Delimited continuations in natural language: quantification and polarity sensitivity. In H. Thielecke, editor, *Proceedings of the Fourth ACM SIGPLAN Workshop on Continuations (CW'04)*, Technical report CSR-04-1, Department of Computer Science, Queen Mary's College, pages 55–64, Venice, Italy, Jan. 2004.

[26] W. W. Tait. Intensional interpretation of functionals of finite type I. *Journal of Symbolic Logic*, 32:198–212, 1967.

[27] N. Zeilberger. Polarity and the logic of delimited continuations. In J.-P. Jouannaud, editor, *Proceedings of the 25th IEEE Symposium on Logic in Computer Science (LICS 2010)*, pages 219–227, Edinburgh, UK, July 2010. IEEE Computer Society Press.

Dependent Session Types via Intuitionistic Linear Type Theory

Bernardo Toninho
Carnegie Mellon University & Universidade Nova de Lisboa
Pittsburgh, PA, USA
btoninho@cs.cmu.edu

Luís Caires
Universidade Nova de Lisboa
Lisbon, Portugal
luis.caires@di.fct.unl.pt

Frank Pfenning
Carnegie Mellon University
Pittsburgh, PA, USA
fp@cs.cmu.edu

Abstract

We develop an interpretation of linear type theory as dependent session types for a term passing extension of the π-calculus. The type system allows us to express rich constraints on sessions, such as interface contracts and proof-carrying certification, which go beyond existing session type systems, and are here justified on purely logical grounds. We can further refine our interpretation using proof irrelevance to eliminate communication overhead for proofs between trusted parties. Our technical results include type preservation and global progress, which in our setting naturally imply compliance to all properties declared in interface contracts expressed by dependent types.

Categories and Subject Descriptors D.3.1 [*Programming Languages*]: Formal Definitions and Theory; F.3.2 [*Logics and Meaning of Programs*]: Semantics of Programming Languages; F.4.1 [*Mathematical Logic and Formal Languages*]: Mathematical Logic

General Terms Languages, Theory

Keywords type theory, dependent types, session types, π-calculus

1. Introduction

We introduce a theory of dependent session types for distributed processes, based on an interpretation of pure linear type theory for a term passing extension of the π-calculus.

The π-calculus is a foundational model for interacting concurrent processes, building on the key ideas of naming, and name mobility. Name mobility overcame essential limitations of previous models, which were expressive enough to capture value passing concurrent computation, but not dynamic allocation and reference passing, as needed to model, e.g., ML-like programming languages and higher-order processes [26, 30]. As for the λ-calculus, the π-calculus was originally presented as an untyped language. This has opened the opportunity for intensive research on various type disciplines, some based on notions of linearity and sharing, inspired by concepts originating in linear logic [24]. More recently, session types have been introduced as a general typing discipline for name passing processes that structure interactions around the notion of sessions [20, 22].

PDPP'11, July 20–22, 2011, Odense, Denmark.

A session connects, via a private communication channel, exactly two subsystems which interact on it in perfect harmony. Interactions within a session always match precisely: when one side sends, the other receives; when one side offers a selection, the other chooses; when one side terminates, the other quits as well. Such discipline is enforced even when session channels are passed along in communications. New sessions may be dynamically created by calling on capabilities of persistent shared servers. Various forms of session types have proven useful to model realistic concurrent interactions in scenarios ranging from service-oriented computing [11] to operating system kernels [15].

In prior work [10], we have discovered a remarkable correspondence between session types and (intuitionistic) linear logic, which offers the first purely logical account of all the key features (both linear and shared) of session types. In this paper, we extend our basic interpretation to cover processes that communicate data values of an underlying functional language, not just pure sessions, and generalize it by introducing dependent types.

Our framework yields a powerful theory of dependent session types in which types may be used to specify not only the dynamics of protocols, but also properties of data received and sent in communications in the style of interface contracts. For generality, we assume data to be defined by terms of some dependent type theory, such as LF [19]. This way, functional terms may be used to represent not only basic data (such as integers, strings, structures, and higher-order functions) but also, quite importantly, proofs of data properties. Such proof terms may also be exchanged in communications, thus modeling a form of proof-carrying certification (cf. [27]), clearly useful for distributed computing. Our development is based on a purely logical foundation, via an interpretation of a standard sequent calculus proof system for linear logic [4], where base types are drawn from an underlying functional type theory [12].

All types in the logical structure are interpreted as some kind of session behavior. Following [10], multiplicative types $A \multimap B$ and $A \otimes B$, correspond to input and output session types $A?.B$, the type of sessions that receive a session of type A and then behaves as B, and $A!.B$, the type of sessions that send a session of type A and then behaves as B, respectively. The exponential type $!A$ is used to type shared channels, associated with replicated servers. As we will see, a session channel of base type $\$\tau$ just carries a basic value N of the appropriate functional type τ. A dependent type $\forall x{:}\tau.B$ types a session process that inputs a value N of type τ, and then behaves as $B\{N/x\}$. Compatibly, a type $\exists x{:}\tau.B$ types a session process that outputs a value N of type τ, and then behaves as $B\{N/x\}$. As an example, consider the process:

$$\mathsf{Up}(x) \triangleq x(n).x\langle n+1\rangle.\mathbf{0}$$

In a classical session type system, this process is given type x : ?int.!int.end, which in our basic linear session type system is rendered $x : \$\mathsf{int} \multimap (\$\mathsf{int} \otimes \mathbf{1})$. Using dependent types we can provide a much more informative interface contract, such as (among many others):

$$\mathsf{UpInterface}(x) \triangleq x : \forall n{:}\mathsf{int}.\forall p{:}(n > 0).\exists y{:}\mathsf{int}.\exists q{:}(y > 0).\mathbf{0}$$

This type specifies that if the process receives a positive amount (on session x), it will send back a positive amount as well. A sample process inhabiting type $\mathsf{UpInterface}(x)$ is

$$\mathsf{UpCert}(x) \triangleq x(n).x(p).x\langle n+1\rangle.x\langle \mathsf{incp}(n,p)\rangle.\mathbf{0}$$

Here, we have used $\mathsf{incp}(n,p)$ to denote a proof term of type $(n+1>0)$, computed by some function

$$\mathsf{incp} : \Pi m{:}\mathsf{int}.(m > 0) \to (m+1 > 0)$$

given n and p. Clearly, process $\mathsf{UpCert}(x)$ mimics $\mathsf{Up}(x)$ defined above, but also explicitly receives and sends proof certificates for the interface properties, thus witnessing the validity, at the appropriate steps, of all properties expressed by dependent types. For example, $\mathsf{UpCert}(x)$, after outputting m, also issues a proof of $(m > 0)$.

Explicitly manipulating proof certificates may be necessary in a distributed setting, but may also turn out redundant in other scenarios. To address this potential issue, again building on purely logical foundations, we explore proof irrelevance [29]. Proof irrelevance allows us to safely mark parts of a type specification that must be respected at runtime, but need not to be explicitly witnessed in the typed process. Irrelevant components A in a type are marked by a bracketing operator $[A]$. So, instead of type $\mathsf{UpInterface}(x)$ for $\mathsf{UpCert}(x)$, we may instead pick type

$$\mathsf{UpInterfaceP}(x) \triangleq x : \forall n{:}\mathsf{int}.\forall p{:}[n > 0].\exists y{:}\mathsf{int}.\exists q{:}[y > 0].\mathbf{0}$$

Then, by applying to the process $\mathsf{UpCert}(x)$ a type-directed erasure map based on $\mathsf{UpInterfaceP}(x)$, we may prune the behavior associated with irrelevant components of the process type. We then get back to the process

$$\mathsf{Up}(x) \triangleq x(n).x\langle n+1\rangle.\mathbf{0}$$

which can still be shown to conform to the rich interface type $\mathsf{UpInterfaceP}(x)$, in a precise sense, since we know the process passed type-checking with the extra information.

Our technical results show that our logical type system enjoys type preservation under reduction in a rather strong sense, and (global) progress, meaning that well typed processes never get stuck. The standard result of type preservation naturally holds in our system (Theorem 3.3). A stronger result, relating reduction in the process world and cut reduction/conversion steps in the sequent calculus world also holds, but is out of the scope of this particular presentation. The progress property (Theorem 3.5), in our setting, implies not only that all communications prescribed by types will succeed, but also that all "assertions" captured by dependent types hold at the appropriate protocol steps.

The presentation is structured as follows: In Section 2 we discuss our interpretation of linear logic as session types, beginning with a session composition principle that is embodied by a sequent calculus cut. We interpret each of the propositions of intuitionistic linear logic as session behaviors, beginning with the multiplicative fragment, followed by atomic propositions, additives and exponentials and, finally, quantifiers, which correspond to input and output of *proof terms*. Section 3 presents the results of type preservation and progress for our type system. Section 4 describes the usage of proof irrelevance as a form of type-directed runtime optimization of processes and Section 5 concludes.

2. Linear Logic as Session Types

In this section, we present our correspondence of quantified linear logic propositions as session types for a term passing π-calculus by interpreting each linear logic proposition as a type describing the session behavior of a particular channel (a summary of the process calculus definition is given in Section 2.9). The interpretation extends the one given in [10] with a functional layer, based on some dependent type theory, giving meaning to base types, and also crucially, with universal and existential dependent type constructors.

We begin by first defining our typing judgment. We start off with a single typing context Δ which is used according to a linear discipline (it is not subject to weakening or contraction). Later in the paper we add new context regions as necessary to account for the full generality of our system. Our type system assigns types to channels. The context Δ records assignments of the form $x : A$, denoting that a process typed under such an assumption expects to be placed in an environment providing the behavior A along channel x. Our typing judgment is: $\Delta \Rightarrow P :: z : A$, meaning that process P implements, on channel z, the session behavior described by A provided it is composed with a process environment that implements the behaviors specified by Δ (linearity imposes that *all* behaviors specified in Δ are completely used by P). We tacitly assume that all channels declared in Δ and the channel z are distinct. We can apply renaming as necessary to satisfy this condition. We always consider processes modulo structural congruence, therefore typing is closed under structural congruence by definition.

In existing presentations of session types [20] a notion of type duality is commonly present, in which the behavior of the inhabitants of a type is in some sense symmetric to the behavior of the inhabitants of its dual (e.g. the output session is dual to the input session, the choice session is dual to the branch session). In our setting a notion of behavioral duality also arises naturally from the additive and multiplicative nature of linear logic propositions. Multiplicative conjunction $\otimes$ and implication $\multimap$ are dual in the sense that using a session of one type is equivalent to implementing a session of the other. The same applies to additive conjunction and disjunction.

2.1 Cut as composition

A fundamental aspect of process calculi is parallel composition. Parallel composition allows for a process to rely on the functionality of another to implement its own. In our typed setting, this means that given a process P that implements behavior A along some channel x, that is, $\Delta \Rightarrow P :: x : A$, we can take a process Q that uses the behavior of type A (and maybe more) to implement the behavior C on z (formally $\Delta', x : A \Rightarrow Q :: z : C$) and compose the two processes so that the composition provides C along z outright. Since we follow a linear typing discipline, Q requires *all* the behavior supplied by P along x and therefore the composition must restrict the scope of x to the two processes. The cognoscenti will have already identified this reasoning principle as a sequent calculus cut, and we thus obtain the rule:

$$\frac{\Delta \Rightarrow P :: x : A \quad \Delta', x : A \Rightarrow Q :: z : C}{\Delta, \Delta' \Rightarrow (\nu x)(P \mid Q) :: z : C}\ \mathsf{cut}$$

When we compose two processes as in the above rule, we do so in order for them to interact with one another. In general, both P and Q may perform some interaction with the outside environment, but the point of composing them together with a shared local name is so they communicate with each other and evolve together to some residual processes P' and Q'. All of these process reductions (interaction with the "outside world" by P, by Q, and interaction between P and Q) can be given meaning through the reduction of cuts in a proof. We thus take the correspondence of principal cut reductions and process reductions as a guiding principle in our design, just as the correspondence between proof reductions and λ-calculus reductions are the guiding principle for the Curry-Howard isomorphism.

We now build up the system, following and extending [10]. We interpret linear logic propositions as types that characterize behaviors of processes as session-based interactions. The grammar of propositions is given by:

$$\begin{array}{lcl} A, B & ::= & \mathbf{1} \mid \$\tau \mid A \multimap B \mid A \otimes B \mid\ !A \\ & \mid & A \mathbin{\&} B \mid A \oplus B \mid \forall x{:}\tau.B \mid \exists x{:}\tau.B \end{array}$$

2.2 Linear implication

The usual way of reading $A \multimap B$ in linear logic is that, given an A, we consume it and produce a B. Alternatively, we can think of $A \multimap B$ as *receiving* something of type A and producing something of type B. We therefore type a channel z with $A \multimap B$ as:

$$\frac{\Delta, x : A \Rightarrow P :: z{:}B}{\Delta \Rightarrow z(x).P :: z{:}A \multimap B} \multimap\mathsf{R}$$

Given a process that performs an input on z, binding it to x and continuing as P, we can type z with $A \multimap B$ if, under the assumption that x provides a behavior of type A, P will use that behavior to provide B along z. We have defined what it means to type a channel with $A \multimap B$, so we must now define what it means to use such a channel:

$$\frac{\Delta \Rightarrow P :: y : A \quad \Delta', x{:}B \Rightarrow Q :: z{:}C}{\Delta, \Delta', x{:}A \multimap B \Rightarrow (\boldsymbol{\nu} y)x\langle y\rangle.(P \mid Q) :: z{:}C} \multimap\mathsf{L}$$

We use a channel of type $A \multimap B$ to produce behavior C along z by first outputting a fresh name y. Since the contract of $x : A \multimap B$ dictates that x expects to receive a session that is to be used as A, we must ensure that such is indeed the case, which we do by having P provide A along y. Having given x a channel of type A, it will now provide behavior of type B, which can be used by Q to provide C along z. We can see that this interpretation is reasonable by composing an instance of $\multimap$R with an instance of $\multimap$L and appealing to our guiding principle of corresponding process reductions with cut reductions (we omit the full typing contexts for brevity):

$$\frac{\dfrac{y{:}A \Rightarrow P :: x : B}{\Rightarrow x(y).P :: x{:}A \multimap B} \quad \dfrac{\Rightarrow Q_1 :: y{:}A \quad x{:}B \Rightarrow Q_2 :: z{:}C}{x{:}A \multimap B \Rightarrow (\boldsymbol{\nu} y)x\langle y\rangle.(Q_1 \mid Q_2) :: z{:}C}}{\Rightarrow (\boldsymbol{\nu} x)(x(y).P \mid (\boldsymbol{\nu} y)x\langle y\rangle.(Q_1 \mid Q_2)) :: z{:}C}$$

$$\longrightarrow \quad \frac{\dfrac{\Rightarrow Q_1 :: y{:}A \quad y{:}A \Rightarrow P :: x{:}B}{\Rightarrow (\boldsymbol{\nu} y)(Q_1 \mid P) :: x{:}B} \quad x : B \Rightarrow Q_2 :: z{:}C}{\Rightarrow (\boldsymbol{\nu} x)((\boldsymbol{\nu} y)(Q_1 \mid P) \mid Q_2) :: z{:}C}$$

We can isolate the process reduction induced by this cut reduction

$$(\boldsymbol{\nu} x)(x(y).P \mid (\boldsymbol{\nu} y)x\langle y\rangle.(Q_1 \mid Q_2)) \longrightarrow (\boldsymbol{\nu} x)((\boldsymbol{\nu} y)(Q_1 \mid P) \mid Q_2)$$

and observe that, modulo structural congruence, it is the expected interaction between an input process $x(y).P$ and output process $x\langle y\rangle.(Q_1 \mid Q_2)$ along a private channel x.

2.2.1 A simple example

Consider we want to describe a bank service in our system. With what we have presented so far, we can specify what is, for the moment, the protocol of a very simple bank process that receives a string encoding a user's identification and an amount that is to be deposited and just terminates:

$$\mathsf{TBank} \triangleq \$\mathsf{string} \multimap (\$\mathsf{nat} \multimap \mathbf{1})$$

We have not yet introduced base types (such as \$string), but we will get into that shortly. The multiplicative unit $\mathbf{1}$, as we show in the following section, denotes the terminated session. An example of a process providing a session of this type on channel x is:

$$x(s).x(n).\mathbf{0} :: x : \mathsf{TBank}$$

This is not *yet* a particularly interesting example. However, as we interpret more linear logic connectives, we can gradually refine our bank specification to describe richer and more interesting features.

2.3 Multiplicative unit

The multiplicative unit of intuitionistic linear logic, written $\mathbf{1}$, is a proposition that is proved using no resources. Dually, using the unit just consumes it, providing no resources. In a process calculus setting, we interpret $\mathbf{1}$ as the terminated session:

$$\frac{}{\cdot \Rightarrow \mathbf{0} :: z : \mathbf{1}} \mathsf{1R} \qquad \frac{\Delta \Rightarrow P :: z : C}{\Delta, x : \mathbf{1} \Rightarrow P :: z : C} \mathsf{1L}$$

We provide a session of type $\mathbf{1}$ with the terminated process (it uses no further ambient resources) and use it (if such is even the appropriate term) by simply erasing. This is one of the two cases where no process reduction takes place in composition, since the inactive process and the scope restriction are erased through *structural congruence*, not through reduction:

$$\frac{\Rightarrow 0 :: x : \mathbf{1} \quad \dfrac{\Rightarrow P :: z : C}{x : \mathbf{1} \Rightarrow P :: z : C}}{\Rightarrow (\nu x)(\mathbf{0} \mid P) :: z : C} \quad \equiv \quad \Rightarrow P :: z : C$$

Note that in terms of behavior duality, $\mathbf{1}$ is self-dual.

2.4 Multiplicative conjunction

Multiplicative conjunction, written $A \otimes B$, means that we must be able to divide our resources (in our interpretation, the sessions available for interaction in the context) in such a way that we can produce both an A and a B. In fact, the rules for $\otimes$ exhibit a deep symmetry with those for linear implication ($\otimes$ is behaviorally dual to $\multimap$ in the manner explained in the introduction of Section 2). We exploit this symmetry and interpret $\otimes$ on the right as output and as input on the left:

$$\frac{\Delta \Rightarrow P :: y : A \quad \Delta' \Rightarrow Q :: z : B}{\Delta, \Delta' \Rightarrow (\boldsymbol{\nu} y)z\langle y\rangle.(P \mid Q) :: z : A \otimes B} \otimes\mathsf{R}$$

Since we need to able to provide both session behaviors A and B, we output a fresh channel y, through which the process P provides a session of type A. Since we are already communicating along z, we use it to provide a session of type B, which is realized by process Q. We use a session of type $A \otimes B$ as follows:

$$\frac{\Delta, y : A, x : B \Rightarrow P :: z : C}{\Delta, x : A \otimes B \Rightarrow x(y).P :: z : C} \otimes\mathsf{L}$$

We input along x, because the contract of $x : A \otimes B$ enforces that an output of a channel which can be used as a session of type A will take place on x, we bind that channel to y, and we can then safely use x as providing type B to provide C along z. The reduction that supports this interpretation is:

$$\frac{\dfrac{\Rightarrow P_1 :: y{:}A \quad \Rightarrow P_2 :: x{:}B}{\Rightarrow (\boldsymbol{\nu} y)x\langle y\rangle.(P_1 \mid P_2) :: x{:}A \otimes B} \quad \dfrac{y{:}A, x{:}B \Rightarrow P :: z{:}C}{x{:}A \otimes B \Rightarrow x(y).Q :: z{:}C}}{\Rightarrow (\boldsymbol{\nu} x)((\boldsymbol{\nu} y)x\langle y\rangle.(P_1 \mid P_2) \mid x(y).Q) :: z{:}C}$$

$$\longrightarrow \quad \frac{\Rightarrow P_2 :: x{:}B \quad \dfrac{\Rightarrow P_1 :: y{:}A \quad y{:}A, x{:}B \Rightarrow Q :: z{:}C}{x{:}B \Rightarrow (\boldsymbol{\nu} y)(P_1 \mid Q) :: z{:}C}}{\Rightarrow (\boldsymbol{\nu} x)(P_2 \mid (\boldsymbol{\nu} y)(P_1 \mid Q)) :: z{:}C}$$

Again, modulo structural congruence, this is exactly the appropriate process reduction, communicating along the private channel x.

2.4.1 A slightly less simple example

The example of 2.2.1 consists of a bank specification that only allows a client to send its user identification, an amount to be deposited and then terminate. Now that we have available the $\otimes$ type, we can slightly enrich our bank to send back to the client a receipt of the deposited amount:

$$\mathsf{TBank} \triangleq \$\mathsf{string} \multimap (\$\mathsf{nat} \multimap (\$\mathsf{nat} \otimes \mathbf{1}))$$

For which we can produce the process:

$$z(s).z(a).(\nu r)z\langle r\rangle.(P_{\mathsf{receipt}} \mid \mathbf{0}) :: z : \mathsf{TBank}$$

where P_{receipt} is a process that will return an appropriate receipt back to the client. In order to give a precise definition of P_{receipt} we need to develop a way of mentioning basic values such as numbers, which we do in the following section.

Note, however, that this is still a rather simplistic bank process in that it only offers deposit operations (which would not leave its clients very happy), and only runs once. Moreover, this specification only really guarantees that the bank will send back a number. Nothing ensures that it really corresponds to the same value that the client wanted to deposit. In the following sections we develop our system to adress each of these issues, ultimately building up to the a dependent linear type theory of sessions.

2.5 Base types and the identity rule

In the previous section we have shown how to interpret linear implication and conjunction as the types of input and output sessions, respectively. Before proceeding to the remaining linear logic connectives, we will assign meaning to base types and interpret the identity axiom of linear logic. As we have hinted at in the previous example, these turn out to be essential for our development.

A base type $\$\tau$ denotes a proposition that can only be ultimately proved from an ambient assumption of that particular type because it cannot be decomposed further. In this sense, $\$\tau$ is an *atom*. Moreover, linear logic only allows us to prove $\$\tau$ if it is our only remaining resource. In previous work [10], since the focus was on interpreting the composite connectives as pure process behavior, no interpretation was given for atomic types. Here, atomic types connect us to another language layer.

Commonly, we want processes to exchange data, such as numbers and strings (indeed, most work on session types takes this for granted and assumes that processes exchange channels and data values [7, 8, 18, 22]). In our approach processes communicate not just names, but also terms of a *functional* language that assigns meaning to the base types of the full calculus and, as we show in Section 2.8, produces the witnesses for universally and existentially quantified types.

Note that while these terms populate base types, the types need not actually be atomic in the term language. Any extra type structure only has meaning in the term language, while from the perspective of the process calculus they are opaque types with no further decomposable structure. Letters M, N range over the terms of this language and we rely on a separate judgment for well-formedness of such terms, written $\Psi \vdash M : \tau$. Ψ is a context region that is reserved for the term language (we may trivially add the context Ψ to all the sequents in the rules we have seen so far, since these do not affect Ψ). Note that τ itself has meaning in the functional language, while in the process calculus all such types are internalized as $\$\tau$.

We refrain from fully specifying the term language to maintain full generality. We instead assume that the term language is defined by some intuitionistic system of natural deduction with the usual properties of substitution and weakening (we could relax the requirement of weakening by considering a typed linear lambda calculus as the term language such as [12], but we refrain from doing so for simplicity of presentation).

We only require two additional rules to fully account for base types and the corresponding terms of the functional language:

$$\frac{\Psi \vdash M : \tau}{\Psi; \cdot \Rightarrow [z \leftarrow M] :: z : \$\tau}\ \$\mathsf{R}$$

The $\$\mathsf{R}$ rule allows us to use terms from the functional language to give meaning to names at base type. The process construct $[z \leftarrow M]$ locates functional term M at name z (we will introduce the operational semantics for this construct shortly). The final missing piece is a rule that takes names of base type from the linear context and places them in the appropriate Ψ context:

$$\frac{\Psi, x : \tau; \Delta \Rightarrow P :: z : C}{\Psi; \Delta, x : \$\tau \Rightarrow P :: z : C}\ \$\mathsf{L}$$

This rule realizes our design to give meaning to base types in the external functional language: given a channel that provides complex session behavior, we successively play out the session down to its basic constituents (which are the types of the functional term language, the terminated session $\mathbf{1}$ or, as we detail later, persistent sessions), at which point, if we are in the presence of a base type, we move it to the context Ψ where it can be further interpreted as needed.

We can now determine what the behavior of the construct in the $\$\mathsf{R}$ rule should be:

$$\frac{\dfrac{\vdash M : \tau}{\Rightarrow [x \leftarrow M] :: x : \$\tau} \qquad \dfrac{x : \tau; \cdot \Rightarrow P :: z : C}{x : \$\tau \Rightarrow P :: z : C}}{\Rightarrow (\boldsymbol{\nu} x)([x \leftarrow M] \mid P) :: z : C}$$

$$\longrightarrow \Rightarrow P\{M/x\} :: z : C$$

where $P\{M/x\}$ is the substitution of term M for variable x in P. The construct $[x \leftarrow M]$ is reminiscent of the applied π-calculus notion of active substitution [1]. In the applied π-calculus, there is no reduction step like the one above, and the substitution is instead silently performed by a structural congruence principle. Although we might have alternatively interpreted this cut-elimination step by a structural congruence (as we have done for multiplicative unit), we prefer not to do so, without any loss of generality, to maintain a crisper correspondence with the dynamics suggested by the proof theory.

2.5.1 Identity as renaming

We have stated that hypotheses denote the existence of ambient names providing certain behaviors. On the logical side, initial sequents $\Psi; x : A \Rightarrow P :: z : A$ allow us to use an assumption directly to prove the conclusion, a rule absent in [10]. We know that x stands for a name or a term of type A, whatever it may be, and we want to make use of x to provide that same A as z. We thus want to *equate* x and z as the *same*, and that is precisely the behavior that process P must implement. For this we introduce a new process construction, $[x \leftrightarrow z]$, meaning that both names are interchangeable, obtaining the rule:

$$\frac{}{\Psi; x : A \Rightarrow [x \leftrightarrow z] :: z : A}\ \mathsf{id}$$

The proof reductions that we obtain in cut elimination can inform us of what the reductions should be:

$$\frac{y : A \Rightarrow [y \leftrightarrow x] :: x : A \quad x : A \Rightarrow P :: z : C}{y : A \Rightarrow (\boldsymbol{\nu} x)([y \leftrightarrow x] \mid P) :: z : C}$$

$$\longrightarrow y : A \Rightarrow P\{y/x\} :: z : C$$

$$\frac{\Rightarrow P :: x : A \quad x : A \Rightarrow [x \leftrightarrow z] :: z : A}{\Rightarrow (\boldsymbol{\nu} x)(P \mid [x \leftrightarrow z]) :: z : A}$$

$$\longrightarrow \quad \Rightarrow P\{z/x\} :: z : A$$

And so interchangeable names will, operationally, be substituted for each other. We are justified in renaming one to the other in a type-safe way. It is possible to replace this construct at any composite type by a process that acts as an intermediary between the ambient session and the provided one, simply acting as a copycat process, until we reach a base type, at which point the two names are equated to refer to the same functional term. This is the computational content of the meta-theoretic proof of admissibility of the identity rule (or *initial* rule) in a sequent calculus.

The two rules above define the reduction of the renaming construct with the proviso that y and z do not occur in P, respectively. In general, we impose the formation restriction that one of the names appearing in the renaming construct must be bound, while the other one must not occur within the remaining scope of the renaming construct, which is enforced by our typing discipline. By adding a structural congruence, $[y \leftrightarrow x] \equiv [x \leftrightarrow y]$, we can summarize the two rules as one:

$$(\boldsymbol{\nu} x)([y \leftrightarrow x] \mid P) \longrightarrow P\{y/x\}$$

2.6 Additive conjunction and disjunction

We now turn our attention to additive conjunction, written $A \mathbin{\&} B$. Additive conjunction represents alternative availability of resources (we are prepared to provide sessions A and B, but can only provide one of them), where the choice of resource A or B is made by the client of $A \mathbin{\&} B$. We thus type a channel with $A \mathbin{\&} B$ if it *offers* a choice between the two behaviors A and B:

$$\frac{\Psi; \Delta \Rightarrow P :: z : A \quad \Psi; \Delta \Rightarrow Q :: z : B}{\Psi; \Delta \Rightarrow z.\mathsf{case}(P, Q) :: z : A \mathbin{\&} B} \;\&\mathsf{R}$$

The process above branches to provide either A or B. If A is selected, the process P provides the necessary session behavior along z, otherwise, process Q provides the session behavior B along z. We can use a channel of type $A \mathbin{\&} B$ by triggering either one of the possible choices:

$$\frac{\Psi; \Delta, x : A \Rightarrow P :: z : C}{\Psi; \Delta, x : A \mathbin{\&} B \Rightarrow x.\mathsf{inl}; P :: z : C} \;\&\mathsf{L}_1$$

$$\frac{\Psi; \Delta, x : B \Rightarrow P :: z : C}{\Psi; \Delta, x : A \mathbin{\&} B \Rightarrow x.\mathsf{inr}; P :: z : C} \;\&\mathsf{L}_2$$

This form of minimal labeled choice is comparable to the n-ary branching constructs of standard session-oriented π-calculi [22]. The behavioral dual of binary branching is binary choice, which corresponds to additive disjunction:

$$\frac{\Psi; \Delta \Rightarrow P :: z : A}{\Psi; \Delta \Rightarrow z.\mathsf{inl}; P :: z : A \oplus B} \;\oplus\mathsf{R}_1$$

$$\frac{\Psi; \Delta \Rightarrow P :: z : B}{\Psi; \Delta \Rightarrow z.\mathsf{inr}; P :: z : A \oplus B} \;\oplus\mathsf{R}_2$$

This means that in order to use a session of type $A \oplus B$ to offer a session behavior of type C, we must be able to offer C for both possibilities of the choice:

$$\frac{\Psi; \Delta, x : A \Rightarrow P :: z : C \quad \Psi; \Delta, x : B \Rightarrow Q :: z : C}{\Psi; \Delta, x : A \oplus B \Rightarrow x.\mathsf{case}(P, Q) :: z : C} \;\oplus\mathsf{L}$$

The reduction we obtain through composition is:

$$\frac{\dfrac{\Rightarrow P_1 :: x{:}A \quad \Rightarrow P_2 :: x{:}B}{\Rightarrow x.\mathsf{case}(P_1, P_2) :: x{:}A \mathbin{\&} B} \quad \dfrac{x{:}A \Rightarrow Q :: z{:}C}{x{:}A \mathbin{\&} B \Rightarrow x.\mathsf{inl}; Q :: z{:}C}}{\Rightarrow (\boldsymbol{\nu} x)(x.\mathsf{case}(P_1, P_2) \mid x.\mathsf{inl}; Q) :: z{:}C}$$

$$\longrightarrow \quad \frac{\Rightarrow P_1 :: x{:}A \quad x{:}A \Rightarrow Q :: z{:}C}{\Rightarrow (\boldsymbol{\nu} x)(P_1 \mid Q) :: z{:}C}$$

and symmetrically:

$$\frac{\dfrac{\Rightarrow P_1 :: x{:}A \quad \Rightarrow P_2 :: x{:}B}{\Rightarrow x.\mathsf{case}(P_1, P_2) :: x{:}A \mathbin{\&} B} \quad \dfrac{x{:}B \Rightarrow Q :: z : C}{x{:}A \mathbin{\&} B \Rightarrow x.\mathsf{inr}; Q :: z{:}C}}{\Rightarrow (\boldsymbol{\nu} x)(x.\mathsf{case}(P_1, P_2) \mid x.\mathsf{inr}; Q) :: z{:}C}$$

$$\longrightarrow \quad \frac{\Rightarrow P_1 :: x{:}B \quad x{:}B \Rightarrow Q :: z{:}C}{\Rightarrow (\boldsymbol{\nu} x)(P_2 \mid Q) :: z{:}C}$$

2.6.1 A slightly less simple example... with choice

We refine our previous bank specification to account for the fact that a bank offers several possible operations to its clients. In particular, we consider the deposit operation of Section 2.4.1 and consulting the account balance:

$$\mathsf{TBank} \triangleq \$\mathsf{string} \multimap ((\$\mathsf{nat} \multimap (\$\mathsf{nat} \otimes \mathbf{1})) \mathbin{\&} (\$\mathsf{nat} \otimes \mathbf{1}))$$

We abstract the details of performing the deposit operation with a function $\mathsf{dep} : \mathsf{string} \rightarrow \mathsf{nat} \rightarrow \mathsf{nat}$ that takes the user identification and the deposit amount and returns the receipt, and the details of obtaining the balance of an account with a function $\mathsf{bal} : \mathsf{string} \rightarrow \mathsf{nat}$ that takes the user identification and returns the balance of the account:

$$\begin{array}{l} z(s).z.\mathsf{case}(z(a).(\nu r)z\langle r\rangle.([r \leftarrow \mathsf{dep}(s, a)] \mid \mathbf{0}), \\ \qquad (\nu b)z\langle b\rangle.([b \leftarrow \mathsf{bal}(s)] \mid \mathbf{0}) :: z : \mathsf{TBank} \end{array}$$

2.7 Replication and exponential

We now develop the technical apparatus to provide an interpretation of the linear logic exponential $!A$. Proof-theoretically, the exponential enables a form of controlled weakening and contraction. More precisely, a proposition $!A$ provides an arbitrary number of copies of A (possibly 0). This means that to prove $!A$, we cannot use *any* linear resource, otherwise we would not be able to use A an arbitrary number of times. To cleanly account for the ability to weaken and contract certain resources, we split the context in an unrestricted zone that is subject to weakening and contraction, which we call Γ, and the linear zone (not subject to weakening or contraction), which we still denote as Δ (this form of context splitting is consistent with Barber and Plotkin's DILL [4]). Variables declared in Γ are called *unrestricted* and are denoted by (u, v, w). As before with the context Ψ, we simply add Γ to all sequents in the rules we have presented so far, since they do not use or change Γ in any way.

We can now assign the type $!A$ to a channel z as follows:

$$\frac{\Psi; \Gamma; \cdot \Rightarrow P :: y : A}{\Psi; \Gamma; \cdot \Rightarrow !z(y).P :: z : !A} \;!\mathsf{R}$$

We represent the *persistent* (or unrestricted) nature of the exponential by using an input-guarded process replication construct. The above process expects an input along z (call it y) to trigger the replication. The received name y will be the one through which P provides the session behavior of type A. Since the input is replicated (and P does not depend on any *linear* sessions), the process is able to provide an arbitrary number of copies of the session behavior A. Note that while we do require the linear context to be empty, we can use any ambient persistent session channel (called *standard* channels in [17]) in Γ to implement a session of type $!A$.

Using a (linear!) channel x of type $!A$ conceptually requires two steps. The first is to unlock the ability for this channel to provide session A multiple times. This is accomplished simply by renaming, taking care to make sure that the new channel $u : A$ is persistent and therefore declared in Γ.

$$\frac{\Psi; \Gamma, u : A; \Delta \Rightarrow P :: z : C}{\Psi; \Gamma; \Delta, x : !A \Rightarrow P\{x/u\} :: z : C}\ !\mathsf{L}$$

The second step is to actually create a fresh channel $y : A$ while retaining the capability to create more in the future, encoded by keeping $u : A$ in the context.

$$\frac{\Psi; \Gamma, u : A; \Delta, y : A \Rightarrow P :: z : C}{\Psi; \Gamma, u : A; \Delta \Rightarrow (\boldsymbol{\nu} y)u\langle y\rangle.P :: z : C}\ \mathsf{copy}$$

This *copy* rule is characteristic of sequent calculi implementing DILL. It is interesting that !L merely renames, while copy outputs a new bound name, being the computationally significant operation.

To follow our program of identifying process reductions with principal cut reductions, we must first observe that our previous composition rule cut cannot properly account for ambient unrestricted assumptions and thus does not completely explain typed composition in its full generality. In fact, if we simply compose the instances of !R and !L using cut:

$$\frac{\dfrac{\Psi; \Gamma; \cdot \Rightarrow P :: y{:}A}{\Psi; \Gamma; \cdot \Rightarrow !x(y).P :: z{:}!A} \qquad \dfrac{\Psi; \Gamma, u{:}A; \Delta \Rightarrow Q :: z{:}C}{\Psi; \Gamma; \Delta, x{:}!A \Rightarrow Q\{x/u\} :: z{:}C}}{\Psi; \Gamma; \Delta \Rightarrow (\boldsymbol{\nu} x)(!x(y).P \mid Q\{x/u\}) :: z{:}C}$$

not only can we not produce a process reduction (which is expected due to the "silent" nature of !L), but we also are unable to produce a proof reduction, since up to this point we have not defined a persistent version of cut. We can fix this by considering a composition rule for unrestricted sessions:

$$\frac{\Psi; \Gamma; \cdot \Rightarrow P :: x : A \quad \Psi; \Gamma, u : A; \Delta \Rightarrow Q :: z : C}{\Psi; \Gamma; \Delta \Rightarrow (\boldsymbol{\nu} u)(!u(x).P \mid Q) :: z : C}\ \mathsf{cut}^!$$

Given a process P that provides a session A along x without using any ambient linear sessions, and a process Q that implements session behavior C along z by (potentially) using the unrestricted ambient session $u : A$ (as well as linear ambient sessions Δ), we may compose Q with P if we prepend a replicated input along u to P, so it may now provide the necessary multiple copies of the session behavior A to produce a process that provides C along z outright. We can now exhibit our correspondence on the copy rule, where the process reduction is matched with a proof reduction obtained by the elimination of a persistent cut:

$$\frac{\Rightarrow P :: x{:}A \qquad \dfrac{u{:}A; x{:}A \Rightarrow Q :: z{:}C}{u{:}A; \Rightarrow (\boldsymbol{\nu} x)u\langle x\rangle.Q :: z{:}C}}{\Rightarrow (\boldsymbol{\nu} u)(!u(x).P \mid (\boldsymbol{\nu} x)u\langle x\rangle.Q) :: z{:}C} \longrightarrow$$

$$\frac{\Rightarrow P :: x{:}A \qquad \dfrac{u{:}A \Rightarrow P :: x{:}A \quad u{:}A; x{:}A \Rightarrow Q :: z{:}C}{u{:}A \Rightarrow (\boldsymbol{\nu} x)(P \mid Q) :: z{:}C}}{\Rightarrow (\boldsymbol{\nu} u)(!u(x).P \mid (\boldsymbol{\nu} x)(P \mid Q)) :: z{:}C}$$

If we now revisit our previous composition of !R and !L, we can observe that the process composition is structurally equivalent to persistent composition (which we know to exhibit the appropriate process reduction when the persistent session u is actually used). Similarly to what happens with $\mathbf{1}$, this is also one of the situations where we witness a proof reduction (of a cut to a persistent cut) that is matched by structural congruence in the process calculus. Note that the proof reductions of the persistent cut are again matched by process reductions (as we have shown above).

This form of composition of unrestricted resources introduces a proof conversion in which the unrestricted resource is "garbage collected" if never used. We can interpret this conversion as extending the standard structural congruence $\equiv$ between processes with the following rule (we will refer to this extended congruence as $\equiv_S$):

$$(\boldsymbol{\nu} x)(!x(y).P \mid Q) \equiv_S Q \text{ if } x \notin \mathit{fn}(Q)$$

While not essential to our development, $\equiv_S$ allows us to provide a more concise statement for some of the theorems of Section 3.

2.7.1 A bank with a persistent service

Having properly defined persistent sessions through linear logic exponentials, we can now have a bank service that persists through multiple sessions, instead of just being available for one usage:

$$\mathsf{TBank} \triangleq !(\$\mathsf{string} \multimap ((\$\mathsf{nat} \multimap (\$\mathsf{nat} \otimes \mathbf{1})) \mathbin{\&} (\$\mathsf{nat} \otimes \mathbf{1})))$$

We modify the bank process to be

$$\begin{aligned} !z(y).y(s).y.\mathsf{case}(&y(a).(\nu r)y\langle r\rangle.([r \leftarrow \mathsf{dep}(s,a)] \mid \mathbf{0}),\\ &(\nu b)y\langle b\rangle.([b \leftarrow \mathsf{bal}(s)] \mid \mathbf{0})) :: z : \mathsf{TBank}\end{aligned}$$

which now receives a session channel (bound to y) and spawns a replica that provides the behavior $\$\mathsf{string} \multimap ((\$\mathsf{nat} \multimap (\$\mathsf{nat} \otimes \mathbf{1})) \mathbin{\&} (\$\mathsf{nat} \otimes \mathbf{1}))$ along y.

We now have what may seem to be a good specification for what a bank process should be. However, if we only consider the type TBank, we are really only describing a persistent service that will receive a string and give a choice between either receiving a number and sending one back or just sending a number. When seen under this light, it becomes less obvious that we should be happy with our specification of what a simple bank process should be. In the next section, we develop a way of refining the specification such that typing will ensure strong guarantees not just on the pure session behavior, but also on the relationships between the actual communicated data. This refinement comes from the universal and existential quantifiers of linear logic, which are interpreted as a form of dependent product and sum, respectively.

2.8 Quantification and term passing

In intuitionistic first-order linear logic we usually consider the quantifiers $\forall x.A$ and $\exists x.A$ as ranging over a single domain that is left unspecified in order to study quantification in a general setting, independent of a particular domain of discourse. We now reconsider the quantifiers as $\forall x{:}\tau.A$ and $\exists x{:}\tau.A$, and therefore focus on quantification where the domain of discourse is *typed* (in particular, with a type τ).

Let us first consider universal quantification. Logic allows us to conclude $\forall x{:}\tau.A$ if by hypothesizing the existence of some element of type τ, labeled by x, we can prove A (which may *depend* on x). In linear logic, the hypothesis $x : \tau$ is given an unrestricted character since it avoids the problematic situation where a proposition may refer to an object that may have already been consumed. Conversely, we use an assumption of $\forall x{:}\tau.A$ by providing an object of type τ, which enables us to use A with the free variable x appropriately instantiated (in type theory this means that A *depends* on a term of type τ). We thus interpret a channel of type $\forall x{:}\tau.A$ as follows:

$$\frac{\Psi, x : \tau; \Gamma; \Delta \Rightarrow P :: z : A}{\Psi; \Gamma; \Delta \Rightarrow z(x).P :: z : \forall x : \tau.A}\ \forall\mathsf{R}$$

Similarly to how in type theory the universal quantifier corresponds to implication, we type the name z with $\forall x{:}\tau.A$ if after performing an input of a *term* of type τ, we can type z with A in the continuation P. We now define how to use a name of type $\forall y{:}\tau.A$:

$$\frac{\Psi \vdash N : \tau \quad \Psi; \Gamma; \Delta, x : A\{N/y\} \Rightarrow P :: z : C}{\Psi; \Gamma; \Delta, x : \forall y : \tau.A \Rightarrow x\langle N\rangle.P :: z : C}\ \forall\mathsf{L}$$

To use an ambient channel x of this type, we must output a functional term of type τ. Upon doing so, x now offers the session A, where the free variable in A has been instantiated with the term N, which we can use in P to provide session C along z.

We choose to use functional terms as the quantifier witnesses because they allow us to refer to the values communicated by processes (which are defined by the same functional language). This allows us to express rich properties of the values communicated by processes (which we will see shortly). Furthermore, it allows us to give a clean and logically based account of processes that exchange proof objects (i.e., the functional terms) which can serve as a form of inspectable proof certificate (vis., a high-level model of proof carrying code [27]).

The reduction for the processes in $\forall$R and $\forall$L is:

$$\dfrac{\dfrac{y{:}\tau; -; - \Rightarrow P :: x{:}A}{\Rightarrow x(y).P :: x{:}\forall y{:}\tau.A} \qquad \dfrac{\vdash N{:}\tau \quad x{:}A\{N/y\} \Rightarrow Q :: z{:}C}{x : \forall y{:}\tau.A \Rightarrow x\langle N\rangle.Q :: z{:}C}}{\Rightarrow (\boldsymbol{\nu} x)(x(y).P \mid x\langle N\rangle.Q) :: z{:}C}$$

$$\longrightarrow \quad \dfrac{\Rightarrow P\{N/y\} :: x{:}A\{N/y\} \quad x{:}A\{N/y\} \Rightarrow Q :: z{:}C}{\Rightarrow (\boldsymbol{\nu} x)(P\{N/y\} \mid Q) :: z{:}C}$$

We now consider existential quantification. Logic allows us to conclude $\exists x{:}\tau.A$ if we can produce a witness of type τ and (potentially) use it to show A (in which x may be free and therefore we need to instantiate the variable x with the witness). Just as universal quantification was interpreted as term input, we interpret existential quantification as its behavioral dual, that is, as term output:

$$\dfrac{\Psi \vdash N : \tau \quad \Psi; \Gamma; \Delta \Rightarrow P :: z : A\{N/x\}}{\Psi; \Gamma; \Delta \Rightarrow z\langle N\rangle.P :: z : \exists x{:}\tau.A}\ \exists\mathsf{R}$$

The term N provides a witness of τ, which is used to instantiate x in the session type A provided by P along z. Using a channel of type $\exists y{:}\tau.A$ is defined as:

$$\dfrac{\Psi, y : \tau; \Gamma; \Delta, x : A \Rightarrow P :: z : C}{\Psi; \Gamma; \Delta, x : \exists y{:}\tau.A \Rightarrow x(y).P :: z : C}\ \exists\mathsf{L}$$

Given that the contract of $x : \exists y{:}\tau.A$ is to output a term of type τ along x and then provide behavior A (with the appropriate instantiation of the variable y), we use a session of existential type by performing an input along x, that is bound in the continuation as y, which then uses the residual behavior A to provide C along z.

The reduction of the process composition is identical to that for sessions of universal quantification type:

$$\dfrac{\dfrac{\vdash N{:}\tau \quad \Rightarrow P :: x{:}A\{N/y\}}{\Rightarrow x\langle N\rangle.P :: x{:}\exists y{:}\tau.A} \qquad \dfrac{y{:}\tau; x{:}A \Rightarrow Q :: z{:}C}{x{:}\exists y{:}\tau.A \Rightarrow x(y).Q :: z{:}C}}{\Rightarrow (\boldsymbol{\nu} x)(x\langle N\rangle.P \mid x(y).Q) :: z{:}C}$$

$$\longrightarrow \quad \dfrac{\Rightarrow P :: x{:}A\{N/y\} \quad x{:}A \Rightarrow Q\{N/y\} :: z{:}C}{\Rightarrow (\boldsymbol{\nu} x)(P \mid Q\{N/y\}) :: z{:}C}$$

We must note that as of this moment in our presentation, our system is not yet a truly dependent type theory of sessions, since we have not yet defined a way in which we can actually have occurrences of the quantified variables in the bodies of types. In logic, this is achieved by allowing atomic propositions p to depend on (typed) variables, that is, to have atomic propositions be predicates on typed objects (e.g. in $\forall x{:}\tau.p(x)$, p is a predicate on objects of type τ). In type theory, predicates correspond to indexed families of types. For instance, $\forall x{:}\tau.p(x)$ defines a type family p indexed by objects of type τ, that is, $p(N)$ is a type for any object N of type τ. We refrain from presenting further insights into the technical aspects of dependent type theories for the sake of brevity, simply noting that their expressive power gives rise to practical and useful solutions to problems that range from foundational aspects [13, 14, 25] to more practical aspects of computer science [28, 31].

In our interpretation, we assume that we can define type families in the functional term language, that is, the functional term language is a dependent type theory in the style of [19, 28]. We thus introduce the final requirement that makes our interpretation a fully dependent type theory of sessions.

2.8.1 A more sophisticated bank service

We now extend our running example of the bank process to a system with a bank and an ATM that interfaces between the bank and its clients. The ATM charges any client a small amount for any operations performed. We therefore specify such an ATM, with the additional caveat that it may only charge at most 2 dollars per operation, and it must provide a proof of such to the client. We begin with the bank specification:

$$\begin{array}{l}\mathsf{TBank} \triangleq\ !(\forall s : \mathsf{string}.\$\mathsf{uid}(s) \multimap \\ \qquad (\forall n : \mathsf{nat}.\$\mathsf{deposit}(s,n) \multimap (\$\mathsf{receipt}(s,n) \otimes \mathbf{1}))\ \&\ \\ \qquad (\exists m : \mathsf{nat}.\$\mathsf{balance}(s,m) \otimes \mathbf{1}))\end{array}$$

By using dependent types at both the session level and at the functional term level, we can provide a refined specification in which the bank receives the user identification and then offers the deposit and balance operations: the former receives a deposit order of n dollars for the specified user s and issues a receipt that refers to s and n (all of which is ensured by typing); the latter simply issues a balance statement that refers to s and an amount m corresponding to the account balance. We use dependent functions dep with type $\Pi s : \mathsf{string}.\Pi n : \mathsf{nat}.\mathsf{deposit}(s,n) \rightarrow \mathsf{receipt}(s,n)$ and bal with type $\Pi s : \mathsf{string}.\Sigma m : \mathsf{nat}.\mathsf{balance}(s,m)$ to implement the bank process ($\pi_i(N)$ denotes the ith projection of N):

$$\begin{array}{l}!z(y).y(s).y(id).y.\mathsf{case}(y(n).y(d).(\boldsymbol{\nu} r)y\langle r\rangle. \\ \quad ([r \leftarrow \mathsf{dep}(s,n,d)] \mid \mathbf{0}), y\langle \pi_1(\mathsf{bal}(s))\rangle.(\boldsymbol{\nu} b)y\langle b\rangle. \\ \qquad ([b \leftarrow \pi_2(\mathsf{bal}(s))] \mid \mathbf{0})) :: z : \mathsf{TBank}\end{array}$$

The ATM client interface specification is (to make matters simpler, we assume the ATM only performs deposits):

$$\begin{array}{l}\mathsf{TATMClient} \triangleq \forall s : \mathsf{string}.\$\mathsf{uid}(s) \multimap \\ \qquad (\forall n : \mathsf{nat}.\$\mathsf{deposit}(s,n) \multimap \exists m : \mathsf{nat}. \\ \qquad \exists p : (\mathsf{n} - 2 \leq \mathsf{m} \leq \mathsf{n}).(\$\mathsf{receipt}(s,m) \otimes \mathbf{1}))\end{array}$$

The client sends its user id, a deposit instruction for some amount n, and the ATM sends back to the client the receipt for the deposited amount, along with a proof object p that guarantees that the amount charged for the deposit is within the bounds imposed by the specification. Note that we can now ensure by typing alone that any well-typed ATM will be guaranteed to *not* overcharge its clients. For the ATM process, we use a function charge of type:

$$\begin{array}{l}\mathsf{charge} : \Pi s{:}\mathsf{string}.\Pi n{:}\mathsf{nat}.\mathsf{deposit}(s,n) \rightarrow \\ \qquad \Sigma m : \mathsf{nat}.\Sigma p : (n - 2 \leq m \leq n).\mathsf{deposit}(s,m)\end{array}$$

The charge function takes the deposit object and issues a new deposit object, providing the necessary proof objects to ensure that the amount charged for the operation is within specification bounds. An inhabitant of type $\mathsf{TATMClient}$ (assuming the bank session is available on channel x) is:

$$\begin{array}{l}z(s).z(id).z(n).z(d). \\ \quad (\boldsymbol{\nu} y)x\langle y\rangle.y\langle s\rangle.(\boldsymbol{\nu} i)y\langle i\rangle.([i \leftarrow id] \mid \\ \quad\ y.\mathsf{inl}; y\langle \pi_1(\mathsf{charge}(s,n,d))\rangle. \\ \qquad (\boldsymbol{\nu} d')y\langle d'\rangle.([d' \leftarrow \pi_2(\pi_2(\mathsf{charge}(s,n,d)))] \mid \\ \qquad\ y(r).z\langle \pi_1(\mathsf{charge}(s,n,d))\rangle. \\ \qquad\quad z\langle \pi_1(\pi_2(\mathsf{charge}(s,n,d)))\rangle. \\ \qquad\qquad (\boldsymbol{\nu} t)z\langle t\rangle.([t \leftrightarrow r] \mid 0))) :: z : \mathsf{TATMClient}\end{array}$$

Note that there are potentially several inhabitants of the type $\mathsf{TATMClient}$, due to the many possible ways in which the communication on the bank session channel x and the client session channel z can be validly interleaved (e.g. the ATM might send the proof objects to the client before sending the deposit message to the bank).

2.9 Summary

We now take a step back and summarize. We have presented a type system of dependent session types for a term passing π-calculus, whose process constructors are given below:

$$\begin{array}{rcl} P & ::= & \mathbf{0} \mid P|Q \mid (\boldsymbol{\nu} y)P \\ & & \mid x\langle y\rangle.P \mid x\langle N\rangle.P \mid x(y).P \\ & & \mid !x(y).P \mid x.\mathsf{inl}; P \mid x.\mathsf{inr}; P \\ & & \mid x.\mathsf{case}(P, Q) \mid [y \leftrightarrow x] \mid [x \leftarrow N] \end{array}$$

The typing rules for our system are summarized in Fig. 1, which is defined modulo structural congruence. Structural congruence is the least congruence on processes defined by the following rules:

$$\begin{array}{ll} P \mid \mathbf{0} \equiv P & P \equiv_\alpha Q \Rightarrow P \equiv Q \\ P \mid (Q \mid R) \equiv (P \mid Q) \mid R & P|Q \equiv Q|P \\ x \notin fn(P) \Rightarrow P \mid (\boldsymbol{\nu} x)Q \equiv (\boldsymbol{\nu} x)(P \mid Q) & (\boldsymbol{\nu} x)\mathbf{0} \equiv \mathbf{0} \\ (\boldsymbol{\nu} x)(\boldsymbol{\nu} y)P \equiv (\boldsymbol{\nu} y)(\boldsymbol{\nu} x)P & [y \leftrightarrow x] \equiv [x \leftrightarrow y] \end{array}$$

The operational semantics for the $[y \leftrightarrow x]$ and $[x \leftarrow N]$ constructs, as informed by the proof theory, consist of channel renaming and term substitution, respectively. The channel renaming construct's behavior is to "re-implement" an ambient session on a different name. The reduction rules for our calculus are summarized below:

$$\begin{array}{l} x\langle y\rangle.Q \mid x(z).P \to Q \mid P\{y/z\} \\ x\langle y\rangle.Q \mid !x(z).P \to Q \mid P\{y/z\} \mid !x(z).P \\ x\langle N\rangle.Q \mid x(z).P \to Q \mid P\{N/z\} \\ (\boldsymbol{\nu} x)([x \leftrightarrow y] \mid P) \to P\{y/x\} \\ (\boldsymbol{\nu} x)([x \leftarrow N] \mid P) \to P\{N/x\} \\ x.\mathsf{inl}; P \mid x.\mathsf{case}(Q, R) \to P \mid Q \\ x.\mathsf{inr}; P \mid x.\mathsf{case}(Q, R) \to P \mid R \\ Q \to Q' \Rightarrow P \mid Q \to P \mid Q' \\ P \to Q \Rightarrow (\boldsymbol{\nu} y)P \to (\boldsymbol{\nu} y)Q \\ P \equiv P',\, P' \to Q',\, Q' \equiv Q \Rightarrow P \to Q \end{array}$$

The term substitution construct is similar to the active substitutions of the applied π-calculus, with the particular differences that active substitutions are persistent and applied by structural congruence, while ours obey a linear discipline and are applied by an actual reduction step. Our term language is also very different from the one in the applied π-calculus, since our terms are defined in a functional language that does not include the notion of process calculus (channel) name, whilst the terms in [1] can contain names. A labeled transition system that characterizes relevant external actions can be defined by a judgment $P \xrightarrow{\alpha} Q$, where α denotes an action that can be silent, an output or input of a (bound) name or of a term:

$$\alpha \quad ::= \quad \tau \mid \overline{(\nu z)x\langle z\rangle} \mid x(y) \mid \overline{x\langle N\rangle} \mid x(N)$$

We now present some of the formal results that we have established for our system.

3. Properties of the type system

In this section we establish the results of type preservation and progress for our type system, following the results of [10]. The proof of type preservation relies on several reduction lemmas that relate process reductions with parallel composition through the cut rule. We illustrate these with the cases for the quantifiers.

Lemma 3.1. *Assume*

(a) $\Psi; \Gamma; \Delta_1 \Rightarrow P :: x : \forall y : \tau.A$ *with* $P \xrightarrow{x(N)} P'$

(b) $\Psi; \Gamma; \Delta_2, x : \forall y : \tau.B \Rightarrow Q :: z : C$ *with* $Q \xrightarrow{\overline{x\langle N\rangle}} Q'$

Then:

(c) $\Psi; \Gamma; \Delta_1, \Delta_2 \Rightarrow (\boldsymbol{\nu} x)(P' \mid Q') :: z : C$

Lemma 3.2. *Assume*

(a) $\Psi; \Gamma; \Delta_1 \Rightarrow P :: x : \exists y : \tau.B$ *with* $P \xrightarrow{\overline{x\langle N\rangle}} P'$ *and*

(b) $\Psi; \Gamma; \Delta_2, x : \exists y : \tau.B \Rightarrow Q :: z : C$ *with* $Q \xrightarrow{x(N)} Q'$

Then:

(c) $\Psi; \Gamma; \Delta_1, \Delta_2 \Rightarrow (\boldsymbol{\nu} x)(P' \mid Q') :: z : C$

We can now state and sketch the proof of type preservation.

Theorem 3.3 (Type Preservation). *If* $\Psi; \Gamma; \Delta \Rightarrow P :: z : A$ *and* $P \to Q$ *then* $\Psi; \Gamma; \Delta \Rightarrow Q :: z : A$

Proof. By induction on the typing derivation. When the last rule is an instance of cut, we appeal to the reduction lemmas, one for each type C of the cut formula (these are of the form of Lemmas 3.1 and 3.2), or to the rules for renaming and substitution. □

To establish progress, a lemma that establishes a contextual progress property is required. First, we define:

$$live(P) \triangleq P \equiv (\boldsymbol{\nu}\overline{n})(Q \mid R) \quad \text{for some } Q, R, \overline{n}$$

where $Q \equiv \pi.Q'$ (π is a non-replicated prefix), $Q \equiv [x \leftrightarrow y]$ or $Q \equiv [x \leftarrow N]$. Given an action label α, we denote by $s(\alpha)$ the subject of the action α (i.e., the name through which the action takes place). We can now establish the contextual progress property (note the use of $\equiv_S$, defined in Section 2.7).

Lemma 3.4. *Let* $\Psi; \Gamma; \Delta \Rightarrow P :: z : C$*. If* $live(P)$ *then there is* Q *such that one of the following holds:*

(a) $P \to Q$,

(b) $P \xrightarrow{\alpha} Q$ *for some* α *where* $s(\alpha) \in z, \Gamma, \Delta$ *and* $s(\alpha) \in \Gamma, \Delta$ *if* $C = !A$,

(c) $P \equiv_S [x \leftrightarrow z]$*, for some* $x \in \Delta$,

(d) $P \equiv_S [z \leftarrow N]$ *for some* N.

Proof. Induction on typing. The proof is similar to that of [10], with more cases when the last rule applied is cut, to account for renaming, term substitutions, and quantifiers. □

Global progress follows directly from Lemma 3.4.

Theorem 3.5 (Progress). *If* $\cdot; \cdot; \cdot \Rightarrow P :: x : \mathbf{1}$*, and* $live(P)$*, then there exists a process* Q *such that* $P \to Q$.

Note that this is the case because P cannot perform any action α with subject x, since $x : \mathbf{1}$.

The guiding principle mentioned earlier allows us to make a stronger formal connection between cut reductions and pi-calculus reductions, but this is beyond the scope of this particular paper (and is straightforward, given the results of [10] and the earlier presented reductions).

4. Proof irrelevance

We now tackle the problem of eliminating some of the communication overhead generated by the exchange of explicit proof objects. Process calculi are a class of languages that allow us to reason about concurrent processes that may or may not be executing in a distributed setting. If such is indeed the case, there is an argument

$$\frac{}{\Psi;\Gamma;x:A \Rightarrow [x \leftrightarrow z] :: z:A}\ \mathsf{id} \qquad \frac{\Psi \vdash M:\tau}{\Psi;\Gamma;\cdot \Rightarrow [z \leftarrow M] :: z:\$\tau}\ \mathsf{\$R} \qquad \frac{\Psi,x:\tau;\Gamma;\Delta \Rightarrow P :: z:C}{\Psi;\Gamma;\Delta,x:\$\tau \Rightarrow P :: z:C}\ \mathsf{\$L}$$

$$\frac{}{\Psi;\Gamma;\cdot \Rightarrow \mathbf{0} :: z:\mathbf{1}}\ \mathsf{1R} \qquad \frac{\Psi;\Gamma;\Delta \Rightarrow P :: z:C}{\Psi;\Gamma;\Delta,x:\mathbf{1} \Rightarrow P :: z:C}\ \mathsf{1L} \qquad \frac{\Psi;\Gamma;\cdot \Rightarrow P :: y:A}{\Psi;\Gamma;\cdot \Rightarrow !z(y).P :: z:!A}\ \mathsf{!R}$$

$$\frac{\Psi;\Gamma,u:A;\Delta \Rightarrow P :: z:C}{\Psi;\Gamma;\Delta,x:!A \Rightarrow P\{x/u\} :: z:C}\ \mathsf{!L} \qquad \frac{\Psi;\Gamma,u:A;\Delta,y:A \Rightarrow P :: z:C}{\Psi;\Gamma,u:A;\Delta \Rightarrow (\boldsymbol{\nu} y)u\langle y\rangle.P :: z:C}\ \mathsf{copy}$$

$$\frac{\Psi;\Gamma;\Delta \Rightarrow P :: z:A \quad \Psi;\Gamma;\Delta \Rightarrow Q :: z:B}{\Psi;\Gamma;\Delta \Rightarrow z.\mathsf{case}(P,Q) :: z:A \,\&\, B}\ \mathsf{\&R} \qquad \frac{\Psi;\Gamma;\Delta,x:A \Rightarrow P :: z:C}{\Psi;\Gamma;\Delta,x:A \,\&\, B \Rightarrow x.\mathsf{inl};P :: z:C}\ \mathsf{\&L_1}$$

$$\frac{\Psi;\Gamma;\Delta,x:B \Rightarrow P :: z:C}{\Psi;\Gamma;\Delta,x:A \,\&\, B \Rightarrow x.\mathsf{inr};P :: z:C}\ \mathsf{\&L_2} \qquad \frac{\Psi;\Gamma;\Delta_1 \Rightarrow P :: y:A \quad \Psi;\Gamma;\Delta_2 \Rightarrow Q :: z:B}{\Psi;\Gamma;\Delta_1,\Delta_2 \Rightarrow (\boldsymbol{\nu} y)z\langle y\rangle.(P \mid Q) :: z:A \otimes B}\ \mathsf{\otimes R}$$

$$\frac{\Psi;\Gamma;\Delta,y:A,x:B \Rightarrow P :: z:C}{\Psi;\Gamma;\Delta,x:A \otimes B \Rightarrow x(y).P :: z:C}\ \mathsf{\otimes L} \qquad \frac{\Psi;\Gamma;\Delta \Rightarrow P :: z:A}{\Psi;\Gamma;\Delta \Rightarrow z.\mathsf{inl};P :: z:A \oplus B}\ \mathsf{\oplus R_1}$$

$$\frac{\Psi;\Gamma;\Delta \Rightarrow P :: z:B}{\Psi;\Gamma;\Delta \Rightarrow z.\mathsf{inr};P :: z:A \oplus B}\ \mathsf{\oplus R_2} \qquad \frac{\Psi;\Gamma;\Delta,x:A \Rightarrow P :: z:C \quad \Psi;\Gamma;\Delta,x:B \Rightarrow Q :: z:C}{\Psi;\Gamma;\Delta,x:A \oplus B \Rightarrow x.\mathsf{case}(P,Q) :: z:C}\ \mathsf{\oplus L}$$

$$\frac{\Psi,x:\tau;\Gamma;\Delta \Rightarrow P :: z:A}{\Psi;\Gamma;\Delta \Rightarrow z(x).P :: z:\forall x:\tau.A}\ \mathsf{\forall R} \qquad \frac{\Psi \vdash N:\tau \quad \Psi;\Gamma;\Delta,x:A\{N/y\} \Rightarrow P :: z:C}{\Psi;\Gamma;\Delta,x:\forall y:\tau.A \Rightarrow x\langle N\rangle.P :: z:C}\ \mathsf{\forall L}$$

$$\frac{\Psi \vdash N:\tau \quad \Psi;\Gamma;\Delta \Rightarrow P : A\{N/x\}}{\Psi;\Gamma;\Delta \Rightarrow z\langle N\rangle.P :: z:\exists x:\tau.A}\ \mathsf{\exists R} \qquad \frac{\Psi,y:\tau;\Gamma;\Delta,x:A \Rightarrow P :: z:C}{\Psi;\Gamma;\Delta,x:\exists y:\tau.A \Rightarrow x(y).P :: z:C}\ \mathsf{\exists L}$$

$$\frac{\Psi;\Gamma;\Delta_1 \Rightarrow P :: x:A \quad \Psi;\Gamma;\Delta_2,x:A \Rightarrow Q :: z:C}{\Psi;\Gamma;\Delta_1,\Delta_2 \Rightarrow (\boldsymbol{\nu} x)(P \mid Q) :: z:C}\ \mathsf{cut} \qquad \frac{\Psi;\Gamma;\cdot \Rightarrow P :: x:A \quad \Psi;\Gamma,u:A;\Delta \Rightarrow Q :: z:C}{\Psi;\Gamma;\Delta \Rightarrow (\boldsymbol{\nu} u)((!u(x).P) \mid Q) :: z:C}\ \mathsf{cut^!}$$

Figure 1. A Dependent Type Theory of Sessions.

to be made that trust between the communicating parties should not be assumed outright. In these scenarios, our system, in which properties of the communicated data are ensured by typing but also witnessed by explicit proof objects that are passed by processes, seems to be a reasonable way of addressing the issue of trust (or lack thereof). A client may not trust the remote server code, but provided the server sends the proof objects, the client may in principle check that the proof objects are valid and thus obtains further assurances on the server.

However, it may not necessarily be the case that the communication of explicit proof objects is required by the parties involved. For instance, the properties in question may be easily decidable, or we have a scenario where we have code residing on the same machine that represents multiple communicating sessions (e.g. an operating system, a file system, etc.), or it may be the case that the communicating parties do indeed exist in a distributed setting, but have established trust by some exterior means. In some of these cases we *can* type-check the process code, and so the proof objects are in principle no longer really needed at runtime. Of course, the system as we have presented so far has really no way of determining if it is really the case that a proof object is not used for its computational content. Luckily, proof theory can help us, with the concept of *proof irrelevance* [3, 29].

Proof irrelevance is a technique that allows us to selectively hide portions of a proof. These "hidden" proofs must exist, but it must also be the case that they can be safely erased from a process at runtime. This means that typing must ensure that these hidden proofs are never required to compute something that is not erased. We internalize this notion of proof irrelevance in the functional term language with a new type, $[A]$ (read *bracket* A), meaning that there is a term of type A, but the term itself can be safely erased before runtime without changing the meaning of the process. We can give a precise meaning to $[A]$ by adding a new introduction form for terms, written $[M]$, meaning that M will not be available computationally. We also add a new class of assumptions $x \div A$, meaning that x stands for a term of type A that is not computationally available. Following the style of [29], we define a promotion operation on contexts that transforms computationally irrelevant hypotheses into ordinary ones:

$$\begin{array}{lcl} (\cdot)^{\oplus} & \triangleq & \cdot \\ (\Psi, x:A)^{\oplus} & \triangleq & \Psi^{\oplus}, x:A \\ (\Psi, x \div A)^{\oplus} & \triangleq & \Psi^{\oplus}, x:A \end{array}$$

We can then define the introduction and elimination forms of proof irrelevant terms:

$$\frac{\Psi^{\oplus} \vdash M:A}{\Psi \vdash [M]:[A]}\ []I \qquad \frac{\Psi \vdash M:[A] \quad \Psi, x \div A \vdash N:C}{\Psi \vdash \mathbf{let}\ [x] = M\ \mathbf{in}\ N : C}\ []E$$

These rules guarantee that a variable of the form $x \div A$ can only be used in terms that are irrelevant (in the technical sense). In such terms, we are allowed to refer to *all* variables, including the irrelevant ones, since the term is not intended to be available at runtime. Terms of bracket type can still be used through the let binding shown above, but the bound variable x is tagged with the irrelevant hypothesis form, to maintain the invariant that no relevant term can use irrelevant variables in a computational manner. Using bracketed types, we ensure that assigned terms are never explored for their computational value, and so can be safely erased at runtime. We first illustrate this with a very simple example and then generalize to our running example of the bank. Consider a very simple process with the following type:

$$\mathsf{T} \triangleq \forall f{:}\mathsf{nat} \to \mathsf{nat}.\forall n{:}\mathsf{nat}.\forall p{:}(n > 0).\$\mathsf{nat} \otimes \mathbf{1}$$

The type describes a process that receives a natural number function f, a natural number n and a *proof* that n is strictly positive (for instance, because f is not defined for 0). It will then reply with a natural number (the result of applying f to n) and terminate. A sample process obeying this specification is:

$$\mathsf{Server} \triangleq x(f).x(n).x(p).(\boldsymbol{\nu} y)x\langle y\rangle.([y \leftarrow f(n)] \mid \mathbf{0}) :: x:\mathsf{T}$$

A sample client that properly interacts with the above process is

$$\mathsf{Client} \triangleq x\langle M\rangle.x\langle 1\rangle.x\langle N\rangle.x(r).[r \leftrightarrow z] :: z : \mathsf{nat}$$

where M must be a term of type $\mathsf{nat} \rightarrow \mathsf{nat}$ and N is a term of type $1 > 0$.

Notice that in this situation, the proof object p in Server only serves the purpose of ensuring a restriction on n, its content is never actually used in a computationally meaningful manner. That is, p is a computationally irrelevant proof object. We can now make use of proof irrelevance to identify that the proof object p in Server can be erased at runtime:

$$\mathsf{T_I} \triangleq \forall f : \mathsf{nat} \rightarrow \mathsf{nat}.\forall n : \mathsf{nat}.\forall p : [n > 0].\$\mathsf{nat} \otimes \mathbf{1}$$

The server process stays the same, while the Client must now send $[N]$ instead of just N:

$$\mathsf{Client_I} \triangleq x\langle M\rangle.x\langle 1\rangle.x\langle [N]\rangle.x(r).[r \leftrightarrow z] :: z : \mathsf{nat}$$

We can define an operation that, given a well-typed process, erases all terms of bracket type and the respective communication actions. This erasure is obviously not type preserving in general, in the sense that the resulting process may no longer be assigned the same type in our system. However, the erasure is to be applied *after* we have ensured that a process is well typed (and therefore abides by whatever specification is defined in its type), but before the code is actually executed. Thus, the erasure is safe because we know that all properties that typing ensured still hold.

In our example above, the erased server and client processes would be:

$$\begin{array}{lcl} \mathsf{T_e} & \triangleq & \forall f{:}\mathsf{nat} \rightarrow \mathsf{nat}.\forall n{:}\mathsf{nat}.\$\mathsf{nat} \otimes \mathbf{1} \\ \mathsf{Server_e} & \triangleq & x(f).x(n).(\boldsymbol{\nu}y)x\langle y\rangle.([y \leftarrow f(n)] \mid \mathbf{0}) :: x : \mathsf{T_e} \\ \mathsf{Client_e} & \triangleq & x\langle M\rangle.x\langle 1\rangle.x(r).[r \leftrightarrow z] :: z : \mathsf{nat} \end{array}$$

The precise definition of the erasure function is standard, since its interaction with the process layer is minimal with the restriction to base types $\$\tau$ only. We therefore elide its formal definition and the companion correctness theorem from this presentation for the sake of brevity.

In our running example of the bank system, if we assume the client trusts the ATM code to not be malicious, we may employ proof irrelevance and write the type of the ATM interface as:

$$\begin{array}{l} \mathsf{TATMClient_I} \triangleq \forall s : \mathsf{string}.\$\mathsf{uid}(s) \multimap \\ \quad (\forall n : \mathsf{nat}.\$\mathsf{deposit}(s, n) \multimap \exists m : \mathsf{nat}. \\ \quad \exists p : [\mathsf{n} - 2 \leq \mathsf{m} \leq \mathsf{n}].(\$\mathsf{receipt}(s, m) \otimes 1)) \end{array}$$

which then allows us to safely erase the communication overhead of the proof object p. To conclude, the technique of internalizing proof irrelevance in bracket types provides a clean and modular way of singling out terms (through their types) that are never used for their computational content. This provides us with the opportunity to erase these terms and minimize communication overheads when appropriate.

5. Concluding Remarks

We have presented an interpretation of intuitionistic linear type theory as a dependent session type system for a π-calculus with value passing. Our framework introduces value passing by interpreting the (higher-order) type structure of an underlying functional dependent type theory as atomic from the process perspective. Dependent types may be used to elegantly specify properties of data exchanged by processes in their session types. Previous work [7] encoded these as assertions built into the session type. In particular, we have shown how certified interface contracts, expressing rich properties of distributed protocols, may be expressed in our framework. Our development provides a new account of dependent session types [8] that is completely grounded in logic, and is free from special-purpose technical machinery that is usually required in this setting.

Our approach naturally addresses challenges not yet tackled by other session type systems, such as the use of proof-based certification in scenarios involving communication between untrusted parties. We have also explored proof irrelevance as a way of singling out proofs that may be safely erased at runtime. We have proven that our system ensures type preservation, session fidelity, and global progress. We do not address the issue of describing infinite protocols through recursive types, since the technical challenges of recursive types are well understood and extending our system with recursive types is straightforward and orthogonal to our development.

Several other connections between the π-calculus and linear logic have been established. A first line of research has investigated the use of linearity in type systems (see, e.g., [9, 18, 23, 24]). These type systems have not developed any interpretation of the pure linear logic connectives as behavioral (session) type operators, a program that we have initiated [10], and extend here to the setting of a much richer dependent linear type theory. A second line of work has investigated operational interpretations of linear logic proofs in the π-calculus and related models (see, e.g., [2, 5, 6, 21]). We may broadly characterize these as applications of the π-calculus as a convenient language for analyzing linear logic proof objects, while our aim is to develop the linear propositions-as-types paradigm as a foundation for distributed, session-based, practical programming languages, with rich interface specifications.

In future work, we plan on extending our program of providing logical explanations to the phenomena of concurrency to multiparty session types, which are a generalization of the binary session types we have given logical meaning in this and prior work. To achieve this, we plan to investigate potential relationships of multi-party sessions to linear modal logic [16], which provides a natural way of reasoning about several principals. Another interesting line of research is the development of appropriate theories of bisimulation and observational equivalence for (dependent) session types and the study of their relationship to forms of logical and proof equivalence. Finally, we also wish to consider a potentially tighter integration of functional and concurrent computation that does not require the two-layer stratification that we have presented in this paper. Ongoing research in concurrent evaluation strategies for functional programs using logical interpretations might provide deeper insights in this particular direction.

Acknowledgments

Support for this research was provided by the Fundação para a Ciência e a Tecnologia (Portuguese Foundation for Science and Technology) through the Carnegie Mellon Portugal Program, under grants SFRH / BD / 33763 / 2009 and INTERFACES NGN-44 / 2009, and CITI.

References

[1] M. Abadi and C. Fournet. Mobile values, new names, and secure communication. In *28th Symposium on Principles of Programming Languages*, POPL'01, pages 104–115. ACM, 2001.

[2] S. Abramsky. Computational Interpretations of Linear Logic. *Theor. Comp. Sci.*, 111(1&2), 1993.

[3] S. Awodey and A. Bauer. Propositions as [types]. *J. Log. Comput.*, 14(4):447–471, 2004.

[4] A. Barber and G. Plotkin. Dual Intuitionistic Linear Logic. Technical Report LFCS-96-347, Univ. of Edinburgh, 1997.

[5] E. Beffara. A Concurrent Model for Linear Logic. *ENTCS*, 155:147–168, 2006.

[6] G. Bellin and P. Scott. On the π-Calculus and Linear Logic. *Theor. Comp. Sci.*, 135:11–65, 1994.

[7] L. Bocchi, K. Honda, E. Tuosto, and N. Yoshida. A theory of design-by-contract for distributed multiparty interactions. In *21st International Conference on Concurrency Theory*, CONCUR'10, pages 162–176. Springer LNCS 6269, 2010.

[8] E. Bonelli, A. Compagnoni, and E. L. Gunter. Correspondence Assertions for Process Synchronization in Concurrent Communications. *J. of Func. Prog.*, 15(2):219–247, 2005.

[9] L. Caires. Logical Semantics of Types for Concurrency. In *International Conference on Algebra and Coalgebra in Computer Science*, CALCO'07, pages 16–35. Springer LNCS 4624, 2007.

[10] L. Caires and F. Pfenning. Session types as intuitionistic linear propositions. In *21st International Conference on Concurrency Theory*, CONCUR'10, pages 222–236. Springer LNCS 6269, 2010.

[11] L. Caires and H. T. Vieira. Conversation types. *Theor. Comput. Sci.*, 411(51-52):4399–4440, 2010.

[12] I. Cervesato and F. Pfenning. A linear logical framework. *Inf. & Comput.*, 179(1), 2002.

[13] R. Constable et al. *Implementing Mathematics with the Nuprl Proof Development System*. Prentice-Hall, 1986.

[14] T. Coquand and G. Huet. The calculus of constructions. *Inf. & Comput.*, 76:95–120, February 1988.

[15] M. Fähndrich, M. Aiken, C. Hawblitzel, O. Hodson, G. C. Hunt, J. R. Larus, and S. Levi. Language support for fast and reliable message-based communication in Singularity OS. In *EuroSys 2006*, pages 177–190. ACM, 2006.

[16] D. Garg, L. Bauer, K. Bowers, F. Pfenning, and M. Reiter. A linear logic of affirmation and knowledge. In *Proceedings of the 11th European Symposium on Research in Computer Security*, ESORICS'06, pages 297–312. Springer LNCS 4189, Sept. 2006.

[17] S. Gay and M. Hole. Subtyping for Session Types in the Pi Calculus. *Acta Informatica*, 42(2-3):191–225, 2005.

[18] M. Giunti and V. T. Vasconcelos. A Linear Account of Session Types in the Pi-Calculus. In *21st International Conference on Concurrency Theory*, CONCUR'10, pages 432–446. Springer LNCS 6269, 2010.

[19] R. Harper, F. Honsell, and G. Plotkin. A framework for defining logics. *J. ACM*, 40:143–184, January 1993.

[20] K. Honda. Types for dyadic interaction. In *4th International Conference on Concurrency Theory*, CONCUR'93, pages 509–523. Springer LNCS 715, 1993.

[21] K. Honda and O. Laurent. An exact correspondence between a typed pi-calculus and polarised proof-nets. *Theor. Comp. Sci.*, 411:2223–2238, 2010.

[22] K. Honda, V. T. Vasconcelos, and M. Kubo. Language primitives and type discipline for structured communication-based programming. In *7th European Symposium on Programming Languages and Systems*, ESOP'98, pages 122–138. Springer LNCS 1381, 1998.

[23] A. Igarashi and N. Kobayashi. A generic type system for the pi-calculus. In *28th Symposium on Principles of Programming Languages*, POPL'01, pages 128–141. ACM, 2001.

[24] N. Kobayashi, B. C. Pierce, and D. N. Turner. Linearity and the pi-calculus. In *23rd Symposium on Principles of Programming Languages*, POPL'96, pages 358–371. ACM, 1996.

[25] P. Martin-Löf. Constructive mathematics and computer programming. In *Logic, Methodology and Philosophy of Science VI*, pages 153–175. North-Holland, 1980.

[26] R. Milner. Functions as processes. *Math. Struct. in Comp. Sci.*, 2(2):119–141, 1992.

[27] G. C. Necula. Proof-carrying code. In *24th Symposium on Principles of Programming Languages*, POPL'97, pages 106–119. ACM, 1997.

[28] U. Norell. *Towards a practical programming language based on dependent type theory*. PhD thesis, Chalmers University of Technology, SE-412 96 Göteborg, Sweden, September 2007.

[29] F. Pfenning. Intensionality, extensionality, and proof irrelevance in modal type theory. In *16th Symposium on Logic in Computer Science*, LICS'01, pages 221–230. IEEE Computer Society, 2001.

[30] D. Sangiorgi and D. Walker. *The π-calculus: A Theory of Mobile Processes*. Cambridge University Press, 2001.

[31] H. Xi and F. Pfenning. Eliminating array bound checking through dependent types. In *Conference on Programming Language Design and Implementation*, PLDI'98, pages 249–257. ACM, 1998.

Linearity and Recursion in a Typed Lambda-Calculus

Sandra Alves
DCC-Faculty of Science & LIACC
University of Porto
sandra@dcc.fc.up.pt

Maribel Fernández
Department of Informatics
King's College London
Maribel.Fernandez@kcl.ac.uk

Mário Florido
DCC-Faculty of Science & LIACC
University of Porto
amf@dcc.fc.up.pt

Ian Mackie
LIX, CNRS UMR 7161
École Polytechnique
mackie@lix.polytechnique.fr

Abstract

We show that the full PCF language can be encoded in $\mathcal{L}_{\mathsf{rec}}$, a syntactically linear λ-calculus extended with numbers, pairs, and an unbounded recursor that preserves the syntactic linearity of the calculus. We give call-by-name and call-by-value evaluation strategies and discuss implementation techniques for $\mathcal{L}_{\mathsf{rec}}$, exploiting its linearity.

Categories and Subject Descriptors F.4.1 [*Mathematical Logic*]: Lambda calculus and related systems

General Terms Languages, Theory

Keywords linear λ-calculus, recursion, PCF

1. Introduction

This paper completes a program of research investigating the power of linear functions, starting from primitive recursion [3], followed by Gödel's System $\mathcal{T}$ [4], and leading to PCF, which we deal with in this paper. Knowing that an argument to a function is used exactly once—i.e., linearly—is a property that a compiler can make use of to optimise code. It is related to several program analyses, for instance, strictness analysis, pointer analysis, effects and resource analysis (see, e.g., [13, 17, 18, 31, 44, 49–51]); computing these analyses gives approximations. Linear functions are also naturally occurring in hardware compilation [22]. Circuits are static (i.e., they cannot be copied at run-time), so linear computations are more naturally compiled into hardware.

Linearity has also applications in other domains. For instance, in the area of quantum computation one of the most important results is the no-cloning theorem, stating that qbits cannot be duplicated. Again, a linear calculus captures this [48]. In concurrent calculi, like the π-calculus [43], a key aspect is the notion of name, and the dual role that names play as communication channels and variables. The linear π-calculus [38] has linear (use-once) channels. This has clear gains in efficiency and on program analysis avoiding several problems of channel sharing. Also, inspired by the works by Kobayashi, Pierce and Turner [38] and the works by Honda [33] on session types, several type systems for the π-calculus rely directly on linearity to deal with resources, non-interference and effects [28, 52].

In this paper we focus on functional computations. We aim at obtaining a linear, universal model of computation that can serve as a basis for the design of programming languages. Our approach is to begin with a linear calculus, and build non-linearity in a controlled way.

Extensions of the linear λ-calculus based on bounded iteration capture interesting classes of programs (see, e.g., [7, 8, 23, 27, 30, 40, 47]). In particular, a linear version of Gödel's System $\mathcal{T}$ which we call System $\mathcal{L}$ captures exactly the class of primitive recursive functions (PR) if iterators use only closed linear functions [16], whereas the same system with a closed reduction strategy [19] has all the computation power of System $\mathcal{T}$ [4]. The latter result shows some redundancy regarding duplication in System $\mathcal{T}$, which can be achieved through iteration or through non-linear occurrences of the bound variable in the body of a function.

Following this work, the question that arises is, what is the minimal extension of the linear λ-calculus that yields a Turing complete system, compatible with the notion of linear function?

From the perspective of recursion theory, Turing completeness can be achieved by adding a minimisation operator working on a first-order linear system (using a set of linear initial functions and a linear primitive recursion scheme) [3]. A similar result is shown in this paper for the linear λ-calculus: an extension of System $\mathcal{L}$ with a minimiser is Turing complete. However, it relies on both iteration and minimisation.

In the context of the simply typed λ-calculus, there is an alternative way to obtain Turing completeness, by adding a fixpoint operator (as it is done in PCF [46]). This approach has been used to extend linear functional calculi (see, e.g., [12, 14, 41, 45]), however, it relies on the existence of a non-linear conditional which throws away a possibly infinite computation in one of the branches. Instead, in this paper, we obtain a Turing-complete linear λ-calculus through the use of an unbounded recursor with a built-in test on pairs, which allows the encoding of both finite iteration and minimisation. More precisely, we define $\mathcal{L}_{\mathsf{rec}}$, a linear λ-calculus extended with numbers, pairs and a linear unbounded recursor, with a closed-reduction strategy. We show that $\mathcal{L}_{\mathsf{rec}}$ is Turing complete and can be easily implemented: we give an abstract machine whose

PDPP'11, July 20–22, 2011, Odense, Denmark.

configurations consist simply of a term and a stack of terms. As an application, we give a compilation of PCF into $\mathcal{L}_{\text{rec}}$.

Several abstract machines for linear calculi are available in the literature (see for instance [39, 42, 50]). The novelty here is that we implement a calculus that is syntactically linear (in the sense that each variable is linear in $\mathcal{L}_{\text{rec}}$ terms) and therefore there is no need to include in the abstract machine an environment (or store in the terminology of [50]) to store bindings for variables.

Summarising, the main contributions of this paper are the following:

- We define $\mathcal{L}_{\text{rec}}$, a linear λ-calculus extended with numbers, pairs and an unbounded recursor, with a closed-reduction strategy. We show some properties regarding reduction (such as subject-reduction and confluence), and prove Turing completeness by encoding the set of partial recursive functions in $\mathcal{L}_{\text{rec}}$.
- We give call-by-name and call-by-value evaluation strategies, and define a simple abstract machine for $\mathcal{L}_{\text{rec}}$, exploiting its linearity.
- We study the interplay between linearity and recursion based on fixpoint combinators, and define an encoding of PCF in $\mathcal{L}_{\text{rec}}$.
- By combining the two previous points, we obtain a new implementation of PCF via a simple stack-based abstract machine.

Related notions of linearity Three notions of linearity have been defined for functional calculi in the literature: syntactical, operational and denotational. Operational linearity means that arguments of functions cannot be duplicated or erased during evaluation (cf. *weak linear terms* [6] and *simple terms* [36]). Denotational linearity is achieved when only linear functions can be defined in the language (see, e.g., [45]). The language defined in [45] is a linear version of PCF in a denotational sense: it has a linear model (linear coherence spaces) but its terms can contain more than one occurrence of the same variable. Finally, syntactical linearity, requires a linear use of variables in terms [34].

Operational linearity has great impact when the control of copying and deleting is important, as it can be used to efficiently implement garbage collection for instance. Note however that checking if a term is operationally linear relies on the evaluation of the term. For the linear λ-calculus, syntactical linearity, which can be statically checked, implies operational linearity. For $\mathcal{L}_{\text{rec}}$, which combines syntactical linearity with closed reduction, the fragment without recursion is operationally linear; erasing and duplication can only be done by the recursor (and moreover, only closed terms can be erased or duplicated in $\mathcal{L}_{\text{rec}}$, thanks to the use of a closed reduction strategy). In linear logic [24] this is done by the use of exponentials, and in other linear calculi [1, 32, 41, 50] by explicit syntactical constructs introduced specifically to perform copy and erase, whereas here we exploit recursion to perform copy and erasing of terms.

Overview of the paper The rest of this paper is structured as follows. In the next section we introduce basic concepts and notations that will be used in the rest of the paper. We give the syntax and type system of $\mathcal{L}_{\text{rec}}$ together with some standard properties in Section 3. In Section 4 we study evaluation strategies and abstract machines. In Section 5 we look at the relation with PCF. Finally, we conclude in Section 6. See [5] for an extended version of this paper with detailed proofs.

2. Background

We assume the reader is familiar with the λ-calculus [9]. In this section we recall the definition of System $\mathcal{L}$ [4], a linear version of Gödel's System $\mathcal{T}$ (for details on the latter see [26]).

The terms of System $\mathcal{L}$ are obtained by extending the terms of the linear λ-calculus [1] with numbers, pairs, and an iterator. Linear λ-terms $t, u, \ldots$ are inductively defined by:

- $x \in \Lambda$,
- $\lambda x.t \in \Lambda$ if $x \in \mathsf{fv}(t)$, and
- $tu \in \Lambda$ if $\mathsf{fv}(t) \cap \mathsf{fv}(u) = \varnothing$.

Note that x is used at least once in the body of the abstraction, and the condition on the application ensures that all variables are used at most once. Thus these conditions ensure syntactic linearity (variables occur exactly once). In System $\mathcal{L}$ we also have numbers generated by 0 and S, with an iterator:

$$\text{iter}\ t\ u\ v \ \text{ if } \mathsf{fv}(t) \cap \mathsf{fv}(u) = \mathsf{fv}(u) \cap \mathsf{fv}(v) = \mathsf{fv}(v) \cap \mathsf{fv}(t) = \varnothing$$

and pairs:

$$\begin{array}{ll} \langle t, u \rangle & \text{if } \mathsf{fv}(t) \cap \mathsf{fv}(u) = \varnothing \\ \texttt{let}\ \langle x, y \rangle = t\ \texttt{in}\ u & \text{if } x, y \in \mathsf{fv}(u) \text{ and} \\ & \mathsf{fv}(t) \cap (\mathsf{fv}(u) - \{x, y\}) = \varnothing \end{array}$$

Since λ and `let` are binders, terms are defined modulo α-equivalence as usual.

Note that when projecting from a pair, we use both projections. A simple example is the function that swaps the components of a pair: $\lambda x.\texttt{let}\ \langle y, z \rangle = x\ \texttt{in}\ \langle z, y \rangle$.

Below we use tuples of any size, built from pairs. For example, $\langle x_1, x_2, x_3 \rangle = \langle x_1, \langle x_2, x_3 \rangle \rangle$ and $\texttt{let}\ \langle x_1, x_2, x_3 \rangle = u\ \texttt{in}\ t$ will be used as abbreviation for the term $\texttt{let}\ \langle x_1, y \rangle = u\ \texttt{in}\ \texttt{let}\ \langle x_2, x_3 \rangle = y\ \texttt{in}\ t$.

System $\mathcal{L}$ uses a closed reduction strategy (first defined by Girard [25] for cut elimination in linear logic, and adapted to the λ-calculus in [19]). This strategy for cut elimination is simple and exceptionally efficient in terms of the number of cut elimination steps. In the λ-calculus, it avoids α-conversion while allowing reductions inside abstractions (in contrast with standard weak strategies), thus achieving more sharing of computation.

The reduction rules for System $\mathcal{L}$ are given in Table 1. Substitution is a meta-operation defined as usual, and reductions can take place in any context.

Note that all the substitutions created during reduction (rules *Beta* and *Let*) are closed (thus, there is no need to perform α-conversions during reduction), and the *Iter* rules are only triggered when the function v is closed. Thanks to the use of a closed reduction strategy, iterators on *open* linear functions are accepted in System $\mathcal{L}$ (since these terms are syntactically linear), and reduction preserves linearity. Normal forms are not the same as in the λ-calculus (for example, $\lambda x.(\lambda y.y)x$ is a normal form), but closed reduction is still adequate for the evaluation of closed terms (if a term has a weak head normal form, it will be reached [4]). Closed reduction can also be used to evaluate open terms, using the "normalisation by evaluation" technique [11] as shown in [19, 20] (in the latter director strings are used to implement closedness tests as local checks on terms).

Although linear, some terms are not strongly normalising. For instance, $\Delta\Delta$ where $\Delta = \lambda x.\text{iter}\ S^2 0\ (\lambda xy.xy)\ (\lambda y.yx)$ reduces to itself. However, the linear type system defined in [4] ensures strong normalisation. System $\mathcal{L}$ has all the power of System $\mathcal{T}$; we refer to [4] for more details and examples.

3. System $\mathcal{L}_{\text{rec}}$: syntax and properties

Since all typable terms in System $\mathcal{L}$ are terminating, it is clear that this system is not Turing complete. In this section we define $\mathcal{L}_{\text{rec}}$, an extension of the linear λ-calculus [1] with numbers, pairs, and a typed unbounded recursor with a closed reduction strategy. We prove that it is Turing complete.

Name	Reduction			Condition
Beta	$(\lambda x.t)v$	$\longrightarrow$	$t[v/x]$	$\mathsf{fv}(v) = \varnothing$
Let	$\mathtt{let}\ \langle x, y\rangle = \langle t, u\rangle\ \mathtt{in}\ v$	$\longrightarrow$	$(v[t/x])[u/y]$	$\mathsf{fv}(t) = \mathsf{fv}(u) = \varnothing$
Iter	$\mathsf{iter}\ (\mathsf{S}\ t)\ u\ v$	$\longrightarrow$	$v(\mathsf{iter}\ t\ u\ v)$	$\mathsf{fv}(v) = \varnothing$
Iter	$\mathsf{iter}\ 0\ u\ v$	$\longrightarrow$	u	$\mathsf{fv}(v) = \varnothing$

Table 1. Closed reduction in System $\mathcal{L}$

The syntax of $\mathcal{L}_{\mathsf{rec}}$ is similar to that of System $\mathcal{L}$, except that instead of a bounded iterator we have a recursor working on pairs of natural numbers. Table 2 summarises the syntax of terms in $\mathcal{L}_{\mathsf{rec}}$. We assume Barendregt's convention regarding names of free and bound variables in terms.

The reduction rules for $\mathcal{L}_{\mathsf{rec}}$ are *Beta* and *Let*, given in Table 1, together with two rules for the recursor shown in Table 3.

Note that the *Rec* rules are only triggered when the conditions hold, thus linearity is preserved by reduction. The conditions on *Beta* and *Let* are orthogonal to the linearity issues (as explained in the previous section, they simply produce a more efficient strategy of reduction) and do not affect the technical results of the paper (we prove that even with these conditions the system is Turing complete).

The *Rec* rules pattern-match on a pair of numbers whereas the usual bounded recursor works on a single number. This is because we are representing both bounded and unbounded recursion with the same operator (as the examples below illustrate). An alternative would be to have an extra parameter of type N in the recursor.

The last parameter of the recursor is used to compute the next pair of numbers; in this way we can program unbounded recursion as well as bounded recursion, as shown below.

3.1 Examples

Bounded iteration Using the recursor we can encode System $\mathcal{L}$'s iterator. Let I be the identity function $\lambda x.x$. We define "iter" in System $\mathcal{L}_{\mathsf{rec}}$ as follows:

$$\text{"iter"}\ t\ u\ v \stackrel{\mathsf{def}}{=} \mathsf{rec}\ \langle t, 0\rangle\ u\ v\ I$$

We will show later that this term has the same behaviour as System $\mathcal{L}$'s iterator.

Projections and duplication of natural numbers We can define projections for pairs $\langle a, b\rangle$ of natural numbers, by using them in a recursor.

$$\begin{array}{lcl} pr_1 & = & \lambda x.\mathtt{let}\ \langle a, b\rangle = x\ \mathtt{in}\ \mathsf{rec}\ \langle b, 0\rangle\ a\ I\ I \\ pr_2 & = & \lambda x.\mathtt{let}\ \langle a, b\rangle = x\ \mathtt{in}\ \mathsf{rec}\ \langle a, 0\rangle\ b\ I\ I \end{array}$$

The following function C can be used to copy numbers:

$$C = \lambda x.\mathsf{rec}\ \langle x, 0\rangle\ \langle 0, 0\rangle\ (\lambda x.\mathtt{let}\ x = \langle a, b\rangle\ \mathtt{in}\ \langle \mathsf{S}a, \mathsf{S}b\rangle)\ I$$

Other mechanisms to erase and copy numbers in $\mathcal{L}_{\mathsf{rec}}$ will be shown later.

Arithmetic functions We can now define some arithmetic functions that we will use in the paper.

- $\mathsf{add} = \lambda mn.\mathsf{iter}\ m\ 0\ n\ (\lambda x.\mathsf{S}x)$;
- $\mathsf{mult} = \lambda mn.\mathsf{iter}\ m\ 0\ (\mathsf{add}\ n)$;
- $\mathsf{pred} = \lambda n.pr_1(\mathsf{rec}\ \langle n, 0\rangle\ \langle 0, 0\rangle\ F\ I)$ where $F = \lambda x.\mathtt{let}\ \langle t, u\rangle = C(pr_2\ x)\ \mathtt{in}\ \langle t, \mathsf{S}\ u\rangle$;
- $\mathsf{iszero} = \lambda n.pr_1(\mathsf{rec}\ \langle n, 0\rangle\ \langle 0, \mathsf{S}\ 0\rangle\ (\lambda x.C(pr_2\ x))\ I)$.

The correctness of these encodings can be easily proved by induction.

Minimisation We can also encode the minimisation operator μ_f used to define partial recursive functions. Recall that if $f : \mathbb{N} \longrightarrow \mathbb{N}$ is a total function on natural numbers, $\mu_f = \min\{x \in \mathbb{N} \mid f(x) = 0\}$.

Let $\overline{f}$ be a closed λ-term in $\mathcal{L}_{\mathsf{rec}}$ representing a total function f on natural numbers. The encoding of μ_f is

$$M = \mathsf{rec}\ \langle \overline{f}0, 0\rangle\ 0\ (\lambda x.\mathsf{S}(x))\ F$$

where $F = \lambda x.\mathtt{let}\ \langle y, z\rangle = C(pr_2 x)\ \mathtt{in}\ \langle \overline{f}(\mathsf{S}y), \mathsf{S}z\rangle$. We prove the correctness of this encoding below. This operator cannot be represented in the strongly normalising System $\mathcal{L}$: μ_f may be undefined, in which case M does not terminate.

3.2 Types for System $\mathcal{L}_{\mathsf{rec}}$

We consider *linear types* generated by the grammar:

$$A, B ::= \mathsf{N} \mid A \multimap B \mid A \otimes B$$

where N is the type of numbers. A type environment Γ is a list of type assumptions of the form $x : A$ where x is a variable and A a type, and each variable occurs at most once in Γ. We write $dom(\Gamma)$ to denote the set of variables that occur in Γ.

We write $\Gamma \vdash_{\mathcal{L}} t : A$ if the term t can be assigned the type A in the environment Γ using the typing rules in Table 4. Note that the only structural rule is Exchange: we are in a linear system. For the same reason, the logical rules split the context between the premises (i.e., the variable conditions in Table 2 are enforced by the typing rules).

All the terms given in the examples above can be typed.

THEOREM 1 (Properties of reductions in $\mathcal{L}_{\mathsf{rec}}$).

1. *If $\Gamma \vdash_{\mathcal{L}} t : T$ then $dom(\Gamma) = \mathsf{fv}(t)$.*
2. *Subject Reduction: Reductions preserve types.*
3. *Church-Rosser: System $\mathcal{L}_{\mathsf{rec}}$ is confluent.*
4. *Adequacy: If $\vdash_{\mathcal{L}} t : T$ in System $\mathcal{L}_{\mathsf{rec}}$, and t is a normal form, then there are $\mathcal{L}_{\mathsf{rec}}$ terms u, s such that:*

$$\begin{array}{lcl} T = \mathsf{N} & \Rightarrow & t = \mathsf{S}(\mathsf{S}\ldots(\mathsf{S}\ 0)) \\ T = A \otimes B & \Rightarrow & t = \langle u, s\rangle \\ T = A \multimap B & \Rightarrow & t = \lambda x.s \end{array}$$

5. *System $\mathcal{L}_{\mathsf{rec}}$ is not strongly normalising, even for typable terms.*

Proof:

1. By induction on type derivations.
2. By induction on type derivations, using a substitution lemma as usual.
3. Confluence can be proved directly, using Martin-Löf's technique (as it was done for System $\mathcal{L}$, see [2]) or can be obtained as a consequence of Klop's theorem for orthogonal higher-order reductions [37].
4. By induction on t.
5. The following term is typable but is not strongly normalisable:

$$\mathsf{rec}\ \langle \mathsf{S}(0), 0\rangle\ 0\ I\ (\lambda x.\mathtt{let}\ \langle y, z\rangle = x\ \mathtt{in}\ \langle \mathsf{S}(y), z\rangle)$$

Another non-terminating typable term is given in Section 3.3.

Construction	Variable Constraint	Free Variables (fv)
0	–	$\varnothing$
$\mathsf{S}\, t$	–	$\mathsf{fv}(t)$
$\mathsf{rec}\ t_1\ t_2\ t_3\ t_4$	$\mathsf{fv}(t_i) \cap \mathsf{fv}(t_j) = \varnothing$, for $i \neq j$	$\cup \mathsf{fv}(t_i)$
x	–	$\{x\}$
tu	$\mathsf{fv}(t) \cap \mathsf{fv}(u) = \varnothing$	$\mathsf{fv}(t) \cup \mathsf{fv}(u)$
$\lambda x.t$	$x \in \mathsf{fv}(t)$	$\mathsf{fv}(t) \smallsetminus \{x\}$
$\langle t, u\rangle$	$\mathsf{fv}(t) \cap \mathsf{fv}(u) = \varnothing$	$\mathsf{fv}(t) \cup \mathsf{fv}(u)$
$\mathtt{let}\ \langle x, y\rangle = t\ \mathtt{in}\ u$	$x, y \in \mathsf{fv}(u), \mathsf{fv}(t) \cap \mathsf{fv}(u) = \varnothing$	$\mathsf{fv}(t) \cup (\mathsf{fv}(u) \smallsetminus \{x, y\})$

Table 2. Terms in System $\mathcal{L}_{\mathsf{rec}}$

Name	Reduction			Condition
Rec	$\mathsf{rec}\ \langle 0, t'\rangle\ u\ v\ w$	$\rightarrow$	u	$\mathsf{fv}(t'vw) = \varnothing$
Rec	$\mathsf{rec}\ \langle \mathsf{S}\ t, t'\rangle\ u\ v\ w$	$\rightarrow$	$v(\mathsf{rec}\ (w\langle t, t'\rangle)\ u\ v\ w)$	$\mathsf{fv}(vw) = \varnothing$

Table 3. Closed reduction for recursion

Axiom and **Structural Rule**:

$$\frac{}{x : A \vdash_{\mathcal{L}} x : A}\ (\mathsf{Axiom}) \qquad \frac{\Gamma, x : A, y : B, \Delta \vdash_{\mathcal{L}} t : C}{\Gamma, y : B, x : A, \Delta \vdash_{\mathcal{L}} t : C}\ (\mathsf{Exchange})$$

Logical Rules:

$$\frac{\Gamma, x : A \vdash_{\mathcal{L}} t : B}{\Gamma \vdash_{\mathcal{L}} \lambda x.t : A \multimap B}\ (\multimap\mathsf{Intro}) \qquad \frac{\Gamma \vdash_{\mathcal{L}} t : A \multimap B \quad \Delta \vdash_{\mathcal{L}} u : A}{\Gamma, \Delta \vdash_{\mathcal{L}} tu : B}\ (\multimap\mathsf{Elim})$$

$$\frac{\Gamma \vdash_{\mathcal{L}} t : A \quad \Delta \vdash_{\mathcal{L}} u : B}{\Gamma, \Delta \vdash_{\mathcal{L}} \langle t, u\rangle : A \otimes B}\ (\otimes\mathsf{Intro}) \qquad \frac{\Gamma \vdash_{\mathcal{L}} t : A \otimes B \quad \Delta, x : A, y : B \vdash_{\mathcal{L}} u : C}{\Gamma, \Delta \vdash_{\mathcal{L}} \mathtt{let}\ \langle x, y\rangle = t\ \mathtt{in}\ u : C}\ (\otimes\mathsf{Elim})$$

Numbers

$$\frac{}{\vdash_{\mathcal{L}} 0 : \mathsf{N}}\ (\mathsf{Zero}) \qquad \frac{\Gamma \vdash_{\mathcal{L}} n : \mathsf{N}}{\Gamma \vdash_{\mathcal{L}} \mathsf{S}\, n : \mathsf{N}}\ (\mathsf{Succ}) \qquad \frac{\Gamma \vdash_{\mathcal{L}} t : \mathsf{N} \otimes \mathsf{N} \quad \Theta \vdash_{\mathcal{L}} u : A \quad \Delta \vdash_{\mathcal{L}} v : A \multimap A \quad \Sigma \vdash_{\mathcal{L}} w : \mathsf{N} \otimes \mathsf{N} \multimap \mathsf{N} \otimes \mathsf{N}}{\Gamma, \Theta, \Delta, \Sigma \vdash_{\mathcal{L}} \mathsf{rec}\ t\ u\ v\ w : A}\ (\mathsf{Rec})$$

Table 4. Type System for System $\mathcal{L}_{\mathsf{rec}}$

3.3 The computational power of System $\mathcal{L}_{\mathsf{rec}}$

We now prove that System $\mathcal{L}_{\mathsf{rec}}$ is Turing complete. First note that although in the linear λ-calculus we are not able to discard arguments of functions, terms are consumed by reduction. The idea of erasing by consuming is related to the notion of Solvability (see [9], Chapter 8) as it relies on reduction to the identity. Using this technique, in [2, 4] it is shown that in System $\mathcal{L}$ there is a general form of erasing. We next apply this technique to System $\mathcal{L}_{\mathsf{rec}}$, generalising the encoding of projections given in Section 3.1.

The term $\mathcal{E}(t, A)$ defined below erases a term t of type A, under certain conditions. In the definition we use a function $\mathcal{M}$ to build a term of a specific type ($\mathcal{E}$ and $\mathcal{M}$ are mutually recursive).

DEFINITION 1 (Erasing). *If $\Gamma \vdash_{\mathcal{L}} t : A$, then $\mathcal{E}(t, A)$ is defined as follows:*

$$\begin{array}{lcl}
\mathcal{E}(t, \mathsf{N}) & = & \mathsf{rec}\ \langle t, 0\rangle\ I\ I\ I \\
\mathcal{E}(t, A \otimes B) & = & \mathtt{let}\ \langle x, y\rangle = t\ \mathtt{in}\ \mathcal{E}(x, A)\mathcal{E}(y, B) \\
\mathcal{E}(t, A \multimap B) & = & \mathcal{E}(t\mathcal{M}(A), B) \\
\textit{and} & & \\
\mathcal{M}(\mathsf{N}) & = & 0 \\
\mathcal{M}(A \otimes B) & = & \langle \mathcal{M}(A), \mathcal{M}(B)\rangle \\
\mathcal{M}(A \multimap B) & = & \lambda x.\mathcal{E}(x, A)\mathcal{M}(B)
\end{array}$$

THEOREM 2. *1. If $\Gamma \vdash_{\mathcal{L}} t : T$ then $\Gamma \vdash_{\mathcal{L}} \mathcal{E}(t, T) : B \multimap B$, for any type B.*

2. $\mathcal{M}(T)$ is closed and typable: $\vdash_{\mathcal{L}} \mathcal{M}(T) : T$.

3. For any type T, $\mathcal{E}(\mathcal{M}(T), T) \rightarrow^* I$.

4. $\mathcal{M}(T)$ is normalisable.

Proof: The first two parts are proved by simultaneous induction on T, as done for System $\mathcal{L}$ [4]. The third part is proved by induction on T. We show the case for the arrow type.

If $T = A \multimap B$ then $\mathcal{M}(T) = \lambda x.\mathcal{E}(x, A)\mathcal{M}(B)$, therefore

$$\begin{array}{cl}
 & \mathcal{E}(\lambda x.\mathcal{E}(x, A)\mathcal{M}(B), A \multimap B) \\
= & \mathcal{E}((\lambda x.\mathcal{E}(x, A)\mathcal{M}(B))\mathcal{M}(A), B) \\
\rightarrow & \mathcal{E}(\mathcal{E}(\mathcal{M}(A), A)\mathcal{M}(B), B) \\
\overset{\text{(I.H.)}}{\rightarrow^*} & \mathcal{E}(I\mathcal{M}(B), B) \rightarrow \mathcal{E}(\mathcal{M}(B), B) \overset{\text{(I.H.)}}{\rightarrow^*} I
\end{array}$$

The last part is proved by induction on T.

$\mathcal{L}_{\mathsf{rec}}$, unlike System $\mathcal{L}$, is not normalising, and there are terms that cannot be erased using this definition. There are even normalising terms that cannot be erased by reduction. For example, consider the following term Y_{N} which represents a fixpoint operator (more details are given in Section 5):

$$Y_{\mathsf{N}} = \lambda f.\mathsf{rec}\ \langle \mathsf{S}(0), 0\rangle\ 0\ f\ (\lambda x.\mathtt{let}\ \langle y, z\rangle = x\ \mathtt{in}\ \langle \mathsf{S}(y), z\rangle)$$

This term is typable (it has type $(\mathsf{N} \multimap \mathsf{N}) \multimap \mathsf{N}$) and is a normal form (the recursor rules do not apply because f is a variable).

However, the term

$$\mathcal{E}(Y_{\mathsf{N}}, (\mathsf{N} \multimap \mathsf{N}) \multimap \mathsf{N}) = \mathsf{rec}\ \langle Y_{\mathsf{N}}(\lambda x.\mathcal{E}(x, \mathsf{N})0), 0\rangle\ I\ I\ I$$

does not have a normal form. On the positive side, closed normalising terms of type N, or tuples where the elements are terms of type N, can indeed be erased using this technique. Erasing "by consuming" reflects the work that needs to be done to effectively dispose of a data structure (where each component is garbage collected).

THEOREM 3. *Let T be a type generated by the grammar: $A, B ::= \mathsf{N} \mid A \otimes B$. If $\vdash_{\mathcal{L}} t : T$ and t has a normal form, then $\mathcal{E}(t, T) \to^* I$.*

Proof: By induction on T. We show the case for $T = A \otimes B$: $\mathcal{E}(t, T) = \mathtt{let}\ \langle x, y\rangle = t\ \mathtt{in}\ \mathcal{E}(x, A)\mathcal{E}(y, B)$. Since t is normalisable then, by Adequacy (Theorem 1), $t \to^* v = \langle u, s\rangle$. Thus $\mathtt{let}\ \langle x, y\rangle = t\ \mathtt{in}\ \mathcal{E}(x, A)\mathcal{E}(y, B) \to^* \mathtt{let}\ \langle x, y\rangle = \langle u, s\rangle\ \mathtt{in}\ \mathcal{E}(x, A)\mathcal{E}(y, B) \to \mathcal{E}(u, A)\mathcal{E}(s, B)$. By I.H. $\mathcal{E}(u, A) \to^* I$ and $\mathcal{E}(s, B) \to^* I$, therefore $\mathcal{E}(u, A)\mathcal{E}(s, B) \to^* II \to I$.

There is also a mechanism to copy closed terms in $\mathcal{L}_{\mathsf{rec}}$:

DEFINITION 2 (Duplication). *Define $D^A : A \multimap A \otimes A$ as:*

$$\lambda x.\mathsf{rec}\ \langle \mathsf{S}(\mathsf{S}\ 0), 0\rangle\ \langle \mathcal{M}(A), \mathcal{M}(A)\rangle\ F\ I$$

where $F = (\lambda y.\mathtt{let}\ \langle z, w\rangle = y\ \mathtt{in}\ \mathcal{E}(z, A)\langle w, x\rangle)$.

THEOREM 4. *If $\vdash_{\mathcal{L}} t : A$ then $D^A\ t \to^* \langle t, t\rangle$.*

Proof: By the definition of $\to$.

The encoding of System $\mathcal{L}$'s iterator, defined in Section 3.1, behaves as expected. System $\mathcal{L}$ is a sub-system of $\mathcal{L}_{\mathsf{rec}}$.

PROPOSITION 1.

"iter" $t\ u\ v \to^* u$	*if* $t \to^* 0$, $\mathsf{fv}(v) = \varnothing$
"iter" $t\ u\ v \to^* v(\text{"iter"}\ t_1\ u\ v)$	*if* $t \to^* \mathsf{S}(t_1)$, $\mathsf{fv}(v) = \varnothing$

If $\Gamma \vdash_{\mathcal{L}} t : \mathsf{N}$, $\Theta \vdash_{\mathcal{L}} u : A$, and $\Delta \vdash_{\mathcal{L}} v : A \multimap A$, then $\Gamma, \Theta, \Delta \vdash_{\mathcal{L}} \mathsf{rec}\ \langle t, 0\rangle\ u\ v\ I : A$ ("iter" $t\ u\ v$ is well typed).

COROLLARY 1. *$\mathcal{L}_{\mathsf{rec}}$ has all the computation power of System $\mathcal{L}$, thus, any System T function can be defined in $\mathcal{L}_{\mathsf{rec}}$.*

We now show that the encoding of the minimiser given in Section 3.1 behaves as expected.

THEOREM 5 (Minimisation in System $\mathcal{L}_{\mathsf{rec}}$). *Let $\overline{f}$ be a closed λ-term in $\mathcal{L}_{\mathsf{rec}}$, encoding the total function f on the natural numbers. The term M encodes μ_f.*

Proof: Consider the non-empty sequence

$$S = f(i), f(i+1), \ldots, f(i+n),$$

such that $f(i+n)$ is the first element in the sequence that is equal to zero. Then one can easily prove by induction on the length of S that:

$$\mathsf{rec}\ \langle \overline{f}\mathsf{S}^i 0, \mathsf{S}^i 0\rangle\ 0\ (\lambda x.\mathsf{S}(x))\ F \to^* \mathsf{S}^n 0$$

Now, let $j = \min\{x \in \mathbb{N} \mid f(x) = 0\}$, and consider the sequence $f(0), \ldots, f(j)$. Therefore $\mathsf{rec}\ \langle \overline{f}0, 0\rangle\ 0\ (\lambda x.\mathsf{S}(x))\ F \to^* \mathsf{S}^j 0$. Note that, if there exists no x such that $f(x) = 0$, then $\mathsf{rec}\ \langle \overline{f}0, 0\rangle\ 0\ (\lambda x.\mathsf{S}(x))\ F$ diverges, and so does the minimisation of f.

COROLLARY 2. *System $\mathcal{L}_{\mathsf{rec}}$ is Turing complete.*

3.4 Unbounded recursion vs. iteration and minimisation

There are two standard ways of extending the primitive recursive functions so that all partial recursive functions are obtained. One is unbounded minimisation, the other is unbounded recursion. For first-order functions (i.e., functions of type level 1), both methods are equivalent, see for instance [10]. Starting from System $\mathcal{L}$ we could add a minimiser, with two reduction rules:

$$\begin{array}{llll} \mu\ 0\ u\ f & \to & u & \mathsf{fv}(f) = \varnothing \\ \mu\ (\mathsf{S}\ t)\ u\ f & \to & \mu\ (f\ (\mathsf{S}\ u))\ (\mathsf{S}\ u)\ f & \mathsf{fv}(ftu) = \varnothing \end{array}$$

and a typing rule

$$\frac{\Gamma \vdash_{\mathcal{L}} t : \mathsf{N} \quad \Theta \vdash_{\mathcal{L}} u : \mathsf{N} \quad \Delta \vdash_{\mathcal{L}} v : \mathsf{N} \multimap \mathsf{N}}{\Gamma, \Theta, \Delta \vdash_{\mathcal{L}} \mu\ t\ u\ v : \mathsf{N}}\ (\mathsf{Min})$$

Then μ_f can be simulated with $\mu\ (f\ 0)\ 0\ f$ and the resulting system (we shall call it System $\mathcal{L}_\mu$) is also Turing complete.

We can encode System $\mathcal{L}_{\mathsf{rec}}$ into System $\mathcal{L}_\mu$, simulating the recursor with iter and μ. Consider the following term:

$$f = \lambda n.pr_1(\mathsf{iter}\ n\ \langle t, t'\rangle\ (w \circ \mathsf{pred}_1))$$

where pred_1 is such that $\mathsf{pred}_1\langle \mathsf{S}(t), t'\rangle = \langle t, t\rangle$. The function f, given n, will produce $pr_1((w \circ \mathsf{pred}_1)^n\langle t, t'\rangle)$. Now consider $(\mu\ t\ 0\ f)$, which will lead to the following sequence:

$$\mu\ t\ 0\ f \to \mu\ f(1)\ 1\ f \to \mu\ f(2)\ 2\ f \to \mu\ f(3)\ 3\ f \to \ldots \to n$$

where n is the minimum number such that $(w \circ \mathsf{pred}_1)^n\langle t, t'\rangle$ produces $\langle 0, t''\rangle$. Now, one can encode $\mathsf{rec}\ \langle t, t\rangle\ u\ v\ w$ as:

$$\mathsf{iter}\ (\mu\ t\ 0\ f)\ u\ v$$

Notice that $\mathsf{rec}\ \langle \mathsf{S}t, t'\rangle\ u\ v\ w$ will iterate v until $w\langle t, t'\rangle$ is equal to zero, and that $\mu\ t\ 0\ f$ will count the number of iterations that will actually be necessary, or will go on forever if that never happens.

$\mathcal{L}_{\mathsf{rec}}$ can be seen as a more compact version of System $\mathcal{L}_\mu$ where the recursor can perform both bounded iteration or minimisation. Yet another way to obtain Turing completeness of typed λ-calculi is via fixpoint operators and conditionals, as done in PCF [46]. We study in Section 5 the relation between $\mathcal{L}_{\mathsf{rec}}$ and PCF.

4. Evaluation strategies

In this section we define two evaluation strategies for System $\mathcal{L}_{\mathsf{rec}}$ and derive a stack-based abstract machine.

Call-by-name The CBN evaluation relation for closed terms in System $\mathcal{L}_{\mathsf{rec}}$ is defined in Table 5. The notation $t \Downarrow V$ means that the closed term t evaluates in System $\mathcal{L}_{\mathsf{rec}}$ to the value V. *Values* are terms of the form 0, $\mathsf{S}t$, $\lambda x.t$ and $\langle s, t\rangle$, i.e., *weak head normal forms* (whnf). Note that System $\mathcal{L}_{\mathsf{rec}}$ does not evaluate under an S symbol, since S is used as a constructor for natural numbers, unlike PCF's succ, which is a function. Also note that no closedness conditions are needed in the evaluation rules for closed terms.

The rule *Let* is given using application to simplify the presentation (in this way, we will be able to reuse this rule when we define the call-by-value evaluation relation below).

The evaluation relation $\cdot \Downarrow \cdot$ corresponds to *standard reduction* to weak head normal form. Recall that a reduction is called standard if the contraction of redexes is made from left-to-right (i.e., leftmost-outermost). It is well known that for the λ-calculus [9], the standard reduction is normalising, that is, if a term has a normal form, then it will be reached. A "standardisation" result holds for closed terms in $\mathcal{L}_{\mathsf{rec}}$, as the following theorem shows.

THEOREM 6. *If $\vdash_{\mathcal{L}} t : T$ (i.e., t is a closed term in $\mathcal{L}_{\mathsf{rec}}$) and t has a whnf, then $t \Downarrow V$, for some V.*

Proof: We rely on Klop's result [35], which states that leftmost-outermost reduction is normalising for left-normal orthogonal Combinatory Reduction Systems (CRSs). A CRS is orthogonal if its rules are left-linear (i.e., the left hand-sides of the rewrite rules contain no duplicated variables) and non-overlapping (there are no critical pairs). A CRS is left-normal if on the left hand-sides of

$$\frac{V \text{ is a value}}{V \Downarrow V}\ Val \qquad \frac{s \Downarrow \lambda x.u \quad u[t/x] \Downarrow V}{s\,t \Downarrow V}\ App \qquad \frac{t \Downarrow \langle t_1, t_2\rangle \quad (\lambda xy.u)t_1 t_2 \Downarrow V}{\texttt{let}\ \langle x, y\rangle = t\ \texttt{in}\ u \Downarrow V}\ Let$$

$$\frac{t \Downarrow \langle t_1, t_2\rangle \quad t_1 \Downarrow 0 \quad u \Downarrow V}{\mathsf{rec}\ t\ u\ v\ w \Downarrow V}\ Rec_1 \qquad \frac{t \Downarrow \langle t_1, t_2\rangle \quad t_1 \Downarrow \mathsf{S}\ t' \quad v(\mathsf{rec}\ (w\langle t', t_2\rangle)\ u\ v\ w) \Downarrow V}{\mathsf{rec}\ t\ u\ v\ w \Downarrow V}\ Rec_2$$

Table 5. CBN evaluation for System $\mathcal{L}_{\mathsf{rec}}$

the rewrite rules, all the function symbols appear before the variables. The λ-calculus is an example of a left-normal orthogonal CRS, as is System $\mathcal{L}_{\mathsf{rec}}$. Therefore, leftmost-outermost reduction is normalising for $\mathcal{L}_{\mathsf{rec}}$. The result follows, since CBN performs leftmost-outermost reduction.

For open terms, the set of weak head normal forms includes more kinds of terms, since, for instance, reduction of an application will be blocked if the argument is open. However, for a given open term one can consider all the free variables as constants and proceed with closed reduction as shown in [19] (see also [11]).

Call-by-value A call-by-value evaluation relation for System $\mathcal{L}_{\mathsf{rec}}$ can be obtained from the CBN relation by changing the rule for application, as usual.

$$\frac{s \Downarrow \lambda x.u \quad t \Downarrow V' \quad u[V'/x] \Downarrow V}{s\,t \Downarrow V}$$

There is no change in the *Rec* and *Let* rules, since they rely on the *App* rule. Unlike CBN, the CBV strategy does not always reach a value, even if a closed term has one (Theorem 6 does not hold for a CBV strategy). For example, recall the term Y_{N} in Section 3.3, and consider the term $(\lambda xy.(\mathsf{rec}\ \langle 0,0\rangle\ I\ \mathcal{E}(x,\mathsf{N})\ I)y)(Y_{\mathsf{N}} I)$. This term has a value under the CBN strategy, but not under CBV. In fact, innermost strategies are normalising in an orthogonal system if and only if the system is itself strongly normalising.

4.1 Stack machine for System $\mathcal{L}_{\mathsf{rec}}$

Intermediate languages that incorporate linearity have well known implementation advantages whether in compilers, static analysis, or whenever resources are limited [12, 39, 41, 50]. Based on these previous works, we finish this section by illustrating how simply System $\mathcal{L}_{\mathsf{rec}}$ can be implemented as a stack machine. We show a call-by-name version, but it is straightforward to modify to other reduction strategies.

The basic principle of the machine is to find the next redex, using a stack $\mathcal{S}$ to store future computations. The elements of the stack are terms in an extension of $\mathcal{L}_{\mathsf{rec}}$ which includes the following additional kinds of terms: $LET(x, y, t)$, $REC(u, v, w)$, $REC'(n, u, v, w)$, where x, y are variables and n, t, u, v, w are $\mathcal{L}_{\mathsf{rec}}$ terms.

The configurations of the machine are pairs consisting of a term and a stack of extended terms. Unlike Krivine's machine or its variants (see for instance [15, 21, 29]) we do not need to include an environment (sometimes called store, as in [50]) in the configurations. Indeed, the environment is used to store bindings for variables, but here as soon as a binding of a variable to a term is known we can replace the unique occurrence of that variable (the calculus is syntactically linear). In other words, instead of building an environment, we use "assignment" and replace the occurrence of the variable by the term.

The transitions of the machine are given in Table 6.

For a program (closed term M), the machine is started with an empty stack: $(M, [\,])$. It stops when no rule can apply.

The use of "assignment" means that there is no manipulation (no copying, erasing, or even searching for bindings) in environments usually associated to these kinds of implementations.

The correctness of the machine with respect to the CBN evaluation relation is proved by induction in the usual way.

THEOREM 7. *If* $\vdash_{\mathcal{L}} t : T$ *and there is a value* V *such that* $t \Downarrow V$, *then* $(t, [\,]) \Rightarrow^* (V, [\,])$.

Proof: By induction on the evaluation relation, using Subject Reduction (Theorem 1) and the following property:
If $(t, \mathcal{S}) \Rightarrow (t', \mathcal{S}')$ then $(t, \mathcal{S} \circ \mathcal{S}'') \Rightarrow (t', \mathcal{S}' \circ \mathcal{S}'')$.
This property is proved by induction on $(t, \mathcal{S})$. Intuitively, since only the top of the stack is used to select a transition, it is clear that appending elements at the bottom of the stack does not affect the computation.

5. Applications

In this section we study the relation between $\mathcal{L}_{\mathsf{rec}}$ and languages with fixpoint operators and in particular with PCF.

5.1 The role of conditionals

Recursive function definitions based on fixpoint operators rely on the use of a non-linear conditional that should discard the branch corresponding to an infinite computation. For instance, the definition of factorial:

$$\mathsf{fact} = Y(\lambda fn.\mathtt{cond}\ n\ 1\ (n * f(n-1)))$$

relies on the fact that cond will return 1 when the input number is 0, and discard the non-terminating "else" branch. Enabling the occurrence of the (bound) variable, used to iterate the function (f in the above definition), in only one branch of the conditional is crucial for the definition of interesting recursive programs. This is why denotational linear versions of PCF [45] allow stable variables to be used non-linearly but not to be abstracted, since their only purpose is to obtain fixpoints.

Fixpoint operators can be encoded in System $\mathcal{L}_{\mathsf{rec}}$: for any type A we define the term

$$Y_A = \lambda f.\mathsf{rec}\ \langle \mathsf{S}(0), 0\rangle\ \mathcal{M}(A)\ f\ W$$

where W represents the term $(\lambda x.\mathtt{let}\ \langle y, z\rangle = x\ \mathtt{in}\ \langle \mathsf{S}(y), z\rangle))$. For every type A, $Y_A : (A \multimap A) \multimap A$ is well-typed in System $\mathcal{L}_{\mathsf{rec}}$. Note that, for any closed term f of type $A \multimap A$, we have:

$$\begin{aligned} Y_A f &= \mathsf{rec}\ \langle \mathsf{S}(0), 0\rangle\ \mathcal{M}(A)\ f\ W \\ &\to^* f(\mathsf{rec}\ (\mathtt{let}\ \langle y, z\rangle = \langle 0, 0\rangle\ \mathtt{in}\ \langle \mathsf{S}(y), z\rangle)\ \mathcal{M}(A)\ f\ W) \\ &\to f(\mathsf{rec}\ \langle \mathsf{S}(0), 0\rangle\ \mathcal{M}(A)\ f\ W) = f(Y_A f) \end{aligned}$$

Although Y_A behaves like a fixpoint operator, one cannot write useful recursive programs using fixpoint operators without a non-linear conditional: if we apply Y_A to a linear function f, we obtain a non-normalisable term (recall the example in Section 3.3). Instead, in System $\mathcal{L}_{\mathsf{rec}}$, recursive functions, such as factorial, can be easily encoded using rec:

$$\lambda n.pr_2(\mathsf{rec}\ \langle n, 0\rangle\ \langle \mathsf{S}(0), \mathsf{S}(0)\rangle\ (\lambda x.\mathtt{let}\ \langle t, u\rangle = x\ \mathtt{in}\ F)\ I)$$

(app)	$(MN, \mathcal{S})$	$\Rightarrow$	$(M, N : \mathcal{S})$
(abs)	$(\lambda x.M, N : \mathcal{S})$	$\Rightarrow$	$(M[N/x], \mathcal{S})$
(let)	$(\mathtt{let}\ \langle x, y\rangle = N\ \mathtt{in}\ M, \mathcal{S})$	$\Rightarrow$	$(N, \mathit{LET}(x, y, M) : \mathcal{S})$
(pair1)	$(\langle N_1, N_2\rangle, \mathit{LET}(x, y, M) : \mathcal{S})$	$\Rightarrow$	$(M[N_1/x][N_2/y], \mathcal{S})$
(rec)	$(\mathsf{rec}\ N\ U\ V\ W, \mathcal{S})$	$\Rightarrow$	$(N, \mathit{REC}(U, V, W) : \mathcal{S})$
(pair2)	$(\langle N_1, N_2\rangle, \mathit{REC}(U, V, W) : \mathcal{S})$	$\Rightarrow$	$(N_1, \mathit{REC}'(N_2, U, V, W) : \mathcal{S})$
(zero)	$(0, \mathit{REC}'(T, U, V, W) : \mathcal{S})$	$\Rightarrow$	$(U, \mathcal{S})$
(succ)	$(S(N), \mathit{REC}'(T, U, V, W) : \mathcal{S})$	$\Rightarrow$	$(V, (\mathsf{rec}\ (W\langle N, T\rangle)\ U\ V\ W) : \mathcal{S})$

Table 6. Stack machine for System $\mathcal{L}_{\mathsf{rec}}$

where $F = \mathtt{let}\ \langle t_1, t_2\rangle = D^{\mathsf{N}}\ t\ \mathtt{in}\ \langle \mathsf{S}\ t_1, \mathsf{mult}\ u\ t_2\rangle$ and D^{N} is the duplicator term defined previously (see Definition 2). Note that, although conditionals are not part of System $\mathcal{L}_{\mathsf{rec}}$ syntax, reduction rules for rec use pattern-matching. In the remainder of this section we show how we can encode in System $\mathcal{L}_{\mathsf{rec}}$ recursive functions defined using fixpoints.

5.2 Encoding PCF in System $\mathcal{L}_{\mathsf{rec}}$

PCF [46] can be seen as a minimalistic typed functional programming language. Let us recall its syntax. PCF is a typed λ-calculus, with a type N for numbers and the constants:

- $n : \mathsf{N}$, for $n = 0, 1, 2, \ldots$
- $\mathsf{succ}, \mathsf{pred} : \mathsf{N} \to \mathsf{N}$
- $\mathsf{iszero} : \mathsf{N} \to \mathsf{N}$, such that

$$\mathsf{iszero}\ 0 \to 0 \qquad \mathsf{iszero}\ (n+1) \to 1$$

- for each type A, $\mathsf{cond}_A : \mathsf{N} \to A \to A \to A$, such that

$$\mathsf{cond}_A\ 0\ u\ v \to u \qquad \mathsf{cond}_A\ (n+1)\ u\ v \to v$$

- for each type A, $Y_A : (A \to A) \to A$, such that $Y_A f \to f(Y_A f)$.

DEFINITION 3. *PCF types and environments are translated into System $\mathcal{L}_{\mathsf{rec}}$ types using $\langle\!\langle \cdot \rangle\!\rangle$:*

$$\begin{array}{rcl} \langle\!\langle \mathsf{N} \rangle\!\rangle &=& \mathsf{N} \\ \langle\!\langle A \to B \rangle\!\rangle &=& \langle\!\langle A \rangle\!\rangle \multimap \langle\!\langle B \rangle\!\rangle \\ \langle\!\langle x_1 : T_1, \ldots, x_n : T_n \rangle\!\rangle &=& x_1 : \langle\!\langle T_1 \rangle\!\rangle, \ldots, x_n : \langle\!\langle T_n \rangle\!\rangle \end{array}$$

Since $\mathcal{L}_{\mathsf{rec}}$ is Turing complete, it is clear that any PCF program can be encoded. We define below an encoding inspired by the encoding of System $\mathcal{T}$ in [4]. We make the following abbreviations, where the variables x_1 and x_2 are assumed fresh, and $[x]t$ is defined below:

$$\begin{array}{rcl} C^{x_1, x_2}_{x:A}\ t &=& \mathtt{let}\ \langle x_1, x_2\rangle = D^A x\ \mathtt{in}\ t \\ A^x_y t &=& ([x]t)[y/x] \end{array}$$

DEFINITION 4. *Let t be a PCF term, with $fv(t) = \{x_1, \ldots, x_n\}$ and $x_1 : A_1, \ldots, x_n : A_n \vdash t : A$. The compilation into System $\mathcal{L}_{\mathsf{rec}}$, is defined as: $[x_1^{A_1}] \ldots [x_n^{A_n}]\langle\!\langle t \rangle\!\rangle$*[1]*, where $\langle\!\langle \cdot \rangle\!\rangle$ is defined in Table 7, and for a term t and a variable x, such that $x \in \mathsf{fv}(t)$, $[x]t$ is inductively defined in the following way:*

$$\begin{array}{rcl} [x](\mathsf{S}\ u) &=& \mathsf{S}([x]u) \\ [x]x &=& x \\ [x](\lambda y.u) &=& \lambda y.[x]u \\ [x^A](su) &=& \begin{cases} C^{x_1, x_2}_{x:A}\ (A^{x_1}_y s)(A^{x_2}_y u) & x \in \mathsf{fv}(s) \cap \mathsf{fv}(u) \\ ([x]s)u & x \notin \mathsf{fv}(u) \\ s([x]u) & x \notin \mathsf{fv}(s) \end{cases} \end{array}$$

[1] We omit the types of variables when they do not play a role in the compilation.

Notice that $[x]t$ (which counts occurrences of the free variable x) is not defined for the entire syntax of System $\mathcal{L}_{\mathsf{rec}}$. The reason for this is that, although other syntactic constructors (like recursors or pairs) may appear in t, they are the outcome of $\langle\!\langle \cdot \rangle\!\rangle$ and therefore are closed terms, where x does not occur free.

Also note that succ is not encoded as $\lambda x.\mathsf{S}x$, since $\mathcal{L}_{\mathsf{rec}}$ does not evaluate under λ or S. We should not encode a divergent PCF program into a normalisable one in $\mathcal{L}_{\mathsf{rec}}$. In particular, the translation of $\mathsf{cond}_A\ (\mathsf{succ}(Y_{\mathsf{N}} I))\ P\ Q$ is $\langle\!\langle \mathsf{cond}_A \rangle\!\rangle\ (\langle\!\langle \mathsf{succ} \rangle\!\rangle(\langle\!\langle Y_{\mathsf{N}} \rangle\!\rangle I))\ \langle\!\langle P \rangle\!\rangle\ \langle\!\langle Q \rangle\!\rangle$, which diverges (if we encode succ as $\lambda x.\mathsf{S}x$, then we obtain $\langle\!\langle Q \rangle\!\rangle$, which is not right).

Regarding abstractions or conditionals, the encoding is different from the one used for System $\mathcal{T}$ in [4]. We cannot use the same encoding as in System $\mathcal{L}$, where terms are erased by "consuming them", because PCF, unlike System $\mathcal{T}$, is not strongly normalising. The technique used here for erasing could have been used for System $\mathcal{L}$, but erasing "by consuming" is preferred when possible (it reflects the work needed to erase a data structure).

Also note that the second case for abstractions in Table 7 uses a recursor on zero to discard the argument, where the function parameter is $\lambda y.\mathcal{E}(\mathcal{E}(y, \langle\!\langle B \rangle\!\rangle \multimap \langle\!\langle B \rangle\!\rangle)x, \langle\!\langle A \rangle\!\rangle)$. The reason for this is that one cannot use x directly as the function parameter because that might make the term untypable, and just using $\mathcal{E}(x, \langle\!\langle A \rangle\!\rangle)$ would make the types work, but could encode strongly normalisable terms into terms with infinite reduction sequences (because $\mathcal{E}(x, \langle\!\langle A \rangle\!\rangle)$ might not terminate). For example, consider the encoding of $(\lambda xy.y)Y_{\mathsf{N}}$.

The translation of a typable PCF term is also typable in System $\mathcal{L}_{\mathsf{rec}}$ (this is proved below). In particular, for any type A, the term $\langle\!\langle \mathsf{cond}_A \rangle\!\rangle$ is well-typed. In Figure 1, we show the type derivation for the encoding of the conditional (we use V to represent the term $\lambda x.(\mathsf{rec}\ \langle 0, 0\rangle\ I\ \mathcal{E}(x, \langle\!\langle A \rangle\!\rangle)\ I)v)$.

The type derivation for V depends on the fact that, if $\Gamma \vdash_{\mathcal{L}} t : A$, then for any type B, we have $\Gamma \vdash_{\mathcal{L}} \mathcal{E}(t, A) : B \multimap B$ by Theorem 2. Note that the recursor on $\langle 0, 0\rangle$ in V discards the remaining recursion (corresponding to the branch of the conditional that is not needed), returning Iv.

We prove that the encoding respects types by induction. To make the induction work, we need to define an intermediate system where certain variables (not yet affected by the encoding) may occur non-linearly. More precisely, we consider an extension to System $\mathcal{L}_{\mathsf{rec}}$, which allows variables on a certain set X to appear non-linearly in a term. We call the extended system System $\mathcal{L}^{+X}_{\mathsf{rec}}$; it is defined by the rules in Table 8 (that is, the typing rules for System $\mathcal{L}_{\mathsf{rec}}$ augmented with weakening and contraction for variables in X). Intuitively, if X is the set of free-variables of t, then $\langle\!\langle t \rangle\!\rangle$ will be a System $\mathcal{L}_{\mathsf{rec}}$ term, except for the variables $X = \mathsf{fv}(t)$, which may occur non-linearly, and $[x_1] \ldots [x_n]\langle\!\langle t \rangle\!\rangle$, will be a typed System $\mathcal{L}_{\mathsf{rec}}$ term. We can prove the following results regarding System $\mathcal{L}^{+X}_{\mathsf{rec}}$.

LEMMA 1. *If $\Gamma \vdash_{\mathcal{L}^{+X}_{\mathsf{rec}}} t : A$, where $dom(\Gamma) = \mathsf{fv}(t)$ and $x \in X \subseteq \mathsf{fv}(t)$, then $\Gamma \vdash_{\mathcal{L}^{+X'}_{\mathsf{rec}}} [x]t : A$, where $X' = X \setminus \{x\}$.*

$$
\begin{array}{lcll}
\langle n\rangle & = & \mathsf{S}^n 0 & \\
\langle \mathsf{succ}\rangle & = & \lambda n.\mathsf{rec}\ \langle n,0\rangle\ (\mathsf{S}\ 0)\ (\lambda x.\mathsf{S}x)\ I & \\
\langle \mathsf{pred}\rangle & = & \lambda n.pr_1(\mathsf{rec}\ \langle n,0\rangle\ \langle 0,0\rangle\ (\lambda x.\mathtt{let}\ \langle t,u\rangle = D^{\mathsf{N}}(pr_2\ x)\ \mathtt{in}\ \langle t,\mathsf{S}\ u\rangle)\ I) & \\
\langle \mathsf{iszero}\rangle & = & \lambda n.pr_1(\mathsf{rec}\ \langle n,0\rangle\ \langle 0,\mathsf{S}\ 0\rangle\ (\lambda x.D^{\mathsf{N}}(pr_2\ x))\ I) & \\
\langle Y_A\rangle & = & \lambda f.\mathsf{rec}\ \langle \mathsf{S}(0),0\rangle\ \mathcal{M}(\langle A\rangle)\ f\ (\lambda x.\mathtt{let}\ \langle y,z\rangle = x\ \mathtt{in}\ \langle \mathsf{S}(y),z\rangle) & \\
\langle \mathsf{cond}_A\rangle & = & \lambda tuv.\mathsf{rec}\ \langle t,0\rangle\ u\ (\lambda x.(\mathsf{rec}\ \langle 0,0\rangle\ I\ \mathcal{E}(x,\langle A\rangle)\ I)v)\ I & \\
\langle x\rangle & = & x & \\
\langle uv\rangle & = & \langle u\rangle\langle v\rangle & \\
\langle \lambda x^A.t\rangle & = & \begin{cases} \lambda x.[x^A]\langle t\rangle & \text{if } x\in \mathsf{fv}(t) \\ \lambda x.(\mathsf{rec}\ \langle 0,0\rangle\ I\ \lambda y.\mathcal{E}(\mathcal{E}(y,\langle B\rangle \multimap \langle B\rangle)x,\langle A\rangle)\ I)\langle t\rangle & \text{otherwise} \end{cases} &
\end{array}
$$

Table 7. PCF compilation into $\mathcal{L}_{\mathsf{rec}}$

$$
\dfrac{t:\mathsf{N}\vdash_{\mathcal{L}} \langle t,0\rangle : \mathsf{N}\otimes\mathsf{N} \quad u:\langle A\rangle\vdash_{\mathcal{L}} u:\langle A\rangle \quad v:\langle A\rangle\vdash_{\mathcal{L}} V:\langle A\rangle\multimap\langle A\rangle \quad \vdash_{\mathcal{L}} I:\mathsf{N}\otimes\mathsf{N}\multimap\mathsf{N}\otimes\mathsf{N}}{t:\mathsf{N},u:\langle A\rangle,v:\langle A\rangle\vdash_{\mathcal{L}} \mathsf{rec}\ \langle t,0\rangle\ u\ V\ I:\langle A\rangle}
$$

$$\vdots$$

$$\vdash_{\mathcal{L}} \mathsf{cond}_A : \mathsf{N}\multimap\langle A\rangle\multimap\langle A\rangle\multimap\langle A\rangle$$

Figure 1. Type derivation for cond_A

Axiom and **Structural Rule**:

$$
\dfrac{}{x:A\vdash_{\mathcal{L}_{\mathsf{rec}}^{+X}} x:A}\ (\mathsf{Axiom}) \qquad \dfrac{\Gamma,x:A,y:B,\Delta\vdash_{\mathcal{L}_{\mathsf{rec}}^{+X}} t:C}{\Gamma,y:B,x:A,\Delta\vdash_{\mathcal{L}_{\mathsf{rec}}^{+X}} t:C}\ (\mathsf{Exchange})
$$

$$
\dfrac{\Gamma\vdash_{\mathcal{L}_{\mathsf{rec}}^{+X}} t:B \quad \text{and } x\in X}{\Gamma,x:A\vdash_{\mathcal{L}_{\mathsf{rec}}^{+X}} t:B}\ (\mathsf{Weakening}) \qquad \dfrac{\Gamma,x:A,x:A\vdash_{\mathcal{L}_{\mathsf{rec}}^{+X}} t:B \quad \text{and } x\in X}{\Gamma,x:A\vdash_{\mathcal{L}_{\mathsf{rec}}^{+X}} t:B}\ (\mathsf{Contraction})
$$

Logical Rules:

$$
\dfrac{\Gamma,x:A\vdash_{\mathcal{L}_{\mathsf{rec}}^{+X}} t:B}{\Gamma\vdash_{\mathcal{L}_{\mathsf{rec}}^{+X}} \lambda x.t:A\multimap B}\ (\multimap\mathsf{Intro}) \qquad \dfrac{\Gamma\vdash_{\mathcal{L}_{\mathsf{rec}}^{+X_1}} t:A\multimap B \quad \Delta\vdash_{\mathcal{L}_{\mathsf{rec}}^{+X_2}} u:A}{\Gamma,\Delta\vdash_{\mathcal{L}_{\mathsf{rec}}^{+(X_1\cup X_2)}} tu:B}\ (\multimap\mathsf{Elim})
$$

$$
\dfrac{\Gamma\vdash_{\mathcal{L}_{\mathsf{rec}}^{+X_1}} t:A \quad \Delta\vdash_{\mathcal{L}_{\mathsf{rec}}^{+X_2}} u:B}{\Gamma,\Delta\vdash_{\mathcal{L}_{\mathsf{rec}}^{+(X_1\cup X_2)}} \langle t,u\rangle:A\otimes B}\ (\otimes\mathsf{Intro}) \qquad \dfrac{\Gamma\vdash_{\mathcal{L}_{\mathsf{rec}}^{+X_1}} t:A\otimes B \quad x:A,y:B,\Delta\vdash_{\mathcal{L}_{\mathsf{rec}}^{+X_2}} u:C}{\Gamma,\Delta\vdash_{\mathcal{L}_{\mathsf{rec}}^{+(X_1\cup X_2)}} \mathtt{let}\ \langle x,y\rangle = t\ \mathtt{in}\ u:C}\ (\otimes\mathsf{Elim})
$$

Numbers:

$$
\dfrac{}{\vdash_{\mathcal{L}_{\mathsf{rec}}^{+\emptyset}} 0:\mathsf{N}}\ (\mathsf{Zero}) \qquad \dfrac{\Gamma\vdash_{\mathcal{L}_{\mathsf{rec}}^{+X}} t:\mathsf{N}}{\Gamma\vdash_{\mathcal{L}_{\mathsf{rec}}^{+X}} \mathsf{S}(t):\mathsf{N}}\ (\mathsf{Succ})
$$

$$
\dfrac{\Gamma\vdash_{\mathcal{L}_{\mathsf{rec}}^{+X_1}} t:\mathsf{N}\otimes\mathsf{N} \quad \Theta\vdash_{\mathcal{L}_{\mathsf{rec}}^{+X_2}} u:A \quad \Delta\vdash_{\mathcal{L}_{\mathsf{rec}}^{+X_3}} v:A\multimap A \quad \Sigma\vdash_{\mathcal{L}_{\mathsf{rec}}^{+X_4}} w:\mathsf{N}\otimes\mathsf{N}\multimap\mathsf{N}\otimes\mathsf{N}}{\Gamma,\Theta,\Delta,\Sigma\vdash_{\mathcal{L}_{\mathsf{rec}}^{+(X_1\cup X_2\cup X_3\cup X_4)}} \mathsf{rec}\ t\ u\ v\ w:A}\ (\mathsf{Rec})
$$

Table 8. Typing rules for System $\mathcal{L}_{\mathsf{rec}}^{+X}$

Proof: By induction on t, using the fact that $x : A \vdash_{\mathcal{L}_{\mathsf{rec}}^{+\emptyset}} D^A x : A\otimes A$.

LEMMA 2. *If* $\Gamma\vdash_{\mathsf{PCF}} t : A$, *then*

$$\langle \Gamma_{|\mathsf{fv}(t)}\rangle \vdash_{\mathcal{L}_{\mathsf{rec}}^{+\mathsf{fv}(t)}} \langle t\rangle : \langle A\rangle$$

where the notation $\Gamma_{|X}$ *denotes the restriction of* Γ *to the variables in* X.

Proof: By induction on the type derivation $\Gamma\vdash_{\mathsf{PCF}} t : A$, as done for System $\mathcal{T}$ in [4].

THEOREM 8. *If* t *is a PCF term of type* A *under a set of assumptions* Γ *for its free variables* $\{x_1,\ldots,x_n\}$, *then* $\langle\Gamma_{|\mathsf{fv}(t)}\rangle\vdash_{\mathcal{L}} [x_1]\ldots[x_n]\langle t\rangle : \langle A\rangle$.

Proof: By induction on the number of free variables of t, using Lemmas 1 and 2.

Using the encodings given above, it is possible to simulate the evaluation of a PCF program in System $\mathcal{L}_{\mathsf{rec}}$. More precisely, if t is a closed PCF term of type N, which evaluates to v under a CBN semantics for PCF [46], then the encoding of t reduces in System $\mathcal{L}_{\mathsf{rec}}$ to the encoding of v, and evaluates under a CBN semantics to a value which is equal to the encoding of v. In Table 9 we recall the CBN rules for PCF: $t \Downarrow_{\mathsf{PCF}} V$ means that the closed term t

$$\frac{V \text{ is a value}}{V \Downarrow_{\mathsf{PCF}} V} \qquad \frac{s \Downarrow_{\mathsf{PCF}} V' \quad V't \Downarrow_{\mathsf{PCF}} V \quad s \text{ is not a value}}{s\ t \Downarrow_{\mathsf{PCF}} V} \qquad \frac{u[t/x] \Downarrow_{\mathsf{PCF}} V}{(\lambda x.u)\ t \Downarrow_{\mathsf{PCF}} V} \qquad \frac{t \Downarrow_{\mathsf{PCF}} 0}{\mathsf{pred}\ t \Downarrow_{\mathsf{PCF}} 0} \qquad \frac{t \Downarrow_{\mathsf{PCF}} n+1}{\mathsf{pred}\ t \Downarrow_{\mathsf{PCF}} n}$$

$$\frac{t \Downarrow_{\mathsf{PCF}} n}{\mathsf{succ}\ t \Downarrow_{\mathsf{PCF}} n+1} \qquad \frac{t \Downarrow_{\mathsf{PCF}} 0}{\mathsf{iszero}\ t \Downarrow_{\mathsf{PCF}} 0} \qquad \frac{t \Downarrow_{\mathsf{PCF}} n+1}{\mathsf{iszero}\ t \Downarrow_{\mathsf{PCF}} 1} \qquad \frac{t \Downarrow_{\mathsf{PCF}} 0 \quad u \Downarrow_{\mathsf{PCF}} V}{\mathsf{cond}_A\ t\ u\ v \Downarrow_{\mathsf{PCF}} V} \qquad \frac{t \Downarrow_{\mathsf{PCF}} n+1 \quad v \Downarrow_{\mathsf{PCF}} V}{\mathsf{cond}_A\ t\ u\ v \Downarrow_{\mathsf{PCF}} V} \qquad \frac{f(Y_A f) \Downarrow_{\mathsf{PCF}} V}{Y_A f \Downarrow_{\mathsf{PCF}} V}$$

Table 9. CBN evaluation for PCF

evaluates to the value V (a value is either a number, a λ-abstraction, a constant, or a partially applied conditional).

LEMMA 3 (Substitution). *Let t be a term in System $\mathcal{L}_{\mathsf{rec}}$.*

1. If $x \in \mathsf{fv}(t)$, and $\mathsf{fv}(u) = \varnothing$, then $\langle t\rangle[\langle u\rangle/x] = \langle t[u/x]\rangle$
2. If $x \in \mathsf{fv}(t)$, then $([x]t)[u/x] \longrightarrow^* t[u/x]$.

Proof: By induction on t.

LEMMA 4. *Let t be a closed PCF term. If $t \Downarrow_{\mathsf{PCF}} V$, then $\langle t\rangle \longrightarrow^* \langle V\rangle$.*

Proof: By induction on the evaluation relation, using a technique similar to the one used for System $\mathcal{T}$ in [4]. Here we show the main steps of reduction for $\mathsf{cond}_A\ t\ u\ v$ where u, v are closed terms by assumption.

- If $t \Downarrow_{\mathsf{PCF}} 0$:

$$\begin{aligned}\langle \mathsf{cond}_A\ t\ u\ v\rangle &= \langle \mathsf{cond}_A\rangle\ \langle t\rangle\ \langle u\rangle\ \langle v\rangle \\ &\overset{\text{(I.H.)}}{\longrightarrow^*} \mathsf{cond}_A\ 0\ \langle u\rangle\ \langle v\rangle \longrightarrow^* \langle u\rangle \overset{\text{(I.H.)}}{\longrightarrow^*} \langle V\rangle\end{aligned}$$

- If $t \Downarrow_{\mathsf{PCF}} n+1$, then we consider v' to be the $\mathcal{L}_{\mathsf{rec}}$ term $(\lambda x.(\mathsf{rec}\ \langle 0,0\rangle\ I\ \mathcal{E}(x,A)\ I)\langle v\rangle)$, in which case:

$$\begin{aligned}\langle \mathsf{cond}_A\ t\ u\ v\rangle &= \langle \mathsf{cond}_A\rangle\ (\mathsf{S}^{n+1}0)\ \langle u\rangle\ \langle v\rangle \\ &\longrightarrow^* \mathsf{rec}\ \langle \mathsf{S}^{n+1}0, 0\rangle\ \langle u\rangle\ v'\ I \\ &\longrightarrow^* I\langle v\rangle \longrightarrow \langle v\rangle \overset{\text{(I.H.)}}{\longrightarrow^*} \langle V\rangle.\end{aligned}$$

For application, we rely on the substitution lemmas above. Note that for an application uv, where u is a constant, we rely on the correctness of the encodings for constants, which can be easily proved by induction. For example, in the case of succ it is trivial to prove that, if t is a number $\mathsf{S}^n 0$ in $\mathcal{L}_{\mathsf{rec}}$ ($n \geq 0$), then $\mathsf{rec}\ \langle t, 0\rangle\ (\mathsf{S}\ 0)\ (\lambda x.\mathsf{S}x)\ I \longrightarrow^* \mathsf{S}^{n+1}0$.

THEOREM 9. *Let t be a closed PCF term. If $t \Downarrow_{\mathsf{PCF}} V$, then $\exists V'$ such that $\langle t\rangle \Downarrow V'$, and $V' =_{\mathcal{L}_{\mathsf{rec}}} \langle V\rangle$.*

Proof: By Lemma 4 $t \Downarrow_{\mathsf{PCF}} V$, implies $\langle t\rangle \longrightarrow^* \langle V\rangle$. By Theorem 6, $\langle t\rangle \Downarrow V'$. Therefore, since $\Downarrow\ \subset \longrightarrow^*$ and the system is confluent (Theorem 1), $V' =_{\mathcal{L}_{\mathsf{rec}}} \langle V\rangle$.

LEMMA 5. *If $t \Downarrow V$ and $t =_{\mathcal{L}_{\mathsf{rec}}} u$, then $u \Downarrow V'$ and $V =_{\mathcal{L}_{\mathsf{rec}}} V'$.*

Proof: By transitivity of the equality relation.

THEOREM 10. *Let t be a closed PCF term. If $\langle t\rangle \Downarrow V$, then $\exists V'$, such that, $t \Downarrow_{\mathsf{PCF}} V'$ and $\langle V'\rangle =_{\mathcal{L}_{\mathsf{rec}}} V$.*

Proof: By induction on the evaluation relation, using Lemma 5. Note that, if t is a value different from a partially applied conditional, the result follows because $t = V'$ and $\langle t\rangle$ is also a value, i.e. $\langle t\rangle = V$, therefore $\langle t\rangle = \langle V'\rangle = V$. If t is an application uv then $\langle t\rangle = \langle u\rangle\langle v\rangle$, therefore $\langle u\rangle\langle v\rangle \Downarrow V$ if $\langle u\rangle \Downarrow \lambda x.s$ and $s[\langle v\rangle/x] \Downarrow V$. If $\langle u\rangle \Downarrow \lambda x.s$, then by I.H. $u \Downarrow_{\mathsf{PCF}} W$, and $\langle W\rangle =_{\mathcal{L}_{\mathsf{rec}}} \lambda x.s$. Note that W is a value of arrow type, which compilation equals an abstraction, therefore $W = \lambda x.s'$, pred, succ, iszero, Y, cond, $\mathsf{cond}\ p$ or $\mathsf{cond}\ p\ q$. We show the case for $\lambda x.s'$ (see [5] for the full proof). If $W = \lambda x.s'$, we have two cases:

- $x \in \mathsf{fv}(s')$: then $\langle W\rangle = \lambda x.[x]\langle s'\rangle =_{\mathcal{L}_{\mathsf{rec}}} \lambda x.s$, therefore $[x]\langle s'\rangle =_{\mathcal{L}_{\mathsf{rec}}} s$. Since $s[\langle v\rangle/x] \Downarrow V$ and $s[\langle v\rangle/x] =_{\mathcal{L}_{\mathsf{rec}}} [x]\langle s'\rangle[\langle v\rangle/x]$ then, by Lemma 3.2 $[x]\langle s'\rangle[\langle v\rangle/x] \longrightarrow^* \langle s'\rangle[\langle v\rangle/x]$, which, by Lemma 3.1, equals $\langle s'[v/x]\rangle$, therefore (by Lemma 5) $\langle s'[v/x]\rangle \Downarrow V''$, and $V =_{\mathcal{L}_{\mathsf{rec}}} V''$. By I.H., $s'[v/x] \Downarrow_{\mathsf{PCF}} V'$ and $\langle V'\rangle = V$, therefore $uv \Downarrow_{\mathsf{PCF}} V'$ and $\langle V'\rangle =_{\mathcal{L}_{\mathsf{rec}}} V'' =_{\mathcal{L}_{\mathsf{rec}}} V$.
- $x \notin \mathsf{fv}(s')$: let v' represent the term $\lambda y.\mathcal{E}(\mathcal{E}(y, \langle B\rangle \multimap \langle B\rangle)x, \langle A\rangle)$. Then $\langle W\rangle = \lambda x.(\mathsf{rec}\ \langle 0,0\rangle\ I\ v'\ I)\langle s'\rangle =_{\mathcal{L}_{\mathsf{rec}}} \lambda x.s$, therefore $(\mathsf{rec}\ \langle 0,0\rangle\ I\ v'\ I)\langle s'\rangle =_{\mathcal{L}_{\mathsf{rec}}} s$. Note that $s[\langle v\rangle/x] = (\mathsf{rec}\ \langle 0,0\rangle\ I\ v'[\langle v\rangle/x]\ I)\langle s'\rangle$ and if $\langle s'\rangle \Downarrow V$, then $(\mathsf{rec}\ \langle 0,0\rangle\ I\ v'[\langle v\rangle/x]\ I)\langle s'\rangle \Downarrow V$, thus, since $s'[v/x] = s'$, by I.H., $s' \Downarrow_{\mathsf{PCF}} V'$ and $\langle V'\rangle =_{\mathcal{L}_{\mathsf{rec}}} V$, therefore $uv \Downarrow_{\mathsf{PCF}} V'$ and $\langle V'\rangle =_{\mathcal{L}_{\mathsf{rec}}} V$ as required.

This completes the proof of soundness and completeness of the encoding.

Note that the terms of the form $\mathsf{rec}\ \langle 0,0\rangle\ I\ t\ I$ used in the encoding of conditionals and λ-abstractions allow us to discard terms without evaluating them. This is a feature of the encoding, otherwise terminating programs in PCF could be translated to non-terminating programs in System $\mathcal{L}_{\mathsf{rec}}$. This differs from the definition of erasing given in Section 3, where terms are consumed and not discarded (in pure linear systems functions do not discard their arguments). However, allowing terms to be discarded without being evaluated, is crucial when defining recursion based on fixpoints.

Once a PCF term is compiled into $\mathcal{L}_{\mathsf{rec}}$ it can be implemented using the techniques in Section 4, thus we obtain a new stack machine implementation of PCF.

6. Conclusions

Our work previously investigated linear primitive recursive functions, and a linear version of Gödel's System $\mathcal{T}$. This paper is the final result in this line of work: it shows how the essential ideas can be extended to general recursion, as found in programming languages. $\mathcal{L}_{\mathsf{rec}}$ is a syntactically linear calculus, but only the fragment without the recursor is operationally linear. The recursor allows us to encode duplicating and erasing, thus playing a similar role to the exponentials in linear logic. It encompasses bounded recursion (iteration) and minimisation in just one operator, thus $\mathcal{L}_{\mathsf{rec}}$ can be seen as an alternative way to recover the power of the λ-calculus within a linear system. It would be interesting to analyse the meaning of this linear recursor in a denotational setting.

The encoding of PCF in $\mathcal{L}_{\mathsf{rec}}$ is type-respecting, and $\mathcal{L}_{\mathsf{rec}}$ seems a potentially useful intermediate language for compilation. The pragmatical impact of these results is currently being investigated within the language Lilac [41]. Other work that is currently being investigated includes the relationship with calculi for computational complexity. For instance, closed construction in System $\mathcal{L}$ gives PR functions [16], but closed construction does not affect $\mathcal{L}_{\mathsf{rec}}$ (the encoding of μ is closed).

References

[1] S. Abramsky. Computational Interpretations of Linear Logic. *Theoretical Computer Science*, 111:3–57, 1993.

[2] S. Alves. *Linearisation of the Lambda Calculus*. PhD thesis, Faculty of Science - University of Porto, April 2007.

[3] S. Alves, M. Fernández, M. Florido, and I. Mackie. Linear recursive functions. In *Rewriting, Computation and Proof*, volume 4600 of *LNCS*, pages 182–195. Springer, 2007.

[4] S. Alves, M. Fernández, M. Florido, and I. Mackie. Gödel's system $\mathcal{T}$ revisited. *Theor. Comput. Sci.*, 411(11-13):1484–1500, 2010.

[5] S. Alves, M. Fernández, M. Florido, and I. Mackie. Linear recursion. *CoRR*, abs/1001.3368, 2010.

[6] S. Alves and M. Florido. Weak linearization of the lambda calculus. *Theoretical Computer Science*, 342(1):79–103, 2005.

[7] A. Asperti and L. Roversi. Intuitionistic light affine logic. *ACM Transactions on Computational Logic*, 3(1):137–175, 2002.

[8] P. Baillot and V. Mogbil. Soft lambda-calculus: a language for polynomial time computation. In *Proc. FOSSACS'04*, volume 2987 of *LNCS*, pages 27–41. Springer-Verlag, 2004.

[9] H. P. Barendregt. *The Lambda Calculus: Its Syntax and Semantics*, volume 103 of *Studies in Logic and the Foundations of Mathematics*. North-Holland, 1984.

[10] U. Berger. Minimisation vs. recursion on the partial continuous functionals. In *In the Scope of Logic, Methodology and Philosophy of Science*, volume 1 of *Synthese Library 316*, pages 57–64. Kluwer, 2002.

[11] U. Berger and H. Schwichtenberg. An inverse of the evaluation functional for typed lambda-calculus. In *Proc. Logic in Computer Science (LICS'91)*, pages 203–211. IEEE Computer Society, 1991.

[12] G. M. Bierman, A. M. Pitts, and C. V. Russo. Operational properties of Lily, a polymorphic linear lambda calculus with recursion. In *Workshop on Higher Order Operational Techniques in Semantics*, volume 41 of *ENTCS*, pages 70–88. Elsevier, 2000.

[13] G. Boudol, P.-L. Curien, and C. Lavatelli. A semantics for lambda calculi with resources. *MSCS*, 9(4):437–482, 1999.

[14] T. Braüner. The Girard translation extended with recursion. In *Computer Science Logic, 8th International Workshop, CSL'94, Kazimierz, Poland*, volume 933 of *Lecture Notes in Computer Science*, pages 31–45. Springer, 1994.

[15] P.-L. Curien. An abstract framework for environment machines. *Theor. Comput. Sci.*, 82(2):389–402, 1991.

[16] U. Dal Lago. The geometry of linear higher-order recursion. In *Proc. Logic in Computer Science (LICS'05)*, pages 366–375, June 2005.

[17] J. Egger, R. E. Møgelberg, and A. Simpson. Enriching an effect calculus with linear types. In *Computer Science Logic, 23rd international Workshop, CSL 2009, 18th Annual Conference of the EACSL, Coimbra, Portugal, September 7-11, 2009. Proceedings*, volume 5771 of *Lecture Notes in Computer Science*, pages 240–254. Springer, 2009.

[18] T. Ehrhard and L. Regnier. The differential lambda-calculus. *Theor. Comput. Sci.*, 309(1-3):1–41, 2003.

[19] M. Fernández, I. Mackie, and F.-R. Sinot. Closed reduction: explicit substitutions without alpha conversion. *MSCS*, 15(2):343–381, 2005.

[20] M. Fernández, I. Mackie, and F.-R. Sinot. Lambda-calculus with director strings. *Applicable Algebra in Engineering, Communication and Computing*, 15(6):393–437, 2005.

[21] M. Fernández and N. Siafakas. New developments in environment machines. *Electr. Notes Theor. Comput. Sci.*, 237:57–73, 2009.

[22] D. R. Ghica. Geometry of synthesis: a structured approach to VLSI design. In *POPL*, pages 363–375, 2007.

[23] J. Girard. Light linear logic. *Inf. and Comp.*, 143(2):175–204, 1998.

[24] J.-Y. Girard. Linear Logic. *Theor. Comp. Sci.*, 50(1):1–102, 1987.

[25] J.-Y. Girard. Towards a geometry of interaction. In *Categories in Computer Science and Logic: Proc. of the Joint Summer Research Conference*, pages 69–108. American Mathematical Society, 1989.

[26] J.-Y. Girard, Y. Lafont, and P. Taylor. *Proofs and Types*. Cambridge Tracts in Theor. Comp. Sci. Cambridge University Press, 1989.

[27] J.-Y. Girard, A. Scedrov, and P. J. Scott. Bounded linear logic: A modular approach to polynomial time computability. *Theoretical Computer Science*, 97:1–66, 1992.

[28] M. Giunti and V. T. Vasconcelos. A linear account of session types in the pi calculus. In *CONCUR*, pages 432–446, 2010.

[29] C. Hankin. *An Introduction to Lambda Calculi for Computer Scientists*, volume 2. College Publications, 2004. ISBN 0-9543006-5-3.

[30] M. Hofmann. Linear types and non-size-increasing polynomial time computation. In *Proc. Logic in Computer Science (LICS'99)*. IEEE Computer Society, 1999.

[31] M. Hofmann and S. Jost. Static prediction of heap space usage for first-order functional programs. In *POPL*, pages 185–197, 2003.

[32] S. Holmström. Linear functional programming. In *Proc. of the Workshop on Implementation of Lazy Functional Languages*, pages 13–32, 1988.

[33] K. Honda. Types for dyadic interaction. In *CONCUR'93*, volume 715 of *LNCS*, pages 509–523. Springer, 1993.

[34] A. J. Kfoury. A linearization of the lambda-calculus and consequences. *Journal of Logic and Computation*, 10(3):411–436, 2000.

[35] J. W. Klop. *Combinatory Reduction Systems*. PhD thesis, Mathematisch Centrum, Amsterdam, 1980.

[36] J. W. Klop. New fixpoint combinators from old. *Reflections on Type Theory*, 2007.

[37] J.-W. Klop, V. van Oostrom, and F. van Raamsdonk. Combinatory reduction systems, introduction and survey. *Theor. Computer Science*, 121:279–308, 1993.

[38] N. Kobayashi, B. C. Pierce, and D. N. Turner. Linearity and the pi-calculus. In *POPL*, pages 358–371, 1996.

[39] Y. Lafont. The linear abstract machine. *Theor. Comp. Sci.*, 59:157–180, 1988.

[40] Y. Lafont. Soft linear logic and polynomial time. *Theoretical Computer Science*, 318(1-2):163–180, 2004.

[41] I. Mackie. Lilac: A functional programming language based on linear logic. *Journal of Functional Programming*, 4(4):395–433, 1994.

[42] I. Mackie. The geometry of interaction machine. In *Principles of Programming Languages (POPL)*, pages 198–208. ACM Press, 1995.

[43] R. Milner, J. Parrow, and D. Walker. A calculus of mobile processes, I. *Information and Computation*, 100(1):1 – 40, 1992.

[44] E. Nöcker, J. Smetsers, M. van Eekelen, and M. Plasmeijer. Concurrent clean. In *PARLE'91*, volume 506 of *LNCS*, pages 202–219. Springer, 1991.

[45] L. Paolini and M. Piccolo. Semantically linear programming languages. In *PPDP*, pages 97–107, Valencia, Spain, 2008. ACM.

[46] G. D. Plotkin. LCF Considered as a Programming Language. *Theoretical Computer Science*, 5:223–255, 1977.

[47] K. Terui. Light affine calculus and polytime strong normalization. In *Proc. Logic in Comp Sci. (LICS'01)*. IEEE Computer Society, 2001.

[48] A. v. Tonder. A lambda calculus for quantum computation. *SIAM J. Comput.*, 33(5):1109–1135, 2004.

[49] P. Wadler. Linear types can change the world! In *IFIP TC 2 Conf. on Progr. Concepts and Methods*, pages 347–359. North Holland, 1990.

[50] D. Walker. Substructural type systems. In *Adv. Topics in Types and Progr. Languages*, chapter 1, pages 3–43. MIT Press, Cambridge, 2005.

[51] K. Wansbrough and S. P. Jones. Simple usage polymorphism. In *Proc. ACM SIGPLAN Workshop on Types in Compilation*. ACM Press, 2000.

[52] N. Yoshida, K. Honda, and M. Berger. Linearity and bisimulation. In *FoSSaCS*, LNCS, pages 417–434. Springer-Verlag, 2002.

Nested Proof Search as Reduction in the λ-calculus

Nicolas Guenot
LIX, École Polytechnique
nguenot@lix.polytechnique.fr

Abstract

We present a system for propositional implicative intuitionistic logic in the *calculus of structures*, which is a generalisation of the sequent calculus to the *deep inference* methodology. We show that it is sound and complete with respect to the usual sequent calculus, and consider a restricted system for a smaller class of formulas. Then, we encode λ-terms with explicit substitutions in these formulas and exhibit a correspondence between proof search in this system and reduction in a λ-calculus with explicit substitutions. Finally, we present a further restriction to allow a correspondence with the standard λ-calculus, and show that we can prove results on λ-calculi by proving results on derivations in the proof systems.

Categories and Subject Descriptors F.4.1 [*Mathematical Logic and Formal Languages*]: Mathematical Logic—Computational logic, Lambda calculus and related systems, Logic and constraint programming, Proof theory

General Terms Theory

Keywords Proof search, Intuitionistic logic, Lambda calculus, Evaluation strategies, Deep inference, Explicit substitutions, Focusing

1. Introduction

This work is oriented towards the connection between structural *proof theory*, a field where the properties of proofs as objects of deductive systems as well as the design of logical rules and transformations applied on proofs are studied, and the design of programming languages, in particular in the setting of the two well-known paradigms of *functional programming* and *logic programming*. Both of these language paradigms have a central connection to logical systems and have greatly benefited from advances made in proof theory over the last decades. The goal of this paper is to show how some recent developments in proof theory can be applied to introduce new ways of reasoning about, and designing, programming languages.

Deep inference. This proof-theoretical methodology [GS01] is an extension of the traditional view of deductive systems such as *natural deduction* and the *sequent calculus*, where inference rules are allowed to be applied deep inside some formula. It has been implemented in several formalisms, and in particular in the *calculus of structures* [Brü03], where no meta-level structure such as a sequent is used, but formulas are directly rewritten by inference rules. As an example, the SKS system for classical logic is an elegant proof system which exhibits a nice top-down symmetry and where all inference rules are atomic, in the sense that they never modify, nor copy, nor erase non-atomic formulas [Brü06]. In this system, inference is not necessarily *shallow*, as illustrated in the following proof:

$$\cfrac{\cfrac{\cfrac{\top}{a \vee \neg a}}{(a \wedge (\neg b \vee b)) \vee \neg a}}{\neg b \vee ((a \wedge b) \vee \neg a)}$$

Moreover, the SKS proof system enjoys a surprisingly simple syntactic cut elimination procedure, which is quite different from the standard proof of the sequent calculus although the cut is defined as an inference rule within the system. The calculus of structures is a versatile tool, and it has also been used to study *non-commutativity* in the setting of linear logic [GS01]. Here we define a proof system for intuitionistic logic, which has not yet been studied thoroughly in this setting.

Functional programming. The λ-calculus is often considered as the theoretical core of the functional programming paradigm, since it provides clean foundations for its main abstraction, the notion of function, as well as the central ideas of bindings, scope and variables. Although it needs to be enriched with various features to be used as a reasonable programming language, it is the home ground for the mathematical study of the evaluation of functional programs, and in particular the study of evaluation strategies [Plo75]. There is a very important line of research on the connection between the proofs of intuitionistic logic and functional programs seen as λ-terms, often referred to as the *Curry-Howard tradition*. Its cornerstone is the correspondence between normalisation of proofs in natural deduction and the β rule expressing the operational behaviour of the λ-calculus.

The Curry-Howard correspondence has been extended later to proofs of the sequent calculus [Her94] and to a decomposition of the λ-calculus through the reification inside the language of the notion of substitution, leading to an extensive literature on explicit substitutions [Kes07]. In this work we will rely heavily on this decomposition of the β-reduction process, since the first correspondence we establish between a system for intuitionistic logic and functional programs is based on a variant of standard λ-calculi that can be found in the literature. However, this nice correspondence can be defined for the usual λ-calculus as well, by using the standard way of recovering plain β-reduction from finer reduction systems. It is important to notice our work does not belong to this tradition, since we are not using any kind of cut, and computation will not be modeled as normalisation of proofs, or as some kind of transformation.

Logic programming. Among modern programming languages, another common way of establishing theoretical foundations for programs consists in using the logical formulas as a language and the process of proving a formula, seen as a program, as the computation associated to this *logic* program. This methodology is often referred to as the *proof-search-as-computation* paradigm, and one can use deductive systems such as the sequent calculus to provide a foundation for such logic programming languages [MNPS91], that can be extended without losing logical purity to advanced features such as modules [Mil89]. This work belongs to this tradition in the sense that we are interpreting formulas of intuitionistic logic as functional programs, and then defining computation as the process of building a proof, even if this is an incomplete proof, in some deductive system.

Contributions. This paper introduces an analysis of functional computation, described by means of a λ-calculus with explicit substitutions, called $\lambda\mathsf{s}$ and based on the following grammar:

$$t, u \ ::= \ x \ \mid \ \lambda x.t \ \mid \ t\ u \ \mid \ t[x \leftarrow u]$$

in a setting of logic programming, where proof search models computation. In Section 2 we present a new proof system for intuitionistic logic in the calculus of structures, called JS, and prove that it is sound and complete with respect to the standard sequent calculus system. The goal is to encode all $\lambda\mathsf{s}$-terms into formulas using the following scheme:

$$\begin{array}{rcl} [\![x]\!] & = & x \\ [\![\lambda x.t]\!] & = & x \to [\![t]\!] \\ [\![t\ u]\!] & = & ([\![u]\!] \to \top) \to [\![t]\!] \\ [\![t[x \leftarrow u]]\!] & = & ([\![u]\!] \to x) \to [\![t]\!] \end{array}$$

and to fit the reduction rules of the calculus with respect to this encoding, we define a restriction of JS, called JLSd, which is sound and comes with a partial completeness result. Then, in Section 3 we establish a precise correspondence between proof search in JLSd and reduction in the rewrite system defining the operational behaviour of our calculus. Properties of $\lambda\mathsf{s}$ and the relation with properties of JLSd are discussed. Finally, Section 4 introduces another restriction based on annotations in the style of *focusing* [And92], called JLSn, shows that this system yields a correspondence with the standard λ-calculus with β-reduction, and proves properties of $\lambda\mathsf{s}$ with respect to the λ-calculus using this correspondence. The relationships between different proof systems and calculi is shown in Figure 1, where arrows indicate which systems simulate other systems — we will also use JLSb, a subset of the JLSd system which is not mentioned here. In the conclusion, we also discuss the possibility of extending this correspondence to the full JS system, which would require to move from the λ-calculus to a calculus with pattern-matching, such as the *pure pattern calculus* [JK09]. It is thus further work to fill the hole in Figure 1 and interpret full JS.

Related work. There is not much work on intuitionistic logic in the setting of deep inference, and most of it is purely on the side of proof theory [Tiu06]. The only computational interpretation of an intuitionistic system in the calculus of structures [BM08] is based on the proofs-as-programs paradigm and cut-elimination. It also uses a different proof system relying on conjunction, and with no switch rule. We have a completely different approach, since we

$$\begin{array}{ccccccc} \mathsf{JS} & \longrightarrow & \mathsf{JLS} & \longrightarrow & \mathsf{JLSd} & \longleftrightarrow & \mathsf{JLSn} \\ \wr & & & & \wr & & \wr \\ ? & & & & \lambda\mathsf{s} & \longleftrightarrow & \lambda \end{array}$$

Figure 1. Proof systems and calculi used in this paper

$$\mathsf{i}\ \frac{B}{(B \to A) \to A} \qquad \mathsf{s}\ \frac{((A \to B) \to C) \to D}{A \to ((B \to C) \to D)}$$

$$\mathsf{w}\ \frac{B}{A \to B} \qquad \mathsf{c}\ \frac{A \to (A \to B)}{A \to B}$$

Figure 2. Inference rules for system JS

use the proof-search-as-computation paradigm. There exists however some work on the encoding of reduction in the λ-calculus with explicit substitutions into proof search [Rov11], also in the setting of deep inference, but we are using here plain intuitionistic logic rather than a variant of linear logic extended with non-commutativity and a renaming operator, and the result here is not restricted to the *linear* fragment of the λ-calculus. The methodology adopted to represent computation is also quite different.

The point of this work is to establish a bridge between functional programming and the methodology of logic programming, which allows for a fine analysis of computation in terms of logic only. A goal would be to get new insights on the evaluation mechanisms of the λ-calculus through the use of proof-theoretical tools, and we can also hope for cross-fertilisation of the two fields if we can transpose results on one side to the other side.

2. Intuitionistic Logic in the Calculus of Structures

The proof systems we present here are all based on a common system JS, which can be seen as an intuitionistic variant of the KSg system [Brü03] for classical logic at the propositional level, using only the implication $\to$ as a connective. In this setting, any inference rule can be applied deep inside a formula, and a derivation is not a tree, but a sequence of rule instances.

We start with a set of *formulas*, denoted by capital latin letters such as A, B, C, and generated from a countable set of *atoms*, denoted by a, b, c and so on, and the truth unit $\top$ by using the binary connective $\to$ for implication. Formally, we have:

$$L \ ::= \ a \mid \top \qquad\qquad A, B \ ::= \ L \mid A \to B$$

and we denote *literals* with letters such as L. Moreover, formulas are usually considered in the calculus of structures through a set of equations, so that *structures* are defined as equivalence classes of formulas generated by the following congruence rules:

$$\top \to A \ \equiv_u \ A \quad \text{and} \quad A \to (B \to C) \ \equiv_a \ B \to (A \to C)$$

Then, the set of inference rules for JS is shown in Figure 2. Being in the setting of deep inference means having the ability to apply inference rules inside some *context*, which is a structure with a hole $\{\ \}$, meant to be filled by a structure. To keep notations simple, we consider only *positive* contexts here, those where the hole is located on the left of an even number of implications, as follows:

$$\xi ::= \{\ \} \mid (\xi \to A) \to B$$

Contexts will be denoted as $\xi\{\ \}$ or $\zeta\{\ \}$, and for example $\xi\{A\}$ is the context ξ where the hole is replaced by a structure or a context A. The inference rules in Figure 2 can only be applied in positive contexts, and any rule r can be instantiated in a context ξ by placing its premise and conclusion inside:

$$(\textit{rule}) \quad \mathsf{r}\ \frac{A}{B} \quad \longrightarrow \quad \mathsf{r}\ \frac{\xi\{A\}}{\xi\{B\}} \quad (\textit{rule instance})$$

We use standard notations for a *derivation* $\mathcal{D}$ from A to B, and a *proof* $\mathcal{D}'$ of B, which is a derivation with $\top$ as premise:

$$\begin{array}{c} A \\ \mathcal{D}\| \\ B \end{array} \qquad \text{and} \qquad \begin{array}{c} \mathcal{D}'\overline{\|} \\ B \end{array}$$

To show that our system is suitable for intuitionistic logic, we prove soundness and completeness with respect to the sequent calculus system shown in Figure 3, that we call $\mathsf{LJ} \cup \{\mathsf{cut}\}$. This requires to translate sequents into structures:

$$[\![\vdash A]\!]_\mathsf{S} \;=\; A \quad \text{and} \quad [\![A, \Delta \vdash B]\!]_\mathsf{S} \;=\; A \to [\![\Delta \vdash B]\!]_\mathsf{S}$$

We use the short notation $\Gamma \to A$ to denote the translation of the sequent $\Gamma \vdash A$, which is sensible because the equation $\equiv_a$ allows to treat $A \to (B \to C)$ as the formula $(A \wedge B) \to C$.

THEOREM 1 (Soundness of JS). *If a structure A is provable in the system* JS, *then the sequent* $\vdash A$ *is provable in* $\mathsf{LJ} \cup \{\mathsf{cut}\}$.

PROOF. The proof is standard, see for example [Brü03]. We proceed by induction on the given proof in JS. For each rule instance with premise $\xi\{A\}$ and conclusion $\xi\{B\}$ we can show by induction on the context that the sequent $\vdash \xi\{A\} \to \xi\{B\}$ is provable in $\mathsf{LJ} \cup \{\mathsf{cut}\}$. Then, we use a cut at each step. □

There is no equivalent of the cut rule in JS, and we thus prove completeness using the cut-free system LJ as a reference.

THEOREM 2 (Completeness of JS). *If some sequent* $\Gamma \vdash A$ *is provable in* LJ, *then the structure* $[\![\Gamma \vdash A]\!]_\mathsf{S}$ *is provable in* JS.

PROOF. By induction on a proof of $\Gamma \vdash A$ in LJ. Almost all cases are straightforward, the only interesting case is actually the left implication rule, shown below:

$$\to_\mathsf{L}\dfrac{\begin{array}{c}\Pi_1 \\ \Gamma \vdash A\end{array} \qquad \begin{array}{c}\Pi_2 \\ \Delta, B \vdash C\end{array}}{\Gamma, \Delta, A \to B \vdash C} \quad \longrightarrow \quad \begin{array}{c} \mathcal{D}_2\overline{\|} \\ \equiv_\mathsf{u}\dfrac{\Delta \to B \to C}{\Delta \to (\top \to B) \to C} \\ \mathcal{D}_1\| \\ \mathsf{s}^*\dfrac{\Delta \to ((\Gamma \to A) \to B) \to C}{\equiv_\mathsf{a}^*\dfrac{\Delta \to \Gamma \to (A \to B) \to C}{\Gamma \to \Delta \to (A \to B) \to C}} \end{array}$$

where the proof $\mathcal{D}_2$ is obtained from Π_2 by induction hypothesis, and the derivation $\mathcal{D}_1$ by plugging the translation of Π_1 into the context $\Delta \to (\{\ \} \to B) \to C$, which is possible because of the deep inference methodology used here. □

Although it is a simple system for a fragment of intuitionistic logic, JS is already too general to represent the λ-calculus with precision in a proof search style. Indeed, no term corresponds to a formula with a compound formula in negative position, such as $(A \to (B \to C)) \to D$, and even if we restrict formulas to images of the translation mentioned in the introduction — and formally defined in Section 3 — we still have problems with inference rules and equations that do not correspond to valid operations of our λ-calculus, as for example:

$$\begin{array}{rcl} \lambda x.t & \longrightarrow & \lambda x.\lambda x.t \\ \lambda x.\lambda y.t & \equiv_a & \lambda y.\lambda x.t \end{array}$$

Thus, we define a restriction of this system, called JLS, where formulas are limited to those where the subformulas in negative position, located on the left of an odd number of implications, can only be atoms, plus some restrictions on the use of the $\top$ unit, as shown in the following grammar:

$$\begin{array}{l} B \;::=\; a \mid a \to B \mid \omega \to B \mid \delta \to B \\ \delta \;::=\; B \to a \qquad \omega \;::=\; B \to \top \end{array}$$

$$\mathsf{ax}\,\dfrac{}{A \vdash A} \qquad \mathsf{cut}\,\dfrac{\Gamma \vdash A \quad \Delta, A \vdash B}{\Gamma, \Delta \vdash B} \qquad \top_\mathsf{R}\,\dfrac{}{\vdash \top}$$

$$\mathsf{weak}\,\dfrac{\Gamma \vdash B}{\Gamma, A \vdash B} \qquad \mathsf{cont}\,\dfrac{\Gamma, A, A \vdash B}{\Gamma, A \vdash B} \qquad \top_\mathsf{L}\,\dfrac{\Gamma \vdash A}{\Gamma, \top \vdash A}$$

$$\to_\mathsf{R}\,\dfrac{\Gamma, A \vdash B}{\Gamma \vdash A \to B} \qquad \to_\mathsf{L}\,\dfrac{\Gamma \vdash A \quad \Delta, B \vdash C}{\Gamma, \Delta, A \to B \vdash C}$$

Figure 3. Inference rules for system $\mathsf{LJ} \cup \{\mathsf{cut}\}$

where B defines the class of *restricted formulas*, that we denote as normal formulas, and δ defines the *blocks*, denoted by greek letters such as δ, κ, μ, which represent explicit substitutions in our encoding. Subformulas defined by ω are called *matchers* and denoted by ω or τ, they represent the argument term in an application. We use contexts to restrict the congruence as well, keeping only the equation $\equiv_a$ on specific positive subformulas:

$$\xi\{\delta \to (\kappa \to A)\} \;\equiv_b\; \xi\{\kappa \to (\delta \to A)\}$$

Finally, the inference rules of the restricted system JLS are given in Figure 4. In this system, the switch rule and the rules of weakening and contraction can only be used to move, erase or duplicate blocks. Moreover, another part of the equation $\equiv_a$ is expressed in the rule xr, which also can only exchange blocks. The identity rule is also restricted, through the condition that the premise cannot be the $\top$ unit, and it only applies on atoms. The new rule isu is a compound rule that embodies the use of an identity on $\top$, and corresponds to the following JS derivation:

$$\mathsf{i}\,\dfrac{(B \to a) \to C}{\mathsf{s}\,\dfrac{((((B \to \top) \to \top) \to a) \to C)}{\equiv_\mathsf{u}\,\dfrac{(B \to \top) \to ((\top \to a) \to C)}{(B \to \top) \to (a \to C)}}}$$

This new inference rule corresponds, through the encoding of λs-terms, to the standard B rule which triggers a β-redex to turn an application into an explicit substitution, to be carried out:

$$(\lambda x.t)\ u \longrightarrow_\mathsf{B} t[x \leftarrow u]$$

This system is clearly not going to be complete, since restrictions are so strong that for example, there is no way of writing a proof of $a \to (a \to \top) \to a$. However, this system can easily be shown sound with respect to its general version JS.

THEOREM 3 (Soundness of JLS). *If there is a derivation from A to B in* JLS, *then there is a derivation from A to B in* JS.

PROOF. Any derivation from A to B in JLS can be immediately converted into a derivation in JS. Indeed, the rules ir, wr, cr and sr are restrictions of the rules of JS, the equation $\equiv_b$ is a restriction of $\equiv_a$ and the xr rule also corresponds to another use of this equation. Finally, any instance of the isu rule can be replaced with a derivation of JS, as it was shown above. □

It is interesting to notice that the identity on the unit $\top$ we use in the derivation corresponding to isu is not even needed in JS, since it will be shown admissible. To preserve the upper bound on the length of proofs during the process, it is useful to consider the system JS', a variant of JS where the usual switch is replaced with a compound rule called *super-switch* [Str03]:

$$\mathsf{ss}\,\dfrac{\xi\{\delta\} \to B}{\delta \to (\xi\{\top\} \to B)}$$

$$\text{ir}\ \frac{B}{(B \to a) \to a} \qquad \text{isu}\ \frac{(B \to a) \to C}{(B \to \top) \to (a \to C)}$$

$$\text{wr}\ \frac{A}{\delta \to A} \qquad \text{cr}\ \frac{\delta \to (\delta \to A)}{\delta \to A}$$

$$\text{xr}\ \frac{A \to (\delta \to B)}{\delta \to (A \to B)} \qquad \text{sr}\ \frac{((\delta \to A) \to L) \to B}{\delta \to ((A \to L) \to B)}$$

Figure 4. Inference rules for system JLS

which is equivalent to a derivation of several switches, so that there are obvious translations between JS and JS'. We can use this alternative system to count a sequence of switches as only one rule instance in the length of a proof.

PROPOSITION 4. *If there is a proof of a structure $\xi\{A\}$ in* JS, *then there is a proof of $\xi\{(A \to \top) \to \top\}$ as well in* JS, *not using an identity on these $\top$ occurrences.*

PROOF. By induction on the length of the given proof $\mathcal{D}$ of A in JS, translated into the JS' system. If $\mathcal{D}$ is of length 0, we replace $\top$ with $(\top \to \top) \to \top$ using $\equiv_u$. Then, in the general case, we use a case analysis on the bottommost rule instance r in $\mathcal{D}$. We can always rewrite the conclusion and use the induction hypothesis to rewrite the premise, but in the case of a switch moving some structure E inside A, where A is $(B \to C) \to D$, we must use an additional switch:

$$\text{s}\ \frac{\xi\{((E \to B) \to C) \to D\}}{\xi\{E \to ((B \to C) \to D)\}}$$

$$\longrightarrow \quad \text{s}\ \frac{\text{s}\ \dfrac{\xi\{((((E \to B) \to C) \to D) \to \top) \to \top\}}{\xi\{((E \to ((B \to C) \to D)) \to \top) \to \top\}}}{\xi\{E \to ((((B \to C) \to D) \to \top) \to \top)\}}$$

which can be rewritten into a super-switch ss instance. Note that in the case of the contraction c, we need to use the induction hypothesis twice, and this is possible because the transformation is length-preserving, thanks to the super-switch. □

Now, we will show that the JLS proof system is actually not so far from being complete with respect to the restricted fragment of intuitionistic logic. In order to do this, we consider a smaller fragment, by imposing more restrictions on structures: only one negative occurrence of each atom is allowed, and all its positive occurrences must appear *in the scope* of this negative occurrence. We use the notation $a \in B$ to denote that some atom a appears in the structure B, and $a \in \xi$ if a appears in the context $\xi\{\ \}$.

DEFINITION 5. *The* (positive) multiplicity *of an atom a in some structure B, denoted by $|B|_a^+$, is the number of occurrences of a in positive position in B. Its* negative multiplicity, *denoted by $|B|_a^-$, is its number of occurrences in negative position in B.*

The formulas of the more restricted class defined here are called *functional structures* because they will be the ones corresponding to λs-terms in the rest of the paper.

DEFINITION 6. *A restricted structure B is said to be* functional *if for any $a \in B$, there is a context $\xi\{\ \}$ and structures C and D such that we have either $B \equiv_b \xi\{a \to C\}$ or $B \equiv_b \xi\{(D \to a) \to C\}$, with $a \notin \xi$, $a \notin D$, $|C|_a^+ \geq 0$ and $|C|_a^- = 0$.*

Then, we can observe that functional structures are not stable under application of inference rules of JLS, in particular under contraction. Therefore we need to tweak our inference rules.

apply wr *on* $(B \to a) \to C$	: *only if* $\lvert C\rvert_a = 0$
apply crn *on* $(B \to a) \to C$	: *only if* $\lvert C\rvert_a \geq 2$
apply xr *on* $(B \to a) \to (C \to D)$	: *only if* $\lvert C\rvert_a = 0$
apply sr *on* $(B \to a) \to ((C \to L) \to D)$	: *only if* $\lvert D\rvert_a = 0$

$$\xi\{(C \to a) \to ((D \to b) \to E)\} \equiv_b \xi\{(D \to b) \to ((C \to a) \to E)\}$$

this equation holds only if we have $|D|_a = 0$ *and* $|C|_b = 0$

Figure 5. Restrictions used to define JLSd from JLS

To be able to use contraction on such structures, we consider the following variation of the cr rule:

$$\text{crn}\ \frac{(B \to d) \to ((B \to a) \to C_{[d/a]})}{(B \to a) \to C}$$

where $C_{[d/a]}$ denotes the same C with exactly one occurrence of the atom a replaced by an occurrence of a fresh atom d. This rule can be shown sound by a induction on proofs. Finally, we define the proof system JLSd as {ir, isu, wr, crn, xr, sr}, with extra conditions on the conclusion of rules and on the congruence, summarised in Figure 5. These conditions ensure that functional structures are stable under application of rules of JLSd, as well as its congruence.

These new restrictions correspond, on the side of our λ-calculus, to the idea that we want to manipulate terms up to renaming of variables, so that no variable name is bound twice, and we can use implicitly α-conversion to change names.

The JLSd system is sound with respect to intuitionistic logic, since we only added restrictions on inference rules of JLS and we observed that the variant rule crn was sound too, and we will now study its completeness. As we already noticed, this system is not complete — the unit $\top$ cannot appear as the premise of a derivation, so that there is no proof *per se* in this system — but we can establish a partial completeness result. We do that in three steps: first we use a subset of the JLSd system, then we deal with some particular weakenings forbidden in JLSd, and finally we build the proof premise $\top$ from a simple formula, by dealing again with weakenings. The goal is to show that if some A is provable in JS, we can build a proof of the shape:

$$\begin{array}{c} \top \\ {\scriptstyle \{\mathsf{wm},\mathsf{iaw}\}}\Big\| \\ B \\ {\scriptstyle \mathsf{JLSb}}\Big\| \\ A \end{array} \qquad (1)$$

A terminating subset of JLSd. We consider the system JLSb, which is defined as JLSd without the isu rule, for which we show that proof search is terminating. To do that, we need a measure on functional structures that will decrease during proof search, and the first part of this measure can be defined in a simple way.

DEFINITION 7. *Given any functional structure A, we can define as follows its* block-complexity, *denoted by $\mathcal{C}(A)$ and its* net size, *denoted by $\mathcal{N}(A)$, using the following induction:*

$$\begin{array}{rcl} \mathcal{C}(a) &=& 0 \\ \mathcal{C}(a \to B) &=& \mathcal{C}(B) \\ \mathcal{C}((C \to \top) \to B) &=& \mathcal{C}(C) + \mathcal{C}(B) \\ \mathcal{C}((C \to a) \to B) &=& \mathcal{C}(C) + \mathcal{C}(B) + \mathcal{N}(B) \end{array}$$

$$\begin{array}{rcl} \mathcal{N}(a) &=& 1 \\ \mathcal{N}(a \to B) &=& 1 + \mathcal{N}(B) \\ \mathcal{N}((C \to \top) \to B) &=& \mathcal{N}(C) + \mathcal{N}(B) \\ \mathcal{N}((C \to a) \to B) &=& \mathcal{N}(B) \end{array}$$

REMARK 8. *The block-complexity is invariant under congruence, namely the equation $\equiv_b$, because the blocks that can be exchanged this way are exactly the substructures that are not counted in the size of a given structure.*

This complexity measure is simply the sum, for each block δ, of the size of the structure in the scope of δ. We can use this to show that the process of building a derivation by applications of inference rules of JLSb terminates — we call this *proof search* although we are building derivations and not proofs.

LEMMA 9. *Proof search in* JLSb *is terminating.*

PROOF. Given some functional structure A, if we apply any inference rule of JLSb on A other than the contraction crn rule, we obtain a functional structure B such that $\mathcal{C}(B) < \mathcal{C}(A)$, as can be checked for the rules ir, wr, xr and sr.

In the case of crn, we can observe that one positive occurrence of an atom has been replaced with an occurrence of some fresh atom. We define for any functional structure F a measure $M(F)$ as the multiset of $|F|_d^+$ for all $d \in F$, under multiset ordering, and with crn we have $M(B) < M(A)$ since $|B|_e^+ < |A|_e^+$ for some $e \in A$, and the introduced atom has a multiplicity of 1 in B.

Finally, we can use an induction on the pair $(M(A), \mathcal{C}(A))$, under lexicographic order, and we reach the case of a structure G such that $(M(A), \mathcal{C}(A)) = (0, 0)$, which means that there is no block δ in G. This implies that no rule of JLSb can be applied on G. □

Moreover, we can prove that the rules JLSb are invertible in JS, so that proof search preserves provability in JS. This means we can use JLSb on a structure A to produce by proof search a B such that A is provable in JS if and only if B is provable in JS.

LEMMA 10. *If there is a proof in* JS *of a functional structure* $\xi\{(B \to a) \to a\}$, *then there is a proof in* JS *for* $\xi\{B\}$.

PROOF. By induction on the length of a given proof $\mathcal{D}$ in JS of $\xi\{(B \to a) \to a\}$, we build a proof of at most the same length for $\xi\{B\}$. If $\mathcal{D}$ has length 2, it uses identities on $((b \to b) \to a) \to a$, and we use the identity on $b \to b$ only. In the general case, we use a case analysis on the bottommost rule instance r in $\mathcal{D}$:

1. If r does not affect this occurrence of $(B \to a) \to a$, we can rewrite the conclusion into $\xi\{B\}$, and use the induction hypothesis to rewrite the premise accordingly.
2. If r only affects a structure inside this occurrence of B, we rewrite the conclusion into $\xi\{B\}$, use the same rule inside a smaller context, and then the induction hypothesis.
3. If r is a contraction c on this occurrence of $B \to a$, we use the induction hypothesis on only one copy of $B \to a$.
4. If r is a switch s moving a structure D on the left of $B \to a$, we can remove it and go on by induction hypothesis:

$$\mathsf{s}\,\frac{\xi\{((E \to B) \to a) \to a\}}{\xi\{E \to ((B \to a) \to a)\}} \quad \longrightarrow \quad \xi\{E \to B\}$$

Notice that there can be no weakening on this $B \to a$ since there would be no a left in negative position to complete the proof. □

LEMMA 11. *If there is a proof in* JS *of some functional structure* $\xi\{(B \to a) \to C\}$, *and* $|C|_a = 0$, *then there is a proof in* JS *for the structure* $\xi\{C\}$.

PROOF. By induction on the length of a given proof $\mathcal{D}$ in JS of $\xi\{(B \to a) \to C\}$, we build a proof of at most the same length for $\xi\{C\}$. If $\mathcal{D}$ has length 2, it uses a weakening and an identity on $(B \to a) \to (c \to c)$, and we use the identity on $c \to c$ only. In the general case, we use a case analysis on the bottommost rule instance r in $\mathcal{D}$:

1. If r does not affect this occurrence of $B \to a$, we rewrite the conclusion into $\xi\{C\}$ and use the induction hypothesis to rewrite the premise accordingly.
2. If r only affects a structure inside this occurrence of B, we rewrite the conclusion into $\xi\{C\}$, use the same rule inside a smaller context, and then the induction hypothesis.
3. If r is a weakening w on this occurrence of $B \to a$, we remove it in the conclusion and the result is immediate.
4. If r is a contraction c on this occurrence of $B \to a$, we can rewrite the conclusion into $\xi\{C\}$ and then use twice the induction hypothesis, which is possible since the first proof obtained has at most the same length as the original.
5. If r is a switch s moving a structure E on the left of $B \to a$, we replace it by a weakening, as shown below:

$$\mathsf{s}\,\frac{\xi\{((E \to B) \to a) \to C\}}{\xi\{E \to ((B \to a) \to C)\}} \quad \longrightarrow \quad \mathsf{w}\,\frac{\xi\{C\}}{\xi\{E \to C\}}$$

and we can go on by induction hypothesis. □

LEMMA 12. *If there is a proof in* JS *of some functional structure* $\xi\{(B \to a) \to ((C \to L) \to D)\}$, *and* $|D|_a = 0$, *then there is a proof in* JS *for the structure* $\xi\{((((B \to a) \to C) \to L) \to D)\}$.

PROOF. By induction on the length of a given proof $\mathcal{D}$ in JS of $\xi\{(B \to a) \to ((C \to L) \to D)\}$ translated to JS', we build a proof of at most the same length for $\xi\{((((B \to a) \to C) \to L) \to D)\}$. If $\mathcal{D}$ has length 3, it uses on $((c \to c) \to a) \to ((a \to b) \to b)$ three identities and we do the same. In the general case, we use a case analysis on the bottommost rule instance r in $\mathcal{D}$:

1. If r does not affect this occurrence of $B \to a$, we rewrite the conclusion into $\xi\{((((B \to a) \to C) \to L) \to D)\}$ and use the induction hypothesis to rewrite the premise.
2. If r only affects a structure inside this occurrence of B, we rewrite the conclusion again, use the same rule inside a smaller context, and then use the induction hypothesis.
3. If r is a weakening w on this occurrence of $B \to a$, we rewrite the conclusion again and use a weakening.
4. If r is a contraction c on this occurrence of $B \to a$, we rewrite the conclusion again and use twice the induction hypothesis, which is possible since the proof obtained the first time has at most the same length as the original.
5. If r is a switch s moving a structure E on the left of $B \to a$, we replace it by a super-switch, as shown below:

$$\mathsf{s}\,\frac{\xi\{((E \to B) \to a) \to ((C \to L) \to D)\}}{\xi\{E \to ((B \to a) \to ((C \to L) \to D))\}}$$

$$\longrightarrow \quad \mathsf{ss}\,\frac{\xi\{((((E \to B) \to a) \to C) \to L) \to D\}}{\xi\{E \to ((((B \to a) \to C) \to L) \to D)\}}$$

and then we go on by induction hypothesis. The case of a super-switch is treated exactly the same way.

In the end, we have a proof in JS' that we can turn into a proof of the same structure in JS by expanding super-switches. □

LEMMA 13. *If there is a proof in* JS *of some functional structure* $\xi\{(B \to a) \to C\}$*, and* $|C|_a \geq 2$*, then there is a proof in* JS *for the structure* $\xi\{(B \to a) \to ((B \to a) \to C)\}$.

PROOF. Such a proof can be obtained as follows:

$$\mathsf{w}\,\frac{\overset{\mathcal{D}\Vert}{\xi\{(B \to a) \to C\}}}{\xi\{(B \to a) \to ((B \to a) \to C)\}}$$

where $\mathcal{D}$ is the given proof of $\xi\{(B \to a) \to C\}$ in JS. □

LEMMA 14. *If there is a proof in* JS *of some functional structure* $\xi\{(B \to a) \to (C \to D)\}$*, and* $|C|_a = 0$*, then there is a proof in* JS *for the structure* $\xi\{C \to ((B \to a) \to D)\}$.

PROOF. This corresponds to the use of the congruence in the JS system, namely the equation $\equiv_a$, so that this is immediate. □

We can use all these lemmas to prove that proof search in JLSb has the interesting property of preserving provability, which will be a crucial argument in our partial completeness result.

LEMMA 15. *For any structures A and B, if there is a derivation from A to B in the* JLSb *system and B is provable in* JS*, then A is provable in* JS.

PROOF. By induction on the length of the given derivation $\mathcal{D}$ from A to B in JLSb. If $\mathcal{D}$ has length 0, the result is immediate since A is B. In the general case, we use a case analysis on the bottommost rule instance r in $\mathcal{D}$, to prove that if there is a proof of its conclusion A in JS, there is a proof of its premise, by either Lemma 10, Lemma 11, Lemma 13, Lemma 14 or Lemma 12. □

Weakening matchers. We consider the following rule, which corresponds to a case of weakening forbidden in JLS:

$$\mathsf{wm}\,\frac{A}{(B \to \top) \to A}$$

Then, we show that this inference rule is complete, in the sense that using it during a proof search cannot turn some provable structure into an unprovable one — it is an *invertible* rule.

LEMMA 16. *If there is a proof in* JS *of some functional structure* $\xi\{(B \to \top) \to A\}$*, then there is a proof of* $\xi\{A\}$ *in* JS.

PROOF. By induction on the given proof $\mathcal{D}$ in JS, we build a proof of $\xi\{A\}$, preserving the upper bound on the length of the proof. If $\mathcal{D}$ has length 1, it uses a weakening on $(B \to \top) \to \top$, and the result is immediate. In the general case, we use a case analysis on the bottommost rule instance r in $\mathcal{D}$:

1. If r does not affect this occurrence of $B \to \top$, we remove it from the conclusion and use the induction hypothesis to rewrite the premise accordingly.
2. If r only affects a structure inside this occurrence of B, we remove this instance and use the induction hypothesis.
3. If r is a weakening w on this occurrence of $B \to \top$, the result is immediate.
4. If r is a contraction c on this occurrence of $B \to \top$, we can rewrite the conclusion and we use twice the induction hypothesis, which is possible since the proof obtained the first time has at most the same length as the original.
5. If r is a switch s moving a structure C on the left of B, we replace it by a weakening, and go on by induction hypothesis:

$$\mathsf{s}\,\frac{\xi\{((C \to B) \to \top) \to A\}}{\xi\{C \to ((B \to \top) \to A)\}} \quad \longrightarrow \quad \mathsf{w}\,\frac{\xi\{A\}}{\xi\{C \to A\}}$$

In this analysis, there is no need to consider the case where r is an instance of the identity i used on $(B \to \top) \to \top$, since we can always remove it from any proof in JS by using Proposition 4. □

Closing the proof. We consider a functional structure where no block and no matcher appears, and observe that it is of the shape $b_1 \to \cdots \to b_n \to a$. Such a structure is provable if and only if there is an i such that b_i is a, and we can use the following inference rule, not to be applied inside a context:

$$\mathsf{iaw}\,\frac{\top}{b_1 \to \cdots \to a \to \cdots \to b_n \to a}$$

which can be applied on a structure of this shape if and only if it is provable, since it is equivalent to many weakenings and one identity instance. Now, we can glue the pieces together to produce a proof of weak completeness, which states that given a functional structure A provable in JS, although there is no proof of A in JLSb nor in JLSd, there is a derivation from a structure B to A in JLSb, such that B can easily be mechanically checked.

THEOREM 17 (Weak completeness of JLSb). *For any given functional structure A, if there is a proof of A in* JS*, then there is a structure B such that there is a derivation from B to A in* JLSb *and a proof of B in* {wm, iaw}.

PROOF. As a first step, we apply Lemma 9 to produce by proof search a derivation $\mathcal{D}_1$ from some structure A_1 to A in the JLSb system. Notice that there can be no block — that is, structures of the shape $(B \to c)$ in negative position — in the structure A_1 since that would imply that at least one inference rule of JLSb could be applied. Moreover, by Lemma 15 we know that if A is provable in JS, then A_1 is provable in JS too. Then, we apply as much as possible the wm rule on A_1 to produce a derivation $\mathcal{D}_2$ from a structure A_2 with no matchers — that is, structures of the shape $(B \to \top)$ in negative position — to A_1. By Lemma 16 we know that if A_1 is provable in JS, then A_2 is provable in JS too. Finally, if A_2 is provable in JS and does not contain matchers, then we can use one instance of iaw to build a proof of the shape described in (1), where the expected derivation from B to A in JLSb is $\mathcal{D}_1$, since this A_1 is provable in {wm, iaw}. □

COROLLARY 18 (Weak completeness of JLSd). *For any given functional structure A, if there is a proof of A in* JS*, then there is a structure B such that there is a derivation from B to A in* JLSd *and a proof of B in* {wm, iaw}.

This result tells us that JLSb is indeed a sensible system to deal with functional structures, and therefore JLSd can also be used. The problem of proving functional structures in the JLSd system is more subtle that in JLSb, since it allows the use of the isu rule which is not invertible, but we can avoid using the wm rule to get a complete proof in some cases. This is not always possible, as shown by the following example proof:

$$\mathsf{wm}\,\frac{\mathsf{iaw}\,\frac{\top}{a \to a}}{(B \to \top) \to (a \to a)}$$

In this case, we cannot use the isu rule if the structure B is not provable in JS, while the complete structure is provable in JS. The JLSd system allows to use the minimal amount of instances of wm to get a proof in JS, but there is no way in general to build a proof from JLSd and the iaw rule only. The class of structures that can be proved using JLSd and iaw only is more behaved than general functional structures, since the structure B in a structure of the shape $(B \to \top) \to C$ is not logically *relevant*.

3. Proof Search as Reduction with Explicit Substitutions

We now consider a λ-calculus with explicit substitutions [Kes07], that we will call λs, and show how its terms can be encoded into logical structures, so that the process of building a derivation in JLSd will simulate the process of applying reduction rules in the λs-calculus. We say *proof search*, although we are not building complete proofs but rather open derivations, to emphasize the relation of this work with the usual *proof-search-as-computation* paradigm [MNPS91].

It is a direct approach, based on incomplete derivations of the proof system, in the sense that if two given structures A and B represent programs such that A can be reduced to B through the operational semantics of the language, there is a derivation from B to A rather than a proof of $A \to B$, as we will see.

Our λ-calculus is very similar to many other calculi with explicit substitutions in the literature, and in particular it borrows its handling of duplication using a linear renaming operation from the *structural λ-calculus* [AK10]. The syntax of λs-terms can be defined by the following grammar:

$$t, u ::= x \mid \lambda x.t \mid t\ u \mid t[x \leftarrow u]$$

where the object $[x \leftarrow u]$, which is called an *explicit substitution*, is a binder for the variable x, so that x is bound in $t[x \leftarrow u]$. Moreover, terms are considered *modulo* α-conversion, so that a variable is always bound at most once in any λs-term. We will need to count the use of variables in a term.

DEFINITION 19. *The* multiplicity *of a variable x in a term t, denoted by $|t|_x$, is the number of occurrences of the variable x in the term t, not including the use of the name x in a binder.*

The reduction rules defining the operational behaviour of the λs-calculus are shown in Figure 6, where the construction $t_{[y/x]}$ denotes the term t where exactly one occurrence of x has been replaced with y. Notice that in the dup rule, the new variable y must of course be fresh to avoid capture by some binder. This system of reduction rules is standard, and is similar to the one of the λes-calculus [Kes07], except in the handling of duplications.

We can now define an encoding of λs-terms into structures. For that, we need to consider a bijection between logical atoms and variables in the calculus, so that to any variable x corresponds an atom also denoted by x.

DEFINITION 20 (Encoding of λs). *The encoding $[\![\cdot]\!]_\lambda$ from λs-terms into structures of the* JLSd *system is defined as follows:*

$$\begin{array}{rcl} [\![x]\!]_\lambda & = & x \\ [\![\lambda x.t]\!]_\lambda & = & x \to [\![t]\!]_\lambda \\ [\![t\ u]\!]_\lambda & = & ([\![u]\!]_\lambda \to \top) \to [\![t]\!]_\lambda \\ [\![t[x \leftarrow u]]\!]_\lambda & = & ([\![u]\!]_\lambda \to x) \to [\![t]\!]_\lambda \end{array}$$

Notice that through this encoding, λs-terms correspond only to functional structures as they were defined for use with the JLSd system — this is of course the reason why we restricted the rules of JS this way. Moreover, the equation on λs-terms allowing to exchange unrelated explicit substitutions exactly corresponds to the equation $\equiv_b$ used on functional structures.

REMARK 21. *It is easy to see that the encoding $[\![\cdot]\!]_\lambda$ defines a bijection between λs-terms and functional structures. Indeed, each shape of structure defined in the grammar for restricted structures corresponds to exactly one construction in the λ-terms syntax, and the extra restrictions for functional structures correspond to the writing of a λs-term with a correct scope structure α-converted to avoid repetition of bindings on the same name.*

$$\begin{array}{rcll}
(\lambda x.t)\ u & \longrightarrow_{\mathtt{B}} & t[x \leftarrow u] & \\[1ex]
x[x \leftarrow u] & \longrightarrow_{\mathtt{var}} & u & \\
t[x \leftarrow u] & \longrightarrow_{\mathtt{rm}} & t & \text{if } |t|_x = 0 \\
t[x \leftarrow u] & \longrightarrow_{\mathtt{dup}} & t_{[y/x]}[x \leftarrow u][y \leftarrow u] & \text{if } |t|_x \geq 2 \\[1ex]
(\lambda y.t)[x \leftarrow u] & \longrightarrow_{\mathtt{lam}} & \lambda y.t[x \leftarrow u] & \\
(t\ v)[x \leftarrow u] & \longrightarrow_{\mathtt{apl}} & t[x \leftarrow u]\ v & \text{if } |v|_x = 0 \\
(t\ v)[x \leftarrow u] & \longrightarrow_{\mathtt{apr}} & t\ v[x \leftarrow u] & \text{if } |t|_x = 0 \\[1ex]
t[y \leftarrow v][x \leftarrow u] & \longrightarrow_{\mathtt{cmp}} & t[y \leftarrow v[x \leftarrow u]] & \text{if } |t|_x = 0
\end{array}$$

$$t[y \leftarrow v][x \leftarrow u] \equiv t[x \leftarrow u][y \leftarrow v] \qquad \text{if } |v|_x = |u|_y = 0$$

Figure 6. Reduction rules and equation for the λs-calculus

We can now state the theorem establishing the correspondence, at the computational level, between the operational behaviour of the λs-calculus and the behaviour of proof search in the JLSd system, where the $\longrightarrow_{\mathtt{R}}$ relation is the reduction defined by the rules of Figure 6, $\longrightarrow^*_{\mathtt{R}}$ is its reflexive and transitive closure, and $\longrightarrow_{\mathtt{S}}$ is the same as the first, where the B rule is not used.

THEOREM 22 (Computational adequacy of JLSd). *For any given λs-terms t and u, there is a derivation from $[\![u]\!]_\lambda$ to $[\![t]\!]_\lambda$ in the* JLSd *system if and only if $t \longrightarrow^*_{\mathtt{R}} u$.*

PROOF. By induction on the reduction steps from t to u. If the reduction path is empty, t and u are the same and the result is trivial because the encoding $[\![\cdot]\!]_\lambda$ is uniquely defined. In the general case, we consider the first step in the reduction, and use the induction hypothesis on the rest of the reduction. We thus simply have to check that there is an inference rule instance in JLSd with premise $[\![u]\!]_\lambda$ and conclusion $[\![t]\!]_\lambda$ if and only if we have $t \longrightarrow_{\mathtt{R}} u$. This is immediately done by observing that each reduction rule corresponds exactly to one case of application of an inference rule of JLSd:

$$\mathsf{isu}\,\frac{(B \to a) \to C}{(B \to \top) \to (a \to C)} \quad \longleftrightarrow \quad \mathtt{B}\,\frac{t[x \leftarrow u]}{(\lambda x.t)\ u}$$

$$\mathsf{ir}\,\frac{B}{(B \to a) \to a} \quad \longleftrightarrow \quad \mathtt{var}\,\frac{u}{x[x \leftarrow u]}$$

$$\mathsf{wr}\,\frac{C}{(B \to a) \to C} \quad \longleftrightarrow \quad \mathtt{rm}\,\frac{t}{t[x \leftarrow u]}$$

$$\mathsf{cr}\,\frac{(B \to d) \to ((B \to a) \to C_{[d/a]})}{(B \to a) \to C} \quad \longleftrightarrow \quad \mathtt{dup}\,\frac{t_{[y/x]}[x \leftarrow u][y \leftarrow u]}{t[x \leftarrow u]}$$

$$\mathsf{xr}\,\frac{c \to ((B \to a) \to D)}{(B \to a) \to (c \to D)} \quad \longleftrightarrow \quad \mathtt{lam}\,\frac{\lambda y.t[x \leftarrow u]}{(\lambda y.t)[x \leftarrow u]}$$

$$\mathsf{xr}\,\frac{(C \to \top) \to ((B \to a) \to D)}{(B \to a) \to ((C \to \top) \to D)} \quad \longleftrightarrow \quad \mathtt{apl}\,\frac{t[x \leftarrow u]\ v}{(t\ v)[x \leftarrow u]}$$

$$\mathsf{sr}\,\frac{(((B \to a) \to C) \to \top) \to D}{(B \to a) \to ((C \to \top) \to D)} \quad \longleftrightarrow \quad \mathtt{apr}\,\frac{t\ v[x \leftarrow u]}{(t\ v)[x \leftarrow u]}$$

$$\mathsf{sr}\,\frac{(((B \to a) \to C) \to e) \to D}{(B \to a) \to ((C \to e) \to D)} \quad \longleftrightarrow \quad \mathtt{cmp}\,\frac{t[y \leftarrow v[x \leftarrow u]]}{t[y \leftarrow v][x \leftarrow u]}$$

Notice that the conditions on the multiplicity of variables in the reduction rules for λs-terms exactly match the restrictions that were imposed on inference rules to define JLSd from JLS. □

This result establishes a tight connection between our restricted intuitionistic system and the λs-calculus. The interesting point is then that a theorem that we prove on derivations of the JLSd system on the logical side also holds in its *computational* form on reduction paths in the λs-calculus. As an example, we can prove that the subsystem $\longrightarrow_{\mathrm{S}}$ terminates.

THEOREM 23. *The reduction subsystem* $\longrightarrow_{\mathrm{S}}$ *terminates.*

PROOF. This is a direct corollary of Lemma 9, considering derivations of JLSb as reduction paths in the $\longrightarrow_{\mathrm{S}}$ subsystem through the correspondence defined by Theorem 22. □

The other way around, if we have some result on reduction in the λs-calculus, then we can directly transpose this result to the logical side. For example, the Church-Rosser property states that the $\longrightarrow_{\mathrm{R}}$ rewriting system is confluent, and we could prove it using the standard method of parallel reductions from Tait and Martin-Löf, see for example [Kes07] — to prove a similar result on derivations of the JLSd system. We would thus obtain a proof of the following proposition.

PROPOSITION 24. *For any structures A, B and C, if there are derivations from B to A and from C to A in* JLSd, *then there is a structure D such that there are derivations from D to B and from D to C in* JLSd.

Moreover, we observed that the class of structures which can be proven by proof search in JLSd without using wm is more interesting than plain functional structures, since this rule does not correspond to a valid rewriting on λs-terms. Also notice that the conclusion of the iaw rule, where no structure of the shape $B \to \top$ appears, is exactly a λs-term in normal form. From this we can derive a characterisation of *weakly normalising* terms.

THEOREM 25. *A* λs*-term t is weakly normalising if and only if there is a proof of $[\![t]\!]_\lambda$ in the* JLSd ∪ {iaw} *system.*

PROOF. First, if the term t is weakly normalising, then there is a u in normal form such that $t \longrightarrow^*_{\mathrm{R}} u$, and by Theorem 22 we have a derivation $\mathcal{D}$ from $[\![u]\!]_\lambda$ to $[\![t]\!]_\lambda$ in JLSd. We can thus use the iaw rule on $[\![u]\!]_\lambda$ to produce a proof of $[\![t]\!]_\lambda$. Then, if there is a proof of $[\![t]\!]_\lambda$ in JLSd ∪ {iaw}, we have such a derivation $\mathcal{D}$ and we can use Theorem 22 the other way around to get a term u in normal form such that $t \longrightarrow^*_{\mathrm{R}} u$. □

It would therefore be interesting to learn more about this class of structures, inside the logic, to get insights on weakly normalising terms in the λs-calculus. Furthermore, an important class is the one of *strongly normalising* terms, for which any reduction path reaches a normal form, and which are often characterised using type systems [LLD+04]. It is not clear whether this class can be characterised through a particular variant of the JLSd system. An interesting problem would then be in defining an efficient procedure to decide whether a given structure is provable in this system, to check if some λs-term is strongly normalising without computing its typing derivation. In particular, this means that we could ensure termination of a program without knowing its type: if this can be done efficiently using an algorithm such as a variant of resolution for a fragment of intuitionistic logic, this is interesting, but it does not ensure that the composition of two well-behaved programs is well-behaved. It is thus unclear what kind of mechanism could take the role of typing in this setting.

The tight correspondence established by Theorem 22 allows for direct reasoning on reduction paths in the λs-calculus, where each step can be handled separately. In particular, if we have a trace of computation corresponding to the reduction of a term t to some term u and another trace for the reduction from u to some term v, composing these traces is immediate and provides a trace of computation from t to v. Contexts can also be handled in a very natural way, as it is done in the calculus of structures.

Moreover, permutations of rule instances, and transformations on derivations in the JLSd system allow for a reorganisation of a reduction path between two given λs-terms. There are strong decomposition results in the calculus of structures [GS10], and results of this kind can be interesting when studying reduction strategies of the λs-calculus. In the following section, we will present a restriction of JLSd yielding such a reduction strategy.

$$\mathsf{ir}\ \frac{B}{(B \to a) \to \Downarrow a} \qquad \mathsf{isu}\ \frac{(B \to a) \to \Downarrow C}{(B \to \top) \to (a \to C)}$$

$$\mathsf{wr}\ \frac{A}{\delta \to \Downarrow A} \qquad \mathsf{cr}\ \frac{\delta \to \Downarrow (\delta \to \Downarrow A)}{\delta \to \Downarrow A}$$

$$\mathsf{xr}\ \frac{A \to (\delta \to \Downarrow B)}{\delta \to \Downarrow (A \to B)} \qquad \mathsf{sr}\ \frac{((\delta \to \Downarrow A) \to L) \to B}{\delta \to \Downarrow ((A \to L) \to B)}$$

Figure 7. Inference rules for system JLSn

4. Focused Proof Search and Reduction Strategies

Following our methodology, there is a direct connection between the cases where an inference rule can be applied on a structure and the reduction strategy implemented by the reduction system chosen for λs-terms. Indeed, we could use a variant of JLSd not using extra conditions on the multiplicity of atoms in the rules, but this would induce highly non-deterministic reduction rules for the λs-calculus. We made the reduction system deterministic by imposing a strategy in the sense that one reduction rule can be applied in only one way, but there is still a non-deterministic dimension in the choice of which redex to pick and reduce, given a λs-terms with several redexes. We now address the question of this choice, which is usually called choosing a *reduction strategy*.

The JLSd system can be restricted further by using annotations on structures in the spirit of focusing [And92], and this can be interpreted on the computational side as restricting the choice of the next redex to be rewritten. This restriction is similar to a standard formulation of *focusing* for intuitionistic logic [LM07], although the deep inference setting used here does not allow the exact same treatment. It should be noted that focusing in the calculus of structures cannot be immediately defined through a translation of usual focusing in the sequent calculus, although there is some work on the topic [Gue10]. For example, there is no separation between branches, and we thus need to duplicate focusing annotations, with copies being moved to different parts of the structure, corresponding to branches.

The inference rules for JLSn are shown in Figure 7, where the syntax of structures is extended with annotations, so that $\xi\{\Downarrow A\}$ is a valid structure for any $\xi\{\ \}$ and A — annotations are only allowed in positive position. Then, the *decision* action is embedded inside the isu rule, which picks a structure on the right of a block of the shape $B \to a$ and forces to move this block inside this structure until its contents, in B, are released by the ir rule. This sequence of rule applications guided by annotations is called a focused *phase*, and we are mainly interested in the structures at the borders of such a phase.

DEFINITION 26. *A functional structure B is said to be* basic *if all the structures in negative position inside B are either atoms or matchers — it contains no block, as $C \to a$ in negative position.*

The point of the JLSn system is then to handle basic structures by choosing a redex for the isu rule, to introduce a block $B \to a$ through this rule, and then maximally use the JLSb subsystem to produce a new basic structure, by removing all the remaining blocks. In particular, we add the restriction that the rule isu is not used on a structure that already contains a focus annotation. It is easy to see that any basic formula corresponds through the encoding $[\![\cdot]\!]_\lambda$ to some pure λ-term, which is a λs-term without explicit substitutions. We can therefore consider the standard rule for β-reduction in the pure λ-calculus:

$$(\lambda x.t)\ u \longrightarrow_\beta t\{u/x\}$$

and show that there is a computational adequacy result between JLSn and this simple rewriting system, through the same $[\![\cdot]\!]_\lambda$ encoding as before. As a first step, we need a lemma explaining the effect of a focusing phase on a structure. In the following, we denote by $\xi\{A\}^+$ a context with several holes filled with the structure A, and by $\xi\{A\}^*$ a context with zero or more holes filled with A. Moreover, the notation $\xi\{a\}^*$ implicitly means there is no occurrence of a in $\xi\{\ \}^*$ except in its holes.

LEMMA 27. *Given any functional structure without annotations, of the shape $\xi\{(B \to \top) \to (a \to \zeta\{a\}^*)\}$, there is a derivation from $\xi\{\zeta\{B\}^*\}$ to this structure in* JLSn.

PROOF. Given a functional structure without annotations, of the shape $\xi\{(B \to \top) \to (a \to \zeta\{a\}^*)\}$ we prove that there is a derivation $\mathcal{D}$ in JLSn such that we have the following situation:

$$\begin{array}{c} \xi\{\zeta\{B\}^*\} \\ \mathcal{D}\| \\ \text{isu}\ \dfrac{\xi\{(B \to a) \to \Downarrow \zeta\{a\}^*\}}{\xi\{(B \to \top) \to (a \to \zeta\{a\}^*)\}} \end{array}$$

We proceed by induction on the size of the context $\zeta\{\ \}^*$ to prove that there is such a $\mathcal{D}$, using a case analysis on its toplevel shape:

1. If $\zeta\{\ \}^*$ is $\{\ \}$, then we can use an identity rule, as shown below, and we are done since we have our derivation $\mathcal{D}$.

$$\text{ir}\ \frac{\xi\{B\}}{\xi\{(B \to a) \to \Downarrow a\}}$$

2. If $\zeta\{\ \}^*$ is C, where the atom a does not appear in C, then we can use a weakening rule, as shown below, and we are also done with the induction:

$$\text{wr}\ \frac{\xi\{C\}}{\xi\{(B \to a) \to \Downarrow C\}}$$

3. If $\zeta\{\ \}^*$ is $(C \to L) \to \theta\{\ \}^+$, then we can use an exchange rule, since the atom a does not appear in C, and then go on by induction hypothesis:

$$\text{xr}\ \frac{\xi\{(C \to L) \to ((B \to a) \to \Downarrow \theta\{a\}^+)\}}{\xi\{(B \to a) \to \Downarrow ((C \to L) \to \theta\{a\}^+)\}}$$

4. If $\zeta\{\ \}^*$ is $(\theta\{\ \}^+ \to L) \to C$, then we can use a switch rule, since the atom a does not appear in C, and then go on by induction hypothesis:

$$\text{sr}\ \frac{\xi\{(((B \to a) \to \Downarrow \theta\{a\}^+) \to L) \to C\}}{\xi\{(B \to a) \to \Downarrow ((\theta\{a\}^+ \to L) \to C)\}}$$

5. If $\zeta\{\ \}^*$ is $(\theta\{\ \}^+ \to L) \to \theta'\{a\}^+$, then we have to use both the exchange and switch rules, after using a contraction rule to duplicate the block $B \to a$, and then go on by using twice the induction hypothesis:

$$\begin{array}{l} \text{xr}\ \dfrac{\xi\{(((B \to a) \to \Downarrow \theta\{a\}^+) \to L) \to ((B \to a) \to \Downarrow \theta'\{a\}^+)\}}{\text{sr}\ \dfrac{\xi\{(B \to a) \to \Downarrow (((B \to a) \to \Downarrow \theta\{a\}^+) \to L) \to \theta'\{a\}^+\}}{\text{cr}\ \dfrac{\xi\{(B \to a) \to \Downarrow ((B \to a) \to \Downarrow ((\theta\{a\}^+ \to L) \to \theta'\{a\}^+))\}}{\xi\{(B \to a) \to \Downarrow ((\theta\{a\}^+ \to L) \to \theta'\{a\}^+)\}}}} \end{array}$$

Notice that if the context $\zeta\{\ \}^*$ had no hole, the weakening rule is applied and no replacement is performed. □

THEOREM 28 (Computational adequacy of JLSn). *For any two λ-terms t and u, there is a derivation from $[\![u]\!]_\lambda$ to $[\![t]\!]_\lambda$ in the* JLSn *system if and only if $t \longrightarrow_\beta^* u$.*

PROOF. By induction on the reduction steps from t to u. If the reduction path is empty, t and u are the same and the result is trivial because the encoding $[\![\cdot]\!]_\lambda$ is uniquely defined. In the general case, we consider the first step in the reduction, and use the induction hypothesis on the rest of the reduction. We thus simply have to check that there is an inference rule instance in JLSn with premise $[\![u]\!]_\lambda$ and conclusion $[\![t]\!]_\lambda$ if and only if we have $t \longrightarrow_\beta u$. To do it, we consider a particular redex, such that t is the term $C[(\lambda x.v)\ w]$ for some context $C[\cdot]$, and show that u is $C[v\{w/x\}]$ if and only if there is a derivation from $[\![u]\!]_\lambda$ to $[\![t]\!]_\lambda$ in JLSn. More precisely, this derivation exactly consists of one phase, where the bottommost rule instance is an instance of isu with premise $([\![w]\!]_\lambda \to x) \to \Downarrow [\![v]\!]_\lambda$, and the premise of the phase is a basic structure which must be $[\![u]\!]_\lambda$, as a direct consequence of Lemma 27. □

COROLLARY 29 (Full composition). *For any given λs-terms t and u, we have $t[x \leftarrow u] \longrightarrow_{\mathsf{S}}^* t\{u/x\}$.*

PROOF. This is a corollary of Lemma 27 considered through the encoding $[\![\cdot]\!]_\lambda$ using Theorem 28. Indeed, the therm $t\{u/x\}$ using an implicit substitution corresponds through $[\![\cdot]\!]_\lambda$ to the structure $[\![t]\!]_\lambda$ where all occurrences of x are replaced with $[\![u]\!]_\lambda$. □

This theorem establishes a precise correspondence between one β-reduction big step, performing an implicit substitution inside the term, and a focusing phase in JLSn. We can now express the relation between the big-step reduction in the λ-calculus and the small-step operational behaviour which is implemented in the λs-calculus, and this corresponds to the study of soundness and completeness of JLSn with respect to JLSd.

THEOREM 30 (Soundness of JLSn). *For two basic structures A and B, if there is a derivation from A to B in* JLSn *then there is a derivation from A to B in* JLSd.

PROOF. Each inference rule in the JLSn system is actually an inference rule of JLSd with focus annotations. Therefore, we just need to remove annotations in the given derivation from A to B in JLSn to produce a derivation from A to B in JLSd. □

The meaning of this theorem, on the computational side, is that any reduction path from t to u in the restricted reduction system of β-reduction can be replaced with a reduction sequence from t to u in the more general $\longrightarrow_{\mathsf{R}}$ rewrite system, which is exactly stepwise simulation of β-reduction by explicit substitutions.

COROLLARY 31 (Simulation of β). *For any λ-terms t and u, if $t \longrightarrow_\beta^* u$ then $t \longrightarrow_{\mathsf{S}}^* u$.*

The other direction of the correspondence between JLSd and JLSn is more interesting, since it indicates that the simulation of β-reduction in the λs-calculus does not rely on the use of a reduction system that would not be sensible.

LEMMA 32. *For a basic structure A, if there is a derivation from A to a structure $\xi\{(B \to c) \to \zeta\{c\}^*\}$ in* JLSd, *there is a derivation of at most the same length from A to $\xi\{\zeta\{B\}^*\}$ in* JLSd.

PROOF. By induction on the context $\zeta\{\ \}^*$. If $\zeta\{\ \}^*$ is $\{\ \}$, then we can use the ir rule and an induction on the given derivation $\mathcal{D}$ to remove the structure $(B \to c)$ and replace c with B. This is similar to the result of Lemma 10, stating the invertibility of the rule ir. In the general case, we use a case analysis on the shape of $\zeta\{\ \}^*$ and in each case an induction on the derivation, as for ir. This induction is a variant of invertibility for the rules of JLSb, which preserves the upper bound on the length of the derivation, and relies on the fact that the given derivation uses these rules because its premise A is a basic structure — and $B \to c$ thus does not appear in A. □

THEOREM 33 (Completeness of JLSn). *Given any two basic structures A and B, if there is a derivation from A to B in the* JLSd *system, there is a derivation from A to B in the* JLSn *system.*

PROOF. By induction on a given derivation $\mathcal{D}$ from A to B in the JLSd system. If $\mathcal{D}$ is of length 0, then A is B and there is a trivial derivation from A to B in JLSn. In the general case, since B is a basic structure, there is no structure of the shape $C \to d$ in negative position in B and the bottommost rule instance must be an instance of the isu rule, and has a structure of the shape $\xi\{(C \to d) \to \zeta\{d\}^*\}$ as premise. Thus, by Lemma 32 there is a derivation $\mathcal{D}_1$ of smaller length than $\mathcal{D}$ from A to $\xi\{\zeta\{C\}^*\}$ in JLSd, and by Lemma 27 there is a derivation $\mathcal{D}_2$ from $\xi\{\zeta\{C\}^*\}$ to B in JLSn. We can then apply the induction hypothesis to $\mathcal{D}_1$ to produce a derivation $\mathcal{D}_3$ and the result is the composition of the two derivations $\mathcal{D}_2$ and $\mathcal{D}_3$. □

On the computational side, this theorem says that the λs-calculus is sensible with respect to the standard λ-calculus. Indeed, a way of defining a reduction system that can simulate β-reduction is to add *too many* possible reductions, thus loosing all good properties. This is not the case here, since we have stated in this theorem the projection of reduction with explicit substitutions inside β-reduction. Notice that in the following corollary, it is important that the given terms t and u are plain λ-terms, and not terms with explicit substitutions.

COROLLARY 34 (Projection in β). *For any λ-terms t and u, if $t \longrightarrow_{\mathsf{s}}^* u$ then $t \longrightarrow_{\beta}^* u$.*

We have now all the elements to compare the standard λ-calculus and the λs-calculus with explicit substitutions only in terms of comparisons between the logical systems JLSn and JLSd that we have defined. Moreover, there are many possible restrictions of the JLSd system that correspond to other λ-calculi or various reduction strategies. For example, we could add restrictions on inference rules of JLSn to enforce a normal order evaluation, so that this variant would correspond exactly to the *call-by-name* weak reduction of λ-terms. Enforcing a *call-by-value* reduction strategy is more complicated, since the required restrictions on inference rules would be less natural, because of the problem of detecting structures that represent values. Notice that using a shallow proof search strategy betrays the idea of using the deep inference methodology, the same way as using a weak reduction strategy *betrays the very spirit of the λ-calculus* [Asp98].

5. Conclusion

We have defined here a deductive system for a small fragment of intuitionistic logic and established a correspondence between the proof search process in this system and computation in the functional programming setting, by means of a λ-calculus with explicit substitutions. This methodology can provide interesting links between results on the logical side, such as the soundness and completeness results of a deductive system, and results in the λ-calculus, such as the simulation of a reduction system in another system.

The use of a deep inference system is essential in the sense that it induces a very elegant correspondence between inference rules and reduction rules, and allows to model a reduction sequence as a derivation from one structure to another in a logical system, so that computation traces can be easily composed. If we want to have this ability, we need to be able to apply inference rules deep inside formulas to handle reductions inside a λ-term, and not reduce the study to weak evaluation strategies only. There is much future work left in this project, and we give now some details on further research directions to be explored.

Extension to full JS. In this paper we have restricted our study to a small fragment of the JS proof system, based on restrictions that are quite artificial from the logical viewpoint, which were only motivated by the structure of our λ-calculus. Although we can still explore the relations between logical and computational notions in this setting, it would surely be interesting to design a correspondence for the full JS system. The question is then to find a meaning for non-atomic formulas in negative position, which could be done with a generic notion of *pattern matching*, as is defined in the pure pattern calculus [JK09]. Indeed, this calculus generalises the notion of λ-abstraction from $\lambda x.t$ into the *case* construct $u \to t$, where the x in negative position is replaced with some arbitrary term u is negative position. This extension is not trivial, since we have to handle explicit pattern matching, and syntactic distinctions between case, application and explicit matching. Moreover, we would still have to restrict JS since we cannot accept some term manipulations, such as the transformation from $u \to v \to t$ to $v \to u \to t$ in the general case. Such an extension would provide a logical background for the pure pattern calculus, allowing to explore the benefits of using the standard proof-theoretical techniques.

Evaluation strategies. Another important direction is the study of different evaluation strategies available in the λ-calculus with explicit substitutions, ranging from highly non-deterministic to highly constrained procedures. It was interesting to notice the connection between the focusing technique and call-by-name, and we can now look for more subtle restrictions which would correspond to known strategies, such as call-by-value. Normal forms for proofs can be used as a source of inspiration for new evaluation strategies, and because of the methodology used here, all the work on improving the efficiency of proof search can be used to improve efficiency in reduction strategies. For example, if we can prove that for a given set of formulas, some restricted system only allows *short proofs* — that is, bound in some way with respect to the size of the formula — it means that we have an evaluation strategy where reduction is also bounded. It might be interesting to translate the question of optimal reduction in this setting.

Variant systems. Many variants of our inference rules can be defined in the calculus of structures, and in particular local rules, which never modify, copy or erase non-atomic formula. Such a local variant of JLSd would induce through our correspondence a calculus where all reduction steps are local, which can be a nice feature in the implementation of a functional language. The problem is that designing a local presentation for intuitionistic logic might be quite difficult, or induce a highly complex system that would not fit our needs [Tiu06].

Classes of λ-terms. There is one aspect of the standard results on λ-terms that has been set aside in this study: the class of *simply-typed*, and weakly or strongly normalising terms, is quite difficult to understand in our proof-search setting. It is unclear if these subsets of the set of all programs make any sense here, since types are usually identified with logical formulas. It would be interesting to provide characterisations, in terms of restricted proof systems, of important sets of terms, such as those that terminate, or those that can be composed while preserving some good properties.

Other logics and calculi. The methodology introduced here is a general notion of correspondence, and could be applied in other settings. As an example, *linear logic* [Gir87] is a refinement of intuitionistic logic that is often presented as a logic of *resources*, as it offers a greater control over duplication and erasure inside its proof system. The interpretation of a system for intuitionistic linear logic could thus provide a basis for the study of λ-calculi with resource operators [KL05]. Moreover, our correspondence could be translated to a classical setting, its computational side taking the form of some *process algebra* rather than a sequential programming language, as suggested by existing work on the encoding of concurrent computation in proof search within the setting of deep inference [Bru02].

Acknowledgements. The paper has greatly benefited from the many interesting comments and useful suggestions made by the anonymous reviewers.

References

[AK10] B. Accattoli and D. Kesner. The structural λ-calculus. In A. Dawar and H. Veith, editors, *CSL'10*, volume 6247 of *LNCS*, pages 381–395, 2010.

[And92] J-M. Andreoli. Logic programming with focusing proofs in linear logic. *Journal of Logic and Computation*, 2(3):297–347, 1992.

[Asp98] A. Asperti. Optimal reduction of functional expressions. In C. Palamidessi, H. Glaser, and K. Meinke, editors, *PLILP'98*, volume 1490 of *LNCS*, pages 427–428, 1998.

[BM08] K. Brünnler and R. McKinley. An algorithmic interpretation of a deep inference system. In I. Cervesato, H. Veith, and A. Voronkov, editors, *LPAR'08*, volume 5330 of *LNCS*, pages 482–496, 2008.

[Bru02] P. Bruscoli. A purely logical account of sequentiality in proof search. In P. J. Stuckey, editor, *ICLP'02*, volume 2401 of *LNCS*, pages 302–316, 2002.

[Brü03] K. Brünnler. *Deep Inference and Symmetry in Classical Proofs*. PhD thesis, Technische Universität Dresden, September 2003.

[Brü06] K. Brünnler. Locality for classical logic. *Notre Dame Journal of Formal Logic*, 47:557–580, 2006.

[Gir87] J-Y. Girard. Linear logic. *Theoretical Computer Science*, 50:1–102, 1987.

[GS01] A. Guglielmi and L. Straßburger. Non-commutativity and MELL in the calculus of structures. In L. Fribourg, editor, *CSL'01*, volume 2142 of *LNCS*, pages 54–68, 2001.

[GS10] A. Guglielmi and L. Straßburger. A system of interaction and structure IV: The exponentials and decomposition. To appear in *ACM Transactions on Computational Logic*, 2010.

[Gue10] N. Guenot. Focused proof search for linear logic in the calculus of structures. In M. Hermenegildo and T. Schaub, editors, *ICLP'10 (Technical Comm.)*, volume 7 of *LIPIcs*, pages 84–93, 2010.

[Her94] H. Herbelin. A λ-calculus structure isomorphic to Gentzen-style sequent calculus structure. In L. Pacholski and J. Tiuryn, editors, *CSL'94*, volume 933 of *LNCS*, pages 61–75, 1994.

[JK09] B. Jay and D. Kesner. First-class patterns. *Journal of Functional Programming*, 19(2):191–225, 2009.

[Kes07] D. Kesner. The theory of calculi with explicit substitutions revisited. In J. Duparc and T. A. Henzinger, editors, *CSL'07*, volume 4646 of *LNCS*, pages 238–252, 2007.

[KL05] D. Kesner and S. Lengrand. Extending the explicit substitution paradigm. In J. Giesl, editor, *RTA'05*, volume 3467 of *LNCS*, pages 407–422, 2005.

[LLD+04] S. Lengrand, P. Lescanne, D. Dougherty, M. Dezani-Ciancaglini, and S. van Bakel. Intersection types for explicit substitutions. *Information and Computation*, 189(1):17–42, 2004.

[LM07] C. Liang and D. Miller. Focusing and polarization in intuitionistic logic. In J. Duparc and T. A. Henzinger, editors, *CSL'07*, volume 4646 of *LNCS*, pages 451–465, 2007.

[Mil89] D. Miller. A logical analysis of modules in logic programming. *Journal of Logic Programming*, 6(1&2):79–108, 1989.

[MNPS91] D. Miller, G. Nadathur, F. Pfenning, and A. Scedrov. Uniform proofs as a foundation for logic programming. *Annals of Pure and Applied Logic*, 51:125–157, 1991.

[Plo75] G. Plotkin. Call-by-name, call-by-value and the λ-calculus. *Theoretical Computer Science*, 1(2):125–159, 1975.

[Rov11] L. Roversi. Linear λ-calculus with explicit substitutions as proof-search in deep inference. Accepted at *TLCA'11*, 2011.

[Str03] L. Straßburger. *Linear Logic and Noncommutativity in the Calculus of Structures*. PhD thesis, Technische Universität Dresden, July 2003.

[Tiu06] A. Tiu. A local system for intuitionistic logic. In M. Hermann and A. Voronkov, editors, *LPAR'06*, volume 4246 of *LNCS*, pages 242–256, 2006.

Author Index

www.ingramcontent.com/pod-product-compliance
Lightning Source LLC
Chambersburg PA
CBHW081523220326
41598CB00036B/6316
* 9 7 8 1 4 5 0 3 1 2 6 8 4 *